Handbook of
Couple and Family
Forensics

WILEY SERIES IN COUPLES AND FAMILY DYNAMICS AND TREATMENT

FLORENCE W. KASLOW, SERIES EDITOR

Handbook of Couple and Family Forensics

A SOURCEBOOK FOR MENTAL HEALTH
AND LEGAL PROFESSIONALS

Edited by
Florence Kaslow

John Wiley & Sons, Inc.

New York • Chichester • Weinheim • Brisbane • Singapore • Toronto

Library of Congress Cataloging-in-Publication Data:

Handbook of couple and family forensics / edited by Florence W. Kaslow.
     p.   cm. — (Wiley series in couples and family dynamics and treatment)
    Includes bibliographical references.
    ISBN 0-471-19129-9 (cloth : alk. paper)
    1. Marital psychotherapy—Law and legislation—Handbooks, manuals, etc.
  2. Family psychotherapy—Law and legislation—Handbooks, manuals, etc.
  3. Family therapists—Legal status, laws, etc.—Handbooks, manuals, etc.
  4. Forensic psychiatry—Handbooks, manuals, etc.   5. Mental health laws—
Handbooks, manuals, etc.   I. Kaslow, Florence Whiteman.   II. Series.
  RA1151.H24 1999
  614'.1—dc21   98-53730
                                               CIP

Printed in the United States of America.

10 9 8 7 6 5 4 3 2 1

Contributors

Stephen J. Anderer, JD, PhD, is an attorney in the Family Law Department at Schnader Harrison Segal & Lewis. His practice includes domestic relations and psychological issues that arise, particularly in child custody and civil competency determination cases. Dr. Anderer has a BA from Yale University, a JD from Villanova University School of Law, and a PhD in clinical psychology from Allegheny University of the Health Sciences. He is a coauthor of *Law for Mental Health Professionals: Pennsylvania,* an APA publication.

Peter Ash, MD, is an assistant professor in the Department of Psychiatry and Behavioral Sciences at Emory University in Atlanta, Georgia. He directs the Psychiatry and Law Service and the fellowship in forensic psychiatry at Emory. He is board certified in general psychiatry, child and adolescent psychiatry, and forensic psychiatry.

Cole Barton, PhD, is a professor of psychology at Davidson College in North Carolina and is also a clinical professor in the Duke University Family Medicine Program. He was a coinvestigator in the kidnap research program with Dr. Chris Hatcher, with continuing research interests in families of abused children and behavioral medicine.

Dorothy S. Becvar, MSW, PhD, is a family therapist in private practice in St. Louis, Missouri. She is the author of *Soul Healing: A Spiritual Orientation in Counseling* and, with her husband, Raphael J. Becvar, of numerous other publications in family therapy. She is a teacher and trainer who has been a member of the faculties of the University of Missouri—St. Louis, St. Louis University, Texas Tech University, Washington University and Radford University, and has presented workshops nationally and internationally on a wide variety of topics.

Stanley L. Brodsky, PhD, received his PhD in clinical psychology from the University of Florida. He served as Chief of Psychology at the U.S. Disciplinary Barracks and was on the faculty of Southern Illinois University before going to the University of Alabama as professor of psychology and coordinator of the psychology-law concentration. He maintains an independent practice of forensic psychology. Dr. Brodsky is editor or author of 10 books, including *Testifying in Court, The Psychology of Adjustment and Well-Being,* and with Stuart Greenberg of *The Civil Practice of Forensic Psychology.*

Loren Brooks, PhD, is a faculty member of St. Mary's College in Moraga, California. For the past 9 years she has been involved in research on the psychological consequences of kidnapping on children and families, trauma secondary to violence, and related forensic issues.

O. Brandt Caudill, Jr., JD, is an attorney licensed in California and the District of Columbia, and a graduate of Georgetown University Law Center. He specializes in the defense of mental health professionals in civil suits and administrative hearings. A member of the California Psychological Association, he has written more than 15 articles on the defense of mental health professionals and has participated in helping various professional associations draft ethical standards. He is coauthor with Dr. Kenneth Pope of *Law and Mental Health Professionals: California,* an APA publication, and with Dr. Lawrence Hedges of *All Therapists at Risk.*

Mary E. Dankoski, MS, has a masters degree in marriage and family therapy from Purdue University Calumet, and is currently a doctoral student in the marriage and family therapy program at Purdue University, West Lafayette, Indiana.

Marion Gindes, PhD, is a clinical and forensic psychologist in independent practice in New York City and Westchester County. She has been working, writing, and teaching in the areas of divorce and child for more than 20 years, and serves as an expert witness in custody, workplace, and gender issue cases. Dr. Gindes is an Adjunct Clinical Supervisor at the Ferkauf Graduate School, Yeshiva University; and has been a faculty member at Brooklyn College of CUNY, Albert Einstein College of Medicine, and Pennsylvania State University. She has been president of the Division of Media Psychology of APA.

Michael C. Gottlieb, PhD, is in independent practice in Dallas, Texas. A board-certified family psychologist (ABPP) and Fellow of the American Psychological Association, he is a clinical associate professor at University of Texas Health Sciences Center and an honorary clinical professor at Texas Woman's University. He is a past president of the Academy of Family Psychology and the Texas Psychological Association, and past chair of the American Board of Family Psychology. He is currently a member of the Board of Trustees of ABPP. His scholarly interests include ethics and professional issues.

Deborah I. Gottschalk, JD, is staff attorney at Community Legal Aid Society, Inc., Wilmington, Delaware, the New Castle County Coordinator for the ACLU-DE Lesbian and Gay Civil Rights Project, and a founding member of both the Delaware Network of Lesbian and Gay Attorneys and the Delaware Coalition Against Domestic Violence Committee on Lesbian, Gay, and Bisexual Concerns. She is a past board member of both AIDS Delaware and the Gay and Lesbian Lawyers of Philadelphia (GALLOP).

Charles G. Guyer II, EdD, is Chief Psychologist with the Perquimans County School System in North Carolina. He holds Diplomates in Counseling and in Family Psychology from ABPP. Dr. Guyer is a Fellow of the American Psychological

Association, the Academy of Family Psychology, the Academy of Counseling Psychology, and the American Society of Clinical Hypnosis. He is a past president of the American Board of Family Psychology, of the Academy of Family Psychology, and of the Academy of Counseling Psychology. Dr. Guyer received the Irving I. Secter Award from the American Society of Clinical Hypnosis for the Advancement of the Science and Practice of Hypnosis.

Chris Hatcher, PhD, was a clinical professor of psychology at the University of California, San Francisco, for most of his academic career, directing the Family Therapy Program for 9 years and a federally funded kidnap research program for 8 years. He was a frequent forensic expert in cases involving violent behavior in both the United States and Canada. Dr. Hatcher passed away in February 1999, while this book was in preparation. Chapter 14 is dedicated to his memory and the trailblazing work he did in the arena of preventing abductions and recovering missing children.

Florence W. Kaslow, PhD, a PhD from Bryn Mawr College, is Director of the Florida Couples and Family Institute and President of Kaslow Associates, a family business consultation firm. She is a visiting professor of psychology at both Florida Institute of Technology and the Department of Psychiatry at Duke University Medical Center. She is the author or editor of 18 books and over 135 journal articles and book chapters. She frequently guest lectures throughout the United States and myriad other countries. Currently Dr. Kaslow is President of both the American Board of Family Psychology (ABPP) and the International Academy of Family Psychology; she was the first president of the American Board of Forensic Psychology and of the International Family Therapy Association, and is board certified in clinical, forensic, and family psychology (ABPP). She is a Fellow of numerous APA Divisions.

Daniel F. Kearns, PsyD, received his PsyD in clinical psychology from the Florida Institute of Technology (Melbourne, Florida) in August 1998, and interned at Vanderbilt Consortium's Veterans Administration Medical Center. He has been active in the development of a model memory clinic funded by the State of Florida, in new models for behavioral medicine. His doctoral research was on MMPI-A assessment with adolescents.

Diana Adile Kirschner, PhD, is a clinical and family psychologist and consultant in private practice in Gwynedd Valley, Pennsylvania. She taught at the Wharton School, Division of Family Business Studies. She is coauthor of *Comprehensive Family Therapy* with Dr. Sam Kirschner, and of several other professional books, and many book chapters.

Sam Kirschner, PhD, of Gwynedd Valley, Pennsylvania, is a psychologist in private practice and a management consultant who specializes in family business consulting. Dr. Kirschner has taught at the Wharton School, Division of Family Business Studies. He is the author or coeditor of several books, including *Psychology and the Media* (APA), and numerous articles, and is a frequent workshop leader.

Stuart B. Klein, JD, is the senior partner in Klein & Klein, P.A., a law firm in West Palm Beach, Florida, where he concentrates on corporate, health care, mental health, and real estate law, and trust and estate planning and litigation. He graduated from the University of Toledo College of Law and then obtained an LLM from the New York University School of Law. Mr. Klein is an adjunct professor at Nova Southeastern University School of Law and the author of several law review articles published in the areas of law and medicine.

Wilhelmina S. Koedam, PhD, is in private practice in North Miami Beach and Cooper City, Florida. She has authored articles on patient behavior with rheumatoid arthritis, patients participating in the Federal Witness Protection Program, and a chapter on dissociative identity disorders. She is currently developing a book regarding postponed parenting. She is a Florida Supreme Court–certified mediator and often conducts custody evaluations.

Kevin T. Kuehlwein, PsyD, is Staff Psychologist, Center for Cognitive Therapy, University of Pennsylvania, and is adjunct associate professor at Hahnemann University of the Health Sciences, in Philadelphia. He is coediter with Hugh Rosen of *Cognitive Therapies in Action: Evolving Innovative Practice* as well as of *Constructing Realities: Meaning-Making Perspectives for Psychotherapy*. He has a chapter in the *Comprehensive Handbook of Cognitive Therapy* on applying cognitive therapy to gay men. He has presented on psychotherapy in the United States and abroad. Dr. Kuehlwein serves on the editorial board of *Cognitive and Behavioral Practice* and has done extensive supervision and training of cognitive therapists, as well as managing a small private practice in Philadelphia.

Marsha Levick, JD, is a graduate of Temple University School of Law. Ms. Levick is an attorney with the Juvenile Law Center in Philadelphia, Pennsylvania, an organization she cofounded to advance the legal rights and interests of children in society. She served as the Legal Director and then Executive Director of the NOW Legal Defense and Education Fund from 1982 to 1988.

Susan P. Limber, PhD, MLS, is Assistant Director of the Institute for Families in Society, University of South Carolina, and assistant research professor of neuropsychiatry and behavioral sciences at USC. She received her graduate degrees in psychology and law from the University of Nebraska—Lincoln. She was a James Marshall Public Policy Fellow for the Society for the Psychological Study of Social Issues. As a public policy fellow, she worked on various issues related to child and family policy at APA in Washington, DC. She was the 1997 recipient of the Saleem Shah Award from the American Psychology-Law Society for early career excellence in law and policy.

Lewis P. Lipsitt, PhD, is professor emeritus of psychology, medical science, and human development at Brown University where he has been on the faculty for 42 years. He holds a research professorship in psychology to conduct a large-scale neuropsychological follow-up of children, now in their mid-30s, originally studied from birth to age 7. Dr. Lipsitt has a BA from the University of Chicago, MS in social and clinical psychology from the University of Massachusetts, and PhD in child psychology from the University of Iowa. He has been a Guggenheim Fellow, a Fellow at the Stanford Center for Advanced Study in the Behavior Sciences, and at London's Tavistock Institute. He won the 1994 American Association for Advancement of Science Lifetime Achievement Mentor Award.

Paul D. Lipsitt, LLB (Boston University), **PhD** (University of Chicago), a psychologist and an attorney, has held faculty appointments at Boston University, Harvard Medical School, and SUNY—Buffalo. Dr. Lipsitt served as Research Director in Law and Psychology at the Law-Medicine Institute, Boston University, and at the Laboratory of Community Psychiatry, Harvard Medical School. In the Massachusetts Department of Mental Health he was Director for Legal Medicine and Court Clinic Director. A Diplomate in Forensic Psychology (ABPP), Dr. Lipsitt is a past president of the American Psychology-Law Society and the American Board of Forensic Psychology. He is a clinical associate and a senior supervisor at the Boston University Student Mental Health Center, and lecturer on psychology at Harvard Medical School.

James R. Oelschlager, PsyD, is the Director of Counseling and Psychological Services at Florida Tech, Melbourne, Florida. He has specialty training in geriatrics and neuropsychology and is an advisory board member to the East Central Florida Memory Disorder Clinic. He presents and writes on the topic of domestic violence and brain injury as a sequelae.

Thomas H. Peake, PhD, ABPP (Clinical), is an approved AAMFT supervisor, a Fellow of APA, a professor of psychology at Florida Tech, and an adjunct professor at the Florida Mental Health Institute. Licensed in three states and England, he has trained health professionals and practiced clinical psychology for over 20 years. His publication and practice areas include brief psychotherapy, clinical training, medical psychology, couples therapy, and his latest book is *Healthy Aging, Health Treatment: Telling Stories.*

Pauline M. Pagliocca, PhD, an assistant professor of psychology at the University of South Carolina, was educated at the University of Massachusetts (BA) and the University of Virginia (MEd, PhD). She completed a clinical internship and an advanced fellowship in psychological trauma at the Cambridge Hospital/Harvard Medical School and served as a postdoctoral research fellow at the Center on Children, Families, and the Law at the University of Nebraska, Lincoln. She was cofounder and director of the Community Crisis Response Team of the Victims of Violence Program at Cambridge Hospital. Her research and clinical interests relate to children and adolescents and the law, and she has conducted studies of delinquency diversion and intervention, decision making in juvenile courts, and truancy.

Kenneth S. Pope, PhD, ABPP, received graduate degrees from Harvard and Yale, chaired the Ethics Committees of the APA and ABPP, and is in independent practice. A charter fellow of the American Psychological Society and a fellow of APA Divisions 1, 2, 12, 35, 41, 42, 44, and 51, he received the APA Award for Distinguished Contributions to Public Service, the APA Division of Clinical Psychology

Award for Distinguished Professional Contributions to Clinical Psychology, the Belle Mayer Bromberg Award for literature, and the Frances Mosseker Award for Fiction. His publications include 10 books and over 100 articles and chapters in peer-reviewed professional journals and books.

Lita Linzer Schwartz, PhD, Distinguished Professor Emerita at Pennsylvania State University, is a Diplomate in Forensic Psychology (ABPP) and writes frequently on matters of family law. In addition to *Alternatives to Infertility: Is Surrogacy the Answer?*, she has coauthored *The Dynamics of Divorce* and *Painful Partings: The Aftermath of Divorce* with Dr. Florence Kaslow, and has also written *Why Give Gifts to the Gifted? Investing in a National Resource.* Dr. Schwartz teaches a course on "Psychology and the Law" at Abington College of Penn State University, and consults privately in child custody cases.

Jane F. Silovsky, PhD, is a clinical instructor in the Department of Pediatrics at the University of Oklahoma Health Sciences Center (OUHSC). She received her PhD in clinical psychology at the University of Alabama, and took specialized graduate training in responding to child maltreatment at the Center on Child Abuse and Neglect at OUHSC. Dr. Silovsky is the codirector of the ADHD Clinic and the Psychosocial Clinic at the Child Study Center of OUHSC. She conducts treatment outcome research on therapies designed for children affected by child maltreatment.

Terry S. Trepper, PhD, is Director of the Family Studies Center at Purdue University Calumet, and professor of psychology and of marriage and family therapy. He is an APA Fellow, an AAMFT Clinical Member and Approved Supervisor, an AASECT Certified Sex Therapist, and a Diplomate of the American Board of Sexology. He is the editor of the *Journal of Family Psychotherapy* (journal of the International Family Therapy Association), and is senior editor for *Haworth's Series on Marriage and the Family.* He is coauthor with Mary Jo Barrett of *Systemic Treatment of Incest: A Therapeutic Handbook, Treating Incest: A Multiple Systems Perspective* with Thorana Nelson, *101 Interventions in Family Therapy,* and *101 More Interventions in Family Therapy.* He has a private practice in family psychology in Northwest Indiana.

Diane J. Willis, PhD, is a professor in the Department of Pediatrics, University of Oklahoma Health Sciences Center and Director of Psychological Services at the Child Study Center. She served 4 years on the U.S. Advisory Board on Child Abuse and Neglect and has testified before Congress on issues related to child maltreatment and American Indians. Dr. Willis consults with IHS and tribes on mental health issues and does extensive training in the area of child maltreatment. She is a Fellow of APA, and the author or editor of 4 books and over 40 articles and chapters.

Robert Henley Woody, PhD (Michigan State University), **ScD** (University of Pittsburgh), and **JD** (Creighton University), is professor of psychology, Director of School Psychology Training, and former Dean for Graduate Studies and Research at the University of Nebraska at Omaha. He is an attorney in private practice. He is a Fellow of the American Psychological Association and the American Association for Marriage and Family Therapy, and holds Diplomates in Clinical Psychology and in Forensic Psychology from ABPP. He is a member of the Florida, Michigan, and Nebraska bars, and a licensed psychologist in Florida and Michigan. He is author of 27 books and approximately 200 articles.

Series Preface

Our ability to form strong and meaningful interpersonal bonds with romantic partners, children, parents, siblings and other relatives is one of the key qualities that defines our humanity. These relationships shape who we are and what we become—they can be a source of great gratification or tremendous pain. Yet only in the mid-20th century did behavioral and social scientists really begin focusing on couples and family dynamics, and only in the last several decades have the theory and findings that emerged from studies on couples and families been used to develop effective therapeutic interventions.

We have made great progress in understanding the structure, function, and interactional patterns of couples and families—and made tremendous strides in treatment. However, as we stand poised at the beginning of a new millennium, it seems quite clear that both intimate partnerships and family relationships are in a period of tremendous flux. Economic factors are changing work patterns, parenting responsibilities, and relational dynamics. Modern medicine has helped lengthen the life span, giving rise to the need for transgenerational caregiving. Cohabitation, divorce, and remarriage are quite commonplace, and these social changes make it necessary for us to rethink and broaden our definition of what constitutes a family.

It is no longer enough simply to embrace the concept of the family as a system. In order to understand and effectively treat the evolving family, our theoretical formulations and clinical interventions must be informed by an understanding of ethnicity, culture, religion, gender, sexual preference, family life cycle, socioeconomic status, education, physical and mental health, values, and belief systems.

The purpose of the Wiley Series in Couples and Family Dynamics and Treatment is to provide a forum for cutting-edge relational and family theory, practice, and research, and also to offer an interdisciplinary venue for exploring areas that overlap several professional disciplines. Its scope is intended to be broad, diverse, and international, but all books published in this series share a common mission—to reflect on the past, offer state-of-the art information on the present, and speculate on, as well as attempt to shape, the future of the field.

FLORENCE W. KASLOW
Florida Couples and Family Institute
Series Editor

Preface

Throughout the course of their life cycle, many families have a variety of reasons for coming into contact with the legal, judicial, or criminal justice systems. Some of these interactions are voluntarily initiated, as when a person wants to accomplish something and needs legal assistance, such as to expedite an adoption, draw up a surrogacy agreement, or draft a will. However, many of the contacts are mandatory—for example, if a juvenile is taken to a police station under suspicion of having committed an offense and needs an attorney to defend him or her, if a divorce action has been entered into which eventually must be filed in court, or if contracts must be drafted for establishing or dissolving a family business. Given that many of these legal issues are perplexing and potentially upsetting to families, they may seek out therapy to help deal with the turmoil, concurrent with their period of legal involvement.

Treatment may be sought that focuses primarily on getting supportive help to buoy them up during a particularly turbulent time. It may be focused on clarification of the issues at hand, providing a sounding board and a place to ventilate and say anything (including derogatory, critical statements about other professionals) without fear of reprisal. However, if the family members are unfamiliar with the adversarial system, they may want information about what to expect and how to comport themselves, how to find a suitable attorney, how to navigate in this unfamiliar terrain, and how to keep their anxiety under control. They may also need assistance in problem solving or encouragement to speak out in their own behalf, as in a domestic violence situation, or if they are professionals against whom malpractice charges have been filed. They will want the therapist to be conversant with legal and judicial processes and procedures so the data provided is accurate; where the therapist is unfamiliar with a specific area, it is incumbent upon him or her to say so and to tell the patients where they can obtain correct information.

Being empathic with their fears, worries, and even terror is essential. Some patients may need medication during a particularly trying period—such as if they are undergoing a criminal investigation by the IRS or if they are embroiled in a particularly bitter child-snatching situation. The clinician must be flexible in the selection of treatment interventions because they must be relevant to the pressing reality problems and the legal and judicial labyrinth in which the family's life has become entwined.

Because of the vast array of complex topics being addressed herein, a concerted effort has been made to have chapters authored by both attorneys and an array of mental health professionals including psychologists, psychiatrists, social workers, and marital and family therapists. Professionals drawn from these various disciplines are often involved with the same clients and must deal with similar issues, albeit from different perspectives. These chapters elucidate the importance of working collaboratively on behalf of "the client's best interest" while respecting that this may be interpreted quite differently by each professional. For example, the lawyer can usually represent only his or her individual client, while the therapist may be concerned about the couple or family as a unit and the impact of each one's behavior on the others. In many situations attorneys, seeking to have their client's position and goals prevail, fight hard for a win–lose outcome. Conversely, therapists emphasize an outcome that is beneficial to all—a win–win resolution. This fundamental disparity in the goals of these two professions often mitigates against collaborative efforts and leads to an essential tension between the two groups of professionals which in some instances is insurmountable.

A striking example in which professional differences may be manifested is the area of child custody. The therapist may be attempting to work with the couple conjointly to share and contribute to the children emotionally and financially, as well as legally and physically, in a way that is constructive and feasible. The therapist's goal is to allow the children to benefit most from what each parent has to offer in an arrangement that is reasonably stable and predictable. Concurrently, the attorneys may be working with their respective clients to mount cases proving that he or she should have primary physical and legal custody while the other parent is relegated to infrequent visitation and yet bears much of the financial responsibility. When this clash of goals occurs, the several professionals involved may be working at cross purposes, adding more havoc to the lives of families that are already experiencing trauma and stress. In other instances, as in the practice of divorce mediation, both lawyer mediators and mental health mediators concur that they are seeking a win–win agreement for the parties.

These tensions, the differing modi operandi, and the shared areas of concern about the client's well-being are amplified in the following chapters. What emerges clearly is that (a) concern for the clients is the primary shared concern; (b) many clients or patients are involved in both the mental health and legal systems concurrently and should not become triangulated between the various professionals nor be able to split them; (c) interprofessional dialogue and educational activities are helpful in promoting mutual understanding; and (d) it is incumbent upon the various professionals to know when they can and cannot work collaboratively, why or why not, and to explain this to the client, if need be.

Parts I to III deal with the psychological issues families may face within a family life cycle development perspective, beginning with the early years and family formation and raising young children, progressing through the middle years of raising adolescents and young adult children, and the later, postlaunching years. Some of the placement of specific chapters in a part is quite arbitrary; for example, one could place preparing a prenuptial agreement in later life before a second or third marriage rather than before the first marriage. And people may write wills at any time during their lives. We have tried to place each chapter where it seemed to belong most logically.

Similarly, an effort has been made to be reasonably inclusive, and yet we are sure some relevant arenas have been omitted—such as treating physicians, thera-pists, or attorneys while they are defendants in malpractice suits. It just is not pos-sible to include every exigency—we selected those that seem to occur with greatest frequency.

Part IV addresses the general forensic and ethical issues and guidelines that cir-cumscribe and impact on mental health practice and practitioners. This material now constitutes part of our requisite core knowledge base. In addition, for those wishing to incorporate or expand their forensic practice, recommendations for the preparation necessary for this demanding, exacting and challenging specialty are included.

We believe this book can be used as a text in family law, forensic psychology, and psychiatry courses, and will be useful to professionals from all law and men-tal health disciplines who are on the front lines of assisting clients to cope with life's transitions and the wonderful and tragic events that bring them to the offices of attorneys and therapists.

My profound appreciation is expressed to the contributing authors whose stel-lar chapters comprise this volume, and to the many colleagues, too numerous to mention individually, who have contributed to my knowledge of family theory and therapy and of forensic psychology. Specific thanks to my secretary, Gladys Adams, who has helped me in an infinite variety of ways to bring this book to fruition; to my husband, Solis Kaslow, who is always so patient and encouraging when I am struggling to write and edit a book; and to my brilliant editor at Wiley, Kelly Franklin, who recognized the need for a definitive *Handbook of Couple and Family Forensics*, an area in which I began teaching 23 years ago.

FLORENCE KASLOW, PhD
Palm Beach Gardens, Florida

Contents

Foreword

Most professionals who work with families, couples, and young children are very much oriented to being helpful and available. Deescalation of conflict is a primary focus. Frequently when psychologists, psychiatrists, social workers, and other family practitioners find that working with the family may entail involvement in legal proceedings, panic sets in.

When family conflict leads to litigation (as it often does) the treating doctor often becomes an "expert" subject to judicial rules, procedures, and expectations beyond his or her training. This leads to considerable stress. Many skillful and talented professionals withdraw from work with families after one or two stressful experiences with unexpected case complexities involving the courts.

This volume essentially takes the fear and confusion out of professional family practice when forensic issues make their appearance. The *Handbook of Couple and Family Forensics* provides an extremely useful guide as to the diverse problems, pitfalls, and opportunities inherent in the interaction between family and couples therapists and the law. This is a reference book that belongs in the readily available bookshelf of all couple and family practitioners and attorneys specializing in family law issues.

THEODORE H. BLAU, PHD
Tampa, Florida

PART ONE

WHEN FAMILIES IN TREATMENT INTERFACE WITH LEGAL AND JUDICIAL SYSTEMS

The Early Years—Family Formation and Young Children

CHAPTER 1

Prenuptial and Postnuptial Agreements

Sunny or Stormy Bellwethers to Marriage or Remarriage

FLORENCE W. KASLOW

THIS BOOK opens with a chapter on prenuptial agreements because they often serve as an overture to marriage and the family. As such, they may be the couple's first contact with the legal system and should be handled as deftly and skillfully as possible so as not to contribute to disillusioning the couple.

This chapter explores the rationale behind prenuptial and postnuptial agreements and their emotional, familial, and legal ramifications. Some guidelines are suggested to help defuse the anguish they stir up in some individuals, as well as to provide warning signs as to when the contents of the prenuptial agreement signal danger ahead. The potential positive aspects of both *psychosocial prenuptial accords* (Kaslow, 1991) and legal antenuptial and postnuptial agreements are addressed. The role of a mental health professional as therapist or mediator when a prenuptial is being considered is also explored.

ATTITUDES TOWARD MARRIAGE

Ideals of personal choice and individual freedom are highly valued in the United States (and in some other Western countries that prize autonomy, self-actualization, and democracy). Pioneers who came to this country disseminated the dream of liberty and equality for all. Dearly held traditions extant in countries from which our ancestors emigrated (and which still prevail today in parts of the world, particularly some Arab nations) in which parents selected their children's future partners based on principles of endogamy (marrying within the tribe or group), homogamy (similarity in background factors such as religion, race, and socioeconomic status), and "goodness of fit" of the two families were considered to be incompatible with

3

notions of autonomy and the right to individual choice. In North America, the practice of entering into marriages arranged by parents, sometimes through matchmakers (as portrayed in such Broadway shows as *Fiddler on the Roof* and *Hello Dolly*), was superseded by young people insisting on choosing their own mate based on *romantic love*. One "fell in love," married the person to whom they were attracted, and embarked on living out the fantasy of "happily ever after."

During the first centuries of this country's existence, practices of paying a bride price or providing a dowry were denigrated by many as old fashioned. Nevertheless, positive relics of this tradition have persisted in modernized versions. Families still contribute by purchasing trousseaus, and engagement and wedding gifts are given to help young couples begin marriage with new wardrobes and some of the material possessions they will need to embark on their lives together. Some families make lavish weddings and the new couple, depending on the financial circumstances of friends and family, might receive quite generous gifts of bonds and checks. But this has come to be considered voluntary, not mandatory. And in previous eras, marriage vows were taken with the belief that the union would exist "'til death do us part"; thus, few couples were worried about specifying how assets would be divided in the event of divorce.

Over time, fewer and fewer prospective bridegrooms have asked future fathers-in-law for their daughter's hand in marriage. By the mid to late 20th century, as an offshoot of the suffragette and feminist movements, daughters in many families no longer viewed themselves as possessions or chattel of their fathers; thus fathers no longer had veto power over their children's choices. Dad might lovingly walk his daughter down the aisle, but she was not his to sell or give away to any man. She was recognized as belonging to herself, and the young couple often became outraged if the two sets of parents wanted to negotiate any agreement.

What has become important is *being in love*, feeling happy with and excited by one another, and being with the person one desires. Consequently, contracts between families have become passé. Permission to marry is necessary only if the young woman is under the legal age of consent; asking the father for the young woman's hand in marriage is today a courtesy and a bow to custom.

In the United States for many decades, perhaps even centuries, the man's verbal proposal of marriage was a sufficient romantic declaration of his intent to love, honor, cherish, and protect. A woman's delighted, willing acceptance was enough to bind their mutual declaration of commitment. They could elope if they wanted to share this special occasion only with each other, or to avoid unwanted family control or feuding, or the turbulence and expense of planning a large wedding. A brief civil or religious ceremony consecrated the union. Nevertheless, the majority of couples still seek parental approval, and their involvement in the wedding festivities, including undertaking some (or all) of the costs. When parents do come together to discuss wedding plans and what each is willing to give to help the new couple get started (i.e., paying for a trousseau, honeymoon, some furniture, or a down payment on a house), usually such promises are given verbally, sealed with a handshake or a hug, and taken on faith. Rarely are these agreements written. If a parent reneges on his or her promises, there may be disappointment, rage, or estrangement. But rarely is legal action taken to enforce verbal promises.

Until the 1950s, marriage vows emphasized a lifelong commitment that was expected to endure "for better or for worse, in sickness and in health." People married young and stayed together for the sake of the children, to avoid the stigma of divorce, and to uphold family and religious expectations regarding the sanctity of marriage that were deeply engrained (Kaslow & Schwartz, 1987). Therefore, divorce rates were relatively low, remarriages occurred only if a spouse had died, and the couple shared in building their assets and paying their bills.

All of this has changed dramatically in the last three decades. More and more individuals now marry in their late 20s or in their 30s. Not only are they less dependent on their parents' desires and dictates emotionally, but also financially. Many have accumulated their own assets and wish to protect these in the event of divorce. They have seen their friends get raw deals in divorces and are not naïve enough to think that all marriages are made in heaven and will last "'til death do us part." They know death of the relationship may occur *before* the death of their partner (Schwartz & Kaslow, 1997).

This group of about-to-marry couples presents a different picture than the couple who get married in their late teens or early 20s and dream of building everything together. They are keenly aware that since the 1960s divorce rates have climbed above the 50% mark before hitting a plateau and beginning to slide downward slightly in 1988; their skepticism has some roots in statistical probability.

Also, remarriage rates have crescendoed to more than 75% for divorcees. Many of those entering second marriages "felt unjustly treated in the divorce settlements and wanted to guarantee that this would not happen again in the event of another divorce. This set the scene for the emergence of modern marital contracts and prenuptial agreements in the United States" (Kaslow, 1991, p. 376).

Thus, despite the fact that premarital agreements have been utilized in the United States for many decades, they did not assume prominence during the courtship/engagement/just-before-first-marriage phase until the late 1970s when expectations about the durability of marriage changed. Prior to then, couples married because they "fell in love" and wanted to spend the rest of their lives together. The assumption was that what each brought into the marriage would be shared; they would build a life together and whatever they acquired would belong to both of them. This was true for the vast majority of couples, unless they came from a family in the upper socioeconomic strata where an emphasis had been placed on protecting premarital assets by excluding them from becoming marital property, particularly if there was parental pressure to do so. In the past two decades prenuptial agreements have received much more attention in the media, and in lawyers' offices, leading to consideration of these by more couples. Consequently, more clients want to discuss their concerns about such contracts in therapists' offices before and after they have been entered into. If they do utilize such a contract, and the marriage is later splitting asunder, they may go to court to see if the agreement can be invalidated.

PRENUPTIAL ACCORDS: A PSYCHOSOCIAL VARIATION

Sager was one of the first in the couples therapy field to discuss marriage contracts (Sager, 1976). He and his colleagues elaborated this theme in the book *Treating the Remarried Family* (Sager et al., 1983), because they deemed the topic to be of great importance. Basically, he used the term *marriage contract* to denote not a formal written agreement but a document that illuminates the conscious and unconscious expectations each party holds for the relationship. Like Sager, and utilizing some of his suggested areas of query (Sager et al., 1983, pp. 355–361), I recommend to couples in premarital therapy, whether before a first or subsequent marriage, that they openly explore together what each desires to give to and receive from their partner. Frequently they are astonished to hear their future mates articulate their hopes and assumptions. Sometimes their two sets of ideas about lifestyle preferences, children, reciprocity, role expectations, and finances are quite disparate. Prior to the discussion in therapy each *assumes* congruence of values and goals because they are "so much in love" or have bonded as "soul mates."

Some individuals recoil at the idea of making their covert desires and expectations overt, as they think that by demystifying their heart's innermost longings they will detract from the romance. They want to maintain a veil of secrecy, and they subscribe to the myth that love conquers all. One or both cling to "the childish belief that because the partner loves him or her, he or she will magically know their every wish and need, and be delighted to attempt to satisfy these. Rarely does this idyllic vision come to fruition; more frequently it leads to frustration, disappointment and fury" (Kaslow, 1991, p. 377), as being in love does not make one's partner clairvoyant or omniscient.

I encourage clients to reveal their hopes, fears, mixed emotions, and ambivalent wishes to each other and to consider their future commitment to one another and to other members of each of their families. This includes, but is not limited to, children from previous unions and sick or elderly parents, as well as other healthy members of their respective families of origin. Each brings along visible and invisible prior loyalties (Boszormenyi-Nagy & Spark, 1973/1984) that will impact on the forthcoming marriage; these will need to be respected and honored. To assume one will not continue to pay child support or alimony, talk to an ex-spouse about the children, or want to be involved in the children's lives is unrealistic, and even destructive. The children from an earlier marriage predate the new relationship; there exist many binding ties, and these necessarily are a part of the new marital package (Kaslow, 1993b), as is amply demonstrated in the following case:

CASE 1—MR. GREEN AND MISS BARKETT: HOW CENTRAL SHOULD HIS CHILDREN BE?

Phil Green was 42 and had been divorced for 6 years. His 16-year-old son, Don, and his 13-year-old daughter, Gina, lived with their mother in another state, and she had primary residential status. He saw them over Easter, Labor Day, and Christmas, and had them every July. He willingly paid child support and had maintained a reasonably good relationship with his children, whom he loved dearly. He was, at the time of his engagement to Julia, very involved in helping Don in his college search process. Although his marital settlement agreement (MSA) did not obligate him to pay for his children's college education (and graduate or professional school costs), he planned to do so. His children were bright, and he wanted to provide them with the best education that he could afford and that they wanted to acquire.

Julia Barkett was 28 years of age and single. She had fallen madly in love with Phil Green, whom she saw as debonair, intelligent, and prosperous. All had gone very well during their 6-month courtship, and she had become absorbed in planning their wedding. Bill wanted his children to play a central role in their wedding and the festivities, and wanted their maternal grandparents, with whom he maintained contact and who were terrific to his children, to be invited. He preferred to postpone their wedding until after the children's Christmas vacation so he would not miss one of his all-too-infrequent visits with them. Julia was perturbed by these preexisting emotional entanglements, and felt that his children's and ex-in-laws' presence would detract from her day to be the star. She convinced Bill that they should go for premarital therapy, hoping the therapist would side with her.

Rapidly it became obvious that they had not discussed their individual assumptions; rather, each had assumed concordance because they enjoyed the same activities, restaurants, friends, and sports. They had loads of fun together. Their sex life was great; they described their being together as a perfect fit. In response to the therapist's questions, Phil said he intuitively thought Julia, who was so affectionate with him, would like and enjoy his children, would welcome them at their home, and would be eager to go on trips with them. His children were old enough to travel with them and not be a burden; also, he planned to have them visit more often than in the past, as soon as he and his future wife had a home suitable for the children's stays. In addition, he envisioned a residence large enough to accommodate friends they might bring along. Consequently, he had agreed to buy a big home with a pool and patio that far exceeded the space needs of just a couple.

Phil's fiancée reacted with chagrin and astonishment at what he conveyed. She had surmised that with her as his lover and best friend he would not need the children as much, and that they would travel alone together on holidays and not be tied down. Her motivation for buying a large manse was that they would be able to entertain friends lavishly, something both enjoyed doing, and in anticipation of soon starting "a real family of our own." Until that moment Phil was unaware that she wanted to have children; she took for granted that he "just knew" that she did and that he, too, wanted a family of their own. His children did not figure significantly in her projections for the future.

The revelation of these divergent life plans evoked great anxiety; each said they needed some time alone to rethink their commitment. Throughout the next 2 months they did a great deal of soul searching and finally decided their love was strong enough to overcome the differences, and so they chose to go ahead with their marriage. Julia said she recognized that Phil was part of a package deal that was acceptable to her and to which she would be graciously responsive. When he realized how important having a child was to her, he expressed willingness to have a second family. The far-reaching impact of this accord for them and for his children was explored thoroughly. They engaged in many truthful dialogues, and each worked toward a *win–win* compromise. Eventually both were satisfied that they had come to understand each other's needs and wishes better through their honest conversations about feelings and expectations. Out of this give-and-take process, each felt jubilant about setting a wedding date, and about life beyond the honeymoon.

THE PSYCHOSOCIAL PRENUPTIAL ACCORD

It is posited here that this kind of process should be engaged in prior to the formulation of a legal prenuptial agreement. What follows details how this might be accomplished.

It has proven useful to request that couples write down (a) their expectations of the marriage regarding such matters as loyalty and fidelity, handling of children, security, and accountability (Sager, et al., 1983); (b) their emotional and physical needs vis-à-vis closeness and distance, power distribution, and styles of communication; (c) their views about external issues that often contribute to marital discord, such as "relationship to respective families of origin, former in-law families, and friends" (Kaslow, 1991); and (d) their attitudes and values about a home; about earning, saving, spending, and contributing money; and toward sexuality. As can be seen in the Green case, many of these issues surfaced in their personal and couple narratives (White & Epstom, 1990) and were the focal concerns brought to therapy.

Some couples find it sufficient to talk about these issues alone together as a first step to resolving differences that could become major problems. Others find it more useful to write down their thoughts separately and then discuss them. If this process reveals incongruities and incompatibilities, which often happens, these issues can then be brought into therapy for resolution. If the clinician believes the couple will run into serious disagreements if they have these dialogues when alone, the entire process can be conducted as part of therapy so they can sort it out with someone objective who can cushion the shock waves *and* be the voice of reason. At times great disparities emerge and the pair may realize that they are happy together as lovers, but that a long-term marriage probably would be a nightmare. Conversely, others who go through this self-revelation and sharing process find that it enriches their capacity for intimacy and mutual appreciation (Schnarch, 1991). They can then formalize their commitment and goals into a pact that I call a *psychosocial prenuptial accord* (Kaslow, 1991).

Their contract may be verbal or written; the latter is preferable so they can peruse it in the future as a reminder of the dream they agreed to pursue together. It should be written with clarity and specificity, and should embody what each wants and is willing to give. When this occurs, following a candid and sincere give-and-take process, the marriage has a good likelihood of being built on a solid emotional and financial foundation.

During the process of negotiating the accord, the couple has a prolonged opportunity to learn how to tune into each other, how to compromise (Dreyfus, 1990), and how to seek a win–win solution (Schwartz & Kaslow, 1997). Developing these skills can enable them to generate a shared model for problem solving that should stand them in good stead when conflicts arise in the future (Lewis, Beavers, Gossett, & Phillips, 1976), and for reconsidering their promises to one another periodically when the need to do so arises. For example, a woman who has stated that she wants to continue her career when they have children and intends to return to work when the baby is 6 weeks to 3 months old may later truly change her mind and want to stay home and care for the baby herself, rather than dropping it off at a nursery. Conversely, a woman who knew she would love mothering and has told her fiance that she would gladly trade her career for it may find that she feels too confined and cannot wait to go back to work. Change of opinions, needs, and wants is inevitable, and each party should do their best to accommodate them. What is untenable and sometimes unforgiveable is when a partner has agreed to something that he or she had no intention of doing—for example, the deliberate deception perpetrated when a woman tells her betrothed that she is eagerly looking forward to motherhood even though she knows in her heart that she does not want children, but realizes he might not marry her if she told him this.

This self-disclosure negotiation process is valid only if both parties conduct themselves with utmost integrity. This entails being willing to allow any hidden agendas to surface and receive attention before the wedding rather than seeping out later and causing grave distress because major issues were kept buried. Interestingly, some couples who write their own wedding vows incorporate portions of what they have included in their psychosocial accord into their ceremony.

Therapists of all theoretical orientations can help couples during the premarriage or pre-remarriage stage of their lives to forge such agreements and to find the discovery process a marvelous channel for getting to know each other better. If such a task-centered process is incongruent with a particular clinician's therapeutic philosophy and style, or if an impasse arises because each party has taken on a strong defensive posture, or the therapist is not adept at the art of negotiation (Fisher & Ury, 1981), a referral to a mediator skilled in helping couples draft personalized (not boilerplate) prenuptial psychosocial accords may be advisable.

Unfortunately, prenuptial documents that emphasize psychosocial considerations have received little coverage. Rather, the traditional antenuptial contract that deals with financial matters and legal rights has been showcased. "Whereas moving toward the former tends to lessen interpersonal barriers and lead to voluntary revelations about the innermost self, thoughts of the latter legal document raise fears and resistances, and often become an obstacle to the pair's ability to achieve closeness and harmony" (Kaslow, 1991, p. 299). It is posited here that *it is feasible and valuable to have the psychosocial premarital accord reached before the couple engages in having a legal antenuptial contract drawn up.*

LEGAL PRENUPTIAL AGREEMENTS

The following discusses some important concerns to be considered in drawing up an antenuptial contract.

BACKGROUND DATA AND STATUTORY PROVISIONS

The National Conference of Commissioners on Uniform State Laws (NCCUSL) approved the Uniform Premarital Agreements Act in 1983, and recommended its adoption in all states (George, 1984). The core provisions of the act define the word *prenuptial*, clarify the elements needed to make it a valid agreement, and delineate what premarriage agreements are not allowed to cover.

In Section 1 of the Model Act, antenuptial agreements are defined as contracts between future partners prepared in contemplation of marriage. Section 2 specifies that the contract must be written and must be signed by both parties. Section

3 indicates that the prenuptial agreement may cover the ownership, use, and disposition of real estate *and* personal property, both during the marriage and in the event of divorce or the death of either partner. The document may include provisions that predetermine the nature and extent of possible future alimony. The act allows such agreements to provide great breadth regarding most issues that the future spouses might want to specify, providing they do not violate public policy (George, 1984, p. 25). Provisos for child support contained in a *prior* marital settlement agreement must be fulfilled. But they cannot predetermine *future* financial responsibility for children of the forthcoming marriage.

In the past 15 years many states have passed modified versions of the Uniform Premarital Agreements Act. Therefore, what may be encompassed in a formal prenuptial contract is partially dictated by state law. Such agreements can delineate a wide array of rights and obligations by containing clauses regarding property disposition in the event of separation, divorce, or death; the creation of a will, trust, or other instrument that will affect the marriage contract; death benefits specified in life insurance policies; and other items that do not go counter to law or public policy.

Most state statutes also elucidate what types of premarital agreements are invalid. Agreements that may subsequently be held to be unenforceable are those that one party signed under duress, ones in which the terms of the agreement later were deemed unconscionable, or ones that were not signed by witnesses. An agreement is *unconscionable* when one party was not given "fair and reasonable" information by the other and did not have adequate knowledge of the other's financial or property interests. Unless there has been full disclosure by both parties, and adequate comprehension of the intent and content of the contract, a sound decision as to whether to sign the pact cannot be made.

CONTENT AND OBJECTIVES

A premarital contract should start with a preamble that articulates the overall intent of the agreement and indicates that it goes beyond planning for the possibility of divorce. On a positive note, it can also serve as a document for taking care of and providing for one another through offering certain strong assurances. This latter goal is enhanced by incorporation of the provisions of the psychosocial accord discussed earlier.

This type of prenuptial agreement also may function as a blueprint drawn up to *protect* one partner's property, income, and other assets from the other in the event of divorce or death. A strong criticism of prenuptial agreements is that they are philosophically in contradiction to the ideal of marriage as being built on commitment, good faith, and a desire to share in all realms of living—emotional, sexual, intellectual, spiritual, and financial. When the process of preparing a prenuptial agreement is undertaken, there seems to be an implicit assumption, which is sometimes accurate, that one person may be marrying the other for monetary gain—that is, "to become instantly wealthier and to have an immediate claim on the other's assets in the case of a divorce. The more affluent party may want to guard him/herself and his/her children and perhaps parents against a greedy newcomer who might not be considerate and fair in a future divorce action"

(Kaslow, 1991, p. 380). Thus, when one partner doubts the other's integrity and motives for getting married to him or her, how the assets would be divided in case of a separation must be predetermined. Some premarital agreements even go so far as mandating the surrender of any right to sharing the fruits acquired by (joint) marital energies (Du Canto, 1991, p. 83).

Such stringent agreements, based on high levels of suspiciousness, do not bode well for the marriage. Conversely, if a psychosocial prenuptial accord has been carefully and compassionately crafted conjointly, the level of mutual trust should be solid and the couple should be able to consider the financial issues in a way that engenders less distrust and tension. It is no wonder that some relationships teeter-totter when the prospect of a prenuptial agreement is introduced into an otherwise affectionate, friendly, and enjoyable relationship.

In the past 15 years I have been consulted by many couples about to embark on second marriages, and numerous others getting ready to divorce who had previously signed antenuptial contracts. A repetitive theme has emerged that reflects much deep-seated conflict, and even rage. The pattern is that some time after the wedding invitations have been sent out, the groom says, "Darling, I need you to sign some papers." He quickly assures her, "It's nothing to worry about; it's only a necessary formality."

If his fiancée is bright, she peruses the document and realizes that, contrary to what he has said, this is quite serious. She notes clauses that protect his assets and minimize her entitlements. Many prenuptial agreements state that in the event of a divorce she may receive a settlement of *x* dollars for each month they were married, and that if her husband predeceases her she will receive a stipulated amount per month for the balance of her life. Said income may be specified as coming from the income of an irrevocable trust established for his children. The document may also specify that upon her death, any assets she has received from him revert to his family; nothing can be given to her children or grandchildren.

The woman is often astonished and distressed at how tightly and painstakingly everything has been predetermined. The idea that he had it drawn up absent any discussion with her, and gave it to her to sign without considering her wishes, strikes her as controlling and self-centered. She looks up and says, "I'm shocked and disturbed that you would do this and in this way; I need to go over it with my attorney." He acts bewildered and denies that this will alter anything. He all too often blurts out, "Don't you trust me? You know I wouldn't do anything to hurt you, or anything that is unfair."

She feels trapped in a "damned if I do and damned if I don't" double bind (Watzlawick, 1963). The tension mounts; she wants neither to antagonize him nor to be too quick to sign a contract that appears not to be in her best interest. She tries to convey—sweetly or angrily—that she would have much preferred if he had broached the subject of wanting a prenuptial agreement and they had then discussed each other's needs and wishes and what they hoped to accomplish, before either had gone to an attorney to formalize an agreement that clearly appeared to favor his interests at the expense of hers. He responds—either angrily or feigning mystification—that he didn't realize she was so self-involved and so interested in acquiring a quick claim on his assets. She may retaliate by accusing him of being stingy, insensitive, and domineering, and of wanting her only as a beautiful trophy wife (if she is substantially younger than he) or as a nurse and caretaker (if he is elderly and infirm).

She becomes plagued with mixed emotions—understanding the implications of his behavior, yet wanting to deny them. With the wedding scheduled in a few weeks, she is torn between breaking off and being embarrassed, or complying with his wishes while seething inside. Time may not permit renegotiation of the contract, and he may be intransigent about changing its substance. Postponing the wedding would be costly and humiliating. In many cases she has been single for a long time and knows there are not many interesting, available men around. Plus she "loves" him and hopes that after they are married, he will come to appreciate her more and become more generous. She may be able to seduce, cajole, or shame him into some minor alterations in the contract, but she refrains from precipitating a major brouhaha that might provoke him into breaking the engagement.

His high-handed intimidation works; she represses her trepidation and hopes she has worried needlessly. Friends and perhaps even her lawyer may have reassured her that the agreement can be declared null and void later if he did not fully disclose all of his assets, or that once they are happily married she can prevail upon him to draw up a postnuptial agreement that, once signed, will supersede the prenuptial agreement and be more to her benefit. Feeling a little more optimistic and a little less betrayed, she decides to take the risk and proceed with the wedding.

Conversely, if Darling is less intelligent than the woman just described, or is quite compliant, she signs the agreement to placate him. He stashes it away (just in case he needs it in the future). For now, she is blissfully unaware of what has occurred and continues to enjoy and trust him. If and when a divorce is imminent, she will try to find the toughest matrimonial lawyer she can to argue that she signed the prenuptial agreement under duress, and to find a loophole to prove that he did not produce full disclosure of assets. Such divorces tend to be ultrabitter and hotly contested.

INTERGENERATIONAL CONCERNS

Some betrothed couples, before a first or second marriage, want to combine all of their assets, as they believe that they should totally commit all they are and have to each other. They look forward to sharing in all realms of their being together. Nonetheless, a dissident note may be introduced by a parent who insists on a prenuptial agreement. Rarely does this occur in families that are poor. They have little to protect and are wrapped up in daily survival tasks. It is on the upper rungs of the socioeconomic ladder that the future disposition of family wealth may be a serious concern. Such families do not want their assets to flow out of the family in the event of divorce, and will band together to prevent this from becoming a possibility.

The engaged couple may come for therapy, deeply distressed over the parent's "intrusiveness" in their affairs. Their dismay is heightened if a parent has threatened to disinherit or disown the engaged son or daughter if the future partner does not sign a prenuptial agreement—prepared by the *parent's* attorney. The couple feels ensnared; they want neither to alienate the parents nor to lose access to the family and its substantial resources. Nonetheless, they do not want to permit their life to be dominated by parental fiats nor have it be overshadowed by pessimism and an aura of distrust. Yet an intelligent, reality-oriented adult child of an affluent family may realize that in light of the high divorce rate, parental fears that the marriage may end in divorce have a 50% chance of being accurate, and he or she may appreciate that the parents (or other relatives) do not want the assets that have been accumulated through decades of hard work and sound investing to be diverted out of the family as part of a divorce settlement. Thus, what seems like a dictatorial stance may emanate from experiential wisdom and intergenerational family loyalty bonds (Boszormenyi-Nagy & Spark, 1973/1984).

Some nonnegotiable demands for prenuptial agreements arise when the engaged son or daughter is involved in a family business (Kaslow & Kaslow, 1991). The soon-to-be in-law child (Horsley, 1996) may be perceived as a potential interloper who could eventually weaken or destroy the corporation by suing for a portion of the assets, including shares of stock, as part of a property settlement. These fears are rooted in reality as this does happen, and not infrequently. Ultimately it also can lead to an attempt at a hostile takeover by the existing in-law child.

All involved should be aware that assets accrued during the duration of the marriage are held to be marital assets that are divisible (Schwartz & Kaslow, 1997). This includes but is not limited to shares in the business, profit sharing and retirement plans, and funds invested in pension plans. Because of all these legal stipulations, caution is warranted from the perspective of the senior generation family members who therefore believe protective measures should be set in place at the outset.

Conversely, to the prospective in-law adult child, the insistence that an antenuptial contract be signed in which he or she renounces any future claim to all business assets is likely to set up an adversarial situation, as it clearly does not express a warm welcome to the family. Rather, it seems to herald that he or she is to be a nonentity in the spouse's family constellation.

The young couple may turn to a therapist or a mediator to arrange a multigenerational session with them and parents who are expressing their concerns so forcefully. (See Framo, 1981, for discussion on conducting multigenerational sessions.) The aim is to "foster greater mutual understanding, respect, and some modicum of trust, and to forge a compromise that is acceptable to all involved parties so that it is a win–win and not a win–lose situation" (Kaslow, 1991, p. 381). If this crisis is not averted, the in-law child will continue to be perceived as an intruder and will grow increasingly resentful. Another consequence is that the son or daughter will feel pulled between two forces competing for his or her loyalty. The parents will believe they need to be vigilant to guard their territory and may later find, as a consequence of what has transpired, that they are expected to be peripheral in the lives of their grandchildren. Such a scenario depletes and destroys family integrity, ties, continuity, and the legacy of love. When financial considerations are allowed to triumph over and eclipse emotional ones, the outcome may be pervasive disharmony and rancor in the extended family system.

Although the shadow of a prenuptial agreement hovering near may run counter to the notion that love conquers all, many financial planners, like attorneys, recommend that such a contract be written. Bernstein (1990) posits that there are advantages to spelling out in advance how property will be divided up in case of divorce.

Courts take into consideration the emotional dilemmas that accompany prenuptial agreements; thus judges are apt to scrutinize such pacts more thoroughly than they would other documents. Those who do not desire that their agreements be open to challenge later are expected to adhere to the following *principles* (Bernstein, 1990, and amplified and revised by the current author):

- Each party should be represented by their own lawyer, and this person should be someone who specializes in the matrimonial field. Sensitive, promarriage lawyers should be sought.
- Full disclosure of all assets should be made. Anything less may constitute fraud.
- The contract should specify the parties' intention regarding whether premarital assets are to be considered joint or separate property. Since statutes mandate that the interest that accrues on premarital property during the marriage may be considered marital property and therefore subject to distribution at the time of divorce, they may want to stipulate their future preference regarding how the enhancement amount will be protected.
- If there is a business involved, the prenuptial agreement should provide for the buyout of one party's stock by the other (*Family Business Review, 1988–1998*). If the new spouse is to be appointed or elected an officer or director in a family business, there should be a clause requiring the future spouse to resign if and when a divorce is sought, and to agree in advance not to cause the business to be liquidated as part of a property settlement.
- The agreement should be discussed, prepared, signed, and notarized several months prior to the wedding. Signing too close to the time of the wedding could later lead to charges of duress, and this could cause the prenuptial agreement to be decreed null and void.
- The parties might also decide to include sections on the following:
    1. Division of financial responsibilities, that is, who is to do and pay for what, and even when and how.
    2. Consequences in case of contract violations.

If either party will be entering the marriage with debts rather than assets (such as debts for college loans or car payments), it is essential that the couple predetermine together who is to repay these, how, and when. Also, if future debts are to be incurred, the couple would be wise to agree in advance on what kinds of items they are willing to purchase on installment or by acquiring loans. Will they cosign loans and purchase a home as joint tenants by the entirety, or will transactions occur in single name? Some discussion of these potentially volatile issues is advisable so that they can cocreate a blueprint for their shared future.

CAN THE PRENUPTIAL AGREEMENT
BE INVALIDATED?

When a divorce is imminent, the aggrieved partner may try to find a loophole to have the premarital contract declared invalid. An antenuptial contract may be declared null and void by the court if it finds it to be unfair, to have not been negotiated in good faith, or to have been entered into under duress (Frumkes & Greene, 1984). Unfair pacts are inequitable ones that place one spouse at a definite disadvantage. Prenuptial agreements must be based on full disclosure of all assets. No misrepresentation, fraud, or coercion is allowable. Nonetheless, it is still quite difficult to have a prenuptial agreement set aside "unless allegations which may include, but are not limited to, fraud, misrepresentation, undue influence or withholding information can be clearly substantiated" (Kaslow, 1991, p. 383).

SAMPLE RELEVANT COURT DECISIONS

- In a *California* case (*Pablano v. Pablano*, 1980), the court invalidated the prenuptial agreement for reasons of fraud and duress. Allegedly the man had told the woman she must sign the contract or he would not marry her. They were living a great distance from her home and she did not want to return home in disgrace, so she capitulated and signed the pact.
- Similarly, in *Norris v. Norris* (1979), a *District of Columbia* court found an agreement to be invalid because it had been signed one hour before the wedding and the woman was not made aware of her future mate's true worth (from Freed, 1984).
- In *Sieg v. Sieg* (1995), the woman had waived all claims to her husband's estate in a premarital agreement. After her husband's death, Mrs. Sieg distributed all of his assets to herself as the sole heir. However, the *Georgia* court decided that Mr. Sieg's mother and sister could have the prenuptial agreement enforced because it was an actual legal settlement agreement. The court upheld a restraining order to prevent Mrs. Sieg from depleting the assets of the estate.
- In *Rider v. Rider* (1995), an *Indiana* court decreed that a premarital agreement that denied the wife maintenance was "unconscionable." Further, the court stated that unconscionability would be determined at the time of divorce. They held that an agreement would not be enforced when it would deprive an ex-mate of the reasonable support she or he could not otherwise obtain.
- In *Ritz v. Ritz* (1995), a *Louisiana* court held a prenuptial agreement to be void merely because one of the witnesses did not sign it until after the ceremony, and then did so outside of the presence of the parties.
- In *New York*, in the same year, the decision went in the opposite direction *In re the Estate of Garbarde* (1995). In this case an appellate court held that a wife was not entitled to have a prenuptial agreement invalidated because of her husband's alleged fraud, particularly because she had signed the contract willingly. Evidence that the agreement had been executed a few brief hours prior to the wedding and that she was not advised that the agreement provided for a waiver of her elective rights was not sufficient to establish evidence of fraud.

Some kinds of stipulations have been found to be unenforceable. For example:

- *In re Marriage of Weiss* (1996), the prenuptial agreement contained a clause that the children would be raised in the Jewish faith. The *California* court held this to be unenforceable because these are religious terms contained in a secular agreement. Such terms are not likely to be upheld in the event of a challenge.

These court cases and the decisions rendered by the several courts in a number of quite different states serve to illustrate that despite the fact that these all initially emanated from the same federal Uniform Premarital Agreement Act (George, 1984), there are variations between the states and sometimes rather definite contradictions, as in the Louisiana and New York decisions alluded to in the foregoing section regarding the necessity of having a witness present at the time of the signing of the agreement.

If the couples alluded to in these court cases had entered into the kind of discussion that is inherent in the process of creating a mutually acceptable prenuptial psychosocial accord, they might have avoided these discordant battles at the time of the dissolution of their marriages. They might then have averted the strife and the financial costs inherent in legal contests, and both parties would have fared better.

MODIFICATION OF PRENUPTIAL AGREEMENTS

An often heard criticism of prenuptials is that, once written and signed, they are nonmodifiable. Du Canto (a past president of the American Academy of Matrimonial Lawyers) posited that "premarital agreements have their weak links in the legal chain, primarily because they do not contain any mechanisms or techniques for change. Often they are written when anxiety over success of a new venture [the marriage] may be high, and forever form an obstacle to the couple's relationship" (1991, p. 83). He suggested that contracts should include a proviso conducive to subsequent alterations so that if the relationship seems likely to last, a revised version that augments what the spouse's share is and will be can be substituted. He suggested another course of action also—a preset time frame of 10 years before the initial prenuptial agreement is "sunset." I have found that for some a happy, pleasurable union of 5 years may be enough to warrant writing a new pact in which the assets are shared more, or to agree that the prenuptial agreement is no longer in effect and to take the legal steps necessary to cancel its existence.

"This option to rewrite the prenuptial by mutual consent based on an enduring and solid marital record certainly has some compelling logic to commend it" (Kaslow, 1991, p. 384).

Sometimes a prenuptial agreement is originally written with a phase-out clause to take effect at the conclusion of 5 or 10 years of marriage; that is, it will automatically cease to exist and the distribution that will occur in the event of death will be specified in a will or trust instead (see Chapter 20 of this book). Should the couple later decide to divorce, at that point the terms of the settlement would be negotiated. Although initially such a time-limited clause may tend to soften the idea of a prenuptial agreement, odious as it is to some, it can boomerang. On various occasions when such phase-out clauses have been in effect, I have seen husbands in shaky marriages rush to file a divorce action so that the decree will be granted prior to the time when the expiration clause in the prenuptial agreement would come into play, rather than staying married and trying to improve the relationship. They resent the prospect of having to share their assets in accordance with equitable distribution laws if a divorce were to occur later (see, for example, Florida Dissolution of Marriage—Children Act, 1982/1992) and are not willing to take that risk. The wife may be baffled about why he refuses to invest time in trying to make the relationship better until she realizes he's racing against a financial time clock. Once again she feels taken advantage of, and sometimes duped or tricked. At that point, a nasty battle to invalidate the prenuptial agreement may ensue.

POSTNUPTIAL AGREEMENTS

As indicated previously, if a couple did not draw up a premarital agreement and later concur that they want a written and binding agreement to specify how their assets will be distributed in the event of death or divorce, a postnuptial agreement is an appropriate document. Also, such a contract can become a substitute for or a modification of an antenuptial agreement, or it can be written so as to ensure that one partner regains control of assets that he or she brought into the marriage and then comingled with the spouse's funds.

Ordinarily the same guidelines prevail that govern prenuptial agreements. Postnuptial agreements differ from prenuptials only in timing; that is, they are promulgated after the couple is married. Generally, postnuptial agreements are upheld in court, and, like prenuptials, they are harder to have invalidated if each spouse has utilized separate legal counsel. The agreement should attest that each person has disclosed all assets and has carefully reviewed the terms. Such pacts should specify how the appreciated value of any property will be dispersed.

Here, too, coercion is unacceptable under law (but may occur unbeknownst to others). I have been the therapist in several cases where I have been aware that a husband or wife had threatened an infirm or rapidly deteriorating mate with abandonment or divorce unless a postnuptial was agreed to and signed, or the will was rewritten in accordance with his or her wishes. Unless the ill spouse has access to an attorney, guardian, or other competent, responsible person, he or she will have no one to tell about the treachery, and the new missive may well be upheld in court.

Sample Relevant Court Decisions

- In *Cook v. Cook*, the *Nevada* court, in 1996, found that a lawyer-husband has a fiduciary relationship to his wife. Therefore, any property settlement agreement he drafts will be subject to close scrutiny to ensure that there has been full and fair disclosure and that no fraud or overreaching has taken place. As a matter of law, the husband had breached those duties when (a) he threatened his wife, telling her not to retain counsel; (b) he kept his law practice without ascribing a value to it; and (c) he failed to give her an income for a certain number of years, while (d) holding her liable for taxes.
- In a fascinating case, the *New York* Court of Appeals rejected a flexible inter-

pretation of the Domestic Relations Law (DRL) on May 8, 1997, ruling that a nuptial agreement is unenforceable unless it complies with the statutory requirement of a "formal acknowledgment," through a certificate provided by a witness (Spencer, 1997). Although both spouses had signed the premarital contract, in which each renounced any claim to the other's property, and there was no claim of fraud or misunderstanding, the court held that the requirement of *DRL* 236B(3) that the agreement be acknowledged by a witness was essential (Spencer, 1997). Further, the justices, in a unanimous decision, opined that a bright-line rule "requiring an acknowledgment in every case is easy to apply and places couples and their legal advisers on clear notice of the prerequisites to a valid nuptial agreement" (Spencer, 1997, p. 1).

In the case under consideration, *Matisoff v. Dobi*, No. 76, Stephen Dobi sought to enforce a postnuptial agreement to disallow any claims by Louise Matisoff to property held in his name when their 13-year marriage ended in 1994 (Spencer, 1997). Originally Ms. Matisoff had insisted on the agreement, which they signed 1 month after their marriage in 1981. Both spouses were then earning about $40,000 per year. Because Mr. Dobi had already had two divorces, she wanted the agreement to protect *her* real property and other assets in the event that their marriage also turned out to be unsuccessful.

But the material circumstances had changed markedly by the time the divorce action was filed in 1992. Mr. Dobi had earned an MBA and joined an investment firm as a stock analyst. His annual salary had jumped to over $400,000. Ms. Matisoff's income was still about $40,000. Her lawyer argued that the contract was *unenforceable because it was not formally acknowledged.*

The trial court concurred, and ruled that the agreement was invalid. The court held that Mr. Dobi's increased earning potential, valued at $2.8 million, *was* marital property. It awarded 40 percent of it to his soon-to-be ex-wife.

The Appellate Division reversed, holding that the "acknowledgment requirement" in *DRL* 236B(3) was not absolute, and that the purpose of preventing fraud had been achieved.

The court not only noted that Ms. Matisoff had initiated the original agreement to protect her own interests, that it was drawn up by her attorney, "that she testified she had signed it, and that she made no claim of fraud" (Spencer, 1997, p. 2), but also pointed out that the spouses maintained separate finances throughout their marriage.

However, subsequently the Court of Appeals stated that the statutory language requiring acknowledgment is clear and precise, and that there is "no exception to the requirement of formal acknowledgment."

The court emphasized that the legislature had "opted for a bright-line rule" rather than a flexible rule that permitted consideration of extenuating circumstances.

- A Common Pleas Court judge in *Pennsylvania*, upholding the terms of a postnuptial agreement, ordered a man to loan his wife $10,000. The agreement specified that Richard Laudenslager should loan this amount to his wife, Marilyn. However, he refused to make the loan when he learned that she had received a loan from someone else; he said this violated their agreement.

In this case, *Laudenslager v. Laudenslager* (PICS No. 96-5670, [C.P. Berks Feb. 27, 1996]), the Judge stated that the agreement was clear and must be enforced. He held that "the essence of the bargain is that Richard is to give Marilyn a loan for the sole purpose of buying a home." He opined, "there is nothing in the agreement which prohibits Marilyn from obtaining another loan at any time"; thus he concluded it was the husband's duty to release the $10,000.

These three cases provide but a glimpse of the range of issues that may be brought to the attention of a court pursuant to upholding or invalidating a post-nuptial agreement. This is another expanding and complex area of legal and judicial practice, and the decisions made have long-term consequences for the future emotional and financial well-being of all involved parties.

GUIDELINES FOR THERAPISTS AND MEDIATORS

With the vast increase in the number of couples considering prenuptial and post-nuptial agreements, therapists and mediators (as well as attorneys) should know as much about these documents as possible in order to maximize their ability to provide information so that a couple can objectively consider the pros and cons for themselves. These professionals may also want to hone their knowledge and skills to help couples formulate what they want contained in such an agreement, if they decide to proceed with creating one, or know who they can refer them to for this type of assistance. Nonlawyers must be careful that they do not inadvertently exceed their competence and practice law instead of forensic psychology (mental health). The following guidelines, which flow from the preceding discussion of expectations, dreams, disappointments, and hurts, may prove valuable to professionals when assisting couples who are negotiating such agreements (Kaslow, 1991):

- *Empathic listening and responding.*   Acknowledge the sensitivity of the concerns to be covered in the agreement. By conveying respect to each of the individuals and fostering a context of mutual consideration and openness, the therapist or mediator can promote an honest exchange about the feelings that are being stirred up, as well as about the substance of the contract.
- *Sensitivity to conscious and unconscious wishes, motivations, intent, and feelings.* It is essential to bring hidden agendas to the surface and to unveil the resistances to self-disclosure. The residuals from a previous marriage, including unresolved relational and financial dilemmas with the prior spouse, must be revealed and handled, and hopefully brought to closure (Kaslow, 1993a).
- *Issues revolving around children from previous relationships.*   Have the couple explore expectations regarding responsibilities to, accountability for, and ideas about sharing of authority pertaining to children from prior marriages (Kaslow, 1993b). Parenting and visitation schedules, children's activities, and financial commitments also merit serious consideration by the couple conjointly.
- *Loyalties and legacies from and to families of origin and extended family members.* It is crucial for the new couple to explore positive and negative emotional,

existential, and financial bonds and obligations to their respective families of origin, and to consider the type of future relationships they envision with them. This may also extend to consideration of relationships with prior in-law families (Horsley, 1996).

* *Utilizing a problem-solving model for reaching decisions.* Through brainstorming numerous alternatives and then selecting what appears to both individuals to be the best solution for each problem or issue, the couple learns how to view their dilemmas together and work toward resolution (de Shazer, 1988), utilizing input from both in a synergistic discussion as they find a win–win solution.

Although lawyers who draft prenuptial and postnuptial contracts can represent only one party and will seek to protect that client's interests, from a humanistic perspective of concern for the long-term well-being of that person in his or her relational context, an abiding commitment to the principle of fairness and an awareness of the guidelines elucidated earlier may help them to write agreements that are less skewed to one side and that do not precipitate as much distrust, angst, and sense of foreboding.

Occasionally a prospective mate is told not to worry about the prenuptial agreement because everything will be taken care of later to their satisfaction in the will. Therefore, it is imperative that therapists and mediators be aware of the fact, as attorneys are, that a will can be altered at any time, unilaterally and secretively, so this guarantee may prove meaningless. Conversely, a prenuptial or postnuptial agreement should be a *bilateral* accord, fashioned by both parties, and it should be stressed that it can be modified only *by mutual consent.* Therefore, it is a safer document for articulating and protecting each person's wishes and needs than a will may be.

SUMMARY AND RECOMMENDATIONS

Prenuptial psychosocial accords and legal agreements are intensely personal instruments and should reflect the idiosyncratic desires, personalities, and circumstances of each specific couple. These missives should be evolved as expressions of the couple's most deeply held wishes, beliefs, dreams, hopes, trepidations, longings, and expectations. Forging such an agreement can be a profoundly enriching experience that augments the couple's knowledge and appreciation of one another, or it can become the battleground for a bitter struggle for control, power, and domination. The contract becomes a blueprint that maps the couple's future together, and so must illuminate and delineate their unique and personal life plan.

This chapter makes a case for good faith and full disclosure on ethical, moral, and emotional, as well as legal grounds, so that the marriage is built on a foundation of trust and honesty, as well as friendship, love, and respect. It is recommended that therapists and mediators working with clients who are dealing with prenuptial and postnuptial agreements familiarize themselves with what the laws and statutes stipulate regarding such agreements, their revisions, and the legal consequences of various actions in order to be better prepared to be of assistance. Likewise, it is important for attorneys to be cognizant of the psychological, social, and emotional issues that undergird, circumscribe, and are precipitated by the prenuptial agreement so they can optimize the beneficial counsel and other services they provide. Coming from a broad, multidisciplinary knowledge base, we should all be able to make a sounder contribution to clients who come for professional consultation and assistance before marrying, and perhaps prevent serious misunderstandings, inequities, and even divorce from erupting.

REFERENCES

Bernstein, M. A. (1990, July). Prenuptial agreements: Saying "Sign here" before "I do." *Alert* (a clients' monthly bulletin). Hallendale, FL, p. 2.

Boszormenyi-Nagy, I., & Spark G. (1973). *Invisible loyalties: Reciprocity in intergenerational family therapy.* New York: Harper & Row. (Reprinted 1984, New York: Brunner/Mazel.)

Cook v. Cook (1996), 912 P. 2d-264 (Nevada).

de Shazer, S. (1988). *Clues: Investigating solutions in brief therapy.* New York: W. W. Norton.

Dreyfus, E. A. (1990, October). Antenuptial agreements revisited: Intimate negotiations. *Independent Practitioner.* Phoenix, AZ: APA Division #42, pp. 27–30.

Du Canto, J. N. (1991, March). Passing your wealth on to others: How to avoid financial pitfalls. *USA Today* (magazine), pp. 82–83.

Family Business Review (1988–1998). Journal of the Family Firm Institute. San Francisco: Jossey-Bass.

Fisher, R., & Ury, W. (1981). *Getting to yes.* Boston: Houghton Mifflin.

Florida Dissolution of Marriage—Children Act, Chapter 82–96 (1982), Chapter 61 (1992 Revision).

Framo J. (1981). The integration of marital therapy with sessions with the family of origin. In A. S. Gurman & D. P. Kniskern (Eds.), *Handbook of family therapy* (pp. 33–158). New York: Brunner/Mazel.

Freed, D. J. (1984). What the states say about prenuptial agreements. *Family Advocate, 6*(3), 26–29.

Frumkes, M., & Greene, C. (1984). How to get an agreement set aside. *Family Advocate, 6*(3) 20–21.

George, C. C. (1984). Marching to a single beat. *Family Advocate, 6*(3), 24–25.

Horsley, G. C. (1996). *In-laws: A guide to extended family therapy.* New York: John Wiley & Sons.

In re Estate of Gabarde (1995), 633 N.Y.C. 2d 878 (N.Y. App. Div.)

In re Marriage of Weiss (1996), 49 Cal. Rptr. 2d 339 (Cal. Ct. App.)

Kaslow, F. W. (1991). Enter the prenuptial: A prelude to marriage or remarriage. *Behavioral Sciences & the Law, 9,* 375–386.

Kaslow, F. W. (1993a). The divorce ceremony: A healing strategy. In T. Nelson & T. Trepper (Eds.), *101 favorite family therapy interventions.* New York: Haworth Press.

Kaslow, F. W. (1993b). Understanding and treating the remarriage family. *Directions in marriage and family therapy, 1*(3), 1–16. New York: Hatherleigh Co., Ltd.

Kaslow, F. W., & Schwartz, L. L. (1987). *Dynamics of divorce: A life cycle perspective.* New York: Brunner/Mazel.

Kaslow, F. W., & Kaslow, S. (1991). Family business: An escalating phenomenon. In S. Zedeck (Ed.), *Work and family.* San Francisco: Jossey-Bass.

Laudenslager v. Laudenslager (1996), PICS #96-5679; C. P. Berks, February 27. In *Pa. Law Weekly,* April 1, 1996.

Lewis, J., Beavers, W. R., Gossett, J. T., & Phillips, V. A. (1976). *No single thread: Psychological health and the family system.* New York: Brunner/Mazel.

Norris v. Norris (1979), D.C., 459A 2d 952.

Pablano v. Pablano (1980), California Ct. Supp., 1st District, July 9, 6 F.L.R. 2753.

Rider v. Rider (1995), 648 N.E. 2d 661 (Ind. Ct. App.).

Ritz v. Ritz (1995), 666 So. 2d 1181 (La. Ct. App.).

Sager, C. J. (1976). *Marriage contracts and couple therapy: Hidden forces in intimate relations*. New York: Brunner/Mazel.

Sager, C. J., Brown, H. S., Crohn, N., Engel, T., Rodstein, E., & Walker, L. (1983). *Treating the remarried family*. New York: Brunner/Mazel.

Schnarch, D. M. (1991). *The sexual crucible: An integration of sexual and marital therapy*. New York: W. W. Norton.

Schwartz, L. L. & Kaslow, F. W. (1997). *Painful partings: Divorce and its aftermath*. New York: John Wiley & Sons.

Sieg v. Sieg (1995), 445 S.E. 2d, 830 (Georgia).

Spencer, G. (1997, May 9). Nuptial agreement invalidated on appeal. From *New York Law Journal*. In Lexus-Nexus Universe summary, pp. 1, 2.

Watzlawick, P. (1963). A review of the double bind theory. *Family Process, 2*, 132–153.

White, M., & Epstom, D. (1990). *Narrative means to therapeutic ends*. New York: W. W. Norton.

CHAPTER 2

Adoption

Parents Who Choose Children and Their Options

LITA LINZER SCHWARTZ

COUPLES CONFRONTED with infertility who wish to have a child often look to adoption as the solution to their unfulfilled desire or altruistic motivation. So do those who wish to improve life for a child from the United States or overseas regardless of whether they have other children. Unlike some biological parenting, this is a very conscious decision, and the prospective adoptive parents must, for their own and for the child's sake, recognize that this is a lifetime commitment.

Infertility can be primary or secondary. *Primary infertility* can be the result of a number of causes, ranging from low sperm count or a vasectomy on the husband's part to an inability to become pregnant or to carry through a pregnancy on the wife's part due to hysterectomy, severe endometriosis, or other factors. *Secondary infertility* refers to those cases in which the couple has had one child successfully and is later unable to sustain another pregnancy. At some point, it becomes apparent that the numerous tests and treatments for infertility are ineffective and the couple must relinquish their hopes for biological parenthood (Daly, 1988). Whether the cause is primary or secondary infertility, sooner or later one member of the couple is likely to ask the other, "What do you think about adopting a child?" That tentative probe leads to a host of other questions and may ultimately bring the couple to someone for professional advice.

In this chapter, the initial focus of discussion is on the major questions prospective adoptive couples must ask themselves regarding a child and their views of the options from which they must choose. A variety of positions held by social service agencies, racial and ethnic groups, lawyers, clergy, and others are then presented because these bear upon the options. State, federal, and international laws are introduced and discussed as they are relevant to the question at hand. From there, the focus is narrowed to deal with the couple and their awareness of immediate and potential issues, their readiness to make the transition to adoptive parenthood, and situations that may bring them to a therapist before, during, and after adopting.

MAJOR ISSUES

Prospective adoptive parents must confront some serious questions and choose from a variety of adoption paths.

INITIAL QUESTIONS

Once a couple begins to discuss the possibility of adoption, several questions arise. Perhaps the first is whether they are related to the prospective adoptee, and if so, what situation has created the need for adoption. There are a few possibilities here:

1. The child's parents have died and someone must take legal and physical custody of the child.
2. The child's mother is unmarried and cannot or chooses not to raise the child.
3. The child's parents feel they cannot raise the child possibly because they have too many other children, or they cannot afford to raise a(nother) child.

In the first case, one member of the couple may be a sibling of one of the child's deceased parents and may feel both a desire and a duty to provide a home for the orphaned child. The couple may be grandparents to the orphan and want to adopt the child. In either situation, if the couple can prove that they have had an in loco parentis relationship with the orphaned child, the courts in many jurisdictions will support the adoption petition, barring any adverse reasons (Oppenheim, 1996). Similarly, if the biological parent has died and a surviving stepparent wishes to adopt the child, courts are likely to permit the adoption if it is perceived to be in the best interests of the child.

The second situation, where the birth mother does not want to rear the child, means that the child will remain with relatives; this may be permitted if the prospective adoptive parents are deemed satisfactory by social service agencies and the court. There are similarities here, however, to *open adoption,* which is another issue with which the adoptive couple must wrestle. This is also true for the third possibility, where a couple feel they cannot raise another child. All three contingencies raise potential problems that may bring the adoptive family to a therapist in future years. The second and third situations may lead the biological parents who have given up a child for adoption to seek therapy immediately or at a later date.

If the adoption is of a nonrelative, the prospective parents must ask themselves whether they have preferences about the age, religion, race, or origin of the child. Will they accept only a healthy newborn from a background similar to their own? Indeed, only a few decades ago, adoption agencies tried to match the background and physical characteristics of the baby and the prospective parents (Schwartz, 1991). The trend toward interracial and international adoptions is a relatively recent phenomenon.

A third issue to be decided is whether the couple wants to have some relationship with the child's biological or *birth* parent(s) (*open adoption*) or no relationship with them (*closed adoption*). Again, only a few decades ago, almost all nonrelative adoptions were closed, with the identifying records sealed. Today, many birth parents who contemplate placing their child for adoption not only want to choose who will adopt their child, but also want to maintain some degree of long-term relationship with the adoptive parents and the child. If the adoption is closed, what rights does the child have in later years to seek to learn the identity of the birth parent(s)? What rights do those biological parents have to remain unknown to the child? If the adoption is open, how much contact will the biological parent(s) have with the child? The contact can range from an annual letter and photo from the adoptive parents to fairly frequent visitation and interaction with the child by the biological parents.

Even as the couple tries to think about these concerns, they must consider to what source(s) they will apply for a child. There are traditional public and private adoption agencies; newer nontraditional agencies; and agencies that specialize in the placement of older children, special needs children, or children from foreign countries (international adoptions). Independent or private adoptions may be arranged through a physician, an attorney, or possibly a member of the clergy. They may also be the result of an advertisement placed by the prospective parents. The guidance of an adoption professional or agency is strongly advised in these latter efforts. International adoptions usually involve an agency that specializes in such arrangements, but caution is needed to determine the legitimacy of the agency. Johnston asserts that "Adoption requires both competent and complete pre-adoption and post-adoption *education*—service which is quite different from individual counseling or mental health services" (1997, p. 3). She further urges that any attorney consulted should be a qualified member of the American Academy of Adoption Attorneys so that legal complications can be averted or minimized.

A final issue of concern is whether the couple are "approvable" by an agency's standards or are in accord with statutory standards. Traditional agency criteria, such as those cited in the following subsection, are more difficult to meet today when couples tend to marry later than was true in the 1950s and 1960s, when both husband and wife are employed outside the home, and when half of first marriages end in divorce, often with subsequent remarriage of one or both of the parties. Even when some of the criteria are relaxed, continuing employment of the wife tends to be a sticky issue with many social workers and courts. Added complications arise when the prospective adoptive parents are a gay or lesbian couple.

PREVAILING POSITIONS AND OPTIONS

Various agencies, jurisdictions, and advocacy groups uphold criteria or take positions on the range of adoption paths available.

Social Service Agencies

Traditional public and private adoption agencies tend to have fairly strict criteria for prospective adoptive parents.

> The ideal candidate is a college educated couple, married at least five years, no prior marriages, proven infertility, practicing Christians [or Jews or other religion, depending on the agency's sponsor], stable employment and health history, a wife who plans to become a full-time mother, both people under age 35. (Ehrenpreis, 1992, p. 2)

Less traditional agencies or lawyers may have less rigid criteria to be met, but they may also charge exorbitant fees for a placement.

Among the factors considered by social service workers in determining the suitability of the adoptive parents are cleanliness of the home, availability of a separate room for the child, presence of other children or other adults in the home, history of prior criminal activity or police reports, income, parental plans for the child's future, and, after placement, interaction between parents and child observed during the worker's home visit. One adoptive mother found the home study process "one of many humbling steps along the grovel train," and further found herself feeling resentful that most "normal" people "haven't had to pass pop quizzes, mid-terms and final exams in order to have a baby" (Wolff, 1997, p.9).

Although social service agencies hold high standards as to the quality and characteristics of prospective parents, they are not always as thorough (or honest) in researching the physical, emotional, or mental health of the baby's birth parents or the child, if past the infancy period, and supplying that information to the adoptive parents. "When agencies intentionally or negligently misrepresent a child's health or background or conceal material information, the adoptive parents may sue for wrongful adoption. Generally, parents allege that they would not have adopted the child had they been told the truth" (Lewis, 1992, p. 75). Unfortunately, no appellate court has "imposed an affirmative duty on adoption agencies to investigate a child's background and medical history, but several courts have stated in dicta that agencies have no such duty, and one court has expressly rejected this claim" (Lewis, 1992, p. 77).

With the prevalence of drug use, alcoholism, HIV, and AIDS, in addition to possible genetic defects, it behooves would-be adoptive parents to be certain of the honesty and thoroughness of the agency (or other source) with which they are dealing. It is difficult enough to be confronted with a child's ordinary illnesses; the surprise of preexisting health problems can jeopardize not only an adoption, but also the adoptive parents' marriage if one parent blames the other for using a less than reputable source.

Whether attempting adoption through a public or private agency or an independent source, the prospective parents need to be aware (or be made aware) of legal processes governing interstate adoptions. In 1960, the Council of State Governments drafted an Interstate Compact on the Placement of Children (ICPC) which has since been enacted into law in all jurisdictions except the District of Columbia and the state of New Jersey (Lippold, 1995). When a child is to be adopted in a state other than its home state, the sending state must inform the receiving state that all of the home state's statutes and rules have been met, and the prospective parents must arrange for a home study by a licensed adoption agency in the receiving state. If all of the ICPC's provisions are not properly met, the adoption may not be permitted to proceed (Lippold, 1995).

Interracial Adoption

Transracial or *interracial adoption* is the term customarily used for cases involving the adoption of African American, Native American, or mixed-race children by white parents. Such adoptions have taken place for several decades, but in 1972, the National Association of Black Social Workers took the position that transracial adoptions were a "form of genocide." Similarly, Native American tribal leaders have protested the placement of their children in nontribal families. Their protest resulted in the passage of the Indian Child Welfare Act of 1978, which gave first preference to native families and tribes in the adoption of Native American children. In each instance, the fear is that the children will lose their ethnic identity and cultural heritage (Schwartz, 1996).

> A renewed interest in transracial adoption has been sparked in recent years by one of the more troubling aspects of the current child welfare system of adoption: a disproportionately large number of black children is waiting for permanent homes. This situation has not arisen because black families are reluctant to adopt; rather, it stems from the fact that the number of black children entering the temporary care system far exceeds the number of available black families. (Esten, 1995, p. 1941)

Proponents of transracial adoption argue that a transracial adoption by loving parents is preferable to long-term foster home or institutional care. These latter alternatives do little to promote a child's self-esteem or sense of well-being.

Even when African American children have been cared for by white foster parents, adoption agencies tend to remove them if these parents want to adopt the children. The children are then placed in black adoptive families, if available. While this may satisfy a racial policy, it may not be in the children's best interests to move them. It was to defuse such situations that the Multiethnic Placement Act was passed in 1994. This prohibits agencies that receive federal funding from using race as the sole criterion in foster or adoption placements.

> The controversy over transracial adoption and the Multiethnic Placement Act illustrates the conflicting issues implicated: the constitutionally protected right to equal protection under the law, the right of a racial minority to protect its ethnic and cultural integrity and influence how its children are raised, and the widely accepted principle that child welfare agencies should make decisions for children bearing in mind the children's best interests. When addressing transracial adoption, it is critical that the great importance of these conflicting issues not obscure the fragility and vulnerability of the primary constituents of the adoption system: the children. (Esten, 1995, p. 1945)

Studies of children involved in transracial adoption offer conflicting conclusions (Curtis, 1996). Some studies showed that the black children were poorly prepared to deal with prejudice and had little identification with the African American community. Other studies indicated that the children were socially well adjusted. What *is* apparent is that white parents contemplating transracial adoption need to be counseled before and after such an adoption. Mental health professionals providing the counseling or therapy should be conversant with the issues and the range of feelings that multiracial families confront in the contexts in which they live.

Even with the best of intentions, the black or mixed-race child raised by white parents may find him- or herself at a loss with reference to ethnic identity. A case in point is Asher Isaacs (1995), biological son of a white mother and an African American father, and the adopted son of white Jewish parents. His adoptive family also had three biological children. They never discussed his obvious differences in appearance from the rest of the family, and saw no need to expose him to any aspects of African American culture, history, or models. He fit in well with his white peers in high school, although he experienced an occasional racial incident, but did not assimilate as easily in college. It was then that he tried to become part of the African American community, succeeding only when he met another bira- cial individual who helped him to gain a sense of his African American identity.

Isaacs points out that black and biracial children have two critical needs: "per- manent placement in a stable and loving family, and an environment which will enable the child to develop a positive racial identity" (1995, p. 131). He urges, as have others, that if a black child cannot be placed with an African American adop- tive family within a reasonable length of time, then placement should be made with a carefully selected white family that will make every effort "to instill that child with a positive racial identity" (p. 131). The critical question then becomes "what constitutes a 'reasonable length of time'?" Each state has its own guidelines for placement, varying from no specified time period to 90 days (Cal. Fam. Code §8708 [Isaacs, 1995, p. 153]). Attempts to avoid the differences in state laws have been made by the National Conference of Commissioners on Uniform State Laws in 1953, 1971, and most recently in 1994, followed by the strong endorsement of the American Bar Association in 1995 (Tenenbaum, 1996). This proposed Uniform Adoption Act is consistent with the provisions of the Multiethnic Placement Act of 1994 with reference to transracial adoption placements (Tenenbaum, 1996). In addition, the search for an appropriate placement means that adoption may take place long after infancy, a concern that is dealt with a bit later in this chapter.

International Adoptions

International adoptions raise some of the same questions as transracial adop- tions. There are many adoptions today by white couples of youngsters from coun- tries such as Guatemala, Korea, Peru, China, India, Vietnam, and Eastern Europe. Such adoptions have averaged fewer than 10,000 such placements per year in the period 1988 to 1994 (Berger, 1995). The children are frequently from the lowest rung of the social ladder and are of mixed blood or are very dark-skinned, limit- ing their placement and opportunities in their home countries. In China, with its one-child-per-family policy, girl babies are placed in orphanages so that couples may go on to have a boy. Thus only girls are available, or older boys, usually with handicaps.

In addition, these children tend to be toddlers or older, not infants, and they may have been subject to malnutrition, abuse, and neglect in their homelands. They have already begun to speak the language of their homeland, adding learn- ing a new language and missing all that is familiar to the adjustments they need to make in the United States. They may or may not be subject to prejudice in their new communities and may never make contact with adult communities from their native land. This obviously differs from the situation confronted by African Amer- ican and some Native American children.

In addition to the personal differences between transracial and international adoptions, there are vast legal differences between the laws governing adoption within a state and those governing adoption between countries. Bartholet (1993), a Harvard lawyer, has written of the difficulties and costs she encountered in her ultimately successful efforts to adopt two children in Peru. Bascom and McKelvey (1997) have written a guidebook to foreign adoptions that focuses on the bureaucratic challenges confronting the would-be parent(s) as well as the special needs of many of the children allegedly available for placement. They also have furnished detailed lists of helpful resource agencies in the United States, together with the caution to be wary of those who would exploit the longing of prospective parents.

International adoption involves laws in the foreign country and our own Immigration and Naturalization Services regulations as well as state laws. There is frequently conflict among these. Sometimes our embassy in a foreign country is required to be involved before the adoption is completed and to issue a passport to the departing child.

The poverty rampant in many countries tempts some mothers to offer their children for overseas adoption—for a price, which contravenes their own country's laws. "The extent of baby-selling cannot be easily determined because it is difficult to distinguish between innocent cash payments to intermediaries or government officials, and a true illicit market for infants" (Berger, 1995, p. 39). This has led some countries to suspend intercountry adoptions (ICAs) or to increase the bureaucratic procedures governing the process (Berger, 1995). The potential profit motive tempts many "agencies" in countries here and abroad to hide significant information about the children or their family histories from prospective parents. It is with an eye to such irregularities and challenges that a uniform international adoption law has been drafted—the Hague Private Law Convention on the Protection of Children and Cooperation in Respect of International Adoption (Lippold, 1995). The Hague Convention not only provides concrete suggestions on how each country should deal with foreign adoptions, but also "calls for worldwide recognition of ICAs as a viable alternative for child placement" (Berger, 1995, p. 45). This is a step in the right direction, but the Convention has a possibly fatal flaw in that the Central Authorities in countries that are supposed to oversee and implement ICAs are frequently unable to deal with ICAs effectively, as when the sending countries are at war or in a state of instability (Berger, 1995). Thirteen countries have adopted the Convention, including some that have been most troublesome in implementing international adoption: Peru, Philippines, and Romania (Elrod & Spector, 1997, p. 773).

Although some of the agencies sponsoring overseas adoptions require parenting classes as well as psychological evaluations, home study visits, and a variety of background checks of prospective parents, sometimes all of these precautions are not enough to protect the children. A particularly sad example of something gone wrong was reported in local daily newspapers: "Adoption goes awry on flight home" (Hays, 1997). An Arizona couple, certified and trained by an adoption agency in their home state, were bringing home two 4-year-old girls from Russia; they repeatedly abused them physically and verbally throughout most of the 10-hour flight from Moscow. Flight attendants and others attempted to intervene, but to no avail. The bewildered and frightened girls screamed and cried for most of the time in flight. Whether the parents were stressed by the adoption process in Russia, frustrated with the girls' lack of understanding of English, or overwhelmed for some other reason was not clear. The outcome, however, seemed likely to be the removal of the children from their care, with the girls either being returned to Russia or, if legally feasible, placed with another family. In either case, the girls were old enough to have this experience register as traumatic, and it surely added to their readjustment tasks. This was hardly in their best interests.

The United Nations Convention on the Rights of the Child (1989) stressed that every child is entitled to a *family environment* within which the child has a right to be guided toward development of his or her "personality, talents and mental and physical ability to their fullest potential" (Article 29, § 1a). This pronouncement appears to support the transfer of children from long-term institutional care to adoptive families. Some provisions of the convention may, however, be in conflict with some federal and state laws. This important statement has yet to be ratified by the United States (Limber & Wilcox, 1996).

Closed versus Open Adoptions

In bygone years, virtually all nonrelative adoptions were closed—the identifying records were sealed when the relinquishment was finalized and the decree of adoption was signed by the court. On the birth mother's part, this meant that no one could learn that she had delivered a baby nor whom she might have identified as the baby's father. For the adoptive parents, this meant that they had no need to fear the appearance of a biological parent on their doorstep with a demand for the return of the child. This confidentiality policy sought to maintain privacy for all parties as well as to promote unity and bonding within the new adoptive family (Schwartz, 1996). It also meant that the child had no way of finding his or her biological forebears, of asking them why they had placed him or her for adoption, or of being aware of the biological family's health history. These questions often surfaced during the child's adolescence or young adulthood.

Open adoptions, on the other hand, are placements in which the biological and prospective adoptive parents meet each other and may have continuing contact. This seems to be reasonable sometimes in cases when the children are adopted at the age of 1 year or older, or when they are adopted by a relative, for there are existing bonds with the birth parents. Open adoption may, however, create the potential for the child to manipulate one or both sets of parents, or it may create questions of who has parental authority. Moreover, where there are adopted children from different biological parents in the same adoptive family, the policy of open adoption can lead to conflicts among the children, or loss of self-esteem if one child's biological parents visit and another's only send a birthday card or ignore the child's existence. In addition, there are likely to be indirect influences on all the children due to contacts between any one of them and that child's set of birth parents (Schwartz, 1993a). Continued contact often causes confusion, denial, and the inability to form a solid attachment to the adoptive family.

Adoption of Special Needs Children

Special needs children are those who are no longer infants, those with physical, mental, or emotional challenges, and others who are regarded as being hard to place. Looking first at those who are older, one has to ask why their placement has been delayed. Have they been in a foster home, or perhaps more than one? If so, what has been their experience there? Why have the foster parents not chosen, or not been permitted, to adopt? How old is the child? Are there siblings who also need adoption? Has the caretaking parent died or been declared unfit as a parent by a court because of substance abuse or a criminal act?

When a child has been placed in foster care because of problems such as abuse or neglect within the biological family, the traditional social welfare position has been to try to rehabilitate the biological parents so that the child can be reunited with them. This has often meant that children remain in the foster care system for years. A bill passed by the U.S. House of Representatives in April 1997 says "the highest priority must be the safety and well-being of children—not family reunification" (Hess, 1997). Further, it would require states to "take legal action to end parental rights involving children under 10 who have been in foster care for 18 of the last 24 months" (Hess, 1997). A similar bill has been proposed in the Senate, and the legislation has been supported by the administration. Enactment of this legislation would clearly make more noninfants available for adoption, and would reduce the trauma that about half a million children currently experience during years of foster care with possible brief returns to their disinterested or abusive biological parents.

Children with physical challenges may have any of a variety of disabilities or health risks, some of which may affect their mental development or their emotional well-being. Some may have problems related to having been exposed to drugs, HIV or AIDS, alcohol, or other hazards during their mother's pregnancy. In other cases, a genetic defect or postnatal illness may have caused hearing, vision, or other physical impairments that will make raising them more of a challenge than some prospective parents are willing to assume.

Mental challenges are those that slow a child's mental development to a significant degree. Children who are profoundly retarded will require total care throughout their lives; those at the level of mild retardation also require extra care, but are able to learn—even if at a slower rate than average—and to take an active part in family life. The lifelong dependency of mentally challenged children often makes it difficult to find caring adoptive parents for them.

Emotionally challenged children are those who have been abused, who have been moved from one home to another so often that they have not been able to develop a sense of trust with any caretakers, or who have some biologically based tendency toward autism, schizophrenia, or other psychologically abnormal behavior that may have been exacerbated by their environment. These are among the most difficult to place for adoption because no one can predict how they will react to yet another set of parents. Most people do not knowingly want to rear a potential arsonist, murderer, or self-destructive individual.

Prospective adoptive parents of such children not only need very careful screening by and full information from the placement source, but also must decide themselves whether they are willing and able to deal with the condition(s) the child has, as well as any future complications that could arise. They may be well advised to discuss their options and the potential consequences of their choice with a knowledgeable therapist before taking the final step. Should a couple decide to move forward with the adoption of a special needs child, they will need a variety of supports, including, possibly, financial aid to cover the child's medical or other therapeutic expenses.

Gay and Lesbian Couples

Gay and lesbian couples, though at present not legally permitted to marry in any state, often perceive themselves as married and may even have a ceremony to seal their mutual commitment. In some states or communities, gays and lesbians are allowed to identify their *life partner* for health and life insurance purposes and share other benefits normally shared by married couples. When it comes to adopting children born to or previously adopted by one of the partners, however, the laws are less clear. The lesbian or gay second parent, with the support of the children's legal parent, petitions "the court for legal recognition of his/her relationship with the children through a court ordered second-parent adoption" (Connolly, 1996, p. 189). Difficulties may arise in having the petition granted, however, as some states have statutes or court rulings that either declare homosexuality illegal or that indicate that homosexuality can be used as a reason to deny custody. Alaska, Massachusetts, New York, and Washington courts, on the other hand, "consider the parent's heterosexual or homosexual activity in custody determinations only if it is shown to adversely affect the child" (Connolly, 1996, p. 190). In fact, New York's adoption statute "specifically prohibits discrimination on the basis of sexual orientation," and a District of Columbia appellate court ruled that an "unmarried *couple* may jointly adopt" (Connolly, 1996, p. 196).

In cases where adoption is permitted, or where the question of visitation has arisen when the gay or lesbian couple parts, some courts have tended to focus on the psychological parenting relationship rather than on a statutory definition of family that they perceive as outdated. The legal picture is so ill-defined, in terms of both statutes and court rulings, however, that a knowledgeable attorney's advice is critical before an adoption is even contemplated.

IMPACT OF THESE ISSUES ON FAMILIES

The mental health professional who is consulted by a couple considering adoption should try to ascertain how cognizant the prospective parents are of the issues just discussed. Part of the professional's role may become that of educator, either directly informing the couple of the issues involved or suggesting sources where they might learn about the challenges as well as the pleasures of adoption. Additional matters for the consultant to raise include the following:

1. How prepared are the clients for the expectations of the person or couple that will be surrendering the child?
2. Can they handle the delays and disappointments common to some local and many overseas adoptions?
3. Are they aware of the possibility of an adoption being overturned?
4. How prepared are they to parent a hard-to-place child?

One of the issues often overlooked is the role of the unmarried biological father and his rights vis-à-vis his child. As the public has learned, from the Baby Jessica and Baby Richard cases particularly, an unmarried father can appear even after an adoption has been legalized and seek to overturn it on the grounds that he was not notified of the impending adoption and had not terminated his parental rights (Schwartz, 1993b; Rosenman, 1995; Resnik, 1996).

In the Baby Jessica case, the birth mother relinquished her rights to the baby about 40 hours after the child's birth in Iowa on February 8, 1991, and the man she named as the father relinquished his rights 4 days later. About 2 weeks later, the would-be adoptive parents, a Michigan couple, filed for the baby's adoption. About the same time, the mother attended a meeting of the Concerned United Birthparents group and changed her mind about giving up her child. Two days later, she informed a former boyfriend that she thought *he* was the baby's father, and within 2 weeks he filed a request to vacate the paternal termination of rights and subsequently filed an affidavit of paternity. Baby Jessica was not yet 2 months old. There were already at least three major issues: (a) a biological mother who had changed her mind before the adoption was final, (b) an unmarried father who did not want to surrender his child, and (c) the complications of an interstate adoption (Weaver-Catalana, 1995).

The next step in this saga took place when Baby Jessica was about eight months old, with the biological father filing proof (99.9% probability) of his paternity and the adoptive parents filing a petition to terminate his rights, citing his unfitness as a parent (based on his record with previous children he had fathered). Two months later, the Iowa court ordered the Michigan couple to surrender the baby to her father within 2 months, but an appeal to the Iowa Supreme Court stayed that order pending the resolution of other proceedings in the case. Meanwhile, the Michigan couple filed a petition in their home state seeking to have the matter decided in Michigan, as that had been the child's home state for all but 3 weeks of her life. A circuit court in Michigan decided that it was in the child's best interests to remain with her adoptive parents. Court hearings continued in both states over a period that lasted in toto almost 2½ years, setting parental rights against the child's best interests. The ultimate result was that Baby Jessica was returned to her birth parents on August 3, 1993. They had married each other about 1 year after setting their claims to her in motion (Weaver-Catalana, 1995).

Baby Jessica was, in a sense, the innocent victim of a war between two sets of parents. For most of her first 29 months of life, she lived with one couple who were her psychological parents in a home that was beset with the anxieties aroused by their legal battles to keep her. At an age when she certainly regarded them as Mommy and Daddy, she was unceremoniously removed from their care and turned over to another couple, complete strangers to her—an event shown on nationwide television.

A second case that occurred at about the same time similarly involved an unmarried couple. Baby Richard was born on March 16, 1991. His mother signed away her parental rights 4 days later, and told the baby's father, who was then in Europe, that the baby had died at birth. Eight weeks after the birth, the father learned that the child was alive and had been placed for adoption. By June, he filed a petition to stop the adoption proceedings, and in September he and the child's mother were married. In December, the adoptive parents filed a petition to adopt and alleged that the birth father was an unfit parent under Illinois law. The case was heard in May 1992, with custody awarded to the adoptive parents—a decision affirmed by the Illinois Appellate Court in August 1993. That court

> emphasized that because the child was the real party in interest, the child's best interests and corollary rights prevailed over the interests and rights of both biological and adoptive parents. Since Richard had spent all but four days of his life with his adoptive parents, the court decided that it would be contrary to Richard's best interests to remove him from their home. (Rosenman, 1995, p. 1859)

The Illinois Supreme Court reversed that decision in June 1994, finding that the father was not unfit, and that, accordingly, his consent to the adoption was necessary and outweighed Richard's best interests. Appeals and decisions continued into 1995, with Baby Richard being returned to the birth parents he had never met on April 30, 1995. Sometime in 1996, the father left the mother (whom he had married at some point after he began his suit to recover their son) and Baby Richard (Nordgren, 1997).

The issue of an unmarried or putative father's rights rests largely on whether he has been involved with the child and acting as a parent, and on how quickly he has acted to protect his constitutional rights. Depending on the court, if he has had other children, his relationship with or support of them may also be considered in determining his "fitness." States differ in how they balance his rights with the child's best interests, and there is considerable conflict between those holding one position or the other. Rosenman (1995) has suggested a number of legislative reforms that would reduce the likelihood of protracted court battles such as were seen in the Baby Jessica and Baby Richard cases.

> First, expedited court decisions and appeals will ensure that the final placement of a child takes place quickly. Second, a putative father registry will allow the putative father to protect his parental rights before the child is placed with adoptive parents, even if the natural mother seeks to conceal the adoption. Third, mandatory preplacement counseling will ensure that the natural mother is giving her informed consent when she places her child for adoption. Fourth, punishing fraud will discourage the natural mother from fraudulently concealing the natural father's identity. By incorporating these reforms, states can ensure that the best interests of the child will be promoted without forcing judges to apply an amorphous, subjective standard on a case-by-case basis. (Rosenman, 1995, p. 1877)

Not only would the child's best interests be protected, and judges' decision making made more consistent, but the adoptive (and birth) parents' stress and grief would be minimized as well.

Resnik (1996) avers that the Uniform Adoption Act previously discussed is inadequate to deal with the problems presented by putative fathers and has proposed an alternative measure: a Statute Clarifying the Rights of Unwed Fathers in Newborn Adoptions (SCRUFNA). Specifically,

> SCRUFNA seeks to effectuate an equitable balancing of the interests of the unwed father, the infant adoptee, the prospective adoptive parent(s), the state, and the birth mother. . . . The best interests of the child are threefold: first the child's interest is in being placed with a parent or set of parents who are committed to loving and caring for her; second is in seeing that this placement is effectuated in an expedient manner; and third, that this placement, once made, is assured of permanency. . . .
> SCRUFNA's second goal is to provide clear, objective guidelines that will enable unwed father cases to be adjudicated quickly thus avoiding the long drawn out disputes which have become characteristics of putative-father-contested adoption cases. (Resnik, 1996, pp. 422–423)

Like Rosenman (1995), Resnik favors a putative father registry and other measures to protect everyone's rights.

Prospective adoptive parents also need to be aware of pressures on and expectations of the couple or individual surrendering a child for placement. The woman has more options from which to choose, including raising the child herself, than was the case in the past. In one study comparing adolescents who placed their babies for adoption with those who became teenaged mothers, it was found that those "who place tend to come from somewhat more well-to-do families and from suburban residences, and to express higher educational aspirations. . . . Those who place are also more frequent attendees of religious services [than those who parent]" (Resnick, Blum, Bose, Smith, & Toogood, 1990, pp. 582–583). A second study, using subjects in maternity residences, found a similar socioeconomic and educational difference between those who intended to place their children and those who did not (Kalmuss, Namerow, & Cushman, 1991). In addition, "twice as many young women who considered adoption as those who did not report that the three scenarios related to the adoptive family (choosing them, meeting them and receiving yearly updates about the baby) would make them more likely to place the baby" (Kalmuss et al., 1991, p. 19).

The young mother may be convinced she wants to place the child until a few days or weeks before delivery, or even a few days or weeks after she has signed papers terminating her parental rights, and then change her mind for any number of reasons. The unmarried father may refuse to give up *his* rights, perhaps because he views the child as proof of his virility. If a couple is waiting for that baby, their disappointment is great.

What can contribute to such a change of heart by the birth mother? In the 1990s, being an unmarried mother (or part of an unmarried couple) is not always the source of personal and family shame that it was a mere 25 to 35 years ago. There have been, until recently, funds from the welfare system to help support the mother and the child. There is open adoption, which enables the mother, in a sense, to have her cake and eat it, too, in that someone else has the primary responsibility (and cost) of raising her child, while she can still have contact. It is possible that the mother may have encountered a social worker, friend, or other source of influence who has encouraged her to rear her child and even admonished her for thinking of giving up the child. If the mother is a young adolescent, the child may be seen as a source of love for her in what is otherwise a loveless world, but the young mother has little recognition of the care and attention needed by the baby. Further, although baby-selling is illegal in all jurisdictions, she (or the father) may try to collect a sizable amount of money for surrendering the child. The change of heart may occur after the placement (and possibly after receiving and spending the money), resulting in the kind of protracted court proceedings described previously, which wreak havoc on the lives of the child and the adoptive parents.

Finally, if the couple is considering adoption of a hard-to-place child, how aware are they of the problems that may be part of the child's "baggage?" Have they had experience with challenged children and their needs? What assets do they perceive in themselves that will be especially helpful to such a child?

ENTER THE THERAPIST

In what ways might these dilemmas and problems be manifested covertly or brought into therapy overtly?

SCENARIO 1

If one or both members of a prospective adoptive couple were in therapy before thoughts of adoption arose, is one partner blaming the other for the infertility or exhibiting less enthusiasm about the possibility of adoption? The stresses of infertility procedures and treatment are enough to generate manic-depressive mood swings even in an emotionally healthy couple and can certainly exacerbate any problems in the individual or couple. If the marriage is already troubled, the adoption, as is also true for children born to a couple, is not a magic cure-all. If one partner is reluctant to adopt, he or she may be unable to overcome that feeling enough to be a caring parent and spouse. If one of these situations is the case, the therapist should certainly help the couple resolve the issue prior to any moves toward adoption.

SCENARIO 2

Is one partner saying to the other, "Adoption is my gift to you, dear?" The therapist here needs to explore why the partner isn't saying that adoption is a gift to *us*, to enrich *our* lives. Again, this may be a facade covering reluctance, or a desire by a husband to keep his wife occupied or satisfied for reasons of his own. In either event, the therapist needs to ask the prospective parents to consider whether it is fair to themselves and to any child they might adopt to go forward with the process under these conditions.

SCENARIO 3

The couple are cognizant of the many issues involved with adoption, and have determined that this *is* their choice, but they are concerned about how they will relate to the adoptee on his or her arrival. The therapist can truthfully say that most adoptive parents welcome their new arrival with all the warmth exhibited by most birth parents. In most cases, even with the negative situations described previously occurring more frequently today than formerly, the adoption moves forward and the little one becomes part of the family emotionally as well as legally. The therapist can explain that it is normal to have a bit of anxiety until the adoption papers are finally signed, but that this should not be allowed to pervade their relationship with the child.

The therapist needs to know how to help patients cope more effectively with the social, legal, and judicial systems and personnel as they consider and then move forward with adoption. A suggestion that the couple attend meetings of a local RESOLVE chapter, or contact that organization for information and support, would be appropriate. The therapist should have some knowledge of the options for arranging an adoption and should be aware of possible complications of open adoptions, transracial and international adoptions, and adoption of challenged or older children. Some basic information about adoption statutes in the home state is likewise essential. If the client is single, or gay or lesbian, the therapist should know at least whether adoption is legally possible for the client under the laws of that state. An additional important resource is a list of attorneys to whom the couple can go for legal information and assistance. The more familiar the therapist is with available sources and resources, obviously, the more helpful the therapist can be to clients.

If the adoptive parents are in therapy prior to the adoption, the therapist can play a critical role in helping them to decide how open they are willing to be with the birth parent(s). Are they comfortable with the idea of inviting the biological mother to their home, or to spend a day with the child? Do they foresee potential problems for the child if there is such an open adoption? How will they explain the biological parent(s) to the child—as a close friend? As an aunt or uncle? As the birthparent? The therapist should not press a decision on the couple, but rather should endeavor to have it fully considered. A thoughtful discussion of the many factors in open adoption that the couple might want to consider is provided for the therapist by Reitz and Watson (1992). The therapist might provide research data to the couple that compares open and closed adoptions.

SCENARIO 4

On the other hand, if the couple comes to therapy as a result of a change of heart on the part of a birth parent prior to the actual adoption or an overturned adoption, there is a real need for grief therapy. (Grief therapy is also appropriate for the biological mother if she is depressed at having surrendered her child for adoption.) There are no funeral services or similar rites for the loss of an anticipated child or one who has been removed from the home, yet the grief is as real as if the child had died. Beyond grief therapy for the prospective or adoptive parents, the therapist may have to help them find a way to explain the loss of the anticipated or adopted child to an older sibling so that that child does not fear being removed from the parents as well. In addition, the therapist can help the couple devise a tactful response to the questions of outsiders who become aware of the situation.

Another role that the therapist may play is that of expert witness, either in a case where foster parents wish to adopt the child they have been caring for (Drotar & Stege, 1988), or in a contested adoption case. The therapist's knowledge of child development, especially the effects of separation in early childhood, can be critical information for the court.

SCENARIO 5

What if the client is the adopted child, not the parents? Although it is quite normal for children ages 5 to 10 to develop some fantasized romance about really being the child of wealthy or noble parents, what is apparent to the adopted child is that there really is another set of birth parents somewhere. Not all adoptees have a problem with their status; some may have only a passing curiosity about their biological forebears. It should not be assumed that *every* adopted child has problems related to adoption, or that every problem an adopted child derives from this circumstance. If the child is in therapy because of problems related to the adoption, however, the therapist should inquire of the adoptive parents what the child has been told about why or how he or she was adopted and proceed from there.

The painful reality to be confronted by adoptees is that their biological parents did not want, or were unable, to find a way of keeping and rearing their own child. The children feel that they were either "not meant to be" or "intolerable," and may spend a large part of a lifetime struggling with whether this means that the biological parents were bad (inadequate) parents, or that they themselves were bad children, causing their unhappiness, thereby deserving abandonment, and so on. (Rosenberg & Horner, 1991, p. 71)

Sometimes the child is teased by other children about lack of resemblance to the adoptive parents, although this becomes less likely in communities where more transracial and international adoptions occur. For younger children, the therapist should be familiar with a number of books written expressly for adopted children and should be able to recommend them. Another possibility, as youngsters approach adolescence, is that the child becomes aware that many children are placed for adoption because they were born to unwed parents, and the child has conflicts about his or her progenitors' promiscuity. This can affect self-esteem and self-image negatively and needs to be dealt with by the parents and the therapist.

SCENARIO 6

In adolescence or young adulthood the client may try to decide whether to search for his or her biological roots. Bertocci and Schecter (1991) report that for some adoptees, there is an empty feeling, a feeling of loss, or questions related to health that they feel can be healed by finding the biological parents. The therapist needs to be able to present possible outcomes of a search and ask the client to try to envision how he or she would feel in each situation, with respect to both the biological parents (and possible siblings) and the adoptive parents. The therapist may also want to determine whether the child has mentioned this desire to the adoptive parents and perhaps have a few sessions with them, if they are anxious or upset by the possible search. The therapist should also be aware of the procedures available to unseal adoption records in the state and, indeed, whether this is permissible in the particular jurisdiction.

SCENARIO 7

At some time after adoption, the parents become disenchanted or disappointed with the child and blame it on the child's heredity. They not only regret having adopted the child, but become rejecting parent figures. The youngster's current or ensuing behavior or emotional turmoil becomes so difficult for the couple to handle that they have him or her institutionalized. It may be that the child truly has psychological problems that cannot be treated on an outpatient basis, but whether this is primarily due to genetic or environmental factors is hard to say. Estimates of adopted children in inpatient psychiatric settings range from 8% to 15%, but this overrepresentation may stem from delayed adoptions, or from greater readiness on the part of adoptive parents to seek professional help (Schwartz, 1996). The therapist may be consulted by the parents to help them deal with their feelings about the failure of their adoption experience.

SUMMARY AND RECOMMENDATIONS

People who choose to enrich their family life by adopting children may have wrestled with the challenge of infertility for many years. They may have sought therapy to reduce the anxiety and distress caused by that unwanted battle. Having at some point turned to thoughts of adoption, they need to be reasonably certain that this is a mutual decision and that they have reflected on the questions that arise from such a decision. They also must be aware of the potential stumbling blocks on the road to successful adoption and where to get help if they need it.

If clients consult them about the possibility of becoming a family via the adoption route, therapists should be well informed so as to guide the clients to decisions that are appropriate for their lives and ultimately are in the best interests of any child they may adopt. Indeed, it is the therapist's responsibility to be knowledgeable or to refer the clients to someone who is. (There are a number of books that provide the needed information, some of which are listed in the references. Other resources are listed in the "Additional Resources" section.)

Among the questions discussed in this chapter are those involving preferences as to the age, sex, race, and special needs of the child; closed versus open adoption; factors considered by social welfare agencies in the approval of prospective parents for adoption; possible disappointments en route to adoption; and the readiness of the couple to parent someone else's biological child. These are matters that need thought and discussion prior to embarking on the search for a child to adopt. Once the prospective parents have made such a decision, they have to seek a source for acquiring a child—either a social service agency or, where permitted, an independent party such as an attorney or physician who has experience with this process and who is recommended as being honest. These are matters with which the therapist should be familiar, at least on the local scene as far as agencies are concerned and at the state level in terms of adoption statutes.

Despite the serious issues discussed here and the possibilities for disappointments and other problems, therapists should be aware that most adoptions have happier outcomes than a number of the situations presented suggest and that most adoptees are loved and guided toward a fulfilling adulthood. Helping an adoptive family to be successful as a family should be the therapist's goal—a goal that brings its reward in the form of a client family terminating treatment when all is going smoothly.

REFERENCES

Bartholet, E. (1993). *Family bonds: Adoption and the politics of parenting.* New York: Houghton Mifflin.

Bascom, B. B., & McKelvey, C. A. (1997). *The complete guide to foreign adoption.* New York: Pocket Books.

Berger, D. (1995). Improving the safety and efficiency of foreign adoptions: U.S. domestic adoption programs and adoption programs in other countries provide lessons for INS reform. *Cornell Journal of Law and Public Policy, 5,* 33–65.

Bertocci, D., & Schecter, M. D. (1991). Adopted adults' perception of their need to search: Implications for clinical practice. *Smith College Studies in Social Work, 61,* 179–196.

Connolly, C. (1996). An analysis of judicial opinions in same-sex visitation and adoption cases. *Behavioral Sciences and the Law, 14,* 187–203.

Curtis, C. M. (1996). The adoption of African American children by whites: A renewed conflict. *Families in Society: The Journal of Contemporary Human Services, 77*(3), 156–165.

Daly, K. (1988). Reshaped parenthood identity: The transition to adoptive parenthood. *Journal of Contemporary Ethnography, 17*(1), 40–66.

Drotar, D., & Stege, E. R. (1988). Psychological testimony in foster parent adoption: A case report. *Journal of Clinical Child Psychology, 17,* 164–168.

Ehrenpreis, T. (1992, Winter). Adoption in the 90's. *Insights into Infertility: A Newsletter, 2,* 12.

Elrod, L. D., & Spector, R. G. (1997). A review of the year in family law: Of welfare reform, child support, and relocation. *Family Law Quarterly, 30,* 765–809.

Esten, D. R. (1995). Transracial adoption and the Multiethnic Placement Act of 1994. *Temple Law Review, 68,* 1941–1995.

Hays, T. (1997, May 31). Adoption goes awry on flight home. *Philadelphia Inquirer,* p. A3.

Hess, D. (1997, May 1). House: Speed up child adoption. *Philadelphia Inquirer,* pp. A1, A21.

Isaacs, A. D. (1995). Interracial adoption: Permanent placement and racial identity—an adoptee's perspective. *National Black Law Journal, 14,* 126–156.

Johnston, P. I. (1997). Who are the "real" adoption professionals? *Resolve National Newsletter, 22*(2), 1, 3, 10.

Kalmuss, D., Namerow, P. B., & Cushman, L. F. (1991). Adoption versus parenting among young pregnant women. *Family Planning Perspectives, 23*(1), 17–23.

Lewis, J. (1992). Wrongful adoptions: Agencies mislead prospective parents. *Trial, 28*(12), 75–78.

Limber, S. P., & Wilcox, B. L. (1996). Application of the U.N. Convention on the Rights of the Child to the United States. *American Psychologist, 51,* 1246–1250.

Lippold, J. M. (1995). Transnational adoption from an American perspective: The need for universal uniformity. *Case Western Reserve Journal of International Law, 27,* 465–503.

Nordgren, S. (1997, January 21). Father of disputed child leaves. *Philadelphia Inquirer,* p. A3.

Oppenheim, E. (1996). Adoption: Where do relatives stand? *Child Welfare, 75,* 471–488.

Reitz, M., & Watson, K. W. (1992). *Adoption and the family system: Strategies for treatment.* New York: Guilford Press.

Resnick, M. D., Blum, R. W., Bose, J., Smith, M., & Toogood, R. (1990). Characteristics of unmarried adolescent mothers: Determinants of child rearing versus adoption. *American Journal of Orthopsychiatry, 60,* 577–584.

Resnik, S. A. (1996). Seeking the wisdom of Solomon: Defining the rights of unwed fathers in newborn adoptions. *Seton Hall Legislative Journal, 20,* 363–431.

Rosenberg, E. B., & Horner, T. M. (1991). Birthparent romances and identity formation in adopted children. *American Journal of Orthopsychiatry, 61,* 70–77.

Rosenman, A. S. (1995). Babies Jessica, Richard, and Emily: The need for legislative reform of adoption laws. *Chicago-Kent Law Review, 70,* 1851–1895.

Schwartz, L. L. (1991). *Alternatives to Infertility: Is surrogacy the answer?* New York: Brunner/Mazel.

Schwartz, L. L. (1993a). The interaction of field theory, family systems theory, and children's rights. *American Journal of Family Therapy, 21,* 267–273.

Schwartz, L. L. (1993b). What *is* a family? A contemporary view. *Contemporary Family Therapy, 15,* 429–442.

Schwartz, L. L. (1996). Adoptive families: Are they nonnormative? In M. Harway (Ed.), *Treating the changing family: Handling normative and unusual events* (pp. 97–114). New York: John Wiley & Sons.

Tenenbaum, J. D. (1996). Introducing the Uniform Adoption Act. *Family Law Quarterly, 30,* 333–343.

United Nations General Assembly. (1989, November). *Adoption of a convention on the rights of the child* (U.N. Doc. A/Res/44/25). New York: Author.

Weaver-Catalana, B. (1995). The battle for Baby Jessica: A conflict of best interests. *Buffalo Law Review, 43*, 583–615.

Wolff, J. (1997). Secret thoughts of an adoptive mother: A fiercely honest look at the emotional complexities in adoption. *Adoptive Families, 30*(2), 8–12.

ADDITIONAL RESOURCES

BOOKS

Brodzinsky, D. M., & Schecter, M. D. (Eds.). (1990). *The psychology of adoption.* New York: Oxford University Press.

Dunn, L. (Ed.). (1993). *Adopting children with special needs: A sequel.* Washington, DC: North American Council on Adoptable Children.

Rosenberg, E. B. (1992). *The adoption life cycle: The children and their families through the years.* New York: Free Press.

U.S. Department of Justice, Immigration and Naturalization Service. (1990). *The immigration of adopted and prospective adoptive children.* Washington, DC: U.S. Government Printing Office (M-249Y).

PERIODICALS

Adoption Quarterly (magazine)
The Haworth Press, Inc.
10 Alice Street
Binghamton, NY 13904-1580

Adoptive Families (magazine)
c/o Adoptive Families of America
2309 Como Avenue
St. Paul, MN 55108

Family Law Quarterly (American Bar Association journal)
750 North Lake Shore Drive
Chicago, IL 60611-4497

Family and Conciliation Courts Review (Association of Family and Conciliation Courts journal)
c/o Sage Publications
2455 Teller Road
Thousand Oaks, CA 91320

The Future of Children: Adoption, 3(1). (1993).
The David and Lucile Packard Foundation
300 Second Street, Suite 102
Los Altos, CA 94022

AGENCIES

American Academy of Adoption Attorneys
Box 33053
Washington, DC 20033

Child Welfare League of America
67 Irving Place
New York, NY 10003

Immigration and Naturalization Service
425 I Street
Washington, DC 20536

RESOLVE
1310 Broadway
Somerville, MA 02144-1731

CHAPTER 3

Surrogacy

The Third Leg of the Reproductive Triangle

LITA LINZER SCHWARTZ

FOR MILLIONS of married couples, the Biblical injunction to "go forth and multiply" is easily obeyed. For thousands of other couples, however, their efforts to do so are thwarted by an unforeseen medical problem leading to infertility. The psychological blow of learning that they may not be able to procreate can be devastating, and the severe effects continue as the couple seeks treatment leading to the desired outcome—a successful pregnancy yielding a healthy child. One reproductive alternative is surrogate motherhood.

The practice of surrogate motherhood is often thought to go back to Biblical times when Sarah, wife of Abraham, could not conceive and so sent him to her handmaid, Hagar, who subsequently bore Abraham's son Ishmael (Genesis 16). Sarah did not raise Ishmael as an adoptive mother; rather, Hagar raised him. Hagar was considered a concubine (legal in those times), not a surrogate mother. In modern surrogate motherhood practice, Sarah, as wife of Abraham, would have adopted Ishmael legally and she would have been regarded as his mother, not Hagar. The same situation arose with Rachel, wife of Jacob, and again involved concubinage, not surrogacy as we know it today (Genesis 30).

Surrogacy involves a third person in the production of a child, either as supplier of the ovum and carrier of the fetus, as carrier of an already fertilized ovum, or as supplier of ova to the prospective mother who will carry the fetus. (In cases where a male [usually anonymous] other than the husband supplies sperm to a woman who can become pregnant and carry the resulting fetus, this is not considered surrogacy but is referred to as *artificial insemination by donor* [AID].)

"What makes a woman a mother—genetic contribution, gestation, or the intent with which the woman contributed her reproductive function?" (Coleman, 1996, pp. 502–503). The term *surrogate mother* is sometimes a misnomer, despite its wide acceptance. A *surrogate* is, by definition, a stand-in or substitute for someone else, and, in one sense, she *is* substituting for someone else during pregnancy. If the

43

woman is the supplier of the ovum, however, she is actually the child's biological mother. Even if she is the carrier of an already fertilized ovum (i.e., the gestational carrier), some courts regard her as the biological mother. The "surrogate," under these circumstances, is the woman who is married to the child's biological father and who will serve as the mother for child-rearing purposes. For the sake of conforming to current usage, however, the woman who carries the fetus (her own ovum or someone else's) will be referred to here as the *surrogate mother*. If the woman donates an oocyte to be fertilized, with the resulting fetus then to be carried by another woman, this is usually done anonymously and would parallel the AID process. Such cases are not a major consideration in this chapter.

It is the presence of this third person as carrier of a fetus in a triangle involving the biological father and his wife that leads to complications even more complex than those associated with adoption. To begin with, the pregnancy is deliberate; indeed, it is a carefully scheduled event. Second, the surrogate mother and the prospective parents sign a contract before any attempts at pregnancy in which certain promises are made, culminating in delivery of the neonate to the parents-to-be.

What complications can arise from such a seemingly straightforward arrangement? First, there may be minimal mention of the surrogate's husband or children, if she has a family. (Generally, the contract specifies that the surrogate's husband must agree to refrain from having intercourse with her during the insemination phase of the planned pregnancy and must subsequently relinquish his paternal rights. This tends to be all that is said with regard to the surrogate's family.) Second, the payment of any incentive funds is legally perceived in many jurisdictions as baby-selling, which is against the law. Third, although the actual termination of parental rights does not occur until after the baby is born, a constantly hovering question is whether the surrogate will still wish to fulfill that portion of her contract after the child's birth. Fourth, there are conflicting legal opinions as to whether the termination of parental rights by the surrogate mother is in the child's best interests. Finally, there are clashes about the right of a woman to use her body as she wishes versus allegations of exploitation of women, especially of those who are relatively poor, to serve as surrogates.

MAJOR ISSUES

Why does a couple choose to seek a child via surrogacy rather than adoption? The motives vary. The wife may not be able to carry a pregnancy because of having had a hysterectomy or other medical problem or procedure that can interfere. She may be able to produce ova which, when fertilized by her husband's sperm, can be transplanted to another woman's womb via in vitro fertilization (IVF) for the duration of the pregnancy. In this arrangement, the third party is a gestational carrier. In some cases, it is the desire of the couple to have at least some genetic tie to their prospective child that motivates this choice. In other situations, the wish for a genetic tie may be stronger: There may be an element of narcissism on the husband's part that he is able to continue his family line through such an arrangement. This was the case with the Stern-Whitehead *Baby M* contract, as William Stern's family had been virtually wiped out in the Holocaust (Schwartz, 1991a). In still other instances, the couple may feel that they are minimizing the possibility of substance abuse effects or HIV infection in the child, which might not be possible in an adoption. A fifth possibility is that the couple perceive surrogacy as an arrangement in which they have more control over their potential parenthood than may be true in adoption. In yet other cases, the couple may have been rejected by adoption agencies because of age or other factors, or may themselves have rejected adoption as an option because of lack of availability of or lengthy wait for a healthy infant. Whichever professional works with the husband and wife should help them clarify their motives before they consider moving forward in the process.

In most surrogacy programs, the woman who will serve as the surrogate mother is evaluated by a mental health professional to ascertain her motives and emotional stability. Some women are fee-oriented; that is, their eyes are on the $10,000 or more to be paid for bearing the child as a way of paying family bills. Others may perceive the delivery of a live child as atonement for a child earlier aborted or given out for adoption. Altruism is a third motive, giving the gift of a child to a childless couple. There are also women who enjoy being pregnant, or who feel that they are demonstrating their femininity through pregnancy, but who cannot or choose not to raise another child (Overvold, 1988; Schwartz, 1991a).

There is a vast difference in motives between a sister or cousin who volunteers to donate ova or carry a fetus for an infertile relative and a stranger who agrees to the arrangement for a cash fee. This may affect the odds of the woman changing her mind after the pregnancy occurs. In all cases, the mental health professional consulted should try to determine whether the prospective surrogate mother has thought through the impact of the pregnancy and the surrender of the resulting baby on herself, her husband, and her children, both short- and long-term.

The therapist's role with either the prospective parents or the prospective surrogate mother is to help the clients deal with these questions from a psychological perspective, and to help them anticipate potential outcomes of any decision made. The issues raised in the following paragraphs should be dealt with in a legal contract and should be handled by a knowledgeable attorney, although the therapist should be sufficiently aware of these issues to be able to mention them to clients.

CHOOSING A SURROGATE

Noel Keane, an attorney in Michigan, began his surrogate mother practice in 1976. Since then, other attorneys and private agencies have developed surrogacy programs (Schwartz, 1991a). The availability of the service is made known through interpersonal communications, advertising, computer network sites, and sometimes publicity in the media. Overvold (1988) listed several surrogacy agencies, with details of their policies and costs. Although some of the data may have changed in the past several years, the information provided can serve as a guideline to prospective parents. Ragoné (1994) included eight established surrogate mother programs in her study, some of which are *open* in the sense that the couple and surrogate meet, select each other, and interact throughout the process. Other programs are *closed*, with selection based on brief biographies and completed questionnaires supplied by all parties. Prospective parents should verify the credentials of any intermediary with some authoritative source like the Family Law section of the American Bar Association, RESOLVE (a national infertility support group), or the Organization for Parents Through Surrogacy (OPTS), before becoming involved in choosing a surrogate or signing any contracts to search for one.

As Overhold (1988) has asserted, there is no one pattern that fits all prospective surrogate mothers. Their motives vary. Reputable intermediaries often have an intake application form that a prospective surrogate completes which provides some information about her motives and state of mind as well as basic biographical and physical information (Ragoné, 1994).

A common criterion for a candidate for the surrogate mother role is that she has previously borne a healthy child. Once committed to finding a surrogate, the couple should make certain that the potential surrogate has also been carefully screened both medically and psychologically. Apart from a complete physical examination, a full medical history should be obtained to determine whether she has any medical disorders or chromosomal abnormalities—for example, diabetes, Rh sensitivity, a recessive gene for a congenital disease, HIV or other sexual disease, alcoholism, or heavy drug usage—that might affect the health of the fetus (American Society for Reproductive Medicine, 1996). It is suggested that the potential surrogate undergo a series of psychological tests, including, for example, the Minnesota Multiphasic Personality Inventory (Ragoné, 1994), and be carefully examined about her motives for participating in a surrogacy arrangement. The psychological evaluation cannot determine with certainty whether a woman will ultimately change her mind about keeping the baby, but it should screen out those who are clearly emotionally unstable. It might also be advisable to interview her husband and children, when applicable, to obtain their views of her action. Once she is selected as a surrogate, it is recommended that the woman participate in monthly or semimonthly support group meetings.

Psychologists must be careful not to play a double role—screening a candidate for surrogate motherhood and acting as her therapist (Tangri & Kahn, 1993). They also need to observe other specific cautions explicated in the *Ethical Principles* of the American Psychological Association (1992) that apply to surrogacy contracts.

RESPONSIBILITIES TO THE SURROGATE

The legal contract that is signed by all parties should spell out all of the responsibilities of each person to the others. A detailed sample contract is included in Ragoné's book (1994). For the couple that will raise the child, these documents typically focus on financial commitments to be made to the surrogate to cover medical expenses, maternity clothing, and lost wages, as well as a life insurance policy for her.

There is also a contractual obligation to take the child after birth. This may lead to problems if the child has birth defects that cause the biological father and his wife to reject the child, even if there is a clause in the contract that obligates them to take the baby. A second possibility is a breach of contract by the couple if the surrogate mother delivers twins and the couple wants only one child (Schwartz, 1991a). (In the latter case, the surrogate and her husband refused to surrender the wanted child, choosing instead to raise the twins themselves. They were awarded custody by the court, and the biological father was not allowed to have visiting privileges [Nowakowski, 1990].)

RESPONSIBILITIES OF THE SURROGATE

The legal contract that is signed before the biological arrangements go forward also should itemize the commitments to be made by the surrogate mother. These typically include that she will not take drugs (other than those prescribed by a doctor), will have appropriate obstetrical care, will not drink alcohol or smoke, and will surrender the baby after birth to the contracting couple. There may be a provision that she will not have intercourse with anyone during the attempts at insemination and that she will not develop an emotional attachment to the baby (Schwartz, 1987). As a practical matter, this last item may be virtually impossible to enforce.

In the opinion of Tangri and Kahn (1993), such parenting contracts should be held illegal regardless of whether they involve financial compensation, as they "do not protect the birth mother's control over her own body and pregnancy. . . . A woman can obviously consent informally to medical, dietary, or other regimens if she wishes to do so; however, making it illegal for contracts to require her to do so discourages practices that put women under the control of others" (p. 273).

One can understand the origin of each viewpoint. The detailed restrictions do, however, appear to some to treat the surrogate as chattel.

SURROGATE'S POSTPARTUM RIGHTS

The legal contract should state whether the surrogate mother will have any rights to interact with the baby after she surrenders her parental rights. Typically, she will never again see the child. Since the Baby M case (Schwartz, 1987, 1988, 1989, 1990, 1991b), however, some surrogate mothers may, like Mary Beth Whitehead, want to have visits or other contacts similar to those in open adoptions. The prospective surrogate needs to consider this both in terms of her own feelings and from the perspective of the child. As in adoptions, the prospective legal parents should also consider this possibility carefully before they embark on this path to parenthood. What will it mean to them in terms of psychological security? What might it mean to the child in the future?

PREVAILING POSITIONS

Our modern concern with surrogate motherhood has evolved within the past 15 to 20 years. Questions about its legal and mental health ramifications were raised early in the 1980s (Howe, 1983; Schwartz, 1984) and both the number and the nature of the arguments escalated very quickly after that. The focus on this practice was intensified when the Baby M case went to the New Jersey courts in 1986 and 1987, and discussion has continued since then in a variety of professional and lay publications.

CONFLICTING VIEWS REGARDING SURROGACY

There are a number of legal and human rights issues that arise from the concept of surrogate motherhood. Arguments about surrogate motherhood in particular are raised not only by attorneys, but also by legislators, mental health professionals, social service agencies, religious authorities, and women's rights activists.

Religious Views

The position of the Roman Catholic Church is that "our official theological teachings prohibit all forms of artificial insemination, in vitro fertilization, and surrogate motherhood. These practices are morally illicit and cannot be justified by the desire to procreate" (Macklin, 1994, p. 34). The Vatican's opposition to surrogate motherhood and other artificial means of reproduction was clearly stated in its document entitled *Instruction on Respect for Human Life in Its Origin and on the Dignity of Procreation: Replies to Certain Questions of the Day* (Ostling, 1987). In 1987, Roman Catholic bishops in New Jersey filed an amicus brief with the state's Supreme Court opposing surrogate motherhood because it promoted "exploitation of women and infertile couples and the dehumanization of babies. In short it traffics for profit in human lives" (McCoy, 1987; Sullivan, 1987).

Jewish law in general opposes surrogate motherhood because it places the surrogate's health and life at risk for no justifiable reason (Gellman, 1988), and may have adverse psychological effects on the infertile wife. Further, a Jewish medical ethicist, Rabbi David Feldman, concluded that "the issues raised by surrogate motherhood pose a clash between two desirable goals: procreation and family. The first should be pursued through alternatives that do not destroy the second" (Feldman, 1987). Another view is that it is a *mitzvah* (a good deed) for a Jewish woman to become a surrogate mother in order to help an infertile couple to have a child, but at the same time, the "rabbis of the Talmud would have considered as null and void a contract to place a baby not yet conceived" (Gold, 1988, p. 122).

In Israel, where Orthodox Judaic views tend to prevail in family law matters, the health minister in 1987 issued regulations that forbade the "implantation of an ovum in a woman who will not be the child's mother" and the transplantation of a donor's ovum "unless it was fertilized by the recipient's husband" (Landau, 1995). The Israeli Supreme Court subsequently declared these regulations invalid as of January 1, 1996, ruling that the subject of surrogate motherhood should be determined by the Knesset through legislation rather than by administrative regulation (Landau, 1995). At the same time, a committee of experts that included lawyers, a psychologist, a sociologist, a medical ethicist (who was also a rabbi and a gynecologist), and a philosopher "issued a 126-page report in which the majority recommended the legalization of surrogate motherhood" (Siegel, 1995). The report included detailed guidelines for implementing a surrogacy arrangement, including a provision that at least one of the prospective parents be an actual biological parent (i.e., supply the ovum or the sperm; Siegel, 1995). A law was passed early in 1996 permitting surrogate motherhood under clearly stated conditions, including many of the committee's recommendations (Fishman, 1996). These include limits on compensation for the woman; a requirement that either the mother (i.e., the husband's wife) or a third party supply the ovum, not the surrogate; provision for the surrogate to change her mind if she decides she wants to keep the baby she carried; and supervision by a committee "comprised of three physicians, a lawyer, a clinical psychologist, a social worker and clergy from the same religion as the parties involved" (Vikhanski, 1996). The first surrogate pregnancy under the new law, using the wife's ova, was reported in July 1997 (Siegel, 1997).

The Qur'an (Koran) "teaches that in the creation of mankind the roles of the males and females in the process are recognized. . . . And it emphasizes, the union should be legitimized through the marriage bond (23:5–6)" (Ebrahim, 1991, pp. 62–63). Thus, implantation of donor eggs, fertilized or not, into the wife's uterus "would be questionable under Islamic law. And the above mentioned religious decree (*fatwa*) of Shaykh Shaltut against artificial insemination with the sperm of a donor, could apply equally, on the basis of analogy, against the adoption of such techniques to correct infertility" (Ebrahim, 1991, p. 63). Surrogate parenting itself, whether in the usual form or as gestational carrier, is similarly against Islamic law both in concept and as a contract for several reasons: (a) it is the "sale" of a free person; (b) the adulterous character of implantation in a third person; and (c) the woman who gives birth to the child is considered to be the mother, thus rendering a child born of a surrogacy contract illegitimate. The conclusion is that "There is no place for surrogate motherhood within the Islamic system, for the evils that would accrue from it will far outweigh any good" (Ebrahim, 1991, p. 65). Even in cases where the gestational surrogate is the woman's mother, as has occurred a few times, Ebrahim (1991) considers the resulting confusion of biological ties to be one of the "evils" that stem from this practice.

An African American theologian (Sanders, 1992) found that few blacks were attracted to surrogacy. Although African American Christians value children as part of family life, she found, upon investigation, that lack of interest in surrogacy and in artificial insemination appeared to stem from three principal sources: "(1) black babies are easier to adopt; (2) the services are prohibitively expensive; and (3) blacks are not solely interested in biological offspring" (p. 1715).

EXPLOITATION VERSUS REPRODUCTIVE AUTONOMY

Should women have the freedom to decide what to do with their own bodies (i.e., reproductive autonomy)? Is surrogate motherhood exploitative of women, especially those who are poor? These are basically the major concerns of those who are for or against the practice. Put another way, "Are women exploited if they are induced by economic incentives to consent to a procedure as invasive and burdensome as surrogacy, or are they patronized by having their consent to that procedure questioned or closely scrutinized?" (Wasserman & Wachbroit, 1992, p. 441). Realistically, the remuneration is very low as an hourly wage and plays a very minor role in the surrogate's act. Ragoné (1996) found that the primary motivation among surrogates she interviewed was the power to give the "ultimate gift," "the gift of life," to a couple. She concluded that surrogacy also provides some women with a feeling that they are doing something important and of social value.

Some feminist groups perceive that poor women are being used as surrogates to serve the desires of the wealthy (Annas, 1988), or are being regarded as nothing more than an almost inanimate means to an end, and condemn this as exploitation (Corea, 1986; Raymond, 1993). Certainly many of those who serve as surrogates do so, at least partially, because of the money they will be paid, and those who seek a surrogate have the money to pay for their services. In the case of those who serve as gestational surrogates, especially, the view of the woman as an "incubator" with no rights to feelings about or wishes for the baby-to-be is a common one. Mental health professionals might ponder the question posed by Heyl (1988): "What does being treated like a piece of machinery for producing a salable product do to the self-esteem of these women, to their relationship with their own children—ones they bear and keep and ones they bear and relinquish?" (p. 13)

On the other side of the argument, there are those who say that a woman should be free to choose pregnancy if she so wishes, whether to raise the child herself or to provide a service for the childless. No one forces a woman to seek out an intermediary who will enable her to become a surrogate mother; she does so voluntarily. She can decline to continue a pending arrangement at any stage prior to signing a contract, and can change her mind even after the baby is born. As Kane (1988) asked, are the reports of exploitation real or magnified?

At this level of discussion, the woman's pre-conception agreement that she will terminate her maternal rights to the baby "may be seen as akin to a similar decision to surrender a baby for adoption in advance of its birth, or as an expression of reproductive autonomy . . ." (Schwartz, 1991b, p. 364). It may also be perceived legally as a violation against the Thirteenth Amendment's prohibition of involuntary servitude (Suh, 1989) because of the restrictions placed on her activities, even though she agrees to them voluntarily. Ethical concerns for the surrogate and the physicians involved have been considered as well by a number of medical associations in the United States and elsewhere (Pretorius, 1994).

ECONOMIC AND LEGAL CONCERNS

There are a number of economic and legal issues relevant to the practice of surrogate motherhood. These include: (a) the legality and enforceability of the surrogacy contract; (b) the payment of fees to the surrogate mother and the intermediary; (c) the applicability of adoption laws to placement of the child; (d) the timing of the surrogate's termination of her parental rights; (e) Constitutional issues; and (f) state laws (Schwartz, 1991a). (A valuable source on international legal views of surrogate motherhood and contracts is Pretorius [1994].)

In an attempt to regulate the outcome of artificial reproductive techniques such as surrogate motherhood, the Uniform Status of Children of Assisted Conception Act was approved by the National Conference of Commissioners on Uniform State Laws in 1988 and adopted by the American Bar Association in 1989 (Yoon, 1990).

> Under the Act, after the parties form the agreement, a petition must be filed in the appropriate court for approval of the arrangement. The court then appoints a guardian *ad litem* for the expected child and a counselor to protect the interests of the surrogate mother. At the hearing, if the court decides that the surrogacy agreement does not adequately protect the interests of all parties, the judge may not approve the petition. (Yoon, 1990, pp. 546–547)

The act also requires that an appropriate child-welfare agency conduct home studies of all parties to the contract as well as counseling all parties.

The Surrogacy Contract

Carefully drawn surrogacy contracts avoid the prohibition against baby-selling by wording any payment of fees as reimbursement for expenses. They also detail the obligations and responsibilities of all parties to the contract. Such a contract is viewed by some as a "collision of public policy and freedom of contract..." (Linzer, 1989, p. 325).

> Because of the fundamental right of a mother to associate and develop a relationship with her child, any surrogacy arrangement that involves a pre-birth or pre-conception agreement to relinquish parental rights and custody should be void and unenforceable. This critical part of the surrogacy contract cannot be upheld without violating the surrogate's constitutional rights of privacy. Applying contract law to surrogacy and insisting that "a deal's a deal" fails to protect the surrogate's fundamental rights, and upholds the contracting couple's rights at her expense. (Rae, 1994, p. 109)

On the other hand, California courts *In re Johnson v. Calvert* (1993), a case involving a gestational carrier who wanted to keep the baby, and New York courts *In re McDonald v. McDonald*, where the husband's sperm had been used to fertilize a female donor's ovum, which was then implanted in his wife's uterus for the pregnancy, both considered what the intentions of the contracting parties were in reaching their decisions. (In the McDonald case, the husband sued for divorce shortly after the birth of twin girls and sought to retain sole custody on the grounds that he alone was the genetic and legal parent.) "The *McDonald* court followed California's lead in holding that where the means of reproduction do not coincide in one woman, she who intended to bring about the birth of a child that she intended to rear as her own, is the natural mother" (Coleman, 1996, p. 510). Although these decisions set a precedent, it does not mean that courts in other states that permit surrogacy will follow the precedent.

Assuming that a surrogacy contract is held enforceable in a specific situation, to what degree does it specify the biological father's responsibilities for child support if the woman does not fulfill the original agreement and he has no visiting rights (i.e., she refuses to terminate her maternal rights or to surrender the child, or is awarded custody by a court)? Does it spell out the woman's rights if the contracting couple (biological father and his wife) refuse to accept the child because the child is handicapped in some way? Who is to support the child or provide medical care for the child if this happens? (Marshall, 1996) In ordinary business-type contracts, there are penalties for not fulfilling a contract (nonperformance) that can range from fines to jail sentences. In surrogacy contracts, however, there are competing considerations, ranging from the Thirteenth Amendment to reproductive autonomy and the individual's right to privacy, that are used to argue against penalties for nonperformance (Schwartz, 1991a). Further, "family-law situations commonly involve two right-holders whose interests conflict" (Schneider, 1990, p. 129). Finally, there are abundant moral and ethical aversions to viewing a baby as a commodity (Kieber, 1992; Radin, 1995; Tangri & Kahn, 1993; van Niekerk, 1995).

Is This Baby-Selling?
There are several questions involved in the economic aspects of surrogate motherhood. Can the intermediary who brings the prospective parents and the prospective surrogate mother together be paid a fee? How large a fee? To what compensation, if any, is the surrogate mother entitled? May the prospective parents pay the surrogate

mother a fee beyond her basic expenses? May they pay her for terminating her parental rights? In toto, is surrogacy baby-selling? If it *is* baby-selling, what does that tell us about the way in which children are perceived? As Radin (1995) asserted, "if we view children as market commodities, it might make the self-conception of those children as persons harder or impossible. In other words, it might impinge on personhood" (p. 136). The view of surrogacy as commodification of children is an ethical as well as a moral question, for some claim "that surrogacy is similar to prostitution in that it reduces women's reproductive labour to a form of alienated and/or dehumanized labour" (van Niekerk, 1995, p. 345).

"Every state has a law against exchanging consideration for obtaining a child" (Radin, 1995, p. 135). Of the four states that have legislation providing for the enforcement of surrogacy agreements (Florida, Nevada, New Hampshire, and Virginia), "Virginia makes it unlawful for a third party to accept compensation for the recruiting or procurement of women to act as surrogates, while Nevada makes it unlawful to pay or even to offer to pay a surrogate anything more than necessary medical and living expenses related to the child's birth" (Coleman, 1996, pp. 503–504).

In those states where surrogacy contracts are legally enforceable, the contract typically specifies a fee to be paid by the couple to the surrogate mother at different points in the contractual period to cover medical expenses, the cost of maternity clothes, and lost wages. In the sample contract included in Ragoné (1994), Clause XVI specifically states: "The consideration paid the Surrogate is intended to compensate her for unforeseen and unanticipated expenses such as travel, child care, lost wages, discomfort, pain and inconvenience by the Surrogate, her Husband (if any) and her family" (p. 146). In addition, the prospective parents are to purchase a short-term life insurance policy on the surrogate's life from the time conception is confirmed to a period a few months after the child is born. The funds provided by the prospective parents, again by contractual agreement, may be set aside in a trust fund when the contract is signed.

The Role of Adoption Laws

The practice in most surrogacy cases (i.e., where the surrogate supplies the ovum) is for the biological father's wife to adopt the child after the surrogate has terminated her maternal rights. This raises the question of evaluating the prospective adoptive mother's fitness to be a mother, just as would be done with any other prospective adoptive parent. In the Baby M case, it was noted that no such evaluation was made of Mrs. Stern (Chesler, 1988).

Adoption laws may also apply in surrogacy cases with respect to confidentiality or openness of adoption records. The Uniform Status of Children of Assisted Conception Act, previously cited, made "brief mention of confidentiality as follows: '(t)he court shall keep all records of the proceedings confidential and subject to inspection under the same standards applicable to adoption'" (Smith, 1992–1993, p. 99). This protects the privacy of the surrogate if that is her wish, as it does for biological mothers of adoptees, but it also permits the child to obtain medical or other needed information if a court deems it appropriate.

An additional question arises if the biological father and his wife, the adoptive mother, subsequently divorce. Who has the right to primary (or sole) custody of the child (Blankenship, Rushing, Onorato, & White, 1993)?

Timing of the Surrogate's Termination of Rights

In adoption, most states have statutes that specify when the biological mother may consent to terminate her parental rights (i.e., how many days after birth). In surrogacy contracts, however, she makes this decision when she makes the initial commitment to become pregnant for the purpose of delivering a child to a couple. Legally, the termination of rights must be confirmed after the birth of the baby. If she changes her mind after delivery, this amounts to nonperformance of her contract and raises the questions previously discussed. When Mary Beth Whitehead did this, the lower court in New Jersey ruled against her, but the appeals court declared that she was in fact the mother of Baby M and voided the adoption by William Stern's wife. The appellate ruling stated that she could not have waived her rights with informed consent prior to the birth of the baby (Blankenship, et al., 1993).

Constitutional Issues

If the surrogacy contract is upheld as enforceable and not contrary to public policy, it may still be void if it infringes on one or another of the parties' constitutional rights. The issues raised include the constitutional prohibition of slavery (the Thirteenth Amendment and the Anti-Peonage Act); the "right to privacy" derived from the Fifth Amendment and applied, for example, to a woman's right to abortion in the famous *Roe v. Wade* case; and "the equally derivative 'right to procreate' with its corollary the 'right to marry' " (Fox, 1993, p. 25). These issues also bear on the woman's reproductive autonomy versus exploitation argument previously discussed.

> The argument that surrogacy should be a constitutional right tries to say that privacy and substantive due process would include the man's right to procreate, and men's right to procreate presumably is not limited to their spouses if the spouses are unable or unwilling to help them procreate. That is a dubious constitutional right. . . . In line with the liberal argument, you could also argue that the woman has a constitutional liberty right to sell whatever she wants to. Or you could argue equal protection: You could say, if we allow sperm donors to donate or even sell, maybe we should allow the commissioned adoption transaction, as an analagous transaction for women. . . .
>
> You could argue that commissioned adoption is not analogous to sperm donation because birth mothers develop a relationship with the unborn child that a man doesn't have with his sperm. You might say there is a constitutional argument prohibiting our forcing someone who is a birth mother to give up a child that she decides she wants to keep, because the substantive due process privacy right is that the birth mother has a right to companionship of her children which can't be overridden by contract. (Radin, 1995, p. 140)

State Laws

According to Robinson (1993), there are several compelling state interests in the surrogate motherhood arrangement:

- Protection against the possible exploitation of poor women.
- Prevention of individuals being bought and sold as property.
- Protection of the family.
- Prevention of disruption of the mother–child bond.
- Protection of the fetus in the event of a mother–fetus conflict.

Varying interpretations of these state interests have led to different laws in different states. Several states impose civil or criminal penalties on persons entering into surrogacy agreements (New York, Utah, Washington, and the District of Columbia), while other states have statutes stating that such agreements are unenforceable (Arizona, Indiana, Louisiana, Michigan, Nebraska, North Dakota, and Tennessee); Coleman, 1996, p. 504). Conversely, the California Supreme Court ruled, in a gestational surrogacy case where the woman who carried the child wanted to keep him, that a surrogacy contract was enforceable and did not violate public policy (Egelko, 1993).

That state laws regarding surrogacy contracts and arrangements vary is apparent. Even within states, as was evident in the Baby M case, an appellate court judge may interpret the state's laws differently from a lower court judge. For any therapist working with prospective surrogate mothers or with prospective parents, it is imperative to know what the law is in their jurisdiction so that the therapist can indicate to the client(s) that there may be a statutory impediment to surrogate motherhood and to recommend working with an attorney knowledgeable about the laws regarding surrogacy in their state of residence.

Parental Rights of the Surrogate Mother Postdelivery

Whether the surrogate mother has any rights of visitation or lesser contact with the baby after she terminates her parental rights depends in part on the contract she originally signed, partly on whether she is a relative of one of the prospective parents, and partly on her postpartum reactions. Under the provisions of most contracts, she will have no further contact with the child or the biological father and his wife after the child is in their care. If the contract provided for a more open arrangement, such as an annual letter or photograph, then she is entitled to those. These differing arrangements resemble those of open and closed adoptions. Only if the surrogate mother does not terminate her rights, as happened in the Baby M case, does she have more influence on the child's care and development, including, perhaps, lengthy visits and a voice in the child's health care, education, and religious upbringing.

In those cases where a family member served as biological mother or as gestational carrier, there is some concern that the biologic elements of familial relationships are rearranged. For example, the grandmother who carries a child for her daughter then becomes the child's mother as well, and the daughter is the child's mother as well as sister to the child. "Instead of merely spreading these elements around, as in extrafamilial surrogacy, it recombines them. The effect is equally subversive: By decomposing the elements of natural parenting, it blurs the boundaries of the nuclear family and diminishes its significance" (Wasserman & Wachbroit, 1992, pp. 438–439). Will mother and daughter each argue "This is *my* child!"? The outcome in any specific family is obviously dependent on the ways in which family members interact.

IMPACT OF THE ISSUES ON THE PARTICIPANTS

When surrogate motherhood was barely underway as an alternative to infertility, a number of questions were posed:

Will the infertile adoptive mother be able to develop the much-desired affectionate relationship with a child born in these circumstances? How will she relate to the child's father? Will jealousy or resentment become overwhelming? . . . Will there be problems for the surrogate mother within her own marriage? (Schwartz, 1984, p. 57)

These questions are still relevant.

TRADITIONAL SURROGACY AND IMPACT ON THE ADOPTIVE MOTHER

If the surrogate mother supplies the ovum, what is the impact on the wife of the parenting couple? The adoptive mother of a baby born as a result of the fertilization of another woman's ovum by the adoptive mother's husband's sperm may rejoice simply because she has a child, just as any other adoptive mother might. In other situations, the baby is a constant reminder of her own infertility. It would be difficult to generalize a single reaction to this situation. However, if she is like most adoptive mothers, she will very quickly bond with the child who has entered her life and will be as affectionate toward him or her as she would be to a child she herself had borne. In those cases where the arrangement is an open one, she may also develop a close relationship with the surrogate mother.

GESTATIONAL SURROGACY AND IMPACT ON THE WIFE

If the wife supplies the ovum and the surrogate carries it to term, what is the impact on the wife? Might the wife have mixed feelings of gratitude and envy? One would expect that a woman who could not carry a pregnancy to term but could supply an ovum to be fertilized with her husband's sperm would feel extremely grateful to the gestational carrier who helped to bring the resulting baby into the world and into her arms. If the carrier is a family member, both women should be counseled beforehand on ways to handle their prospective double relationship in the most positive manner. If the gestational surrogate is a stranger, can her 9 months of total care for the fetus be viewed as just a commercial convenience?

HUSBAND-WIFE RELATIONSHIPS

In what ways might the surrogacy arrangement affect the husband's relationship with his wife, and hers with him? The ineffective treatments for infertility prior to embarking on a surrogacy arrangement may increase the feelings of frustration and, to a degree, helplessness that beset any couple that wants to have children but cannot. The strain may be exacerbated if one member of the couple wants to follow the surrogacy route and the other would prefer adoption or some other path. It is at this point that a therapist can be helpful in exploring the reasons for their preferences while reducing the strains in the marital relationship.

THE SURROGATE AND HER FAMILY

What is the impact of the surrogacy arrangement on the *surrogate's* family? Her husband cannot have intercourse with her while attempts at insemination are being made; her children will experience her pregnancy but be deprived of the excitement of a new half-sibling; and her parents, the baby's maternal grandparents, will not be allowed to enjoy a new grandchild. Odds are that her children may be most in need of psychological support. It is surely difficult for children to understand how their mother (and father) can, in their eyes, give away a baby. It may also create anxiety in the surrogate's children that *they* may be given away, too. Much depends on the age of the surrogate's children at the time and the way in which their mother's motives are explained to them.

The maternal grandparents, who may not have been informed or consulted about their daughter's surrogacy role beforehand, may well feel deprived of a pleasure they feel should be theirs. This can cause resentment and anger, which may escalate to an estrangement between them and their daughter. At that point, one can only hope that someone urges all parties to seek therapy to mend the family's relationships.

The surrogate herself may be viewed by some as an inanimate incubator, although she is risking her health and well-being during pregnancy and delivery. Women who serve as gestational surrogates may be especially criticized by some "because their pregnancies are viewed more negatively than usual. Not only is she pregnant, but she's pregnant 'with someone else's child' who has no genetic link to her—for money" (Raymond, 1993, p. 68). Psychotherapy for the surrogate can be an appropriate means of helping her to deal with such negative views.

SURROGACY MEETS THERAPY

There are a number of ways in which surrogacy may interact with therapy. Perhaps the couple are in marital counseling because of their difficulty in dealing with infertility and its effect on their relationship, or maybe it is just the wife who is seeking help to maintain her self-esteem in the face of her inability to conceive or bear a child. Although the expectation that every woman will have children is not quite as strong a social belief and pressure as it was in the 1940s and 1950s (Schwartz, 1991a), the individual may feel that she is a failure as a wife and a woman if she can not, and therefore she may seek help. She may also feel that she is being pushed into agreeing to a surrogacy contract to salve her husband's needs rather than to meet their joint desire to parent a child. Matters may have deteriorated to the point that he has said something like, "If you really loved me, you would do this." At this juncture, the therapist needs to help each party to see the other's point of view, for the marriage itself may well be at risk, or the wife's self-doubts may make it difficult for her to function effectively.

A second possibility is that the couple, or the wife, is having a problem dealing with ambivalent feelings—gratitude and resentment, for example, toward the surrogate mother. Although the prospective parents appreciate the gift she is nurturing for them, there may also be negative feelings because she is doing something the wife cannot do. The therapist can guide the couple to understand and resolve this inherent conflict in the least damaging ways.

A third situation that may arise is that children born of the surrogacy arrangement later enter therapy and want to know more about their origins, or have to resolve residual anger toward their adoptive mother for not being their biological mother. Maybe a child has been taunting her mother about this, as teenagers may do when seeking any way to vent their hostility about rules imposed by parents. In this scenario the therapist might indicate the need for some family therapy sessions. Helping the youngster learn about the surrogate mother may be beyond the therapist's scope, as the records are often sealed. The therapist can, however, explore with the youngster why this is so important, and how much she or he was wanted by her or his psychological and adoptive mother, and what might be possible when the youth is an adult.

Children of surrogacy may be quite upset to realize that they were the "product" of a commercial surrogacy arrangement, and be devastated to learn that their biological mothers did not want to raise them. In response to this, the therapist might portray the surrogate "as an altruistic actor who understood the parents' plight and helped them by conceiving and carrying the child to term" (Smith, 1993, p. 77). Some of this difficulty might be averted if the therapist is working with the parents when the child is very young. The therapist can guide them in developing age- and situation-appropriate responses to the question every child asks, "Where did I come from?" (Bernstein, 1994; Glazer, 1990; Pruett, 1992).

It is equally possible that the surrogate mother is depressed about or is suffering belated regrets at having borne a child only to give the baby to someone else. It is not enough for the therapist to remind the woman that she voluntarily chose to enter such an agreement; she needs empathy and understanding. The therapist needs to help her to find ways to deal with her grief rationally and effectively.

Finally, the client may be a child of the surrogate mother. The child may be anxious about being turned away from his or her family, or distraught because she or he is unable to interact with a child who is a half-sibling. What the therapist imparts will be dictated in part by both the maturity of the client and by the arrangements in the specific situation as revealed by the surrogate mother.

WHAT THE THERAPIST NEEDS TO KNOW

It should be apparent from the preceding discussions of ethical, religious, and legal issues in this chapter that the therapist should have at least some familiarity with different religious perspectives and with the legal status of surrogacy in the state of practice so that misinformation is not given. The therapist active in this area of practice should also have a list of reliable legal referrals available to offer to the client.

If, as in the Baby M case, the surrogate mother refuses to surrender the child or demands partial custody, the therapist will need to provide support to the parent couple and help them deal with the ensuing legal battles. Should they never have the opportunity of raising the baby, the therapist will have to move toward grief therapy, just as if they had lost a child at birth or soon after.

In cases where the parenting couple divorce, the therapist will have the task of dealing not only with the psychological problems stirred up by divorce, but also with the potential loss of custody by the adoptive mother because courts tend to favor biological relationships over psychological ones. It might be most productive in this situation for the therapist to refer the patients for family mediation (Schwartz & Kaslow, 1997).

THERAPEUTIC INTERVENTIONS

At different times and with different clients, the therapist may be called upon to play a variety of roles vis-à-vis surrogate parenting. Sometimes the therapist will be a teacher, albeit one who steers clients toward appropriate or needed sources of information. At other sessions, the therapist will be the one to help the clients confront their feelings, questions, and doubts with respect to becoming involved in a surrogacy contract. Once they are committed to such an arrangement, the therapist may help clients deal with their relationship with the surrogate mother and prepare for parenthood, and the therapist may also provide grief therapy if the outcome is other than the planned or hoped-for one. Yet another role for the therapist may be to assist the court in determining what is best for the child (Schwartz, 1991b).

If the client is the child born of a surrogacy arrangement, the therapist again may serve as teacher as well as counselor. In one role, the therapist may satisfy the child's curiosity about surrogate motherhood or gestational carriers, whichever is appropriate. In a second role, the therapist may act in the more traditional sense of helping the child deal with fantasies, hostilities, or other problems which may or may not be relevant to surrogacy. (As noted in the preceding chapter on adoption, the therapist should not assume that *all* problems the child experiences stem from the surrogacy arrangement.)

Should the client(s) be from the surrogate mother's family, either her husband or her children, or even the maternal grandparents, the therapist's task may revolve around their anxiety with respect to her pregnancy or their conflict with the commitment she has undertaken. If it is the latter, this may involve the use of mediation techniques between the mother and the client(s), in an effort to reduce areas of conflict within the parameters of the signed contract.

SUMMARY AND RECOMMENDATIONS

As should be apparent from the preceding discussion, surrogacy is an alternative to infertility that raises many legal, ethical, psychological, and religious questions. It poses potential difficulties that adoption does not, not the least of which is the legality and enforceability of surrogacy contracts in a given state. If a husband and wife decide, after appropriate investigation and therapy, that this is the path to parenthood for them, they may still need psychological support both during the ensuing pregnancy and after they become parents. If there is a negative outcome after the birth, grief therapy is appropriate, just as may be warranted in any great loss or disappointment.

Because surrogate motherhood in all of its formats is still a relatively new reproductive technology, the first recommendation to a family therapist is to learn as much as possible about its implications, restrictions, and potentials for positive and negative outcomes. Second, with reference to working with clients who have infertility problems, it is recommended that the therapist become familiar with RESOLVE, a national support organization for couples with infertility problems, and find out if there is a local chapter in the community that clients can contact. A third recommendation, useful for a variety of problems and not just cases involving surrogacy, is that the therapist become acquainted with trained family mediators who can be called upon to assist in resolving a dispute related to surrogacy when necessary.

The critical issues in this facet of reproductive technology are information about the procedure and its ramifications, and the motives of the participants. Assuming that all goes well, and it apparently has in most such arrangements, the new parents can take on the joys and anxieties of any other parents, perhaps with added zest because of the thoughtfulness and self-examination that has preceded their decision.

REFERENCES

American Psychological Association (1992). Ethical principles of psychologists and code of conduct. *American Psychologist, 47,* 1597–1611.

American Society for Reproductive Medicine (1996). *Third party reproduction: A guide for patients* (pamphlet). Birmingham, AL: Author.

Annas, G. J. (1988, April/May). Death without dignity for commercial surrogacy: The case of Baby M. *Hastings Center Report, 18,* 20–23.

Bernstein, A. C. (1994). *Flight of the stork* (Rev. ed.). Indianapolis, IN: Perspectives Press.

Blankenship, K. M., Rushing, B., Onorato, S. A., & White, R. (1993). Reproductive technologies and the U.S. courts. *Gender & Society, 7*(1), 8–31.

Chesler, P. (1988). *Sacred bond: The legacy of Baby M.* New York: Times Books.

Coleman, M. (1996). Gestation, intent, and the seed: Defining motherhood in the era of assisted human reproduction. *Cardozo Law Review, 17,* 497–530.

Corea, G. (1986). *The mother machine.* New York: Perennial Library.

Ebrahim, A. F. M. (1991). *Abortion, birth control, & surrogate parenting: An Islamic perspective.* Indianapolis, IN: American Trust Publications.

Egelko, B. (1993, May 21). Surrogate birth contract is upheld by Calif. high court. *Philadelphia Inquirer,* p. A16.

Feldman, D. M. (1987, Summer). The Jewish response to surrogate motherhood. *Women's League Outlook, 57*(4), 9–10.

Fishman, R. H. B. (1996, March 16). Surrogate motherhood becomes legal in Israel. *Lancet,* p. 756.

Fox, R. (1993, Spring). Babies for sale. *Public Interest, 111,* 14–40.

Gellman, M. (1988). "I'll take the head": The ethics of surrogate motherhood. *Journal of Reform Judaism, 35*(2), 7–11.

Genesis. (1965). *The holy scriptures.* Philadelphia: Jewish Publication Society.

Glazer, E. S. (1990). *The long-awaited stork: A guide to parenting after infertility.* Lexington, MA: Lexington Books.

Gold, M. (1988). *And Hannah wept: Infertility, adoption, and the Jewish couple.* Philadelphia: Jewish Publication Society.

Heyl, B. S. (1988). Commercial contracts and human connectedness. *Society, 25*(3), 11–16.

Howe, R-A. W. (1983). Adoption practice, issues, and laws, 1958–1983. *Family Law Quarterly, 17,* 173–197.

In re Baby M., 525 A.2d 1128 (N. J. Super. Ct. Ch. Div. 1987).

In re Baby M., 537 A.2d 1227 (N. J. 1988).

In re Johnson v. Calvert, 851 P.2d 776 (Cal. 1993).

In re McDonald v. McDonald, 608 N.Y.S.2d 477 (App.Div. 1994).

Kane, E. (1988). *Birth mother: The story of America's first legal surrogate mother.* New York: Harcourt, Brace, Jovanovich.

Kieber, K. B. (1992). Selling the womb: Can the feminist critique of surrogacy be answered? *Indiana Law Journal, 68,* 205–232.

Landau, A. F. (1995, July 24). Surrogate motherhood a Knesset matter. *Jerusalem Post.*

Linzer, P. (Ed.). (1989). *A contracts anthology.* Cincinnati, OH: Anderson Publishing.

Macklin, R. (1994). *Surrogates and other mothers: The debates over assisted reproduction.* Philadelphia: Temple University Press.

Marshall, A. (1996). Choices for a child: An ethical and legal analysis of a failed surrogate birth contract. *University of Richmond Law Review, 30,* 275–302.

McCoy, C. R. (1987, July 16). Surrogate parenting assailed. *Philadelphia Inquirer,* pp. 1-B, 4-B.

Nowakowski, P. (1990, July). How could I let them separate my twins? *Redbook,* pp. 38–41.

Ostling, R. (1987, March 23). Technology and the womb. *Time,* 58–59.

Overvold, A. Z. (1988). *Surrogate parenting.* New York: Pharos Books.

Pretorius, D. (1994). *Surrogate motherhood: A worldwide view of the issues.* Springfield, IL: Charles C. Thomas.

Pruett, K. D. (1992). Strange bedfellows? Reproductive technology and child development. *Infant Mental Health Journal, 13,* 312–318.

Radin, M. J. (1995). What, if anything, is wrong with baby selling? *Pacific Law Journal, 26,* 135–145.

Rae, S. B. (1994). *The ethics of commercial surrogate motherhood: Brave new frontiers?* Westport, CN: Praeger.

Ragoné, H. (1994). *Surrogate motherhood: Conception in the heart.* Boulder, CO: Westview Press.

Ragoné, H. (1996). Chasing the blood tie: Surrogate mothers, adoptive mothers and fathers. *American Ethnologist, 23,* 352–365.

Raymond, J. G. (1993). *Women as wombs: Reproductive technologies and the battle over women's freedom.* New York: HarperCollins.

Robinson, C. (1993). Surrogate motherhood: Implications for the mother-fetus relationship. *Women & Politics, 13,* 203–224.

Sanders, C. J. (1992). Surrogate motherhood and reproductive technologies: An African American perspective. *Creighton Law Review, 25,* 1707–1723.

Schneider, C. E. (1990). Surrogate motherhood from the perspective of family law. *Harvard Journal of Law & Public Policy, 13,* 125–131.

Schwartz, L. L. (1984). Adoption custody and family therapy. *American Journal of Family Therapy, 12*(4), 51–58.

Schwartz, L. L. (1987). Surrogate motherhood I: Responses to infertility. *American Journal of Family Therapy, 15,* 158–162.

Schwartz, L. L. (1988). Surrogate motherhood II: Reflections after "Baby M." *American Journal of Family Therapy, 16,* 158–166.

Schwartz, L. L. (1989). Surrogate motherhood III: The end of a saga? *American Journal of Family Therapy, 17,* 67–72.

Schwartz, L. L. (1990). Surrogate motherhood and family psychology/therapy. *American Journal of Family Therapy, 18,* 385–392.

Schwartz, L. L. (1991a). *Alternatives to infertility: Is surrogacy the answer?* New York: Brunner/Mazel.

Schwartz, L. L. (1991b). Psychological and legal perspectives on surrogate motherhood. *American Journal of Family Therapy, 19,* 363–367.

Schwartz, L. L., & Kaslow, F. W. (1997). *Painful partings: Divorce and its aftermath.* New York: John Wiley & Sons.

Siegel, J. (1995, July 18). Ticking of biological clocks helped to alter stand on surrogacy. *Jerusalem Post.*

Siegel, J. (1997, July 29). First surrogate pregnancy here announced. *Jerusalem Post.*

Smith, P. (1992–1993). Regulating confidentiality of surrogacy records: Lessons from the adoption experience. *University of Louisville Journal of Family Law, 31,* 65–103.

Suh, M. M. (1989). Surrogate motherhood: An argument for denial of specific performance. *Columbia Journal of Law and Social Problems, 22,* 357–396.

Sullivan, J. F. (1987, July 19). Bishops file brief against surrogate motherhood. *New York Times,* p. 28.

Tangri, S. S., & Kahn, J. R. (1993). Ethical issues in the new reproductive technologies: Perspectives from feminism and the psychology profession. *Professional Psychology, 24,* 271–280.

van Niekerk, A. (1995). The ethics of surrogacy: Women's reproductive labour. *Journal of Medical Ethics, 21,* 345–349.

Vikhanski, L. (1996, April). Israel legalizes surrogate motherhood. *Nature Medicine, 2*(4), 372.

Wasserman, D., & Wachbroit, R. (1992). The technology, law, and ethics of in vitro fertilization, gamete donation, and surrogate motherhood. *Clinics in Laboratory Medicine, 12*(3), 429–448.

Yoon, M. (1990). The Uniform Status of Children of Assisted Conception Act: Does it protect the best interests of the child in a surrogate arrangement? *American Journal of Law & Medicine, 16,* 525–553.

ADDITIONAL RESOURCES

Organization for Parents through Surrogacy (OPTS)
National Headquarters
7054 Quito Court
Camarillo, CA 93012

RESOLVE
1310 Broadway
Somerville, MA 02144-1731

CHAPTER 4

Foster Parenting

JANE F. SILOVSKY and DIANE J. WILLIS

As WE approach the 21st century the challenge to our citizens will be to develop safety nets for all families, reduce the incidence of poverty and violence in our society, and prevent child maltreatment, substance abuse, and prenatal substance exposure (Willis & Silovsky, 1998). The National Commission on Family Foster Care (NCFFC; 1991) reported that, in the United States, one in four babies is born to a mother with no history of prenatal care. The number of drug-exposed infants has increased threefold from 1985 to 1997, and homicide is the number-one cause of injury-related deaths among infants. Twenty percent of our children live below the poverty level, with Hispanics, Native Americans, and African Americans reaching poverty levels of 39% to 50%. Many of the children affected by poverty, substance abuse, and family violence become involved in the child protection service system and are cared for by foster families.

Foster parenting children in the United States is a huge voluntary effort by those who accept children into their homes. The number of children residing in family foster care has increased over the last decade, and now approaches about 500,000 (Child Welfare League of America, 1998; Rosenfeld et al., 1997). In California, children placed in out-of-home care increased 83% from 1985 to 1990 (Child Welfare Research Center, 1991) and the number of children in California being placed in foster homes rose from 33,285 in 1984 to 84,000 in 1994 (Barth, Courtney, Needell, & Johnson-Reid, 1994). As the number of children needing foster care has increased, the number of available foster homes has decreased. In 1987 there were approximately 147,000 foster homes nationwide, but 3 years later the number had been reduced to 100,000 (Chamberlin, Moreland, & Reid, 1992). Child protection services (CPS) have begun to rely more on kinship care (i.e., relatives of the children provide the foster care). In 1990, an analysis of 29 states indicated that 31% of children removed from their parents were placed in kinship care (Kusserow, 1992).

Appreciation is expressed to Jan L. Culbertson, PhD, and Rebecca McNeese, JD, Oklahoma City, for reviewing this manuscript and offering constructive editorial and legal assistance.

Children entering the foster care system have had more complex adjustment problems in recent years than in previous years, as suggested by a report of the U.S. Advisory Board on Child Abuse and Neglect (1990). The Board noted that low income and poverty conditions still account for a large number of children entering care but that substance abuse and all of the activities (including fetal substance exposure) associated with substance abuse account for much of the increase in CPS caseloads. Indeed, neglect is the highest reported type of maltreatment that accounts for foster care placement, with at least three-fourths of these cases attributed to substance abuse (Klee, Kronstadt, & Zlotnick, 1997). Current estimates suggest that 50% to 80% of families reported to CPS have a substance abuse problem.

Foster children often have complex social, emotional, behavioral, and developmental treatment needs, due in large part to the impact of events that led to the out-of-home placement (e.g., child abuse). There are additional influences emanating from the process of foster care. The experience of out-of-home care "involves separation, usually through court procedures; placement of the child in a foster home; planning for the parents and the child; rehabilitative activities to meet plan requirements; efforts to maintain contact between parents and children during placement, and, . . . eventual reunification of the family," or other long-term placement (Hubbell, 1981, p. 71). Due to the nature of foster care, issues of separation, loss, feelings of abandonment, safety, trust, and integration with a new family further complicate treatment planning for the children. Thus, the huge increase in the number of children needing foster care makes an enormous impact on CPS workers, the courts, foster placements, and mental health facilities.

Foster parents (and mental health professionals providing care for the family and foster children) should be educated about the procedures of juvenile court, civil court, and criminal court, about their rights as foster families in the court procedures, and on the availability of court-appointed advocates for the children. Professionals must be cognizant of the adjustment and treatment needs of children in foster care and of the policies and procedures of the foster care system. This chapter provides background information regarding types of foster homes, treatment needs of children in care, the judicial procedures in foster care, and other issues important to professionals providing services for children in foster care.

FOSTER FAMILIES

Couples decide to become foster parents for many reasons, including their interest in children's well-being, belief in community service, desire for companionship, inability to adopt or have children, desire to test out parenthood, need for more income, religious beliefs, and previous relationship with a specific child (U.S. Department of Health and Human Services, 1993). Many families wish to provide a safe home to children in need and become licensed foster parents. Each state has developed procedures for licensing foster families. The screening and evaluation consist of, but are not limited to, checking police records and health records and conducting home investigations (Benedict, Zuravin, Brandt, & Abbey, 1994). Families who pass the evaluation are then licensed to provide care for an identified number of children of specified ages (such as being licensed to provide care to two infants).

Foster families provide care for children in a home environment when it is determined that the children were harmed or were in potential danger if they remained with their caregivers. Being raised and cared for in a homelike environment has been assumed to be more beneficial and preferred over institutional care, such as that offered in group homes.

Recommendations for foster care in the 1990s made by the Child Welfare League of America and the National Foster Parent Association list specific responsibilities for the foster family to provide a nurturing, safe, and consistent family environment (NCFFC, 1991). Foster families are charged with providing for the children's physical, mental, recreational, cultural, and spiritual needs, using a positive approach and nonphysical discipline. Promoting and supporting the relationship between children *and their families* (i.e., the family from whom the child was removed) is specifically recommended. Information regarding children's progress towards goals is to be provided to the CPS worker, and foster families are to participate in judicial hearings relevant to the child's well-being (NCFFC, 1991). The foster parents are also considered to be advocates for the specific needs of the children.

The NCFFC (1991) strongly recommends a team approach that includes the foster family in developing treatment plans, communicating about the children's and family's progress, and supporting transitions to permanent placements. A frequent concern of foster families is that they do not have adequate information about the children's history and needs, which leaves them unprepared to provide appropriately for a specific child. The team approach facilitates educating and directly assisting those who have the most direct care of the children, that is, the foster parents.

TYPES OF FOSTER HOME PLACEMENTS

Depending on the children's needs and the availability of foster homes, children may be placed in one of the following types of foster homes: emergency foster homes, specialized or therapeutic foster homes, nonrelative foster homes, and relative foster homes (kinship care). *Emergency foster homes* provide immediate, short-term placement (although children may remain longer than anticipated due to difficulty in finding longer-term foster care placement). Emergency foster care is an important substitution for group shelters that are not desirable for some children (e.g., infants). *Specialized (therapeutic) foster care* may be required for children with physical disabilities or behavioral and emotional problems (Harling & Haines, 1980). Foster parents who have received specialized training provide therapeutic care for these children. Otherwise, children may be placed in *foster homes* or in *kinship care,* monitored by public or private agencies.

Each placement decision should integrate an understanding of the child's attachment to and relationship with significant caregivers and the impact of separation from these caregivers on the child's well being. For children's development, maintaining a secure attachment with their caregiver is critical; disruptions to primary attachment relationships may interfere with their ability to form trust in relationships, hindering long-term adjustment. Policies related to the different types of foster care homes directly impact children's attachment and adjustment. Emergency foster homes, like shelters, are designed to be short term, with many children soon experiencing a change in placement to another foster home, rather than returning to their parent(s) residence.

Limits are also placed on the length of time of placement in specialized or therapeutic foster homes. The foster parents in these home are required to have had additional training to address the children's special needs (e.g., implementing medical treatments or providing for emotional needs). The youngsters are evaluated to determine their requirements and plans are developed to address their needs. The foster parents are to work with a team of professionals to implement the treatment plan. Because of the intensity of services, the number of children allowed in each therapeutic foster home is limited. Residence in these homes is often contingent on the determination of continued need for specialized care or indicated by a specific length of time (e.g., 1 year). Such specialized care is much more expensive than the traditional foster care home (e.g., the family may receive more than double the payment). The higher payment is dependent on whether the child is determined to be in need of specialized care. States' policies differ regarding whether the children can remain in the specialized home after improvement; if so, the foster family would have to agree to a lower payment for care. Unfortunately, this may mean that a child with emotional disturbances who improves (perhaps in part due to the relationship developed with the foster family) is then in danger of being moved to another foster home. Each change in placement has a potential negative impact on the child's ability to become attached to others.

KINSHIP CARE

During the 1980s, state placements of deprived children in a relative's home dramatically increased (Rosenfeld et al., 1997; Scannapieco & Hegar, 1995). Perhaps as many as 30% to 50% of children in legal custody of the state reside with extended family members, and placement with appropriate family members is often given precedence over placement in nonrelative foster homes (Berrick, Barth, & Needell, 1994). It is important to remember that extended families have provided direct care for children throughout the world and throughout the centuries (Berrick et al., 1994).

CPS agencies have traditionally used nonrelative families to provide foster care. However, their availability has decreased over the last three decades as more women have joined the work force and fewer homes have caregivers available to provide care for children. At this same time, there has been an increase in the number of children in the custody of the state. Two legal rulings likely further spurred the transition to using relative's homes. In 1979, the U.S. Supreme Court ruled in *Miller v. Yovakim* that relative care homes must be allowed the opportunity to receive foster care payments, should they qualify for a foster care license (Berrick, et al., 1994). Further, the Adoption Assistance and Child Welfare Act (P.L. 96-272) of 1980 emphasized the need for permanency planning and family preservation.

There are at least minimal requirements for relatives to qualify for kinship placement, with investigations including background checks (to ensure that they do not have a felony conviction for crimes against a child, spousal abuse, rape, sexual assault, or homicide), case studies, and an evaluation of the home. Some states require a full licensing assessment of the family, with the same standards for all foster care homes. Those states that require licensure of the kinship care homes may lose potential relative placements due to factors such as inadequate housing (Scannapieco & Hegar, 1995), thereby impacting the long-term adjustment of the children. Many families living below the poverty level cannot meet the requirements for licensure (such as limitations on the number of children in each bedroom), making placement with relatives impossible. (Scannapieco & Hegar, 1995).

Kinship care families, in comparison to nonrelative foster families, typically are offered fewer services, including respite care, support groups, and training (Berrick et al., 1994). They also tend to have less contact with the CPS worker and to receive less direct assistance from CPS than nonrelative foster homes. Despite the fact that placement in kinship homes may be consistent with family preservation goals, these families are in need of more services and are less likely to receive such services. Enhanced services and training are needed before an honest comparison of kinship homes and nonrelative foster care can be made (Berrick et al., 1994).

The United States General Accounting Office reported that, in 1995, children in kinship care were less likely to receive needed health services (Rosenfeld et al., 1997). Berrick et al. (1994) found that nonrelative foster families received over $100 per month more than kinship foster families for each of the children in their care. In addition to the financial pressure is the stress of unplanned parenthood. Nonrelative foster parents often volunteer for the service while preparing for parenthood (U.S. Department of Health and Human Services, 1993), whereas kinship care families may be pressed into the position without preparation (Berrick et al., 1994). Although they may have raised children, caregivers in the kinship homes often have not been expecting to care for young children at the time in their life they are pressed into service, and they may be emotionally and financially unprepared to care for children.

There are concerns regarding the use of relatives for foster parenting. The knowledge that their children are provided for in a relative's home may lower the parent's motivation to fulfill the treatment plan, which itself may appear a daunting task to a parent with complex long-term problems such as drug abuse, poverty, or depression (Hubbel, 1981). Some child protection services have reported that parents often do not have the motivation to change their behavior unless their children are removed from their home, thus increasing the use of foster care homes. Strategies for motivating parental behavior change do not necessarily require the removal of children from their care (see Prochaska, Norcross, & DiClemente, 1994). Decisions to change children's residential placement are better made when they are focused on the health and well-being of the child, rather than as an incentive for parental behavior change.

Another concern regarding kinship placement is that the conditions related to the maltreatment of the child may be present in the home of the relatives. However, this assumption has not been supported by research (Berrick et al., 1994). Research suggests that children placed in kinship care remain in that home longer and are less likely to have a change in placement than are children in nonrelative foster homes. However, children in kinship care who are returned to their parents are less likely to be removed again. The availability of relatives to provide temporary care may indicate a better social support network for the family, and this in turn could contribute to a better outcome (Courtney, 1995).

Greater contact between children and their families during foster placement has been associated with a higher likelihood of ultimate return to the parent(s). Visitation with the parents is often allowed to occur with greater frequency in kinship care placements, with the kinship home guardians providing supervision. Non-kinship foster parents may be reluctant to supervise visitation, or the CPS agency's policies may not allow them to provide supervision. Visits then become dependent on the busy, and often restricted, schedule of the CPS worker. However, the kinship relationship may bring pressure to allow contact between the child and parent that is contradictory to the court order, such as allowing unsupervised contact (Rosenfeld et al., 1997).

CHILDREN IN FOSTER CARE AND THE LEGAL AND JUDICIAL SYSTEM

Under the *parens patriae* doctrine, states are given the duty of protecting their underaged citizens and are to act in the "best interest of the child" (Portwood & Reppucci, 1994). For the protection and treatment of the children, their custody may be transferred to the CPS agency, and many of these children are placed in foster care homes. Placement of children in state's custody most typically occurs through juvenile court, after a child is found to be *deprived* due to child maltreatment, *delinquent* due to criminal behavior of the child, *in need of supervision* due to repeated status offenses, or *in need of treatment* due to emotional problems (Myers, 1992). Decisions are made regarding legal custody of the child by the juvenile court judge based on recommendations provided by CPS workers.

Children who are subject to maltreatment may be involved in two or more court arenas. These may include *juvenile court, criminal court,* and *civil court* (known sometimes as *family court* or the *domestic relations division* of the court). In juvenile and criminal courts, the state (represented by the district attorney or county attorney) has the burden of proof, but the evidence presented in the two courts must reach different standards. In criminal court, the state must prove its case against the defendant *beyond a reasonable doubt.* In juvenile court, the state must prove that the child is deprived by a *preponderance of the evidence* and by *clear and convincing evidence* if termination of parental rights is sought. (Note: If the Indian Child Welfare Act is applicable to the case, the federal government must prove its case for deprivation of a child by clear and convincing evidence, and if termination of parental rights is sought, the burden is beyond a reasonable doubt.) The district attorney or county attorney, when making decisions regarding the filing of a case, must evaluate the evidence in a case in light of these burdens of proof (R. McNeese, personal communication, August 1998). The state's interest in the juvenile court and criminal court arenas is also different. In criminal court, the state has many goals, including punishment of the offender and deterence of others from committing the same offense. In juvenile court, the state's interest is the protection of the child (R. McNeese, personal communication, August 1998).

Factors common in child maltreatment cases complicate and challenge criminal prosecution of these cases. Child sexual abuse occurs predominantly in secret, with no witnesses (Bross, 1987). Testimony of young children (with the victim being the only witness) is often questioned, with limited acceptability of the testimony of children under 5 years of age. Issues related to children's memory and the veracity of their testimony have provoked great controversy (see Ceci & Bruck, 1993; Saywitz & Goodman, 1996), and this complicates criminal prosecution of these cases. In addition, the process of disclosure may be followed by denial and recantation, which further challenges prosecution (Berliner & Elliott, 1996). Difficulty in clearly defining and gaining specific evidence of harm complicates the criminal prosecution of child neglect and emotional abuse cases. Rather than committing acts that directly cause harm to a child, child neglect involves the omission of acts necessary for care. However, there is no clear line demarcating when the omission of care reaches the extent that harm is brought to the child. Emotional abuse may not be considered a criminal offense in some states because of the challenge of proving that the parent committed a specific act that caused specific harm to the child.

In addition to involvement in the juvenile and criminal court arenas, the child may be the subject of proceedings in domestic relations court or civil court. A child maltreatment case can raise issues of custody between the parents (especially in cases where the parents are divorced). In child maltreatment cases, a child may be removed from the home of one parent and placed in the physical care of the other parent. The state agency can continue to retain legal custody of the child in spite of the actual physical placement of the child. Unless immediate termination of parental rights is sought by the state, the initial treatment plan will be directed toward family reunification and correction of the conditions that caused the removal of the child. Although the nonoffending parent may sue for custody in domestic relations court, these actions are often postponed until the juvenile court has ended its involvement with the family. (See Chapter 13 for a detailed description of forensic issues in child custody cases. For details regarding court procedures [e.g., emergency removal and adjudication] and roles of professionals involved in these cases, see Bross [1987], Hardin [1985], Myers [1992], and Portwood and Reppucci [1994].)

BEST INTEREST OF THE CHILD AND FAMILY REUNIFICATION

Courts refer to the *best interest of the child* as the core principle guiding their decisions regarding children. However, there are no clear guidelines on how courts should determine what is in the "best interest" of the child. Professionals and litigants involved in cases often have different appraisals of the needs of children and contrasting perceptions of the effects that placement may have on the short-term and long-term adjustment of children. It is not surprising that children become attached to their foster families, and this bond poses a dilemma for the court, which is faced with defining the best interest of the child and which cannot punish a family (and the child) for delayed court proceedings. *Bonding* and *attachment* are not legal terms, and courts are reluctant to rely on mental health experts (Gross, 1984) who often provide contradictory testimony in cases. Loose guidelines regarding what constitutes the "best interest" have caused wide variations in treatment and difficulty in implementing plans.

It is impossible to evaluate the best interest of individual children without assessing the impact of other individuals involved, including other children such as siblings and foster siblings. Some of the factors to be considered are the following:

1. The length of time the child has been separated from the parents.
2. The adverse effect on the development of youngsters caused by disruption of an established stable relationship.
3. The desirability of raising siblings together whenever possible.
4. The fitness of the parties seeking custody (*In re Donna W.,* 284 Pa. Super. 338. 425 A.2d 1132, 1981, cited in Gross, 1984, p. 512).

However, there are no definitive strategies for balancing these and other issues. As a result, the best-interest standard is often applied according to the beliefs and values of the particular judge, rather than based on any exact law and policies.

Assessment of the child's best interest may change over the time in which the child remains in the legal custody of the state. Numerous factors lengthen the time that children remain outside of their parents' homes. Delays in court decisions and in the court process may be due to the family's failure to follow and complete a treatment plan. However, overcrowded court systems, and large caseloads of all the professionals involved (district attorneys, public defenders, CPS workers, etc.) also delay court procedures. There are more professional sanctions against making a wrong decision than there are rewards for making a right one, leading to further delays in permanency decisions for the children (Hubbell, 1981).

Due to concern about the length of time children were remaining in the foster care system separated from their families, permanency planning has become an integral part of care for children in state custody (Fein, Maluccio, Hamilton, & Ward, 1983). The Adoption and Safe Families Act of 1997 (P.L. 105-89; Child Welfare League of America, 1997) strengthens the requirements for permanency planning even further. For children who have been in foster care for 15 out of the most recent 22 months, states must immediately act on a permanency plan, including parallel initiation of proceedings for termination of parental rights and identifying and finalizing adoption. However, exceptions to these requirements can be made in any of the following circumstances:

1. At state's option, a child is being cared for by a relative.
2. The state agency documents in the case plan . . . a compelling reason why filing is not in the best interest of the child.
3. The state agency has not provided to the child's family, consistent with the time period in the case plan, the services deemed necessary to return the child to a safe home (Child Welfare League of America, 1997, p. 3).

In their review of the literature, Fein et al. (1983) found that intensive family case work services and case planning were effective in shortening the length of time foster children spent in out-of-home placements.

States are required by law to provide clear plans for families to correct conditions that led to the removal of the child, with the goal of reunifying families (as indicated in P.L. 96-272). The Adoption and Safe Families Act of 1997 (P.L. 105-89) provides states with exceptions to the family reunification requirements for cases in which the child maltreatment is considered to involve "aggravated circumstances" (e.g., torture, abandonment, chronic abuse, and sexual abuse). Reunification exceptions also include situations in which the parent's rights have been terminated with regard to another child when the parent committed murder or voluntary manslaughter of another of his or her children, or when the parent committed a felony assault resulting in bodily injury to another of his or her children (Child Welfare League of America, 1997). Children's health and safety continues to be paramount in the decisions of the court.

Intensive short-term service implementation with families in which family reunification remains the treatment goal has been found to be more effective in reaching this goal than standard case management (Walton, Fraser, Lewis, Pecora, & Walton, 1993). The intensive services focus on family-centered care, provision of specific needed services (e.g., food stamps, transportation assistance, and medical treatment), enhancing access to supporting resources, and teaching skills important for parenthood and maintaining a household. In another project, Sisto (1980) developed a staff training program that taught a decision-making model that provided intensive permanency planning combined with direct parent–child interventions to help parents learn problem-solving skills and to exercise self-control. There is a need to advocate for permanency planning from the day the child has been removed from the home with a true service coordinator for the family, and the foster family should be viewed as part of the team. Without specific planning and service delivery, children remain in foster homes longer, without a sense of stability, or they may be returned to their families without appropriate services and support—placing at further risk their emotional and behavioral adjustment and their ability to form trusting relationships with others.

REPRESENTATION OF AND ADVOCACY FOR CHILDREN IN FOSTER CARE

Children in foster care may become lost in the system, resulting in extended stays in foster homes for prolonged periods without clear permanency planning (Fein et al., 1983). Additional efforts to provide for checks and balances and representation of the children have been created, including guardians *ad litem* (Sivan & Quigley-Rick, 1991), court-appointed special advocates (CASA) organizations, and citizen review boards (also known as foster care review boards; Jennings, McDonald, & Henderson, 1996).

Determination of the child's ability to make "adequately considered decisions" (Hubbell, 1981, p. 17) influences the attorney's job to advocate for the child's self-reported needs and interests or to advocate the attorney's own understanding of the child's best interest. Role conflict may arise when the attorney's assessment of the best interest of the child contrasts with the child's stated interest, in cases where the child is able to demonstrate judgment in decisions (Lightfoot, 1988; Sivan & Quigley-Rick, 1991). The American Academy of Matrimonial Lawyers (1995) provides standards for attorneys representing children in custody proceedings that may facilitate defining their roles and responsibility.

The duty of a guardian *ad litem* is to investigate the case to determine the child's needs, represent the child by defending his or her legal rights, explain the process to the child, and provide recommendations to the court (Sivan & Quigley-Rick, 1991). Guardians *ad litem* may have access to all records relevant to the case and may investigate at their own discretion. In a survey of 48 randomly selected guardians *ad litem*, the vast majority reported that they interviewed the child

(85%), reviewed the file (77%), and contacted the CPS worker and other professionals (71%). Only 24% reported visiting the child in his or her own home placement, and it was unclear whether they interviewed the foster parents. It would be prudent for the guardian *ad litem* to contact the foster family (Bross, 1987), who will have critical information about the children's every day functioning. In addition, foster parents often know information that the child has shared with them that may not have been disclosed in the initial investigation. Communicating with the child's guardian *ad litem* may facilitate the foster parents' empowerment to help the child in their care and enhance the representation of the child.

In some communities, CASAs are utilized rather than guardians *ad litem*. CASAs are volunteers from the community who may or may not have formal legal training, but who may receive training in the juvenile court legal system and the effects of maltreatment on children. CASAs have access to court records and can report directly to the judge regarding the findings of their investigations. In some jurisdictions, referrals for a CASA worker can be initiated by foster parents.

Citizen review boards are often comprised of community citizens and professionals appointed by a judge to review and monitor case material and make recommendations to the court. Citizen review boards are often multidisciplinary teams including lawyers, physicians, and mental health professionals, as well as citizens from the county or district. The board is often given access to court documents and to professionals involved in the case, and it provides opinions to the judge. Although contradictory evidence exists, the results of a study comparing cases randomly assigned to citizen review teams or to control conditions (no citizen review) suggest that the cases reviewed by the teams remain in state's custody for shorter amounts of time (Jennings, McDonald, & Henderson, 1996). Foster families and mental health professionals may participate or provide direct information to the citizen review board.

STATUS OF THE FOSTER FAMILY

The status of *foster* changes the roles and responsibilities of the caregivers, impacting everyday decisions regarding the care of the children. Key issues include: Who is ultimately responsible for the child when there are many people involved in the child's life (e.g., judge, CPS worker, foster parents, CASA, as well as the child's biological parents)? When there are disagreements among the multiple caregivers, who makes final decisions regarding the care of the child? What are the rights of the foster parents, who are providing everyday care for the child? What knowledge are they given regarding the child's history and current functioning? All of us are aware of the difficulties that arise when divorced parents have to make joint decisions about the care of their child. These struggles are multiplied as the number of individuals making decisions about the child increases, with the added complexities of the bureaucracies involved.

Responsibility, rights, and decisions regarding a child's care become quite divided when the child is placed in foster care (Hardin, 1985). The foster parent and the foster care agency (public or private) are responsible for the everyday care of the child (Hardin, 1985). However, many decisions that are normally considered routine cannot be made without permission from the state, often through the CPS worker. Even a decision to cut the hair of the child may have to be postponed until approval is given by the biological parents, who may refuse to permit the haircut because this is one of the few decisions these parents may still be able to make. The state, not the foster parent, can give consent for treatment of the child, give consent to release information, and decide on school placement. Children in state's custody often have exceptional mental health, physical, and social needs—placing additional demands on those in the parenting role. It can be incredibly stressful for families, who are responsible for the care and well-being of the children, if they are not given the right to make independent decisions, especially emergency ones. Through advocacy by the National Organization for Foster Families, the rights of foster parents have received greater recognition than was the case before, but they vary depending on specific state laws. Federal legislation is also impacting foster parents' rights. For example, P.L. 105-89 requires foster parents (including kinship care parents) to be given notice of court reviews with the opportunity to be heard.

INVESTIGATIONS OF FOSTER FAMILIES FOR ALLEGATIONS OF CHILD MALTREATMENT

Foster families may be more likely than nonfoster families to be investigated for alleged child maltreatment, particularly physical abuse and neglect (Benedict et al., 1994). Based on such investigations, the rates of substantiated child maltreatment are lower in foster families than in community samples of nonfoster families (Benedict et al., 1994). Thus, children in foster homes are considered to be at lower risk for physical abuse than the general population of children in the community. The higher rate of reporting has been hypothesized to be due to the fact that these families are more closely supervised than the average family in the community. Differences in standard of care could also cause increased reporting of foster families. In many states corporal punishment is not allowed in foster homes, and foster families may be reported to child protection services for such behavior. Further, dynamics related to the reasons the children were placed in foster care may increase the risk of reporting child maltreatment (Benedict et al., 1994).

The experience of being suspected of and investigated for child maltreatment can be incredibly stressful for the foster family, and can affect the family's relationships with both the children in foster care and the social service agency. To investigate allegations of child maltreatment, NCFFC (1991) recommends a team evaluation with CPS workers, supervisory staff, a representative from the foster parent association, and a consultant from an outside child-placing agency. The NCFFC also recommends providing liability coverage for CPS caseworkers and foster families who may be sued for taking actions within the scope of the agency. Support for the foster family during the investigation is strongly recommended (Carbino, 1991), and has been provided by some foster care associations.

THERAPEUTIC ISSUES OF FOSTER CHILDREN AND THEIR FAMILIES

Many children placed in foster care have multiple unmet needs that should be dealt with in a timely manner. The health of children entering foster care may not be as good as that of children in healthy, stable homes. For example, one investigator surveyed preschool foster children and found that 60% exhibited developmental delays, 35% had chronic medical problems, 15% had a birth defect, and 15% were of short stature (Simms, 1989). Acute and chronic health problems, developmental delays, and emotional problems are 3 to 7 times greater among foster care children than among other children in families living in poverty (Rosenfeld et al., 1997). Further, children in foster care have been found to have "a much higher rate of asthma, anemia, vision and dental problems, and developmental delays than American children in general" (Dubowitz, 1990, p. 37, reported in Berrick et al., 1994).

In addition, children who have experienced or witnessed maltreatment often have social, emotional, behavioral, cognitive, and academic problems. Research demonstrates that repeated exposure to marital violence and conflict not only constitutes a form of psychological abuse (Hart & Brassard, 1987), but also leaves children more behaviorally reactive and subject to emotional and behavioral adjustment problems (Margolin, 1998). In a review of the literature on the educational needs of abused and neglected children, Trocmé and Caunce (1995) found that the children showed marked delays in language and intellectual development, attention, readiness to learn, and delays in socioemotional development (p. 101). Children who have been sexually abused may show hormonal or cortisol dysregulation (Trickett & Putnam, 1998), immunological dysfunction (DeBellis, Burke, Trickett, & Putnam, 1996), inappropriate sexual behavior and sexual activity (Kolko, Moser, & Weldy, 1990), and internalizing and externalizing behavior problems (Deblinger, McLeer, Atkins, Ralphe, & Foa, 1989; Friedrich, Beilke, & Urquiza, 1987; Trickett & Putnam, 1998).

Although placement in foster homes strains the attachment process between biological parents and children, many maltreated children have been found to be insecurely attached to their biological mothers (Crittenden, 1985a, 1985b) and to exhibit either anxious/ambivalent, avoidant, or disorganized/disoriented behavior toward their mother at times of separation and reunion (Lyons-Ruth, Connell, & Zoll, 1989). Galinsky, Howes, Kontos, and Shinn (1994), in their study of children in family child care and relative care, found that only half of the children they studied were securely attached to their providers. Since many of these children were placed in relatives' homes, the security of the attachment relationship is of concern. This presumes to leave half of the children *unattached* to any significant adult. Galinsky et al. (1994) reported that parents and providers agreed that "when the care that children receive is sensitive, responsive, and of better quality, children are more likely to be securely attached to their providers and achieve higher levels of cognitive competence" (p. 26). Why is the attachment relationship important? Whether the attachment is to a foster parent, a relative, or a natural parent, the attachment relationship helps the child learn:

1. Trust, and the nature of others (i.e., whether they are responsive, nurturing, and interested versus harsh, disinterested, unresponsive, and emotionally unavailable).
2. His or her own nature (i.e., that he or she is lovable, worthy of being cared for, competent in eliciting care, safe and secure enough to explore the environment).
3. Empathy—the ability to perceive and care about other people's needs, feelings, and ideas.

A secure attachment relationship serves as an emotional buffer for the child and as one of the *protective factors* that can help to counteract many of the *risk factors* present in the child's life. Whatever the circumstances that brought the child into foster care, there is considerable evidence that mothers who abuse their children are more negative, punitive, and interfering when interacting with their children than are nonabusing mothers. This hampers the attachment relationship (Belsky, Rovine, & Taylor, 1984; Crittenden, 1985a; Crittenden & Ainsworth, 1989; Sroufe, 1988).

Indeed, attachment relationships are critically important in predicting later socioemotional competence in children (Cicchetti & Carlson, 1989; Sroufe, 1988). Thus, the foster parents' first challenge is in easing the anxiety or fear of the child who is entering their home. The foster parents need to be accessible, sensitive to the child, and appropriately responsive to the child's behavioral cues. Because a number of foster children will exhibit disorganized behaviors, great patience, love, kindness, and flexibility will be needed as the foster parents begin the process of integrating the child into their home. Because of the child's marginal or problematic attachment relationships, good foster parents must make a deep emotional investment in the child, and this may initiate a deep attachment of the child to them. This commitment to each other will likely be temporary, and there will be loss and grieving by both the child and the family when they are separated.

As a result of the many physical, developmental, and mental health symptoms exhibited by foster children, the Child Welfare League of America and the American Academy of Pediatrics (1994) recommend that all foster children have prompt physical examinations; comprehensive developmental, educational, and mental health assessments; routine health care; and a health "passport" that follows them wherever they are placed. The NCFFC's report (1991) recommends that complete records of medical and health services be provided, including a copy of the child's birth certificate, immunization record, and other important documents. Unfortunately, these recommendations are rarely followed, hindering the ability of the foster family to meet and advocate for the child's needs.

Thus, foster parents need to be alerted to the medical and mental health needs of children in their care so that they are prepared to meet these needs (Rosenfeld et al., 1997). Payments for care have been found to be inadequate to meet the complex needs of foster children (Ward, 1995). In addition, there are other barriers to raising children in foster care (e.g., difficulty finding providers who accept Medicaid). Unfortunately, foster families often have limited information about the children in their care and are unprepared to meet their emotional and behavioral needs. Sexualized behavior of the children and other behavior problems are of particular concern, because they are one of the primary reasons children are removed from foster care homes (U.S. Department of Health and Human Services, 1993).

MEDICAL, EDUCATIONAL, AND MENTAL HEALTH TREATMENT ISSUES

Because children entering foster care often have health, education, and socioemotional problems, the foster parent will often be the primary advocate for the child and will be transporting children to appointments. Following through on all medical or health-related appointments is essential. Unfortunately, it has been found that many foster children entering foster care still do not receive adequate health care.

Halfon and Klee (1992) found that 34% had not been properly immunized and 32% still had unmet health needs after placement (U.S. General Accounting Office, 1995).

School-aged children must be enrolled in school. Often, an educational evaluation assists in identifying education needs. Success in school will do much to enhance the child's feelings of self-worth and self-confidence. Often foster children will need remedial assistance because of the emotionally unstable environment in which they resided or due to a prior lack of educational opportunities. The foster parents are important advocates to facilitate proper placement of the child and to obtain necessary services.

Children who enter foster care may require therapy. Depression and learned helplessness are symptoms often overlooked in the foster child (Zimmerman, 1988). Teaching foster parents how to provide opportunities for foster children to gain some control over their environment and to learn to recognize that they can be in charge of some aspects of their lives and behavior will help alleviate the helplessness demeanor that some foster children exhibit. Zimmerman (1988) offers several suggestions for assisting the child who is depressed or feels helpless, such as teaching the child specific skills or providing social skills training so that they have success in interacting and playing with peers.

Another aspect of treatment may focus on reactive attachment disorders. Prior to treatment the therapist will want a full history detailing placement and attachment background, why the child was removed from home, and what permanency plans are in place. The therapist will want to work closely with the foster parents on ways to enhance the child's security, trust, and attachment relationship. (See James [1994] and Delaney [1997] on treatment of attachment problems in children who have experienced trauma.)

As stated previously, children who present with disruptive or oppositional behaviors, aggressive behaviors, and sexually acting out behaviors need specialized treatment. These behaviors frequently lead to changes in residential placement if the foster parents are not trained in strategies of prevention and response. Critical to reducing these problematic behaviors is an alliance between the foster parents and the therapist.

Foster parents often need consultation and assistance on issues related to behavior. Children who have experienced substance exposure or other abuse may exhibit disruptive oppositional-defiant or overactive behaviors. Infants may be irritable, colicky, and exhibit sleep disturbances due to substance exposure; foster parents then need guidance on how to soothe, massage, or swaddle the infant to quiet it and to help regulate its nervous system. Young children (ages 2 to 7) who present with aggressive and oppositional-defiant problems secondary to abuse benefit from Parent–Child Interaction Therapy (PCIT; Urquiza & McNeil, 1996). PCIT facilitates the development of positive relationships between foster parents and children by teaching the parents play-therapy skills that use considerable positive reinforcement, apply appropriate disciplinary skills that are free from corporal or coercive punishment, and make use of time out as opposed to negative statements and negative reinforcement.

Young children with more serious developmental and emotional disorders benefit from group or therapeutic preschool programs that offer developmental services such as speech therapy, physical therapy, social skills training, play therapy, and more normalized developmental programming as opposed to a strictly play-therapy group (Culp, Little, Letts, & Lawrence, 1991; Oates, Gray, Schweitzer, Kempe, & Harmon, 1995). (Other intervention strategies for ameliorating negative developmental consequences of child maltreatment can be found in Trickett and Schellenbach [1998].) Foster parents who focus on strengthening a child's socio-emotional competencies and social skills do much to enhance the child's overall development. Strengthening a child's sense of self-worth and confidence enables that child to benefit more from school and in his or her interactions with others.

Foster Children and Their Impact on Foster Families

Very little research has been done on the foster family as a system and fewer than five studies have looked at the impact of fostering on the foster parents' own children. In one small sample study ($N = 8$), children of foster parents all felt they had lost something during the foster care experience: their parents' time and attention, family closeness, and their place in their family (Twigg, 1994, p. 307). Twigg reported that he was surprised at the amount of anger the foster parents' own children felt toward their parents. Use of qualitative research designs, which employ methods such as asking open-ended questions to obtain qualitative information, may be helpful in beginning to understand more about the impact of foster care on the biological children of foster parents.

In a much better controlled study with a larger sample size, Poland and Groze (1993) found that 57% of the foster parents believed that fostering had had a positive impact on their family. Seventy percent of the children liked having foster siblings, but almost half of them did not like the changes that had occurred in their home as a result of the foster siblings. The foster parents and their children agreed that fostering produced both positive and negative influences on their lives. If foster parents spent equal time with their own children, provided explanations about fostering to their children, and were responsive to questions their children had about foster children, the experience was more acceptable and positive. Poland and Groze (1993) felt that caseworkers visiting the foster home should spend more time talking to the biological children of the foster parents, should be available to respond to their questions about fostering, and should provide more training inclusive of the children prior to the first foster child placement. The training could include an explanation of realistic ways the home would change with the addition of a foster child, such as sharing mother and dad, or mother and dad appearing to be more lenient with the foster child.

THERAPEUTIC ISSUES IN
WORKING WITH FOSTER FAMILIES

Those who decide to become foster parents need more intensive training than has been given in the past. Prospective foster parents would likely benefit from inter-disciplinary training whereby legal professionals would discuss the applicable laws, mental health professionals would discuss the effects of abuse or neglect on the educational and psychosocial functioning of the child, health professionals would discuss health-related issues, and social workers would discuss rules and regulations of the CPS agency and their role in investigation and case management. Using experienced foster parents to discuss issues they have confronted while fostering has been useful.

Foster parents would benefit from specialized training in behavioral management of disruptive and oppositional behaviors. Training in PCIT for the 2- to 7-year-old foster child and managing aggressive behaviors in the older child might prevent children being moved from home to home due to disruptive behavior. Within this framework, training to manage sexual behavior problems would also be warranted because these kinds of behaviors put other children in the home at risk.

Supervisory visits by the caseworker to the foster home would be more effective if time were spent with the whole family, including the foster parents' own children. This would help the worker assess the degree of integration of children into the home and whether the foster parents' natural children were experiencing difficulties such as anger or feeling left out.

Time spent training foster parents about the importance and necessity of visitation with natural parents will be time well spent. Foster parents (as well as caseworkers) need to understand that regular parent–child visits are the "strongest prediction of the childs' return to the natural parents' care" (Simms, 1991, p. 352). Children in foster care generally look forward to visiting with their parents, but may exhibit anxiety before and after the visits (Rosenfeld et al., 1997). These can be stressful for both the foster parents and the children. It has often been reported by foster parents that the children act out after visits with their parents; yet foster parents must be supportive, or at least neutral, in their reactions to the natural parents and must also have the knowledge and skills to deal with the child's reactions to the visits. Foster parents must be educated about the loyalty and attachment children often feel toward their parents, even toward severely abusive parents (Rosenfeld et al., 1997).

SUMMARY AND RECOMMENDATIONS

As we think about strengthening the foster care system we must also advocate ways to strengthen families, to reduce the incidence of substance abuse through early prevention programs in the public schools and through community, state, and national education campaigns. Violence in our country, including child maltreatment and domestic violence, accounts for a large number of the children entering the foster care system—whether it is secondary to the stress of poverty, to poor parenting, or to substance abuse. This chapter reviews the different types of foster homes, the treatment needs of children entering care, and the judicial procedures in foster care. From this review we make the following recommendations:

1. To strengthen foster parents, we must elevate and broaden the types of pre-service and ongoing training that is provided parents. Interdisciplinary training may be the best method of training due to the numerous areas of information that must be covered (legal, psychological, agency regulations, impact of fostering on the family, managing difficult behaviors, etc.).
2. Foster parents must have clearly defined roles with identifiable competencies and supports as recommended by the National Commission on Family

Foster Care (1991). Indeed, foster parents might well be considered professionals—thus elevating the prestige of being a foster parent and, hopefully, altering the way they are viewed by agency personnel.

3. Physical and mental health needs of children entering care must be addressed within the first month. A complete medical examination is warranted, psychological and educational assessments must be scheduled, and the child's treatment needs must be addressed.

4. It is evident from reviewing the literature on foster parenting that few studies meet rigorous research guidelines. There is a need for more sophisticated longitudinal research on the psychological impact of foster care on children, attachment issues, effective treatment methods for children and their parents, and on the impact of fostering on the foster child and on children of the foster parents.

The challenge of the 21st century will be to reduce the incidence of child maltreatment and to strengthen families. Another challenge will be to find and recruit outstanding foster parents for our nations' children in need and to provide both appropriate treatment for the children and training and respect for the foster parents.

REFERENCES

American Academy of Matrimonial Lawyers. (1995). *Representing children: Standards for attorneys and guardians ad litem in custody or visitation proceedings with commentary.* Washington, DC: Author.

American Academy of Pediatrics, Committee on Early Childhood, Adoption and Dependent Care. (1994). Health care of children in foster care. *Pediatrics, 93,* 335–338.

Barth, R. P., Courtney, M., Needell, B., & Johnson-Reid, M. (1994). *Performance indicators for child welfare services in California.* Berkeley: University of California, Child Welfare Research Center.

Belsky, J., Rovine, M., & Taylor, D. J. (1984). The Pennsylvania infant and family developmental project III: The origins of individual differences in infant-mother attachment: Maternal and infant contributions. *Child Development, 55,* 718–728.

Benedict, M. I., Zuravin, S., Brandt, D., & Abbey, H. (1994). Types and frequency of child maltreatment by family foster care providers in an urban population. *Child Abuse & Neglect, 18*(7), 577–585.

Berliner, L. & Elliott, P. M. (1996). Sexual abuse of children. In J. Briere, L. Berliner, J. A. Bulkley, C. Jenny, & T. Rerd (Eds.), *The APSAC handbook on child maltreatment.* Thousand Oaks, CA: Sage.

Berrick, J. D., Barth, R. P., & Needell, B. (1994). A comparison of kinship foster homes and foster family homes: Implications of kinship foster care as family preservation. *Children and Youth Services Review, 16,* 33–63.

Bross, D. C. (1987). *Defining child abuse and neglect from a legal perspective.* In D. C. Bross & L. F. Michaels (Eds.), *Foundations of child advocacy.* Colorado: Bookmakers Guild.

Carbino, R. (1991, March–April). Advocacy for foster families in the United States facing child abuse allegations: How social agencies and foster parents are responding to the problem. *Child Welfare League of America, 70*(2), 131–149.

Ceci, S. J. & Bruck, M. (1993). The suggestibility of child witnesses. *Psychological Bulletin, 113,* 403–439.

Chamberlin, P., Moreland, S., & Reid, K. (1992). Enhanced services and stipends for foster parents: Effects on retention rates and outcomes for children. *Child Welfare, 71*(5), 387–404.

Child Welfare League of America. (1997). *Summary of the adoption and safe families act of 1997* (P.L. 105-89). Washington, DC: Author.

Child Welfare League of America. (1998). *Children '98: America's promise: Children need protection more than ever.* Washington, DC: Author.

Child Welfare Research Center. (1991). *Child welfare symposium on multi-state foster care study: California data.* Berkeley: University of California, School of Social Welfare Family Studies, Welfare Research Group.

Cicchetti, D. & Carlson, V. (Eds.). (1989). *Child maltreatment: Theory and research on the causes and consequences of child abuse and neglect.* New York: Cambridge University Press.

Courtney, M. E. (1995). Reentry to foster care of children returned to their families. *Social Service Review, 69,* 226–241.

Crittenden, P. M. (1985a). Maltreated infants: Vulnerability and resilience. *Journal of Child Psychology and Psychiatry, 26,* 85–96.

Crittenden, P. M. (1985b). Social networks, quality of child-rearing, and child development. *Child Development, 56,* 1299–1313.

Crittenden, P. M., & Ainsworth, M. D. (1989). Child maltreatment and attachment theory. In D. Cicchetti & V. Carlson (Eds.), *Child maltreatment: Theory and research on the causes and consequences of child abuse and neglect* (pp. 432–463). New York: Cambridge University Press.

Culp, R. E., Little, V., Letts, D., & Lawrence, H. (1991). Maltreated children's self-concept: Effects of a comprehensive treatment program. *American Journal of Orthopsychiatry, 61,* 114–121.

DeBellis, M. D., Burke, L., Trickett, T. K., & Putnam, F. W. (1996). Antinuclear antibodies and thyroid function in sexually abused girls. *Journal of Traumatic Stress, 9,* 369–378.

Deblinger, E., McLeer, S. V., Atkins, M. S., Ralphe, D., & Foa, E. (1989). Post-traumatic stress in sexually abused, physically abused, and nonabused children. *Child Abuse and Neglect, 13,* 403–408.

Delaney, P. J. (1997). *Festering changes: Testing attachment-disordered foster children.* Ft. Collins, CO: Walter J. Corbett.

Dubowitz, H. (1990, August). *The physical and mental health and educational status of children placed with relatives: Final report.* Unpublished manuscript. Baltimore: University of Maryland Medical School.

Fein, E., Maluccio, A., Hamilton, V. J., & Ward, D. E. (1983). After foster care: Outcomes of permanency planning for children. *Child Welfare League of America, 62*(6), 485–558.

Friedrich, W. N., Beilke, R. L., & Urquiza, A. J. (1987). Children from sexually abusive families: A behavioral comparison. *Journal of Interpersonal Violence, 2,* 391–402.

Galinsky, E., Howes, C., Kontos, S., & Shinn, M. (1994). *The study of children in family child care and relative care.* New York: Families & Work Institute.

Gross, M. (1984). Custody conflicts between foster and birth parents in Pennsylvania. *Social Work,* 510–515.

Halfon, N. G. & Klee, L. (1992). Mental health service utilization by children in foster care in California. *Pediatrics, 89,* 1238–1244.

Hardin, M. (1985). Families, children, and the law. In J. Laird and A. Hartman (Eds.), *A handbook for child welfare practice* (pp. 213–236). New York: Free Press.

Harling, P., & Haines, J. (1980). Specialized foster homes for severely mistreated children. *Children Today,* 16–18.

Hart, S. N., & Brassard, M. R. (1987). A major threat to children's mental health: Psychological maltreatment. *American Psychologist, 42,* 160–165.

Hubbell, R. (1981). *Foster care and families: Conflicting values and policies*. Philadelphia: Temple University Press.

James, B. (1994). *Handbook for treatment of attachment–trauma problems in children*. New York: Free Press.

Jennings, M. A., McDonald, T., & Henderson, R. A. (1996). Early citizen review: Does it make a difference? *Social Work, 41*, 224–231.

Klee, L., Kronstadt, D., & Zlotnick, C. (1997). Foster care's youngest: A preliminary report. *American Journal of Orthopsychiatry, 67*, 290–299.

Kolko, D. J., Moser, J. T., & Weldy, S. R. (1990). Medical/health histories and physical evaluation of physically and sexually abused child psychiatric patients: A controlled study. *Journal of Family Violence, 5*, 249–267.

Kusserow, R. (1992). *Using relatives for foster care*. Washington, DC: U.S. Department of Health and Human Services, Office of the Inspector General.

Lightfoot, J. H. (1988). Children's rights, lawyers' roles. *Family Advocate: A Practical Journal by the ABA Family Law Section, 4*(2), 4–5.

Lyons-Ruth, K., Connell, D. B., & Zoll, D. (1989). Patterns of maternal behavior among infants at risk for abuse: Relations with infant attachment behavior and infant development at 12 months of age. In V. Carlson & D. Cicchetti (Eds.), *Child maltreatment: Theory and research on the causes and consequences of child abuse and neglect* (pp. 464–493). New York: Cambridge University Press.

Margolin, G. (1998). Effects of domestic violence on children. In P. K. Trickett & C. J. Schellenbach (Eds.), *Violence against children in the family and the community* (pp. 57–101). Washington, DC: American Psychological Association.

Myers, J. E. B. (1992). *Legal Issues in Child Abuse and Neglect*. London: Sage.

National Commission on Family Foster Care. (1991). *A blueprint for fostering infants, children, and youths in the 1990's* (pp. 4–5). Washington, DC: Child Welfare League of America and National Foster Parent Association.

Oates, R. K., Gray, J., Schweitzer, L., Kempe, R. S., & Harmon, R. J. (1995). A therapeutic preschool for abused children: The KEEPSAFE Project. *Child Abuse & Neglect, 19*, 1379–1386.

Poland, D. C., & Groze, V. (1993). Effects of foster care placement on biological children in the home. *Child and Adolescent Social Work Journal, 10*, 153–164.

Portwood, S. G., & Reppucci, N. D. (1994). Intervention versus interference: The role of the courts in child placement. In J. Blacher (Ed.), *When there's no place like home: Options for children living apart from their natural families*. Baltimore: Paul H. Brookes.

Prochaska, J. O., Norcross, J. C., & DiClemente, C. C. (1994). *Changing for Good*. New York: Avon Books.

Rosenfeld, A., Pilowsky, D. J., Fine, P., Thorpe, M., Fein, E., Simms, M., Halfon, N., Irwin, M., Alfaro, J., Saletsky, R., & Nickman, S. (1997, April). Foster care: An update. *Journal of American Academy of Child and Adolescent Psychiatry, 36*(4), 448–457.

Saywitz, K. J., & Goodman, G. (1996). Interviewing children in and out of court: Current research and practice implications. In J. Briere, L. Berliner, J. Bulkley, C. Jenny, & T. Reid (Eds.), *The APSAC handbook on child maltreatment*. Thousand Oaks, CA: Sage.

Scannapieco, M., & Hegar, R. L. (1995). Kinship care: Two case management models. *Child and Adolescent Social Work Journal, 12*(2), 147–156.

Simms, M. D. (1989). The foster care clinic: A community program to identify treatment needs of children in foster care. *Journal of Developmental and Behavior Pediatrics, 10*, 121–128.

Simms, M. D. (1991, September). Foster children and the foster care system, Part II: Impact on the child. *Current Problems in Pediatrics*, 345–369.

Sisto, G. (1980). An agency design for permanency planning in foster care. *Child Welfare, 59*, 103–111.

Sivan, A. B., & Quigley-Rick, M. (1991). Effective representation of children by the guardian *ad litem:* An empirical investigation. *Bulletin of the American Academy of Psychiatric Law, 19,* 53–61.

Sroufe, L. A. (1988). The role of infant caregiver attachment in development. In J. Belsky & T. Nezworski (Eds.), *Clinical implications of attachment* (pp. 18–38). Hillsdale, NJ: Erlbaum.

Trickett, P. K., & Putnam, F. W. (1998). Developmental consequences of child sexual abuse. In P. K. Trickett & C. J. Schellenbach (Eds.), *Violence against children in the family and the community* (pp. 39–56). Washington, DC: American Psychological Association.

Trickett, P. K. & Schellenbach, C. J. (1998). *Violence against children in the family and the community.* Washington, DC: American Psychological Association.

Trocmé, N., & Caunce, C. (1995). The educational needs of abused and neglected children: A review of the literature. *Early Child Development and Care, 106,* 101–135.

Twigg, R. S. (1994). The unknown soldiers of foster care: Foster care as loss for the foster parents' own children. *Smith College Studies in Social Work, 64,* 297–311.

U.S. Advisory Board on Child Abuse and Neglect. (1990). *Child abuse and neglect: Critical first steps in response to a national emergency.* Washington, DC: U.S. Department of Health and Human Services.

U.S. Department of Health and Human Services. (1993). *The national survey of current & former foster parents.* Washington, DC: Author.

U.S. General Accounting Office. (1995). *Health needs of many young children are unknown and unmet* (GAO/HEHS-95-114). Washington, DC: U.S. General Accounting Office.

Urquiza, A. J., & McNeil, C. B. (1996). Parent-child interaction therapy: An intensive dyadic intervention for physically abusive families. *Child Maltreatment, 1,* 134–144.

Walton, E., Fraser, M. W., Lewis, R. E., Pecora, P. J., & Walton, W. K. (1993, September–October). In-home family-focused reunification: An experimental study. *Child Welfare League of America, 72*(5), 473–487.

Ward, J. (1995). Specialized foster care: One approach to retaining good foster homes. *The Connection, 11*(1), 10–11. Seattle, WA: National CASA.

Willis, D. J., & Silovsky, J. F. (1998). Prevention of violence at the societal level. In P. K. Trickett & C. J. Schellenbach (Eds.), *Violence against children in the family and the community.* Washington, DC: American Psychological Association.

Zimmerman, R. B. (1988). Childhood depression: New theoretical formulations and implications for foster care services. *Child Welfare League of America, 67,* 37–47.

CHAPTER 5

Physical and Sexual Abuse

TERRY S. TREPPER and MARY E. DANKOSKI

CHILD PHYSICAL and sexual abuse are among the most perplexing problems seen by therapists. Not only are the cases usually complex clinically, with multiple family members involved and many vulnerabilities to be assessed and treated, but the involvement of so many external systems makes clinical case management extremely difficult. An understanding of these outside forces, along with plans to use them to therapeutic advantage, can facilitate counseling abusing families. Also, understanding the roles and functions of each external system will make any clinical forensics the therapist may be involved with somewhat easier.

The degree and magnitude of the problem of physical and sexual abuse is determined in a number of ways. First, there is the official national database maintained by the National Clearinghouse on Child Abuse and Neglect (part of the U.S. Department of Health and Human Services). There are also state and local records, which may differ from the national databases because of reporting requirement differences. There are also various epidemiological studies that appear in publications like the *American Journal of Public Health*. Finally, there are clinical studies that may offer post hoc data and information on unreported cases. All of these can change dramatically, so clinicians preparing forensic reports should obtain the most current information available and not rely on even recent articles and reports which, with publication lag time, may be several years old when they are presented.

WHAT CONSTITUTES ABUSE?

One of the difficulties in working with child abuse cases is that definitions of abuse are vague. One reason that there is not one accepted standardized definition of abuse is that there is not an agreed-upon standard of optimal parenting (Gelles, 1987). This makes it hard to develop agreed-upon standards of unacceptable or incorrect parenting. What is considered abusive, then, is often a reflection of one's value judgments. Frequently, what therapists believe is abusive would not be legally determined as abusive and not considered so by the parents.

The government's definition of child abuse was first stated in the federal Child Abuse Prevention and Treatment Act in 1974 (PL 93-237; cited in Gelles, 1987):

> the physical or mental injury, sexual abuse, negligent treatment, or maltreatment of a child under the age of eighteen by a person who is responsible for the child's welfare under circumstances which would indicate that the child's health or welfare is harmed or threatened hereby.

This definition leaves many specifics unsaid. For example, what specifically constitutes "mental injury" is ambiguous.

In addition to this federal guideline, the definition of abuse varies from state to state. For example, in Indiana, child abuse is defined as when "the child's physical or mental health is seriously endangered due to injury by the act or omission of the child's parent, guardian, or custodian" (Indiana Statute 31-6-4-3 [a][2], cited in *Burns Indiana Statutes Annotated*, 1987). Just across the state line in Illinois, an abused child is defined as a "child whose parent or immediate family member, or any person responsible for the child's welfare (a) inflicts, causes to be inflicted, or allows to be inflicted upon such child physical injury, by other than accidental means, which causes death, disfigurement, impairment of physical or emotional health, or loss or impairment of any bodily function, or (b) inflicts excessive corporal punishment" (Illinois Department of Children and Family Services, 1982). Child neglect is also hard to define, and difficult to prove from a legal standpoint. Reber (1985) states that "child neglect has come to be used for other less than obvious physical forms of maltreatment such as improper attention to health, diet, clothing, education, socialization, etc. The term encompasses maltreatment which results more from omission . . . than commission" (p. 188).

Despite these guidelines, therapists are left in the position of developing their own personal distinctions as to what constitutes physical abuse and neglect. The extreme cases are often clear, as evidenced in shocking displays of abuse and neglect in news reports. However, as mandated reporters, therapists must decipher the more vague situations for themselves. Where is the line between spanking and abuse? The line between raising your voice at a child and emotional abuse? At what age can children be left unsupervised and for how long? Clinically, many therapists make distinctions about what constitutes abuse by assessing the intention of the adult and the effects on the child, using clues such as physical marks left on the child, as well as emotional marks such as excessive fear of the adult. These criteria, however, may not be upheld in court or by protective services.

Likewise, sexual abuse is also ambiguously defined both legally and clinically. Finkelhor (1986) reviewed several studies to examine differences in operational definitions of sexual abuse. He found that many studies differ in whether to consider "noncontact abuse" (such as exhibitionism) in addition to "contact abuse" in definitions. Including incidents involving peers as offenders in definitions of abuse also varies, which is especially important in studies of adolescent victims and sibling abuse. The age difference that exists between the victim and perpetrator is one criterion that affects the decision to categorize a relationship as abusive. Finkelhor (1986) believes there should be a 5-year age difference between the victim and perpetrator when the victim is under 12, and a 10-year difference for victims ages 13 to 16 as a guideline for gauging the power differential and exploitation of the younger child.

Drawing from the work of Russell (1984), Trepper and Barrett (1989) use the following criteria to clinically define sexual abuse: "touching or fondling of the genitals or body parts, or prolonged kissing, with the intent to sexually arouse either the child or the adult, as well as overt sexual contact like, intercourse, oral-genital contact, or manual stimulation of the genitals" (pp. xvi–xvii). Other behaviors may be recognized as sexually abusive, for example, deliberately intending to sexually arouse the child by showing him or her pornography.

If the preceding behaviors are initiated by a family member, it is considered *incestuous abuse*. Just as the specific legal definitions of incest vary from state to state, *clinical* definitions may be different. We do not doubt that children having sex with parents constitutes incestuous abuse. But is sexual abuse by an uncle who is visiting from his home across the country more incestuous than abuse committed by a trusted friend of the family? The clinical issue in terms of incestuous abuse may be more the closeness of the relationship, the amount of trust placed in the adult, and the degree of nurturing that the adult usually provides the child. That is, what matters is whether the adult and the child share *functionally* those factors which characterize a *family*.

To summarize, the definitions surrounding abuse are somewhat complicated. DeKraai and Sales (1991) recommend that therapists specifically need to know: (a) the particular professions included in the statute as mandatory reporters (i.e., some states specify what disciplines, and whether they have to be licensed); (b) what type of abuse is targeted (e.g., present physical, mental, and sexual abuse; past abuse; or imminent abuse); (c) whether the statute requires direct observation or any knowledge of the abuse, and whether one has to see marks; (d) what the penalties are for not reporting child abuse, and whether the state offers immunity from liability for good-faith reporting. Obtaining this information in advance of working with abusing families is essential.

WHAT CONSTITUTES A FAMILY?

As previously mentioned, the abuse may have been perpetrated by someone who is not legally defined as a family member, but who is considered to be family in terms of the emotional bonds between that person and the child victim. Many people, especially ethnic minorities, have broader conceptualizations of family (e.g., kin networks; Schwartz, 1993). If a member of this larger family perpetrated the abuse, its impact may be similar to that if a member of the nuclear family had committed the behavior because of the trust and emotional bond between the child and the offending adult.

The client's concept of family has important treatment implications as well. Including kinship members, godparents, grandparents, and stepparents in therapy may be extremely useful in some cases. It is important to determine the client's conceptualization of family to plan treatment and assess the impact of the abuse. Many abused children are also placed in foster homes, and how this impacts on the child's sense of family must also be included in evaluations and treatment. In some cases, child protective services (CPS) may attempt to contact and include biological parents who, prior to their involvement with the CPS system, had no contact with the child. Schwartz (1993) recommends assessing family boundaries, the parents' marital status, the age of the child, and the client's cultural tradition when probing for the client's conceptualization of family.

UNDERSTANDING EXTERNAL SYSTEMS INVOLVED IN ABUSE CASES

A number of public systems are involved in abuse cases, and their roles may conflict.

CHILD PROTECTIVE SERVICES (CPS)

Child protective services (CPS) agencies, called various names in different locales, have the primary state-mandated duty of protecting children from abuse. Under this broad umbrella come specific charges, including: (a) conducting timely investigations (usually within 24 to 72 hours) when charges of abuse are lodged against a family member; (b) providing case management services if the investigation deems that the child was likely abused or is at risk for abuse, such as monitoring compliance with therapy and court orders related to living arrangements; (c) referring cases to the prosecutor's office for criminal investigation; (d) referring family members for therapy services; and (e) supporting and managing foster care, if applicable.

Therapists need to be cognizant of a couple of issues that may make working with CPS difficult. First, CPS has multiple functions, and there may be more than one case manager involved with a family during the duration of the case. Second, the caseloads for most CPS workers are extremely high, making it difficult for them to maintain sufficient contact at times. Third, CPS workers, by training and mandate, will try to err on the side of the continued safety of the child, even at the expense of early family reunification with a low-risk family.

On the other hand, CPS, because of its many functions, has a great deal of power that can be utilized in therapy. For example, because CPS can affect the criminal justice component (e.g., by deciding whether to send the case to the prosecutor, or by reporting to the court whether the family has been compliant with therapy), caseworkers can put pressure on family members to attend and cooperate with treatment. This can be especially important in therapy with abusing parents, for whom denial is a powerful defense mechanism but one that is usually amenable to treatment.

CRIMINAL JUSTICE SYSTEM

The criminal justice system's role is to investigate, prosecute, try, and punish abuse cases which are criminal in nature. The names may vary in different regions, but generally the systems involved with abuse cases include the following:

1. The *police*, whose job it is to investigate child abuse complaints, to possibly arrest a suspected child abuser, and to enforce any court mandates regarding the family once the matter is under court jurisdiction.

2. The *prosecutor's office*, which further investigates the family and determines whether to file criminal charges. If charges are filed, the prosecutor will gather the evidence and try the criminal case for the state.
3. The *courts,* including *criminal court,* which tries cases where criminal charges have been filed, and *family court,* which hears evidence and determines if the child is at risk, makes decisions regarding temporary or permanent wardship of the child or other children potentially at risk, and decides on cases where recommendations for termination of parental rights are made.
4. The *attorney* or *guardian* ad litem, who is court appointed and represents the interests of the children under consideration.

MENTAL HEALTH SERVICES

It is a very common practice for family physical and sexual abuse cases to be referred for mental health services, either for the victim, the abuser, or the entire family. Therapy may merely be suggested as appropriate or it can be mandated. In some locales, CPS has the flexibility to defer a referral for criminal prosecution of abusing family members and offer instead an *informal adjustment.* In this situation, the abuser or family is referred for intensive mental health counseling for a period of time. If significant change occurs, and the risk of further abuse is deemed low, then the case is not referred for criminal prosecution. On the other hand, if the abuser or family is *not* cooperative, or the risk to continued child abuse is significant, the case will proceed to the prosecutor's office. This offers important flexibility for CPS, and provides a powerful incentive for the abuser and the family to cooperate in therapy and to change their behavior.

The role of the mental health professional in family abuse cases is to: (a) assess the level of risk for further abuse; (b) assess the psychological states of the victims, abusers, and other involved family members; (c) provide counseling services to family members based on the assessment; (d) provide family therapy and other counseling services, if possible and desirable, to work toward family reunification in a safe, nonabusive environment; and (e) decrease the likelihood of future abuse by reducing vulnerabilities to abuse (Trepper & Barrett, 1989).

It should be added that, it is usually *not* the role of mental health practitioners to determine whether the abuse actually took place, especially if one or more of the family members involved denies that it did. Our assessment procedures are not designed to make that determination. At best, clinical and family psychologists may be able to assess the degree and magnitude of the individual and systemic vulnerabilities to abuse. The ultimate determination of whether, in cases of denial by the alleged abuser, abuse actually occurred is the role of the court.

Mental health services can include the entire range of health care, from individually oriented outpatient counseling to long-term residential treatment. Within that range, individual counseling, couples therapy (especially in cases of domestic violence), family therapy (especially when reunification is the goal), and group therapy (especially in same-sex abuser groups; Geffner, Barrett, & Rossman, 1995) are all likely to be required. It is our experience that, because of the complexity and intensity of family abuse cases and the likelihood that multiple levels and modes of therapy will be needed, these services are best provided by a comprehensive mental health center, preferably one that specializes in the treatment of abuse in families.

THE SCHOOLS

An often neglected system, but one that is extremely important, is the schools. Teachers or counselors know children well enough to notice subtle changes in attitude and behavior and be alert to signs of abuse. The school often makes the initial report to CPS, and will be able to help in the ongoing assessment of the progress of the child during the very precarious periods that usually follow that report. The appropriate school personnel should be kept apprised of the progress of the case throughout, so they can make the necessary educational and social adjustments necessary to support the social service and mental health efforts and stabilize the child in the school environment.

CONFLICTING GOALS AND OBJECTIVES

Conflict is inherent in a process that forces multiple systems to work together on a single problem, particularly when those systems hold different perspectives. While ultimately each system wants to protect children from abuse, the roles and tasks of each vary. For example, while the formal goal of therapy may be family reunification, the goal of prosecution may be to win a conviction against the abuser and have him or her sentenced to prison, thus further alienating family members. Another example is when CPS or the court expects and wants the mental health counselor to determine whether abuse actually occurred, when the primary training and role of the therapist is to provide counseling to ameliorate the individual and systemic vulnerabilities to abuse.

It is best when representatives of the various systems can, early in the progression of the case, meet to agree on common goals for the family, to clarify each other's roles, and to develop a systematic intervention plan. In practice, however, this rarely happens. Instead, the systems usually move along, doing their respective jobs, often with minimal communication with each other. When these systems *do* work together, it is our experience that there is less stress on the family, including the child victim, and the outcomes are better. Others in the field also maintain that collaboration within and between agencies is best for all involved (Peck, Sheinberg, & Akamatsu, 1995; Sheinberg, True, & Fraenkel, 1994; Westman, 1996).

IMPACT OF THE VARIOUS SYSTEMS ON THE FAMILY

Intervention by external systems obviously affects a family in various ways.

CHILD ABUSE REPORTING

In the past few years, more and more states have instituted a system to ensure that child abuse is reported quickly. In the past, child abuse was underreported, partially because the prevailing attitudes were to "mind one's own business," and partially because there were often negative consequences to the reporter. The current systems are usually two-pronged. First, there is a mandatory reporting component, so that *by law* someone who suspects child abuse *must* report it. In some states, the law limits this requirement to certain professionals who come in contact with children; in others it is required of all adults. Second, telephone hotline systems are increasingly common; with these, someone who suspects child abuse can anonymously make a report.

The benefits of these programs are obvious. They have helped change the cultural view of child abuse from being "someone else's business" to being a problem that is everyone's concern. These procedures also make it rather easy to report abuse and, coupled with a fairly rapid investigation, they can get children out of unsafe situations much more rapidly. The mandatory reporting laws have also taken any ambiguity out of the decision about whether a professional should report suspected child abuse, because there are criminal consequences for not reporting. Finally, these two factors combined usually result in decisions erring on the side of protecting an abused or potentially abused child.

There is a downside, unfortunately, to these requirements. Because of the desire to err on the side of protection, combined with the anonymity of much of the reporting, sometimes child abuse reports are made as tools of harassment or retaliation, or are made by someone with a hidden agenda. Such agendas might include long-standing family resentments harbored toward a sibling or adult child by an extended family member, or a desire to change a custody decision by an estranged spouse. Usually well-trained investigators are able to sort through those situations, but in some cases children who are not being abused are taken from their homes and put in foster placement during long-term investigations; such an arbitrary removal can be detrimental to child and parent alike. There can also be the unconscious belief by some caseworkers that even if child abuse is not clearly present, *something* must be going on, or the complaint would not have been filed.

MANDATED REMOVAL OF FAMILY MEMBERS FROM THE HOME

Once abuse is discovered, a series of actions follows that places the various systems in interaction with each other. One of the first actions is a decision about how to keep the child safe from further abuse during the intervention period. This is usually first accomplished by the mandated removal of a family member from the home. This can take various forms, each done for a different reason, each with benefits and potential problems: (a) removal of the abuser, (b) removal of the child, (c) removal of both, and (d) removal of neither.

Removing the abuser from the home makes the most "logical" sense, because it makes for the least trauma to the child victim, and alternately causes the most discomfort to the person who should have to endure it. The problem is that, in many families, it cannot always be guaranteed that the abuser will not surreptitiously return. This often happens without the knowledge of the caseworker or therapist, and often the family members themselves support the return of the abuser, despite the CPS decision. This not only puts the child victim at further risk, but forces family members to lie to the very people with whom they should be developing therapeutic trust. Another problem is the burden of economic hardship when the abuser has to maintain a second residence.

A second option is to remove the child victim and other at-risk children from the home and place them in foster care. Because of the problems inherent with removing the abuser, this option is now the one most often used. It has the benefit of assuring that the child will not be further abused within the family. It also has the added benefit of encouraging the nonabusing parent to cooperate more fully with CPS and therapy, because doing so may help get the child back home sooner.

Of course, the negatives to this option are quite serious, and are often horrific from the perspective of the child. Having to leave the comfort and familiarity of his or her own home to live with strangers can be frightening and feel punitive; that is, he or she has been extricated from the family as if the problem were his or her fault. The trauma of being separated is usually unsettling and detrimental. It is not unheard of for children to be abused in foster placement, although this is now unusual given increased training and support for foster families. Also, the child may get to visit the nonabusing parent only for short, supervised visits on an infrequent basis. Being removed from the home may feel like punishment to the child, while the intent is merely to maintain his or her safety. While no child enjoys being abused, and many are quite happy to be out of an abusive environment, many children report that the removal and placement is *worse* than the abuse they suffered, and that if they had to do it over again, would not report their abuse.

A third option, used quite infrequently, is to remove both the abuser and the child victim from the home. This occurs in those specific situations where the abuse has been particularly severe, both the abuser and nonabusing parent deny that it has occurred, and the nonabuser is deemed unable to protect the child or the other children from further abuse. The benefit is the absolute confidence that no further abuse will occur within the family during the intervention period. The same negatives would apply as previously described.

An alternative to each of these options is to remove *no one* from the home. Instead, families at risk are offered a variety of intensive treatment options that ensure the maximum amount of outside involvement and ongoing assessment, while causing the least disruption to the family. One such option that is gaining in popularity is in-home therapy and support services, which works to reduce the vulnerabilities to abuse in vivo (Barton, Baglio, & Braverman, 1994; Washburn, 1994). This, of course, is in addition to any individual therapy that is required for the abuser and the child victim. This option offers the least disruption to the family, does not force the child to live in a foster home, provides the family with therapy at home where structural problems may be easier to observe and ameliorate, and allows for intensive ongoing assessment of the likelihood for further abuse. The major negative is that with the abuser and victim still living together, there is always a chance of further abuse. It is for this reason that this option is suggested only after a thorough assessment has determined that further abuse under supervision is unlikely.

IMPACT ON THE FAMILY AND THE CHILD VICTIM

Sometimes, in their zeal to protect children, social service systems appear to forget that the very process that is designed to protect the child victim from further abuse may actually feel abusive to a child. The crisis of discovery and the way the investigation is handled can worsen the trauma experienced by abused children (Elwell & Ephross, 1987; Maddock & Larson, 1995). This chapter has already addressed the situation in which the child is removed from the home and put in foster placement, usually with strangers with their own rules, roles, and systems (an exception is the situation in which the child can be placed with extended family members, which may lessen the trauma to the child). This can be extremely frightening, and can impose a great sense of loss on the child. An ironic outcome often occurs: The child, as a result of the placement, becomes depressed or acts out. He or she is then referred for therapy, where the therapist determines that the child is experiencing these symptoms as a result of being abused, and if the symptoms persist, the therapist may recommend that the child not be reunified with the family until the abuse issues are "resolved." Of course, being abused would be one reason for the symptoms, but it is equally likely that the *placement* would be a major reason for them.

Families often find themselves in other dilemmas and contradictions when they are referred for therapy. For example, if the accused parent is denying the abuse, the nonoffending parent is placed in the position of choosing between the spouse and the child (Lipovsky, 1991). Many clients appear resistant to therapy, but Ackerman, Colapinto, Scharf, Weinshel, and Winawer (1991) remind therapists that these families present for therapy under conditions that make "resistance" seem understandable—that is, they did not choose their therapist, and in fact, their therapist was chosen by the "enemy" (CPS); they are expected to discuss problems that they didn't define; and acknowledgment of this problem could increase the possibility of prosecution and removal of the children from the home. In fact, the requirement of an admission of guilt for therapy to be considered successful has been discussed by some as a potential violation of the Fifth Amendment, which states that a person cannot be forced to be a witness against him- or herself in a criminal case (Levine & Doherty, 1991; Smith-Bell & Winslade, 1994), especially when the termination of parental rights hangs in the balance.

It cannot be overstated that the process of discovery and the intrusion into the lives of the family members can be extremely difficult for a family where physical or sexual abuse has occurred. With people being removed from the home, caseworkers scrutinizing all activities, the threat of impending criminal prosecution, the potential for the abusive parent to be jailed, and ultimately the threat of dissolution of the family, it is no wonder that families appear "resistant" to the process. Of course, that resistance can be seen as indicative of the "abusive nature" of the family. This tautological response affects not only the child victim. The lives of the nonabusing parent, the other siblings, and the extended family members are changed forever. Our goal should be to try to reduce the likelihood of further abuse while not inadvertently imposing *more* pain and suffering.

DIFFICULTY EXTRICATING FROM THE EXTERNAL SYSTEMS

One of the most troubling dilemmas for families who have come under the scrutiny of CPS, the courts, and the mental health systems is how to get out from under that scrutiny. If the process always worked as it should, the family would receive mental health services and, if the abuse had stopped and was assessed as being unlikely to reoccur (by virtue of most of the major vulnerabilities to abuse being ameliorated) then reunification would be effectuated. Then, within a reasonable period of time, all systems would end their involvement. In reality, once a family comes under the observation of quasi-legal or legal external systems, there is a tendency for those systems to maintain control for longer periods of time than may be necessary. Also, behaviors and aspects of the family's life may be intruded upon which, had there not been the report of child abuse, would not have been grounds for governmental scrutiny or intervention.

As an example, we recently became aware of a case in which CPS had custody of an abused child, and the caseworker reported to the court that the family's house was not clean enough, even though there were no sanitation or hygiene concerns. The family contested this, stating that their house was as clean as it could be given that five children lived there with one single mother (the sexually abusing father having been removed from the home). The caseworker saw this challenge by the mother as her unwillingness to cooperate in her own rehabilitation (it should be noted that the child had been abused by the father, not the mother), and suggested ongoing CPS custody, a suggestion which was accepted by the court. While there may have been extenuating circumstances particular to the case, this is not an unusual situation, and it illustrates how difficult it can be for a family to get out of a system once in it.

EFFECT ON CLINICAL SERVICES

All of these issues can obviously affect therapists' clinical practice. Most clinicians are used to working with individuals who are openly seeking therapy and are cooperative, where privacy and confidentiality are paramount, and where the presenting problem does not provoke extreme personal feelings on the part of the therapist. The treatment of physical or sexual abuse cases requires working with an entire family system that is mandated for therapy, where one or more members are usually hostile and appear highly resistant. A multitude of agencies and people need to know the details of the therapy, so confidentiality is at a minimum. In addition, the presenting problem is so horrific—the abuse of a child—that strong personal reactions may be evoked in the therapist. These factors, plus those discussed in the following sections, make working with family abuse cases particularly challenging, and require special training and supervision so that one can intervene appropriately.

WHO IS THE CLIENT?

One of the first questions raised by all of the systems involved is: "Who is the client?" (Korner, 1990). Few agencies have the resources to provide an individual therapist to each family member in need—and frankly, many would question the efficacy of doing so, given the profound impact on the entire family system. Is the client the child? Is it the abuser? Is it the nonabusing parent? Is it the entire family? Is it CPS or the courts? The answer, in our opinion, is that *all* of the individual members and subsystems, as well as the family as a whole, are the client, at least from a clinical perspective, and that there are obligations to the impinging external systems. We understand that individual agency requirements may mandate separate files for each member, with separate diagnoses, but these are administrative rather than clinical realities. For the therapist receiving a referral for a family abuse case, the reality should be that he or she is the *family's* therapist.

Considering the whole family as the client offers a number of advantages. First, it allows for more thorough, accurate, and complete assessment of the multiple vulnerabilities to abuse. While it is tempting to consider child abuse to be the product of a pathological *individual*, there is clear clinical and empirical evidence that there are multiple factors that contribute to abuse in the family (e.g., Finkelhor, 1980; Larson & Maddock, 1986; Maddock & Larson, 1995; Simons, Whitbeck, Conger, & Chyi-In, 1991; Trepper & Barrett, 1989; Trepper, Niedner, Mika, & Barrett, 1996).

Second, seeing the family as the client allows the therapist to join with all members, even those who do not initially show symptoms or problems but who may do so later, facilitating later interventions with them. Third, it permits the therapist to intervene at a systemic level to help change, for example, a dysfunctional family structure which may have made the children more vulnerable to abuse.

None of this should suggest that needed services to individuals, such as the child victim, should be ignored. Quite the contrary, viewing the family as the client allows the therapist to provide more comprehensive services than does just seeing the child alone. Some have argued that treating the family as a whole in physical or sexual abuse cases may indirectly send the message that the responsibility of the abuse rests with the entire family, the nonoffending parent, or even the child victim (e.g., Avis, 1986; Bograd, 1984; James & MacKinnon, 1990). However, viewing the family as the client should not in any way imply to the family, or anyone else, that the *responsibility* for the abuse lies with them. No serious family systems theorists or therapists would absolve the perpetrator of moral responsibility or blame other members for the abuse (Maddock & Larson, 1995).

TYPES OF THERAPY INDICATED

Child physical and sexual abuse cases are, without doubt, some of the most complex and perplexing cases to treat. Given the number of external systems involved, the number of people who are affected both by the abuse and by disruption in the family, the severity of the presenting problem, and the potential severity of effects on individual family members, it is our opinion that these cases are best treated in a comprehensive family abuse treatment program, preferably within a community mental health system which offers the full range of outpatient and inpatient services. We believe that attempting to treat a family in which child physical or sexual abuse has occurred in an independent practice can be very demanding and draining for the therapist. Also, unless the practitioner has many supportive resources such as an emergency service network and access to group therapy for abusers, child victims, and nonabusing parents, he or she may not be able to provide some of the key services necessary for effective treatment.

Family Therapy

Family therapy should be the cornerstone of treatment. It encompasses the ability to do a complete family evaluation, assessing the multiple vulnerabilities present in the family (Maddock & Larson, 1995; Trepper & Barrett, 1989). These vulnerabilities include *socioenvironmental factors*, such as gender issues, chronic family stress, and social isolation; *family-of-origin factors*, such as incidences of abuse in previous generations and strong family themes regarding rigid male and female roles; *family systems factors*, such as family structure, communication, abusive style, and function of the abuse; and *individual psychological factors*, such as cognitive distortions, personality disorders, or sexual fantasies or paraphilias (Trepper et al., 1996).

Family therapy also offers all members access to assessment of critical needs (e.g., severe depression on the part of the child victim, continued risk for extra-familial abuse by the abuser, etc.). It allows the therapist to intervene more easily with external systems, such as the schools and CPS, in a more informed way. Finally, and most important from a clinical perspective, it offers the best hope for changing the family structure, communication patterns, and problem-solving deficits that may have increased the family's dysfunctional behaviors, and it will help reduce the likelihood of further abuse.

Family therapy need not include the entire family for each session. In fact, most programs have specific guidelines about when to include particular family members. For example, the abuser and the child victim should *never* be brought into the same session when the offending parent is denying the facts of the abuse. This would put the child in an uncomfortable position, perhaps even leading to an unwarranted recanting of the facts. Family therapy should also include *others*, such as foster parents, grandparents, and anyone else who might have an impact on the case. Subsystems, such as the parents or siblings, will usually have sessions alone to emphasize certain clinical points, for example, the importance of boundaries.

Individual Therapy

All comprehensive family-based programs treating child physical and sexual abuse include individual therapy for child victims, abusers (if they are willing and not incarcerated), the nonabusing parent, and non-abused siblings. Given limited resources, usually not all family members have weekly individual therapy, and it becomes a matter of who has the most need or the most likelihood of benefiting from individual sessions. It is most helpful if the individual therapy is integrated with the family therapy. For example, a theme being developed in family sessions, such as the importance of clear boundaries and the unacceptability of physical intrusion on any person, can be punctuated in the individual therapy. There are times when it is most useful to have separate therapists for different family members, particularly if counselors in an agency have specialties that can be utilized, such as working with children or sex abuse perpetrators. At all times, it is essential that the individual therapists coordinate their work with the family therapist, so that family members do not triangulate their counselors or pit them against each other, a frequent defense mechanism used by distressed, dysfunctional families.

Group Therapy

Group therapy is an extremely useful modality for sexual abuse cases, and whenever possible it should be used as part of the family's overall treatment endeavor. Specialized groups most commonly focus on abusing parents, child victims, and nonabusing parents. These groups are usually a combination of psychoeducational and emotionally focused components. For example, a leader of a group for physically abusing parents may didactically present the four types of denial commonly present (i.e., denial of facts, of awareness, of responsibility, and of impact; cf. Trepper and Barrett, 1989) for the first hour, and then have the group members discuss the times they were in each type of denial, how it felt, and the impact it may have had on others.

Couples Therapy

In many abuse cases, clinicians may find couples therapy sessions to be quite useful to help strengthen the marital dyad, which in turn serves as a foundation for further systemic changes. Couples therapy may also help to clarify serious marital issues, which may be one of the primary precipitants of abuse. (For a complete discussion on the multiple vulnerabilities to family abuse, cf. Trepper & Barrett, 1986; 1989, pp. 20–27.) Sometimes these issues are resolvable, and sometimes they are not. In the latter case, one outcome may be a decision on the part of the couple to divorce, which may in the long run be the most advantageous for the couple and the family (Schwartz & Kaslow, 1997). In any event, couples sessions allow the pair to explore their relationship in a safe and objective environment, without involving the children, which in turn increases the clarity of boundaries within the family.

IMPORTANT GOALS OF THERAPY

There are a number of possible goals in the treatment of family violence, depending upon the desire of the family, the realities of the legal situation, and the limitations of therapy itself. First and foremost, and overriding all others, is the goal of protecting the child and the other children in the home from further abuse. This is no gratuitous goal; it has an impact on all other goals and clinical decisions. For example, the abusing and nonabusing parents may have as their goal quick reunification. However, they may both be denying the facts of the abuse. In that case, intermediate goals, such as having them admit to the abusive behavior and accept responsibility, apologize and make amends (Trepper, 1986; Madanes, 1990), and support the abused child's statements, would have to be reached and achieved before the reunification goal could be worked on (Powell & Ilett, 1992).

Beyond admission of the facts and accepting responsibility, there are many other goals that are common in therapy for family abuse cases. Once the factors that made the family vulnerable to abuse have been identified, preferably with members of the family, then specific goals are set to reduce those proclivities. For example, if one of the systemic vulnerabilities to sexual abuse by extended family members was that the family had a chaotic structure with few rules, parents rarely in charge, and people in and out of the house, then one of the primary clinical goals would be to improve that structure through the use of structural family therapy interventions (Minuchin, 1974; Beavers & Voeller, 1983; Maddock & Larson, 1995). If one of the vulnerabilities was that the family was isolated from their community, with few external resources, then the goal would be to encourage them to reconnect with community resources, their church, or civic, athletic, or other groups.

Goals are commonly set with the individuals within the family. For physically abusing family members, these might include anger management, improved parenting skills, and alternatives for tension relief. Goals for sexually abusing family members would include these plus sexual fantasy reduction, control of inappropriate sexual impulses, reducing cognitive distortions surrounding sexual abuse, and fostering changes in attitudes and interpersonal behaviors. Goals for nonabusing parents often center around improving their abilities to protect their children (e.g., through assertiveness training interventions), to notice signs of abuse, and to improve their relationships with abused family members.

One dilemma that may occur in any family therapy, and is especially of concern with family abuse cases, is when different family members have divergent goals. For example, it may be the goal of a sexually abused teenage girl to never see her abusing stepfather again, while it may be her mother's goal to work toward reunification because she is unwilling to end the relationship with her husband, especially while he is working to make changes in therapy, is financially supporting the children, or is doing both. There are different ways to handle a situation like this. First, the therapist may try to work with the girl and the mother (along with other members of the family) individually to see if a mutual goal can be established. It may be that the issue for the girl is safety from abuse, and if mechanisms were in place where she could feel safe, then she could agree to live in the same house. Another solution we have seen to these disparate goals is for the mother and stepfather to live separately until the daughter leaves home, so that the child victim is not further victimized.

THE ROLE OF THE THERAPIST

The role of the therapist should be clarified early in the intervention process, and not only with the family itself, but with the other systems. It is best if therapists are *not* placed in an investigative or punitive role. Greenberg and Shuman (1997) maintain that the roles of therapists and forensic evaluators are quite different. Therapists clearly need to know their limits. That does not mean therapists should ignore signs of continued abuse or fail to report families who are not cooperative in therapy to CPS or the courts. It does mean that the role of investigating ongoing abuse or whether the family is complying with the rules of the court should rest with CPS, and the role of punishment for failure to comply with court orders should rest with the courts. The family, not the therapist, has the ultimate responsibility for persuading the systems involved that the children will be safe with them (Ackerman et al., 1991).

Not only are therapists often expected to act as forensic investigators by CPS or the courts, but they are often called on to testify in court when working with abuse cases. It is important for clinicians to clarify such issues as what type of information will be sought and whether they will serve as a fact or opinion witness (Vesper & Brock, 1991; also see Chapter 23). When called to testify in termination of parental rights hearings, therapists are often asked questions about what constitutes adequate parenting, the services required to change parenting skills, the indicators of progress in abuse cases, and the meaning of noncompliance (Azar, Benjet, Fuhrmann, & Cavallero, 1995). Therapists are also often requested to prognosticate about the likelihood of future violence, and therapists are expected to know the research about the unreliability and near impossibility of making accurate predictions of dangerousness (Azar et al., 1995; Powell & Ilett, 1992; Vesper & Brock, 1991).

Throughout the treatment process, therapists must clarify issues of confidentiality and communication with external systems. In most cases, therapists and clients understand that the sanctity of confidentiality is a foundation for a trusting therapeutic relationship, as is specified in the ethical principles of psychologists and of marriage and family therapists (American Psychological Association, 1992;

American Association for Marriage and Family Therapy, 1991). Therapists know that they are legally required to break the bonds of confidentiality when they suspect child abuse or neglect (e.g., see the APA Ethical Principles of Psychologists, Standard 5.01, 5.02, and 5.05, American Psychological Association, 1992; and the AAMFT Code of Ethics, Standard 2.1, American Association for Marriage and Family Therapy, 1991). There are no hard and fast rules about what is confidential and what is not. Clearly, CPS workers and the courts need information about the client's attendance in therapy, treatment goals, progress, and risk for further violence. However, many caseworkers expect to have access to any and all information while others rely on written or verbal reports from therapists; this allows therapists to exclude information that is clinically significant, but not necessarily relevant to the courts, such as *specific* marital problems discussed by the nonoffending parent. Further, clients know that what their therapists tell their caseworkers is often extremely influential in determining the outcome of their cases, and they may feel caught in the bind between discussing issues in therapy and not wanting their cases to "look bad." Clinicians working with different subsystems and individuals in the family should also discuss confidentiality and secrets with each member of the family to avoid being triangulated. Because the confidentiality issue in abuse cases is unique and vague, it is essential that therapists discuss this principle overtly with their clients and with CPS case workers.

It is highly recommended that clinicians develop and use detailed informed-consent forms, which, while always important, are crucial when working with multiple systems. The purpose of informed consent is to provide at least a degree of legal protection for the therapist, demonstrating a good-faith effort to explain all aspects of any treatment program prior to beginning. It also serves to provide important, detailed information about the program to all members of the family, while serving as a vehicle for a comprehensive discussion of all elements of the treatment program. Finally, it has a therapeutic function by clarifying the role of the therapist, and immediately suggests that the therapist is in charge of the clinical aspects of the case. The informed-consent form is *in addition* to release-of-information forms, request-for-information forms, and formal treatment plans.

Although there are many possible ways to organize such forms, all of them should include at least the following information:

- Client's name and any identifying clinic number.
- Type of treatment to be provided (e.g., outpatient individual counseling; group therapy).
- If the treatment is part of a comprehensive program, what all of the elements of the program are, how these elements interrelate to the treatment goals, and what the expected outcomes of each of the elements are.
- Expected duration of each treatment modality.
- The limits of confidentiality.
- What procedures the therapist will follow if information on additional child abuse episodes is obtained.
- What types of reports may be written to which agency and with what degree of participation from the client.

• Client's rights, including freedom to terminate treatment at any time, and what consequences may apply in exercising those rights (e.g., the therapist will report the client's decision to the appropriate agencies and offices involved with the case).

The informed-consent form should be given to clients to read and sign before treatment commences, and the therapist should discuss all parts of it to make certain it is understood. When doing family therapy, each adult member of the family should read and sign a copy, and one should be signed by the legal guardian of any minor children.

This clarification of roles, through initial discussions and the signing of an informed-consent form, allows therapists to do what they do best, and that is *to work to ameliorate the vulnerabilities to abuse.* Not unlike any other therapy, this is best accomplished in a cooperative relationship with the family and its individual members. That cooperative stance can be seriously eroded when the therapist is put into the role of an agent of the court or of CPS, as perceived by the family. While not quite an ally—that is, the therapist should not be seen as someone who will support the family no matter what—the therapist should be seen as being generally supportive of the family members and their goals.

The Role of the Forensic Assessor

We highly recommend that the family's therapist not act as the forensic assessor, although in smaller communities where agency budgets are meager there is a temptation to ask one clinician to serve both functions. The role of the forensic assessor is to provide information to the court which establishes truth within the parameters of the law, a job that requires fact finding, the collection and interpretation of evidence. Historically, the forensic assessor has relied primarily on individual assessments of the abused child and offending parent, using the traditional assessment tools of clinical interviews, objective and projective personality tests, and specialized procedures and inventories (Wakefield & Underwager, 1988; Walker, 1988b), although the validity of reliance on single tests is not supported by the literature (Lanyon, 1993). More recently these evaluations have become more expansive to include a complete systemic assessment, or what Maddock and Larson (1995) call an *ecological assessment.* Even under the best conditions, with a wide-ranging clinical investigation, where data is obtained from the broadest array of sources, the assessment of truthfulness, which is the primary question to be answered by forensic assessors, can only *sometimes* be made with great confidence (Hall & Crowther, 1991; Lanyon, 1993).

A complete ecological assessment can provide a framework upon which the forensic evaluator can organize the data, and make more sense of the complex case for the court. More important, since no one "test" can provide the answer to the most common question the court will ask—"Did abuse occur?"—the ecological assessment offers a more complete package of information from which the court can make its decision.

A complete evaluation should always include the following (for a complete discussion on the forensic assessment of abuse, cf. Maddock & Larson, 1995; Robin, 1991; Wakefield & Underwager, 1988; Walker, 1988a):

Individual pathology should be determined using clinical interviews, objective personality and pathology tests such as the Minnesota Multiphasic Personality Inventory (MMPI) or Millon Clinical Multiaxial Inventory (MCMI), and projective tests such as the Rorschach, to determine the presence and degree of conditions that may influence the commission of child abuse (such as antisocial personality disorder, narcissistic personality disorder, etc.). It should be noted, however, that many abuse perpetrators and victims show no elevations on standardized tests (Goeke & Boyer, 1993; Maddock & Larson, 1995; McAnulty, Adams, & Wright, 1994).

Physiological measures, such as a polygraph and penile plethysmograph, which may provide external, nonreactive measures to support information gathered during the clinical interview, should also be utilized. There is a possibility of false positives and negatives with both tests, especially with well-guarded or antisocial personality individuals, which would limit their use and further suggest that they be used only as part of a more complete evaluation (Gardner, 1992).

Procedures with children, such as the use of anatomically correct dolls (Walker, 1988b), and the Event Drawing Series (Burgess & Hartmann, 1993), which is a structured method to have young children *draw* the traumatic event, are often used in forensic assessment as a vehicle for a complete clinical interview with the child. However, caution must be exercised to use these only while carefully following procedures that reduce the likelihood of assessor bias. Also, the assessor should be aware that there is *not* a strong empirical basis for using these methods as single-item procedures (Lanyon, 1993; Wakefield & Underwager, 1988).

Family assessment is considered a critical part of an ecological evaluation. Maddock and Larson (1995) recommend that the following areas be addressed: (1) *assess the boundaries* between the family and its community, intergenerationally, interpersonally, and intrapsychically; and (2) *assess the meaning or functions of the abuse*—that is, whether it is *affection-based*, *erotic-based*, (for incestuous abuse), *aggression-based*, or *rage-based*. While a number of assessment schema exist in family therapy (e.g., Beavers and Voeller, 1983; Olson, Russell, & Sprenkle, 1989), there are very few psychometrically sound instruments that measure family functioning or that can reliably differentiate clinical and nonclinical families. One exception is the Family Assessment Device (FAD) (Epstein, Baldwin, & Bishop, 1983; Stevenson-Hinde & Akister, 1995), which has been shown to possess the requisite psychometric properties to be used in forensic assessment. It yields seven scale scores on the dimensions of problem solving, communication, roles, affective responsiveness, affective involvement, behavior control, and general functioning.

The forensic assessor, in the absence of clear medical evidence or a direct admission by the allegedly offending parent, should put together a composite picture from the ecological assessment from which to draw a conclusion. The advantage of the ecological assessment is that there are more sources of information from which a conclusion can converge. A stronger case is made for the likelihood that abuse occurred when the parent, the child, and the family system as a whole can be shown to be highly vulnerable.

SUMMARY AND RECOMMENDATIONS

As suggested throughout this chapter, treating physically and sexually abusing families can be extremely difficult, not just because of the clinical complexity of the cases, but because of the involvement of so many different external systems. Based on our experience and the experience of others who specialize with this population, we suggest the following to help therapists to intervene more effectively:

- *Become familiar with the agencies involved with abuse cases.* Therapists treating family abuse cases will *always* need to have some contact with some other agencies. It is crucial that the therapist know all of the agencies potentially involved, and if possible, develop close, professional relationships with the individuals who represent these agencies.
- *Develop a comprehensive treatment program.* Because of the complexity of physical and sexual abuse cases, it is most prudent to offer services within a comprehensive treatment program, which offers family, individual, and group therapies along with psychological diagnostic services. In addition, emergency services should be available, along with staff who are competent in providing crisis assessment and intervention (including inpatient hospitalization if necessary). It is not recommended that independent practitioners working alone treat family abuse cases unless they are connected with a comprehensive treatment program.
- *Clarify the role of the therapist.* When working with other agencies, it is essential that the role of the therapist be clarified. Hopefully, the therapist can stay in the role of supportive counselor more than that of investigator or police officer. Those roles are better performed by others, and such a demarcation allows the therapist to focus on the task of ameliorating the vulnerabilities that contributed to the abuse in the family.
- *Intervene with all relevant "families."* Therapists will have the most success in achieving clinical goals when they can assess and intervene with all the "families" involved with the case. This may include all members of the nuclear family (defined as anyone living in the home, including paramours). It would also include "families" that are often forgotten, but that may have a profound impact on the outcome, including foster families, extended families, biological parents not living with the child, and even close friendship groups. Although this may seem overwhelming, there is so much potential for splitting among these various families that it is imperative to include them and to attempt to set and achieve agreed-upon goals.

Treating physically and sexually abusing families is without doubt one of the most challenging clinical opportunities a therapist may have. These cases can be extremely demanding and often difficult, with a myriad of external systems and people involved. However, with knowledge of these systems, a basic knowledge of the law, and the structure of a comprehensive treatment program, they can turn into the most rewarding of cases.

REFERENCES

Ackerman, F., Colapinto, J. A., Scharf, C. N., Weinshel, M., & Winawer, H. (1991). The involuntary client: Avoiding "pretend therapy." *Family Systems Medicine, 9*(3), 261–266.

American Psychological Association. (1992). *Ethical principles of psychologists.* Washington, DC: Author.

American Association for Marriage and Family Therapy. (1991). *AAMFT code of ethics.* Washington, DC: Author.

Avis, J. M. (1986). Feminist issues in family therapy. In F. Piercy & D. Sprenkle (Eds.), *Family therapy sourcebook* (pp. 213–242). New York: Guilford Press.

Azar, S. T., Benjet, C. L., Fuhrmann, G. S., & Cavallero, L. (1995). Child maltreatment and termination of parental rights: Can behavioral research help Solomon? *Behavior Therapy, 26,* 599–623.

Barton, K., Baglio, C. S., & Braverman, M. T. (1994). Stress reduction in child-abusing families: Global and specific measures. *Psychological Reports, 75,* 287–304.

Beavers, W. R., & Voeller, M. N. (1983). Family models: Comparing and contrasting the Olson Circumplex model with the Beavers system model. *Family Process, 22,* 85–98.

Bograd, M. (1984). Family systems approaches to wife battering: A feminist critique. *American Journal of Orthopsychiatry, 54*(4), 558–568.

Burgess, A. W., & Hartmann, C. R. (1993). Children's drawings. Special Issue: Clinical recognition of sexually abused children. *Child Abuse and Neglect, 17,* 161–168.

Burns Indiana statutes annotated (1987). Charlotteville, VA: Michie.

DeKraai, M. B., & Sales, B. D. (1991). Liability in child therapy and research. *Journal of Consulting and Clinical Psychology, 59*(6), 853–860.

Elwell, M. E., & Ephross, P. H. (1987). Initial reactions of sexually abused children. *Social Casework,* 109–116.

Epstein, N. B., Baldwin, L. M., and Bishop, D. S. (1983). The McMaster Family Assessment Device. *Journal of Marital & Family Therapy, 19,* 171–180.

Finkelhor, D. (1980). Risk factors in the sexual victimization of children. *Child Abuse and Neglect, 4,* 265–273.

Finkelhor, D. (1986). *A sourcebook on child sexual abuse.* Beverly Hills, CA: Sage.

Gardner, R. A. (1992). *True and false accusations of child sex abuse.* Cresskill, NJ: Creative Therapeutics.

Geffner, R., Barrett, M. J., & Rossman, B. R. (1995). Domestic violence and sexual abuse: Multiple systems perspectives. In Richard H. Mikesell, Don-David Lusterman, & Susan H. McDaniel (Eds.), *Integrating family therapy: Handbook of family psychology and systems theory* (pp. 501–517). Washington, DC: American Psychological Association.

Gelles, R. J. (1987). What to learn from cross cultural and historical research on child abuse and neglect: An overview. In R. J. Gelles & J. B. Lancaster (Eds.), *Child abuse and neglect: Biosocial dimensions.* Hawthorn, NY: Adline De Gruyter.

Goeke, J. M., & Boyer, M. C. (1993). The failure to construct an MMPI-based incest perpetrator scale. *International Journal of Offender Therapy and Comparative Criminology, 37,* 271–277.

Greenberg, S. A., & Shuman, D. W. (1997). Irreconcilable conflict between therapeutic and forensic roles. *Professional Psychology: Research and Practice, 28*(1), 50–57.

Hall, G. C., & Crowther, J. H. (1991). Psychologists' involvement in cases of child maltreatment: Additional limits of assessment methods. *American Psychologist, 46*(1), 79–80.

Illinois Department of Children and Family Services (1982). Abused and Neglected Child Reporting Act. Springfield, IL: Author.

James, K. & MacKinnon, L. (1990). The "incestuous family" revisited: A critical analysis of family therapy myths. *Journal of Marital and Family Therapy, 16*(1), 71–88.

Korner, S. (1990). Evaluating child sexual abuse: Who is the client? *Psychotherapy in Private Practice, 8,* 1–11.

Lanyon, R. I. (1993). Assessment of truthfulness in accusations of child molestation. *American Journal of Forensic Psychology, 11,* 29–44.

Larson, N. R., & Maddock, J. W. (1986). Structural and functional variables in incest family systems: Implications for assessment and treatment. In T. S. Trepper & M. J. Barrett (Eds.), *Treating incest: A multiple systems perspective* (pp. 27–44). New York: Haworth Press.

Levine, M., & Doherty, E. (1991). The fifth amendment and therapeutic requirements to admit abuse. *Criminal Justice and Behavior, 18*(1), 97–112.

Lipovsky, J. A. (1991). Disclosure of father-child sexual abuse: Dilemmas for families and therapists. *Contemporary Family Therapy, 13*(2), 85–101.

Madanes, C. (1990). *Sex, love, and violence: Strategies for transformation.* New York: W. W. Norton.

Maddock, J. W., & Larson, N. R. (1995). *Incestuous families.* New York: W. W. Norton.

McAnulty, R. D., Adams, H. E., & Wright, L. W. (1994). Relationship between MMPI and penile plethysmograph in accused child molesters. *Journal of Sex Research, 31,* 179–184.

Minuchin, S. (1974). *Families and family therapy.* Cambridge, MA: Harvard University Press.

Olson, D. H., Russell, C. S., & Sprenkle, D. H. (Eds.), (1989). *Circumplex model: Systemic assessment and treatment of families.* New York: Haworth Press.

Peck, J. S., Sheinberg, M., & Akamatsu, N. N. (1995). Forming a consortium: A design for interagency collaboration in the delivery of service following the disclosure of incest. *Family Process, 34,* 287–302.

Powell, M. B., & Ilett, M. J. (1992). Assessing the incestuous family's readiness for reconstitution. *Families in Society, 73*(3), 417–423.

Reber, A. S. (1985). *Dictionary of Psychology.* New York: Penguin Books.

Robin, M. (Ed.), (1991). *Assessing child maltreatment reports: The problem of false allegations.* New York: Haworth Press.

Russell, D. E. H. (1984). The prevalence and seriousness of incestuous abuse: Stepfathers vs. biological fathers. *Child Abuse and Neglect, 8,* 15–22.

Schwartz, L. L. (1993). What is a family? A contemporary view. *Contemporary Family Therapy, 15*(6), 429–442.

Schwartz, L. L., & Kaslow, F. W. (1997). *Painful partings: Divorce and its aftermath.* New York: John Wiley & Sons.

Sheinberg, M., True, F., & Fraenkel, P. (1994). Treating the sexually abused child: A recursive, multimodal program. *Family Process, 33,* 263–276.

Simons, R. L., Whitbeck, L. B., Conger, R. D., & Chyi-In, W. (1991). Intergenerational transmission of harsh parenting. *Developmental Psychology, 27*(1), 159–171.

Smith-Bell, M. & Winslade, W. J. (1994). Privacy, confidentiality, and privilege in psychotherapeutic relationships. *American Journal of Orthopsychiatry, 64*(2), 180–193.

Stevenson-Hinde, J., & Akister, J. (1995). The McMaster model of family functioning: Observer and parental ratings in a nonclinical sample. *Family Process, 34,* 337–347.

Trepper, T. S. (1986). The apology session. In T. S. Trepper & M. J. Barrett (Eds.), *Treating incest: A multiple systems perspective.* New York: Haworth Press.

Trepper, T. S., & Barrett, M. J. (1986). Vulnerability to incest: A framework for assessment. In T. S. Trepper & M. J. Barrett (Eds.), *Treating incest: A multiple systems approach.* New York: Haworth Press.

Trepper, T. S., & Barrett, M. J. (1989). *Systemic treatment of incest: A therapeutic handbook.* New York: Brunner/Mazel.

Trepper, T. S., Niedner, D., Mika, L., & Barrett, M. J. (1996). Family characteristics of intact sexually abusing families: An exploratory study. *Journal of Child Sexual Abuse, 5,* 1–18.

Vesper, J. H., & Brock, G. W. (1991). *Ethics, legalities, and professional practice issues in marriage and family therapy.* Needham Heights, MA: Allyn & Bacon.

Wakefield, H., & Underwager, R. (1988). *Accusations of child sexual abuse.* Springfield, IL: Charles C. Thomas.

Walker, L. E. (1988a). *Handbook on sexual abuse of children.* New York: Springer.

Walker, L. W. (1988b). New techniques for assessment and evaluation of child sexual abuse victims: Using anatomically correct dolls and videotape procedures. In L. E. Walker (Ed.), *Handbook on sexual abuse of children.* New York: Springer.

Westman, J. C. (1996). The child advocacy team in child abuse and neglect matters. *Child Psychiatry and Human Development, 26*(4), 221–234.

Washburn, P. (1994). Advantages of a brief solution oriented focus in home based family preservation services. *Journal of Systemic Therapies, 13,* 47–58.

PART TWO

WHEN FAMILIES IN TREATMENT INTERFACE WITH LEGAL AND JUDICIAL SYSTEMS

The Middle Years—Raising Adolescents and Young Adults

CHAPTER 6

Privacy Rights of Minors

MARSHA LEVICK

MENTAL HEALTH professionals treating families must be cognizant not only of the rights to privacy and confidentiality that the family members possess collectively as a unit, but also of each individual family member's right to privacy. Thus, in the treatment of adolescent family members, the therapist must recognize that adolescents themselves possess individual rights to privacy and confidentiality which, under certain circumstances, encompass their communications with the therapist. At the same time, these privacy rights of minors may occasionally appear to conflict with the therapist's obligations to other family members or third parties. This chapter addresses the privacy rights of minors in the therapeutic relationship.

THE RIGHT TO PRIVACY GENERALLY

The makers of our Constitution undertook to secure conditions favorable to the pursuit of happiness. They recognized the significance of man's spiritual nature, of his feelings and of his intellect. They knew that only a part of the pain, pleasure and satisfactions of life are to be found in material things. They sought to protect Americans in their beliefs, their thoughts, their emotions and their sensations. They conferred, as against the Government, the right to be let alone—the most comprehensive of rights and the right most valued by civilized men (*Olmstead v. United States*, 1928).

In *Olmstead*, U.S. Supreme Court Justice Brandeis first recognized more than 60 years ago that the Constitution protects an individual's "right to be let alone." Without grounding it in any particular provision of the U.S. Constitution, Justice Brandeis heralded the sanctity of the individual's right to be protected in his or her beliefs, thoughts, and emotions from unwanted and uninvited intrusion by the government. Subsequent to Justice Brandeis' now famous dissent in *Olmstead*, the Supreme Court has, in several cases decided since, elevated this right to a fundamental constitutional right to privacy which the Court has said derives from several different express guarantees of individual freedom in the Constitution.

This newly articulated right to privacy was first officially recognized by the U.S. Supreme Court in 1965 in *Griswold v. Connecticut* (1965). In *Griswold,* the Supreme Court struck down a statute which made it a crime to give medical advice and information to married persons about contraception and to prescribe contraceptive drugs or devices for the couple's use. Although the Court acknowledged that the Constitution does not specifically mention a right of privacy, the Court concluded in *Griswold* that various provisions of the Constitution, such as the right of association contained in the First Amendment, the Fourth Amendment's protection against unreasonable searches and seizures, and the Fifth Amendment's right against self-incrimination, create zones of privacy worthy of constitutional protection in and of themselves. More recently, the Court has characterized the right of privacy as deriving from the Fourteenth Amendment's concept of "personal liberty and restrictions upon state action" (*Roe v. Wade,* 1973). Whether rooted in various provisions of the Constitution or the Fourteenth Amendment alone, this constitutional right of privacy has been held to extend to two types of interests: the individual's interest in avoiding disclosure of personal matters, and the individual's interest in independence in making certain kinds of important decisions (*Whalen v. Roe,* 1977). The latter decisions have encompassed matters relating to marriage, procreation, contraception, family relationships, child rearing, and education.

For example, in a series of cases involving the reproductive rights of both men and women, single or married, the Supreme Court has recognized a right to privacy, which excludes the state from intruding into these decisions. Among the individual and personal "procreative" or "reproductive" decisions protected by this zone of privacy, according to the Court, are individual decisions relating to marriage (*Loving v. Virginia,* 1967), procreation (*Skinner v. Oklahoma,* 1942), contraception (*Eisenstadt v. Baird,* 1972), abortion (*Roe v. Wade,* 1973), family relationships (*Prince v. Massachusetts,* 1944), and childrearing and education (*Pierce v. Society of Sisters,* 1925).

With respect to the individual's privacy interest in guarding against the disclosure of personal information, the Constitution does not provide an absolute protection against disclosure; disclosure may be required if the government interest in disclosure outweighs the individual's privacy interest (*United States v. Westinghouse Electric Corp,* 1980). In determining whether information is entitled to privacy protection, courts have looked at whether the type of information sought is within an individual's reasonable expectations of privacy; the more personal and intimate the information, the greater the expectation that it will not be open to public disclosure. Thus, in weighing the competing interests of the individual and the government, courts consider, among other things, the type of record and nature of the information requested, the harm to the relationship in which the information was generated if the information is disclosed, the adequacy of safeguards to protect against unauthorized disclosure of the information, the degree of need for access to the information, and whether there is a statute, articulated policy, or other acknowledged public interest favoring access and disclosure.

As a general matter, medical records, which often contain intimate facts of a personal nature, are considered well within the ambit of materials entitled to privacy protection (*United States v. Westinghouse,* 1980). Information about a person's physical and emotional state of health is information that is ordinarily considered "part of the private enclave" where individuals conduct their private lives. (*Murphy v. Waterfront Commission*, 1964). In recognition of the particularly private nature of medical information, this data is treated differently in many legal contexts than other kinds of personal information. For example, the federal discovery rules impose a higher burden on parties seeking the release of medical and mental health information than other records and information under the Federal Rules of Civil Procedure [compare Fed. R. Civ. P. with Fed. R. Civ. P. 26(b)]. Medical files are also the subject of a specific exemption under the Freedom of Information Act [5 U.S.C. §552(b)(6) (1976)]. The exceptional treatment accorded medical records is a reflection of the special nature of this information under the law.

The disclosure of medical information is not, however, absolutely prohibited. The state's responsibility for the health of its citizens has justified the disclosure of certain types of medical information when necessary to help the state carry out those responsibilities. Disclosure of medical information pursuant to statutory reporting requirements regarding venereal disease, child abuse, fetal deaths, certain abortion-related information, and injuries caused by deadly weapons have all been upheld as proper exercises of the state's concern for the public health (*Whalen v. Roe*, 1977).

PROTECTION OF RIGHTS OF MINORS

The rights to privacy described in the preceding have all originated in cases involving adults challenging state intrusion into matters or decisions they deemed private. As a general principle, minors' constitutional rights historically have been deemed more limited than those of adults because of their presumed immaturity and lessened capacity to exercise judgment and control over certain important aspects of their lives to the same degree as adults. Specifically, the Supreme Court has articulated three factors that warrant distinguishing between the constitutional rights of minors and those of adults: (1) the peculiar vulnerability of children; (2) their inability to make critical decisions in an informed, mature manner; and (3) the importance of the parental role in childrearing (*Bellotti v. Baird;* 1979).

In fact, the Supreme Court has long recognized that the right of parents to assert authority over their minor children is encompassed within the *parents'* liberty interests protected by the Fourteenth Amendment (*Pierce v. Society of Sisters*, 1925). The Court's recognition of parents' interests in exercising control over many aspects of their children's lives is consistent with society's view generally that parental consent and involvement in their children's decision making is critical to minors' well-being. State laws requiring parental consent for certain kinds of medical treatment or for a minor to marry, for example, are designed to foster and support parental authority.

At the same time, the Court has also recognized that "if parental control falters, the State must play its part as parens patriae." (*Schall v. Martin*, 1984). Thus, the Court has also repeatedly acknowledged the State's heightened interest in the protection of children (*Prince v. Massachusetts*, 1944; *Bellotti v. Baird*, 1979).

However, while plainly holding that the Constitution gives parents as well as the state greater authority to regulate the lives of children than would be permissible for adults alone, the Court has also recognized that minors possess rights of their own to control certain important decisions in their lives, free from interference by either their parents or the state. "Constitutional rights do not mature and come into being magically only when one attains the state-defined age of majority. Minors, as well as adults, are protected by the Constitution and possess constitutional rights" (*Planned Parenthood of Central Missouri v. Danforth*, 1976).

The Supreme Court has described "the question of the extent of state power to regulate conduct of minors not constitutionally regulable when committed by adults [as] a vexing one" (*Carey v. Population Services International*, 1977). Nevertheless, minors plainly possess constitutional rights, including the right to privacy protected by the Fourteenth Amendment and other provisions of the Bill of Rights. Having recognized more than 50 years ago that "the power of the state to control the conduct of children reaches beyond the scope of its authority over adults" in *Prince v. Massachusetts* (1944), the Court has tried to balance the competing interests of the minor and the state by allowing state restrictions of minor's privacy rights only where they serve a significant state interest that is not present in the case of an adult.

Against this backdrop, the Court has carved out a constitutional protection for minors' privacy rights that reflects their different status under the Constitution. In the area of *reproductive rights*, for example, the Court has held that states may not impose a blanket provision requiring the consent of a parent or other person in loco parentis as a condition for abortion of an unmarried minor during the first 12 weeks of pregnancy (*Planned Parenthood of Central Missouri v. Danforth*, 1976). At the same time, however, the Court has upheld the right of states to impose a parental consent requirement if it also provides the young woman with a confidential and expeditious proceeding through which she may obtain a waiver of the parental consent requirement (*Bellotti v. Baird*, 1979). Commonly referred to as a *judicial bypass procedure*, this proceeding must permit a young woman to obtain an abortion without the consent of her parents if she demonstrates that she is mature enough to consent to the procedure on her own or if the abortion is found to be in her best interests.

In addition, while the Court has upheld statutes requiring parental consent provided that the minor has the opportunity to obtain a waiver of the requirement, the Court has also overturned state efforts to circumscribe minors' reproductive rights based upon generalized assumptions about particular minors' capacities to make such decisions. In *City of Akron v. Akron Center for Reproductive Health* (1983), the Court invalidated a city ordinance requiring the consent of one parent or a court order before the performance of an abortion on any woman under the age of 15. Finding that constitutional protections were not limited only to women aged 16 and 17, the Court held that the State "may not make a blanket determination that *all* minors under the age of fifteen are too immature to make this decision or that an abortion may never be in the minor's best interests without parental approval." Likewise, the Court has held that a state may not impose a blanket prohibition on the distribution of contraceptives to minors (*Carey v. Population Services International*, 1977).

Laws governing the extent to which the right to privacy protects minors from compelled or unwanted disclosures of their confidential communications and information have also been adapted to reflect minors' generally more limited rights to control their lives to the same degree as adults. In the context of the rights of minors and adults to access mental health services and to control release of their mental health records, laws usually afford the minor more limited rights to seek and obtain treatment for themselves without parental knowledge or consent.

The precise contours of minors' right to access mental health services themselves are found in the myriad of state laws nationwide that regulate minors' rights in this area. Many states recognize children's right to voluntarily seek mental health treatment absent parental consent in a manner that grants minors greater control over the initiation of mental health treatment than is available in the area of medical or physical health. These laws regulate whether minors may consent to mental health treatment on their own, whether the mental health provider is obligated to notify the parent that the minor has sought and is receiving treatment, and whether the information obtained from the minor during the course of the therapeutic relationship must be kept confidential by the therapist or whether it may be shared with the parent. Where the minor's parents are divorced, state law also guides the therapist in determining whether one or both parents are entitled to information regarding the minor's mental health treatment.

Therapists treating minors must familiarize themselves with the particular mental health laws in their state, as well as state laws regarding the legal consequences of various custody arrangements following divorce, before proceeding to provide mental health services to a minor without parental consent, or before releasing information to a parent regarding the minor's course of treatment without the minor's consent. The sampling of the mental health laws of 13 states in Table 6.1 reveals a range of statutory responses to the issue of minors' rights to both initiate mental health treatment on their own and maintain the confidentiality of their treatment, whether inpatient or outpatient. Table 6.1 shows how various states regulate parental consent to the inpatient and outpatient mental health treatment of minors.

SUMMARY AND RECOMMENDATIONS

This partial survey of state laws regulating a minor's right to consent to mental health treatment illustrates the states' recognition of the need to balance the juvenile's right to privacy in treatment with the sovereignty of parental authority. It also shows how the exact scope of the minor's ability to access services varies from state to state, for both inpatient and outpatient treatment.

States obviously vary in their view of the age at which juveniles may consent to mental health treatment, with some granting children as young as 12 the authority to consent to outpatient mental health counseling. Where access to outpatient treatment without parental consent is granted, the access is often limited to a small number of sessions before the therapist is required to inform the parent of the minor's attendance. Most statutes permitting outpatient treatment require the practitioner to seek parental or guardian consent after 6 sessions or 30 calendar days unless he or she believes that obtaining consent would not be in the best interest of the minor's well-being or would greatly inhibit or interfere with treatment. The practitioner's determination of what would be in the best interests of his or her minor client carries a great deal of weight in the balancing test between minor and parent rights. As reflected in a number of statutes, practitioners may

Table 6.1 Sample State Statutes on Minors' Rights to Treatment

State	Inpatient	Outpatient	Other
Arizona Revised Statutes Annotated §36-518 (1997)	A minor may be admitted to a mental health agency by the written application of the parent, guardian or custodian of the minor after the following has occurred: (1) a psychiatric investigation that carefully probes the child's social, psychological, and developmental background; (2) an interview with the child by the medical director of the mental health agency; (3) explanation to the child's parent or guardian regarding the program or evaluation or treatment; (4) exploration of alternatives to inpatient treatment; and (5) determination that the child needs an inpatient evaluation that cannot be accomplished in a less restrictive setting.		
California Welfare & Institutions Code §5585.53 (1997) Family Code §6924 §6929 (1994)	Every effort shall be made to obtain the consent of the minor's parent or legal guardian prior to treatment and placement of the minor. Inability to obtain the consent of the minor's parent or legal guardian shall not preclude the involuntary treatment of a minor who is determined to be gravely disabled or a danger to himself or herself or others.	A minor who is 12 years of age or older may consent to mental health treatment or counseling on an outpatient basis, if both the following conditions are satisfied: (1) the minor is mature enough to participate intelligently in outpatient services; (2) the minor would present a danger to self or others without mental health treat-	A minor who is 12 years of age or older may consent to medical care and counseling relating to the diagnosis and treatment of a drug or alcohol related problem. The treatment plan shall include involvement of the minor's parent or guardian, as determined by the service provider. Replacement narcotic abuse treat-

ment may not be provided without parental or guardian consent. It is the intent of the Legislature that the state shall respect the right of a parent or guardian to seek medical care for a drug or alcohol problem of a minor child when the child does not consent to the medical care or counseling and nothing is construed to eliminate this right.

ment or is the alleged victim of incest or child abuse. A professional person offering residential shelter services shall make his or her best efforts to notify the parent or guardian of the provision of services. The mental health treatment or counseling of a minor shall include involvement of the minor's parent or guardian unless in the opinion of the provider such involvement would be inappropriate. The minor's parents or guardian are not liable for payment for services unless services are rendered with the participation of the parent or guardian.

Treatment may be provided without consent if: (1) requiring consent would cause the minor to reject treatment; (2) the provision of such treatment is clinically indicated; (3) the failure to provide such treatment would be seriously detrimental to the minor's well-being; (4) the minor has knowingly and voluntarily sought such treatment; and (5) in the opinion of the provider, the minor is mature enough to participate in treatment. Minor is required to provide written

Connecticut General Statutes Annotated §17a-682 §19a-14c (1997)

A parent or legal guardian of a minor may make an application for voluntary admission directly to a treatment facility operated by the Department of Mental Health and Addictive Services. Requests for discharge from the treatment facility may be made by the parent or legal guardian if he or she was the original applicant.

(Continued)

Table 6.1 *(Continued)*

State	Inpatient	Outpatient	Other
Connecticut *(Continued)*		statement. After the sixth session of outpatient treatment, provider shall notify minor that parental consent is required to continue treatment, unless such a requirement would be detrimental to the minor's well-being. In such cases, the provider may continue treatment and review this determination every sixth session thereafter. No provider may notify a parent or guardian nor disclose any information regarding treatment without consent of the minor.	
Florida Statute §394.4625 §394.4784	A facility may receive for observation, diagnosis, or treatment any individual age 17 or under for whom an application is made by his or her parent or guardian pursuant to §394.467. A facility may also receive for evaluation, diagnosis, or treatment any individual age 17 or under who makes express and informed consent only after a hearing to verify the voluntariness of the consent.	When any minor 13 years of age or older experiences an emotional crises to such a degree that he or she perceives the need for professional assistance, he or she shall have the right to request, consent to, and receive mental health diagnostic and evaluative services. Such services shall not exceed two visits during any 1-week period in response to a crisis situation before parental consent is required for further services.	

(Continued)

Idaho Code §66-318
(1997)

The director of any mental health facility may admit as a voluntary patient: (1) any person 18 years of age or older; (2) any individual 14 to 18 years of age with notification of parent or guardian; (3) emancipated minors; (4) any individual under 14 years of age upon application of the individual's parent or guardian. Parents or guardians may apply for the release of a minor and the facility will release the minor within 3 days.

Illinois Compiled Statutes
Annotated 405 ILCS 5/3-503
405 ILCS 5/3-501 (1997)

Any minor may be admitted to a mental health facility for inpatient treatment upon application to the facility director. The application may be executed by a parent or guardian, or by a person in loco parentis.

Any minor 12 years of age or older may request and receive counseling services or psychotherapy on an outpatient basis. The consent of his or her parent or guardian shall not be necessary to authorize outpatient counseling. The minor's parent or guardian shall not be informed of such counseling without the consent of the minor unless the facility director believes such disclosure is necessary. If the director intends to disclose the fact of counseling, the minor shall be so informed. However, until the consent of the minor's parent or guardian is obtained, outpatient counseling to a minor under the age of 17 years shall be limited to not more than 5 sessions.

Table 6.1 *(Continued)*

State	Inpatient	Outpatient	Other
Michigan Statutes Annotated §14.800(498j) (1997)	The parent or guardian of a minor admitted to a hospital shall be requested to give written consent to the treatment of the minor and for the release of information from agencies involved in treatment prior to hospitalization. If consent cannot be obtained, the director may proceed as warranted by the situation and the best interests of the minor.		
New Jersey Statutes Annotated 4:74-7A (1997)	A minor shall be institutionalized only upon court order in accordance with prescribed procedures, except that any minor 14 years of age or over may request admission to an institution for psychiatric treatment provided the court enters an order approving the admission. If an order approving a voluntary admission is entered, the minor may discharge himself or herself in the same manner as a voluntarily admitted adult.		
New York Consolidated Laws Art. 9 §9.13 Art. 33 §33.21 Art. 21 §21.11 (1983)	If the person is under 16 years of age, the person may be received as a voluntary patient only on the application of the parent or legal guardian or if the	In providing outpatient mental health services to a minor, the consent of parents or guardians shall be required in nonemergency situations,	If in the judgment of a physician parental or guardian involvement and consent would have detrimental effect on the course of treatment of a

114

person is over 16 and under 18 years of age, the director may admit such person as a voluntary patient on his or her own application or on the application of the person's parent or legal guardian. Voluntarily admitted patients may release themselves unless there are reasonable grounds for belief that involuntary care is needed, in which case, the director may retain the patient for a period not to exceed 72 hours from receipt of such notice.

except as provided below: (a) no consent required if the mental health practitioner determines that the minor is (i) knowingly and voluntarily seeking services that are (ii) clinically indicated and necessary to the minor's well-being and either: (i) requiring consent would have a detrimental effect on the course of treatment, or (ii) a parent or guardian refuses to consent and treatment is necessary and in the best interests of the minor. A practitioner may provide an initial interview without parental or guardian consent to determine whether the above criteria exist.

minor who is voluntarily seeking treatment for alcohol abuse, alcoholism, substance abuse or substance dependence, or if a parent or guardian refuses to consent to such treatment and the physician believes that such treatment is necessary for the best interests of the child, such treatment may be provided to the minor by a licensed physician on an inpatient or outpatient basis without the consent or involvement of the parent or guardian. Minor must sign form indicating that treatment is voluntarily sought.

Ohio Revised Code Annotated §5122.02 §5122.04 (1997)

An application for voluntary admission to a mental health facility may be made by a parent or guardian on behalf of a minor.

Upon the request of a minor 14 years of age or older, a mental health professional may provide outpatient mental health services, excluding the use of medication, without the consent or knowledge of the minor's parent or guardian. The parent or guardian shall not be informed of the services without the minor's consent unless the mental health professional treating the minor determines that

(Continued)

Table 6.1 (*Continued*)

State	Inpatient	Outpatient	Other
Ohio (*Continued*)		there is a compelling need for disclosure based on a substantial probability of harm to the minor or to other persons, and if the minor is informed of the mental health professional's intent to inform the parent or guardian. Services provided shall be limited to not more than 6 sessions or 30 days, whichever occurs sooner. At this time, the mental health professional shall terminate services or with consent of minor, notify the parent or guardian to obtain consent for further outpatient treatment.	
Pennsylvania Statutes Title 50 §§7201-7206 (1997)	Any person 14 years of age or over who believes that he or she is in need of treatment and substantially understands the nature of voluntary treatment may submit himself or herself to examination and treatment. A parent or guardian to a child less than 14 years old may subject such child to examination and treatment, and in so doing shall be deemed to be acting for the child. Upon application for treat-		

ment by a minor 14 years or over but less than 18 years, the director of the facility shall promptly notify the minor's parents or guardian and inform them of the right to be heard upon the filing of an objection. If a minor under the age of 14 years old wishes to withdraw from treatment, his or her release must be effected by a parent or guardian.

South Dakota Codified Laws §27A-15-5 (1998)

A minor may be immediately admitted to an inpatient psychiatric facility by the minor's parent if: (1) the minor is seriously emotionally disturbed; (2) minor displays either seriously impaired contact with reality or manifests long-term behavioral problems or suffers from severe anxiety, depression, eating or sleeping disturbances, extreme sadness, or maladaptive dependence on parents; (3) minor needs and is likely to benefit from inpatient treatment; (4) less restrictive means have failed and are unlikely to meet the minor's treatment needs; and (5) parents have exercised informed consent to inpatient treatment of the minor.

(Continued)

Table 6.1 (Continued)

State	Inpatient	Outpatient	Other
Wisconsin Statutes Annotated §51.13 §51.14 §51.47 (1997)	Admission of a minor under 14 years of age to an approved inpatient mental health treatment facility shall be executed by a parent who has legal custody of the minor or the minor's guardian. Minor's refusal to consent shall be noted on the face of the application. If a minor 14 years of age or older wishes to be voluntarily admitted to an approved inpatient treatment facility but a parent or guardian refuses to execute the application for admission or cannot be found or if there is no parent with legal custody, the minor or someone acting on the minor's behalf may petition the court to exercise jurisdiction. If the court determines that the parent or guardian is unreasonably withholding consent or cannot be found, it shall approve the admission pending hearing on the petition.	Either a minor 14 years of age or older or his or her parent or guardian may petition the mental health review officer in the county in which the parent or guardian has residence for a review of a refusal of either the minor or his or her parent or guardian to provide informed consent for outpatient mental health treatment. The review officer or court may issue a written order stating that informed consent is not required if all of the following are found: (1) informed consent is unreasonably withheld; (2) the minor is in need of treatment; (3) the particular treatment sought is appropriate for the minor and is the least restrictive treatment available; and (4) the treatment is in the best interests of the minor.	Except as provided elsewhere, any approved physician or health care facility may render preventive, diagnostic, assessment, evaluation or treatment services for the abuse of alcohol or other drugs to a minor 12 years of age or over without obtaining the consent of or notifying the minor's parent or guardian. Consent is required in the following circumstances: before any surgical procedure unless the procedure is essential to preserve the life or health of a minor; before administering any controlled substance to the minor except to detoxify; before admitting the minor to inpatient treatment unless the admission is to detoxify for ingestion of alcohol or other drugs; if the period of detoxification extends beyond 72 hours after the minor's admission as a patient, only if the facility then offers inpatient therapy or treatment which is appropriate for the minor's needs. The minor has the right to be discharged within 48 hours of his or her request.

provide treatment without consent if requiring consent would compel the minor to reject services, or if, in the opinion of the practitioner, the minor is mature enough to participate in treatment.

With regard to inpatient treatment, states also employ a variety of approaches. Some states permit parents to "voluntarily" admit minors of any age, until they are 18; some allow children above a certain age, such as 14 or 16, to admit and discharge themselves as if they were adults.

In addition, as with consent, the degree to which states mandate the disclosure of a minor's counseling and other mental health records to a parent reflects a balancing of the competing interests at stake: the parent's traditional authority over the minor as otherwise permitted by law, the rights of the minor to protect and maintain the confidentiality of his or her treatment, and the ability and desire of mental health professionals to safeguard patients' records even when their patients are minors. Often, the ability to control access to the information follows the ability to provide consent. To the extent that minors of any age can give effective consent to treatment, even for a limited time period, these minors can generally limit disclosure of their records. As reflected in Table 6.1, where the minor is granted even a limited right to initiate treatment, therapists are typically precluded from releasing any information to the parent or guardian regarding treatment without the consent of the minor.

REFERENCES

Bellotti v. Baird (1979), 99 S. Ct. 3035, 443 U.S. 622.
Carey v. Population Services International (1977), 97 S. Ct. 2020, 431 U.S. 678.
City of Akron v. Akron Center for Reproductive Health (1983), 103 S. Ct. 2481, 462 U.S. 416.
Eisenstadt v. Baird (1972), 92 S. Ct. 1029, 405 U.S. 438.
Griswold v. Connecticut (1965), 85 S. Ct. 1678, 381 U.S. 479.
Loving v. Virginia (1967), 87 S. Ct. 1817, 388 U.S. 1.
Murphy v. Waterfront Commission (1964), 84 S. Ct. 1594, 378 U.S. 52.
Olmstead v. United States (1928), 48 S. Ct. 564, 277 U.S. 438.
Pierce v. Society of Sisters (1925), 45 S. Ct. 571, 268 U.S. 510.
Planned Parenthood of Central Missouri v. Danforth (1976), 96 S. Ct. 2831, 428 U.S. 52.
Prince v. Massachusetts (1944), 64 S. Ct. 784, 321 U.S. 804.
Roe v. Wade (1973), 93 S. Ct. 1409, 410 U.S. 959.
Schall v. Martin (1984), 194 S. Ct. 2403, 467 U.S. 253.
Skinner v. Oklahoma (1942), 62 S. Ct. 1110, 316 U.S. 535.
United States v. Westinghouse Electric Corp. (1980), 638 F.2d 570 (3d Cir.).
Whalen v. Roe (1977), 429 U.S. 587, 97 S. Ct. 896.

CHAPTER 7

Sexual Harassment and Stalking

WILHELMINA S. KOEDAM

CLINICIANS ARE likely to encounter individual and family cases that are referred to treatment due to allegations of sexual harassment in the workplace and in academe. These cases may be self-referred or be referred by an attorney, a family physician, an employee assistance program coordinator, or a friend. Often the victim of sexual harassment is unable to return to work or school as symptoms of depression or anxiety may permeate the victim's life and profoundly affect the significant people in the victim's life. To understand the ramifications of harassment, the therapist must be conversant with the legal definitions, the legal history, and the social history of sexual harassment; these are reviewed in the first section of this chapter. A description of sexual harassment and its characteristics follows. Victim responses and the psychological effects of harassment on the individual, the family, the community, and the victim's physical health and work performance are also discussed. Issues encountered in the therapy of victims and their families or significant others are highlighted.

Stalking or obsessional following is an area of increasing concern for those in law enforcement and for therapists in terms of its effects on individuals, families, and communities. Stalking cases are primarily highlighted in the news when celebrities and political figures are victims. Yet, the majority of stalking cases are found in domestic situations. The high incidence of domestic stalking is both staggering and frightening. To provide a knowledge base regarding this phenomenon, the legal definitions, legal history, and social history of stalking are reviewed. Descriptions and characteristics of the stalker as well as the psychological and social impact of stalking follow. Next there is a discussion of therapeutic issues in stalking cases.

An examination of the similarities and differences in treating victims of sexual harassment and stalking is presented, as the clinician must be aware of these distinctions in order to treat the victim most effectively. The clinician should also be aware of legal and law enforcement issues to better assist the victim, who will be dealing with the legal system and possibly the law enforcement community during the time that he or she is in treatment.

SEXUAL HARASSMENT

Sexual harassment is a pervasive and endemic problem in this country. Some studies report that a majority of women experience sexual harassment at some time in their lives, the statistics ranging from 35% to 90% (Giuffre & Williams, 1994; Tata, 1993). There is also an awakening recognition of sexual harassment of men by men and women (Berdahl, Magley, & Waldo, 1996). As pervasive as this problem appears now, it is probable that therapists and attorneys will continue to see an increase in these type of cases. As a result, these two disciplines should cooperate to deal with this problem in work and academic settings.

LEGAL DEFINITIONS OF SEXUAL HARASSMENT

There are two categories of harassment that are generally recognized due to the Equal Employment Opportunities Commission (EEOC) Guidelines on Sexual Harassment (1980) and the 1986 Supreme Court decision in *Meritor Savings Bank, FSB v. Vinson et al.* (106 S. Ct. 2399, 1986). The first type of sexual harassment is *quid pro quo* or *conditional* harassment, and the second type is *hostile environment harassment.* Quid pro quo harassment is often the type of harassment that becomes the focus of workplace complaints and litigated harassment cases.

Quid Pro Quo Harassment

Quid pro quo or conditional harassment is characterized by requiring an individual to submit to sexual requests as a condition of continued employment or in return for some promised benefit (i.e., future employment benefits, promotions, or satisfactory performance ratings) or the removal of a threat to do harm (Charney & Russell, 1994; Thacker, 1996; Thacker & Gohmann, 1996). Quid pro quo harassment is coercive in that the benefits offered by the harasser are amplified by the consequences of nonsubmission to his or her sexual advances. This harassment requires a difference in power between the harasser and the victim (Bargh & Raymond, 1995; Berdahl et al., 1996; Charnay & Russell, 1994). Other key elements are that the victim must perceive the harasser's behavior as *unwelcome* (Fitzgerald, Swan, & Fischer, 1995; Thacker, 1996; Weiner, 1995), and there must be a chronic, ongoing pattern of these behaviors as opposed to an isolated incident (Fitzgerald et al., 1995; Thacker, 1996).

Hostile Environment Harassment

Hostile environment harassment is defined in terms of the perceptions of the individual claiming the harassment. For example, sexual jokes, sexual comments, asking for dates, or derogatory comments based on the gender of the individual may or may not be construed as hostile depending on the perspective of the recipient of these behaviors. In a work setting, hostile environment harassment is defined as behavior that is pervasive and severe enough to alter the individual's work environment because it creates an abusive working atmosphere which affects the victim's work and personal life (Gutek & O'Connor, 1995; Thacker, 1996; Weiner, 1995).

Gender-Based Harassment

Gender-based harassment is distinguished in the courts from sexual harassment as harassment based on sex or gender in which the offending conduct is directed solely toward persons of one gender, but the conduct is not sexual in nature (Hadley & Chuzi, 1995). Hadley and Chuzi state that harassment based on the sex of the victim is not limited to unwelcome verbal conduct or physical contact; it also encompasses other discriminatory behaviors, such as berating an individual for errors, criticizing work performance, excessively strict accounting of work absenteeism and lateness, either taking away duties or overburdening an individual, forbidding conversation with coworkers, refusal to instruct or cooperate in a team setting, or suggesting that an individual quit his or her job. If any of the aforementioned behaviors are directed at individuals because of their sex by employers, supervisors, or coworkers, this behavior qualifies as gender-based sexual harassment.

LEGAL HISTORY OF SEXUAL HARASSMENT

There have been laws against sexual harassment in the United States since the 1960s. This prohibition was first legislated by Title VII of the Civil Rights Act of 1964, which reads:

> It shall be an unlawful employment practice for an employer—(1) to fail to refuse to hire or to discharge any individual or otherwise to discriminate against any individual with respect to his compensation, terms, conditions, or privileges of employment, because of such individual's race, color, religion, sex, or national origin; or (2) to limit, segregate, or classify his employees or applicants for employment in any way which would deprive or tend to deprive any individual of employment opportunities or otherwise adversely affect his status as an employee, because of such individual's race, color, religion, sex, or national origin. (42 U.S.C., Section 703)

A similar act was enacted regarding sexual harassment in educational settings through Title IX of the Education Amendments of 1972. These issues were even more clearly defined by the guidelines presented by the EEOC (1980). These guidelines serve as the standard by which sexual harassment is defined in work, educational, political, and military settings. The EEOC regulation states:

> Unwelcome sexual advances, requests for sexual favors, and other verbal or physical conduct of a sexual nature constitute sexual harassment when (1) submission to such conduct is made either explicitly or implicitly a term or condition of an individual's employment, (2) submission to or rejection of such conduct by an individual is used as the basis for employment decisions affecting such individual, or (3) such conduct has the purpose or effect of unreasonably interfering with the individual's work performance or creating an intimidating, hostile, or offensive working environment. (29 CFR Sec. 1604.11)

The legal standard set forth by the U.S. Supreme Court in *Meritor Savings Bank, FSB v. Vinson et al.* (1986, p. 67) further refined the standard by defining harassment as "sufficiently severe and pervasive to alter the conditions of employment and create an abusive working environment" (Charney & Russell, 1994; Thacker, 1996; Wiener, 1995; Woody & Perry, 1993).

Legal controversy continues in the struggle to define when behavior is construed as *unwelcome* in these cases because the perception of the behavior as unwelcome is determined by the victim's testimony and credibility. Social science and the legal literature have yet to define clearly the standard of welcomeness in these cases (Burns, 1995; Wiener, 1995). Fitzgerald et al. (1995) posit a position that the legal community mistakenly pigeonholes victims into two roles: the *silent tolerator*, whose failure to speak out is seen as *welcoming* the harassment, and the *instigator in kind*, who goes along with the situation and is seen as consenting to the harassment. Another legal controversy stems from the term *reasonable person*. The EEOC guidelines (1980) attempt to define harassment by a standard that says that the *unwelcome* sexual conduct must *unreasonably* interfere and create a hostile or abusive work environment. Gutek and O'Connor (1995) cite various cases (e.g., *Rabidue v. Osceola Refining Co.*, 1986/1987; *Radtke v. Everett*, 1993), in which the standard to ascertain harassment is met by the judgment of a *reasonable person*. In *Ellison v. Brady* (1991) the Ninth District Court of Appeals held that

> a female plaintiff states a prima facie case of hostile environment sexual harassment when she alleges conduct which a *reasonable woman* would consider sufficiently severe or pervasive to alter the conditions of employment and create an abusive working environment. (p. 879)

There are a number of studies that explore gender differences in the perception of sexual harassment which postulate that there are significant differences between men and women as to which types of behaviors they perceive as constituting sexual harassment (Fitzgerald & Omerand, 1991; Gutek & O'Connor, 1995; Jaschik-Herman and Fisk, 1995; Sheffey & Tindale, 1992; Tata, 1993). Not only at issue is how the courts or the social sciences operationalize a definition of *reasonable*, but also the fact that the courts continue to vacillate between the *reasonable woman* and *reasonable person* standards, as evidenced 2 years after the landmark *Ellison v. Brady* (1991) in the *Harris v. Forklift Systems* (1993) case. In *Harris*, the issue was whether the individual suffered psychological trauma as a result of hostile environment sexual harassment. The Supreme Court returned to the term *reasonable person* in determining that the behavior of the harasser at Forklift Systems was not severe enough for a *reasonable person* to perceive that a hostile or abusive environment was created, and therefore it was deemed that the plaintiff did not suffer sexual discrimination under Title VII (Gowan & Zimmermann, 1996). Weiner (1995, p. 170) suggests adopting a new nongender legal perspective in using "the *reasonable victim approach* to the severity and pervasiveness test." This would adopt the EEOC recommendation that courts "consider the victim's perspective and not stereotyped notions of acceptable behavior" (EEOC, 1980, p. 388).

The complexity and subjectiveness of perception and credibility in these cases make them difficult ones for attorneys and mental health care professionals. As the courts continue to redefine the concepts and the media continue to highlight the high rate of these behaviors in individuals' work and academic life experiences, clinicians should continue to stay abreast of legal decisions pertaining to sexual harassment. The continuous legal reinterpretation of standards and terminology challenges the victim and the treating clinician in psychologically resolving the emotional trauma resulting from the sexual harassment. In addition, these reinterpretations may also affect the victim's potential to remedy the offense in a court of law and possibly gain financial remuneration for the economic, psychological, and physical effects of suffering this trauma.

SOCIAL HISTORY OF SEXUAL HARASSMENT

Brief histories of sexual harassment in a number of social realms follow.

Academia

The best known case of sexual harassment in the realm of academia was highlighted in October 1991 in the testimony of law professor Anita Hill, who alleged that the then nominee for the U.S. Supreme Court, Clarence Thomas, had created a hostile environment with inappropriate sexual overtones 10 years previously when she worked under his supervision at the EEOC. During the hearings she asserted that she had remained silent as she was fearful that speaking out would jeoperdize her career and derail her professional success in the future. The issues surrounding sexual harassment came to the national forefront during the 1991 Senate hearings investigating her charges against Thomas (Charney & Russell, 1994; Fitzgerald, Swan, & Fischer, 1995; Jaschik-Herman & Fisk, 1995). Despite the charges, Clarence Thomas was confirmed as a justice of the Supreme Court.

Charney and Russell (1994, p. 10) cite a July 1991 *Time* magazine interview of Dr. Frances Conley, a neurosurgeon who resigned from Stanford University due to her belief that she suffered 25 years of "gender insensitivity." They report that Dr. Conley expressed similar reasons to those given by Anita Hill for not addressing the issue of sexual harassment at the time the trauma was occurring. It is interesting to note that Dr. Conley's allegations were in a major news journal, *Time*, 3 months prior to Anita Hill's allegations, yet the American public only really took notice when a political person, Supreme Court justice nominee Clarence Thomas, was under scrutiny, thus highlighting the media's and the public's tendency to be more responsive to celebrities, famous people, and politicians than to the average citizen.

Numerous studies explore the presence of sexual harassment in academic settings; such behaviors may affect both students and colleagues in this environment in terms of grades; projects; recommendations for grants, scholarships, or graduate programs; and passing or failing classes, all of which also fall under the rubric of workplace harassment (Barak, Fisher, & Houston, 1992; Fitzgerald et al., 1988; Komaromy, Bindman, Haber, & Sande, 1993; McCormick, 1985; Rubin & Borgers, 1990).

Politics

One of the most notorious sexual harassment cases in the political arena was that of U.S. Senator Bob Packwood of Oregon, who was investigated by the Senate

Ethics Committee in 1995 for sexually harassing a number of his subordinates. Packwood was forced to resign his position as a U.S. senator rather than face censure by the Senate Ethics Committee.

A more shocking development was the allegation by Paula Corbin Jones, a former Arkansas state employee, of sexual harassment by the sitting president of the United States, Bill Clinton. Jones alleged that Clinton sexually harassed her and misused his political power while he was governor of Arkansas, at a governors' conference in Little Rock in 1991. On January 13, 1997, the U.S. Supreme Court heard arguments in the case of *William Jefferson Clinton v. Paula Corbin Jones* (*Economist*, 1997). Jones' case was dismissed in March 1998 for insufficient evidence, and was settled out of court later that year.

The president was under investigation during much of 1998 for allegations of sexual harassment against a former unpaid White House intern, a 21-year-old college graduate named Monica Lewinsky, who alleged she began an 18-month affair with the president in 1995. This information came to light during questioning of Lewinsky by the attorneys representing Paula Jones in her case against President Clinton. Four additional women accused President Clinton of sexual harassment or of having extramarital affairs. There were additional allegations that President Clinton and Vernon Jordan, a Washington lawyer and friend of the president's, urged Lewinsky to lie about the sexual harassment, which would constitute obstruction of justice. These allegations led to the president's impeachment in the House of Representatives and trial in the Senate.

The purported attempt to silence Lewinsky is similar to what happens in many trauma cases, such as when incest is committed—the perpetrator often attempts to coerce the victim into lying or not disclosing the incident in order to protect him- or herself.

From a sociological and historical perspective, it is interesting to note that President John F. Kennedy allegedly engaged in similar sexual behavior during his tenure in the White House in the early 1960s, yet that behavior was tacitly accepted by the American public and press. Clinton ultimately apologized to the American people for his sexual transgressions.

Military Services

The advent of women in the military and in military academies was highlighted by the emergence of sexual harassment and rape charges, as evidenced by the 1992 Tailhook incident in the Navy (Culbertson, Rosenfeld, Booth-Kewley, & Magnusson, 1992) and by the 1997 resignation of a female cadet at Virginia Military Institute due to harassment. Charges in the news media of sexual harassment in the military, such as the discovery of sexual abuse cases at the U.S. Army Ordinance Center in Aberdeen, Maryland, caused the Army to take a survey that showed a consistent level of harassment in this branch of the military (Walters, 1997).

Workplace

The most common setting associated with sexual harassment is the workplace. The literature indicates that 35% to 90% of women report experiencing some form of sexual harassment on the job. The literature is replete with many studies about sexual harassment in the workplace. Issues regarding ethnicity, gender, and previous experience are discussed in an article by Gowan and Zimmermann (1996). Workplace gender-related jokes (Hemmasi, Graf, & Russ, 1994), assumptions that specific jobs are assigned to a specific sex, and the vulnerability of individuals working in temporary positions (Rogers & Henson, 1997) are a sampling of issues presented in these studies. Work correlates such as intergender contact, females in traditionally male jobs, and blue-collar versus white-collar settings (Ragins & Scandura, 1995) are a few additional areas of study.

The following sections focus on definitions of the behaviors and characteristics associated with sexual harassment, as well as the psychological implications of the trauma of sexual harassment; victim response styles; effects on the individual victims, their families, and the community; and the clinical treatment of victims.

CATEGORIES OF SEXUAL HARASSMENT

Tata (1993) cites a 1980 study by Till which categorizes sexual harassment in a continuum of five levels of severity:

> The five categories are (a) *gender harassment,* or generalized sexist remarks and behavior; (b) *seductive behavior,* or offensive but sanction-free sexual advances; (c) *sexual bribery,* or solicitation of sexual activity by promise of rewards; (d) *sexual coercion,* or solicitation of sexual activity by threat of punishment; and (e) *sexual assault,* or gross sexual imposition. (Tata, 1993, pp. 200–201)

These categories encompass quid pro quo, hostile environment, and gender-based harassment. Fitzgerald et al.'s (1988) development of the Sexual Experiences Questionnaire was based on Till's categories of sexual harassment. Studies suggest that gender harassment and seductive behaviors may be less likely to be perceived as sexual harassment than sexual bribery or sexual coercion (Tata, 1993). Tata's study indicated that the individual's perception of sexual harassment are influenced by the category of harassment, based on Till's continuum of severity; that is, the individuals perceived a clearer and more consistent definition of what behavior was sexually harassing as one continues further along the severity continuum of categories. The gender of the victim was also significant, as males were less likely to define a behavior as sexually harassing than female subjects were. The greater the hierarchal difference between the individual and the harasser, the greater the assignation of harassment.

ANTECEDENTS OF SEXUAL HARASSMENT BEHAVIORS

Theories of the antecedents of sexual harassment behaviors include the sex-role spillover model developed by Gutek and Morasch (1982), based on role model theories which state that sex-role spillover involves the inappropriate extension of gender roles to the workplace. This may refer to stereotypically female gender-role behavior, including passivity, nurturance, and dependency, and to viewing women as sexual objects who are expected to accept sexual overtures and comments. They also posit that female workers are perceived as women first and colleagues second, and that women may be more comfortable in "typical" female roles in and out of work settings. They discuss three different job types: (a) *traditionally female jobs* such as secretary or nurse, (b) *nontraditional jobs* such as mechanic or police officer, and (c) *integrated jobs* such as realtor or banker, which are jobs that are held by both men and women, and there are therefore no longer societal expectations that the job is generally held by either gender. According to the results of their study, they propose that sexual harassment is least likely to occur in integrated jobs. Sheffey and Tindale (1992) studied how job context affects behaviors deemed appropriate between men and women. They found that a job which is thought to fall within the range of traditionally female occupations influences perceptions of work roles and gender behaviors: For example, in female occupations, sex and work roles were less differentiated and sexual behaviors were assessed as more acceptable. They found that integrated jobs result in fewer sexual harassment allegations. Sheffy and Tindale's results are basically consistent with sex-role spillover theory, although their study indicates that the job type in terms of status differences generates a different set of behaviors that are considered acceptable sexual behavior, in that the larger the status difference the more sexual behavior is tolerated.

A study conducted by Ragins and Scandura (1995) found only limited support for the overall theory; instead they found that women in traditionally male blue-collar occupations reported significantly more sexual harassment than women in traditionally male white-collar occupations. In traditionally female occupations, sex and work roles were less differentiated and sexual behaviors were assessed as more acceptable. Women in nontraditional jobs reported more sexual harassment, which may be a result of difficulty in defining appropriate behavior; therefore, ambiguous behaviors are more likely to be interpreted as sexually harassing. They found that reports of sexual harassment in integrated jobs were relatively low.

Another hypothesis is that some men resent the "intrusion" of women into domains they see as theirs and purposely seek to make them uncomfortable as a way of driving them out of the workplace. They may be even more uncomfortable if a woman's job places her in a position of authority over them and they resent having to take orders from a female.

Work-setting influences are noted in the research literature. In a study focusing on restaurant workers, Guiffre and Williams (1994) found that race and ethnic context may influence the perception of harassment, as may the sexual orientation of the harasser. Women in blue-collar jobs reported more harassment than women in white-collar jobs but were less likely to display assertive responses to this harassment as they may believe they have to be tough and it goes with the territory; they may experience fears of physical retaliation (Ragins & Scandura, 1995); or they simply may not feel as powerful as women in white-collar jobs.

Rogers and Henson (1997) reported that many temporary clerical workers not only believe they have to engage in sex role expectations of deference in terms of subservient behavior, but they also perceive themselves as especially vulnerable because they are temporary workers who are dependent on an agency that is hired by employers. Temporary clerical workers report that they feel the agency's loyalty may lie with the employers who pay the fees to the agency; therefore, they feel they may be blackballed and jeopardize their future employment possibilities if they report sexual harassment.

The contact hypothesis states that "harassment is not a function of gender role expectations; harassment is viewed as a result of contact with individuals of the opposite gender" (Ragins & Scandura, 1995, p. 431). This theory holds that the more contact that exists between members of different sexes, the more likely sexual harassment will occur simply due to opportunity. Ragins and Scandura attempted to study both sex-role spillover and the contact hypothesis and found no support for the contact hypothesis.

Power as an antecedent of harassment is the focus of an article by Bargh and Raymond. They propose that there is an "automatic mental link between power and sex association which is why there is an 'unconscious misuse of power' in those men who are likely to sexually exploit or rape" (Bargh & Raymond, 1995, p. 87). Perceived power and hierarchical status on the part of harasser and victim are the focus of a number of studies in this field and are discussed in greater detail under "Factors Influencing Individual Responses to Sexual Harassment" (Berdahl et al., 1996; Giuffre & Williams, 1994; Kidder, Lafleur, & Wells, 1995).

SPECIFIC BEHAVIORS AS SEXUAL HARASSMENT

The Sexual Experiences Questionnaire designed by Fitzgerald et al. (1988) attempts to measure and operationalize a definition of behaviors as sexual harassment within the five categories proposed by Till. Sexual harassment can include behaviors on a continuum, such as sexual remarks, unrelenting requests for dates, whistles, staring, sexual propositions not linked to employment, unwanted non-sexual touching, sexual propositions linked to job status, unwanted sexual touching, and sexual assault (Charnay & Russell, 1994). Frazier, Cochran, and Olson (1995) included sexual jokes, stereotype jokes, suggestive looks, unwanted sexual letters and calls, unwanted cornering, and pressure for sex or dates in their study of lay definitions of sexual harassment.

FACTORS INFLUENCING INDIVIDUAL RESPONSES TO SEXUAL HARASSMENT

Thacker (1996) discusses the importance of the nature of the working relationship between the harasser and the victim, such as a supervisor and subordinate or coworker dyad. The issue of hierarchical placement of the harasser is often perceived as critical in the response of the victim; the more powerful the harasser is perceived to be in the organizational structure of the workplace, the less control and power the victim believes he or she has in terms of stopping the harassment (Frazier et al., 1995; Tata, 1993; Thacker, 1996; Thacker & Gohmann, 1996).

Studies of gender differences, as previously discussed, find that men are less likely to define gender harassment or seductive behavior as offensive, although these gender differences disappear when men perceive that sexual bribery, sexual coercion, or sexual assault has happened to them or when they observe it happening to another (Tata, 1993).

There is a noticeable dearth in the literature of any studies that discuss seductive behavior or dress on the part of the victim as contributing to the phenomenon. It is interesting to note that in the *Miami Herald* (April 19, 1998, p. 2a), Helen Gurley Brown and other feminists decried the cases brought by women against President

Clinton as "setting the cause of women back by 8,000 years." These pioneers in equality stated that they had fought hard for all equality, including sexual equality, and were appalled at women portraying themselves as "helpless pitiful victims."

Duration of harassment is significant; it has been found that the more chronic the harassment the victim suffers, the more likely that she or he will report dissatisfaction with work and exhibit a significant physical and emotional deterioration (Thacker & Gohmann, 1996). Thacker (1996) states that victims may become more passive as the harassment continues if initial attempts at avoidance or going along fail. Passive responses may also occur if the victim attempts to complain but the complaints are ignored by the appropriate authority. The victim may believe she or he cannot restore lost control and become increasingly passive.

The gender of the victim was also found to be significant in Thacker's (1996) study, in that males appeared to find social-sexual behavior appropriate in the workplace and were therefore less likely to file complaints or display refusal behaviors. Berdahl et al. (1996) studied men and sexual harassment. They found that unwanted sexual attention from both men and women was mentioned more than any other form of harassment. The second most frequent category was gender harassment in the form of negative stereotyping of men and negative feedback for men who deviated from traditional male roles. Men also reported sexual harassment if they believed that women were being favored for promotions and raises. The report also discusses issues regarding women abusing their power and privilege over men. In this study, men stated that although they may try to avoid the harasser, they also reported a higher likelihood of taking action in the form of lodging a complaint or confronting the harasser.

RESPONSES TO SEXUAL HARASSMENT

Victims' responses to sexual harassment range from passive to assertive—the victim may submit to harassment, ignore it, avoid or confront the harasser, change jobs or classes, report the harassment within the organization, or seek legal recourse. Charney (1994, p. 13) reports that assertive responses to harassment tend to be very low.

Fitzgerald et al. (1995) propose a system of coding responses based on a survey of actual sexual harassment victims. The responses were divided into ten strategies, which are classified as internally focused or externally focused. *Internally focused strategies,* which concentrate more on means to manage cognition and emotions related to the harassment, include *endurance, denial, detachment, reattribution,* and *illusory control. Externally focused strategies,* which focus on problem solving, include *avoidance, appeasement, assertion, seeking institutional or organizational relief,* and *seeking social support* (Fitzgerald et al., 1995, p. 119). The most commonly implemented types of internally focused strategies are to ignore the harassment and do nothing (endurance) or pretend its not occurring (denial). These researchers also report that almost half of the respondents attempted avoidance as an externally focused strategy. The more severe the harassment, the more likely that an assertive response would ensue. Fitzgerald et al.'s study focused on the question, "Why didn't she just report him?" Their research indicates that the respondents did not report because they believed that nothing would be done, or they were fearful of retaliation, of not being believed, of hurting their career, or of being shamed and humiliated. These overwhelmingly powerful fears prevented them from reporting. In addition, the tremendous emotional and economic costs of initiating a lawsuit far outweighed the perceived potential gains (Fitzgerald et al., 1995, p. 123). Rogers and Henson (1997), in their study of temporary clerical workers, reported a set of responses which includes complaining to the agency, confronting the harasser, ignoring the harasser, or leaving the agency. Again, the fears of retaliation, of disbelief, of agency loyalty to the client company rather than to the worker, and of being blackballed by the agency prevented many temporary workers from assertive responses to sexual harassment.

Thacker (1996) looked at responses to sexual harassment in light of Wicklund's (1974) reactance or learned helplessness theory, that individuals will attempt to restore lost control only if they believe they have the freedom to act as they choose. The results indicate that higher-level supervisors were more likely to engender avoidance or going along responses, and the longer the duration of the harassment, the more likely that the victim would display avoidance or going along responses.

Two more studies looked at other responses to sexual harassment. Kidder et al. (1995) discuss an *agenda shift* in which the original encounter was not sexual in nature; rather, it was a professional relationship with an employer, physician, or educator. The women in the study reported not recognizing the shift and often blamed themselves for the nature of the encounter. Williams and Cyr (1992) discuss the escalating commitment of a relationship in terms of adaptation level theory, in which people adapt to a given level of stimulation. In this paradigm the individual may not be aware of gradual increases in the intensity of sexual harassment, as it may be mild early on. Due to gradual compliance with the interactions, even though they intensify and although the victim may become uncomfortable with the harasser's behavior, the victim may behave in ways to maintain the relationship, which creates a self-perpetuating level of commitment. Once this escalating commitment trap has begun, it is very difficult for the individual to extricate herself from the relationship, especially as the harasser attributes her behavior to welcomeness or desire.

PSYCHOLOGICAL EFFECTS OF SEXUAL HARASSMENT

Psychological effects of sexual harassment encompass the individual victim, the victim's family, the individual's physical health, the individual's work performance, and the community.

Woody and Perry (1993) cite several studies that indicate that there are long-term psychological effects as sequelae of sexual harassment. These effects encompass clinical symptoms such as post-traumatic stress reactions, stress, low self-esteem, and depression, including shock, emotional numbing, lack of affect, day- and nightmares, flashbacks, and anxiety. Woody and Perry (1993 pp. 139–140) cite Pauldi and Barickman's (1991) Sexual Harassment Trauma Syndrome, which has five categories:

1. *Emotional reactions.* Anxiety, shock, denial, anger, fear, frustration, insecurity, betrayal, embarrassment, confusion, self-consciousness, shame, powerlessness, guilt, and isolation.

2. *Physical reactions.* Headaches, sleep disturbances, lethargy, gastrointestinal distress, hypervigilance, dermatological reactions, weight fluctuations, nightmares, phobias, panic reactions, genitourinary distress, respiratory problems, and substance abuse.
3. *Change in self-perception.* Negative self-concept or self-esteem, lack of competency, lack of control, isolation, hopelessness, and powerlessness.
4. *Social, interpersonal relatedness, and sexual effects.* Withdrawal, fear of new people or situations, lack of trust, lack of focus, self-preoccupation, change in social network patterns, negative attitudes and behavior in sexual relationships, potential sexual disorder associated with stress and trauma, and changes in dress or physical appearance.
5. *Career effects.* Changes in study and work habits, loss of job or promotion, unfavorable performance evaluation, drop in academic or work performance because of stress, lower grades as punishment for reporting sexual harassment or for noncompliance with sexual advances, absenteeism, withdrawal from work and school, and changes in career goals.

A number of studies reflect on the individual psychological and physical effects of sexual harassment. Fitzgerald et al. (1995, p. 124) characterize sexual harassment from a cognitive perspective as a stressful life event in which the harassment produces such a high level of stress that it exceeds the individual's internal resources to cope and endangers his or her well-being. They incorporate such factors as frequency, duration, and degree of offensiveness as well as such individual factors as previous victimization, perceived threat, and economic vulnerability in determining the psychological severity of the harassment. The effects of loss of personal control result in psychological trauma regardless of gender, and the concomitant psychological symptoms previously discussed lead to a worsening of the individual's physical or emotional condition as well as his or her feelings about and commitment to work (Thacker & Gohmann, 1996). Charney and Russell (1994, p. 13) state that 90% of victims of sexual harassment suffer significant emotional distress, such as anger, depression, fear, self-doubt, tearfulness, anxiety, irritability, loss of self-esteem, and feelings of humiliation or alienation, vulnerability, and helplessness. They discuss physical symptomology, which includes headaches, weight loss, sleep disorders, and respiratory or urinary tract infections.

The impact on the family of the sexually harassed victim's state of mind and behavior is a significant issue as the individual begins to exhibit psychological and physical symptoms. The entire family is disrupted. If the individual exhibits marked depression, withdrawal, irritability, or anxiety, the spouse and children are greatly affected by the change in conjugal and parenting interaction. In addition, if the individual begins to avoid going to work, the economic structure of the family may also be seriously impacted. Woody and Perry (1993) discuss the impact on the family structure and the importance of family therapy for victims of sexual harassment. They highlight the importance of family therapy with the sexual harassment victim and his or her family or significant other. They postulate that the family group is the most powerful "composite of potentially positive influences." As the family is in a state of disarray as a result of the harassment of the victim, the techniques they suggest encompass allaying intrafamilial misgivings, such as blame or guilt, and creating constructive commitments to unification. The importance of empowerment is discussed in a therapeutic model of reconstructing the self-concept and developing coping skills. Clearly, the therapist should not make recommendations on legal issues or pursuit of civil rights; when these issues arise, the client should be referred to an attorney. The client may choose to use legal proceedings as a mechanism for moving toward resolution and better emotional health.

The fallout of sexual harassment may spread to the work organization and the community. Concerns such as poor work performance, increased absenteeism, increases in worker errors, and accidents are evident. Stress and its concomitant medical effects, worker turnover, workers using sick leave to avoid harassment, workers' financial problems and increasing debts, and workers' difficulty in forcing themselves to look for other jobs and therefore becoming jobless affect the workplace as well as the community at large, as there are potentially larger pressures on the community to financially support this disenfranchised group of workers (Gehry, Hateley, Rose, & Stoner, 1994; Tata, 1993; Thacker & Gohmann, 1996).

THERAPEUTIC ISSUES

Therapeutic issues in treating victims of sexual harassment encompass not only the requisite clinical skill and knowledge of trauma recovery, but also workplace considerations and awareness of legal issues on the part of the treating clinician. In a comprehensive consideration of the treatment of sexual harassment victims, Charney and Russell (1994) discuss a paradigm of treatment which they feel differs significantly from traditional psychiatric treatment. They state that in 1994 only 12% of victims sought professional help. An assumption that the victim's presenting instability is a result of the harassment as opposed to a premorbid state is critical in the initial stage of treatment, or the clinician may revictimize the individual. Focusing on empowerment and attitudes that may prevent further victimization, such as discarding beliefs that women are helpless and irresponsible and men are powerful and responsible, are vital. As expected, establishing trust and a therapeutic alliance are difficult in these cases; therefore, discussing and creating safety is critical for the therapy to continue. Empathic emotional support for processing, comprehension, and abreaction is also a key element. These authors state that group counseling is helpful as it allows the individual to validate his or her feelings, understand the experience, develop support and new coping skills, and bounce career and academic options off other group members. Individual therapy focuses on these issues as well as on the effect on the individual's self-evaluation, coping style, trauma symptomology, and conflicts. Charney and Russell only recommend medication when there is a psychiatric diagnosis and it is needed to sustain the intervention. They also discuss the necessity of being aware of grievance procedures and the psychological impact of implementing these procedures. The importance of keeping detailed notes without speculation, including quotations from the victim, are important as there may later be legal proceedings in which the clinician's records may be subpoenaed.

Evidently the arena of treating sexual harassment is a challenging one for the clinician, as it entails psychological, legal, and political considerations for and to the individual, the family, the work organization, and the community at large. Yet the interface also creates a unique opportunity for treatment and ultimately for improvement of workplace male–female relationships.

STALKING OR OBSESSIONAL FOLLOWING

Stalking or obsessional following has become a focal point of the media in the past two decades. There is increased media coverage of celebrity stalkings, as well as the more common news reports of domestic violence cases in which a spurned spouse or former lover has stalked and often harmed the victim. In a comprehensive review of stalking, McAnaney, Curliss, and Abeyeta-Price (1993, pp. 822–824) include a list of kinds of stalkers which spans obsessed fans, divorced or separated spouses, ex-lovers, rejected suitors, neighbors, coworkers, classmates, gang members, former employees, disgruntled defenders, and complete strangers. The scope and dimension of the issue of stalking becomes frighteningly real. As there is a great possibility of violence and little ability for the individual to stop the perpetrator's behavior, stalking is an even more difficult treatment, legal, and law enforcement issue than sexual harassment.

LEGAL DEFINITIONS OF STALKING

In 1990 California passed the first antistalking statute, which defined stalking as follows:

> Section 646.9(a) makes it a crime for anyone who "willfully, maliciously, and repeatedly follows or harasses . . . makes a credible threat with the intent to place that person in reasonable fear for his or her safety . . ." [FN138] "Harassing" is defined as a "knowing and willful course of conduct directed at a specific person which seriously alarms, annoys, torments, or terrorizes the person, and which serves no legitimate purpose."[FN139] "Course of conduct" is defined as a "pattern of conduct composed of a series of acts over a period of time, however short, evidencing a continuity of purpose"[FN 140] A "credible threat" is "a . . . threat . . . made with the intent and the apparent ability to carry out the threat so as to cause the person who is the target of the threat to reasonably fear for his or her safety . . ."[FN 141]. (Diavco, 1995 p, 8)

The definitions in the statutes encompass six primary areas that are necessary to constitute stalking for purposes of civil or criminal prosecution. (McAnaney et al., 1993):

1. *Stalking.* The perpetrator must follow another person.
2. *Repeatedly following.* The behavior of following an individual must be observed multiple times for it to qualify as stalking.
3. *Harassing.* The individual being followed must feel that the behavior is threatening in nature. This may include telephone harassment, although this behavior must fit into a criterion which causes the victim to perceive him- or herself as being annoyed, harassed, or terrorized.
4. *Course of conduct.* There must be a pattern of conduct over time with a clear, evident purpose.
5. *Harm to the victim.* The pattern of behavior must cause severe emotional distress.
6. *Credible threat.* The stalker must have the ability to carry out the threat in order for the behavior to be considered stalking.

Meloy and Gothard (1995, p. 258) define stalking as "the willful, malicious, and repeated following and harassing of another person that threatens his or her safety." They highlight that the criminalization of stalking is a result of the ineffectiveness of court injunctions such as restraining orders to protect individuals from both the threat of and actual physical harm and the terror associated with stalking.

LEGAL HISTORY OF STALKING

In an interesting review of the history of stalking and the law, McAnaney et al. (1993) review stalking laws back to 15th century England and the passage of a law in 1429 wherein sending a threatening letter to a person was part of the offense of burning and was then defined as a separate offense of treason. In the 1700s the sending of "nondemanding threatening" letters was considered a felony. Criminal law in the 1800s in England did not encompass many of the behaviors that are now deemed criminal. (For a more comprehensive examination of this history see McAnaney et al., 1993.)

California enacted the first antistalking law in recent legal history in 1990 as a result of the murders of Theresa Saldano in 1982, Rebecca Schaeffer in 1989, and the murders of four women in Orange County in a space of 5 weeks despite the restraining orders issued against their harassers (Diavco, 1995; McAnaney et al., 1993; Morin, 1993). Since the hallmark statute in California, more than 20 other states have adopted antistalking legislation (Morin, 1993; Salame, 1993). A number of the authors just cited discuss the ineffectiveness of antistalking legislation in that restraining orders are difficult to enforce as the order must be served (oftentimes the victim does not know the identity of the stalker), the officer must catch the offender in the act (frequently police do not arrive until after the stalker has left the premises), and the time delay and cost of obtaining a restraining order often allow the stalker to carry out the act before the restraining order can actually be issued (Diavco, 1995). Diavco also discusses the fact that the penalties for the act of stalking are not effective as a deterrent because the penalties are too mild; for example, "California Penal Code section 646.9 (a) states that violation is punishable by up to one year in the county jail or a fine up to one thousand dollars, or both" (Diavco, 1995, p. 8). She reports that the 1994 changes to the Penal Code Section 646.9 lowered the threshold, increased the penalty, and added a mental health provision for the treatment of the defendant.

It is clear in a review of these articles that the legal system, both at the state and federal levels, has a long way to go in order to establish legislation that will help in protecting the victims of stalkers. "Categories of Stalking," the subsection on the psychological characteristics of the stalker, makes it clearer why stalking is such a difficult legal and law enforcement issue.

SOCIAL HISTORY OF STALKING

The current social history of stalking is highlighted by the fact that celebrity, political, domestic, and stranger stalking is fast becoming an area of increased focus in the arenas of media, law enforcement, legislation, law, and psychology. The daily newspapers, radio, television, and Internet are replete with news stories of murders and injuries as a result of stalking, especially in domestic violence cases. Yet, the more rare cases of celebrity or political stalking gain the most media attention in headline stories.

Celebrity and Political Stalking

Celebrity stalking has gained the most media notoriety due to the aforementioned murders of actresses Rebecca Schaeffer and Theresa Saldano, as well as stories of celebrities who have survived being stalked, such as Michael Jackson, Michael Landon, Cher, David Letterman, and Katarina Witt, to mention a few (Morin, 1993). The 1981 stalking and shooting of President Ronald Reagan by John Hinckley, Jr. to attract the attention of actress Jodie Foster, and the tragic 1997 death of England's Princess Diana, who was ostensibly stalked by media paparazzi from numerous countries, highlight the predominance of stalking of celebrities and have brought this issue to the foreground. Dietz and his colleagues have studied the phenomenon of stalking of members of the U.S. Congress and of Hollywood celebrities (Dietz, Matthews, Van Duyne, et al., 1991; Dietz, Matthews, Martell, et al., 1991). They found that in the case of political figures, the stalking is more focused on issues of power and violence, whereas in celebrity stalking, the issue is more often unrequited romance. Another study reviewed Secret Service information regarding cases of stalking related to the White House (Shore et al., 1985). A review of the demographics and diagnoses of these cases indicates that the stalkers tend to be single, white males with a diagnosis of paranoid schizophrenia.

Domestic Stalking

Domestic stalking is the more common form of stalking that tragically fills local television and radio newscasts and print media. This type of stalking is generally defined in the domestic violence literature or in the law enforcement arena as a "domestic dispute." These cases account for the majority of stalking cases. Here the stalker is known to the victim and is generally an ex-spouse or a spurned lover who is unwilling to accept the rejection, becomes obsessed with the former love, and will often harm or kill rather than be without that person or allow that person to begin a life with someone else.

Stranger Stalking

Stranger stalking of a noncelebrity is less commonly discussed as the individual is unable to identify the stalker; no doubt some murder victims in unsolved cases have been killed by stalkers. In these cases the victim is really unprotected as the individual cannot afford to hire bodyguards as a celebrity can. As the stalker is unknown, the victim cannot identify him or her to have a restraining order served.

CATEGORIES OF STALKING

McAnaney et al. (1993) discuss stalker profiles. *Erotomania* or *de Clerambault's syndrome* is defined in the *Diagnostic and Statistical Manual of Mental Disorders, Fourth Edition* (*DSM-IV*; American Psychiatric Association [APA], 1994) as the presence of a persistent "erotic delusion that one is loved by another." A distinction is highlighted in that erotomania is a delusional disorder in which one believes him- or herself to be loved by the individual, whether that individual even knows of his or her existence, with the additional criterion of a diagnoses of psychosis. This contrasts with de Clerambault's syndrome, in which one believes that the object of the obsession initiated the relationship but does not exhibit psychosis (Meloy, 1989; Segal, 1989). These types of obsessive stalkers are often the ones who stalk celebrities and political figures, although stalkers of strangers often fall into this group as well.

Borderline erotomania, a term coined by Meloy (1989, p. 480), creates a distinction between delusional process and a "gross disturbance of attachment or bonding, but not necessarily a loss of reality testing." Meloy highlights the legal case of John Hinckley, Jr. There was no evidence that Hinckley had delusional beliefs that Jodie Foster loved him; rather, he was obsessed with the fact that she did not care for him, and so chose to attempt to assassinate Ronald Reagan to draw attention to himself so she would notice him. Meloy further distinguishes the two forms of erotomania in that the nature of the attachment is different. In *delusional erotomania*, the meaning and the emotions tied to the relationship have no basis in reality. On the other hand, in *borderline erotomania* there is some history of interpersonal engagement—it can be as minute as a glance or a smile or can range across the spectrum of relationships to include the intensity of a terminated intimate relationship. These individuals "view separation as abandonment, and rejection by the object evokes abandonment rage" (Meloy, 1989, p. 481). Identity disturbance is exhibited by the chaotic attachment to the objects of their love, in that they desperately wish for affection yet may destroy the object of affection. An individual with a borderline erotomania may vacillate between loving or idealizing and hating or devaluing the object of obsession. Meloy further discusses the characterological traits of erotomania to include narcissism, dependency, hysteria, paranoia, and psychopathy, all which may contribute to the potential of violence toward the object of obsession.

The third profile, the *former intimate stalker*, falls into the domestic violence domain and tends to be the type of stalker who acts out his or her violent behavior; these cases constitute much of the stalker data of crime statistics. McAnaney et al. (1993, p. 838) cite 1990 FBI statistics which report that 4% of male homicide victims were killed by former lovers or spouses, 30% of female homicides victims were killed by former husbands or spouses, and 90% of the females killed by former lovers or spouses were stalked before they were murdered. These individuals have a history of an emotional dependence on the obsessional object that is disrupted when the relationship ends. The individual tends to be ambivalent regarding this dependency and is unable to tolerate the panic, pain, and abandonment anxiety when the relationship is terminated. This level of emotional distress can cause the individual to see new persons in the former lover's life as obstacles to reconciliation. The stalker may target his or her rage, jealousy, frustration, and violent tendencies toward that new person and also the former lover.

The fourth profile that McAnaney et al. (1993) discuss is the *sociopathic stalker*; this category encompasses the serial killer and the serial rapist. This group is distinguished by the facts that they do not appear to wish to have a personal relationship with the victim and that they tend to create an "ideal victim"—they find individuals to fit the criteria and victimize those chosen individuals. Ted Bundy of Florida, Jeffrey Dahmer of Milwaukee, and David Berkowitz (Son of Sam) of New

York City are examples of serial rapists and murderers who typed individuals they did not know to rape, maim, and kill.

Zona, Sharma, and Lane (1993) studied a forensic sample of case files which focus on obsessional subjects from the Threat Management Team of the Los Angeles Police Department. They defined an obsessional subject as "an individual who establishes an obsessional, or abnormal long-term pattern of threat or harassment directed toward a specific individual. By obsessional we mean persistent thoughts, impulses or images that result inevitably in some act in relationship to the victim" (Zona et al., 1993, p. 896). These researchers divided obsessional subjects into three categories:

1. *The erotomanic,* who is an individual with a delusional belief that he or she is passionately loved by another. The erotomanic believes this delusion for years and rejects any evidence to the contrary. As the erotomanic may repeatedly attempt to contact his or her love object, he or she may be known by the law enforcement community due to complaints lodged by the victim.
2. The *love obsessional,* who may also be unknown to his or her victim, does not necessarily believe the object of obsession loves him or her. He or she may engage in behaviors to gain the attention of the love object in the belief that if given a chance, that individual will love him or her, as in the John Hinckley/Jodie Foster example previously presented. This individual may vacillate between loving and hating the love object. In addition, the love obsessional tends to have several additional delusions and psychiatric symptoms (Diavco, 1995; Zona et al., 1993). This individual is described in Meloy's nosology as the *borderline erotomanic.*
3. The *simple obsessional,* who has a history of a relationship with the victim. This "prior relationship may vary in degree from customer, acquaintance, neighbor, professional relationship, to date and/or lover." In all of these cases, obsessional activities begin either after the relationship had gone sour or after the perception by the stalker that he or she has been mistreated. The stalker usually begins a campaign either to rectify the schism or to seek some type of retribution (Zona et al., 1993, p. 896). Diavco (1995) reports that one in five women attacked by a former spouse or lover have reported repeated incidents of violence prior to the severe attack. She states that the simple obsessional is more likely to make threats and follow through with those threats, injuring the target or the target's property, than are the love obsessional or the erotomanic. These individuals tend to exhibit the same behaviors as domestic violence subjects, according to Diavco. The simple obsessional is categorized by McAnaney et al. (1993) as the *former intimate stalker.*

ANTECEDENTS OF STALKING BEHAVIORS

Theories of the antecedents of stalking behaviors include theories that the stalker may present with psychobiological disorders; chemical imbalances such as schizophrenia; endocrine disorders such as Cushing's syndrome, Addison's disease, and gonadal hormone dysfunction; brain lesions; or diffuse brain damage (McAnaney et al., 1993, p. 844). Cognitive and emotional problems including abandonment;

early borderline personality development; history of emotional, mental, and physical abuse; physical and emotional neglect; and incest and sexual abuse are also prevalent. Stalking behaviors include persistent following; repeated attempts at face-to-face contact such as showing up at the victim's home or work; telephone or letter harassment; sending packages or flowers; and verbal and physical threats and acts against the victim, the victim's significant others, or the victim's family.

FACTORS INFLUENCING INDIVIDUAL RESPONSES TO STALKING

Factors that influence the individual's response to stalking vary depending on the type of stalker the victim is dealing with as well as the victim's resources, such as ability to hire bodyguards, move, or change jobs. The effectiveness of law enforcement in protecting the individual may be dependent on whether the identity of the stalker is known and how much pathology the stalker exhibits as a truly delusional or psychotic stalker. He or she will not be deterred by the mere existence of a restraining order. The level of the severed relationship and the subsequent access the stalker has to the victim are major factors in these cases. Former lovers and spouses generally have greater leverage in gaining access to the victim, especially if they share children. These factors certainly influence the amount of control that potential victims may be able to assert in terms of attempting to protect themselves, to have the stalker apprehended, or to incarcerate the stalker and create a sense of safety.

RESPONSES TO AND PSYCHOLOGICAL EFFECTS OF STALKING

Victims tend to be more passive than assertive as most victims attempt to avoid the stalker at all costs, such as by changing phone numbers, addresses, and jobs. Most victims of stalking exhibit symptoms of terror and Post-Traumatic Stress Disorder (PTSD). As defined in the *DSM-IV* (American Psychiatric Association, 1994) the individual may have recurrent distressing recollections of the event, diminished interest in activities, nightmares, dissociative phenomena, restricted range of affect, sleep disturbance, appetite disturbance, hypervigilance, exaggerated startle responses, physical ailments such as headaches, and gastrointestinal disorders. In addition, the individual may exhibit depression, anxiety, panic disorders, substance abuse, obsessive-compulsive behaviors, superstitious behaviors, or dissociative disorders.

Members of the stalking victim's family not only have to deal with the victim's emotional response to the stalker but they are also at significant risk, as stalkers may transfer their rage and retribution onto the loved ones of the victim in order to control or punish him or her. The entire family structure and family life may be disrupted, uprooted, and subject to terror. The community at large is also greatly affected by the preponderance of violence in society and the uncontrollable and unpredictable nature of stalkers of both the psychotic and nonpsychotic genres.

THERAPEUTIC ISSUES

It is interesting to note that the preponderance of the literature on stalking and erotomania deals with the treatment of the perpetrator. It appears that the traditional approaches to the treatment of PTSD, affective disorders, and chemical dependency are assumed to be the best treatment paradigms available for the victims. Instead, I believe protocols or recommendations for the treatment of these victims are to be sought in the domestic violence literature. Interestingly, these two bodies of related materials are not cross-referenced in the computer searches. It is important for the clinician to be aware of both bodies of literature in treating these victims of terror.

SUMMARY AND RECOMMENDATIONS

The focus of the clinical literature in the area of *sexual harassment* is on the treatment of the victim, and there are few if any clinical studies on the treatment of the harasser. Conversely, both the clinical and legal literature on *stalking* or *erotomania* focus almost exclusively on the treatment of the perpetrator. The effect of stalking on the victim and the subsequent treatment of victims is rarely mentioned in these bodies of literature. As previously indicated, material on the treatment of stalking victims is likely to be found in the domestic violence literature. The treating clinician must be aware of all three areas of study and be familiar with the legal issues and litigation in sexual harassment cases and antistalking legislation in order to understand and treat patients optimally and help them in their encounters with law enforcement, the telephone company, and legal and medical personnel. It is evident that this is a complex area of treatment. Clinicians must be careful to acknowledge the need to refer patients to the legal and law enforcement community and must support their efforts, so as to not overstep our professional skills and boundaries and possibly harm patients in an effort to be helpful.

REFERENCES

American Psychiatric Association. (1994). *Diagnostic and statistical manual of mental disorders* (4th ed.). Washington, DC: Author.

Barak, A., Fischer, W., & Houston, S., (1992). Individual difference correlates to the experience of sexual harassment among female university students. *Journal of Applied Social Psychology, 22*, 17–37.

Bargh, J., & Raymond, P. (1995). The naive misuse of power: Nonconscious sources of sexual harassment. *Journal of Social Issues, 51*(3), 85–96.

Berdahl, J., Magley, V., & Waldo, C. (1996). The sexual harassment of men? Exploring the concept with theory and data. *Psychology of Women Quarterly, 20*, 527–547.

Burns, S. (1995) Issues in workplace sexual harassment law and related social science research. *Journal of Social Issues, 51*(1), 193–207.

Charney, D., Russell, R. (1994). An overview of sexual harassment. *American Journal of Psychiatry, 151*(1), 10–17.

Civil Rights Act, Title VII (1964), 42 U.S.C. 2000e *et seq.*

Culbertson, A., Rosenfeld, P., Booth-Kewley, S., & Magnusson, P. (1992). *Assessment of sexual harassment in the Navy: Results of the 1989 Navy-wide survey* (TR-92-11). San Diego, CA: Navy Personnel Research and Development Center.

Diavco, N., (1995). California's anti-stalking statute: Deterrent or false sense of security? *Southwestern Law Review*, (389), 1–28.

Dietz, P., Matthews, D., Van Duyne, C., Martell, D., Parry, C., Stewart, T., Warren, J., & Crowder, J. (1991). Threatening and otherwise inappropriate letters to Hollywood celebrities. *Journal of Forensic Science, 36*, 1445–1468.

Dietz, P., Matthews, D., Martell, D., Stewart, T., Hrouda, D., & Warren, J., (1991). Threatening or otherwise inappropriate letters to members of the United States Congress. *Journal of Forensic Science, 39,* 185–209.

Education Amendments, Title IX (1972), 42 U.S.C., Section 703.

EEOC guidelines on sexual harassment. (1980). *Federal Register, 45*(72), 25025.

Economist. (1997, January 18), Scandal in the second term, monkey business? *The Economist,* 21–23.

Ellison v. Brady (1991), 924 F.2d 872 (9th Cir.).

Fitzgerald, L. F., & Omerod, A. J. (1991). Perceptions of sexual harassment: The influence of gender and context. *Psychology of Women Quarterly, 15,* 281–294.

Fitzgerald, L. F., Shullman, S. L, Bailey, N., Richards, M., Swecker, J., Gold, A., Omerod, A. J., & Weitzman, L. J. (1988). The incidence and dimensions of sexual harassment in academia and the workplace. *Journal of Vocational Behavior, 32,* 152–175.

Fitzgerald, L. F., Swan, S., & Fischer, K. (1995). Why didn't she just report him? The psychological and legal implications of women's responses to sexual harassment. *Journal of Social Issues, 51*(1), 117–138.

Frazier, P., Cochran, C., & Olson, A. (1995). Social science research on lay definitions of sexual harassment. *Journal of Social Issues, 51,* 21–37.

Gehry, F., Hateley, B. J., Rose, S., & Stoner, M. (1994, August). *American Behavioral Scientist, 37,* 1122–1137.

Giuffre. P., & Williams, C. (1994, September). Boundary lines labeling sexual harassment in restaurants. *Gender and Society, 8*(3), 378–401.

Gowan, M., & Zimmerman, R. (1996). Impact of ethnicity, gender, and previous experience on juror judgments in sexual harassment cases. *Journal of Applied Social Psychology, 26*(7), 596–617.

Gutek, B. A., & Morasch, B. (1982). Sex ratio, sex-role spillover, and sexual harassment of women at work. *Journal of Social Issues, 38,* 55–74.

Gutek, B. A., & O'Connor, M. (1995). The empirical basis for the reasonable woman standard. *Journal of Social Issues, 51*(1), 151–166.

Hadley, E. C., & Chuzi, G. M. (1995). *Sexual Harassment: Federal Law* (pp. 1–5). Dewey Publications.

Harris v. Forklift Systems (1993), U.S. Sup. Ct. 63 FEP Cases 255.

Hemmasi, M., Graf, L., & Russ, G. (1994). Gender-related jokes in the workplace: Sexual humor or sexual harassment? *Journal of Applied Social Psychology, 24*(12), 1114–1128.

Jaschik-Herman, M., & Fisk, A. (1995). Women's perceptions and labeling of sexual harassment in academia before and after the Hill-Thomas hearings. *Sex Roles, 33*(5/6), 439–458.

Kidder, L., Lafleur, R. A., & Wells, C. (1995). Recalling harassment, reconstructing experience. *Journal of Social Issues, 51*(1), 53–67.

Komaromy, M., Bindman, A., Haber, R. J., & Sande, M. A. (1993). Sexual harassment in medical training. *New England Journal of Medicine, 328,* 322–326.

McAnaney, K., Curliss, L., & Abeyeta-Price, C. (1993). From imprudence to crime: Anti-stalking laws. *Notre Dame Law Review, 68,* 819–909.

McCormick, A. (1985). The sexual harassment of students by teachers: The case of students in science. *Sex Roles, 13,* 21–32.

Meloy, J. R. (1989). Unrequited love and the wish to kill: The diagnosis and treatment of borderline erotomania. *Bull. Menninger Clinic, 53,* 477–492.

Meloy, J. R., & Gothard, S. (1995, February). Demographic and clinical comparisons of obsessional followers and offenders with mental disorders. *American Journal of Psychiatry, 152*(2), 258–263.

Meritor Savings Bank, FSB v. Vinson et al. (1986), 106 S. Ct. 2399.

Morin, K. (1993). The phenomenon of stalking: Do existing state statutes provide adequate protection? *San Diego Justice Journal, 1,* 123–162.

Paludi, M. A., & Barickman, R. B. (1991). *Academic and workplace sexual harassment*. Albany, NY: SUNY Press.

Rabidue v. Osceola Refining Company, 803 F.2d 611 (6th Cir. 1986), *cert. denied*, 481 U.S. 1041 (1987).

Radtke v. Everett (1993), 61 FEP Cases 1644 (Mich.)

Ragins, B., & Scandura, T. (1995). Antecedents and work-related correlates of reported sexual harassment: An empirical investigation of competing hypotheses. *Sex Roles, 32*(7/8), 429–455.

Rogers, J. K., & Henson, K. D. (1997). "Hey, why don't you wear a shorter skirt?" Structural vulnerability and the organization of sexual harassment in temporary clerical employment. *Gender and Society, 11*(2), 215–237.

Rubin, L. J., & Borgers, S. B. (1990). Sexual harassment in universities during the 1980's. *Sex Roles, 23,* 397–411.

Salame, L. (1993). A national survey of stalking laws: A legislative trend comes to the aid of domestic violence victims and others. *Suffolk University Law Review, 27,* 67–111.

Segal, J. (1989, October). Erotomania revisited: From Kraepelin to DSM-III-R. *American Journal of Psychiatry, 146*(10), 1261–1266.

Sheffey S., & Tindale, S. (1992). Perceptions of sexual harassment in the workplace. *Journal of Applied Social Psychology, 22*(19), 1502–1520.

Shore, D., Filson, R., Davis, T. S., Olivos, G., DeLisi, L., & Wyatt, R. J. (1985, March). White House cases: Psychiatric patients and the Secret Service. *American Journal of Psychiatry, 142,* 308–312.

Tata, J. (1993). The structure and phenomenon of sexual harassment: Impact of category of sexually harassing behavior, gender, and hierarchal level. *Journal of Applied Social Psychology, 23*(3), 199–211.

Thacker, R. (1996). A descriptive study of situational and individual influences upon individuals' responses to sexual harassment. *Human Relations, 49*(8), 1105–1122.

Thacker, R., & Gohmann, S. (1996). Emotional and psychological consequences of sexual harassment: A descriptive study. *The Journal of Psychology, 13*(4), 429–446.

Walters, N. (1997, September 12). Sexual harassment pervasive in the army, panel finds. *Miami Herald*, p. 1.

Wicklund, R. (1974). *Freedom and reactance*. New York: John Wiley & Sons.

Wiener, R. (1995). Social analytic jurisprudence in sexual harassment litigation: The role of social framework and social fact. *Journal of Social Issues, 51*(1), 167–180.

Williams, K., & Cyr, R. (1992). Escalating commitment to a relationship: The sexual harassment trap. *Sex Roles, 27*(1/2), 47–72.

Woody, R. H., & Perry, N. W. (1993). Sexual harassment victims: Psycholegal and family therapy considerations. *The American Journal of Family Therapy, 21*(2), 135–144.

Zona, M., Sharma, K., & Lane J. (1993). A comparative study of erotomanic and obsessional subjects in a forensic sample. *Journal of Forensic Science, 38,* 894–903.

CHAPTER 8

Psychological and Legal Issues in Abortion

SUSAN P. LIMBER and PAULINE M. PAGLIOCCA

A WOMAN's decision about the resolution of her pregnancy is complex and frequently stressful. Whether her decision is based on moral or religious beliefs, personal circumstances, or medical advice, she may consult a mental health professional at any time—whether initially, as she considers her options, or later, as she examines the consequences of her decision. Counseling may be sought whether the woman chooses to carry her pregnancy to term or to abort.

This chapter focuses on the legal and psychological context of abortion. At some point during their practice, most mental health professionals (MHPs),[1] regardless of their discipline or work setting, are likely to provide consultation or counseling services to women and adolescent girls before, during, or after pregnancies that result in abortion. In order to provide competent intervention, it is essential that clinicians be well informed about the myriad laws regulating abortion, current research related to the decision-making process, and the psychological impact of the pregnancy and abortion experience.

THE ABORTION CONTEXT

Although the number of abortions performed in the United States each year has declined steadily since 1990, and is at its lowest rate since 1977 (Henshaw, 1998), abortion remains a fairly common medical procedure for women and adolescent girls. According to the most recent figures released by the Centers for Disease Control, which collects abortion data from state reporting systems, 1.27 million abortions were performed in 1994 (Alan Guttmacher Institute, 1997a). The Alan Guttmacher Institute, which provides a more complete source of information on abortion from its nationwide surveys of all abortion providers, reported that approximately 1.37 million abortions were performed in 1996; approximately 26% of all pregnancies in that year were terminated by abortion (Henshaw, 1998). In

142

1996, the abortion rate was 23 abortions per 1,000 adolescent girls and women (ages 15 to 44) (Henshaw, 1998), lower than any year since 1975.

CHARACTERISTICS OF WOMEN OBTAINING ABORTIONS

Abortions are sought by women with very diverse personal, social, and socioeconomic circumstances (Russo, Horn, & Schwartz, 1992). Nevertheless, the likelihood of obtaining an abortion is higher among particular subgroups of women. The most comprehensive information on the characteristics of abortion patients comes from a 1994 to 1995 national survey of 9,985 women obtaining abortions at 13 hospitals and 87 nonhospital facilities (Henshaw & Kost, 1996). A number of these characteristics are relevant to the later discussion concerning women's decision making about abortion and their experiences vis-à-vis the abortion process.

Age

The majority of women obtaining abortions are young; 54% are under the age of 25; 22% are teenagers. Only 24% are age 30 or older (Henshaw & Kost, 1996).

Marital and Parental Status

Most women obtaining abortions (64%) have never been married. Indeed, never-married women are nearly 5 times as likely as women who are married (and are not separated) and 3 times as likely as women who are divorced to have abortions. Women who cohabit with a partner (to whom they are not married) are 4 times as likely to obtain an abortion as women who are not cohabiting. Abortion also is more common among women who already have a child. Women with four or more children are particularly likely to obtain abortions. Approximately two-thirds of women terminating pregnancies indicate that they intend to have additional children (Henshaw & Kost, 1996).

Ethnicity

Although white women obtain the majority of abortions (61%), their abortion rate is significantly below that of women of other races (Henshaw & Kost, 1996). Black women are nearly 3 times as likely as white (non-Hispanic) women to obtain abortions, and the rate of abortions for Hispanic women is approximately twice that of non-Hispanic women (Henshaw & Kost, 1996).

Socioeconomic Circumstances

Women who obtain abortions are disproportionately from families with low annual incomes (less than $15,000). The poorest of these women—women on Medicaid—are twice as likely as non–Medicaid recipients to have abortions (Henshaw & Kost, 1996).

Religious Background

Women who report no religious identification obtain abortions at approximately 4 times the rate of women who claim a religious affiliation. The abortion rate for Catholics is approximately 29% higher than for Protestants; the abortion rate for born-again Christian or evangelical Christian women is far below the rate for other women (Henshaw & Kost, 1996).

In sum, those personal characteristics that are associated with high rates of abortion include being young, being unmarried or separated, cohabiting while unmarried, having four or more children, being of a minority race, having a low income, and being covered by Medicaid. As Henshaw and Kost note, "with the exception of cohabitation, [these characteristics] suggest a lack of financial and social resources and, perhaps, a lack of control over one's life (1996, p. 146).

LEGAL ISSUES

A woman seeking an abortion must not only contend with practical and personal issues surrounding her decision, but must also make and carry out her decision within the context of a complex web of state and federal legislation and court rulings which regulate the conditions under which she may obtain an abortion. It is critical that therapists have a basic understanding of the trends in the law so that they may help their clients to navigate the various state and federal restrictions on abortion, assist their clients with the often arduous decision-making process, and provide support to them during and after the pregnancy decision.

THE LEGALITY OF ABORTION

Prior to the 19th century, abortions that were performed before the "quickening" of the fetus—the stage in pregnancy when the fetus makes movements that can be felt by the mother—were legal. However, because of the health risks involved in performing abortions, by 1900 all states had passed laws that prohibited abortion except in the most extreme circumstances (Merz, Jackson, & Klerman, 1995). In the late 1960s and early 1970s, a sea change occurred in legislatures across the country, as 17 states modified or repealed their laws governing abortion and nearly every other state in the nation introduced similar laws (Alan Guttmacher Institute, 1997b).

In 1973, the U.S. Supreme Court invalidated most of the remaining restrictions against abortion when it struck down state laws in Georgia (*Doe v. Bolton*, 1973) and Texas (*Roe v. Wade*, 1973). The Court ruled that a woman has a constitutionally protected right to terminate her pregnancy without state interference, at least in the early stages of pregnancy (loosely defined as the first trimester). During the second trimester of pregnancy (prior to the fetus' viability), a state may impose restrictions on abortion only if these restrictions are reasonably related to the protection of the woman's health. Once a fetus is viable, the Court acknowledged that a state may have a compelling interest in the unborn child and could limit or prohibit abortion entirely, except in those instances when the health or life of the mother is in danger.

In the two decades after this landmark decision, states have adopted laws that place increasing restrictions on the conditions under which an individual may obtain an abortion, and the Supreme Court has ruled on the legality of such provisions on at least 19 separate occasions. The pace of lawmaking and the volume of litigation pertaining to abortion has been staggering. Following, we provide a brief review of recent trends in state laws regulating abortion and resulting Supreme Court decisions. Because laws can change rapidly, this review is intended to give only a snapshot of current legal trends. It is not meant to provide detailed state-specific information pertaining to abortion laws.[2]

PROCEDURE-SPECIFIC BANS AND LATE-TERM ABORTIONS

In recent years, a number of states have enacted laws to ban specific surgical procedures (most commonly, intact dilation and extraction [D&X]) that are used for late-term abortions (Alan Guttmacher Institute, 1997b, 1997c; Sollom, 1997). In 1995, Ohio became the first state to outlaw D&X procedures, imposing criminal penalties on physicians who failed to comply with the law. (This law is not currently in force, as it has been enjoined by a state court.) The U.S. Congress passed a similar bill in 1996 to outlaw such procedures (dubbed *partial-birth abortions*), but the measure was defeated by a presidential veto. Legislators in numerous other states have considered partial-birth abortion bills that would impose criminal or civil penalties against physicians who conduct D&X or saline abortions, although such laws are currently enforced in only six states (Indiana, Mississippi, South Carolina, South Dakota, Tennessee, and Utah; Alan Guttmacher Institute, 1998). Typically, states that do enforce procedure-specific bans provide exceptions when a woman's life is endangered. To date, the U.S. Supreme Court has not ruled on the constitutionality of this recent spate of late-term, procedure-specific bans, although it invalidated several state provisions against saline abortions in 1986, ruling that the determination of the abortion procedure must be made by the attending physician in light of the medical facts of the case (*Thornburgh v. American College of Obstetricians and Gynecologists*, 1986).

INFORMED CONSENT/WAITING PERIOD

A number of state laws mandate that women receive specific types of information before being permitted to obtain an abortion.[3] Often referred to as *informed-consent laws*, these state regulations typically require that physicians or counselors provide a woman with verbal or written information pertaining to fetal development, prenatal care, and adoption (National Abortion and Reproductive Rights Action League [NARAL], 1997; Sollom, 1997). The Supreme Court has indicated that there are limits to the type of information that is permissible, however. In *Thornburgh v. American College of Obstetricians and Gynecologists* (1986), the Court invalidated provisions of a Pennsylvania law that required physicians to give their patients antiabortion information that included pictures of fetuses at various stages of development.

Frequently, this informed-consent requirement is paired with a mandatory waiting period, such that a woman must wait a certain period of time (typically 24 hours) after receiving such information before she may obtain an abortion.[4] In a 1992 decision, the U.S. Supreme Court upheld a Pennsylvania law that required physicians to provide such information 24 hours prior to performing an abortion, but the Court left open the possibility that an informed-consent law could be struck down if it could be shown to seriously affect a women's access to abortion (*Planned Parenthood of Southeastern Pennsylvania v. Casey*, 1992).

SPOUSAL CONSENT OR NOTIFICATION

Ten states currently have laws that require a woman to notify or obtain consent from her husband prior to obtaining an abortion (NARAL, 1997). However, in 1992, the U.S. Supreme Court found such a law unconstitutional (*Planned Parenthood of Southeastern Pennsylvania v. Casey*), rendering these state laws unenforceable.

BANS ON ABORTION COUNSELING

Currently, five states have laws that prevent state employees (or employees of organizations that receive state funds) from counseling or referring women for abortion services (Louisiana, Michigan, Missouri, North Dakota, and Pennsylvania; NARAL, 1997). These laws are frequently dubbed *gag rules* by their detractors. Similarly, the federal government has prohibited employees of agencies that receive funds under Title X of the Health Services Act (which makes grants to public and nonprofit agencies that offer family planning efforts) from providing abortion counseling, referrals, or information (Bullis, 1991). These federal prohibitions have been upheld by the Supreme Court (*Rust v. Sullivan*, 1991).

FUNDING OF ABORTION

State and federal laws have placed limits upon the financing of abortion services, by restricting or prohibiting Medicaid or insurance coverage for abortion procedures. Since 1977, the U.S. Congress has limited the availability of Medicaid funds for abortion by adding a version of the *Hyde Amendment* to the annual funding bills for the U.S. Department of Health and Human Services. Under this amendment, federal Medicaid funds will pay for abortion services only if the life of the woman would be endangered if the pregnancy were carried to term or if the pregnancy is the result of rape or incest. The U.S. Supreme Court has upheld the constitutionality of the Hyde Amendment (*Harris v. McRae*, 1980). Despite the cutoff of federal funds for abortion, 17 states currently use their own state medical assistance programs to fund abortions for low-income women under most circumstances (Alan Guttmacher Institute, 1998; NARAL, 1997; Planned Parenthood Federation of America, 1994; Sollom, 1997).

LEGAL ISSUES PERTAINING TO MINORS

Although the U.S. Supreme Court has not been entirely clear about the extent of adolescents' right to abortion, it has ruled that minors have a constitutional right to obtain abortions (*Planned Parenthood of Central Missouri* [PPCM] *v. Danforth*, 1976) and that states must not restrict this right unless the restrictions further significant state interests (*PPCM v. Danforth*, 1976; *H. L. v. Matheson*, 1981). The primary restrictions that states have placed upon adolescents' right to obtain abortions are parental consent and notification requirements.

In a line of decisions beginning in 1976, the Supreme Court has attempted to define the parameters of a state's power to require a parents' involvement in a minor daughter's abortion decision. The Court has ruled that although states may not grant parents absolute veto power over their daughter's pregnancy decision (*Bellotti v. Baird*, 1979; *City of Akron v. Akron Center for Reproductive Health*, 1983), they may require parental consent or notification as long as the state also provides the minor an alternative to parental involvement (*H. L. v. Matheson*, 1981; *Hodgson v. Minnesota*, 1990; *Ohio v. Akron Center for Reproductive Health*, 1990; *Planned Parenthood Association of Kansas City, Missouri, v. Ashcroft*, 1983; *Planned Parenthood of Southeastern Pennsylvania v. Casey*, 1992). Under this alternative provision, which is commonly referred to as a *judicial bypass*, a minor may obtain permission for an abortion from a judge without informing her parents. A judge must authorize the abortion if he or she determines either that the young woman is mature enough to make the decision for herself or that it would be in her best interest to have an abortion (*Bellotti v. Baird*, 1979). Currently, 15 states enforce laws that require minors to obtain a parent's consent before obtaining an abortion,[5] while 14 states enforce laws requiring the notification of a minor girl's parent[6] (3 states require notification of both parents; several permit notification of a grandparent or sibling in lieu of a parent; Alan Guttmacher Institute, 1998). These requirements may be waived in circumstances where a physician determines that an adolescent's health is in immediate danger without the abortion. Further, a number of states permit waivers of these requirements when an adolescent informs the physician that she has been abused or neglected.

PSYCHOLOGICAL ISSUES AND ABORTION

Within this legal labyrinth, many women and adolescents face decisions about continuing or terminating their pregnancies. Such decisions, the conditions in which they are made, the abortion experience itself, and the role of significant others all have potential implications for women's psychological well-being and adjustment.

Psychological Issues and Research Related to the Decision-Making Process

Deciding whether to terminate a pregnancy may be a conflictual experience for many women. To assist clients in making such decisions, clinicians must have a good understanding of women's reasons for obtaining abortions and the role of significant others in this process.

Why Women Obtain Abortions

The reasons that women give for seeking abortions are varied and complex. Moreover, their rationales vary as a function of their age (adults versus minors), marital status, and status as mothers (Russo et al., 1992; Torres & Forrest, 1988). The most recent and comprehensive assessment of women's reasons for obtaining abortions was conducted by Torres and Forrest in 1988. Their study, which involved a national sample of 1,900 abortion patients at 30 different medical facilities, revealed that the abortion decision is quite complicated. Most women provided more than three reasons for obtaining an abortion. The most common reasons included concerns that: (a) having a baby could change her life (76%), (b) she could not afford a baby (68%), (c) she had problems with a current relationship or wanted to avoid single parenthood (51%), (d) she was unready for responsibility (31%), (e) she did not want others to know she was pregnant (31%), and (f) she was not mature enough or was too young to have a child (30%). These responses highlight the particular importance of the women's developmental level or life stage, her interpersonal relationships, and the socioeconomic circumstances surrounding her decision making about abortion (Russo et al., 1992). Although some differences in reasoning were observed for different subgroups of women (primarily adults versus minors and married versus unmarried women), race and poverty status were unrelated to their abortion rationale (Torres & Forrest, 1988).

A reanalysis of this data set was conducted by Russo et al. (1992) to examine in more detail women's personal versus situational reasons for abortions. Findings revealed that minors seek abortions for personal reasons related to both their developmental level and their relationships with others. Three-quarters of young women under the age of 18 indicated that they were not ready for child rearing, primarily because they did not believe that they were mature enough to have a child. Among the situational reasons that minors cited for seeking abortions were their educational circumstances (37%), their inability to afford a child (28%), social disapproval (14%), and issues related to their partner (e.g., concern that the relationship might dissolve; 12%). Among adults, differences in rationales emerged depending upon the woman's parental and marital status. For example, women who already had children were likely to say that their childbearing was completed or that their children needed them. Nonmothers and nonmarried women were more likely to cite educational reasons for their abortion decision or to indicate that they were too young or not mature enough to have a child. Some reasons, however, were important to all groups of women. Regardless of marital or parental status, more than one in three women indicated that they could not afford to have a baby. In addition to the reasons cited for terminating an unwanted pregnancy, women sometimes decide to terminate a pregnancy that was originally "wanted and meaningful" (Adler et al., 1992, p. 1202). A woman may opt for an abortion due to pressure from a significant other, such as a parent (7% of Russo et al.'s sample, 1992) or partner (23% of Russo et al.'s sample, 1992; David, 1994), or upon learning that the fetus has a medical or genetic defect (13% of Russo et al.'s sample, 1992; Adler, 1992; Dagg, 1991).

Where Women Turn for Assistance with the Decision

Whatever a woman's reasons for terminating her pregnancy, rarely does she make this decision alone. Research describing decision making has consistently suggested that women routinely consult significant others in determining whether to seek abortion (Bracken, Klerman, & Bracken, 1978; Lewis, 1980; Miller, 1992; Plutzer & Ryan, 1987; Ryan & Plutzer, 1989; Smith & Kronauge, 1990). For example, in a study of 924 pregnant married women whose husbands were the coconceivers, 93.7% reported that they had informed their husbands of their intent to terminate the pregnancy (Smith & Kronauge, 1990). In another study involving women of various marital statuses (Plutzer & Ryan, 1987; Ryan & Plutzer, 1989), 89.5% indicated that they had told their coconceivers of the pregnancy, with fewer (82.5%) telling them of their subsequent abortion. A closer look at these data reveal that married women were somewhat more likely to inform their coconceivers than were other women. This research further examined more closely reasons that some married women (less than 8%) did *not* inform their husbands of their pregnancy. Three primary explanations for choosing this option emerged: (a) The husband was not the coconceiver (the woman had been involved in an extramarital affair or had been raped), (b) the couple was experiencing marital problems (e.g., marital rape, separated since conception, pregnancy might further jeopardize an already tenuous relationship), or (c) the woman feared that her husband might insist on her bringing the pregnancy to term.

In a study of young, never-married pregnant women, Bracken et al. (1978) compared those seeking abortion with those attending their first prenatal care appointment. Consistently, women intending to give birth were more likely to have discussed their pregnancy with significant others than were those who intended to abort. The most likely "consultants" for both groups were partners (delivery, 93.3%; abortion, 83.2%) and best girlfriends (delivery, 86.2%; abortion, 68.0%). Mothers were next most likely to be consulted by those giving birth (82.8%), while physicians were in that position for those choosing abortion (50.9%). Clergy appear to have played an insignificant role in decision making for both groups (delivery, 14.5%; abortion, 3.0%). Unfortunately, the list of potential consultants in this study did not include counselors other than physicians and clergy, so we do not know whether any of these women had conferred with mental health professionals.

In addition to spousal notification and consent laws having been found unconstitutional (*Planned Parenthood of Southeastern Pennsylvania v. Casey,* 1992), they would appear to be superfluous based on the consistent findings that married women voluntarily inform their husbands. Likewise, single women routinely discuss their pregnancy decisions with their coconceivers, and both married and unmarried women consult with significant others.

Consistent with the research describing decision making by adults, results from a number of studies have suggested that adolescents consult other individuals extensively about abortion decisions and most voluntarily involve their parents (Ashton, 1980; Finken & Jacobs, 1996; Griffin-Carlson & Mackin, 1993; Limber, 1992; Resnick, Bearinger, Stark, & Blum, 1994; Rosen, 1980). For example, in a study with 184 adolescents obtaining abortions, Resnick et al. (1994) observed that although only 13% of adolescents consulted a parent when they first suspected that they were pregnant (compared with 57% who notified their male partner and 43% who consulted friends), 57% informed one or both parents once the pregnancy had been confirmed (compared with 83% who notified male partners and 50% who notified friends). When asked at the time of abortion to identify the individual who was the most helpful in their pregnancy decision making, adolescents cited their male partners (32%) and mothers (28%) first, followed by friends (20%), and counseling services (9%).

Younger adolescents appear quite likely to involve adults (Resnick et al., 1994)—and, in particular, a parent—in their pregnancy decisions (Griffin-Carlson & Mackin, 1993; Limber, 1992; Torres, Forrest, & Eisman, 1980). In addition to age, the degree of emotional and financial independence, as well as the quality of family communication, appear to be closely linked to adolescents' decisions to confide in parents about ending a pregnancy (Griffin-Carlson & Mackin, 1993). Adolescents who do not voluntarily consult their parents consider themselves more mature. In addition, they are financially more independent, more likely to live outside the family home, and more likely to describe their family communication as closed on the topic of sex (Griffin-Carlson & Mackin, 1993).

It should be emphasized that those adolescents who do not involve their parents in a pregnancy decision do not lack guidance from others. The vast majority of adolescents indicate that they consult several individuals about such decisions (Finken & Jacobs, 1996; Limber, 1992; Resnick et al., 1994), and those who do not consult parents involve other adults (e.g., grandparents, aunts or uncles, or counselors) in the decision-making process (Limber, 1992; Resnick et al., 1994). The minority of teens who decide not to notify a parent about a pregnancy may have good reasons for doing so. A pregnant adolescent may believe that a parent would react violently to the news of her pregnancy or that a parent might try to force her to make a decision contrary to her wishes (Limber, 1992; Melton & Pliner, 1986). A recent study of pregnant adolescents revealed that 25% had histories of being subject to sexual or physical abuse (Berenson, SanMiguel, & Wilkinson, 1992). Over half of these abuse incidents involved family members.

How Their Decisions Are Influenced by Others

Consultations with significant others about decisions as serious as those pertaining to pregnancy have the potential to be highly emotionally charged. Curiously, very little research has been conducted to examine what, if any, effect such consultation has on adolescents' and women's thinking about abortion. Initial evidence suggests that significant others (partners or parents) may exert a powerful influence on adolescents' decisions, however. For example, in a study by Eisen and colleagues (Eisen, Zellman, Leibowitz, Chow, & Evans, 1983), over one-third of the young women who agreed that they should carry the pregnancy to term subsequently had abortions. In three-quarters of these cases, the adolescents had indicated that one or more significant others (primarily their partners or mothers) had strongly supported their having an abortion. Further, in a study involving hypothetical pregnancy dilemmas, Limber (1992) observed that parental influence significantly affected the strength of adolescents' decisions. Adolescents were likely to indicate that they would conform to their parents' wishes, regardless of whether the influence was proabortion or propregnancy.

PSYCHOLOGICAL ISSUES RELATED TO THE ABORTION EXPERIENCE

Researchers have examined not only the decision-making process regarding the termination of pregnancy but also psychological issues related to the abortion experience. In 1989, Nancy Adler testified before Congress on behalf of the American Psychological Association (APA) on the psychological effects of abortion. That testimony (Adler, 1989) and subsequent reviews of the research literature conducted by APA's expert panel on abortion (Adler et al., 1990, 1992) concluded that, although abortion may be distressing, it does not present serious psychological danger for most women. Studies of women's emotional reactions to abortion generally fall into two broad categories, one focusing on psychopathology, and the other adopting a stress-and-coping perspective.

Psychopathological Perspective

Viewing abortion as a traumatic event, reports focusing on psychopathological responses to abortion have tended to rely primarily on anecdotal case studies, self-selected samples of postabortion women, or descriptions of hypothesized disorders, with little empirical support (e.g., Bagarozzi, 1994; McAll & Wilson, 1987; Speckhard, 1987; Speckhard & Rue, 1992). Recent proponents of this position have suggested that a considerable number of women experience Post-Traumatic Stress Disorder (PTSD) as a result of their abortion experience (Bagarozzi, 1994). Within this view, Speckhard and Rue (1992) have proposed postabortion syndrome (PAS) as a subtype of PTSD that lies along a continuum of disorders between postabortion distress (PAD) and postabortion psychosis (PAP). Although these authors outline diagnostic criteria for PAS, their rationale does not provide sufficient support to warrant this being established as a distinct disorder, instead seeming only to offer abortion as one potential psychosocial stressor that may contribute to the development of PTSD. They go to some length to compare the criteria and course of PAS to those for PTSD, as described in the *Diagnostic and Statistical Manual of Mental Disorders, Third Edition, Revised* (*DSM-III-R*; American Psychiatric Association [APA], 1987). If their approach were to be operationalized, it would appear that a potentially endless number of stressor-specific diagnoses might replace the more general diagnostic category of PTSD. The variables cited as those predisposing women to PAS are essentially the same as those found in a number of abortion outcome studies (discussed following) to be among the negative mild to moderate psychological sequelae experienced by some women. Although proponents of PAS argue strongly that this abortion-induced disorder is not adequately diagnosed in clinical practice, no compelling scientific basis for its existence has yet been offered (David, 1994; Russo & Zierk, 1992). Instead, their assessment of abortion *decisions* as "maladaptive" appears to serve as the principal foundation for their work.

Regardless of whether postabortion syndrome is eventually demonstrated to be a valid psychiatric disorder, researchers and clinicians have consistently found that a minority of women who have had abortions meet with considerable emotional distress. As is later discussed, mental health professionals should not minimize or ignore such experiences, but rather should seek to understand them in order to intervene effectively on behalf of their clients.

Stress-and-Coping Perspective

In contrast to the view of abortion as a traumatic experience resulting in serious and widespread psychopathology is the more common perspective of both unwanted pregnancy and abortion as "potentially stressful life events, events that pose challenges and difficulties to the individual but do not necessarily lead to psychopathological outcomes. Rather, a range of possible responses, including growth and maturation as well as negative affect and psychopathology, can occur" (Adler et al., 1992, p. 1197). Often, such views also emphasize the relatively short duration of negative psychological sequelae that do not necessarily result in long-term, serious distress (Adler et al., 1992; Cohan, Dunkel-Schetter, & Lydon, 1993; Miller, 1992; Mueller & Major, 1989; Russo & Zierk, 1992). And frequently, significant improvement in psychological status has been cited following induced abortions (Adler, 1975; David, 1994; Lazarus, 1985; Osofsky & Osofsky, 1972). For example, Lazarus (1985) reported that 76% of his sample felt relieved, and Osofsky and Osofsky (1972) found that 65% experienced positive emotions immediately following induced abortion. (See Adler et al., 1992; and Dagg, 1991 for more extensive reviews.) This line of research has been cited as methodologically stronger than that supporting the view of abortion outcome as pathological (Wilmoth, de Alteriis, & Bussell, 1992), and generally supports the position that although most women feel some level of stress related to abortion, there is no evidence of a widespread, abortion-induced, psychological disorder (Adler et al., 1990; Koop, 1989; Russo & Zierk, 1992). When examined along with the psychopathology-supportive literature, however, this literature offers compelling documentation of the negative emotional impact that the resolution of an unwanted pregnancy through abortion can have for a *minority* of women and yields support for assessing women's reactions within a broader context of stress and coping.

Research equating abortion with other life stressors generally has been based on the work of Lazarus and Folkman (1984), emphasizing the roles of appraisal and coping in examining a woman's postabortion adjustment. From this perspective, a woman's response is influenced by her appraisal of the significance of the pregnancy and of abortion, appraisal of her personal and social coping resources, and her actual use of coping efforts (Major & Cozzarelli, 1992). Within this view, responses to unwanted pregnancy and abortion are comparable to those involved in confronting any stressful life event, and do not require any unique understanding or specialized therapeutic intervention. The following subsections review the circumstances surrounding abortion that have been suggested as risk factors for evaluating reactions of individual women and adolescents and discuss their implications for psychological intervention.

WHO RESPONDS NEGATIVELY TO ABORTION: IMPLICATIONS FOR MENTAL HEALTH PROFESSIONALS

Psychosocial and other factors identifying those at risk for negative emotional reactions following abortion have been outlined in several reviews of research findings (e.g., Adler, 1992; Adler et al., 1990; Dagg, 1991; Major & Cozzarelli, 1992). Rather than focus on the details of the research, we attempt to alert clinicians to findings that have implications for assessment and treatment. (For a more detailed discussion of the research, see Adler et al., 1992, Dagg, 1991, and Major & Cozarelli, 1992, and the specific studies discussed therein.) This discussion does not advocate any specific theoretical model of intervention, preferring instead to focus on circumstances and variables to which MHPs should attend while assisting clients contending with the impact of decisions about pregnancy and abortion. Although, as previously discussed, evidence of the psychological sequelae of abortion does not warrant a large scale, public health response (Koop, 1989), clinicians are generally more concerned with those individuals who in large studies may appear at the outer limits and beyond the range of the average participant. In the case of pregnancy and abortion, the women who walk into a therapist's office seeking assistance are likely to exhibit some combination of the following risk factors.

Demographic and Social Factors

Research has identified demographic and social circumstances associated with negative psychological sequelae following abortion. For example, younger, never-married women who do not have children (variables that may be correlated with one another) have been found to be at higher risk for problematic adjustment (Bracken, Hachamovitch, & Grossman, 1974; Adler, 1992). The quality of available social support and the woman's experience during the decision-making process also may be relevant factors.

Characteristics of the Pregnancy

Circumstances surrounding the pregnancy itself have also been noted as influential. Both the degree to which the pregnancy was wanted and the reasons for termination can affect a woman's emotional well-being. For example, women who wanted to have a child are more likely to be distressed by an abortion than those for whom the pregnancy was unwanted (Miller, 1992). In cases of therapeutic abortion (i.e., the pregnancy is terminated because of genetic defects or other medical complications), women generally experience more adverse reactions than when abortion occurs for psychological reasons (Adler, 1992; Dagg, 1991). The decision may be particularly difficult for a woman who chooses abortion for medical reasons but otherwise would have carried the pregnancy to term. When a pregnancy is wanted, a woman may experience the abortion as a loss. Congleton and Calhoun (1993) suggest that a lack of ability or opportunity to discuss such feelings may serve as a risk factor for negative adjustment, and they report that postabortion counseling that allows for expressing such feelings, grieving, and dealing with guilt fosters psychological relief. But are expression and grieving necessary?

With regard to coping with irrevocable loss, Wortman and Silver (1989) dispel a number of myths that MHPs may wish to reconsider when working with postabortion clients. For example, contrary to both popular belief and clinical lore: (a) although feelings of sadness and depressed mood may be common, universal distress and depression are not; (b) absence of grief is not necessarily problematic and does not necessarily result in delayed grief; (c) failure to "work through" the loss is not necessarily maladaptive, and early, intense effort to do so may actually be predictive of later difficulty; (d) no optimum length of time for recovery from loss has been identified; and (e) some individuals may not recover from loss or find satisfactory meaning in the experience (Wortman & Silver, 1989). Considering these research-based findings, clinicians may benefit from a reexamination of their own beliefs about abortion as loss and their expectations of client behavior.

The stage during the pregnancy during which the abortion took place also can affect a woman's reactions. Most abortions (approximately 90%; Henshaw, Koonin, & Smith, 1991) take place during the first trimester of the pregnancy and do not result in significant distress for most women. For those that take place during the second trimester, however, the situation appears to be quite different; many of these women experience greater levels of distress (e.g, Adler, 1975; Kaltreider, 1973). Clinicians should inquire not only about the length of gestation, but also about the reasons for waiting to terminate the pregnancy. For example, was the decision based on new medical information? Was the woman ambivalent about the pregnancy and therefore avoided making the decision for as long as possible? Did her relationship with her partner change? Did his level of support of the pregnancy change? Was she coerced into aborting a wanted pregnancy? Was an adolescent's delay due to compliance with state laws (e.g., a judicial bypass procedure) or concern about parental notification? Information about the length of gestation may provide clues to other factors that contribute to the woman's emotional experience.

Preexisting Emotional Difficulties

In addition to characteristics of the pregnancy, a woman's emotional well-being prior to pregnancy has been cited as an important factor in adjustment (Russo & Zierk, 1992). As such, postabortion reactions should be assessed within a broader context of prior style of coping with life stress, including the pregnancy, rather than in a context restricted to the abortion experience. For therapists, this point has important implications regardless of the point at which treatment might occur. For example, in working with a client who has recently learned that she is pregnant, assessment should address her usual ability to cope with stress, considering her likelihood of adjusting to her various choices, including motherhood, adoption, and abortion. Unfortunately, few studies have compared these three options as they relate to women's well-being when the pregnancy is unwanted. Those that have (e.g., Russo & Zierk, 1992; Zabin, Hirsch, & Emerson, 1989) suggest that adult and adolescent females who have abortions fare better psychologically than women who give birth and raise their children. For an adolescent, the decision to give birth and raise a child can affect multiple areas of her life, including physical and psychological health, educational attainment, subsequent economic status, marital dissolution, multiple pregnancies and births, and relationships with family members (for reviews see Coley & Chase-Lansdale, 1998, and Marecek, 1986). Thus, the stress associated with motherhood and the client's current emotional state should be considered in assisting her with decisions about an unwanted pregnancy.

For women seeking counseling *following* abortion, clinicians should also assess emotional status prior to pregnancy, even when postabortion adjustment has been identified as the presenting problem. Given that serious emotional reactions following abortion are not routine, knowledge of the psychological context of both the pregnancy and the abortion may contribute to a better understanding of poor adjustment. As previously discussed, considering abortion as comparable to other life stressors, evaluation for treatment need not follow any specialized abortion-related protocol.

Individual Coping

As with any potentially stressful event, a woman's coping style and skills influence her reactions to unwanted pregnancy and abortion. A considerable amount of research has examined the role of a woman's attribution for her pregnancy—that is, does she blame her pregnancy on some global aspect of her own character or personality (e.g., general irresponsibility), on a more specific, controllable behavior (e.g., failure to use birth control), on another person (e.g., her partner), on her situation at the time, or on chance? (See Major & Cozzarelli, 1992, for a summary.) In one study, 87% of women engaged in self-blame, particularly regarding some aspect of their own behavior that led to the pregnancy. Attributions that focus on controllable events, such as one's own behavior, are related to higher self-efficacy for coping and to positive adjustment. Conversely, blaming the pregnancy on one's own character, combined with low expectations for coping with the abortion, are related to poor adjustment, including depression (Mueller & Major, 1989). Although therapists may be tempted to focus on changing a woman's attributions, especially when she engages in characterological self-blame, research suggests that interventions designed to change negative expectations of how she will cope may have a stronger effect on emotional adjustment, particularly depression (Major & Cozzarelli, 1992; Major, Mueller, & Hildebrandt, 1985; Mueller & Major, 1989). Such an approach may be particularly effective when providing treatment prior to abortion and should be considered along with preabortion counseling that focuses on future choices and use of birth control.

Another aspect of coping—the use of approach/acceptance versus avoidance/ denial strategies—also has implications for therapeutic intervention (Cohen & Roth, 1984; Congleton & Calhoun, 1993). Approach strategies include "talking about [the abortion], thinking of ways to prevent it from happening again, . . . trying to deal with feelings about it," and taking appropriate action to ameliorate the situation. Avoidance strategies include "trying not to talk about the abortion, staying away from reminders of it, . . . avoiding letting oneself get upset about it when reminded," thus providing a way of modulating the degree of distress experienced at any given point (Cohen & Roth, 1984, p. 140). Cohen and Roth found that women undergoing abortion could not be classified exclusively as either "approachers" or "avoiders." Instead most women used both strategies, resulting in a combination coping style. Women who scored high on the avoidance or denial dimension, however, were more depressed and anxious following the abortion than those who scored low. Those who were high approachers experienced a significant decrease in anxiety shortly after the abortion, while low approachers did not. Thus, although women use both approach and avoidance strategies, and each is potentially useful in coping with stress, high reliance on avoidance does not decrease abortion distress over time. (See Major, Richards, Cooper, Cozzarelli, & Zubek, 1998, for similar findings.) Cohen and Roth (1984) suggest that matching counseling style to coping style may influence overall adjustment. For example, with high approachers, therapy that provides a great deal of information and an opportunity to discuss thoughts, feelings, and behavior may be more effective than the usual educational approach alone. Alternatively, for low approachers, the usual educational approach appears to have little impact on anxiety and may offer too much information at a point when they cannot take advantage of it. Thus, the timing of providing such information may need to be adjusted.

Decision-Making Context

Research has also addressed the relationship between postabortion adjustment and aspects of the decision-making context, including conflict related to a woman's own moral and religious beliefs, perceived social support, and social conflict related to the decision. Women who have difficulty making abortion decisions also tend to have greater difficulty with postabortion adjustment. (See Major & Cozzarelli, 1992, for a summary of relevant research.) Difficulty with decision making may be due to any of the situations just listed, as well as to numerous other risk factors (e.g., wanting a child or negative assessment of coping abilities). For a given client, individual risk factors can affect each other, sometimes compounding an already stressful experience. Three decision-related factors are discussed individually in the following, although they frequently coexist and influence each other.

Personal Beliefs.   Some women have difficulty making decisions about abortion (either elective or therapeutic) because of personal or religious beliefs. Such beliefs do not need to be strongly held to be influential. Conklin and O'Connor (1995) found that women who have had an abortion and only weakly endorsed the belief that a fetus is human scored lower on multiple measures of well-being, as compared to women with similar beliefs who have not had abortions and women who have had abortions but did not view the fetus as human. Thus, this discrepancy between attitude (i.e., the fetus is human) and behavior (i.e., having an abortion) may cause considerable distress for some clients.

Therapists, too, may have personal or religious beliefs regarding pregnancy and abortion—for example, the belief that abortion is morally wrong under any circumstances, or that abortion is the appropriate alternative for any pregnant adolescent. When such views have the potential to interfere with their ability to assist clients in making their own responsible, autonomous decisions, therapists should consider referring the client to another clinician or treatment setting, or making their views explicit to the client (Lindsay, 1997). (See Scott, 1986, for further discussion specific to counseling adolescents.)

Social Support.   To fully understand a woman's psychological response to abortion, Bracken et al. suggest that clinicians must consider the "social and interpersonal milieu in which the [abortion] decision was made" (1974, p. 155). Support seeking, as a coping strategy, generally has been found to be beneficial for women seeking abortion (Major & Cozzarelli, 1992; Major et al., 1998). For older women (ages 23 to 44), perceived support from male partners has been demonstrated to be more highly related to positive adjustment than support from parents, whereas for adolescents and younger women (ages 14 to 22), the reverse appears to be true (Bracken et al., 1974). But, Major et al. (1990) found that this relationship between support and adjustment may not be a simple one. Rather than observing a direct connection between perceived social support and postabortion emotional adjustment, they concluded that perceived social support from significant others serves as a resource that affects a woman's appraisal of her own ability to cope, which in turn affects her emotional well-being.

Effective counseling will assist a woman in appraising and enhancing her ability to cope with both emotional and practical issues related to the abortion. Research findings (e.g., Major et al., 1990; Major et al., 1998) suggest that improved self-efficacy will result in more positive coping. But, given research findings of the positive relationship between social support and postabortion adjustment, what role should counseling play in encouraging a woman to seek support when deciding about an unwanted pregnancy? This issue may be understood more fully by examining social conflict, another component of the decision-making context.

Social Conflict.   Although most women faced with decisions about pregnancy receive high levels of support when they seek it, a minority of women do not. Instead, they may experience a lack of support, direct conflict, or coercion either to have an abortion or to continue with the pregnancy. Women who perceive those whom they tell as being nonsupportive have poorer emotional adjustment, especially depression, than those who do not tell anyone and those who tell but perceive others as being supportive (Major et al., 1990; Major et al., 1998; also see Major & Cozzarelli, 1992, for a summary). Thus, simply consulting others does not guarantee positive support. In some cases, social contact can serve as an additional source of stress for women considering abortion, resulting in poorer outcomes than if they had not sought support (Major et al., 1990).

Given research findings about the potential benefits of social support and the negative effects of social conflict, how should therapists proceed? Clearly, not all close social contacts are created equal in providing needed support. Rather than offering any wholesale advice about the value of social support, therapists should encourage clients to assess potential sources for their availability and likelihood of offering positive support. In some cases, not confiding in a partner or particular family members may be the wisest choice for promoting a woman's emotional well-being. Whether or not to seek assistance, and from whom to seek it, are questions that should be addressed on an individual basis with clients.

Special Issues in Treatment of Adolescents. Questions regarding social support and social conflict can take on a legal twist when counseling adolescents. As previously noted, MHPs must be familiar with the relevant laws (e.g., parental notification and consent), referrals for legal counsel, and referrals for medical care (including abortion) in the jurisdictions in which they practice (Scott, 1986). Regardless of whether parental notification or consent is required, clinicians must assess the likelihood that an adolescent client will receive parental support. Thus, both legal and interpersonal factors should guide intervention (Scott, 1986). Involvement of parents may undermine a young woman's ability to cope with her decision and subsequent adjustment when she perceives them to be unsupportive, or likely to insist upon a particular resolution of the pregnancy (Major et al., 1990). Conversely, young women who receive support from their parents for their decision making (especially when such support is not accompanied by any opposition) fare better in adjusting to their choice (Bracken et al., 1974). In this regard, clinicians might be more objective than adolescents in assessing the degree of parental support, especially in the face of such an important personal, medical, and legal decision.

Coupled with a therapist's clinical interest in enhancing a client's social support is an ethical interest in protecting her from undue coercion in deciding about her pregnancy. An adolescent may experience pressure either for or against abortion from her parents, as well as from the putative father. Practitioners can assist a client in considering her alternatives and making a carefully deliberated choice, thus supporting both legal and clinical concerns. Legally, consent for abortion requires that the choice be made voluntarily; clinically, "consent" involves both a psychological need for autonomy and a developmental need to accept responsibility for choices made. (See Scott, 1986, for further discussion.) Thus, legal and clinical goals go hand in hand.

Related to the question of parental supportiveness is that of the legality of providing counseling in the absence of parental knowledge and consent. Although minors legally can seek medical and psychological treatment independently in some jurisdictions for some purposes (e.g., contraception, pregnancy, sexual abuse, sexually transmitted diseases, and substance abuse; Gustafson & McNamara, 1987), this may not extend to pregnancy-related counseling that takes place in settings other than family planning clinics. Thus, clinicians in other settings, including schools, should consult state laws to determine if such treatment can be undertaken without parental permission and must address the issue of parental consent with minor clients (e.g., see Corrao & Melton, 1988; Jacob-Timm & Hartshorne, 1998). Clinicians should also bear in mind that even in states in which minors have a legal right to consent to abortion, they may not have a similar legal right to consent to mental health treatment (Scott, 1986).

Related to parental support and involvement is the legal protection of the confidentiality of any therapeutic relationship with a minor client (Jacob-Timm & Hartshorne, 1998; Scott, 1986). Confidentiality is held as a "universal ethical concept in mental health" and is incorporated into the ethical codes of all mental health professional organizations in the United States (Swenson, 1993) and may also be governed by state law in some cases. Special considerations may apply to all therapeutic relationships with minors, but assume a special urgency related to the timing of a young woman's decision about abortion. For example, therapists should assess the advisability of involving a client's parents even if she can legally seek treatment independently, considering the practical and emotional support that may be gained. In some jurisdictions, and in some treatment settings, parents may have access to their children's mental health records even when their consent to treatment is not required (Scott, 1986). Therapists should consult the ethical codes of their professional organization, relevant state statutes, and guidelines for addressing the meaning and limits of confidentiality (e.g., Gustafson & McNamara, 1987; Taylor & Adelman, 1989) before beginning therapeutic intervention with minor clients. They also should be prepared to address issues of confidentiality directly with clients, including any weighing of a minor's interest in receiving timely treatment against parents' interest in overseeing the care of their children (Pagliocca, Melton, Weisz, & Lyons, 1995).

Postabortion Factors

Much of the research reviewed in the preceding has examined women's reactions either immediately following the abortion procedure or after only a few weeks or months. The limited research that has evaluated emotional adjustment to the abortion after a relatively long period (e.g., 8 years, Russo & Zierk, 1992; 2 years, Zabin et al., 1989) has demonstrated that adults and adolescents who had abortions continue to be better adjusted in terms of educational attainment, economic status, and psychological well-being, in comparison to their counterparts who either gave birth or were not pregnant. In both studies, the negative long-term adjustment experienced by a small number of abortion participants was attributed to subsequent unwanted pregnancies, rather than to the abortion itself. Russo and Zierk (1992) stress the importance of focusing therapeutic efforts on preventing future unwanted pregnancy through accurate information about contraception and "education and career development programs for young women that enhance self-esteem and increase access to coping resources associated with employment and income" (p. 278). These recommendations are consistent with others that seek to strengthen a woman's sense of self-efficacy and control, as previously discussed, and suggest a role for clinicians beyond the therapy office, including program development in schools and other community settings.

Findings of these long-term studies support the observation that women generally do not experience negative psychological sequelae associated with abortion. It has been suggested, however, that over time, some women may reexamine their earlier abortion experience in light of subsequent life events (Major & Cozzarelli, 1992). For example, Lemkau (1988) suggested that later difficulty becoming pregnant or loss of a child may lead a woman to attribute the cause to an earlier abortion. Likewise, Congleton and Calhoun (1993) speculated that later changes in beliefs about the fetus or about the morality of abortion (related to change in religious affiliation) may lead a woman to reconstruct her earlier experience. Despite such accounts, therapists should be mindful that the limited, existing research does not support such attributions.

SUMMARY AND RECOMMENDATIONS

Although abortion rates have been declining for nearly a decade, abortion remains a common procedure for many women in the United States. It is not known what percentage of women who seek therapy have previously undergone an abortion or are deciding whether to terminate a pregnancy. However, it is likely that at some point in their clinical practice, most therapists will provide mental health services to a woman prior to, during, or following a pregnancy that results in an abortion.

In order to assist women who may be grappling with a pregnancy decision, it is critical that clinicians understand the legal landscape in which such decisions must be made. As noted, there are numerous state and federal restrictions on the conditions under which a woman may obtain an abortion. These restrictions not only vary significantly across states, but also change with some regularity (particularly in regard to conditions under which minors may obtain abortion). Although this chapter provides a summary of current law, clinicians are encouraged to consult their local professional associations or family planning organizations about specific laws in their state.

In order to support a woman in making a pregnancy decision or adjusting to its aftermath, practitioners also should familiarize themselves with relevant research and clinical literature. As intimated throughout this chapter, however, psychological counseling related to pregnancy and abortion need not involve any specialized techniques. Rather, as with any identified psychosocial problem for which an individual seeks treatment, intervention should be guided by sound theoretical and empirical findings, thorough assessment and understanding of the specific client, professional ethical codes and standards, and laws governing clinical practice. This chapter discusses all of these as they relate to decision making and emotional adjustment in the realm of pregnancy and abortion.

Abortion is a highly charged topic that brings to the fore strong personal, moral, and religious beliefs—for both client and therapist. Clinicians who do not feel comfortable discussing such issues with clients or who believe that their personal views (whether prolife or prochoice) may unduly influence treatment have an ethical obligation to refer clients to sources that can provide appropriate treatment.

NOTES

1. The terms *mental health professional* (MHP), *counselor, clinician,* and *therapist* are used interchangeably and do not refer to any particular professional discipline. Likewise, the terms *counseling* and *therapy* are used generically to refer to mental health treatment.

2. To obtain current information about the status of state laws concerning abortion, clinicians are encouraged to contact the following organizations: the Alan Guttmacher Institute, www.agi-usa.org; or Planned Parenthood of America, www.plannedparenthood.org.

3. Currently, such laws are in effect in 20 states: Alaska, California, Connecticut, Idaho, Indiana, Kansas, Louisiana, Maine, Minnesota, Mississippi, Nebraska, Nevada, North Dakota, Ohio, Pennsylvania, Rhode Island, South Carolina, South Dakota, Utah, and Virginia (Alan Guttmacher Institute, 1998).

4. The following states have mandatory waiting periods coupled with informed-consent laws: Idaho (24 hours), Indiana (18 hours), Kansas (24 hours), Louisiana (24 hours), Mississippi (24 hours), Nebraska (24 hours), North Dakota (24 hours), Ohio (24 hours), Pennsylvania (24 hours), South Carolina (1 hour), South Dakota (24 hours), and Utah (24 hours; Alan Guttmacher Institute, 1998).

5. Currently, 15 states require a parent's consent for a minor to obtain an abortion: Alabama, Indiana, Kentucky, Louisiana, Massachusetts, Michigan, Mississippi, Missouri, North Carolina, North Dakota, Pennsylvania, Rhode Island, South Carolina, Wisconsin, and Wyoming.

6. Currently, 14 states require parental notification for a minor to obtain an abortion: Arkansas, Delaware, Georgia, Idaho, Iowa, Kansas, Maryland, Minnesota, Nebraska, Ohio, South Dakota, Utah, Virginia, and West Virginia.

REFERENCES

Adler, N. E. (1975). Emotional responses of women following therapeutic abortion. *American Journal of Orthopsychiatry, 45,* 446–454.

Adler, N. E. (1989). *The medical and psychological aspects of abortion on women.* Testimony on behalf of the American Psychological Association before the Subcommittee on Human Resources and Intergovernmental Relations. Committee on Government Operations, 101st Congress, 1st session, March 16, 1989.

Adler, N. E. (1992). Unwanted pregnancy and abortion: Definitional and research issues. *Journal of Social Issues, 48,* 19–35.

Adler, N. E., David, H. P., Major, B. N., Roth, S. H., Russo, N. F., & Wyatt, G. E. (1990). Psychological responses after abortion. *Science, 248,* 41–44.

Adler, N. E., David, H. P., Major, B. N., Roth, S. H., Russo, N. F., & Wyatt, G. E. (1992). Psychological factors in abortion: A review. *American Psychologist, 47,* 1194–1204.

Alan Guttmacher Institute (1997a, February 7). CDC data show drop in abortion. *Washington Memo,* 1.

Alan Guttmacher Institute (1997b). *Issues in brief: Late-term abortions: Legal considerations.* New York: Author.

Alan Guttmacher Institute (1997c). States rush to prohibit later-term abortion method. Internet: 206.215.210.6/pubs/journals/SRHM039703.html.

Alan Guttmacher Institute (1998, February). *The status of major abortion-related laws in the states.* New York: Author.

American Psychiatric Association. (1987). *Diagnostic and statistical manual of mental disorders* (3rd ed., rev.). Washington, DC: Author.

Ashton, J. R. (1980). Patterns of discussion and decision-making amongst abortion patients. *Journal of Biosocial Science, 12,* 247–259.

Bagarozzi, D. A. (1994). Identification, assessment and treatment of women suffering from post traumatic stress after abortion. *Journal of Family Psychotherapy, 5,* 25–54.

Bellotti v. Baird (1979), 443 U.S. 622.

Berenson, A. B., SanMiguel, V. V., & Wilkinson, G. S. (1992). Prevalence of physical and sexual assault in pregnant adolescents. *Journal of Adolescent Health, 13,* 466–469.

Bracken, M. B., Hachamovitch, M., & Grossman, G. (1974). The decision to abort and psychological sequelae. *The Journal of Nervous and Mental Disease, 158,* 154–162.

Bracken, M. B., Klerman, L. V., & Bracken, M. (1978). Abortion, adoption, or motherhood: An empirical study of decision-making during pregnancy. *American Journal of Obstetrics and Gynecology, 130,* 251–262.

Bullis, R. K. (1991). "Gag rules" and chastity clauses: Legal and ethical consequences of Title X and AFLA for professionals in human sexuality. *Journal of Sex Education and Therapy, 17,* 91–102.

City of Akron v. Akron Center for Reproductive Health (1983), 462 U.S. 416.

Cohan, L. C., Dunkel-Schetter, C., & Lydon, J. (1993). Pregnancy decision making: Predictors of early stress and adjustment. *Psychology of Women Quarterly, 17,* 223–239.

Cohen, L., & Roth, S. (1984). Coping with abortion. *Journal of Human Stress, 10,* 140–145.

Coley, R. L., & Chase-Lansdale, P. L. (1998). Adolescent pregnancy and parenthood: Recent evidence and future directions. *American Psychologist, 53,* 152–166.

Congleton, G. K., & Calhoun, L. G. (1993). Post-abortion perceptions: A comparison of self-identified distressed and nondistressed populations. *International Journal of Social Psychiatry, 30,* 255–265.

Conklin, M. P., & O'Connor, B. P. (1995). Beliefs about the fetus as a moderator of post-abortion psychological well-being. *Journal of Social and Clinical Psychology, 14,* 76–95.

Corrao, J., & Melton, G. B. (1988). Legal issues in school-based behavior therapy. In J. C. Witt, S. N. Elliot, & F. M. Gresham (Eds.), *Handbook of behavior therapy in education* (pp. 377–399). New York: Plenum Press.

Dagg, P. K. B. (1991). The psychological sequelae of therapeutic abortion—Denied and completed. *American Journal of Psychiatry, 148,* 578–585.

David, H. P. (1994). Reproductive rights and reproductive behavior: Clash or convergence of private values and public policies. *American Psychologist, 49,* 343–349.

Doe v. Bolton (1973), 410 U.S. 179.

Eisen, M., Zellman, G. L., Leibowitz, A., Chow, K., & Evans, J. R. (1983). Factors discriminating pregnancy resolution decisions of unmarried adolescents. *Genetic Psychology Monographs, 108,* 271–273.

Finken, L. L., & Jacobs, J. E. (1996). Consultant choice across decision contexts: Are abortion decisions different? *Journal of Adolescent Research, 11,* 235–260.

Griffin-Carlson, M. S., & Mackin, K. J. (1993). Parental consent: Factors influencing adolescent disclosure regarding abortion. *Adolescence, 28,* 1–11.

Gustafson, K. E., & McNamara, J. R. (1987). Confidentiality with minor clients: Issues and guidelines for therapists. *Professional Psychology: Research and Practice, 18,* 503–508.

Harris v. McRae (1980), 448 U.S. 297.

Henshaw, S. K. (1997). Teenage abortion and pregnancy statistics by state, 1992. *Family Planning Perspectives, 29,* 115–122.

Henshaw, S. K. (1998). Abortion incidence and services in the United States, 1995–1996. *Family Planning Perspectives, 30,* 263–270, 287.

Henshaw, S., Koonin, L. M., & Smith, J. C. (1991). Characteristics of women having abortions, 1987. *Family Planning Perspectives, 27,* 54–59.

Henshaw, S. K., & Kost, K. (1996). Abortion patients in 1994–1995: Characteristics and contraceptive use. *Family Planning Perspectives, 28,* 140–147, 158.

H. L. v. Matheson (1981), 450 U.S. 398.

Hodgson v. Minnesota (1990), 497 U.S. 417.

Jacob-Timm, S., & Hartshorne, T. S. (1998). *Ethics and law for school psychologists* (3rd ed.). New York: John Wiley & Sons.

Kaltreider, N. B. (1973). Psychological factors in mid-trimester abortions. *Psychological Medicine, 4,* 129–134.

Koop, C. E. (1989, December 11). *The federal role in determining the medical and psychological impact of abortion on women* (H. R. 101-392). Washington, DC: U.S. Government Printing Office.

Lazarus, A. (1985). Psychiatric sequelae of legalized first trimester abortion. *Journal of Psychosomatic Obstetrics and Gynecology, 4,* 141–150.

Lazarus, R., & Folkman, S. (1984). *Stress, appraisal, and coping.* New York: Springer.

Lemkau, J. P. (1988). Emotional sequelae of abortion. *Psychology of Women Quarterly, 12,* 461–472.

Lewis, C. C. (1980). A comparison of minors' and adults' pregnancy decisions. *American Journal of Orthopsychiatry, 50,* 446–453.

Limber, S. P. (1992). Parental notification in cases of adolescent abortion: Parental consultation and the effects of parental influence upon adolescents' pregnancy decisions. Unpublished doctoral dissertation, University of Nebraska—Lincoln.

Lindsay, J. W. (1997). Crisis counseling with pregnant teens. In T. N. Fairchild (Ed.), *Crisis intervention strategies for school-based helpers* (pp. 370–398). Springfield, IL: Charles C. Thomas.

Major, B., & Cozzarelli, C. (1992). Psychosocial predictors of adjustment to abortion. *Journal of Social Issues, 48,* 121–142.

Major, B., Cozzarelli, C., Sciacchitano, A. M., Cooper, M. L., Testa, M., & Mueller, P. M. (1990). Perceived social support, self-efficacy, and adjustment to abortion. *Journal of Personality and Social Psychology, 59,* 452–463.

Major, B., Mueller, P., & Hildebrandt, K. (1985). Attributions, expectations and coping with abortion. *Journal of Personality and Social Psychology, 48,* 585–599.

Major, B., Richards, C., Cooper, M. L., Cozzarelli, C., & Zubek, J. (1998). Personal resilience, cognitive appraisals, and coping: An integrative model of adjustment to abortion. *Journal of Personality and Social Psychology, 74,* 735–752.

Marecek, J. (1986). Consequences of adolescent childbearing and abortion. In G. B. Melton (Ed.), *Adolescent abortion: Psychological and legal issues* (pp. 96–115). Lincoln, NE: University of Nebraska Press.

McAll, K., & Wilson, W. P. (1987). Ritual mourning for unresolved grief after abortion. *Southern Medical Journal, 80,* 817–821.

Melton, G. B., & Pliner, A. J. (1986). Adolescent abortion: A psycholegal analysis. In G. B. Melton (Ed.), *Adolescent abortion: Psychological and legal issues* (pp. 1–39). Lincoln, NE: University of Nebraska Press.

Merz, J. F., Jackson, C. A., & Klerman, J. A. (1995). A review of abortion policy: Legality, Medicaid funding, and parental involvement, 1967–1994. *Women's Rights Law Reporter, 17,* 1–61.

Miller, W. B. (1992). An empirical study of the psychological antecedents and consequences of induced abortion. *Journal of Social Issues, 48,* 67–93.

Mueller, P., & Major, B. (1989). Self-blame, self-efficacy, and adjustment to abortion. *Journal of Personality and Social Psychology, 57,* 1059–1068.

National Abortion and Reproductive Rights Action League (1997). *Who decides? A state-by-state review of abortion and reproductive rights.* Washington, DC: National Abortion and Reproductive Rights Action League Foundation.

Ohio v. Akron Center for Reproductive Health (1990), 497 U.S. 502.

Osofsky, J. D., & Osofsky, H. (1972). The psychological reaction of patients to legalized abortion. *American Journal of Orthopsychiatry, 42,* 48–60.

Pagliocca, P. M., Melton, G. B., Weisz, V., & Lyons, P. M., Jr. (1995). Parenting and the law. In M. H. Bornstein (Ed.), *Handbook of parenting. Vol. 3: Status and social conditions of parenting* (pp. 437–457). Mahwah, NJ: Erlbaum.

Planned Parenthood Association of Kansas City, Missouri v. Ashcroft (1983), 462 U.S. 476.

Planned Parenthood of Central Missouri v. Danforth (1976), 428 U.S. 52.

Planned Parenthood Federation of America (1994). *Medicaid funding for abortion.* New York: Author.

Planned Parenthood of Southeastern Pennsylvania v. Casey (1992), 505 U.S. 833.

Plutzer, E., & Ryan, B. (1987). Notifying husbands about an abortion: An empirical look at constitutional and policy dilemmas. *Sociology and Science Research, 71,* 183–189.

Resnick, M. D., Bearinger, L. H., Stark, P., & Blum, R. W. (1994). Patterns of consultation among adolescent minors obtaining an abortion. *American Journal of Orthopsychiatry, 64,* 310–316.

Roe v. Wade (1973), 410 U.S. 113.

Rosen, R. H. (1980). Adolescent pregnancy decision-making: Are parents important? *Adolescence, 15,* 43–54.

Russo, N. F., Horn, J. D., & Schwartz, R. (1992). U.S. abortion in context: Selected characteristics and motivations of women seeking abortions. *Journal of Social Issues, 48,* 183–202.

Russo, N. F., & Zierk, K. L. (1992). Abortion, childbearing, and women's well-being. *Professional Psychology: Research and Practice, 23,* 269–280.

Rust v. Sullivan (1991), 500 U.S. 173.

Ryan, B., & Plutzer, E. (1989). When married women have abortions: Spousal notification and marital interaction. *Journal of Marriage and the Family, 51,* 41–50.

Scott, E. S. (1986). Legal and ethical issues in counseling pregnant adolescents. In G. B. Melton (Ed.), *Adolescent abortion: Psychological and legal issues* (pp. 116–137). Lincoln, NE: University of Nebraska Press.

Smith, H. W., & Kronauge, C. (1990). The politics of abortion: Husband notification legislation, self-disclosure, and marital bargaining. *Sociological Quarterly, 31,* 585–598.

Sollom, T. (1997). State actions on reproductive health issues in 1996. *Family Planning Perspectives, 29,* 35–40.

Speckhard, A. C. (1987). *The psycho-social aspects of stress following abortion.* Kansas City, MO: Sheed & Ward.

Speckhard, A. C., & Rue, V. M. (1992). Postabortion Syndrome: An emerging public health concern. *Journal of Social Issues, 48,* 95–119.

Swenson, L. C. (1993). *Psychology and law for the helping professions.* Pacific Grove, CA: Brooks/Cole Publishing.

Taylor, L., & Adelman, H. S. (1989). Reframing the confidentiality dilemma to work in children's best interests. *Professional Psychology: Research and Practice, 20,* 79–83.

Thornburgh v. American College of Obstetricians and Gynecologists (1986), 476 U.S. 747.

Torres, A., & Forrest, J. D. (1988). Why do women have abortions? *Family Planning Perspectives, 20,* 169–176.

Torres, A., Forrest, J. D., & Eisman, S. (1980). Telling parents: Clinic policies and adolescents' use of family planning and abortion services. *Family Planning Perspectives, 12,* 284–292.

Wilmoth, G. H., de Alteriis, M., & Bussell, D. (1992). Prevalence of psychological risks following legal abortion in the U.S.: Limits of the evidence. *Journal of Social Issues, 48,* 37–66.

Wortman, C. B., & Silver, R. C. (1989). The myths of coping with loss. *Journal of Consulting and Clinical Psychology, 57,* 349–357.

Zabin, L. S., Hirsch, M. B., & Emerson, M. R. (1989). When urban adolescents choose abortion: Effects on education, psychological status and subsequent pregnancy. *Family Planning Perspectives, 21,* 248–255.

CHAPTER 9

Legal and Psychological Issues Confronting Lesbian, Bisexual, and Gay Couples and Families

KEVIN T. KUEHLWEIN and DEBORAH I. GOTTSCHALK

THIS CHAPTER enumerates some of the legal issues facing same-sex couples and families, and explores the interface between these legal and psychological issues. Suggestions for therapists working with lesbian, bisexual, or gay clients likely to be affected by these problems are offered. (Note that throughout this chapter, the terms *lesbian, gay,* and *same-sex* are used interchangeably.) The legal issues discussed apply equally to bisexual persons when they are in a same-sex relationship. Anyone can experience discrimination in housing, employment, or public accommodations because of actual or perceived sexual orientation. Therefore, these issues may apply to some heterosexual clients as well.

OVERVIEW

One of the most upsetting and unsettling experiences about being a lesbian, gay, or bisexual person in the United States today is that their experiences are often disqualified, misunderstood, or ignored by the larger heterosexual society. Segal (1996) relates a good example:

> The next question [on the questionnaire] was "what relationship is that person to me?" That question always gets me since Tony and I really don't like any of the titles society has to offer. . . . As I was pondering this issue, the man took pity on me and said that there was a list of possible titles to choose from. So we looked at the list. It was a whopping three-columns long . . . but nothing that depicted a relationship consisting of two people of the same sex. I found myself getting angry—angry at the arrogance to just ignore our relationships as though they didn't exist. . . . Then I asked him if he ever had to fill out forms like these and how he'd feel if the forms made him feel as though his relationship was second class. He told me that he understood

where I was coming from, but that he only takes down the information. "By the way, how long have you been married?" I asked him. "Eight years," he replied. "You?" he asked. "Almost 16 years," I said. He just nodded.

Same-sex love for each other is delegitimized in a variety of ways. Society often denies, dismisses, or disallows other experiences that are remarkably similar if not sometimes identical to those of heterosexuals (e.g., the desire to be a parent, raising a child, and maintaining an intimate, partnered relationship). Indeed, the current language itself makes it awkward to adequately describe two equal, same-sex parents (e.g., the "non–birth mother," the "biological father"). The larger heterosexual society and its language proscribe, distort, or limit key aspects of lesbian and gay experiences, probably because the realities of lesbian and gay life challenge and enlarge traditional ideas along several important axes: What is a family? What are the appropriate roles of the sexes in society? What is love? Who can and should raise children?

The inability of heterosexual society to adequately understand and fully accommodate to the realities of lesbian and gay life means that this experience frequently is legally unprotected. Legally, therefore, same-sex couples and families do not enjoy rights equal to those of heterosexuals in key areas because existing laws do not cover their experiences. Moreover, because few heterosexuals are fully aware of society's institutionalized dislike of lesbians, bisexuals, and gays, they rarely realize and fully sympathize with sexual minorities' serious lack of rights. They also fail to appreciate the very real economic and psychological implications for both same-sex couples and their families (here the term, *families* is used to mean couples who have any children). For example, discrimination on the basis of sexual orientation is illegal in 9 states, Washington, DC, and about 200 municipalities across the United States. This means, however, that in the vast majority of the country it is still *entirely legal* to reject an applicant for a job or an apartment for which he or she is otherwise qualified solely because of the person's sexual orientation (American Civil Liberties Union [ACLU], 1996). As the ACLU notes, without this basic protection from discrimination, gays and lesbians do not have "that basic right to be equal participants in the communities in which they live" (1996, p. 3).

LEGAL PROBLEMS

Gay men and lesbians do not have most of the basic legal rights that most people in the United States take for granted (Monahan, Facciolo, Bhaya, & Gottschalk, 1997). Perhaps most important, same-sex couples are not permitted to marry under civil laws. This leaves same-sex families without a host of related protections, especially in the areas of child custody, support, domestic violence, health benefits, foreign partner immigration, taxes, and inheritance. There is also no common-law right to sue accorded same-sex partners in case of the injury or death of the other partner (Berzon, 1988). Second, national laws that prohibit discrimination in housing, public accommodations, and employment do not include sexual orientation as a protected category. Third, sodomy statutes in 19 states make most lesbian and gay people technically criminals if they express their love in normal, physical ways. Central to the thesis of this chapter, these sodomy laws are used to justify discrimination against lesbians and gays in employment and cus- tody situations (Rubenstein, 1995; Rivera, 1987).

Some of the legal protections that civil marriage and antidiscrimination laws afford—unavailable to lesbians and gay men—are especially poignant when one partner in a relationship suffers a debilitating illness (e.g., AIDS or cancer) or acci- dent. A variety of federal and state laws protect people with disabilities from dis- crimination. This may or may not help a lesbian or gay man facing discrimination on the job or in obtaining medical services. For example, an HIV-positive gay man will be protected from or have recourse if discriminated against in employment because of his illness. However, he is protected from actions taken by his employer due only to his illness. Absent local laws or protective employer policies, his boss can still fire him for being gay.

Because of the absence of civil same-sex marriage, furthermore, the sick per- son's same-sex partner often cannot take time off from work to care for him or her. The recently passed Family and Medical Leave Act does not, unfortunately, cover lesbian and gay families. In asking for time off, well partners may therefore face the thorny decision of whether to disclose their sexual orientation to a potentially hostile employer. Finally, same-sex couples are rarely covered by bereavement leave policies.

The Sharon Kowalski case is a clear example of the trauma that can ensue with- out same-sex marriage provisions (Curry, Clifford, & Leonard, 1996). She and her partner, Karen Thompson, lived together for 4 years in a clearly spousal relation- ship. Yet after a bad auto crash in 1988, Sharon was left with severe brain injuries, unable to speak. Thompson wanted to nurse Sharon at home, but Sharon's parents placed her in a nursing home and prevented contact between the two partners. Following a painful, almost 10-year legal battle, Thompson was finally permitted to bring her lover home.

SAME-SEX MARRIAGE

In recent years the concept of same-sex marriage has become a topic of public debate. Although many religious denominations increasingly allow and perform same-sex unions, these relationships are not recognized under civil law as are heterosexual marriages. Civil marriage creates a legal relationship automatically affording each partner property rights, inheritance rights, child support and visi- tation rights, the ability to make medical decisions about the care of the partner, the ability to seek a protection from abuse order, and alimony rights. Many employers recognize civil marriages for purposes of health insurance, life insur- ance, pension plans, and family leave policies. Civil marriage is also recognized by the federal government for the purposes of filing joint income tax returns and obtaining social security benefits. It therefore represents far more than simple legal recognition of the couple's commitment to each other, but comes with a host of other important related rights and privileges.

The idea of civil recognition of same-sex marriages became a potential legal reality because of the success of a lawsuit filed in Hawaii in 1991. This case, *Baehr v. Miike* (1996), is based upon sex discrimination protections in the Hawaii Constitution. Although there has been no final determination by the Hawaii Supreme Court that same-sex marriages must be allowed in Hawaii, the case has had and could still have a tremendous impact on the rest of the country. Under the "full faith and credit" clause of the U.S. Constitution, each state is required to recognize all contracts, including marriages, that are validly created in another state.

In response to the possibility that same-sex marriages will become legal in Hawaii or any other state, the federal government and many worried state legislatures have enacted preemptive bills. These prohibit the recognition of same-sex marriages, even if those marriages are legal in the state where they were performed. The 1996 federal law prohibiting the recognition of same-sex marriages, the Defense of Marriage Act, stipulates that same-sex marriages will not be recognized by the federal government for purposes of joint income tax filing, social security, or immigration (Anders, 1999).

Domestic Partnership

The concept of *domestic partnership* has emerged from the same-sex marriage debate. What domestic partnership is exactly depends upon the definition in the law or policy that creates the domestic partnership. For example, an employer's domestic partnership policy may grant employees' same-sex partners equal rights to the same health benefits and medical and bereavement leave policies that heterosexual spouses enjoy. Alternatively, a governmental entity can create a mechanism to register domestic partnerships and provide to registered partners such rights as hospital visitation, the ability to make medical decisions on behalf of an incapacitated partner, inheritance rights, property rights, and child custody and support rights. How domestic partnership benefits compare to the rights enjoyed by heterosexual married couples depends on the individual situation, but the result for the same-sex couple is usually a piecemeal approach that, at best, does not provide full parity.

Legal Implications of the Ban on Same-Sex Marriage

Because neither gay men nor lesbians can marry in the United States and because very few have access to any sort of domestic partnership policy through the workplace, their families have no *automatic* legal protections. This leads to a host of potential economic, psychological, and practical problems throughout their relationships and after they end, either by the death of one partner or by dissolution. Many of the monetary penalties amount to a substantial de facto tax on lesbian and gay families with two-woman households being especially economically disadvantaged (McCandlish, 1987; see Table 9.1 for a summary of these economic burdens). In addition, unless the children are adopted by the second parent, he or she has no authority to act on their behalf (e.g., authorizing necessary medical procedures) and no parental claims to the children if the biological parent dies or dissolves the relationship.

Given these negative social, vocational, and economic implications, it is a significant sign of commitment when two men, and even more so, two women, form a same-sex union.

Table 9.1   Monetary Penalties for Same-Sex Couples and Families Compared to Heterosexual Counterparts

- Greater taxes during life via inability to file joint income tax
- Greater taxes to surviving spouse in partner's death
- No access to Social Security benefits in partner's death
- Domestic partnership benefits, where available, taxed
- Higher health insurance premiums because partners and children not covered under each other's health plans
- Higher auto insurance premiums because partners not covered under each other's plans
- Loss of partner's pension money after death of partner
- Greater lawyer fees and court costs to retain custody or visitation of the children (if any) from a prior heterosexual marriage
- Additional legal fees for consulting lawyers to draw up extra documents clarifying and protecting the relationship
- Additional expenses to retain control of jointly purchased property after one partner's death
- Less likely to advance as far professionally due to inability to socialize as expected with coworkers if closeted

Lesbian and Gay Parenting Issues

Six to seven and a half million children in the United States live with at least one gay or lesbian parent (Blau, 1996; Rivera, 1987). Many of these children were born in heterosexual unions that later terminated because one or both spouses realized their same-sex orientation (see Schwartz & Kaslow, 1997). In fact, both Masters and Johnson (1979) and the more extensive Bell and Weinberg (1978) studies on homosexuality found that approximately one-fourth of their sample participants had previously been married. Often gay and lesbian parents faced with divorce and custody battles have legitimate fears that their sexual orientation will be used against them by their former spouses to limit custody and visitation (Rivera, 1987). The mere presence of same-sex orientation can legally disqualify someone as an adequate parent (Rubenstein, 1995). Because court battles can be so expensive, lesbian and gay parents sometimes acquiesce to more of their ex-spouses' demands than they would otherwise need to, so as to avoid litigation. Nationally, there have been several well-publicized cases in which a gay man or lesbian has lost custody to objectively less fit and more distant relatives solely because of his or her sexual orientation. One such case is *Bottoms v. Bottoms* (1995).

Sometimes gay and lesbian parents are denied overnight visits with their children or visitation when a same-sex partner is present, although unmarried heterosexual couples rarely need to meet these conditions. This places the same-sex couple under much higher scrutiny than the heterosexual ex-spouse. It is worth noting that original child custody decisions are seldom appealed because the legal standards for doing so are rather high and because these types of trials are especially costly when gay and lesbian parents can find the rare lawyer who will take this type of case (Rivera, 1987).

Even if the gay or lesbian parent retains custody and enters into a new long-term relationship, potential legal problems remain. These problems are identical for children who have been conceived through artificial insemination (Pies, 1987). Unless the same-sex couple lives in a jurisdiction that allows coparent adoptions, the nonbiological parent will always be a legal stranger to the child. (A *coparent adoption* is one in which the nonbiological parent of the child adopts the child and becomes a parent with equal standing to the biological parent.) Without coparent status, the nonbiological parent has no right to custody or visitation of the child if the relationship breaks up or the biological parent dies. The child's blood relatives, who may be actual strangers to the child, can then intervene and can move the child out of state as well as deny visitation to the nonbiological parent, a crushing event for any parent.

Even with both parents alive and the relationship intact, the gay family faces obstacles that a heterosexual family does not. Like the same-sex spouse, the child has no claim to the nonbiological parent's health insurance or inheritance in case of his or her death unless the employer or local government has a provision for domestic partnership that extends to the child. Also, the nonbiological parent will be considered a legal stranger to the child by doctors, hospitals, and even schools.

While some jurisdictions allow same-sex couples to adopt, many allow only married couples or single people to do so. If a same-sex couple decides to adopt, and only one parent is considered the adoptive parent, the nonadoptive parent is again a legal stranger to the child, and the family faces the problems previously enumerated.

Finally, the lack of legal recognition of same-sex families often makes the dissolution of the family more difficult. Issues involving property, support, and children are likely to be more complicated. This is because family courts have no jurisdiction to decide custody and visitation rights or to supervise property division, as gay and lesbian relationships are not included in the legal definition of a family. Because the nonbiological parent is a legal stranger to the child, he or she has no right to custody or visitation and, conversely, no obligation to pay child support. Major purchases, such as houses and cars, will not be considered joint property unless both names are on the ownership documents. A partner who has given up a career to raise a child, therefore, will have no automatic right to alimony, even if that partner's previous career had put the other partner through professional school. Finally, in the event of domestic violence, the battered partner may not qualify for a civil order of protection against the batterer.

Some of these problems can be addressed through the legal system, either before or after the problem develops. Couples who are financially able can hire a lawyer to draft a myriad of legal documents to create and clarify some of these rights and responsibilities. Legal fees for these services range from a few hundred to several thousand dollars. For example, wills and trusts can direct the distribution of property upon the death of a partner, but they cannot help the surviving partner to avoid inheritance taxes. Couples can draft powers of attorney and advanced health care directives to stipulate who is to make medical decisions on their behalf if they are unable to do so themselves. Parents can create guardianships and draft wills that express their desire that the nonbiological parent become the sole custodian of the child if the biological parent is unable to care for the child. Of course, parents who are able to take advantage of coparent adoptions can avoid these legal hoops.

EMPLOYMENT, HOUSING, AND PUBLIC ACCOMMODATIONS

Health benefits and family leave policies clearly overlap into the employment arena. In addition to these concerns, gay men and lesbians are unprotected from employment discrimination without a state or local law granting such protection, an employer with an inclusive nondiscrimination policy, or perhaps a collective bargaining agreement that includes such a policy. These being rare events, the vast majority of lesbian and gay people in the workplace are unprotected. Indeed, the nation's largest employer, the U.S. military, *requires* discrimination against avowed lesbians and gays (Shilts, 1993). The fear of losing a job compels many gay people to hide their sexual orientation and private lives from coworkers. This means withdrawing from personal conversations, changing pronouns when discussing a weekend's activities, and going alone or bringing a false date to company events.

The fear of employment discrimination can also affect the avenues of relief a person may choose when confronted with these family dilemmas. Especially in smaller communities, a person may realistically fear a court fight over custody if it means that court personnel and possibly friends and colleagues will learn of the person's sexual orientation. The potential loss of a job is also a weapon that a former, or soon to be former, heterosexual or same-sex spouse can use to discourage or scare a person from seeking to enforce what legal rights they have. One may simply need to threaten to "out" the other person to his or her boss to convince him or her to forgo a fight.

Similarly, there is no national protection against discrimination in housing and public accommodations. This means that unless the state or other local government body has enacted specific protective laws—which is unusual—it is legal to refuse to rent or sell a house to someone because of their actual or perceived sexual orientation. *Public accommodations* refers to services offered by restaurants, hotels, and other businesses. Thus, a hotel or conference center could legally refuse to host an event involving lesbian or gay content. Fortunately, several states and many municipalities have enacted laws that prohibit discrimination based on sexual orientation in employment, housing, and public accommodations. While many more private and public employers have recently enacted employment policies that are protective of the rights of their lesbian and gay employees, the vast majority of lesbian and gay Americans remain unprotected.

SODOMY STATUTES

While public discussion and opinion have been gradually expanding basic civil rights protections to lesbians and gays, 19 states still have laws prohibiting sodomy between consenting adults. Sodomy laws were upheld by the U.S. Supreme Court in the case of *Bowers v. Hardwick* (1986). In addition to criminalizing consensual behavior, sodomy laws have been used to justify employment discrimination against lesbians and gays (*Shahar v. Bowers* (1996).

Antigay and -lesbian zealots argue that a person who is violating a state law cannot be charged with enforcing state laws (e.g., as a police officer or lawyer in an attorney general's office). This same logic is sometimes used in custody cases, such as *Bottoms v. Bottoms* (1995), where the court in part based its decision on the mother's perceived violation of the criminal law. Although many legally naïve people in states with sodomy laws are completely unaware of them, "it would be the rare judge that did not consider the admission of regular violations of the laws as tantamount, at a minimum, to a showing of bad moral character" (Mohr, 1988, p. 56).

CURRENT LEGAL TRENDS

Fortunately the legal tide may be changing. Ten years after *Bowers v. Hardwick* (1986), the Supreme Court struck down Colorado's Amendment 2 in *Romer v. Evans* (1996). Amendment 2 was an attempt by the Colorado electorate to deny lesbians and gays equal protection of the law by repealing previously enacted legal protections from discrimination in employment, housing, public accommodations, health insurance, health and welfare services, and private education. Three cities in Colorado had previously enacted laws prohibiting discrimination based on sexual orientation in some of these arenas. This statewide referendum sought to strike down these laws and preempt any similar types of civil protections. However, the Supreme Court said that Amendment 2 was unconstitutional because the only rationale of the amendment was "animus toward the class it affects" and a "desire to harm a politically unpopular group."

Thus, for now, lesbians and gay men who do not have generous employers or do not live in a jurisdiction with inclusive civil rights laws face the daily possibility of allowable legal discrimination in housing, employment, and public accommodations. Moreover, people who currently enjoy these protections risk losing them if they change jobs or move, or if their employers or local governments change those current protections.

In addition, gay men and lesbians must struggle, sometimes at significant financial and emotional cost, to build and maintain a secure family structure. Because laws and practices vary from city to city, employer to employer, and even year to year, people with legal questions should not make any assumptions, about legal protections in their particular situation. Rather, they should actively investigate them.

PSYCHOLOGICAL IMPLICATIONS
OF LEGAL DIFFERENCES

Consider a brief summary of the underlying messages that American society communicates to lesbian and gay couples and families via the legal differences previously described.

1. Your relationship or family does not count and is quite unlike a heterosexual marriage or family.
2. Your sexuality and love for each other indicate that you are not able to parent as well as the least competent heterosexual parent.
3. You are less than a full human being, so do not expect full civil rights.

PSYCHOLOGICAL IMPACT OF THE METAMESSAGES OF LEGAL DIFFERENCES

These legal differences can affect the couple or family in several ways psychologically.

1. The legal status difference may be activated by a specific problem and thereby *generate* problems when everything had been fine beforehand.
2. The legal status difference may be activated by a specific event and thereby *exacerbate* problems generated via other means.
3. There may be a legal status difference with nothing *specifically* negative happening at the moment, but the couple or family are adversely affected by their *awareness* of legal vulnerability. Partners' cognizance of their vulnerability can generate problems by fostering a sense of instability or a reemergence of internalized heterosexism.
4. There may be a legal status difference without any current crisis around this difference, and the couple may be only dimly aware—if at all—of the lack of protections. This difference, however, creates important unseen vulnerabilities within the couple or family. When they therefore later encounter real problems (e.g., death or illness of one member of the couple), their legal position is compromised and they typically handle the crises poorly.

HOW LEGAL PROBLEMS PRESENT IN THERAPY

Some clients will actually verbalize these sorts of legal tensions as presenting problems and seek to find ways (via problem solving or stress management) to deal more effectively with them. More commonly, couples present with problems that are significantly triggered or affected by these stressors. The therapist's task here is to search for the problematic surplus meanings generated in the family by these legal circumstances, seek to bridge to meanings held by others in the family, and discuss whether they should seek legal counsel.

Diminished Security

All of these legal pressures can exert a large psychological and economic toll on same-sex couples and families across many dimensions. One's sense of security is frequently diminished either by experiencing actual incidents of discrimination or by hearing of other antilesbian or -gay incidents. Many heterosexual therapists do not realize the extent to which trust and a sense of security—building blocks of any good relationship—become compromised in same-sex couples and families due to their more precarious legal position.

Loss of Parent Identity or Role

A lesbian or gay man who has constructed an important part of her or his identity around parenting and then loses ongoing contact with the children loses not only the children and those relationships—painful enough—but also a key personal role that has served important needs of self-definition and growth. These, therefore, constitute multiple losses. The fact that the children and their relationships with their absent lesbian or gay parent suffer as well only compounds the pain. The children lose touch with a parent at what are often critical junctures in their lives. Moreover, children often poorly understand what is occurring and may construct their own self-negative explanations for why their biological parents are fighting. One man related to one of the authors his incredible, prolonged stress around custody issues. Most upsetting to him was that the ex-wife, no matter what her psychological problems and mistreatment of the children, always had the legal upper hand: She knew that the courts would typically be hostile to the father's sexual orientation. The father's stable, two-parent household was repeatedly judged not to be a "normal" family. Her one-parent situation, on the other hand, was judged to be "more suitable," despite the fact that she was diagnosed several times as having a very unstable personality disorder. In fact, she had one of the children's three dogs euthanized while the children were at the father's house. At another time, she changed her phone number to an unlisted one without revealing this to the father. Because the court was unresponsive to his repeated requests for an emergency hearing, the frantic father was unable to contact his young children for 6 months. The father reported how these events significantly interfered with his ability to relate optimally not only with the children, but also with his partner, especially because the courts forbade certain affectionate behaviors between the two cofathers in their own house.

Many individuals who have divorced or separated from their former heterosexual or same-sex partners are not lucky enough to have a current spouse as a psychological buffer against the pain, loss, confusion, and doubt of a child custody case that is going poorly. In these cases, a therapist and lesbian and gay support groups can be important lifelines during times of crisis.

Greater Tension in Relationships

Typically, these problems show up as increased tension within the couple or family. Legal problems may elicit anger or resentment between them because of a sense that they have fewer options available to them in housing, careers, or even behavior. This often creates a sense of loss of control or of being trapped, especially if only one partner can be openly lesbian or gay at work. "[I]n most areas of the United States, lesbians and gays . . . are left, in effect, legally naked if they choose to come out publicly. . . . Without such minimal legal protection—and often confronted by employers who frown upon them—gay and lesbian people must constantly negotiate how open to be about their sexual orientation in all realms of life" (Rubenstein, 1995, p. 336). There are typically, however, many positive mental health benefits both to oneself and to one's relationships to being more openly lesbian or gay (Miller, 1987; Berzon, 1990). The couple or family then may experience an uncomfortable, dysfunctional tension between choosing to further their psychological well-being (by being "out") or their financial or physical well-being (by being "in"; Malyon, 1982). Legal restrictions often force other types of unfortunate sacrifices for the sake of the relationship. For example, a former colleague of one of the authors met her current partner of 8 years overseas, but her partner cannot legally stay in the United States because of the current policy barring same-sex marriage. A further source of much stress within this relationship is that the foreign partner cannot now leave to go visit relatives outside the United States, because to do so means being unable to reenter the country. These types of wrenching tensions and sacrifices are not uncommon.

It is both inhibiting and draining always to self-monitor public behavior with one's partner. One client—11 years into a gay relationship—remarked after returning from a largely lesbian and gay resort, "It's so wonderful to be there. I felt like I could be myself for the first time." The lack of spontaneity within same-sex relationships due to self-monitoring is a common casualty of the lack of legal protections.

Differential Parent Status

Where the children in a same-sex family are not adopted and are biologically related to only one parent, it is often difficult for the nonbiological parent to feel like a real or fully equal parent. Similar in some respects to heterosexual stepparenting, lesbian and gay parenting also involves important distinctions: "The non-biological parent(s) may be repeatedly confronted by the painful reality of being unacknowledged as a 'real' parent by family, friends, community, and society at large. Even the child may question whether the nonbiological parent is a 'real' parent because of the pressure for children to have one identifiable mom and one identifiable dad" (Pies, 1987, p. 169). During times of conflict within the couple, the biological parent may also invoke his or her blood relationship to the child as a way of asserting parental supremacy when the two parents disagree over how to handle an issue with the child. The children also may be more likely to pit the parents against each other and refuse to fully acknowledge the authority of the non-biological parent. This, naturally, can become a negative cycle that builds upon itself. The therapeutic task here can be for both partners to respectfully clarify and reflect on their feelings regarding this unequal status when it arises so they can decide together how to embody their stated attitudes toward parenthood and equality.

Greater Problems Handling Crises

It is still surprisingly prevalent for same-sex families to be somewhat ignorant of missing legal protections until they are personally affected. A spouse who has only recently come out, for example, may not understand his or her inability to assert any legal rights toward the partner if he or she becomes disabled, comatose, or hospitalized for other reasons. Likewise, some non–birth mother lesbians who have raised children together with the birth mother have never fully considered how to retain a connection with the children if the relationship breaks up. Many of these women later suffer enormous pain when they realize that they are a legal stranger to their children following the dissolution of the relationship with the birth mother and therefore are extremely vulnerable to the birth mother's whims regarding future contact with the children. Frequently feelings are so intense and blissful at the time of the decision to have a child that neither parent explores the unthinkable: "What would happen to our relationship with the child if we split up or one of us died?" Non–birth mothers therefore often lose complete contact with their children, which is comparable to—if not worse than—losing a young child through death. It is easy to understand how these types of problems can lead couples to stagnate or regress developmentally in their relationship out of fear.

An approach here could be for the therapist to ask questions (discussed later in this chapter) to elicit reflection on these legal issues and help develop problem-solving strategies *before* these issues reach the crisis stage. Sharing the information in Table 9.2 with same-sex couples early in therapy can also help them explore weak spots and work to change them.

Diminished Cohesion and Security within the Couple or Family

Because the states disavow the legitimacy of the same-sex couple and do not therefore protect it (e.g., erecting certain hurdles to discourage its quick dissolution when tempers are high) a same-sex couple often has a less distinct relationship than heterosexuals do. There are no built-in markers (like a wedding) for when the relationship officially began, no societal sanction of its existence, and no standard ritual providing for community acknowledgment and support of the couple. In terms of the cohesion difficulty, Decker (1984) observes that some men who had been heterosexually married prior to a gay relationship "noticed that the same kinds of little problems that they used to tolerate with their wives, now in a gay relationship, seemed to take on much greater meaning because the relationship seemed so much less socially protected" (p. 44). The *internal* bonding of the couple, therefore, may often be the only glue holding it together. These messages from society can lead some frustrated couples unwittingly to enact heterosexist assumptions about the failure of same-sex relationships to endure. (See the material on rituals to increase bonding and commitment in the "Increased Need and Opportunity for Couple or Family Self-Definition" subsection.)

In a book on same-sex relationships, Berzon (1990) draws upon Cass's (1979) psychosocial model of the development of a positive lesbian and gay identity. She notes that the interactions members of a couple have with the larger world as they explore their internal and external lesbian or gay experience are paramount in helping them move to the next developmental step. If members of a couple repeatedly experience negative events occurring to themselves or to others (e.g., news reports), this progression is compromised—they may remain stuck at an earlier stage of self-acceptance. This further complicates their full engagement with significant others. A therapist working with such a couple or family can help them more self-consciously seek to increase their exposure to positive experiences via books, movies, and structured (established, purposeful lesbian or gay groups) or unstructured group experiences (socializing with other couples). In this way they can broaden their experience and put those negative past experiences into a more balanced context, thus diminishing those negative events' salience and interference with developmental growth.

NECESSARY THERAPIST KNOWLEDGE AND GENERAL THERAPEUTIC TASKS

The couples and family therapist must be aware of the realities of the world of gay and lesbian clients. In addition he or she should know of a few good external legal and bibliotherapy resources to help clients confront and work through certain tasks. First among these is to help the same-sex couple or family identify current and potential future legal problems.

Therapists should keep abreast of the legal protections as they pertain to same-sex couples and families in their practice areas (See Table 9.2 for a summary). The therapist should also understand how laws adversely affect the process and quality of interactions within the couple and family. For example, a therapist might explore with them their thoughts about some of the necessary emotional ingredi-

Table 9.2 Problems for Lesbians and Gays in Comparison with Heterosexuals

Type of Issue	Problem	Exceptions	Legal Trends
Housing	No federal law bans discrimination in renting or sale of real estate on basis of sexual orientation.	Some states and cities have protection based on sexual orientation.	Positive in larger cities, but protections are subject to removal via periodic ballot measures. Dozens of states have voted on ballot initiatives such as these.
Employment	No federal law bans discrimination in hiring, firing, or promotion on basis of sexual orientation. In case of divorce, the heterosexual ex-spouse can therefore essentially threaten to "out" the lesbian, gay, or bisexual one at work so as to get him or her to agree to inequitable arrangements. The largest employer (the military) explicitly *requires* discrimination against lesbian and gay people. If a service member or applicant does not reveal his or her same-sex orientation, chances for dismissal or rejection are reduced, but not eliminated. Investigations still occur.	10 states, the District of Columbia, over 200 municipalities, and hundreds of universities and businesses prohibit job discrimination.	See preceding. Individual companies, however, are moving in positive direction.
Marriage	No state allows same-sex marriage.	None.	Many states have taken preemptive legal steps to disallow recognition of same-sex marriages performed in other states as well as clarifying ambiguous language in current laws to prevent future same-sex marriage. Unclear how constitutional these are.

Funeral arrangements	Without written instructions by the deceased, his or her blood relatives can take over possession of the body, dispose of it how they wish, and decide the funeral and burial arrangements.	Domestic partnership laws can give registered partners the power to make these decisions.	Generally positive, but very slow.
Child custody	Many courts have decided that the same-sex orientation of a parent per se renders him or her unfit to parent. Many courts consider same-sex orientation to be a negative factor and therefore award custody to the heterosexual parent. In some cases children have been successfully taken from the lesbian or gay parents entirely by a more distant relative.	Some states have ruled that sexual orientation per se is irrelevant.	Generally in positive direction.
Inheritance	In case a partner dies without a will, there is no provision for the property passing to the surviving lesbian or gay partner. In fact, a lesbian or gay partner may forfeit even jointly purchased property if the partner dies because of the lack of a legal relationship with the deceased.	Domestic partnership laws can give registered partners some rights here.	Generally positive, but very slow.
Medical decisions	Hospitals do not consider same-sex partners to be family or next of kin. A partner can therefore be barred from visiting an injured loved one in the hospital. A well partner also cannot automatically make important medical decisions for an incapacitated, injured partner.	Domestic partnership laws can give registered partners some rights here. Also, additional legal documents can give partners the power to make these decisions.	Generally positive, but very slow.
Death of partner	The surviving partner has no common-law right to sue on behalf of the deceased.	None.	No change.

(Continued)

177

Table 9.2 (Continued)

Type of Issue	Problem	Exceptions	Legal Trends
Visitation of children	Courts often rule against the divorced lesbian or gay parent having extended or overnight visits by their own children because of the parent's sexual orientation.	Some states have ruled that sexual orientation per se is irrelevant.	Generally in positive direction.
Domestic violence	States do not recognize same-sex partners as spouses and therefore offer fewer protections in case of domestic violence.	Some civil protection from abuse statutes have been interpreted to include same-sex couples.	Generally positive, but very slow.
Immigration	Due to the ban on same-sex marriage, foreign nationals cannot become U.S. citizens via their committed relationship with a citizen. In most cases, it is difficult or impossible for a lesbian or gay partner to obtain permanent residency.	None.	No change.
Employment benefits	Few employers offer spousal benefits to same-sex partners of employees. Uninsured same-sex partners therefore may have to pay for their own and their children's benefits or the children may be covered only by the birth parent's benefits, which may be less extensive than the other parent's benefits. Same-sex domestic partner benefits are taxed, whereas heterosexual ones are not.	Over 100 private institutions (some of the largest firms and universities in the U.S.) and scores of municipalities provide at least some benefits for partners of lesbian and gay employees.	More employers are offering some sort of domestic partner benefits.

Adoption and foster care	Some states (e.g., Florida) explicitly ban adoption and/or foster parenting by lesbian or gay individuals and couples.	Some states allow gay and lesbian couples to adopt or foster parent. Others allow gay or lesbian single people to adopt.	Generally positive, but very slow.
Sex	19 states still criminalize "sodomy," which is defined in most cases to include common homosexual and heterosexual acts, but which is used to justify discrimination only against lesbians and gays.	31 states do not criminalize sodomy.	Several states are examining their sodomy laws, but some have recriminalized it in recent years.
Taxes	Same-sex couples cannot file their federal income tax jointly and are therefore subject to higher tax penalties. Inheritance taxes are much higher for surviving same-sex partners because they are not considered spouses. Property purchased by the couple is not protected from being part of the deceased's estate, to be divided among blood relatives. See also employment benefits, preceding.	None.	No change.

NOTE: Given that the preceding data is always subject to change with legislative change and judicial rulings, the reader should always consult up-to-date legal sources (e.g., a lawyer) for timely legal information relevant to his or her particular situation.

ents for optimal development and growth of relationships—such as sense of trust, security, intimacy, respect, self-esteem, and sense of efficacy—and how these are each affected by various legal decisions.

Therapists treating gay men and lesbians should recognize the following legal terms and know what problem each is designed to address: *durable power of attorney for health care, durable power of attorney for finances, will, living will, domestic partnership, coparenting,* and *guardianship.* Although the therapist need not have legal expertise, clinicians who work with this population should have a list of legal resources available for clients. This might include a few books that clients can consult to understand and rectify their own vulnerabilities in their relationships (see Curry et al., 1996; Hunter, Michaelson, & Stoddard, 1992). It might also include, for those with computers and Internet access, a list of a few Web sites that can point them in the correct direction to answer questions they may have and educate them further about areas of vulnerability (see the "Additional Resources" section). A good place for any therapist to begin is to order the short ACLU briefing paper, *Lesbian and Gay Rights* (ACLU, 1996). This can be ordered in bulk to be distributed to clients. Therapists should also develop a referral relationship with a few good lesbian and gay lawyers who are knowledgeable about and comfortable with these issues. If specific legal questions arise, therapists should urge clients to contact an attorney, because even the best reference book quickly becomes obsolete as new laws are enacted or new court decisions are announced.

CREATING A MEANING-MAKING FOCUS

It is important to emphasize that these clients are *not* simply reacting to external problems. Indeed, many of their difficulties result from an interaction between the hostile legal environment and their own internal cognitive structures, which construct more or less functional meanings from these problems. A central task for the therapist is to help the couple or family better appreciate the meanings they assign to problems and—in addition to rectifying legal problems and weaknesses—to search for ways to negotiate these meanings so that they are more adaptive. It is essential, for example, to help clients not overgeneralize about their problems and not feel that everybody in society hates them, that things will always be this bad, or that there is something wrong with them because these frustrating things are happening to them or their family. It is incumbent upon every therapist to elicit, explore, and help clients both to evaluate and to undo these types of dysfunctional beliefs that often result from repeated societal mistreatment and inequity.

It can also be key to help clients better anticipate and take appropriate legal action in areas that could lead to problems so as to prevent later crises. A good initial interview session could include time to discuss how each member of the couple or family views both the partner and parental relationships. Next the therapist can inquire how these relationships are reflected and protected on paper. This can be done either verbally or via questionnaire. The therapist can introduce this by saying something like the following:

> I'm sure you're both aware that society does not acknowledge or validate your relationship with each other or the children as the two of you do. I'm going to ask you a series of questions to prompt your thinking about the relationship and awareness of

any vulnerabilities we can address before they become problematic. These questions can also then help us explore if there are some specific steps—both legal and symbolic—that you might want to consider taking to further express and protect these relationships. Some symbolic steps might include coming up with your own rituals to mark your commitment to each other and to the children. They could also include more organized political steps you could take to try to change the larger, heterosexist system. People often feel more empowered by better understanding these issues and taking steps to strengthen their own position and that of other lesbian and gay people through legal action and by agitating for social change. What do you both think?

The therapist could then discuss the following questions:

1. How do you define your relationship with your partner?
2. How do you define your relationship with your children?
3. How do you define your partner's relationship with the children?
4. Which of the following steps have you already taken to clarify or support your relationship legally?
   - Establishing a joint financial arrangement (e.g., bank account).
   - Drawing up papers that will allow your partner to inherit the house directly in case of your death.
   - Drawing up a will and naming your partner as chief beneficiary.
   - Drawing up protections on paper so that your partner (not your parents) could make appropriate medical decisions on your behalf in a crisis.
   - Drawing up protections on paper so that your partner (instead of your family of origin) could make appropriate financial decisions on your behalf in a crisis.
   - Drawing up papers declaring that you and your partner are equal coparents to the children.
   - Drawing up papers appointing you or your partner guardian of the children if the other dies first.
   - Drawing up papers appointing someone else guardian of the children if you both die together.
   - Drawing up written instructions about what should happen to your body in case of death.
   - Drawing up written instructions (i.e., a Living Will) about what you would like to happen to you medically in case of irreversible coma or terminal illness.

These are good questions to raise to get the couple or family to think about how they define themselves, but not to force them to define themselves in any particular way. The main idea here is to ensure that they have an agreement about their stated wishes and have made legal and economic provisions in case of future problems.

INCREASED NEED AND OPPORTUNITY FOR COUPLE OR FAMILY SELF-DEFINITION

The problems enumerated in this chapter suggest both a need and an opportunity for the couple or family members to provide their own self-definitions of who they are and to strengthen their relationship more mindfully. The therapist at this stage works to clarify and legitimize the couple's or family's relationships. Foremost is for the therapist to ascertain the couple or family's self-perception of the relationships that exist: How committed are they to each other? How do they view their roles regarding the children? Where do they see the relationship heading several years from now? The answers to these questions are then compared with the actualities of the situation. The clients and therapist together can then probe whether the couple or family needs to address any discrepancies by taking legal, economic, or symbolic actions. If the therapist senses, for example, that the couple needs a more formal acknowledgment of their relationship by both themselves and the larger community, he or she may want to suggest that the couple explore or invent their own rituals to celebrate their mutual commitment. These could be as simple or complex as the couple desires. Some couples probably will simply draw up legal papers that make their commitment clear. If they have been "married" for awhile already, but without having undergone a public ritual, planning and holding such a ceremony can help them acknowledge their partnership as an important entity separate from outsiders and to commit to each other in the presence of a supportive, validating community of friends and family (see Sherman, 1992; Uhrig, 1984; Butler, 1997). The therapist can help them construct a meaning for this along the lines of asserting their devotion to each other in the face of society's contrasted disavowal. The clinician can also help the couple understand the need to periodically examine and update their written legal and economic status as their relationship evolves. Helping each couple and family explore and appreciate positive aspects of their position (e.g., the crusading nature of their struggle for self-definition; the way their relationships enlarge the concepts of *family* and *marriage* in this society) can also bring a sense of purpose to what may often seem their mundane, personal efforts to survive and thrive as a lesbian or gay couple or family.

Another therapeutic task for a same-sex family can be to meet with other like families to advocate for legislative change on these issues. This often provides an opportunity for families to meet and exchange practical ideas and solutions. It not only reduces their sense of isolation and stigma, but also tends to increase self-esteem and bonding as they talk about and work on these ideas together. Hosting a monthly letter-writing campaign might be another good ritual by which the couple or family could better address their frustrations on key issues. A further good activity is joining a local or national group (see the "Additional Resources" section) that provides both information and advocacy on these issues. Partners can also work within their companies to lobby for domestic partnership benefits (see Frank & Holcomb, 1990).

DEFUSING DYSFUNCTIONAL SYMBOLIC MEANINGS SURROUNDING LEGAL PROBLEMS

Clients' idiosyncratic beliefs about their relationships and legal situations often interfere with optimal functioning and problem solving. Some of the more dysfunctional (often unspoken) beliefs relevant to legal issues are sometimes unrealistically positive ones: We love each other, so nothing will go wrong with this relationship; my in-laws are very accepting, so there will not be any problems if something happens to my partner; I have just as much right to my children as my ex-partner and I am sure the judge will see that; I am sure that if my partner and I ever did split up, we would be able to handle everything maturely. These beliefs involve, to a large extent, ignorance or denial of very real vulnerabilities in a heterosexist society which is especially prejudiced about the relationships between lesbians and gays and children—even between lesbians and gays and their own children. Any couple, therefore, should be more fully aware of the legal vulnerabilities inherent in same-sex relationships at this time and take certain steps relatively early on to safeguard each partner's rights concerning property, the relationship, and the children.

Dysfunctional meanings can likewise become attached to negative legal events. It is common for people to draw larger than necessary negative conclusions about what is happening. For example, Nancy has a current partner who wants to have children. Nancy, however, lost all contact with her first child a few years after she and the biological mother split up. After unofficially and amicably sharing custody with Nancy for several years, the birth mother became uncomfortable with the closeness that her daughter and her ex-lover had developed, and she stopped the visits. The judges have not allowed Nancy any contact with the daughter although she and the birth mother jointly decided to bear and raise the child. After many unsuccessful court battles, Nancy became very depressed and disconsolate. Not only does she very much miss her little girl and the important relationship they had, but she feels less trusting in general. Therefore it is harder for her to engage in subsequent deep, intimate relationships. Here the task for the therapist is to help both Nancy and her current partner understand and appreciate the depth of Nancy's loss and how her feelings need to be acknowledged. After her fears are addressed she can then freely decide whether to embark on the parenting path again. It may also be pertinent to explore whether Nancy has learned, at painful cost, the necessary legal steps to protect her rights as a parent. Recognition of this could help Nancy realize that she need not be as vulnerable as before. Also important to examine could be the overgeneralized meanings (e.g., I can't trust *anybody*) that Nancy may have constructed following her own nightmarish experience. Unexplored, these issues might block future happiness in the area of intimacy. Explored, they could help both women mindfully take the next step toward parenting, but this time without naïveté. A good therapist will help clients express and understand when they have carried painful life lessons too far in terms of their application to inappropriate partners or situations.

Related types of dysfunctional meaning can arise from custody, employment, or housing discrimination. When clients receive repeated messages of inferiority, exclusion, and inadequacy from the outside world—especially from the legal front to which they turn for redress—this can demoralize them and lead them to reawaken and reinvigorate largely dormant heterosexist beliefs. Therapists should keep in mind that all humans always strive to make sense of their world. When a series of events suggest that the majority of people see lesbians and gays as unworthy or incapable in arenas such as employment, housing, or parenting, this can weaken clients' sense of adequacy, worth, and integrity. These repeated implicit or explicit messages can cause clients to doubt themselves, their ability to parent, or their equal rights as citizens. A client may begin to believe, "Maybe they are right; maybe I am not as good a parent as his birth mother." Sharon Bottoms' partner, for example, conveys how she struggles with internalized guilt: "A part of me knows

I'm not guilty. Another part knows I am" (Henry, 1993, p. 67). It is unsurprising, given this woman's terrible dilemma, that the couple put any further thoughts of children on hold and that she, herself, considered moving out as a solution to the custody problem.

Likewise, legal problems can often greatly increase the tension within the couple or family in various ways. This can lead members of the couple or family to become frustrated and negative with each other more easily. An important task for the therapist in such cases is to highlight the contributing role of the legal discrimination here and redirect or reinterpret these negative feelings and thoughts by bridging between members of the family:

> I'm guessing that underneath all that anger the two of you are feeling toward each other right now, you're *both* angry that society has put you in this frustrating position of not being able to work or live wherever you want. Perhaps by attacking each other you're acting out the dysfunctional script that the heterosexist society offers you: "Gay relationships don't last." How about if together we try to write a new script— one that will acknowledge and validate your commitment to each other, but will also place in that larger context those inevitable disagreements that occur between any two people?

PROVIDING FURTHER INFORMATION

Clients may have access to many varied resources. Encouraging them to seek out and attend same-sex parenting or other support groups can help them feel less isolated. It can also provide a forum in which to receive and provide social and psychological validation, and a way to benefit from the accumulated wisdom and experience of others. There are enormous numbers of local and national groups for lesbian and gay people, several for same-sex parents, and even ones for children in lesbian and gay families (see the "Additional Resources" section). In addition, an increasingly huge number of resources relevant to lesbians, gays, and bisexuals exists online for those clients with computers and modems. Virtual communities can help otherwise psychologically or geographically isolated couples and families to join together, providing key support and information rapidly when in-person assistance is unavailable (see "Additional Resources"). There are also increasing opportunities for same-sex couples and families to vacation or to attend retreats with lesbian and gay peers.

It is quite important, of course, that the couples and family therapist educate him- or herself about the special problems and needs of same-sex couples and families. A heterosexual therapist can regularly (e.g., monthly) scan lesbian, gay, and bisexual news in print (e.g., the quarterly magazine *In the Family*) or on the Internet. He or she may also ask questions of lesbian, bisexual, and gay friends and colleagues, as well as occasionally read literature reflecting the daily frustrations, struggles, dreams and joys of being a same-sex couple or family in today's society (e.g., Gunderson & Morris, 1996; Tessina, 1989; Louganis & Marcus, 1995). Indeed, as the American Psychological Association has suggested (1986), health professionals should help remove the social stigma connected with homosexuality in the public's eye.

SUMMARY AND RECOMMENDATIONS

It is important that therapists working with couples and families be increasingly aware of and comfortable in responding to the unique needs of lesbian, bisexual, and gay couples and families. This client population undergoes numerous special stresses related to their inferior legal and social status in today's American society, and clients may thereby also undergo different psychosocial developmental patterns related to this legal vulnerability. These legal and economic stressors often interact with beliefs already present in the members of gay or lesbian couples to generate dysfunctional meanings. The astute therapist will seek to educate him- or herself about the very real legal challenges facing same-sex couples and families. He or she will also strive to understand how these challenges (as well as their positive resolution) can affect optimal psychological functioning. Helping clients to develop a greater awareness of these legal challenges and to take effective action on them, preferably before they become full-fledged crises, can enable clients to feel more powerful and effective. These challenges also offer clients an important opportunity for better reflecting on, clarifying, and solidifying their relationships by taking certain symbolic and concrete steps to protect and acknowledge those relationships. Such examination may not only exert positive effects on their own relationships. It may also propel clients toward effecting positive social change as well as increase their positive exchange with lesbian and gay peers struggling with similar issues. In these ways same-sex couples and families may strengthen their place internally and externally in today's society. They might quite possibly even engender changes that could make the world a better place for their children and all sexual minorities.

REFERENCES

American Civil Liberties Union. (1996). *Lesbian and gay rights* (ACLU Briefing Paper No. 18). New York: Author.

American Psychological Association, Committee on Lesbian and Gay Concerns. (1986). *APA policy statement on lesbian and gay issues.* Washington, DC: Author.

Anders, C. (1999, January). *Lesbian and gay rights during President Clinton's second term* (working paper). The Citizen's Commission on Civil Rights. Retrieved March 6, 1999 from the World Wide Web: www.aclu.org/congress/lg011599a.html.

Baehr v. Miike (1996), 910 P.2d 112.

Bell, A. P., & Weinberg, M. S. (1978). *Homosexualities: A study of diversity among men and women.* New York: Simon & Schuster.

Berzon, B. (1990). *Permanent partners: Building gay and lesbian relationships that last.* New York: Plume.

Blau, M. (1996, June/July). Gay parents: Another kind of family. *Child Magazine.*

Bottoms v. Bottoms (1995), 249 Va. 410.

Bowers v. Hardwick (1986), 478 U.S. 186.

Butler, B. (Ed.). (1997). *Ceremonies of the heart: Celebrating lesbian unions.* Seattle, WA: Seal Press Feminist Publications.

Cass, V. C. (1979, spring). Homosexual identity formation: A theoretical model. *Journal of Homosexuality, 4,* 219–235.

Curry, H., Clifford, D., & Leonard, R. (1996). *A legal guide for lesbian and gay couples* (9th ed.). Berkeley, CA: Nolo Press.

Decker, B. (1984). Counseling gay and lesbian couples. In R. Schoenberg, R. S. Goldberg, & D. A. Shore (Eds.). *Homosexuality and social work* (pp. 39–52). New York: Haworth Press.

Frank, M., & Holcomb, D. (1990). *Pride at work: Organizing for lesbian and gay rights in unions.* New York: Lesbian & Gay Labor Network.

Gunderson, S., & Morris, R. (1996). *House and home.* New York: Dutton.

Henry, W. A. (1993, September 20). Gay parents: Under fire and on the rise. *Time, 142*(12), 66–68.

Hunter, N. D., Michaelson, S. E., & Stoddard, T. B. (1992). *The rights of lesbians and gay men: The basic ACLU guide to a gay person's rights* (3rd ed.). Carbondale, IL: Southern Illinois University Press.

Louganis, G., & Marcus, E. (1995). *Breaking the surface.* New York: Random House.

Malyon, A. K. (1982). Psychotherapeutic implications of internalized homophobia in gay men. In J. C. Gonsiorek (Ed.), *Homosexuality & psychotherapy: A practitioner's handbook of affirmative models* (pp. 59–69). New York: Haworth Press.

Masters, W. H., & Johnson, V. E. (1979). *Homosexuality in perspective.* Boston: Little, Brown.

McCandlish, B. M. (1987). Against all odds: Lesbian mother family dynamics. In F. W. Bozett (Ed.), *Gay and lesbian parents* (pp. 23–38). New York: Praeger.

Miller, B. (1987). Counseling gay husbands and fathers. In F. W. Bozett (Ed.), *Gay and lesbian parents* (pp. 175–187). New York: Praeger.

Mohr, R. D. (1988). *Gays/Justice: A study of ethics, society, and law.* New York: Columbia University Press.

Monahan, J. T., Facciolo, D. J. J., Bhaya, S., & Gottschalk, D. I. (1997, June). Gay and lesbian civil rights: Marriage is not enough. *Delaware Lawyer, 10,* 12, 13, 31–35.

Pies, C. (1987). Considering parenthood: Psychosocial issues for gay men and lesbians choosing alternative fertilization. In F. W. Bozett (Ed.), *Gay and lesbian parents* (pp. 165–174). New York: Praeger.

Rivera, R. R. (1987). Legal issues in gay and lesbian parenting. In F. W. Bozett (Ed.), *Gay and lesbian parents* (pp. 199–227). New York: Praeger.

Romer v. Evans (1996), 116 S. Ct. 1620.

Rubenstein, W. B. (1995). Lesbians, gay men, and the law. In R. C. Savin-Williams, W. R. Savin, & K. M. Cohen (Eds.), *The lives of lesbians, gays, and bisexuals: Children to adults* (pp. 331–343). New York: Harcourt Brace College.

Schwartz, L. L., & Kaslow, F. W. (1997). *Painful partings: Divorce and its aftermath.* New York: John Wiley & Sons.

Segal, M. (1996, February 2–8). The language of the form. *Philadelphia Gay News, 20*(15), 2. Philadelphia: Masco Communications.

Shahar v. Bowers (1996), 78 F.3d 499.

Sherman, S. (1992). *Lesbian and gay marriage: Private commitments, public ceremonies.* Philadelphia: Temple University Press.

Shilts, R. (1993). *Conduct unbecoming: Gays and lesbians in the U.S. military.* New York: St. Martin's Press.

Tessina, T. (1989). *Gay relationships: How to find them, how to improve them, how to make them last.* Los Angeles: Jeremy P. Tarcher.

Uhrig, L. J. (1984). *The two of us: Affirming, celebrating and symbolizing gay and lesbian relationships.* Boston: Alyson Publications.

ADDITIONAL RESOURCES

Note that because resources on the Internet change so rapidly, there is no assurance that all of the web pages listed will remain at these addresses. One should, however, still be able to access them or similar resources by using search engines to locate these topic words and phrases.

TOPIC	CURRENT URL OR ADDRESS
American Civil Liberties Union: Civil rights organization	www.aclu.org
American Psychological Association: Lesbian and gay parenting	www.apa.org/pi/parent.html
Children of Lesbians and Gays Everywhere	www.colage.org
Gay and Lesbian Parents Coalition, International	P.O. Box 50360 Washington, DC 20091 (202) 583-8029 No Web page
Human Rights Campaign: U.S. lesbigay civil rights organization	www.hrcusa.org
In the Family: The Magazine for Gays, Lesbians, Bisexuals and Their Relations	Family Magazine, Inc. 7302 Hilton Avenue Tacoma Park, MD 20912 (301) 270-4771 E-mail: Lmarkowitz@aol.com
National Journal of Sexual Orientation Law: Online law journal	sunsite.unc.edu/gaylaw
Nolo Press: Legal information for spouses and partners	www.nolo.com/ChunkSP/ sp.index.html
Support groups for gay and lesbian parents	www.welcomehome.org/ rainbow.html
Versus Law: self-research legal library	www.versuslaw.com
Zoe family web page: Lesbian couple	members.aol.com/zoefamily/ index.html

CHAPTER 10

Delinquency and Criminality

PAUL D. LIPSITT and LEWIS P. LIPSITT

The first few years of life provide the critical opportunity for a decent start. Such a beginning greatly increases the odds for lifelong learning, good health, the acquisition of constructive skills, and the development of pro-social behavior. It is a period when children form the initial human attachments that powerfully shape their possibilities for having decent and fulfilling relationships with others. During these years of growth and development, children need dependable caregivers who will nurture, protect, and guide them . . . (Hamburg, 1997, p. 12).

INTRODUCTION

The "critical opportunity for a decent start" (Hamburg, 1997) is a privilege to which an increasing number of children and adolescents in our society do not have easy access. Sometimes the "dependable caregivers who will nurture, protect, and guide them" are absent or incapable. The youth then moves into harm's way, and the reparative task for society and the delinquent often falls to the court system and forensic psychologists.

The identification of antisocial behavior and conduct disorders, the implementation of effective programs of prevention and treatment, and the careful study of the developmental and legal consequences of juvenile delinquency all depend upon clear nomenclature and reliable diagnosis. The limitations of the *Diagnostic and Statistical Manual of Mental Disorders, Fourth Edition* (DSM-IV; American Psychiatric Association [APA], 1994) in recognizing the dynamics and impact of family relationships upon children's behavior are highlighted in Kaslow (1996). In the foreword to this volume on relational diagnosis and dysfunctional family patterns, David Reiss (p. xiii) raises the caveat that *DSM-IV* is not a diagnostic system and classifies disorders without reference to underlying causes. An awareness of the importance of family relationships expands the context for diagnosis and intervention beyond the intrapersonal and organic level.

In the same volume, Alexander and Pugh (1996) explore intervention within the family context for both early-onset and adolescent-onset pathways of behavioral disorders. Alexander and Pugh point out that *DSM-IV* labels should include proper developmental information to improve the richness of diagnosis (p. 220). An appreciation by the clinician of the conditions that promote the onset of criminal activities, including scientific knowledge of societal and familial factors, will aid in the enlistment of the mental health and legal systems in providing opportunities for appropriate behavior change. Multiple causality is common, and there is ample research pointing to the importance of involving the family in effecting children's behavioral change (Dodge, 1993).

This chapter explores the ways in which the crimes of young offenders, and the perpetrators themselves, are dealt with by the U.S. judicial system, and could perhaps be handled better. This chapter also discusses (a) the known origins of antisocial lifestyles, (b) the progress made in recent years toward helping youngsters avert the disastrous consequences of an early developmental pathway to criminality, and (c) the social conditions that seem to lead some youngsters inexorably to delinquency as a natural adjustment to adverse life conditions. Study of the developmental and legal consequences of juvenile delinquency requires collaborative expertise from the fields of law, psychology, and child development.

An excellent historical perspective on the origins and conduct of the rather close liaison that now exists between psychology and the law may be found in Tapp's (1976) wonderful contribution in the *Annual Review of Psychology*.

SOME ORIGINS OF DELINQUENCY

The Chicago sociologist Clifford Shaw (1930), a major figure in the documentation of the natural histories of juvenile delinquent careers, proposed a social psychological understanding of the development of criminality. He and his colleagues described, using information written especially for them by delinquents themselves, the process of indoctrination of youngsters into delinquent pathways, and he claimed that the processes are, for many, the same as those involved in the socialization of nondelinquent or conforming individuals (Shaw & Moore, 1931).

Shaw emphasized the role of elders in determining the delinquency choices of young people. The child, in this view, has a need to relate to older boys (males were studied, mostly), who guide him much as if he were an apprentice in the caring hands of a competent role model. The older boy rewards the younger child for engaging, initially as an amateur, in *guided* antisocial behavior, and the child is made increasingly comfortable in his role as an apprentice, then as an accomplice.

The juvenile's peer associates, in Shaw's view, eventually provide strong support for the antisocial behavior. The misdemeanors in which the child engages are admired by his friends and mentors. Shaw's presumptions, which constitute a working model for the development in the street of a criminal career, have been reaffirmed and validated recently by the studies of Wolfgang (1989), also in Chicago.

The *developmental shaping* process suggested by Shaw came, in a sense, before its time. The Shaw scenario calls attention to the context in which children are reared, and especially emphasizes a social reward system that capitalizes on the young child's dependency upon other individuals (Bandura & Walters, 1963; Weisz, 1996). In conforming families, the significant and rewarding others are usually parents or other family members; they have control of the incentives that, in an effective learning environment, help to set the stage for collaborative prosocial goal seeking. On the other hand, in children reared in environments where the major incentives are controlled by individuals who are outside of the family and are involved in illegal behavior, youngsters are more likely to adopt the behaviors and lifestyle of those who provide access to rewards for antisocial behavior.

A major presumption of this chapter, increasingly subscribed to by modern society, is that "the child is father of the man" (Wordsworth, 1904). This basic proposition, central to Freudian theory and originating in the writings of numerous philosophers, notably John Locke, insists that, regardless of other factors that may influence developmental destinies, the history of the individual is cumulatively determinative in human development. This is supported in great measure by much of the literature on children's learning and socialization processes (Bandura & Walters, 1963; Sears, Maccoby, & Levin, 1975), showing that early experiences are developmental precursors, and indeed can be *causes* of subsequent behavior.

The supposition that earlier experience is powerfully ascendent in determining later development and behavior does not mean that later life experiences have little or no impact. Michael Lewis (1997), for example, finds so much evidence for developmental *turnarounds* (our term) that he regards the presumption of early developmental determinism as scientifically risky. He claims that this widely held assumption may actually be a deterrent to progress in public policy on behalf of individuals who are adversely affected by their early environment. Later experiences, and even major developmental shifts in adult attitudes and behavior, are not uncommon and suggest that negative childhood "determinants" are reversible.

We submit here that the apparent codeterminacy of later with earlier experience, and especially rehabilitative interventions designed to have a constructive psychological and behavioral impact on negatively affected individuals, provide the best evidence that lifetime accumulations of experience multideterminatively affect developmental outcomes. This realization carries with it a public policy mandate that society and the legal system not give up on individuals who have had a bad start. Many delinquent youngsters are not inevitably doomed to a life of crime and other antisocial behaviors, because of protective factors that impinge on their lives even in the face of initial vulnerability (Werner & Smith, 1982).

Generations of successful cases of psychotherapy, behavior modification, and family intervention provide convincing demonstrations not only of the prepotent quality of early experience, but also of the substantial efficacy, even under very challenging conditions, of some remediation techniques (Albee & Gullotta, 1996; Kazdin, 1989; McCord & Tremblay, 1992). Our major message in this regard is that much research remains to be done to find the most efficacious interventions for different kinds of developmental dysfunction (Osofsky, 1997).

The successful stories of turnarounds honor much more than the difficulties inherent in altering the psychological dispositions created in youngsters by adverse early environments. Some vulnerable youngsters, at risk due to adverse early circumstances, are nonetheless beneficiaries of a modicum of positive experience, including special attachments to respected adults, such as a grandparent or teacher. These individuals sometimes capitalize on those positive aspects of their early lives to make reform a reasonable goal and outcome (McCord & Tremblay, 1992).

Comparative studies of well-documented remediation programs, like those of Patterson, Reid, and Dishion (1992), can provide the knowledge base required to guide further advances in the treatment of antisocial individuals. The study and refinement of methods of social control of delinquent youth have occurred at a rapid rate in the past two decades. Current knowledge about behavioral development offers some direction toward effective intervention by the juvenile justice system. For example, earlier rather than later intervention for families seems to lower the risk of return to an environment that spawns deviance (Patterson, DeBaryshe, & Ramsey, 1989; Kazdin, 1996).

LEGAL AND PSYCHOLOGICAL APPROACHES TO DELINQUENCY AND CRIMINAL BEHAVIOR

Controlling crime, protecting the public, and helping delinquent youth are major concerns of our society. The prospect of reducing juvenile delinquency is especially full of opportunities for collaboration between the fields of psychology and the law. The combined talents of the developmental and forensic psychologist, especially in combination with a receptive court system, bear promise.

The courts, human service agencies, criminologists, and correctional psychologists are presently involved in addressing the unacceptable, antisocial behavior of unprecedentedly large numbers of delinquents and criminals. The task of addressing the issues and abating the problem rightfully falls to the state, and particularly the courts. In turn, the courts increasingly look to forensic and correctional psychologists, as well as other child development specialists, for guidance in understanding the origins of delinquency and in the disposition of individual cases (Levine & Levine, 1992; Meehl, 1970).

For more than 100 years, the judicial system of the United States has made a distinction in court procedures between interventions with children and with adults (Behrman, 1996). This adjustment in the way in which the criminal system deals with juvenile crime stemmed from a heightened interest in and concern for child welfare. At the turn of the 20th century, a movement began to correct the then often Dickensian disregard for children and to explore the impact of adverse environmental conditions on their growth and development. Child development and child welfare institutes were founded in major U.S. cities to bring children and adolescents in from the streets and provide them with educational opportunities and with companionship and guidance from adults interested in their well-being. Many social work and social welfare programs enlarged their curricula to include the study of children, of child development, and of rehabilitative processes for youngsters who had "gone astray." As early as 1880, service institutions like Wiley House in Allentown, Pennsylvania, were founded to provide shelter for "unruly and odd" children. This refuge and treatment site, now called Kidspeace, has recently been rededicated as a national center for the better understanding and rehabilitation of "all children in crisis." Early in the history of such services, those cared for in such facilities were often defined as children and youth likely to embark upon a delinquent course of behavior, eventuating in an adult criminal career (Blumstein, Cohen, & Farrington, 1988). Such facilities now are designed, however, to serve a wide spectrum of youngsters with disabilities, psychological disorders, educational insufficiencies, and conditions of sociopathy.

When "settlement houses" were founded in various locations throughout the United States, often under the aegis of humanitarian social workers (such as the famous Hull House founded in Chicago by social reformer and community worker Jane Addams), the involvement of increasing numbers of forensic professionals ensued. Dr. William Healy, a psychiatrist and director of the Juvenile Psychopathic Institute of Chicago, began providing clinical services to the first juvenile court in the United States in 1909 (Healy, 1915, 1922). Stressing the importance of individualization in understanding and treating children, Healy's clinic emphasized the need to gather sufficient data to aid "in the development of a science of conduct." The stream of reform leading to the establishment of juvenile courts sprang from laws against cruelty to children and philanthropic social services on behalf of "street urchins, waifs, and wayward and misdemeanant children" (Rosenheim, 1962).

Soon after, in 1913, Dr. Healy was joined by Dr. Augusta F. Bronner, a psychologist. In 1917, Drs. Healy and Bronner came to Boston, where they organized and directed the Judge Baker Foundation Guidance Clinic (today called the Judge Baker Children's Center), modeled after the Chicago Institute. The mandate of this clinic from its inception was to aid social agencies, schools and families in examining "problem children," focusing on the developmental history of juvenile delinquency and emphasizing "home conditions and family relations" (Glueck & Glueck, 1934, pp. 46–51).

Experts in sociology and psychology began addressing more intensively the prospects that effective remediation of delinquency might be brought about by scientifically and clinically validated methods of intervention. Addressing the extant sociolegal system of retribution and punishment, these experts brought to the table the view that some unfortunate children are aberrant in having acquired antisocial patterns of behavior, but are capable of change (Loeber & Dishion, 1983; Patterson, 1992; Patterson et al., 1989).

Patterson and his colleagues at the Oregon Social Learning Institute focused their research and intervention efforts on family behavioral training to effect reduction of delinquent behavior. Family management practices were identified and training was introduced, both by telephone and by onsite monitoring of family interaction. The family interactive variables that were identified included discipline, problem solving, parental monitoring, and acceptance. Poor parental monitoring was found to be associated with youngsters' delinquent lifestyle and police contact. Inept parental discipline was linked with delinquent lifestyle (Patterson & Stouthamer-Loeber, 1984). The transformation of their findings from research data into a training program has produced impressive reductions in deviant, antisocial behaviors. The Patterson researchers as well as other behavioral scientist interventionists continue to refine intervention techniques, focusing on distinctive domains of behavior. Intervention in the area of family interaction and children's cognitions has resulted in behavioral change in the conduct disorder category (Kazdin, 1993). A multifaceted approach, which includes intervention in the family, at school, and with peers, is currently being studied with children in the early grades who have been identified as being at high risk (Coie & Jacobs, 1993; Reid, 1993). Many studies in this fertile arena are now directed toward sorting out the effectiveness of various strategies for different types of offenses, in relation to the age of the offenders and to diverse familial characteristics.

Since the first court clinics opened, juvenile justice has operated on the assumption that disposition of cases should be tailored to the particular problems at hand (Levine & Levine, 1976), and should include consideration of the life circumstances of the youngster as well as the offense committed.

With these advances, procedures for dealing with offenses of youngsters were introduced so that children's cases would be heard in a forum separate from the criminal courts. The new focus was to be geared to the psychological needs of the offender and his or her rehabilitation, rather than concentrating on a punitive disposition of the case based on the criminal offense. There was a new expectation that the child or youth would help coestablish and work toward goals of behavioral change.

In attempting to promote this "child saving" philosophy and implement an altered course of action based on it, a change in judicial procedures was needed. Most of the safeguards of civil liberties, routinely accorded to adults in the criminal justice system, had to be relaxed. This involved eschewing basic due process considerations in exchange for an approach of *parens patriae* (the state acting on behalf of or in place of the parents). The courts were obliged to assume the posture of a good parent concerned primarily for the health and welfare of the child.

With the implementation of the new judicial safeguards for children, the American juvenile court system was granted jurisdiction over children, usually up to age 18, dealing with two categories of delinquent behavior: (a) status offenses, which are within the province of the court primarily for the well-being of the immature individual, and which include behaviors seen as inappropriate for children, such as drinking, smoking, and truancy from school; and (b) offenses that would be crimes if committed by an adult, but are seen in children as behaviors that can be changed through interventions and controls within the judicial system because of the youngster's presumed malleability and educability, thus avoiding the stigmatizing label of criminal offender.

The challenge, from the inception of the new juvenile justice system to this day, has been to achieve remediation while simultaneously preventing the compounding of adversities in the child's life and reputation. This has been attempted through reliance on both the impact of legal involvement and a range of therapeutic interventions geared toward behavioral change, more positive socialization, and enhancement of psychological well-being.

Recent trends suggest that a dampening of the early optimism of this juvenile justice philosophy may have occurred, perhaps due to the realization that existing programs reach too few children who are in need of them, and that the success rate among those reached is less than optimal. The rising pessimism with regard to effectively addressing juvenile delinquency is directly related to the public perception, found as well among some professional personnel, of increased and more violent delinquent behavior by young people, and a seemingly higher incidence of crimes committed by ever-younger age groups. Moreover, many youngsters who commit crimes against people and property also engage in substance abuse. Drugs and alcohol are utilized by young children with increasing frequency. For many psychologists and other human service providers, this has renewed the challenge to pioneer fresh intervention strategies and to improve upon promising existing techniques.

The forensic specialist in the mental health field tries, through assessment, evaluation, and advice, to help the court by calling upon research findings and other available resources to implement objectives on behalf of the child that are consistent with the juvenile justice philosophy. The overriding objective is to divert the child from a life of crime through early, effective intervention rather than having to resort to incarceration or other punitive consequences as sequelae to the destructive behavior.

At the same time, the advent of children's rights must be recognized and integrated into assessment and evaluation procedures. The recommendations of the forensic psychologist must take into account due process rights provided by the Constitution and interpreted by the U.S. Supreme Court. Since the 1967 enunciation by the U.S. Supreme Court of juveniles' due process rights (*In re Gault*, 1967), major changes have occurred in the relationship between the child and the state, including the right to an attorney, the right to cross-examination, the right to confront witnesses, and the right of appeal. One year before the Gault case was heard, the same Court first recognized the right of a juvenile to a full hearing in order to determine the appropriateness of transfer to the adult court for a serious felony (*Kent v. United States*, 1966).

If a youngster is beyond a particular age (usually 14 years), a transfer from the juvenile to the adult court may be considered when the charge involves a serious offense. In such cases, the maturity of the juvenile and amenability to treatment in the juvenile justice system will be factors in the court's decision whether to transfer. The juvenile's psychosocial history will inevitably be an important part of the clinician's assessment, along with the juvenile's current mental status.

Kent v. United States (1966) has provided guidelines for constitutional and due process safeguards to guarantee fairness when a transfer or waiver of juvenile jurisdiction is under consideration. The trend since the 1960s to invoke procedural safeguards leaves juvenile court judges less discretion in some cases to consider the psychological state or degree of impairment of the offender. Recent legislation in some states has extended adult jurisdiction to juveniles over age 14 who are charged with capital offenses (e.g., Acts and Resolves of Massachusetts, 1996). Emphasis on *amenability to treatment* under the transfer statutes has been replaced by emphasis on *present and long-term public safety*. The reduction in discretion to consider rehabilitative opportunities applies to cases involving first and second degree murder.

STAGES OF ACTION BY THE JUVENILE JUSTICE SYSTEM

The relationship between the court and attorneys, on the one hand, and the forensic clinician, on the other, requires that both the structure and procedures of the judicial system and the nature of human development, particularly the development of criminal patterns of behavior, be considered together. Following are the stages that exist within the judicial system with respect to the way the system will impinge upon the child or youth once the offense has allegedly occurred and the youth has been apprehended. Some of the remarks here have the quality of *advisories*.

APPREHENSION BY POLICE

When a youth is identified as the alleged perpetrator of a delinquent act, the police may hold the accused in a juvenile detention facility pending a preliminary hearing. It is customary for identified parents to be notified immediately of the circumstances.

Clinical issues at this point include the minor's capacity to understand his or her right to remain silent or confess voluntarily. Parents or caretakers might be apprised at this juncture of the nature of the antisocial or deviant behavior, and of its possible connection with a mental disorder. At this time the police should provide information about the child's whereabouts and offer the opportunity for the parents to participate in the procedure from its inception.

The first opportunity for consideration of diversion from the juvenile court, at the discretion of the police, may be at this stage of apprehension and interrogation. At this time, the police would have the option to consider a voluntary placement or plan in collaboration with the parents, to avoid the commencement of a judicial process. This option will likely depend on the seriousness of the offense and the appropriateness of alternative resources and family support.

The clinician, in consultation with the police and the parents, and predicated on the evaluation of the child, may aid in determining at this stage whether the best interests of the child and the community are served through the juvenile justice system or an alternative. Options that may be available include commitment by the parents to closer monitoring, referral to family and children's services, or, if property damage has been involved, an agreement for arrangements for restitution. The forensic clinician must be sensitive at this time to factors that could influence the police decision, such as socioeconomic and minority status of the family, and the availability of reasonable alternative resources in contrast to the more formalized engagement with the court. At this stage, the stability of the child's family, school, and community will be relevant in assessing the risk of subsequent antisocial behavioral problems.

INITIAL DETENTION HEARING

At this stage, the court will make the decision to either release the child to his or her parent(s) or other suitable caretaker, pending an intake hearing, or to detain him or her pending such a hearing. Assessing the behavioral and other characteristics of the child and family will aid in this determination. Assurances of appearance in court, likelihood of danger to self or others, and adequate parental supervision are important considerations at this time. The forensic clinician can aid the defense attorney as well as the court in assessing the risk factors as part of the decision-making process.

Lipsitt, Lelos, & Gibbs (1985), in a study of detained youngsters, found that 92% of them are routinely returned to their homes after disposition. Therefore, a novel program of detention avoidance was developed. Working with the entire family in the home during the period that constitutes detention, a wide range of support is provided. While avoiding prehearing incarceration, family dynamics and social service needs are explored and initiated. At this juncture, help may be provided in very practical ways to reduce family problems contributing to the delinquency. Steps may be taken to assure adequate housing, nourishment, and parental guidance and supervision. Having the child at home during this period offers the opportunity to assess the child's strengths, weaknesses, and needs, particularly within the context of the family and the school.

PRELIMINARY HEARING—INTAKE

The purpose of the intake procedure, usually presided over by a magistrate or probation officer, is to determine, after an evaluation of the child and the circumstances of the apprehension, whether to proceed with a delinquency petition or to select an alternative plan of intervention. This procedure is the last one prior to formal petition for a delinquency charge, and it offers an opportunity for the involvement of a forensic clinician to evaluate the various options in conjunction with the juvenile and his or her family, as well as with the attorney for the juvenile.

FORMAL HEARING AND ADJUDICATION

As in a trial in adult court, the facts relevant to the alleged delinquent behavior are examined to determine the truth of the allegations. Civil rights and due process procedures are respected and followed, including the right to an attorney, the right to confrontation with accusing witnesses, the right to cross-examination, and, in some jurisdictions, the right to a jury trial.

The hearing is generally not open to the public or the media. In contrast with the adult court, insanity is not an acceptable defense because, theoretically, intentionality is not an element for exoneration for the juvenile as it could be for an adult. Neither is diminished capacity a relevant issue at this stage of the proceedings. Impaired mental state and other deficits are considered and are dealt with in the dispositional stage. However, recognition of mental disorder at earlier stages may offer the option of referral to the mental health system.

DISPOSITION—OUTCOME

The forensic clinician has the greatest opportunity to offer expertise and impact during the dispositional, outcome stage of the court process. If the individual is adjudicated a delinquent, the court must assess the most appropriate intervention toward the goal of maximizing opportunity for behavioral change and the minimizing of future delinquent and antisocial behaviors.

The input that the judge receives regarding the psychological and social factors in the youth's background and current mental status can be critical determinants of the court's dispositional order. Amenability to treatment and availability of suitable community resources are determinative factors in the decision-making process. A range of potential interventions may include the utilization of any of a variety of settings, from returning the youth to the family home to placement in a secure facility. The level of deprivation of liberty will depend on the availability and character of family support and the collaboration of the family in shaping the desired opportunity for change.

At this stage, the evaluation and opinion regarding prospects for family training and rehabilitation of the youngster must be invoked (Patterson, 1992). Clinical assessment as to whether the youth is a "socialized delinquent" like the youngsters studied by Shaw, or has a character or behavior disorder (Kazdin, 1996), will be of inestimable value to the court.

Within the court system, the probation department will provide input through a review of past offenses and other background information considered relevant to the court. The forensic clinician may make valuable contributions in interpreting the dynamics of the behavior associated with the alleged crime within the context of the family, school, community, and peer relationships. Consideration of the other environmental factors that impinge on the youth's behavior and emotional state will be useful in aiding the court in considering intervention options.

Unlike the adult criminal court, where guidelines determine the relationship between the offense and the punishment, the goal of the juvenile court is to give the court wide latitude to intervene. The interventions of choice are those that are individualized for the best interests of the child within a framework of ensuring protection to the community.

TOWARD UNDERSTANDING DELINQUENT BEHAVIOR

The influence of the family as a factor in the antisocial behavior of the child, and the potential of the family to be a significant resource in remediating or rehabilitating the delinquent youngster, have been described or delineated time and again in the research and clinical literature. As Alexander and Pugh (1996) have observed, in conceptualizing the significance of behavior disorders, the primacy of family relationships is critical for a research model as well as for intervention strategies. Of special importance is the frequent collusion of other members of the family, parents in particular, by condoning the negative behaviors of the youth with Oppositional Defiant Disorder, including failure to censure the adolescent's substance abuse.

The Alexander and Pugh (1996) thesis is consistent with the work that Patterson and his colleagues have carried on for the past 25 years (Loeber & Dishion, 1983; Patterson, 1992; Patterson et al., 1989; Patterson et al., 1992). They have examined the development of antisocial behavior, conducting research and devising a model to understand the forerunners of antisocial acts. Ineffective parenting, and the family context in which the child is reared, are regarded by these investigators as central in accounting for delinquency and criminality as a developmental outcome.

Patterson et al. (1989) concluded, based on extensive research involving hundreds of families from which delinquent children have emerged, that family interaction processes are critical for understanding the origins of delinquent behavior and for strategizing interventions designed to reduce the incidence of delinquent, antisocial behavior. Their results support the contention that parents of antisocial children typically have provided little positive involvement with the child, offer poor monitoring and supervision, and utilize harsh and inconsistent discipline.

Inept parents encourage aversive behaviors in their children. Family factors that are conducive to this type of juvenile behavior pattern include a history of criminality in the family, dispute resolution through punishment (especially physical punishment), and a high level of rejection of the child by the family. The resulting response patterns by the child or adolescent become escape mechanisms which have the consequence of terminating "intrusions" by other family members. Examples of such behavior patterns range from verbal outbursts, to destruction of property, to physical attacks. An important aspect of family training in such situations is to teach members of the family skills in setting limits without resorting to physical punishment, and helping to shift the targeted person (the delinquent) from making antisocial to making prosocial responses.

Patterson and his colleagues have described ways in which some families essentially *train* children to perform antisocial acts. They describe how coercive behavior by the child becomes functional in terminating aversive (i.e., annoying) intrusions by other family members. Later, in school and with peers, these antisocial acts have negative consequences for academic performance and acceptance by normal (nonantisocial) peer groups. The Patterson team postulates, contrary to earlier existing notions about the causes of school misbehavior, that academic failure and peer rejection are the consequences rather than the causes of antisocial behavior. Wilson and Herrnstein (1985) argue that intervention studies often succeed in improving the academic skills of antisocial youth while failing to reduce the antisocial behavior.

It follows from the data of Patterson's group that parental management training can positively change high-risk youth in several spheres of their lives. The target children in these studies were simultaneously taught academic and social relations skills. Success in this effort is tied to the developmental age of the youngster; greater effectiveness of the remediation procedure, for example, is achieved with preadolescents than at later ages. There is relevancy here for the judicial system in that many youths, unfortunately, do not come to the attention of the court system until antisocial behavior has become entrenched (Patterson, Capaldi, & Bank, 1991). Moreover, judges often dispose of cases of younger first offenders without a treatment plan. When the court is dismissive of the destructive behavior, especially in the case of a first offense, this can be seen by the offender as devaluing the importance of the transgression.

Judges who consider only the offense, to the exclusion of the early remedial opportunities based on diagnostic and risk elements, may err in disposing of the case without a supervisory or treatment plan. Successful rehabilitation at the time of the next offense may become much more challenging than ordering more direction and structure at the time the youth first comes to the attention of the court. At the same time, the judicial decision must delicately weigh the available intervention opportunities to avoid unwarranted deprivation of liberty, on the one hand, and the possibility of seriously exacerbating the youth's oppositional tendencies, on the other. To engage the family in the process, rather than usurp parents' rights, may be both therapeutically and judicially sound.

Youths starting criminal careers in childhood and early adolescence are at greater risk of becoming chronic offenders than are late-starting offenders (Farrington, 1983; Kazdin, 1989, 1996; Loeber, 1982). Farrington found that boys first apprehended between ages 10 and 12 later averaged twice as many juvenile adjudications as late starters (Farrington, Ohlin, & Wilson, 1986). Moreover, Patterson et al. (1991) have found that early antisocial behavior covaries with a wide variety of family variables, such as argumentativeness and oppositional relationships, and predicts later delinquency.

Factors related to the risk of continued delinquency, then, have been identified. The further task is to develop a method of identifying individuals who should receive intensive and early intervention to head off a very likely negative outcome. No single condition, either of the offender or of the offender's history, environment, or current disposition, has been identified by investigators to predict an outcome. Instead, a constellation of historical, personality, and social context variables are found, in most studies, to conspire in significantly predicting outcomes. Because of low base rates for delinquency, even powerful composites of risk factors have been found in structural analyses to yield high rates of false positives (Blumstein et al., 1988; Farrington, 1997; Farrington et al., 1986; Rutter & Giller, 1984). This is unfortunate from the standpoint of society's need to identify with clarity those youngsters who are likely to become or continue to be delinquent. On the other hand, the fact that many youngsters whose predictive conditions and early behavior *seem* to dispose them to an antisocial way of life do not inevitably become criminals speaks to the power of resiliency in development (Garmezy & Rutter, 1983).

Deviance of a child within a family, particularly if it leads to arrest and a delinquency charge, will likely destabilize the entire family. Emotions may range from anger toward the child to a projection of blame onto the police, courts, and other agencies that are intruding on the family's privacy. Denial, rationalization, and avoidance are natural accompaniments of the process of adaptation to the stress, as well as feelings of hopelessness. Such draining of emotional resources and energy and diversion from productive endeavors often is followed by catastrophic financial consequences.

If the family does suffer seriously from the chain of events described, a systems approach to family dynamics may provide a framework for family therapy. For example, a "good" sibling sometimes responds to the behavior of her deviant sister or brother, expressing hate and anger in resentment of the attention her wayward sibling receives from the parents. The nondeviant child may also feel a sense of responsibility, and try protecting the parents from the stress of the prevailing conflict. This "parentification" of the child can rob her of age-appropriate developmental activities at school and in peer relationships.

One kind of response involving the family, taken from tribal customs and called *restorative justice*, shifts responsibility for resolving conflict from the state back to the communities, to families, and to individuals. This acknowledges and tends to reinforce families and communities as the cornerstones of society. This model has been developed and tried with some success in Canada (Stuart, 1996).

When crimes are committed that shock the community, as with violence perpetrated by children on children, intense emotional responses ensue, and these are frequently reflected in and intensified by the accompanying media reports. Murder and other heinous crimes, especially when committed by young children, evoke extreme reactions from the community. A public cry for new legislation to stiffen the laws and relegate juveniles to the adult court often follows. At this point, thoughtful approaches must be appropriated to offer rehabilitation models, even as the expected reactions of rage and desire for revenge and retribution surface.

THE COMORBIDITY OF JUVENILE DELINQUENCY

Juvenile delinquency raises many questions as to whether antisocial behavior and engagement in illegal activities by children and youth is symptomatic of, or at least signals, other psychological problems that may underlie, or even cause, the criminal behavior. There is evidence that delinquency co-occurs with other conditions, both individual characteristics and familial and other contextual factors (McCord & Tremblay, 1992).

van der Kolk (1987) has found that early childhood trauma, and especially brain injury, is a precursor of Attention Deficit Hyperactivity Disorder (ADHD). He has reviewed the psychobiology of memory related to post-traumatic stress, and provides strong evidence that early traumatic experiences may permanently change the physiology of the individual, such that ordinarily innocuous stimuli may be misinterpreted as potential threats (van der Kolk, 1994). Other studies have also shown that ADHD often co-occurs with antisocial and delinquent behavior (Kazdin, 1996; Luthar, Burack, Cicchetti, & Weisz, 1996). Conversely, a study at the National Center for State Courts has found that learning-disabled youth are no more likely to commit delinquent acts than are other youth, based on self-reports and police contacts. Thus there is some ambiguity in the literature as to the applicable nomenclature and the subtleties of co-occurrence in regard to juvenile delinquency.

Lipsitt, Buka, & Lipsitt (1990) found, in a longitudinal study, that at ages 4 and 7 years future juvenile delinquents achieve significantly lower IQ scores than children in the same cohort who do not later come to the attention of the juvenile court. While lower IQ early in life appears to be a vulnerability factor for delinquency, the fact is that most children with lower IQs do not develop delinquent behavior.

The differences of findings in this area are based largely on data on *adjudicated* delinquents. Perhaps this difference is the result of a perception of judges and others of a need for more involvement by the courts. The relevance of academic and vocational skills as predictors, as pointed out by Melton, Petrila, Poythress, & Slobogin (1997), may lie in self-esteem and mastery issues. Increasing social skills and social perception may improve interpersonal relationships, thus setting the stage for a prosocial rather than an antisocial behavioral pattern. Regardless of the reason for these differences in findings and the variation of opinion regarding them, involvement of a forensic clinician as a consultant in aiding the attorney during the preparation of such cases appears to be well justified to explore options for alternative dispositions. If for no other reason, the epidemiologic co-occurrence, even comorbidity, of learning disabilities, conduct disorders, and Oppositional Defiant Disorder would seem to demand this. Quay (1986) has identified several statistically robust constellations of relevant symptom patterns in children, including that for aggressive conduct disorder.

Kazdin (1989) has observed that family interaction patterns and parental dysfunction are particularly relevant in addressing options for intervention for serious antisocial behavior of children. The consideration must be to avoid further harm and act in the best interest of the child.

Tuma (1989) has reported that *atypical* practical interventions, such as job counseling, remedial education, and aid in managing money, are effective in the therapeutic setting and on clinical follow-up. Without these specific interventions, more traditional methods such as separation from the community and family do not typically improve behavior when the child returns to the home and to the community base, which originally contributed to spawning the offending behavior. This observation is consistent with Patterson's finding that the effectiveness of intervention depends upon involvement with the family and in the community where the juvenile will interact with parents and peers.

Patterson et al. (1989) present a paradigm for the experiential acquisition of an antisocial, oppositional, and aggressive pattern of behavior in juveniles. This involves poor parental discipline and monitoring, leading to conduct problems, resulting in rejection by nondelinquent peers and academic failure. This causes the child to gravitate toward a deviant peer group, thus increasing the likelihood of delinquent behavior.

LEGAL ISSUES RELATED TO CONFIDENTIALITY

Confidentiality is a cornerstone of the therapeutic relationship, recognized in the statutes of all 50 states. A recent case before the U.S. Supreme Court (*Jaffee v. Redmond*, 1996) recognized the importance of confidentiality in the relationship between clinicians and patients. However, in both the juvenile and adult courts, confidentiality is waived when an assessment is undertaken for the court. In psychologically evaluating an individual, a warning, preferably in writing, must always be given that the information may be available to the court, and informed-consent issues become relevant. If the clinician is retained by the attorney, the clinician should inform the juvenile that the report will be conveyed to the lawyer and become available to others.

The clinician must also receive guidance from the young person's attorney regarding disclosures to the child's parents. If the interests of the child are not consistent with the parental position, an adversarial relationship may exist between them, obligating the clinician to respect boundaries of confidentiality. The forensic clinician must be aware of the potential for conflictual or multiple relationships when assuming treatment of the youngster on whom he or she has conducted an evaluation (American Psychological Association, 1992). The clinician working in the legal system must be especially sensitive to the danger of merging roles. For example, if an evaluation is requested either by the court or by the attorney for the juvenile, this evaluation clearly should not be undertaken by someone who has been the juvenile's psychotherapist. Moreover, when the situation is reversed, and the clinician is asked, after evaluation, to continue to treat the juvenile, generally it would be considered both clinically and ethically inappropriate to do so. The possibility of a violation of ethics in maintaining multiple roles, as well as interference in a positive clinical relationship, may be compromised in such instances.

In rare circumstances, the unavailability of other qualified clinicians, or some other unavoidable contingency, may be sufficient to overcome the prohibition, and such a relationship may be acceptable. The defense of such a referral should be documented and, if possible, approved by the court.

SUMMARY AND RECOMMENDATIONS

The original *parens patriae* (state in place of the parents) role of the juvenile court has given way in recent times to an emphasis on the due process rights of children. Maintaining the original rehabilitative philosophy of the juvenile court now requires that the forensic psychologist be able to muster the strengths and cooperation of the family and community context to achieve those developmental goals.

The collaboration of psychologists with experts in criminal law has a rather short history, as Meehl (1970) pointed out. This collaboration has facilitated the introduction of a social welfare philosophy to the juvenile court that would avoid most of the procedures of the adult system. The rationale was adopted that the best interest of the child is of paramount importance. This informality in the name of *parens patriae* has now given way to the recognition and honoring of the same due process considerations accorded adults. Because of these rights, the clinician must ascertain the proper procedures for informing the youth of his or her rights, and provide warnings concerning confessions and to whom his or her statements will be revealed.

The American juvenile is entitled to the procedural safeguards of the criminal court, including the right to counsel and cross-examination, the privilege against self-incrimination, and the right to appellate review. A succession of cases has provided the substance of a paradigmatic shift in the treatment of juvenile criminals relative to the procedures for adults.

The David and Lucile Packard Foundation (1996) recently commissioned its Center for the Future of Children to study and make recommendations for society's recommitment to the U.S. juvenile court system, especially to strengthen its capacity to serve children and families. We are in agreement, and can do nothing better, in conclusion, than to repeat those recommendations here:

1. Juvenile courts should be at the level of the highest trial court of general jurisdiction in each state.
2. All judges and other judicial officers serving in a juvenile division or juvenile court should have intensive and ongoing training, not only in the statutory and case law governing delinquency, status offense, and dependency matters, but also in child development, cultural factors, resources for families, the court's relationship with and duties relating to child welfare agencies, and research findings regarding rehabilitative interventions.
3. Juvenile court judges should serve in the juvenile court division for at least 2 to 3 years.
4. All courts should work to better coordinate case processing by different branches of the general court that handle family-related matters, including the juvenile court.
5. Juvenile courts should encourage development and use of more alternative dispute resolution techniques.
6. Every youth referred to juvenile court for formal processing in delinquency matters should be represented by trained counsel from the time of the detention hearing through the court process.
7. The determination as to whether a minor charged with a serious crime should be transferred to the criminal court for trial as an adult is best made by judicial hearing.

8. Communities should ensure that a range of dispositional alternatives, providing a continuum of sanctions from community service and supervised probation to incarceration of juvenile offenders, is available to respond to juvenile crime; particular attention should be given to those models that have shown, through evaluation, success in reducing recidivism.

9. The first line of response to status offenders should be community and public services designed to help children and their families. Court intervention should occur only after services have been offered but have not been successful, or if the child's behavior continues to pose a threat to his or her safety or well-being.

10. In each state and locale, every effort should be made to assess the data system needs of juvenile courts and child welfare agencies and to address these needs in a coordinated and complementary manner.

11. Every juvenile court in the country should work with local child welfare agencies to improve effectiveness in providing abused and neglected children safe and permanent homes in a timely manner as specified by law.

12. Juvenile court judges should be educators and spokespersons in their communities on behalf of abused and neglected children. Judges should advocate for adequate court resources and community systems to respond promptly and appropriately to child abuse and neglect.

REFERENCES

Acts and Resolves of Massachusetts. (1996). An act to provide for the prosecution of violent offenders in the criminal courts of the Commonwealth (Vol. 2, pp. 898–912).

Albee, G., & Gullotta, T. P. (Eds.). (1996). *Primary prevention works: Vol. 6. Issues in children's and families' lives.* Thousand Oaks, CA: Sage.

Alexander, J. F., & Pugh, C. A. (1996). Oppositional behavior and conduct disorders of children and youth. In F. W. Kaslow (Ed.), *Handbook of relational diagnosis and dysfunctional family patterns* (pp. 210–224). New York: John Wiley & Sons.

American Psychiatric Association. (1994). *Diagnostic and statistical manual of mental disorders* (4th ed.). Washington, DC: Author.

American Psychological Association. (1992). *Ethical principles of psychologists and code of conduct.* Washington, DC: Author.

Bandura, A., & Walters, R. H. (1963). *Social learning and personality development.* New York: Holt, Rinehart and Winston.

Behrman, R. E. (Ed.). (1996). *The future of children: The juvenile court.* Los Altos, CA: Center for the Future of Children; Packard Foundation.

Blumstein, A., Cohen, S., & Farrington, D. P. (1988). Criminal career research: Its value for criminology. *Criminology, 26,* 1–35.

Coie, J. D., & Jacobs, M. R. (1993). The role of social context in the prevention of conduct disorder. *Development and Psychopathology, 5,* 263–275.

Dodge, K. A. (1993). The future of research on the treatment of conduct disorder. *Development and Psychopathology, 5,* 311–319.

Farrington, D. P. (1983). Offending from 10 to 25 years of age. In K. T. Van Dusen & S. A. Mednick (Eds.), *Prospective studies of crime and delinquency* (pp. 17–37). Boston: Kluwer-Nijhoff.

Farrington, D. P. (1997). The challenge of teenage antisocial behavior. In M. Rutter (Ed.), *Psychosocial disturbances in young people: Challenges for prevention* (pp. 83–130). New York: Cambridge University Press.

Farrington, D. P., Ohlin, L. E., & Wilson, J. Q. (1986). *Understanding and controlling crime: Toward a new research strategy.* New York: Spring-Verlag.

Garmezy, N., & Rutter, M. (Eds.). (1983). *Stress, coping, and development in children.* New York: McGraw-Hill.

Glueck, S., & Glueck, E. T. (1934). *One thousand juvenile delinquents: Their treatment by court and clinic.* Cambridge, MA: Harvard University Press.

Hamburg, D. A. (1997). *A perspective on Carnegie Corporation's Program, 1983–1997.* New York: Carnegie Corporation of New York.

Healy, W. (1915). *The individual delinquent: A text-book of diagnosis and prognosis for all concerned in understanding offenders.* Boston: Little, Brown.

Healy, W. (1922). *The practical value of scientific study of juvenile delinquents* (U.S. Children's Bureau Publication No. 96). Washington, DC: U.S. Government Printing Office.

In re Gault (1966), 387 U.S. 1.

Jaffee v. Redmond (1996), 116 S. Ct. 1923.

Kaslow, F. W. (Ed.) (1996). *Handbook of relational diagnosis and dysfunctional family patterns.* New York: John Wiley & Sons.

Kazdin, A. E. (1989). Developmental psychopathology: Current research issues and direction. *American Psychologist, 44,* 180–187.

Kazdin, A. E. (1993). Treatment and conduct disorder: Progress and directions in psychotherapy research. *Development and Psychopathology, 5,* 277–310.

Kazdin, A. E. (1996). Conduct disorder across the life span. In S. S. Luthar, J. A. Burack, D. Cicchetti, & J. R. Weisz (Eds.), *Developmental psychopathology: Perspectives on adjustment, risk, and disorder* (pp. 248–272). New York: Cambridge University Press.

Kent v. United States (1966), 383 U.S. 541.

Levine, M., & Levine, A. (1976). *A social history of the helping professions: Clinic, court, school and community.* New York: Appleton-Century-Crofts.

Levine, M., & Levine, A. (1992). *Helping children: A social history.* New York: Oxford University Press.

Lewis, M. (1997). *Altering fate: Why the past does not predict the future.* New York: Guilford Press.

Lipsitt, P. D., Buka, S., & Lipsitt, L. P. (1990). Early intelligence scores and subsequent delinquency: A prospective study. *American Journal of Family Therapy, 18,* 192–200.

Lipsitt, P. D., Lelos, D., & Gibbs, M. P. (1985). A family oriented alternative to pre-trial detention of juveniles. *American Journal of Family Therapy, 13,* 61–66.

Loeber, R. (1982). The stability of antisocial and delinquent child behavior: A review. *Child development, 53,* 1431–1446.

Loeber, R., & Dishion, T. J. (1983). Early predictors of male delinquency. *Psychological Bulletin, 94,* 68–99.

Luthar, S. S., Burack, J. A., Cicchetti, D., & Weisz, J. R. (Eds.). (1996). *Developmental Psychopathology: Perspectives on adjustment, risk, and disorder.* New York: Cambridge University Press.

McCord, J., & Tremblay, R. (Eds.). (1992). *Preventing antisocial behavior: Interventions from birth through adolescence.* New York: Guilford Press.

Meehl, P. E. (1970). Psychology and the criminal law. *University of Richmond Law Review, 5,* 1–30.

Melton, G., Petrila, J., Poythress, N., & Slobogin, C. (1997). *Psychological evaluations for the courts: A handbook for mental health professionals and lawyers* (2nd ed., pp. 417–440). New York: Guilford Press.

Osofsky, J. D. (Ed.). (1997). *Children in a violent society.* New York: Guilford.

Packard Foundation. (1997). The juvenile court [Executive summary]. *The Future of Children, 6*(3). Los Altos, CA: Author.

Patterson, G. R. (1992). Developmental changes in antisocial behavior. In R. D. Peters, R. J. McMahon, & V. L. Quincy (Eds.). *Aggression and violence throughout the life span* (pp. 52–82). Newbury Park, CA: Sage.

Patterson, G. R., Capaldi, D., & Bank, L. (1991). An early starter model for predcting delinquency. In D. J. Pepper & K. H. Rubin (Eds.), *The development and treatment of childhood aggression* (pp. 139–168). Hillsdale, NJ: Erlbaum.

Patterson, G. R., DeBaryshe, B. D., & Ramsey, E. (1989). A developmental perspective on antisocial behavior. *American Psychologist, 44,* 329–335.

Patterson, G. R., Reid, J. B., & Dishion, T. J. (1992). *Antisocial boys.* Eugene, OR: Castalia.

Patterson, G. R., & Stouthamer-Loeber, M. (1984). The correlation of family management practices and delinquency. *Child Development, 55,* 1299–1307.

Quay, H. C. (1986). Classification. In H. C. Quay & J. Werry (Eds.), *Psychopathology disorders in childhood* (3rd ed.) (pp. 1–34). New York: John Wiley & Sons.

Reid, J. B. (1993). Prevention of conduct disorder before and after school entry: Relating interventions to developmental findings. *Development and Psychopathology, 5,* 243–262.

Rosenheim, M. K. (1962). *Justice for the child.* New York: Free Press of Glencoe.

Rutter, M., & Giller, H. (1984). *Juvenile delinquency: Trends and perspectives.* New York: Guilford Press.

Sears, R. R., Maccoby, E. E., & Levin, H. (1957). *Patterns of child rearing.* Evanston, IL: Row, Peterson.

Shaw, C. (1930). *The jack-roller.* Chicago: University of Chicago Press.

Shaw, C., & Moore, M. E. (1931). *The natural history of a delinquent's career.* Chicago: University of Chicago Press.

Stuart, B. (1996). Circle sentencing in Canada: A partnership of the community and the criminal justice system. *International Journal of Comparative and Applied Criminal Justice, 20.*

Tapp, J. L. (1976). Psychology and the law: An overture. *Annual Review of Psychology, 27,* 359–404.

Tuma, S. M. (1989). Mental health services for children: The state of the art. *American Psychologist, 44,* 188–199.

van der Kolk, B. A. (1987). The compulsion to repeat the trauma: Re-enactment, revictimization, and masochism. *Psychiatric Clinics of North America, 12,* 389–411.

van der Kolk, B. A. (1994). The body keeps the score: Memory and the evolving psychobiology of post-traumatic stress. *Harvard Review of Psychiatry, 1,* 4.

Weisz, J. R. (1996). Effects of interventions for child and adolescent psychological dysfunction: Relevance of context, developmental factors, and individual differences. In S. S. Luthar, J. A. Burack, D. Cicchetti, & J. R. Weisz (Eds.), *Developmental psychopathology: Perspectives on adjustment, risk, and disorder* (pp. 3–22). New York: Cambridge University Press.

Werner, E. E., & Smith, R. S. (1982). *Vulnerable but invincible.* New York: McGraw-Hill.

Wilson, J. Q., & Herrnstein, R. (1985). *Crime and human Nature.* New York: Simon & Schuster.

Wolfgang, M. E. (1989). *From boy to man: From delinquency to crime.* Chicago: University of Chicago Press.

Wordsworth, W. (1904). My heart leaps up when I behold. *Wordsworth's original poems* (p. 277). Boston: Houghton Mifflin.

CHAPTER 11

Spouse Abuse

CHARLES G. GUYER II

THERE HAVE been few studies that clearly separate spouse abuse from other forms of domestic abuse (e.g., child abuse, elder abuse, and abuse of other persons living in the home). A scan of the literature indicates that there have not been any clear distinctions as to what constitutes physical abuse, emotional abuse, or sexual abuse. In other words, it is unclear at what point a verbal altercation becomes verbal abuse or a physical touch becomes physical abuse. This chapter defines physical abuse as pushing, slapping, grabbing, or any other more severe form of physical touch (e.g., hitting, kicking, biting, etc.). Straus (1993) used a similar definition to define child physical abuse. Rosenberg (1984) has defined emotional abuse as verbal assaults on a person's character, threats to kill oneself, to coerce another, or to commit homicide.

It is also not easy to determine what relationship defines a spouse. *Spouse* is used here to convey a married partner or significant other living in the same home.

The term *domestic abuse* is now in more common usage than the term *spouse abuse*. This term is broader and includes all members of a household. This chapter focuses on the male–female relationship in the family. It must be kept in mind, however, that men who batter their spouses may also physically abuse children (Ross, 1996). It has also been posited that women who are physically abused by their partners may be at higher risk for abusing their children (Gayford, 1975; Stark & Flitcraft, 1988; Walker, 1984). Some studies have suggested that an equal number of men and women are abused by their spouses (Straus, 1993; Vivian & Langhinrichson-Rohling, 1994). Most authors, however, agree that in male–female physical abuse, the female is the one who is at greater risk for physical harm (Cantos, Neidig, & O'Leary, 1994). Men are generally physically larger in build and have more muscle mass than women. Thus, a man generally is more capable of inflicting severe physical damage on a woman than vice versa. When one person physically attacks another person in our society, it is generally viewed as a clear violation of the law. The person who has perpetrated the attack is usually arrested and placed in jail.

Spouse abuse has not historically been viewed by our society as a criminal offense. Rather, it has often been looked on as a family problem. Domestic abuse complaints are usually handled by agencies who view themselves as social agencies, not law enforcement agencies (e.g., the Department of Social Services, or the Department of Public Welfare). Even when the police are called in on a domestic violence complaint, they prefer to handle it through mediation rather than arrest. Some police view women's claims that they have been battered by their spouses as noncredible and unworthy of police time (Balknap, 1995; Rigakos, 1995). Even marital rape is viewed as a lesser crime in our society than stranger rape (Whatley, 1993).

ETIOLOGY OF DOMESTIC VIOLENCE

A wide array of theories have been put forth to explain the causes of domestic violence. These range from theories involving neurological damage (Krakowski & Czobor, 1994), to sociological theories (Wilson, Johnson, & Daly, 1995), and psychological determinants (Barnett, Martinez, & Bluestein, 1995; Elbow, 1977; Holtzworth-Munroe and Stuart, 1993; Mott-McDonald, 1979; Murphy & O'Farrell, 1994; Pan, Neidig, & O'Leary, 1994; Saunders, 1993, 1994; Walker 1979, 1984, 1988, 1994b, 1995, 1996; Walker & Edwell, 1987). Each set is briefly explicated in the following subsections.

NEUROLOGICAL THEORIES

Neurological damage resulting from head injury has long been thought to play a part in violent behavior. Krakowski and Czobor (1994) studied 38 psychiatric inpatients who were persistently violent in the hospital setting. Their data confirmed that there is a positive correlation between violence and neurological impairment. Rosenbaum, Hoge, Adelman, and Warnken (1994) applied this concept to men who were abusive to their wives. They studied 53 partner-abusive men, 45 maritally satisfied men, and 32 maritally discordant men who were nonviolent. These men were all evaluated for past head injury by a physician who was not informed of group membership and history of aggression. This research confirmed that head injury is a significant predictor of a man being a batterer.

SOCIOLOGICAL THEORIES

Sociological theories indicate that domestic violence occurs across all social strata and in all ethnic groups and cultures. Kantor, Jasinski, and Aldarondo (1994) present evidence that shows that Hispanic families are not different from Anglo American families in the number of reported battering incidents. Saunders (1995) presents similar data for the African American community. Native American families are not exempt from domestic violence problems, and exhibit no more reported spouse abuse than any other group per capita (Chester, Robin, Koss, Lopez, & Goldman, 1994). The military is another subculture that has been studied extensively concerning the incidence of spouse abuse. I served as a psychologist in the U.S. Navy from 1983 until 1988. During that time, the military was expending great sums of money to determine how to best deal with domestic abuse. Dr. Peter Neidig was contracted by the Marine Corps to develop a program for its drill instructors at Parris Island, South Carolina, during that period. There was concern that Marine Corps drill instructors were under more stress than the military population in general. Those stationed at the Parris Island Branch Medical Clinic were forced to become adept at diagnosing and intervening in domestic abuse situations. Schwabe and Kaslow (1984) found that the military, because of its concerns about domestic violence, established child advocacy centers in 1978. In 1979, spouse abuse prevention and treatment were included as another focus of these centers. This led to a greater reporting of incidences of abuse than may have been true in the civilian sector. The research data indicates that the military, in general, does not show a higher rate of domestic violence than the population at large (Mollerstorm, Patchner, & Milner, 1992).

It has even been hypothesized that modernization of the world has increased the frequency of domestic violence due to the pressures of daily life. Morley (1994) attempted to test this hypothesis. She found that there were no significant differences in wife beating between the rural natives and the urban dwellers of Papua, New Guinea. Goeckermann, Hamberger, and Barber (1994) conducted a study of differences in spouse abuse between rural and urban areas in the United States. They, too, found no significant difference between the two groups. Thus, it does not appear that urbanization and industrialization have a great deal of impact on domestic violence.

The search for some clue as to the etiology of domestic violence has led researchers to study the difference between common-law marriages and traditional marriages (Wilson, Johnson, & Daly, 1995) and to study violence among the homeless (Browne, 1993). These two areas of investigation have yielded little new information.

The use of alcohol has long been associated with violence of all types. Murphy and O'Farrell (1994) studied male alcoholics who were physically aggressive toward their wives and compared them to their nonaggressive counterparts. They found that two key patterns of alcohol use were associated with spouse abuse: (a) binge drinking was linked with coercive marital conflicts, and (b) the earlier the onset of alcoholism, the more likely the man was to abuse his spouse. Maritally aggressive men were younger and exhibited more binge drinking, a higher prevalence of arrests, more verbal aggression, a more severe alcohol problem, earlier alcoholism onset, more diagnosed alcoholics among their male biological relatives, less maternal alcohol use, less confidence in their ability to manage interpersonal conflict without drinking, and a stronger belief that alcohol causes marital problems. Several other studies have confirmed the association between violence and alcoholism (Bradford & McLean, 1984; Senchak & Leonard, 1994).

PSYCHOLOGICAL THEORIES

Many different psychological theories may help account for the occurrence of domestic violence. These theories often look at the individual's emotional and personality makeup and the existence of mental illness. Barnett et al. (1995) examined the idea that maritally violent men are more jealous than maritally nonviolent men. Their results found that jealousy does not seem to be a primary precipitating factor in wife battering.

Greene, Coles, and Johnson (1994) examined psychopathology and its relationship to expression of anger. Their goal was to confirm previous distinctions of personality types among abusive individuals and to examine the relationship between these types and anger. They found that there were four clusters of interpersonal violence offenders. The most pathological cluster type reported the highest level of total anger experience, while the histrionic cluster type reported the lowest anger expression. This would provide tentative support for a positive relationship between psychopathology and anger, as well as for the distinction between overcontrolled and undercontrolled subtypes of interpersonal violence offenders. It appears that the overcontrolled group is more abusive.

Hiday (1995) has taken issue with the idea that the presence of mental illness actually increases violence. There is the acknowledgment that the evidence does suggest a modest association between active major mental disorders and violence; however, a case is built that social context establishes the socialization and environmental conditions that are causal in both violence and the development of mental disorders. Hiday posits a causal model which links social stratification with both mental illness and violence through the structured types of strains, events, situations, and personal interactions that individuals experience as an integral part of daily life. There have been many attempts to create a typology of male batterers (Elbow, 1977; Holtzworth-Munroe & Stuart, 1993; Mott-McDonald, 1979). Saunders (1992) also attempted to derive a typology of men who batter their spouses. He concluded that there was not a strong enough statistically significant relationship to make firm statements concerning typologies of batterers. He ended his article encouraging clinicians to recognize that there is no single profile of men who batter.

In spite of repeated failures to establish a profile of the male batterer, many researchers have continued with this quest. Pan et al. (1994) did find that when they compared mildly physically aggressive men to men who were more severely physically aggressive, those who were more physically aggressive earned lower incomes, were more likely to report alcohol and drug problems, and had more marital discord and depressive symptomatology.

There is perhaps only one common truism among those attempting to determine the potential for domestic abuse, and that is the fact that *being abused as a child is a strong predictor of becoming an abuser as an adult.* Saunders (1994) suggests that there may actually be a more consistent risk marker for abusive relationships. He feels that being abused as a child coupled with witnessing violence in the family of origin is the most potent risk factor for men becoming batterers.

It does appear that the prediction of violent behavior is best made based on past acts of violence and not from general personality traits (Monahan, 1981). Wolfe (1985) reviewed the literature on child physical abuse and concluded that the study of underlying personality attributes and traits has not yielded patterns associated with child abusers.

Currently, the theory of battering relationships that has gained the most credibility among mental health professionals is that of the *battered woman syndrome* (Walker, 1979). The definition of this syndrome has become broadened over the years. It now includes descriptions of the dynamics of battering relationships and describes how many battered women experience a group of symptoms that are similar to those of Post-Traumatic Stress Disorder (PTSD) as outlined in the *Diagnostic and Statistical Manual of Mental Disorders, Fourth Edition* (*DSM-IV*; American Psychiatric Association, 1994). Herein, PTSD is placed under the broad heading of anxiety disorders. To receive the diagnosis of PTSD, a person must meet criteria outlined in the *Quick Reference to the Diagnostic Criteria from DSM-IV* (American Psychiatric Association, 1994b, pp. 209–211).

A cycle of violence in battering relationships has been identified by Walker (1996). She views this as consisting of three main phases: (a) a period of building tension, (b) the acute battering incident or explosion, and (c) a period of loving contrition. It is possible to graph this cycle in specific relationships by taking the details from four abusive incidents. Walker believes it is important to use the first battering incident that can be remembered, the last one that occurred prior to the interview, one of the worst incidents, and a typical battering incident. She also points out that a couple's cycle may change over time due to external circumstances (e.g., pregnancy, a young infant in the house, teenagers, loss of one's job, involvement in a treatment program, or involvement with the legal system).

Walker (1979, 1984, 1996) has adapted Seligman's (1975) theory of learned helplessness to aid in explaining the battered woman's behavior of remaining in a relationship in which she is repeatedly placed at physical and emotional risk. The concept of learned helplessness suggests that battered women lose the capacity to perceive that their actions will have any impact in protecting them from what they see as a noncontingent relationship between response (their behavior) and outcome (being physically abused or not). The cycle of violence in which the woman finds herself reinforces to her that a given behavior may work during one phase, but not during another. This leads the battered woman to rely on coping styles that appear to be valid time after time. Many strategies that would appear successful to the casual observer have not worked for her in the past. Often the batterer will stalk the woman and continue to abuse her even when she physically leaves the home. Seligman's theory is a learning theory, and suggests that the man's violent behavior is learned and thus can be unlearned. The woman's ineffective coping styles are also learned and can be unlearned and replaced with more effective responses. This makes the learned helplessness model an optimistic one to most theorists.

ASSESSING THE MALE BATTERER

A word of warning: Do not enter the assessment process assuming that an individual is guilty. Allow the man's innocence or guilt to unfold during the assessment process. Remember, harm can be done if you find an innocent person to be guilty of a crime. Ceci and Bruck (1995) suggest throughout their book that many innocent people have been imprisoned due to professionals from all disciplines entering into cases with preconceived notions of guilt on the part of the accused. These professionals then consciously or unconsciously set about building cases to fit their preconceived notions. Spiegel (1986, 1998, 1990) graphically describes his own experience of being falsely accused of child abuse, with the accompanying horror and pain this brought into his personal life as well as his professional life as a psychologist.

This tendency of some mental health professionals to enter into assessment of alleged abusers with preconceived notions of guilt has contributed to the formation of "family rights" groups. These groups go by several names (e.g., the Family Independent Strike Force, Families Against Court Tyranny, and the False Memory Syndrome Foundation); all have the sole stated purpose of discrediting and eventually eliminating the mental health professions (Brown, Scheflin, & Hammond, 1998; Scott, Scheflin, & Wester, 1998; Spiegel, 1998).

In most states, it is the function of the Department of Social Services (DSS) to orchestrate the gathering of information (possibly with the help of the sheriff's department or the police department) concerning allegations of spouse abuse and child abuse. DSS is not a legal agency; it is not empowered to arrest anyone. A social worker representing DSS can go before the judge and request a court order that requires a person to do certain things. The court order, however, is enforced by a law enforcement agency. The social worker generally gathers data from physicians (who may have treated the battered woman in the emergency room). They interview witnesses who have observed altercations that have occurred in public view; they may interview family members, and may visit the home at unexpected times to observe how the family interacts. The DSS staff also may request that a psychologist or a psychiatrist interview either one or both members of the pair. At the end of the investigation, the social worker is the individual who has all of the data concerning the family (Saunders, 1994), and is the one who makes recommendations to the court.

The use of structured interview techniques and questionnaires is the method of choice for gaining insight into who may engage in violence and who may not (Feldhause, Koziol-McLain, Amsbury, Norton, & Lowenstein, 1997; Hughs, 1996; Lanza, Kayne, Pattison, Hicks, & Islam, 1994; Rhodes, 1992; Smith et al., 1994). This approach provides an opportunity to gain a clear understanding of the individual's history and any involvement in previously violent acts or exposure to a violent home situation as a child. Some data indicate that professional clinicians are no more accurate in predicting violence than are nonclinicians (Minzies & Webster, 1995). Patient self-reports, collateral reports, and clinical judgments about potential for abuse were found to be the most important predictors of violence in a study carried out by Lidz, Mulvey, and Gardner (1993).

The Minnesota Multiphasic Personality Inventory (MMPI) is one of the most studied instruments in the prediction of violence and potential child or spouse abuse. Henderson (1982) studied the MMPI protocols of 87 male nonviolent offenders ages 21 to 56 and compared them to 105 male violent offenders of the same age range. She found no statistically significant differences between the two groups. Fraboni, Cooper, Reed, and Saltstone (1990) examined offense data and MMPI profiles for 67 men who had been remanded by the courts to a psychiatric hospital forensic unit for partial assessment. The men were classified as violent offenders (charged with assault, robbery, sexual assault, and degrees of homicide) or as nonviolent offenders (charged with breaking and entering, uttering threats, and fraud). Their findings indicate that neither of the *two* commonly employed MMPI codes discriminated between the violent and nonviolent offenders. These codes are labeled *psychopathic deviance* and *schizophrenia*. This piece of research is quite significant due to the fact that the characteristics found in the MMPI profiles studied represent many of the characteristics that clinicians have anecdotally attributed to men who batter women.

O'Sullivan and Jemelka (1993), in a study of 94 randomly selected male offenders with a mean age of 31 who had achieved codes on the MMPI that have historically been associated with violence, found that these scores were *not* a good predictor of violent behavior. This lends support to the findings of Fraboni et al. (1990). Many other researchers have also reached the conclusion that the MMPI is not a good predictor of violent behavior (Chick, Loy, & White, 1984; Langevin, Wright, & Handy, 1990; Truescott, 1990).

Research attempting to find a specific MMPI code for the male batterer has also met with failure (Else, Wonderlich, Beatty, Christie, & Staton, 1993; Hale, Zimostrand, Duckworth, & Nicholas, 1988). Hale et al. (1988) investigated the observations of many clinicians that men who batter tend to minimize and externalize blame for violent behavior (Ganley & Harris, 1978; Walker, 1979), to feel inadequate and dissatisfied with themselves (Walker, 1979), and to have strong tendencies toward various addictions (Walker, 1979). Hale et al. hypothesized that persons who achieve a profile on the MMPI on the scales labeled *depression* and *psychopathic deviance* would reflect these traits. Graham (1990) stated that when these persons come to the attention of mental health professionals, it is usually after they have been in trouble with their families or the law. The research of Hale et al. did *not* support the existence of an MMPI profile that could be called a batterer's profile.

Else et al. (1993) attempted to characterize personality traits and psychological and cognitive characteristics of men who batter women in order to distinguish them from nonbatterers. They compared a group of 21 batterers with a group of nonbatterers, using the MMPI and its personality disorder scales (MMPIPDS). They also developed a hostility and direction of hostility questionnaire, which they implemented. The two groups were matched on several demographic variables and on their scores on the Revised Michigan Alcoholism Screening Test, along with three cognitive measures and three measures of affective disturbance. This study found *no* significant differences between men who batter and men who do not batter on these measures.

A variety of other standardized psychological tests have been studied to determine how well they predict violence. The Wechsler scales have fared as poorly as the MMPI in their ability to predict violent behavior (Cornell & Wilson, 1992; Nussbaum, Choudhry, & Martin-Doto, 1996; Roszkowski, 1984).

It has been proposed that persons who score higher on the performance subscales of the Wechsler intelligence tests are more prone to violent acting-out behavior. Cornell and Wilson (1992) attempted to research this hypothesis. They studied 149 juveniles ages 12 to 17 who were convicted of serious crimes. They required a discrepancy of 12 IQ points, with the performance IQ being greater than the verbal IQ on the Wechsler Intelligence Scale for Children—Revised (WISC-R) or the Wechsler Adult Intelligence Scale—Revised (WAIS-R). Their findings indicate that the Wechsler scales do *not* differentiate violent from nonviolent offenders.

It has also been proposed that a low similarities subtest score, relative to other subtests on the Wechsler scales, is associated with violent behavior. Roszkowski

(1984) subjected this hypothesis to empirical scrutiny and found that a low similarities subtest score compared to other subtest scores does *not* differentiate violent from nonviolent behavior. He concluded his article by pointing out that his study was at least the fourth piece of research to yield the same findings.

Nussbaum et al. (1996) examined 30 violent and nonviolent mentally disordered offenders to determine if they could be differentiated on the basis of cognitive impulsivity components, locus of control, abstract and concrete intelligence, and three potentially relevant MMPI scales. Their results indicate that these variables *do not* readily distinguish between groups of violent and nonviolent mentally disordered offenders.

Empirical research data concerning the Rorschach Ink Blot Test and the Thematic Apperception Test (TAT) is largely nonexistent. The majority of articles written concerning the Rorschach and TAT tests present anecdotal data. These articles simply report Rorschach protocols and TAT stories of persons who have committed violent acts (Greiner & Nunno, 1994; Kaser-Boyd, 1993; Pollak & Gilligan, 1983; Sally & Teiling, 1984). Two studies have attempted to empirically evaluate the use of the Rorschach in predicting violence. A study by Coram (1995) and another by Hughes, Deville, Chalhoub, and Romboletti (1992) have yielded data which suggests that the Rorschach may be helpful in predicting violence. Coram is quick to point out, however, that these are tentative findings which have little support to draw from in the general literature.

It becomes apparent that the most reliable and efficient method of assessing the male batterer is through a structured interview that evaluates specific markers of violence in the family of origin, past behavior, and present behavior. Standardized psychological testing appears to add little or no information concerning men who batter. Batterers may actually appear emotionally healthier on standardized psychological tests than their battered female partner does (Ayoub, Grace, Paradise, & Newberger, 1991).

ASSESSING THE BATTERED WOMAN

There is evidence to suggest that when battered women develop psychological problems, they are the direct result of battering (Stark, Flitgraft, & Frazier, 1979). Abused women, when compared with nonabused women, do not report higher rates of past psychopathology. These women and maritally discordant women did report higher rates of emotional abuse as children than maritally satisfied nonabused women (Cascardi, O'Leary, Lawrence, & Schlee, 1995). It appears that victimization by one's mother when growing up predicts marital perpetration, whereas victimization from the father predicts marital victimization (Langhinrichsen-Rohling, Neidig, & Thorn, 1995).

The battered woman's emotional turmoil is escalated by some of the nonviolent tactics used by men who batter. Many of these tactics resemble those used against prisoners of war. The batterer often isolates the woman, blames her for the abuse, falsely accuses her of infidelity, and puts such labels on her as *crazy, stupid,* or *whore* (Walker, 1984). He may also make death threats, especially if the woman tries to leave the relationship. When a battered woman learns that her partner wants custody of the children, her stress level may become overwhelming, because her goal in leaving him is often to protect the children (Chesler, 1987). This pattern of symptoms that make up the battered woman syndrome closely resembles the symptoms of PTSD (Figley, 1986; Walker, 1994b).

Gellen, Hoffman, Jones, and Stone (1984) administered the MMPI orally to 10 conjugally abused females ages 19 to 42 in a residential treatment center and to 10 nonabused females matched for age, race, and socioeconomic status. They found that the abused women scored significantly higher on the scales that measure hypochondriasis, depression, hysteria, psychopathic deviance, paranoia, schizophrenia, and social introversion. The authors maintain that to expect logical, goal-directed, and independent behavior from these women is not consistent with this MMPI profile. They point out that this profile suggests a similarity with the construct of learned helplessness. These authors note that their results confirm the findings of previous studies which showed that women in abusive relationships manifest disordered personalities. Thus, they recommend that these women be treated in a psychotherapeutic relationship concurrent with treatment for the male abuser to bring about constructive change within the relationship. Perrin, Van-Hasselt, Basilio, and Hersen (1996) were interested in testing the hypothesis that battered women manifest a profile on the MMPI-Keane scale that is similar to that of persons suffering with PTSD. These authors studied 69 battered women who were assigned to PTSD-positive and PTSD-negative groups and then were compared on measures of PTSD, distress, social support, and history of abuse in and out of the battering relationship. Their findings are ambivalent and suggest that the Keane scale is only mildly sensitive in distinguishing battered women.

Rosewater (1982, 1985a, 1985b, 1987) suggests that when battered women are administered the MMPI, their average profile shows features that are consistent with borderline personality disorder and schizophrenia. Unlike Gellen et al. (1984), she does not believe that this represents major psychopathology. She believes, instead, that these scores reflect the fact that battered women have been severely traumatized and fear the recurrence of violent behavior.

Battered women may appear to others (e.g., police, social service workers, lawyers, and judges) to be unstable, nervous, inarticulate, or angry (Crites & Coker, 1988). Many women, in an attempt to deal with the trauma in their lives, turn to alcohol or drugs. Psychological tests like the MMPI MacAndrew scale, which assesses alcoholism, may show that the battered woman is an alcoholic or a drug addict. If psychological testing is implemented at all in assessing battered women, it is clear that this must be undertaken with extreme caution. This is particularly important given that our society often asks why so many women allow themselves to be battered. There is a tendency in this environment to victimize the victim (Ryan, 1975).

ASSESSING THE ABUSIVE RELATIONSHIP

The ideal situation for the assessment of domestic violence is to have a well-informed mental health professional who is able to evaluate the entire family utilizing structured interviews (Walker, 1996), questionnaires (Bodin, 1996), or rating scales (Milner, 1986; Milner & Gold, 1986).

PROCEDURE FOR ASSESSMENT OF DOMESTIC VIOLENCE

Determine the referral source. If the referral source is a social agency (e.g., DSS, Child and Youth Services, a community hospital, etc.), then one should set up an appointment with the referring person. In this meeting, an attempt is made to gather all information that has been compiled (e.g., medical, legal, etc.). It is helpful to learn if there is a history of contact with other community agencies. If it is not possible to have an interview with the referring person, then it is important to gather as much information as possible over the telephone and to note the specific referral questions. This allows for a clearer evaluation so that the examiner can respond to the specific questions.

As a programmatic example, the University of North Carolina at Chapel Hill has a Child Mental Health Evaluation Program. This program requires that psychologists and psychiatrists who assess battered women, abused children, or batters directly state their opinions as to whether abuse has occurred. It is also deemed important to establish whether the assessment is being carried out as part of an overall evaluation (e.g., one piece that will be weighed by the referral source along with information from other assessors). This is generally the case when a referral comes from DSS, which will usually gather information from many sources (e.g., medical, legal, etc.). The psychological assessment will be viewed in the context of the overall picture. When the evaluation is court ordered, the judge may or may not have access to as broad a scope of information as DSS can present.

Next, meet with the woman who is allegedly an abuse victim. It is best that this evaluation be carried out separately from the session with the man. It is easier to get more information in these individual interviews, and the safety of the woman is likely to be better protected.

- *Make sure that the woman signs an informed consent for treatment.* The informed consent agreement should make clear to the individual the limits of confidentiality. This must be explained in such a way that she totally understands what can remain confidential and what cannot. If the case is court ordered, be sure to explain in detail that all information will go back to the judge. If the case is referred by DSS, explain that a report containing most of the information will go back to a social worker for that agency. Further, explain the policies of the clinic or practice in which the evaluation is being conducted.

  In my office, I give a brochure to the patients so that they can review it and fully understand the policies and procedures of the office. If minor children are involved, the custodial parent or guardian should sign an informed consent. One should also consider having children between the ages of 13 to 17 sign this form, as they are party to the transaction. I have found that the woman feels more secure going through the informed-consent process, as she knows exactly what will be done with the information she presents. She also gains a sense that she is being respected, which is vital for her self-concept, particularly if she has been abused and tormented.

- *Conduct a structured clinical interview.* This interview may include collecting information under the following headings:
  1. Presenting problem and referral source
  2. Primary care physician—name, telephone number, and street address

3. Mental status examination
4. Medical history
5. Psychological history
6. Social history
7. Legal history
8. Substance abuse screen (history and current data)
9. A working diagnosis using the *DSM-IV*, Axis I through V
10. Medical and psychiatric consultation, when required
11. Development of a safety plan with verbal rehearsal and the homework to actually rehearse the safety plan between this meeting and the next meeting (for the woman and possibly for the man)
12. Treatment plan

Goals of treatment

Objective outcome measures

Planned interventions

Date of next appointment

How to contact the evaluator, therapist or backup person in case of an emergency, 24 hours a day, 7 days a week

The patient then signs the plan, as does the doctor.

- *Assessment of lethality is important and must be accomplished on the first meeting with the woman or man.* Walker and Sonkin (1994) have offered the following questions for assessing lethality (current author's adaptation):

1. Is the frequency of the man's use of violence escalating?
2. Is the severity of the man's violence escalating?
3. What is the frequency of alcohol intoxication and drug use?
4. Is the frequency of alcohol and drug use escalating?
5. Has the man threatened to harm the children?
6. Has the woman threatened to harm the children?
7. Has the man threatened to kill the woman or others?
8. Has the woman threatened to kill the man or others?
9. Has the man forced or threatened to force sexual acts on the woman?
10. Has the man made suicide threats or attempts?
11. Has the woman made suicide threats or attempts?
12. Are easily accessible weapons kept in the home, and have these been used in fights?
13. Is there psychiatric impairment in the man?
14. Is there psychiatric impairment in the woman?
15. What is the proximity of the man and the woman—how close do they both work and live together?
16. What is the level of the man's need for control of contact around the children?
17. What is the level of the woman's need for control of contact around the children?
18. What are the current life stresses that the man is experiencing?
19. What are the current life stresses that the woman is experiencing?
20. Does the man have a criminal history?
21. Does the woman have a criminal history?

22. What is the man's attitude towards violence, specifically violence against women?
23. What is the woman's attitude towards men being dominant over women, and what is her view of men being physical with women?
24. Is there a new relationship in the man's life?
25. Is there a new relationship in the woman's life?

- *Assess the learned helplessness variables.* Walker (1984, 1994b, 1996) has arranged these into seven factors so that the current relationship can be assessed and issues from childhood that arose in the family of origin can be assessed. (The following version is built on Walker's ideas, with revisions and additions made by the author.)

LEARNED HELPLESSNESS VARIABLES FROM THE RELATIONSHIP

1. The pattern of violence often escalates in frequency and severity and follows the violence cycle: (a) period of building tension, (b) acute battering incident or explosion, and (c) period of loving contrition.
2. Sexual abuse and coercion occur within the relationship.
3. Power and control factors, including intrusiveness, overpossessiveness, jealousy, and isolation, occur.
4. There are direct and indirect threats to kill the woman or her family.
5. There is psychological torture (Walker, 1997).

   Isolation
   - The woman may be locked in a house, room, or closet.
   - The woman may be tied up with ropes, chains, handcuffs, or other forms of restraint.
   - The woman may be forced to live in remote, isolated settings so that she has no contact with a support system and is unable to verify information given to her by the man.
   - The man may force the woman to move frequently as a means of keeping her from establishing a support system.
   - The man may totally control the woman's social contacts so that she has little ability to interact with her family or friends.
   - The man may monitor telephone calls, mail, and other forms of communication.

   Degradation
   - The woman may be cursed at, called names and generally put down verbally.
   - The woman may be depreciated and told that she is of no worth to the man or anyone else.
   - The woman may be humiliated both in public and in private.
   - The woman may be forced into prostitution or sex acts with others.
   - The woman may be forced to be involved with pornography in any number of ways.
   - The woman may be repeatedly rejected either emotionally, intellectually, socially, or sexually.

   Denial of reality
   - The man may continually deny the woman any power or feelings of competency.

- The woman may be told, convinced, or badgered into believing that she is mentally ill.
- The man may habitually lie to the woman and manipulate her.

Forced physical distress or exhaustion

- The woman may be forced into servitude by the man.
- The man may make obsessive demands for cleanliness in all areas.
- The man may consistently interfere with the woman's sleep patterns so that she is unable to gain a reasonable amount of rest.
- The man may make certain that the woman's eating habits and nutrition are poor.
- The woman may be allowed no personal time.

Alcohol or drug administration

- The woman may be forced to use alcohol and other drugs against her will.
- The woman may be forced to sell or distribute drugs or other illegal substances.
- The woman may be forced into a dependence upon drugs or alcohol.

Monopolizing of perceptions

- The man may exhibit pathological jealousy.
- The man may attempt to control each and every activity the woman engages in.
- The man may manifest complete and total economic control over the woman.
- The man may involve himself with an obsessive surveillance of the woman's activities.
- The man may refuse to discuss or negotiate on any topic with the woman.

Violence correlates, including abuse

- The man may engage in violence against other people. This effectively intimidates the woman and causes her to be fearful of leaving the relationship.
- The man may engage in violence against children, both his own and other people's. This also intimidates the woman and causes her to be fearful of leaving, because she may not be certain that she can take the children with her.
- The man may engage in violence against family pets, specifically pets that belong to the woman. This is done as a means of intimidation and for sadistic pleasure.
- The man may engage in violence toward inanimate objects (e.g., putting his fist through a wall, throwing furniture, or other explosive behavior). This is done for intimidation and the release of tension.

Escalation of violence when the man uses alcohol or drugs

LEARNED HELPLESSNESS VARIABLES FROM CHILDHOOD (FAMILY OF ORIGIN)

1. The man or woman has witnessed or experienced abuse in his or her childhood home.
2. The man or woman has been a victim of sexual abuse, molestation, or incest.
3. The man or woman has experienced critical factors of noncontrol.
   There has been early parent loss through death, divorce, or separation.
   The family has made many frequent moves.

There has been alcohol or drug abuse by one or both parents.

The family has experienced some kind of severe trauma.

4. The man or woman has been exposed to rigid traditionalism, sex-role-stereotyped behaviors, or fundamentalist religious beliefs.

5. The man or woman has experienced personal chronic health problems, or another member of the family was chronically ill and family activities centered around caring for that person.

- *It is important to assess stalking behavior if the couple is living apart.* See Chapter 7 for a full discussion on this topic. The following are some common domestic violence stalking acts (Walker, 1997):

1. The stalker may mail cryptic cards or other cryptic messages.

2. The stalker may break windows, or enter the partner's home and vandalize it.

3. The stalker may take the partner's mail.

4. The stalker may leave things such as flowers on the partner's doorstep or at the partner's workplace.

5. The stalker may make frequent telephone calls to the partner and hang up.

6. The partner may notice that the stalker has her or him under constant surveillance.

7. The stalker may file numerous pleadings and court cases as a way of harassing the partner.

8. The stalker may continually disregard visitation limitations and dare the partner to do something about it.

Assess each member of the relationship individually, using the preceding protocol. When one examiner sees both spouses, it is easier to get an overall view of the family.

In summary, a review of the literature suggests that the use of standardized psychological testing is *not* appropriate in assessing domestic violence. A more effective model is that of a structured interview which assesses family history, personal history, lethality, stalking behavior, and a review of the variables of learned helplessness (Walker, 1996, 1997).

TREATMENT

A family that is involved with physically violent behavior often enters the health care system during the second phase of the cycle of violence (Walker, 1996). This is when there has been an acute battering incident. The first health care professional to assess the presence of violence is likely to be a nurse (Campbell, Harris, & Lee, 1995; Henderson & Ericksen, 1994; Yam, 1995), a physician (Archer, 1992; Plichta, 1992; Richardson & Feder, 1996; Sassetti, 1993; Steiner, VanSickle, & Lippmann, 1996), or a dentist (Dym, 1995). Even when the abused woman or the batterer is already in psychotherapy, the therapist may not have been aware of the presence of physical abuse. However, as Aldarondo and Straus (1994) state, when the presence of abuse is brought to the attention of the therapist, the first consideration must be the safety of the battered woman. If her life, or the life of anyone else, is in danger, then the woman and any children in the home must be placed in a *safe house* or shelter, or some other protective action must be taken.

Through the years, the approach most often pursued when abuse is identified has been couples therapy, family therapy or mediation (Saunders, 1994). Serra (1993) points out that the use of family therapy in cases involving violence is now questioned as to its appropriateness. Many systemic models assume equal power among family members and equal responsibility for the cause of the family problem (Berk, Berk, Loseke, & Rauma, 1983). Some traditional family therapy models create a presumption for attributing coresponsibility among the various members of the family for the criminal act committed by the batterer. Yet society does not assign power equally to both genders. This along with the fact that the man is generally physically larger and stronger than the woman makes the idea of coresponsibility unrealistic in domestic abuse cases (Avis, 1989; Wylie, 1989). It has also been questioned whether it is really possible to examine power as a circular interaction in which both spouses take part, because it is not clear how such a framework can contain the experiences of both those who wield the power and those who are subjected to the power (Dell, 1989). Feminist family therapists have also asked how systemic-relational categories are conducive to dealing with moral issues raised in family therapy around abusive behaviors (Goldner, 1992; Goldner, Penn, Sheinberg, & Walker, 1990). Abuse is often seen as arising from poor communications or alcoholism. When a counselor uses systemic models, battered women and their children may actually be placed at greater risk for abuse. The patriarchal structure of the family is supported, and, consequently, there is increased risk of the female being abused (Yllo, 1984). Conjoint sessions also are perceived as risky in that the mother or children may reveal continued abuse or a genuine desire for the father to leave the family (Bograd, 1984). The result may be that the family is left unprotected from the man's rage after the counseling session.

Serra (1993) and Giles-Sims (1983) both believe that the concerns voiced in the preceding can be overcome and that a systemic approach to abusive relationships is possible and can be employed with a successful outcome.

Divorce mediators often use similar principles, as do systems-oriented therapists. Walker and Edwell (1987) concluded that abusive men are unlikely to put their children's needs ahead of their own. Mediators may not realize that battered women have such a great fear and terror that it is not possible to ever equalize the power differential within the relationship (Jaffe, Wolfe, & Wilson, 1990). Most mediators hold that mediation offers no way to enforce any agreements that are achieved in the sessions, and there is no guarantee that what is revealed to the mediator will be held in confidence by the parties if they decide to litigate (Woods, 1985).

There are those who believe that a mediator who recognizes the abuse can work out a "no-abuse" contract, refer the abuser for appropriate individual or group treatment, and conduct a safe mediation without compromising the integrity or needs of the abused spouse (Erickson & McKnight-Erickson, 1988). They have detailed a protocol for mediation when abuse is a factor in the relationship (pp. 82–115).

Individual treatment for both the batterer and the abused woman appears to be the most efficacious method of intervention. These separate treatments often should be augmented by group therapy.

Treatment of the Male Batterer

There has been little scientific evaluation of the various innovative treatment approaches to help men who batter end their violent ways. Recidivism rates for male batterers after treatment (all kinds) are high, ranging from 15% to 40% with follow-up of more than 1 year (Saunders & Azar, 1989). This recidivism rate for batterers is actually higher than recidivism rates for men who are involved with incestuous relationships and sexual abuse of children; those range from 14% to 28% (McCary & McCary, 1982). This may be due to the fact that society is much less accepting of sexual abuse of children, and more legal consequences are instituted. Many batterers leave treatment programs prematurely even when they are legally mandated to attend (Saunders & Parker, 1989). Many theoretical models have been applied to the individual treatment of men who batter. Early on, the most popular approaches were psychoeducational ones that dealt directly with the batterers' anger and their sense of entitlement that women must meet men's needs (Pence & Paymar, 1993). These programs are now being supplemented and replaced with a wide array of therapeutic models. Cogan and Porcerelli (1996) have developed an object relations model for treating both batterers and abused women in individual psychotherapy. Lore and Schultz (1993) have taken ideas from comparative psychology to suggest that humans are exquisitely sensitive to subtle social cues and that if these cues can be specifically identified for batterers, they could be used to reduce the frequency of individual violent acts. Wallace and Nosko (1993) take this theory to the treatment room by focusing on shame in their group treatment program with batterers. They feel that this is best handled in a group setting, and their program places a great deal of emphasis on the batterer confessing his worst incident of violence.

In working with batterers over the past 15 years, I have evolved a program which borrows heavily from my work with incest offenders (Guyer & VanPatten, 1995), because I see many similarities between incest offenders and batterers. First, both groups have broken the law. Second, there is no clear personality profile of an incest offender or a batterer (the best predictor of each behavior stems from having been abused as a child and having observed abuse in the family of origin). Third, the people that the batterer and the incest offender perpetrate their acts upon are family members in a powerless role. Fourth, these persons rarely seek psychotherapy or other help on their own. Fifth, the incest offender and the batterer tend to project blame for their actions onto the victim or environmental circumstances. Sixth, they feel little true empathy or remorse for their behaviors.

Groth and Birnbaum (1979) clearly state that the treatment of sexual offenders relies heavily on the threat of legal action if these men do not comply with the treatment regimen. The Minnesota police experiment found that batterers eliminated their physically abusive behavior after the replication of an arrest. This staging of an arrest (not a real arrest) had a great impact on changing these men's behavior. The fear of the legal system does improve the effectiveness of treatment with batterers (Sherman & Berk, 1984). These same authors point out that most communities now either require or encourage mandatory arrest and at least one overnight stay in jail, followed by interventions such as reduction in bond, if the man's use of violence is assessed as low and he agrees to attend (and follows through with) an offender-specific psychological treatment program.

SEVEN-STAGE TREATMENT PROGRAM FOR MALE BATTERERS

1. In this stage of the program, it is imperative that the legal system be involved. The batterer must clearly understand that he has broken the law. He is made aware of the fact that if he were to physically abuse anyone but his wife, he would be charged with assault. He is also informed that if he does not continue in treatment and if his physically abusive behavior does not cease, he will be immediately returned to the court system, where the judge has the option to sentence him as the court sees fit.

2. In this stage the man is confronted with the fact that he is totally responsible for his abusive acts and with the reality that because he is physically larger and stronger than his wife or children, he could seriously injure them, and that this certainly would entail jail time. He is also made aware that any type of stalking or harassing behavior toward his wife will not be tolerated and that such acts will mean the immediate termination of his therapy program and a return to the courts for disposition.

3. This stage of the intervention involves a traditional cognitive-behavioral model where the batterer is taught techniques for effectively coping with the stress in his life and methods for dealing with obsessional thoughts and compulsive behavior. He is also trained in appropriate conflict management techniques. This cognitive-behavioral model, when implemented with sex offenders, has been shown to be followed by much lower recidivism rates than other therapeutic interventions. As pointed out earlier, therapeutic interventions with sex offenders have a general recidivism rate of 14% to 28% (McCary & McCary, 1982). With exposure to cognitive-behavioral approaches, recidivism rates fall to 5% to 15% (Traven, Bluestone, Coleman, Culler, & Melella, 1986; Traven, Bluestone, Coleman, & Melella, 1986). It is anticipated that a similar reduction in recidivism rates will be found for male batterers using this program.

4. This stage involves having the batterer enroll in a parenting program (whether he is a parent or not). In my clinical experience and according to some research data, there is support for the contention that men enrolled in parenting classes decrease their physical abuse of everyone in the family (Novaco, 1975; Schinke, Schilling, Barth, Gilchrist, & Maxwell, 1986; Stacey & Shupe, 1984). My preference is for the systematic training for effective parenting (STEP) model (Dinkmeyer & McKay, 1976).

5. In this stage a hypnotherapeutic intervention model is implemented. Araoz (1979, 1982) has pointed out the many similarities between cognitive-behavioral therapies and hypnotically based interventions. He also suggests that in circumstances where cognitive-behavioral techniques are effective, hypnotically based techniques may be even more effective. The hypnotic intervention that I use involves seven steps, as follows.

    Step 1. The batterer begins treatment by being introduced to the hypnotic procedures that will be utilized. Once he understands completely what this entails and agrees to engage in the treatment, he signs an informed-consent form for the use of hypnotherapy. A sample of this consent form can be found in Hammond et al. (1995, pp. 50–51).

Step 2.   The batterer becomes proficient in the development and the use of hypnotic imagery techniques (Guyer, 1991). This is accomplished through heterohypnosis and self-hypnosis. The batterer is asked to practice self-hypnosis on his own twice each day. He also practices heterohypnosis twice a week in the therapist's office.

Step 3.   The batterer is involved in working with imagery specifically designed to explore his motivation for physically abusive behavior (e.g., exploring self-concept issues, anxieties, fears, etc).

Step 4.   This part of the hypnotherapeutic intervention is devoted to age regression (Kroger & Fezler, 1976) with particular emphasis on any history of physical abuse or of observing physical abuse in the family of origin. At this juncture, relevant family-of-origin issues are brought to the forefront and dealt with while the batterer is in a trance, and they may also be worked on later using cognitive-behavioral therapy when he is in a waking state.

Step 5.   The batterer's inner child is reeducated (Araoz, 1982). This is accomplished by regressing the batterer to his childhood (usually to a time when some form of physical abuse occurred in the family). This may be a very cathartic experience for the batterer, and the therapist may observe heightened emotional expression in him at this point. When the batterer is in a regressed state, the batterer as a child is introduced to the woman he abused (in adulthood) as a child. The images of the two children are given suggestions for becoming friends, caring for one another, protecting one another, and seeing one another as equals. The images of the two children are then merged into one child. This often allows for a great deal of therapeutic work on the batterer's feelings of male–female power issues. It also allows the opportunity to work through any sexual confusion or difficulties in dealing with the female side of his personality, as outlined by Carl Jung (Hall & Lindzey, 1957, p. 84).

When this merger is accomplished so that the new unitary child is the batterer as a child, he is reintroduced to the scene as an adult. The adult batterer in trance gives advice and guidance to the batterer as a child and through this experience attempts to educate the batterer as a child so that he does not again enter and repeat new battering behaviors or offenses. The adult batterer is then removed from the scene, and the batterer as a child is progressed slowly back to the adult batterer's current chronological age. Posthypnotic suggestions for empathy, caring, understanding, and the equality of men and women are made during the progression to the adult batterer's current age.

Step 6.   This portion of the intervention entails an age progression to a time in the future when the batterer accepts responsibility for his behaviors, nonviolently handles conflict with his partner, and has no obsessive thoughts. Posthypnotic suggestions are given for confidence, decreased need to manipulate others, decreased need for power or control, ego-strengthening, and normal nonviolent interaction with his spouse, children, and others.

Step 7.   The batterer is reoriented to the therapeutic setting, where he is once again engaged in cognitive-behavioral psychotherapeutic techniques.

6. Once the batterer has reached a point where he is perceived by the therapist as being willing to interact in a rational, caring, and empathetic way with his wife, a joint session is scheduled. This is a recontracting session. New agreements are made concerning how the man and the woman will interact together in their new relationship. New expectations for one another are established and actually spoken or written down. What is acceptable behavior and what is not acceptable is made totally clear. It is reiterated to the man that physical abuse is illegal and not acceptable—and if it recurs, he can still go to jail, and his wife has every right to leave the marriage. Both parties are made aware that should the time ever come, the woman will have the therapist's total support in leaving the marriage, as well as the backing of social and legal agencies. Shamai (1995) has suggested that the use of rituals (e.g., putting the old relationship in a box and burying it) may help work through old feelings and make tangible a start of a new relationship. In my experience this does help some couples to begin afresh.

7. In this stage the therapeutic alliance is ended. The couple is told that should they ever need to reenter therapy, they are welcome to do so, and should feel free to contact the therapist for other help, should the need arise. This is done without fostering undue dependency.

TREATMENT FOR THE BATTERED WOMAN

Treatment for the battered woman must be designed to help her survive by being as safe as possible (Aita, 1993; Walker, 1995, 1996). Many current approaches to the treatment of battered women are based on a feminist therapy model and focus on trauma theory, safety, reempowerment, validation, exploring options, cognitive clarity, and judgment (Walker, 1996).

It is just as important for the battered woman to know that the legal system and the police are available if she needs them as it is for the batterer to know that the law will punish him if he physically assaults her. The public and the legal system are becoming more aware of domestic violence through high-profile court cases like the O.J. Simpson case. The police in most communities now take women's reports of domestic violence much more seriously than was the case prior to 1995. This trend can be used by the therapist to offer a woman more of a feeling of power and control. Most battered women do exhibit symptoms of PTSD (Figley, 1986; Walker, 1994b). Therefore, it is reasonable to apply PTSD therapeutic methods. The cognitive-behavioral model has gained popularity in this area in recent years. This model maintains appropriate boundaries between the battered woman and the therapist, and helps structure an egalitarian relationship so that the battered woman is treated as an equal in establishing the treatment plan. Due to the anxiety symptoms of PTSD, the implementation of relaxation methods might be in order. The woman might be given a relaxation tape that she can listen to at home. This tape might be cut in the therapist's voice or the woman's own voice and combined with easy-listening music (Guyer & Guyer, 1984).

Many believe that group therapy is the preferred treatment for PTSD and that it aids in building trust and a strong support system (Williams, 1980). Some group theorists believe that the implementation of nonverbal group exercises hastens this building of trust and strengthens the group cohesiveness (Bates & Johnson, 1972; Guyer & Matthews, 1981; Morris & Cinnamon, 1975). A homogeneous group made up of survivors of trauma has been shown to be a successful form of treatment (Marafiote, 1980). Rosewater (1982, 1985a, 1985b, 1987) has found that the majority of psychological symptoms exhibited by abused women are the direct result of the trauma. When this is the case, discussion in a self-help group made up of trauma survivors is often enough to provide the woman with what she needs to return to a healthy lifestyle. When the abused woman is in need of more in-depth therapy to deal with issues from her family of origin, this can be undertaken by the therapist (Kaslow, 1995).

A great deal has been written about the treatment of survivors of abuse, and various successful therapeutic approaches are described in the literature. I highly recommend viewing Walker's survivor therapy videotape (1994a), in which she demonstrates methods for dealing with survivors of abuse.

To reiterate, I have found that ending therapy with a joint session during which the couple makes a new contract for their relationship (if they are going to remain together) adds needed closure to the process.

ETHICAL ISSUES

Domestic violence is clearly against the law; therefore, it is dealt with by the police as a crime. Any laws governing this crime must be taken into consideration by the mental health professional who is assessing or treating a domestic violence case.

There is no clear method for determining whether a case is to be considered a forensic psychology case or a family psychology case. As mentioned previously, one must assess where the referral originated.

During the four years when I chaired the Ethics Committee for the American Society for Clinical Hypnosis (ASCH), we rewrote the ASCH Code of Ethics. This gave me the occasion to review several different professions' codes of ethics (e.g., dentistry, medicine, and podiatry). The only professional ethical code that mentions forensic work at length is that of the American Psychological Association (APA). Dr. Thomas Nagy, chair of the committee that developed the 1992 revision (APA, 1992), points out that nowhere does the APA Ethics Code define "forensic activities," and that with one possible exception, there are no separate or higher standards for forensic work than for any other professional work carried out by psychologists (Nagy, personal communication, January 9, 1998). The one possible exception would be more thorough recordkeeping so that it would stand up to the scrutiny of a judicial forum. Nagy states that the committee developed this section on forensic activities to give psychologists guidance when they are retained by attorneys, plaintiffs, or defendants in civil or criminal suits or in any other role involving litigation or formal legal proceedings.

Psychologists and psychiatrists are not detectives. They should not attempt to be supersleuths. It is important to stay within the limits of one's training when gathering information. (Scott et al., 1998).

Apparently any work carried out by a psychologist could be considered forensic, because clinical notes themselves can be considered legal documents by the courts. A line must be drawn somewhere in determining what is a forensic case. I, therefore, recommend viewing a case as forensic when it is directly ordered by the courts; requested by a judge; referred by the police, another law enforcement agency, or a lawyer; or when the patient is already directly involved in litigation at the time of referral. Referrals from social agencies (e.g., DSS, Department of Vocational Rehabilitation, Department of Disability Determination Services, etc.) are once removed from the courts and generally are not forensic. In these cases, the social agency is an information-gathering entity that will collect data from many sources (e.g., medical, mental health, legal, etc.) and make a recommendation to the courts after weighing this information. The social agency is the entity that acts in a forensic capacity.

Informed consent is imperative. This is true in working with any individual in any way. It is important to explain to them the procedures that will be involved, how these procedures are generally carried out, the limits of confidentiality, and any other pertinent information that may be governed by local, state, or federal laws. The person should then sign an informed-consent form for treatment. When children are involved in the assessment or treatment process in any way, the custodial parent or guardian should sign an informed-consent form for the treatment of a child under the age of 18. When an assessment is court ordered, it must be explained to the person that the court will have full access to all information gathered.

When a mental health professional is ordered by the court to assess spouse abuse, it is preferable to speak with the judge personally and request that the consent order name him or her specifically, and that it clearly state that any individual deemed necessary by the clinician will be made accessible to be interviewed or evaluated; that any cancellations of an established appointment must be made within 24 hours prior to the appointment; that the usual doctor–patient privilege does not hold; that the person will sign a release form allowing the therapist or evaluator to receive medical records, school records, military records, or any other legal records that may be pertinent; that the judge will decide who will be responsible for payment of the evaluation; that any history of previous litigation will be made available to the evaluator; and that each party will attempt to establish an appointment with the clinician within a reasonable time frame. I recommend writing out a protocol for court-appointed evaluations and requesting that it be signed by all persons involved and their attorneys. By following these procedures, the mental health professional is placed in an objective role and can support an unbiased position when required to offer testimony in court. If the mental health professional has prepared a thorough and clear report, the lawyers and the judge will have read it and will have specific questions. It is important to answer these questions as directly and honestly as possible.

When the mental health professional treating a patient is subpoenaed to court, it is important that he or she inform all parties involved of the relationship to the patient. One should convey to the court and to both lawyers that the professional's opinion is not unbiased, and that the professional's answers to questions may reflect concern for the patient.

SUMMARY AND RECOMMENDATIONS

Spouse abuse is defined as pushing, slapping, grabbing, or any other severe form of physical touch (e.g., kicking, biting, etc.). *Emotional abuse* is defined as verbal assaults on a person's character, or threats to kill oneself or another person. It is accepted by practitioners and researchers that domestic violence has reached epidemic proportions in this country.

There are many theories about what causes domestic violence. These theories range from sociological and psychological to biological. There is no profile of a batterer or of a battered woman that has been proven valid. Domestic violence knows no cultural, racial, educational, or economic boundaries.

Assessment of the male batterer is difficult to undertake due to the fact that no specific personality variables have been identified; therefore, standardized psychological testing is of little or no help in assessing the batterer or predicting violent behavior. The most effective means of assessment is utilization of a structured interview. This structured interview must assess any history of abuse as a child, the current use of drugs or alcohol, history of violence as an adult, history of having observed violence in the family of origin, negative attitudes towards women, and current needs for power and control. Implementing the model developed by Walker (1996) for assessing lethality and learned helplessness is imperative in evaluating the batterer.

Assessment of the battered woman also is most successfully carried out through a structured clinical interview. Psychological testing must be used with caution due to the fact that the battered woman may actually appear more emotionally dysfunctional than is in reality the case. It has become an accepted fact that battered women exhibit symptoms of PTSD. The model developed by Walker (1996) for assessing lethality and assessing learned helplessness once again is an effective tool.

Family systems therapy is not generally considered to be the treatment of choice in domestic violence cases due to the lack of protection for the battered woman and children, and the lack of attribution of responsibility to the batterer.

A seven-stage approach to treating male batterers entails: (a) legal involvement, (b) confrontation with the batterer regarding owning responsibility for his behavior, (c) traditional cognitive behavioral approaches, (d) enrollment of the batterer in a parenting program (regardless of whether he has children), (e) hypnotherapeutic intervention, (f) a conjoint meeting where the batterer and his spouse recontract their relationship, and (g) preparation for termination of therapy.

Treatment of the battered woman follows a more traditional approach. Safety is of the utmost importance. First, a safety plan is devised and rehearsed. Second, the effects of trauma are dealt with, utilizing traditional therapeutic approaches for treating PTSD. Then, any deeper problems or psychological issues are dealt with, utilizing traditional therapeutic interventions. Due to the fact that group work has long been recognized as successful in the treatment of trauma, the woman is referred to a homogeneous psychotherapy group or to a self-help group. It is hoped that the involvement with a group will allow her to establish a good support system. Finally, preparation for termination of therapy is carried out.

Ethical issues in the treatment of domestic violence involve determining what legal guidelines the state has established. It is also important to assess whether a case is forensic. Generally, a case is forensic if it is directly involved with the court system (is court ordered, is referred by a lawyer, is already involved in litigation, or is referred by a law enforcement agency). Social agencies are viewed as once removed from the legal system, so cases they refer are not ordinarily considered forensic.

When a case is court referred, it is important to speak with the judge and clarify what is expected of the psychologist's side and what is expected from the judge's side. In these cases, one must maintain objectivity and remain neutral. When subpoenaed to court for a case with which one is already involved, it is important to clarify that the therapist is not objective and can not be considered to be so by the court.

It is imperative that the practitioner working with domestic violence situations have each person involved sign an informed-consent form for treatment. This agreement should explain to each person involved the limits of confidentiality, what procedures they will go through, how these procedures will be carried out, and who will be involved in performing the procedures.

It is hoped that through utilizing the interventions described herein, the transmission of violence will be broken, at least for the given families involved. This will mean that future generations of those particular families will not have to deal with the same issues of trauma and violence. Hopefully, factors in the larger societal context that are conducive to breeding violence will also come under scrutiny and be reduced. Clinicians must be knowledgeable not only about the laws relevant to domestic violence but also about how the experiences of being abusive or abused and coming in contact with the legal and judicial systems impact on individuals' attitudes, values, and behaviors, and how these are likely to be manifested in therapy.

REFERENCES

Aita, J. A. (1993). Women at risk of family violence. *Nebraska Medical Journal, 78*(3), 52–58.

Aldarondo, E., & Straus, M. A. (1994). Screening for physical violence in couple therapy: Mythological, practical, and ethical considerations. *Family Process, 33*(4), 425–439.

American Psychiatric Association. (1994a). *Diagnostic and statistical manual of mental disorders (4th ed.)*. Washington, DC: Author.

American Psychiatric Association. (1994b). *Quick reference to the diagnostic criteria from DSM-IV*. Washington, DC: Author.

American Psychological Association. (1992). Ethical principals of psychologists and code of conduct. *American Psychologist, 47*, 1594–1611.

Araoz, D. L. (1979). *Hypnocounseling* (Eric Document Reproduction Service No. Ed. 182, 624).

Araoz, D. L. (1982). *Hypnosis and sex therapy*. New York: Brunner/Mazel.

Archer, L. A. (1992). Empowering women in a violent society: Role of the family physician. *Canadian Family Physician, 40*, 974–976, 979–980, 983–985.

Avis, J. M. (1989). Integrating gender into the family therapy curriculum. *Journal of Feminist Family Therapy, 1*(2), 3–24.

Ayoub, C. C., Grace, P. F., Paradise, J. E., & Newberger, E. H. (1991). Alleging psychosocial impairment of the accuser to defend oneself against a child abuse allegation. *Child and Youth Services, 15*, 191–207.

Balknap, J. (1995). Law enforcement officers' attitudes about the appropriate responses to woman battering. *International Review of Victimology, 4*(1) 47–62.

Barnett, O. W., Martinez, T. E., & Bluestein, B. W. (1995). Jealousy and romantic attachment in maritally violent and non-violent men. *Journal of Interpersonal Violence, 10*(4), 473–486.

Bates, M. B., & Johnson, D. J. (1972) *Group Leadership: A manual for group counseling leaders*. Denver: Love Publishing.

Berk, R. A., Berk, S. F., Loseke, D. R., & Rauma, D. (1983). Mutual combat and other family violence myths. In D. Finkelhor, R. J. Geles, G. T. Hotaling, & M. A. Straus (Eds.), *The dark side of families: Current family violence research* (pp. 197–212). Beverly Hills, CA: Sage.

Bodin, A. M. (1996). Relationship conflict—verbal and physical: Conceptualizing an inventory for assessing process and content. In F. W. Kaslow (Ed.), *Handbook of relational diagnosis and dysfunctional family patterns* (pp. 371–373). New York: John Wiley & Sons.

Bograd, M. (1984). Family systems approaches to wife battering: A feminist critique. *American Journal of Orthopsychiatry, 54,* 558–568.

Bradford, J. M., & McLean, D. (1984). Sexual offenders, violence and testosterone: A clinical study. *Canadian Journal of Psychiatry, 29*(4), 335–343.

Brown, D., Scheflin, A. W., & Hammond, D. C. (1998). *Memory, trauma, treatment, and the law.* New York: W. W. Norton.

Browne, A. (1993). Family violence and homelessness: The relevance of trauma histories in the lives of the homeless. *American Journal of Orthopsychiatry, 63*(3), 370–384.

Campbell, J. C., Harris, M. J., & Lee, R. K., (1995). Violence research: An overview. *Scholarly Inquiry for Nursing Practice, 9*(2), 105–126.

Cantos, A. L., Neidig, P. H., & O'Leary, K. D. (1994). Injuries of women and men in a treatment program for domestic violence. *Journal of Family Violence, 9*(2), 113–124.

Cascardi, M., O'Leary, K. D., Lawrence, E. E., & Schlee, K. A. (1995). Characteristics of women physically abused by their spouses and who seek treatment regarding marital conflict. *Journal of Consulting and Clinical Psychology, 63*(4), 616–623.

Ceci, S. J., & Bruck, M. (1995). *Jeopardy in the courtroom: A scientific analysis of children's testimony.* Washington, DC: American Psychological Association.

Chesler, P. (1987). *Mothers on trial: The battle for children and custody.* Seattle, WA: Seal Press.

Chester, B., Robin, R. W., Koss, M. P., Lopez, J., & Goldman, D. (1994). Grandmother dishonored: Violence against women by male partners in American Indian communities. *Violence and Victims, 9*(3), 249–258.

Chick, G. E., Loy, J. W., & White, W. E. (1984). Differentiating violent and non-violent opiate-addicted reformatory inmates with the MMPI. *Journal of Clinical Psychology, 40*(2), 619–623.

Cogan, R., & Porcerelli, J. H. (1996). Object relations in abusive partner relationships: An empirical investigation. *Journal of Personality Assessment, 66*(1), 106–115.

Coram, G. J. (1995). A Rorschach analysis of violent murderers and non-violent offenders. *European Journal of Psychological Assessment, 11,* (2)81–88.

Cornell, D. G., & Wilson, L. A. (1992). The PIQ > VIQ discrepancy in violent and non-violent delinquents. *Journal of Clinical Psychology, 48*(2), 256–261.

Crites, L., & Coker, D. (1988). What therapists see that judges might miss: A unique guide to custody decisions when spouse abuse is charged. *Judges Journal, 27*(2), 9–13, 40–43.

Dell, P. F. (1989). Violence in the systemic view: The problem of power. *Family Process, 28,* 1–14.

Dinkmeyer, D., & McKay, G. (1976). *Parents handbook: Systematic training for effective parenting.* Circle Pines: American Guidance Services.

Dym, H. (1995). The abused patient. *Dental Clinics of America, 39*(3), 621–635.

Elbow, M. (1977). Theoretical considerations of violent marriages. *Social Case Work, 58,* 515–526.

Else, L. T., Wonderlich, S. A., Beatty, W. W., Christie, D. W., & Staton, R. D. (1993). Personality characteristics of men who physically abuse women. *Hospital and Community Psychiatry, 44*(1) 54–58.

Erickson, S. K., & McKnight-Erickson, M.S. (1988). *Family mediation casebook.* New York: Brunner/Mazel.

Feldhause, K. M., Koziol-McLain, J., Amsbury, H. L., Norton, I. M., & Lowenstein, S. R. (1997). Accuracy of three brief screening questions for detecting partner violence in the emergency department. *Journal of the American Medical Association, 277*(7), 1400–1401.

Figley, C. (Ed.) (1986). *Trauma and its wake.* New York: Brunner/Mazel.

Fraboni, M., Cooper, D., Reed, T. L., & Saltstone, R. (1990). Offense type and two-point MMPI Code Profile: Discriminating between violent and non-violent offenders. *Journal of Clinical Psychology, 46*(6), 774–777.

Ganley, A., & Harris, L. (1978). *Domestic violence: Issues in designing and implementing programs for male batterers.* Paper presented at the American Psychological Association, Toronto, Canada.

Gayford, J. J. (1975). Wife battering: A preliminary survey of 100 cases. *British Medical Journal, 1,* 194–197.

Gellen, M. I., Hoffman, R. A., Jones, M., & Stone, M. (1984). Abused and non-abused women: MMPI profile differences. *Personnel and Guidance Journal, 62*(10), 601–604.

Giles-Sims, J. (1983). *Wife battering: A systems theory approach.* New York: Guilford Press.

Goeckermann, C. R., Hamberger, L. K., & Barber, K. (1994). Issues of domestic violence unique to rural areas. *Wisconsin Medical Journal, 93*(9), 473–479.

Goldner, V. (1992). Making room for both/and. *The Family Therapy Networker, 16*(2), 55–61.

Goldner, V., Penn, P., Sheinberg, M., & Walker, G. (1990). Love and violence: Gender paradoxes in volatile attachments. *Family Process, 29,* 243–364.

Graham, J. R. (1990). *MMPI-2: Assessing personality and psychopathology.* New York: Oxford University Press.

Greene, A. F., Coles, C. J., & Johnson, E. H. (1994). Psychopathology and anger in interpersonal violence offenders. *Journal of Clinical Psychology, 50*(6), 906–912.

Greiner, N., & Nunno, J. (1994). Psychopaths at Nuremberg? A Rorschach analysis of the records of the Nazi war criminals. *Journal of Clinical Psychology, 50*(3), 415–429.

Groth, A. N., & Birnbaum, H. J. (1979). *Men who rape: The psychology of the offender.* New York: Plenum Press.

Guyer, C. G. (1991). Hypnosis in the treatment of behavior disorders. In W. C. Wester & D. J. O'Grady (Eds.), *Clinical hypnosis with children* (pp. 150–164). New York: Brunner/Mazel.

Guyer, N. P., & Guyer, C. G. (1984). Implementing relaxation training in counseling emotionally healthy adolescents: A comparison of three modes. *American Mental Health Counselors Association Journal, 6,* 79–87.

Guyer, C. G., & Matthews, C. O. (1981) Nonverbal warm-up exercises with adolescents: Effects on group counseling. *Small Group Behavior, 12*(1), 55–67.

Guyer, C. G., & VanPatten, I. T. (1995). The treatment of incest offenders: A hypnotic approach: A brief communication. *The International Journal of Clinical and Experimental Hypnosis, 42*(3), 266–273.

Hale, G., Zimostrand, S., Duckworth, J., & Nicholas, D. (1988). Abusive partners: MMPI profiles of male batterers. *Journal of Mental Health Counseling, 10*(4), 214–224.

Hall, C. S., & Lindzey, G. (1957). *Theories of personality* (p. 84). New York: John Wiley & Sons.

Hammond, D. C., Garver, R. B., Mutter, C. B., Crasilneck, H. B., Frischholz, E., Gravitz, M. A., Hibler, N. S., Olson, J., Scheflin, A., Spiegel, H., & Wester, W. C. (1995). *Clinical hypnosis and memory: Guidelines for clinicians and for forensic hypnosis.* Des Plaines, IL: American Society for Clinical Hypnosis.

Henderson, A. D., & Ericksen, J. R. (1994). Enhancing nurses' effectiveness with abused women: Awareness reframing, support, and education. *Journal of Psychosocial Nursing and Mental Health Services, 32*(6) 11–15.

Henderson, M. (1982). An empirical classification of violent and non-violent offenders using the MMPI. *Personality and Individual Differences, 4*(6), 671–677

Hiday, V. A. (1995). The social context of mental illness and violence. *Journal of Health and Social Behavior, 36*(2), 122–137.

Holtzworth-Munroe, A., & Stuart, G. L. (1993). Typologies of male batterers: Three subtypes and the differences among them. *Psychological Bulletin, 116*(3), 476–497.

Hughs, D. J. (1996). Suicide and violence assessment in psychiatry. *General Hospital Psychiatry, 18*(6), 416–421.

Hughes, S. A., Deville, C., Chalhoub, M., & Romboletti, R., (1992). The Rorschach human anatomy response: Predicting sexual offending behavior in juveniles. *Journal of Psychiatry and the Law, 20*(3), 313–333.

Jaffe, P. G., Wolfe, D. A., & Wilson, S. K. (1990). *Children of battered women.* Newbury Park, CA: Sage.

Kantor, G., Jasinski, J., & Aldarondo, E. (1994). Sociocultural status and incidence of marital violence in hispanic families. [Special issue: Violence against women of color]. *Violence and Victims, 9*(3), 207–222.

Kaser-Boyd, N. (1993). Rorschachs of women who commit homicide. *Journal of Personality Assessment, 60*(3), 458–470.

Kaslow, F. W. (1995) *Projective genogramming.* Sarasota, FL: Professional Resource Press.

Krakowski, M., & Czobor, P. (1994). Clinical symptoms, neurological impairment and prediction of violence in psychiatric in-patients. *Hospital and Community Psychiatry, 45*(7), 711–713.

Kroger, W. S., & Fezler, W. D. (1976). *Hypnosis and behavior modification: Imagery conditioning.* Philadelphia: J. B. Lippincott.

Langevin, R., Wright, P., & Handy, L. (1990). Use of the MMPI and its derived scales with sex offenders: II. Reliability and criterion validity. *Annals of Sex Research, 3*(4), 453–486.

Langhinrichsen-Rohling, J., Neidig, P., & Thorn, G. (1995). Violent marriages: Gender differences in levels of current violence and past abuse. *Journal of Family Violence, 10*(2), 159–176.

Lanza, M. L., Kayne, H. L., Pattison, I., Hicks, C., & Islam, S. (1994). Predicting violence: nursing diagnosis versus psychiatric diagnosis. *Nursing Diagnosis, 5*(4), 151–158.

Lidz, C. W., Mulvey, E. P., & Gardner, W., (1993). The accuracy of predictions of violence to others. *Journal of the American Medical Association, 269*(8), 1007–1011.

Lore, K., & Schultz, L. A. (1993). Control of human aggression: A comparative perspective. *American Psychologist, 48*(1), 16–25.

Marafiote, R. (1980). Behavioral strategies in group treatment of Vietnam veterans. In T. Williams (Ed.), *Post-traumatic stress disorders of Vietnam veterans* (pp. 49–69). Cincinnati, OH: Disabled American Veterans.

McCary, J. L., & McCary, S. T. (1982). *McCary's human sexuality* (4th ed.) Belmont, CA: Wadsworth.

Milner, J. S. (1986). *The child abuse potential inventory manual,* De Kalb, IL: Psytec.

Milner, J. S., & Gold, R. G. (1986). Screening spouse abusers for child abuse potential. *Journal of Clinical Psychology, 42,* 169–172.

Minzies, R., & Webster, C. D. (1995). Constriction and validation of risk assessments in a six year follow up of forensic patients: A tri-dimensional analysis. *Journal of Consulting and Clinical Psychology, 63*(5), 766–778.

Mollerstorm, W., Patchner, M. A., & Milner, J. S. (1992). Family violence in the Air Force: A look at offenders in the role of the family advocacy program. *Military Medicine, 157*(7), 371–374.

Monahan, J. (1981). *Predicting violent behavior: An assessment of clinical techniques.* Beverly Hills, CA: Sage.

Morley, R. (1994). Wife beating and modernization: The case of Papua, New Guinea [Special issue: Family violence]. *Journal of Comparative Family Studies, 25*(1), 25–52.

Morris, K. T., & Cinnamon, K. M. (1975). *A handbook of nonverbal group exercises.* Springfield, IL: Charles C. Thomas.

Mott-McDonald Associates (1979). The report from the conference on intervention programs for men who batter. Washington, DC: U.S. Department of Justice.

Murphy, C. M., & O'Farrell, T. J. (1994). Factors associated with marital aggression in male alcoholics. *Journal of Family Psychology, 8*(3), 321–335.

Novaco, R.W. (1975). *Anger control: The development and evaluation of an experimental treatment.* Lexington, MA: D. C. Heath.

Nussbaum, D., Choudhry, R., & Martin-Doto, C. (1996). Cognitive impulsivity, verbal intelligence, and locus of control in violent and non-violent mentally disordered offenders. *American Journal of Forensic Psychology, 14*(1), 5–30.

O'Sullivan, M. J., & Jemelka, R. P. (1993). 34/43 MMPI code type in an offender population: An update on levels of hostility and violence. *Psychological Assessment, 5*(4), 493–498.

Pan, H. S., Neidig, P. H., & O'Leary, K. D. (1994). Predicting mild and severe husband-to-wife physical aggression. *Journal of Consulting and Clinical Psychology, 62*(5), 975–981.

Pence, E., & Paymar, M. (1993). *Working with men who batter: The Duluth model.* New York: Springer.

Perrin, S., VanHasselt, V. B., Basilio, I., & Hersen, M. (1996). Assessing the effects of violence on women in battering relationships with the Keane MMPI-PTSD Scale. *Journal of Traumatic Stress, 9*(4), 805–816.

Plichta, S. (1992). The effects of woman abuse on health care utilization and health status: A literature review. *Women's Health Issues, 2*(3), 154–163.

Pollak, S., & Gilligan, C. (1983). Differing about differences: The incidence and interpretation of violent fantasies in women and men. *Journal of Personality and Social Psychology, 45*(5), 1172–1175.

Rhodes, N. R. (1992). The assessment of spousal abuse: An alternative to the conflict tactics scale. In C. Viano (Ed.), *Intimate violence: Interdisciplinary perspectives* (pp. 27–35). New York: Hemisphere.

Richardson, J., & Feder, G. (1996). Domestic violence: A hidden problem for general practice. *British Journal of General Practice, 46,* 239–242.

Rigakos, G. S. (1995). Constructing the symbolic complaint: Police subculture and the non-enforcement of protection orders for battered women. *Violence and Victims, 10*(3), 227–247.

Rosenbaum, A., Hoge, S., Adelman, S., & Warnken, W. (1994). Head injury in partner-abusive men. *Journal of Consulting and Clinical Psychology, 62*(6), 1187–1193.

Rosenberg, M. S. (1984). *The impact of witnessing interparent violence on children's behavior, perceived competence, and social problem solving abilities.* Unpublished doctoral dissertation, University of Virginia, Charlottesville.

Rosewater, L. B. (1982). *The development of an MMPI profile for battered women.* Unpublished doctoral dissertation, Union Graduate School, Cincinnati, Ohio.

Rosewater, L. B. (1985a). Feminist interpretations of traditional testing. In L. B. Rosewater & L. E. Walker (Eds.), *Handbook of feminist therapy: Women's issues in psychotherapy.* New York: Springer.

Rosewater, L. B. (1985b). Schizophrenic, borderline or battered? In L. B. Rosewater & L. E. Walker (Eds.), *Handbook of feminist therapy: Women's issues in psychotherapy.* New York: Springer.

Rosewater, L. B. (1987). The clinical courtroom application of battered women's personality assessments. In D. Sonkin (Ed.), *Domestic violence on trial* (pp. 86–96). New York: Springer.

Ross, S. M. (1996). Risk of physical abuse to children of spouse abusing parents. *Child Abuse and Neglect, 20*(7), 589–598.

Roszkowski, M. J. (1984). Validity of the similarities ratio as a predictor of violent behavior: Data from a mentally retarded sample. *Personality and Individual Differences, 5*(1), 117–118.

Ryan, W. (1975). *Blaming the victim.* New York: Vantage Books.

Sally, R. D., & Teiling, P. A. (1984). Dissociated rage attacks in a Vietnam veteran: A Rorschach study. *Journal of Personality Assessment, 48*(1), 98–104.

Sassetti, M. R. (1993). Domestic violence. *Primary Care: Clinics and Office Practice, 20*(2), 289–305.

Saunders, D. G. (1992). A typology of men who batter: Three types derived from a cluster analysis. *American Journal of Orthopsychiatry, 62*(2), 264–275.

Saunders, D. G. (1993). Domestic violence. In R. Ammerman & M. Hersen (Eds.), *Assessment of family violence* (pp. 208–235). New York: John Wiley & Sons.

Saunders, D. G. (1994). Child custody decisions in families experiencing woman abuse. *Social Work, 39*(1), 51–59.

Saunders, D. G., & Azar, S. T. (1989). Treatment programs for family violence. In L. Ohlin & M. Tonry (Eds.), *Family violence: Crime and justice, a review of research.* (Vol. 11, pp. 481–546). Chicago: University of Chicago Press.

Saunders, D. G., & Parker, J. C. (1989). Legal sanctions and treatment follow through among men who batter: A multivariate analysis. *Social Work Research and Abstracts, 25*(3), 21–29.

Saunders, M. (1995). Long term physical complications of battering: Afrocentric intervention of the ancestors. *Journal of Cultural Diversity, 2*(3), 75–82.

Schinke, S. P., Schilling, R. F., Barth, R. P., Gilchrist, L. D., & Maxwell, J. S. (1986). Stress-management intervention to prevent family violence. *Journal of Family Violence, 1*(1), 13–26.

Schwabe, M. R., & Kaslow, F. W. (1984). Violence in the military family. In F. W. Kaslow & R. I. Ridenour (Eds.), *The military family: Dynamics and treatment* (pp. 125–146). New York: Guilford Press.

Scott A., Scheflin, A. W., & Wester, W. C. (1998). *Presentation on forensics in mental health.* American Society of Clinical Hypnosis Annual Conference, Fort Worth, Texas.

Seligman, M. P. (1975). *Learned helplessness: On depression, development and death.* New York: John Wiley & Sons.

Senchak, M., & Leonard, K. (1994). Attributions for episodes of marital aggression: The effects of aggression severity and alcohol use. *Journal of Family Violence, 9*(4), 371–381.

Serra, P. (1993). Physical violence in the couple relationship: A contribution toward the analysis of the context. *Family Process, 32*(1), 21–33.

Shamai, M. (1995). Using rituals in couple therapy in cases of wife battering. *Journal of Family Therapy, 17*(4), 383–395.

Sherman, L. W., & Berk, R. A. (1984). The specific deterrent effects of arrest for domestic assault. *American Sociological Review, 49,* 261–272.

Smith, J. E., Czicman, S. P., Early, J. A., Green, P. T., Lauck, D. L., Lindsay, K., Oblaneczynski, C., & Smochek, M. R. (1994). Validation of the defining characteristics of potential for violence. *Nursing Diagnosis, 5*(4), 159–164.

Spiegel, L. D. (1986). *A question of innocence.* Darsippany, NJ: Unicorn.

Spiegel, L. D. (1990). The phenomenon of child abuse hysteria: The case for a new kind of expert testimony. *Issues in Child Abuse Accusations* (2), 17–26.

Spiegel, L. D. (1998). Expert witness—justice on trial: An expert's view of the justice system and the forces which drive it. *The Forensic Examiner, 7*(3&4), 15–18.

Stacey, W. A., & Shupe, A. (1984). *The family secret: Family volence in America.* Boston: Beason Press.

Stark, E., & Flitcraft, A. (1988). Women and children at risk: A feminist perspective on child abuse. *International Journal of Health Services, 18,* 97–118.

Stark, E., Flitcraft, A., & Frazier, W. (1979). Medicine, patriarchal violence: The social construction of a "private" event. *International Journal of Health Services, 9,* 461–493.

Steiner, R. P., VanSickle, K., & Lippmann, S. B. (1996). Domestic violence: Do you know when and how to intervene? *Post Graduate Medicine, 100*(1), 103–106.

Straus, M. A. (1993). Physical assaults by wives: A major social problem. In R. J. Gelles & D. R. Loeske (Eds.), *Current controversies on family violence* (pp. 67–87). Newbury Park, CA: Sage.

Traven, S., Bluestone, H., Coleman, E., Culler, K., & Melella, J. (1986). Pedophilia: An update on theory and practice. *Psychiatric Quarterly, 57*(2), 89–103.

Traven, S., Bluestone, H., Coleman, E., & Melella, J. (1986). Pedophilia types and treatment perspectives. *Journal of Forensic Science, 31*(2), 614–620.

Truescott, D. (1990). Assessment of overcontrolled hostility in adolescence. *Psychological Assessment, 2*(2), 145–148.

Vivian, D., & Langhinrichson-Rohling, J. (1994). Are bidirectionally violent couples mutually victimized? A gender sensitive comparison. *Violence and Victims, 9*(2), 107–124.

Walker, L. E. A. (1979). *The battered woman.* New York: Harper & Row.

Walker, L. E. A. (1984). *The battered woman syndrome.* New York: Springer.

Walker, L. E. A. (1988). Spouse abuse. In A. Horton & J. Williamson (Eds.), *Abuse and religion: When praying isn't enough* (pp. 13–20). Lexington, MA: D. C. Heath.

Walker, L. E. A. (1994a) The abused woman: A survivor therapy approach [Videotape, 89 min]. New York: Newbridge Professional Programs.

Walker, L. E. A. (1994b). *Abused women and survivor therapy: A practical guide for the psychotherapist.* Washington, DC: American Psychological Association.

Walker, L. E. A. (1995). Current perspectives on men who batter women: Implications for intervention and treatment to stop violence against women [Comment on Gottman et al., 1995]. *Journal of Family Psychology, 9*(3), 264–271.

Walker, L. E. A. (1996). Assessment of abusive spousal relationships. In F. W. Kaslow (Ed.), *Handbook of relational diagnoses and dysfunctional family patterns* (pp. 338–356). New York: John Wiley & Sons.

Walker, L. E. A. (1997). *Presentation on domestic violence.* Florida Psychological Association Conference, Fort Lauderdale, Florida.

Walker, L. E. A., & Edwell, G. E. (1987). Domestic violence and determination of visitation and custody in divorce. In D. J. Sonkin (Ed.), *Domestic violence on trial: Psychological and legal dimensions of family violence* (pp. 127–154). New York: Springer.

Walker, L. E. A., & Sonkin, D. J. (1994). *Jurismonitor stabilization and empowerment programs.* Denver, CO: Endolor Communications.

Wallace, B., and Nosko, A. (1993). Working with shame in group treatment of male batterers. *International Journal of Group Psychotherapy, 43*(1), 45–61.

Whatley, M. A. (1993). For better or worse: The case for marital rape. *Violence and Victims, 8*(1), 29–39.

Williams, T. (1980). *Post-traumatic stress disorders of the Vietnam veteran.* Cincinnati, OH: Disabled American Veterans.

Wilson, M., Johnson, H., & Daly, M. (1995). Lethal and non-lethal violence against wives [Special issue: Focus on the violence against women survey]. *Canadian Journal of Criminology, 37,* 331–361.

Wolfe, D. A. (1985). Child abusive parents: An empirical review and analysis. *Psychological Bulletin, 97*(3), 462–482.

Woods, L. (1985). *Mediation: A backlash to women's progress on family law issues in courts and legislatures.* Unpublished paper, National Center on Women and Family Law, New York. (Available from National Center on Women and Family Law—799 Broadway, Room 402, New York, 10003).

Wylie, M. S. (1989). Looking for the fence posts. *The Family Therapy Networker, 13*(2), 22–33.

Yam, M. (1995). Wife abuse: Strategies for a therapeutic response. *Scholarly Inquiry for Nursing Practice, 9*(2), 147–158.

Yllo, K. (1984). Patriarchy and violence against wives: The impact of structural and normative factors. *Journal of International and Comparative Social Welfare, 1,* 16–29.

CHAPTER 12

Divorce and Its Sequelae

A Psycholegal Perspective

FLORENCE W. KASLOW

ALMOST INVARIABLY, the process of divorce is painful and arduous for all involved. It entails a series of losses and the accompanying grief and guilt; often a great deal of blaming of the other partner intermingled with self-reproach; the compelling need to make many major changes in where and how one lives; and coping with the knowledge that the dream, internalized early, of getting married and living "happily ever after" has been shattered. If there are children, the process is even more complex and overwhelming; although one may divide assets in half, or at least equitably, children are not property and cannot be divided. Yet they need to be shared, and frequently the needs of the various family members regarding parenting and visitation are not synchronous.

STAGES AND PHASES OF THE DIVORCE PROCESS

In numerous prior articles and books, I have elaborated a divorce process (Kaslow, 1984, 1994, 1995) that has three major stages—pre-, during, and postdivorce—and seven major phases, focusing on different aspects and issues (Schwartz & Kaslow, 1997):

1. Emotional
2. Legal
3. Economic and financial
4. Coparental and visitation
5. Extended family, friends, and colleagues (community)
6. Spiritual or religious
7. Psychic (healing and closure)

These phases do not occur in an invariable sequence nor in discrete categories; they are intertwined and overlapping. But for purposes of analysis, understanding, and providing optimally useful therapeutic interventions or legal counsel, it is useful to be cognizant of each of these complex facets (Schwartz & Kaslow, 1997). This chapter also posits that legislators should take the total process and its seque-lae into consideration when writing new laws or revising existing ones concerned with divorce and child custody. Further, it is hoped that family court judges increasingly will be mindful not only of the legal and economic aspects of divorce, but of the underlying emotional dynamics, the posturing and positioning of dis-putants and their attorneys as they seek to achieve their own aims, sometimes motivated by greed or by an overwhelming desire to punish or retaliate against their partner, as they make their choices regarding the parenting plan and the other provisos of the marital settlement agreement (MSA). It is recognized that donning black judicial robes does not, ipso facto, endow judges with the kind of wisdom about family dynamics and processes and child development that they need to make the Solomonic decisions embodied in divorce decrees.

The word *parenting* is used herein moreso than *custody*, because the latter term denotes ownership and parents do not *own* their children—that is, they are not possessions but people with their own separate thoughts, feelings, needs, and wishes. Conversely, the term *parenting* implies responsibilities and privileges as well as rights, and conveys the importance of providing loving nurturance as well as setting realistic limits, both basic ingredients of the parenting role. Conceptual-izing in terms of which parent will carry which responsibilities according to their strengths, skills, and availability and in relation to a specific child's needs provides a very different foundation for deciding a child's residential time with each parent than being determined to battle over which parent deserves more time with or control over the child. (See later in this chapter for more on the custody phase, and also Chapter 13.)

This chapter primarily focuses on the portion of Stage 2 during divorce that encompasses the legal, economic, and coparental issues, as this is the substantive part that is most germane to this volume. However, to place this in context, and make it more anchored and meaningful, a previously developed table that depicts the larger divorce process is included. Table 12.1 has been revised for this volume from Kaslow and Schwartz (1987), based on additional clinical experience and feedback from colleagues.

It is important to note that predictable feelings (Column 3 in Table 12.1) or affec-tive responses are associated with each phase along the pathway from the moment one makes a definitive decision to divorce or is informed by one's spouse that a divorce is going to occur, regardless of whether one wants it. The emotions may include an ambivalent mixture of many of those listed, and can fluctuate rapidly from anger to relief and back. There are, of course, some exceptions to what is being described here. In couples who have been married a relatively short time, in which both rapidly realize that they have made a mistake, and in which there are no children, the divorce process can occur quickly and without the intensity and anguish usually associated with a marital relationship splitting asunder. Another scenario that may produce a departure from the typical feelings and behaviors exhibited occurs when there has been long-term physical or emotional abuse, which will finally come to an end, and one eagerly anticipates a calmer period minus the fear and turbulence. Thus, it is essential to know what feeling states and expression of these can be expected, and when and why variations may occur, if one is the attorney, mediator, or therapist.

Column 4 in Table 12.1 encapsulates many of the tasks that need to be attended to, accomplished, or mastered during the divorce process if it is to culminate ultimately in an acceptable resolution so that each party and the children can continue to grow and build a good-quality life postdivorce. There are a multitude of major decisions to be made and implemented, such as whether the couple should keep or sell the marital home. If they keep it, who will live in it, and, perhaps, for how long? Who will pay the mortgage and the repair bills? What will the arrangements be for alimony and child support, for sharing parenting, for spending holidays, for seeing grandparents, for child care? Will either adult need to work more or less than they have in the past? What if a new, better paying job requires relocation? What should they tell friends, relatives, and people at work, including the boss? And all of this needs to take place in exactly the same time frame during which they are experiencing angst, duress, unhappiness, and uncertainty. Their ability to make rational, wise choices that will stand them in good stead for many years to come may be overshadowed by pain, fear of the unknown, the desire for retribution, and pressure from others, including attorneys, to achieve certain ends—such as "getting all you can," or "giving as little as possible," emphasizing the financial gains to be had in a win–loss battle rather than also considering the emotional scars left from such wrangling, the loss of self respect as one resorts to deceit and chicanery against someone they once loved, and the fallout on the children they jointly conceived. It is no surprise that given this confluence of forces, many poor decisions are made that permeate the lives of all involved family members long into the future, to everyone's regret. Knowledgeable, fair-minded, and empathic professionals can create the space and milieu for diminishing animosities and antagonisms so that the final settlement agreement is a sound win–win one that all concerned can live with long into the future. These split families continue to exist, albeit in a binuclear form, with both parties still related through their mutual children (Ahrons, 1983; Ahrons & Rogers, 1987).

When children have been conceived or adopted by a couple, the divorce is never complete and final. There will be serious occasions, such as when a child has to have surgery, or ostensibly happy events, such as an offspring's wedding, when the former couple will need to be at the same place at the same time, and they should ultimately be able to do so in a civil and even cordial manner if they truly care about the best interests of their children and do not want to wreak further consternation and havoc on their children's lives by perpetuating earlier rancor or pressure to take sides in a loyalty contest or controversy (Boszormenyi-Nagy & Spark, 1973/1984). Also, each will continue to see images of their former partner in the children's appearance and actions. And they will continue to share an attachment to and financial responsibility for their offspring. The fundamental question to be addressed is how all of this can be achieved in the most constructive, positive manner.

THERAPEUTIC OPTIONS

Column 5 in Table 12.1 delineates what may be the treatment of choice at a specific period on the divorce trajectory. This is predicated on a family systems theory con-

Table 12.1 Dialectic Model of Stages in the Divorce Process

Phase	Stage and Aspects	Feelings	Behaviors and Tasks	Therapeutic Approaches	Mediation Issues
Predivorce: A time of deliberation	1. Emotional divorce	Disillusionment Dissatisfaction Alienation Anxiety Disbelief Denial Despair Dread Anguish Ambivalence Shock Emptiness Anger Chaos Inadequacy Low self-esteem Loss Depression Detachment	Avoiding the issue Sulking and/or crying Confronting partner Quarreling Withdrawing (physical and emotional) Pretending all is fine Attempting to win back affection Asking friends, family, clergy for advice Changing residence for one or both partners	Marital therapy (one couple) Couples group therapy Individual therapy Divorce therapy	Contemplation of mediated versus litigated divorce. Deciding which is best option.
During divorce: A time of legal involvement	2. Legal divorce	Self-pity Helplessness Fear of loneliness Apprehension about future	Consulting an attorney or mediator Accepting that divorce is probably inevitable Filing for legal divorce Bargaining Screaming Threatening Attempting suicide	Family therapy Individual adult therapy Child therapy	Set the stage for mediation orientation session. Ascertain parties' understanding of the process and its appropriateness for them.

3. Economic/financial divorce	Confusion Fury Sadness, Loneliness Relief Vindictiveness Greed	Separating physically Considering financial settlement Determining amount of child support and/or alimony Deciding on custody/visitation schedule	Children of divorce group Child therapy Adult therapy	Define the rules of mediation. Identify the issues and separate therapeutic issues from mediation. Focus on parental strengths, children's needs and formulating best possible coparenting and residential arrangement.
4. Coparental divorce/issues of residence and contact	Concern for children Ambivalence Numbness Uncertainty Fear of loss	Grieving and mourning Telling relatives and friends Reentering work world (unemployed woman) Feeling empowered to make choices Possible relocation Arranging child care	Same as preceding, plus family therapy	Negotiate and process the issues and choices. Reach agreement. Analyze and formalize agreement. Take to attorneys for finalizing and filing.

(Continued)

Table 12.1 (*Continued*)

Phase	Stage and Aspects	Feelings	Behaviors and Tasks	Therapeutic Approaches	Mediation Issues
	5. Social/community/ extended family issues	Indecisiveness Optimism Resignation Excitement Curiosity Regret Sadness	Dealing with others' reactions Interpreting changes to extended family Finalizing divorce Reaching out to new friends Undertaking new activities Stabilizing new lifestyle and daily routine for children Exploring new interest and possibly taking new job	Adults and adolescents Individual therapy Singles group therapy Children Child play therapy Children's group therapy Sibling system therapy	
	6. Spiritual/religious divorce	Self-doubt Desire for church approval Fear of God's displeasure or wrath	Gaining church acceptance Having a religious divorce ceremony Making peace with one's spiritual self	Divorce ceremony for total family Adult therapy Pastoral counseling Children—same as preceding	

Postdivorce: A time of exploration and reequilibration	7. Psychic divorce	Acceptance Self-confidence Energetic Improved self-image Wholeness Exhilaration Independence Autonomy	Resynthesis of identity Completing psychic divorce Seeking new love object and making a commitment to some permanency Becoming comfortable with new life style and friends Helping children accept finality of parents' divorce and their continuing relationship with both parents	Parent–child therapy Family therapy Group therapies Children's activity group therapy Individual therapy	Return to mediation when changed circumstances warrant a renegotiation of the agreement.

SOURCE: For earlier versions see Kaslow (1984, 1988, 1995), Kaslow and Schwartz (1987), and Schwartz and Kaslow (1997). Table periodically revised and expanded; updated for this chapter, 1999. Copyright © 1984 by F. W. Kaslow.

241

ceptualization of trying to take into account the needs and interests of each member of the divorcing family while simultaneously being concerned about the total separating unit as an interacting group. Thus, different family subsystems may be seen together at various times—such as the separating couple, a parent–child dyad, or the sibling generation. For example, when the task of the couple is to further solidify their pulling away from each other, individual therapy may be warranted. When a young child is worried and needs to express his or her rage and distress, play therapy may constitute the most efficacious intervention. An adolescent may do best with individual verbal psychotherapy interspersed with occasional sessions with either or both parents to relate his or her anger, anguish, dislike of the arguments, and fears about the future to them. Sometimes a short-term problem-solving children of divorce group may offer the most supportive help and teach coping strategies to children ages 5 through 17, grouped together by age (Kessler & Bostwick, 1977; Roizblatt, Garcia, Maida, & Moya, 1990). Recommendations for treatment should be tailored to the specific family, and should take into consideration their needs, personalities, symptomatology, and goals. They should not be channeled into one model or paradigm which assumes that one type of therapy is preferable for everyone.

LEGAL ASPECTS AND ISSUES

The final column in Table 12.1 addresses legal issues. For a marriage to occur in the United States, a document must be issued by the civil authorities that gives legal recognition to the union and serves as a contract of commitment. Therefore, the actual marriage ceremony may be performed by a justice of the peace or other duly designated civil official. In addition, the couple may opt to have a religious ceremony to solemnize their vows and have it performed by a minister, priest, or rabbi so that the marriage is also religiously sanctioned and recognized. But the religious ceremony is insufficient without obtaining and signing the necessary civil documents; the reverse is not true, in keeping with the doctrine of separation of church and state.

In addition to the civil and religious marital contracts a couple may make and sign, they may also write a prenuptial agreement (see Chapter 1). All of these documents contribute to the evolution and structure of the relationship the couple will build. Thereafter the state, through the courts, will not intervene in the couple's or their family's lives if they pay their taxes and do not come to the court's attention because someone brings charges against them or because they enter into an action that brings them under the court's jurisdiction, such as a divorce. Here again, a religious divorce (such as an annulment in the Catholic church or a *get* in Orthodox Judaism; Schwartz & Kaslow, 1997) may be a requirement within one's religion before one can remarry, but is not sufficient for one to be considered divorced in the eyes of the state—one must also acquire a civil, legal divorce.

Civil law, which includes family law, is partially derived from criminal law. As such, it embodies the concepts that there must be both a guilty and an innocent party, or a perpetrator and a victim, and that the party judged to be guilty should be punished or made to pay some kind of damages to the aggrieved or harmed victim. Undergirding this belief system is Aristotelian logic, which is based on the supposition that causality is linear. When extended for application and utilization in divorce cases, this has traditionally meant that one partner has had to bear the total blame for what went awry in the marriage—that is, to be held responsible for the demise of the couple's earlier wedded bliss.

LITIGATED DIVORCES

Once women were no longer held to be possessions of their husbands (Nineteenth Amendment to the Constitution, 1920) and were granted recognition as separate parties under law entitled to rights of their own, a shift occurred from the presumption that fathers should have possession, and therefore custody, of their children, to a standard of *maternal preference*. Many forces had coalesced for this to occur after centuries of patriarchal dominance and entitlement. These factors included: the psychoanalytic deluge brought to America by analysts trained in Germany, which emphasized the importance of the formative early childhood years and the essential nature of the mother–child bond for the child's healthy development (Brenner, 1955; Freud, 1933/1964); the translation of this psychological, child lifecycle development concept into the legal doctrine of the tender years—that is, that an infant or young child belongs with his or her mother until age 7 unless there are compelling reasons for this not occurring, such as severe mental illness or prostitution; and the transformation of U.S. society from a predominantly agrarian economy, where fathers worked at home on the farm and extended families lived together, so that a grandmother or an aunt was available if the mother was gone, to a primarily industrial society in which people lived in urban areas in small nuclear family units. With industrialization, men went to work for long hours in plants and factories, leaving the women at home to care for the children alone.

The easy accessibility to kinfolk diminished, as did the father's time with his wife and children. For approximately the next five to six decades, children almost invariably stayed with their mothers after divorce, because mothers had become the major nurturing parent. And because the husband/father was the only or primary wage earner, women's lawyers tended to seek to prove the husband guilty of something in an adversarial divorce action to win a larger settlement for her and retain her dignity if she was the rejected and deserted party. Men deemed guilty became the payer partners of child support and frequently of permanent spousal support or alimony (the terms are used interchangeably). The objective of most women and their attorneys was to garner the biggest possible settlement; few minimum and maximum parameters existed. Conversely, the aim of the men and their attorneys was to protect and retain as large a portion of the assets as was possible. The war over the division of tangible and intangible property was sometimes fought for many years in extended, deleterious legal battles which were costly in time, energy, and money. Such acrimonious conflagrations produced bitterness, pettiness, and vituperative behaviors; they interfered with both parties' ability to reach closure to the relationship and to move forward to a more fulfilling life beyond divorce. Divorce battlefields were strewn with emotional casualties.

When a man wanted and thought he deserved to be the custodial parent, or wanted to seek retribution against his wife by taking the children away from her, he was almost invariably advised by his attorney not to waste the time and money to mount a court fight because he probably would not stand a chance to win. The maternal preference principle guided judges' decisions. (The movie *Kramer v. Kramer* demonstrated the centrality of the concept of the tender years and the principle of maternal preference.)

During this time frame, from about 1920 to 1970, if both spouses wanted a divorce they could not say so and file by mutual consent. Divorce implied that one party to the dispute was at "fault," or guilty as previously described. Divorces were not granted on a "no-fault" basis; thus, concurrence was considered an illegal collusion. Nonetheless, as the only route to getting a divorce, couples in these circumstances resorted to deciding between them who would file for divorce, who would be presented as the guilty party, and what the "grounds" would be. Truth had to pale if "justice," under the extant laws, was to prevail. Suitable grounds included, depending on the state of jurisdiction, adultery, alcoholism, mental cruelty (usually by the man at that time), mental illness, and prostitution. If someone wanted out of the marriage badly enough, he or she might admit to a behavior that had never occurred. A man might pay lifelong alimony as a consequence; a woman might forfeit spousal support in return for being granted her exit papers from an intolerable marriage.

Society in general, including judges as its mandated representatives, often went along with the idea that men had a permanent obligation to continue supporting their ex-wives. Women usually believed they had a right to this income based on having borne and raised their ex-husbands' children, having kept their homes for them, and perhaps for having assisted or enabled them to build their careers or given up their own. When husbands could not afford this perpetual encumbrance or did not wish to have it placed on them by the court, they abandoned their wives and children and disappeared. Those who could afford to do so settled in other countries and used whatever artifice was necessary to escape detection. Few of these laws, or the behaviors employed to circumvent or comply with them, were family-friendly.

The 1970s and early 1980s saw a third major shift in the prevalent legal and psychological mind-set regarding custody, child support, alimony, and property distribution. The doctrine of the necessity of considering the "best interest of the child," originally articulated by Justice Brandeis in 1925 and reintroduced by Goldstein, Freud, and Solnit (1973) some 45 years later, had finally taken hold (Florida Dissolution of Marriage—Children Act, 1982/1992). Ideally, this meant that the child's needs and interests were to be given primary consideration and, as interpreted by child advocates and many mental health professionals, if a child's needs and a parent's rights and wishes conflicted, the child's needs were to receive top priority. This has occurred only to a limited extent because many children have no voice or representation in adversarial divorce proceedings (and frequently do not need it) unless there is a court-appointed child advocate or guardian *ad litem*—which is a rarity except in the most contentious cases.

THE ADVENT OF MEDIATION

Given the disastrous course and outcome of hundreds of thousands of divorces after World War II, many therapists and lawyers sounded a clarion call for something different—searching for a more humane, equitable, and benign pathway to and beyond divorce. The quest was taken up by O. James Coogler, an attorney based in Atlanta, Georgia, who underwent his own horrific divorce in the 1970s and realized that there had to be a better way to terminate a marriage legally. He embarked on a crusade to evolve such a process and fashioned the modern divorce mediation movement. His seminal book, *Structured Mediation in Divorce Settlement* (Coogler, 1978), was hailed enthusiastically by those who were seeking an alternative strategy for making marital dissolution a more peaceful, growth-oriented process. Lawyers, therapists, and clergy, among other professionals who heard and read about his work, went to be trained by him in what was almost an apprentice model. Quickly Coogler and his followers formed the Family Mediation Association (FMA), and many of his original trainees became the first group of trainers to initiate others who thought mediation was a promising alternative dispute-resolution approach for couples splitting apart. This group included John Haynes (1981, 1982) and Steven Erickson (Erickson & Erickson, 1988), both of whom have remained active and respected trainers for the past two decades. In a few years the Academy of Family Mediators replaced FMA, with Haynes as its first president. (The politics of the field are not germane to this chapter and so are omitted.) The vast majority of mediators were and still are drawn from the ranks of those with degrees in law or one of the mental health professions, although by the late 1980s several graduate programs emerged that grant degrees in mediation.

The cardinal principles of mediation that were articulated at the outset in Coogler's work have subsequently been refined and expanded by many of the leaders in the field (see, for example, Folberg & Milne, 1988; Gold, 1992; Kaslow, 1988, 1990; Marlow, 1992; Marlow & Sauber, 1990). These include the following:

- Negotiating in good faith
- Making full disclosure of assets
- Empowering both parties to speak on their own behalf
- Believing in the clients' ability to know their own and their children's best interests and to make wise decisions on their own behalf
- Seeking a win–win collaborative and equitable agreement
- Sharing of the cost of the mediator's services
- Giving real attention to the best interests of the child
- Assuring that either party or the mediator can terminate the process if they do not believe it is progressing in a positive and fair direction.

These principles were congruent with the evolving principles of "no-fault" divorce, which was becoming more prominent throughout the United States and had overshadowed the earlier reliance on "fault" divorce.

Ideally, negotiations within mediation were to occur between the two separating partners and the mediator, who was to function as a neutral and objective third party in the settlement conference, fostering understanding, encouraging bargaining and tradeoffs, enhancing good will, and forging miniagreements on each issue discussed. The context was to be the safe sanctuary of the mediator's office or another neutral place. Many mediators have held to the original philosophy and ideals and continue to practice what Erickson and McKnight call *client-centered mediation* (1998, 2000), a structured, empathic, and focused conflict-resolution approach for arriving at agreement. The mediator encourages the parties to brainstorm solutions to each issue being discussed and may suggest additional options. Mutuality, consideration, and being respectful are emphasized.

Another philosophy and approach in the widening spectrum of possibilities is *transformative mediation*. The progenitors of this approach, Bush and Folger (1994), believe that the promise mediation holds out is that it can help the parties transform their relationship so that they can listen to and hear each other better and can interact to bring about a positive postdivorce relationship. It is predicated on the belief that clients are well informed about themselves and can be well intentioned toward each other. Transformative mediation seeks to help participants strive for wholeness and for healthy lives; in this sense it embodies many of the same goals as do some schools of psychotherapy. It is a less structured and more free-flowing mediation style than the client-centered approach (Erickson & McKnight, 2000), but has in common with it a commitment to empowering and encouraging the clients to take charge of their lives and make the decisions that will shape their futures rather than turning this role over to lawyers or a judge.

Others have departed markedly from the original paradigm. There is another school of mediation dubbed *muscle mediation*. Those who utilize this approach go beyond presenting possible options to putting pressure on the disputants to make specific decisions. This detracts from the client's right to self-determination and, in this author's opinion, goes counter to the very respectful basic precepts of mediation.

In some states, most notably Florida, mediation has become increasingly legalized and legalistic in the past decade, and much less a field that values mediators drawn from the mental health disciplines. In Florida, court-based mediators, as well as those who receive referrals from court mediation services, are expected to be certified as mediators by the Florida Supreme Court, and must be recertified every 2 years. Some jurisdictions urge that the parties' respective attorneys attend and participate in the mediation sessions, which often means that the mediator may end up mediating between the attorneys and not between the divorcing spouses, as in the following case:

> Mr. G had initiated the request for mediation in mid-1998. He said his wife, from whom he had been physically separated for over a year, would come, albeit reluctantly. Although in the 17 years in which I have mediated I have held to the policy of having each party pay a percentage of the fee, based on income and assets, Mrs. G declared belligerently in the first session, "I have no money and I will not pay." He volunteered to pay the whole amount (as he claimed he had to do for everything else). When Mrs. G remained rigid in her stance about all issues during three sessions, and insisted on using the time to be critical and sarcastic to her husband, I indicated that little progress was being made and perhaps mediation was not a good solution for them. Mr. G was adamant that he wanted to continue with this method, so I suggested we have the next session with their attorneys present. A month later his lawyer's office called to arrange for this. During this conference, her attorney was unable to get her to agree to any compromises. He, too, was combative in attitude and conveyed that he was against mediation. Several times he implied this was a waste of time and he wanted to get on with the real proceedings. When at the end of the first joint session the attorneys asked me to mediate their fees, as Mrs. G's lawyers

believed the husband should pay these in toto, and he refused (and I learned two lawyers had already dropped her as a client for nonpayment of fees), which I do not deem to be a valid role for a mediator, nor did I think Mrs. G would be satisfied without her "day in court," I indicated that I could not continue to be involved in this case. As of this writing, the predivorce war continues—outside of mediation.

Having lawyers present often makes for a more cumbersome and costly process and is not in keeping with the original spirit of mediation, which promoted empowering people who are trying to avoid an adversarial situation with one another to speak and act on their own behalf as equals at the negotiating table. Such mediations tend to be more hostile, to occur under the pressure and stress of meeting specific legal dictates of preset court dates, and to be characterized by less cooperation than are true client-centered mediations. The latter are geared toward designing an agreement that two people and their significant others, particularly their children, will perceive as their own positive map for the future. Voluntary mediations are more concerned about promoting emotional well-being than conforming to legalities. In addition, in states like Florida, where financial affidavits are to be attached to the memorandum of understanding that goes to the attorneys for finalization into a marital settlement agreement, the process resembles the discovery aspect of an adversarial divorce more than the voluntary full-disclosure and good-faith provisos of client-centered mediation.

Some arbitrators have added divorce mediation to the list of activities in which they engage. Often they try to accomplish as much as possible by nonbinding voluntary arbitration. However, sometimes the contract includes a clause giving the arbitrator the authority to make the decisions on any issues on which the couple cannot reach agreement. This may include a stipulation that the arbitration will be binding. For those individuals who do not wish to take full responsibility for what happens to them so that they can fall back on blaming someone else, such as a judge or an arbitrator, passing final decision-making authority onto another often is preferable, and so binding arbitration is accepted en route to divorce.

In light of the current variations in the philosophy and practice of mediation, only a few of which have been described here, it behooves mediators to tell consumers what their orientation is so that the clients can decide if the mediator's approach is concordant with what they are seeking. If this information is not offered, the client should feel free to inquire about the mediator's philosophy and style, as well as about fees and how and when they are to be paid. Generally, what transpires in mediation is confidential, and the only fact a mediator may have to report to the court in court-connected mediations is whether the couple attended the scheduled mediation sessions. No records akin to therapy notes are kept; the mediator only records the miniagreements made in each session regarding parenting and visitation, child support, spousal support, and property settlement. Because many mediators do everything in triplicate, and request that the parties bring three copies of their financial records and statements, everyone involved has copies of whatever they need throughout the deliberations. The parties are free to provide these to their attorneys whenever they see fit to do so, or to ask that the mediator send a summary of the miniagreements reached in each session, as well as the final memorandum of understanding, to their respective lawyers.

Fortunately, when mediation is the pathway taken to negotiate the divorce agreement, many mediators strongly emphasize the importance of assessing the children's needs and how these are likely to change over the course of a child's normal development. For example, they might point out that an 8-year-old child who now looks forward to going to his or her father's home every other Friday night after school may wish to have that schedule modified in a few years when he or she enters high school and Friday night is the time for football games and other special peer group activities in the community. If the parents listen to the child and try to accommodate these predictable requests, the minor alteration needed to change visitation from Friday night to Saturday morning and the return from Sunday night to Monday morning will be made easily and smoothly. No legal action will be necessary. If, however, the couple is still embroiled in warfare when this change is requested, the father may interpret this request as a demand and a rejection and the result of the mother's continuing efforts at "parental alienation syndrome" (Gardner, 1989; Palmer, 1988).

Children need to derive some sense of security from having a schedule that is reasonably predictable, yet allows for flexibility if the parents need to occasionally switch when a child will be in residence with them. This can be emphasized in mediation when the couple are discussing where the primary and secondary residences will be (see, for example, Florida, 1982/1992), how and when transfers from one parent to the other will occur, and how to ensure that they will be neither too frequent nor traumatic. The adults can be encouraged to respect each other's parenting skills and to reinforce the image that each is and will remain a loving and involved parent who will not openly denigrate the other parent to the children.

Many mediators will advise parting parents, based on their sound knowledge of child development, that it is wise to minimize the number of disruptions and changes the children have to contend with at any one time. They may tell them that sometime in the future the child may want to spend more time with the non-residential parent for such reasons as to get to know him or her better, or to have a greater opportunity to identify with the same-sex parent. Reassurance that this often occurs around early adolescence may offset the shock if and when it occurs and may help make them receptive to renegotiating the agreement later without the further shock of the child precipitating a crisis by getting into trouble (i.e., by using drugs, truanting, developing anorexia or bulimia, attempting suicide, or committing a delinquent act) in order to have his or her needs attended to. It is not unusual for mediators to recommend including annual major conferences between the ex-spouses to review what is happening in their child's life and to consider modifications if they appear warranted. In the event that they cannot discuss current concerns and their resolution with each other, a clause should be inserted that provides for a return to mediation as the next option to be pursued before they enter into a legal battle.

ECONOMIC CONSIDERATIONS

Closely tied into concerns about parenting, residence, and visitation is the issue of child support. Generally, North American society recommends that children be maintained at the same level postdivorce as predivorce. Except in very wealthy families, this is not possible; when the family income has to be split and shared by two households, neither will have as much as they did before the family breakup (Wallerstein & Kelly, 1980). Questions about what child support covers, how often it is to be paid, and whether it is to be reduced partially during periods of time when the children are living with the nonresidential payer parent for more than a week at a stretch need to be considered calmly, with the mediator amenable to providing information, if requested, about how other couples have handled these matters successfully. In jurisdictions where there are child support guidelines (see Figure 12.1) these should be utilized to keep the discussions tied to the legal expectations and to minimize escalation of controversy about what is a realistic amount to be paid.

Child support and the other financial aspects to be addressed are part and parcel of the legal issues that must be resolved during the settlement phase. Nonetheless, it is important to bear in mind that the conclusion of the legal and economic phases are not coterminous. The legal divorce ends the day the final decree is signed and meted out by the judge. The economic divorce is not over until the following conditions are met:

1. The period for payment of *child support* has expired. Thus, if a couple were divorced in 1995 and the youngest child was age 3 at the time, child support would continue to be paid by the more affluent ex-spouse to the less affluent parent, if he or she is designated the primary parent, until 2010, in most states, and perhaps 2013 in New York, where the age of legal majority is 21 rather than 18 years. If there have been extenuating circumstances, such as a mentally retarded or severely physically handicapped child, the payment of child support may continue in perpetuity. Child support ends when no funds for this purpose are sent from the payor spouse, most often the ex-husband, to the recipient spouse, usually the ex-wife. If money is provided directly to the child after that, or if the parents decide to cover college tuition or other post–high school expenses by sending payments directly to the educational institution, they are no longer subsumed under the category of child support.
2. The time allotted for payment of alimony or *spousal support* runs out. In the United States until the last few decades, as previously indicated, spousal support was usually permanent. It did not end until either partner died or the recipient spouse remarried. Thus if a couple got divorced when the woman was age 45 and both lived into their 70s, the ex-husband often continued supporting his former spouse for more years than he had been actually married to her. Multitudes of men believed this to be unfair; they had a continuing obligation to an ex-wife but she had none to them, especially after the children were grown. If the man remarried, he often was supporting two women—how strange to be mandated to commit economic bigamy when legal bigamy remains impermissible!

As more and more women sought equality in all arenas of life and entered the workforce to express and fulfill their competence and independence, more and more men began to convey disgruntlement with the dictum of permanent alimony. If divorce is no longer to be seen as a contest between a guilty and an innocent party, and takes place within the context of a no-fault stipulation, then permanent alimony becomes an anathema except for women who are incapacitated and cannot work or those who are in their senior years and are probably

Florida Child Support Guidelines Worksheet

Step 1: To Determine Monthly Gross Income	Father	Mother
1. Actual Gross Income (Schedule A)		
2. Imputed Monthly Income pursuant to F.S. 61.13, Section 3(2) (b).		
3. Total Gross Income (Add 1 and 2)		

Step 2: To Determine Monthly Net Income		
4. Total Deductions (Schedule B)		
5. Net Income: (Subtract 4 from 3)		
6. Combined Monthly Net Income of both parents		

Step 3: To Determine Child Support Amount		
7. Determine applicable amount for number of children (Schedule C)		
8. Child care cost incurred due to employment or job search or education calculated to result in employment or to enhance current employment income of either parent reduced by 25%. Limited to cost for quality care from licensed source.		
9. Health insurance costs ordered pursuant to §61.13 (1) (b)		
10. Total needed child support: Add lines 7, 8 and 9.		
11. Each parent's mathematical proportion of support; divide the parent's monthly net income (Line 5) by the combined monthly net income (Line 6)		
12. Child support shares: (Multiply Line 10 by Line 11)		
13. Adjustment to support award (Schedule D)		
14. MONTHLY CHILD SUPPORT OBLIGATIONS OF PARENTS		
15. CHILD SUPPORT RANGE (±5%)		

Schedule A	Father/Mon.	Mother/Mon.

Average gross *monthly* income shall include the Following:
  a. Gross salary or wages (AFDC excluded).
  b. Bonuses, commissions, allowances, overtime, tips & similar payments.
  c. Business income from sources such as self-employment, partnership, close corporations, and/or independent contracts (gross receipts minus ordinary and necessary expenses required to produce income).
  d. Disability Benefits.
  e. Worker's Compensation.
  f. Unemployment Compensation.
  g. Pension, Retirements or Annuity Payments.
  h. Social Security Benefits.
  i. Spousal support from a previous marriage.
  j. Interest and Dividends.

Figure 12.1 Child support determination guidelines.

Florida Child Support Guidelines Worksheet

Schedule A	Father/Mon.	Mother/Mon.
k. Rental Income (Gross receipts minus ordinary and necessary expenses required to product income).		
l. Income from Royalties, Trusts or Estates.		
m. Reimbursed expenses and in kind payments to the extent that they reduce personal living expenses.		
n. Gains derived from dealing in property (Not including non-recurring gains).		
o. Itemize any other income of a recurring nature or factor considered		
TOTAL GROSS INCOME		

Schedule B	Father/Mon.	Mother/Mon.
The trier of fact shall deduct the following from Gross Income:		
a. Federal, state & local income taxes (corrected for filing status and actual number of withholding allowances).		
b. F.I.C.A. or self-employment tax (annualized).		
c. Mandatory Union Dues		
d. Mandatory Retirement		
e. Health insurance payments, excluding payments for coverage of minor child.		
f. Court ordered support payments for other children actually paid.		
TOTAL DEDUCTIONS		

Schedule D	Fathers Share	Mothers Share
1. Extraordinary medical, psychological, educational or dental expenses.		
2. Independent income of the child.		
3. The payment of both child support and spousal support to the obligee or payment of regular support to parent in need.		
4. Seasonal variations in one or both parents' incomes or expenses.		
5. The age of the child, taking into account the greater needs of older children.		
6. Special needs that have traditionally been met within the family budget even though the fulfilling of those needs will cause the support to exceed the proposed guidelines.		
7. The particular shared parental arrangement, such as where:		
a. The children spend a substantial amount of time with the secondary residential parent, thereby reducing the financial expenditures incurred by the primary residential parent, or		

(Continued)

251

Florida Child Support Guidelines Worksheet

Schedule D	Fathers Share	Mothers Share
b. The refusal of the secondary residential parent to become involved in the activities of the child, or		
c. Giving due consideration to the primary residential parent's homemaking services, or		
d. Visitation for more than 28 consecutive days.		
8. Total available assets of the obligee, obligor, and the child.		
9. Impact of the IRS dependency exemption and waiver of that exemption.		
10. Application of the child support guidelines requiring payment of 55% of gross income for child support obligation from a single support order.		
11. In a proceeding for increased support, subsequent children and income of other parent may be considered.		
12. Any other adjustment which is needed to achieve an equitable result which may include, but not be limited to, a reasonable and necessary existing expense or debt.		
TOTAL ADJUSTMENTS		

Figure 12.1 (*Continued*)

unemployable. Many states added short-term temporary or rehabilitation alimony as alternatives; a ruling designating temporary alimony usually mandates it from 3 to 10 years, long enough for the youngest child to enter school so the mother doesn't feel she needs to be home all day and can return to school en route to upgrading her skills and earning potential, or can return directly to work. Unfortunately, many women still do not have the ability to earn enough to cover the amount lost when alimony is discontinued.

As Weitzman (1985) has shown, women's and children's economic situations worsen after divorce: They tend to move downward in the socioeconomic scale. Men tend to stay at the same level, or spurt upwards again. Obviously, we still have not arrived at a modus operandi that is fair to both ex-husbands and ex-wives. Although many of the postdivorce quarrels that explode are ostensibly about the children, underneath are the seething financial tensions that flow, like hot lava, from disagreements over who is entitled to what and whether child support and spousal support can and should be renegotiated or how to get a recalcitrant ex-spouse to pay what he (or she) owes in arrears (Palmer & Tangel-Rodriguez, 1995) short of sending him or her to prison, thereby cutting off the potential source of future income. This is a terrible quagmire in which all too many people get stuck.

3. The division of assets has to be finalized before the divorce decree is granted. The property settlement, once concluded and signed, cannot be renegotiated. Thus, it must be crafted carefully and thoughtfully. When a couple have little or nothing to divide, each will remain at the poverty level. They still have to

arrive at some agreement on how they will defray their debts and meet the cost of daily life in order to survive. For those who have accrued various kinds of assets, they need to agree on how to divide both these and their liabilities. This must be done within the framework of the laws of the state in which they reside. The majority of states mandate that there should be *equitable* distribution of property. *Equitable* means *fair*, not equal, and this leaves room for negotiation over entitlement, the value of what each contributed to the marriage, about future earning potential, and the receipt of inheritances. Other states, most notably California, adhere to a *community property* presumption; that is, the assets are coowned equally and must be equally divided—regardless of special needs or contributions. Each asset does not need to be divided in half, but the total of the two halves disbursed must be the same. All of this should be done with knowledgeable consideration of the tax implications of how things are divided in order to maximize the amount of resources that will remain with the parties rather than being paid out in taxes (or to the various professionals involved with the couple).

Thus, there are three legs to the financial picture—child support, alimony, and the property settlement. They should be deliberated so as to achieve a total balanced package, although each portion may need to be negotiated incrementally and then reviewed in light of the totality.

In those situations where assets are plentiful and the woman has a good deal of financial savvy or an expert financial advisor, she may be wise to opt for a larger up-front settlement in lieu of long-term alimony. Then she can invest what she has wisely in a business, in real estate, or in securities, and perhaps derive more income than she would receive from spousal support. It keeps her from being permanently financially dependent and negatively tied to her ex-mate. And once the money is hers, it cannot be taken back. Conversely, if she is counting on alimony for the next 20 to 30 years and the ex-husband dies in 5 years, the support she has assumed will continue will evaporate instead.

For the man who can manage it, a lump-sum larger settlement can also be advantageous. He can be through with alimony much sooner, ending the resentment many men feel about having to continue to pay for the rest of their lives. He is then freer to invest himself financially and emotionally in the new postdivorce life he is building. He may also be able to reach a compromise in which in return for his providing and paying a substantial up-front settlement, she gives up all claims to his pension or retirement plan. For many men, knowing that this asset remains untouched provides a sense of relief.

It is important to emphasize that if the woman is the wealthier party through her earnings, dividends from investments, or inheritances, and she is the one paying child support or alimony, the same concepts, assumptions and considerations apply. In this sense, the decisions should be gender neutral.

THE PSYCHOSOCIAL CONTEXT

It is essential that all professionals involved keep in mind that all of the negotiations and decisions are being made when most of the divorcing pairs are experiencing feelings including extreme pain, anger, hurt, disappointment, grief, bewilderment, uncertainty, and resentment (see Table 12.1). Yet they are expected to act rationally because the choices they make will shape their futures, and those of their children, other significant family members, and perhaps future partners, for years to come. How they act toward each other will also impact on their postdivorce relationship and on whether they will continue to harbor animosity and a desire to retaliate for the narcissistic and other wounds they have inflicted on each other, or will eventually be able to move beyond anger and reach a point of some acceptance and even forgiveness—that is, complete the spiritual (if that is important to them; Kaslow, 1993a) and psychic closure end phase of the divorce process. Whether they behave in ways that promote self-respect and respect of the other party will also influence their ability to be in the same place at the same time when their children have athletic events or artistic school performances, graduate from high school and college, get married, have babies, and celebrate other significant life events, or in times of stress, as when a child has surgery. If the rift is exacerbated by nastiness or chicanery during the divorce proceedings, it will impede everyone's postdivorce recovery and ability to get divorced without ruining the rest of their lives (Margulies, 1992; Schwartz & Kaslow, 1997).

During the time the details of the divorce settlement are being hammered out, either in mediation, arbitration, or litigation, the couple will often be subjected to opinions from others, solicited or unsolicited. They may be besieged by input from their parents, friends, or colleagues as to what they should or should not do or agree to. Although these gratuitous opinions may be offered by people intending to be helpful, they can add to the confusion. Rather, the parting individuals should listen most to their own inner thoughts, feelings, and desires and sort out what suits them and their situation, as this is uniquely theirs and not fully knowable to anyone else.

Throughout the legal phase and beyond, various forms of therapy, as delineated in Table 12.1, can be most beneficial to the members of the disbanding family—separately or in various combinations. Therapy provides a haven for expressing the entire gamut of feelings, rational and irrational: the vacillating and debilitating moods, the sense of failure and loss of self-esteem, the desire for retaliation and punishment of an errant spouse, and the hopes and dreams for the future. Ideally, the therapist helps the patients to consider the options that can be available as they move toward fashioning a sound agreement, and keeps the focus on making the process as constructive and growth-oriented as is possible under the circumstances.

Many divorcees report that the three most difficult days in the divorce process are: (a) the day they tell or are told by their partner that the marriage is over and a divorce is inevitable; (b) the day one of them moves out of the marital home, lending additional credence to the fact that the marriage is irretrievably broken; and (c) the day of the final court hearing.

It is ironic that on the happy day of a wedding friends and family assemble to celebrate with the new couple, signify support of their union, and wish them well. Usually there are more people wanting to attend the ceremony and reception than either the bride or groom would prefer to have present. Yet the very unhappy day of the finalization of divorce (even if it is tinged with feelings of relief, and particularly if it ends an abusive, turbulent, or unbearable marriage) is usually a very lonely one when the party goes alone to court, accompanied solely by his or her attorney, perhaps to face not only an unknown and unpredictable judge, but also the spouse from whom he or she is pulling apart. This is a day when close friends and relatives should rally around and volunteer to go along to court in a support role and perhaps out for lunch or dinner afterwards to mark what is also a monumental turning point and transition event that should not be spent in isolation. Children might be included, too, as this particular D-Day is also a significant occasion in their lives.

It is important that therapist, mediator, and lawyer fees be paid in full to add another note of closure; that all documents that need to be transferred into one name are properly handled; and that any other legal aspects be wrapped up as soon as possible.

LIFE BEYOND DIVORCE

For adults who are reasonably healthy and resilient, it takes from 2 to 5 years to feel optimistic and confident again and to shift from living in and ruminating about the past, or the there and then, to focusing on the present, or the here and now, as well as to planning for the future. It takes this long for any needed relocations and job changes to occur; for the parenting and visitation schedule to be operating smoothly and to everyone's satisfaction; for the individuals to be dating again if they desire to do so; and for someone to risk being willing to trust again. During this time period, the psychological tasks to be accomplished include rebuilding one's self-esteem and self-confidence, looking and feeling better physically, feeling good about one's skill and ability as a single parent, achieving acceptance over what has occurred, and often reactivating old or developing new hobbies, activities, and friendships.

If someone no longer feels comfortable in the predominantly couples world they inhabited while married, they will need to make new friends among single peers—those who were never married or who are divorced or widowed. They are apt to share more in common in terms of concerns about single parenting, visitation glitches, vacations, and interests. Some divorcees retain many of their married friends and continue to be included by them in social events while also building a network of single friends. Each individual has to discern what works for him or her, that is, where they feel most comfortable and stimulated.

Remarrying very quickly is generally not advisable. In less than 2 years there is usually insufficient closure on the prior marital relationship and too much of the hurt and animosity may spill over onto the new loved one. Also, if the new relationship predated the divorce and the affair was one of the triggers prompting the divorce, one needs to make certain that the lover will also be the right spouse when the clandestine, forbidden-fruit facet no longer is operative. Also, fierce resentment from the children is more likely when the new partner is perceived as someone who helped to break up their family.

The vast majority of divorcees do decide to try again and opt to remarry within the initial 5-year postdivorce period. As previously indicated, it is wise for persons contemplating remarriage to show their intended spouse the marital settlement agreement because they are legally and, hopefully, morally committed to fulfilling it in terms of continuing financial and emotional involvement with the children of the prior marriage(s) (Kaslow, 1993b). They also have an ethical and existential obligation to do so because the parental role predates the new union. Thus, all involved parties should be cognizant of the fact that although one may be legally divorced from an ex-spouse, one is never legally or financially divorced from one's children.

Despite the complexities of the remarriage family, many do find great satisfaction in this new life after divorce—as do those who choose to remain single because they like the freedom and independence it affords.

In the words of the immortal bard, Shakespeare (Parrott & Telfer, 1931, pp. 426–427), in divorce as in marriage:

> *This above all;*
> *To thine own self be true*
> *And it must follow, as the night the day,*
> *Thou canst not then be false to any man.*
> —ACT I, SCENE V, HAMLET

REFERENCES

Ahrons, C. R. (1983). *The binuclear family: Parenting roles and relationships.* Unpublished paper.

Ahrons, C. R., & Rodgers, R. H. (1987). *Divorced families: A multidisciplinary developmental view.* New York: W. W. Norton.

Boszormenyi-Nagy, I., & Spark, G. (1973). *Invisible loyalties: Reciprocity in intergenerational family therapy.* New York: Harper & Row. (Reprinted 1984, New York: Brunner/Mazel.)

Brenner, C. (1955). *An elementary textbook of psychoanalysis.* New York: International Universities Press.

Bush, R. A., & Folger, J. P. (1994). *The promise of mediation.* San Francisco: Jossey-Bass.

Coogler, O. J. (1978). *Structured mediation in divorce settlement.* Lexington, MA: D. C. Heath.

Erickson, S., & Erickson, M. (1988). *Mediation casebook.* New York: Brunner/Mazel.

Erickson, S., & McKnight, M. (1998, July 8). Academy of Family Mediators Pre-Conference Workshop, San Francisco, California.

Erickson, S., & McKnight, M. (2000). *A practitioner's guide to mediation.* New York: John Wiley & Sons (in press).

Florida Dissolution of Marriage—Children Act, Chapters 82–96 (1982); Chapter 61 (1992 revision).

Folberg, J., & Milne, A. (1988). *Divorce mediation.* New York: Guilford Press.

Freud, S. (1964). *New introductory lectures on psychoanalysis.* (J. Strachey, Trans. & Ed.). New York: W. W. Norton. (Original work published 1933.)

Gardner, R. A. (1989). *Family evaluation in child custody mediation, arbitration and litigation.* Cresskill, NJ: Creative Therapeutics.

Gold, L. (1992). *Between love and hate: A guide to civilized divorce.* New York: Plenum Press.

Goldstein, J., Freud, A., & Solnit, A. (1973). *Beyond the best interests of the child.* New York: Free Press.

Haynes, J. M. (1981). *Divorce mediation.* New York: Springer.

Haynes, J. M. (1982). A conceptual model of the process of family mediation: Implications for training. *American Journal of Family Therapy, 10*(4), 5–16.

Kaslow, F. W. (1984). Divorce mediation and its emotional impact on the couple and their children. *American Journal of Family Therapy, 12*(3), 58–66.

Kaslow, F. W. (1988). The psychological dimension of divorce mediaton. In J. Folberg & A. Milne (Eds.), *Divorce mediation: Theory and practice* (pp. 83–108). New York: Guilford Press.

Kaslow, F. W. (1990). Divorce therapy and mediation for better custody. *Japanese Journal of Family Psychology, 4,* 19–37. (In English.)

Kaslow, F. W. (1993a). The divorce ceremony: A healing strategy. In T. Nelson & T. Trepper (Eds.), *101 Favorite family therapy interventions* (pp. 341–345). New York: Haworth Press.

Kaslow, F. W. (1993b). Understanding and treating the remarriage family. *Directions in Marriage and Family Therapy, 1*(3), 1–16.

Kaslow, F. W. (1994). Painful partings: Providing therapeutic guidance. In L. L. Schwartz (Ed.), *Mid-life divorce counseling* (pp. 67–82). Alexandria, VA: American Counseling Association.

Kaslow, F. W. (1995). The dynamics of divorce therapy. In R. H. Mikesell, D. D. Lusterman, & S. H. McDaniel (Eds.), *Integrating family therapy: Handbook of family psychology and systems theory* (pp. 271–283). Washington, DC: American Psychological Association.

Kaslow, F. W., & Schwartz, L. L. (1987). *Dynamics of divorce: A life cycle perspective.* New York: Brunner/Mazel.

Kessler, S., & Bostwick, S. (1977). Beyond divorce: Coping skills for children. *Journal of Clinical Child Psychology, 6,* 38–41.

Margulies, S. (1992). *Getting divorced without ruining your life.* New York: Simon & Schuster.

Marlow, L. (1992). *Divorce and the myth of lawyers.* Garden City, NY: Harlan Press.

Marlow, L., & Sauber, S. R. (1990). *The handbook of divorce mediation.* New York: Plenum Press.

Palmer, N. S. (1988). Legal recognition of the parental alienation syndrome. *American Journal of Family Therapy, 16*(4), 361–363.

Palmer, N. S., & Tangel-Rodriguez, A. (1995). *When your ex won't pay: Getting your kids the financial support they deserve.* Colorado Springs, CO: Pinon Press.

Parrott, T. M., & Telfer, R. S. (1931). *Shakespeare's Hamlet* (pp. 426–427). New York: Charles Scribner's Sons.

Roizblatt, A., Garcia, P., Maida, A. M., & Moya, G. (1990). Is Valentine still doubtful? A workshop model for children of divorce. *Contemporary Family Therapy, 12*(4), 299–310.

Schwartz, L. L., & Kaslow, F. W. (1997). *Painful partings: Divorce and its aftermath.* New York: John Wiley & Sons.

Wallerstein, J. S., & Kelly, J. B. (1980). *Surviving the breakup: How children and parents cope with divorce.* New York: Basic Books.

Weitzman, L. J. (1985). *The divorce revolution: The unexpected social and economic consequences for women and children in America.* New York: Free Press.

CHAPTER 13

Child Custody

MARION GINDES

THE HIGH rate of divorce among American couples and the increasingly diverse lifestyles people choose have highlighted the questions of who is responsible for the children, where they should live, and, even, what constitutes a family.

The issue of child custody does not exist when biological parents live together and share in the rearing of their children. Similarly, when parents who do not live together resolve how they will raise their children, custody does not become a conflictual issue. Custody as a family crisis emerges when parents or other parental figures are in conflict regarding the care of the child or children. (Throughout this chapter, *child* and *children* are used interchangeably.) From a family perspective, divorce and subsequent child custody disputes dramatically alter the original family structure for the parents and child as well as for members of the extended family. A new family configuration emerges, which affects the development and psychological well-being of all the parties.

While most disputes involving custody of a child occur when married parents seek a divorce or when nonmarried parents dissolve their relationship, other situations may also precipitate clashes over custody, or, at times, over access and visitation. Increasingly, grandparents are requesting access to children when it has been denied. A previously uninvolved parent may reappear and demand a role in the child's life. Following the dissolution of a second marriage, a stepparent may seek visitation with a stepchild. Adoptive parents may be challenged by biological parents (see Chapter 2). In some cases, the state or family members may seek to wrest custody from a parent they consider unfit. Disputes concerning the visitation of noncustodial parents with their children may escalate into legal battles over custody, if the noncustodial parents see the court system as their only recourse for attaining visitation.

The variety and complexity of familial connections that involve the custody of children can be illustrated most clearly through a series of case vignettes.

Sally's mother died at childbirth. Her father was devastated and did not think he could take care of her. His sister, Joan, who lives 250 miles away from him, brought the newborn Sally to live with her, her husband, and their three children. Sally has been raised as one of their own. After visiting Sally twice a year for 3 years, Sally's father, who is remarrying, now wants Sally to live with him and his new wife 3,000 miles from Joan and her family. Joan reports that she has nightmares about Sally waking in the middle of the night and not knowing where she is. She also fears that Sally will think that they did not love her. Joan and her husband are advised to let Sally go with her father. A visitation plan is worked out so that Sally can become more comfortable with her father and become acquainted with her stepmother before going to live with them.

Alice and Seth separated after 11 years of marriage. They have three children, ages 5, 7, and 10. They both work during the day. Seth would like the children to live with him because he considers himself more stable than Alice and he has greater financial resources. He also contends that his mother, who is a young retiree, can care for the children when he is not available, whereas Alice would have to continue the after-school programs that the children are in now. He would rather have his children taken care of by a relative than by a stranger. Alice maintains that Seth was never involved in the children's care when they were together. She believes that he has filed for custody to punish her for ending the marriage and to avoid providing child support. The children say that they want to live with both their parents. Attempts at negotiation and mediation have failed.

Two-year-old Emily's parents had a brief relationship but never married. Emily's mother alleges that her father neglects her, and returns her from visits with dirty clothing and scratches on her arms. Following the mother's court petition, the father must have someone supervise his visits with Emily. He claims that the mother is inventing the stories. A home visit reveals significant differences in the lifestyles of the mother and the father. The mother's home is spotless, yet she apologizes for its messiness. The child is kept on a specific schedule and the home environment is calm and quiet. The father lives with his father, his mother, and his brother. During the home visit, friends and relatives dropped by, all of whom interacted with Emily in an expansive and affectionate way. The father's home environment is somewhat disorganized, lively, and crowded. The mother sees this atmosphere as detrimental to the child and says that she will go to court until the father no longer can see the child. The father wants to have the child on a regular basis without supervision. There is no indication of neglect on the father's part.

The mother and father were both addicted to drugs. They separated when their son was 6 months old, at which point, the mother returned to her parents' home. The mother soon left but the child stayed with his maternal grandparents, who raised him until he was age 3. The father has "reformed" and now wants his child. The father is from an educated, financially comfortable family. The grandparents are uneducated, poor, unskilled laborers. The father, who now has the child, wants to terminate the grandparents' visits with the child, who is now age 7.

Custody becomes a legal matter when one or both of the parties involved brings the conflict to the courts, as indicated in the last three examples preceding. Once the legal arena is entered, the care and responsibility for the child are transformed from a private family matter to a legal proceeding. The court then has the right to decide who is the most suitable guardian for the child.

The term *child custody* encompasses both legal and physical custody. When the court awards *legal custody*, it gives a parent or guardian the right to make decisions regarding the child's welfare, education, and health care (Buehler & Gerard, 1995; Stahl, 1994). That parent or guardian has the legal responsibility for the child. *Physical custody*, in contrast, determines where the child will reside. Custody also presupposes financial and emotional responsibility for the child. A noncustodial parent may have financial obligations in the form of child support and, certainly, should have an emotional commitment to the child's well-being.

Psychologists and other mental health professionals are increasingly asked to participate in court-related proceedings as evaluators. They may also be brought into a case because of prior contact with one of the parties as a treating therapist or because a therapeutic intervention has been mandated by the court. These discrete roles for psychologists have distinct constraints and characteristics within the legal system as well as within the ethical codes for psychologists.

Although this chapter primarily focuses on custody within the context of parents who are divorcing or severing their relationship, most of the considerations discussed apply to other circumstances surrounding disputed parental rights as well. Because no two custody situations are identical, the particular contexts and variables must be taken into account when evaluating a specific situation. The critical legal and psychological issues are addressed and the current views within the field are presented. The implications for the child's psychological health as well as the implications for the role of the therapist are discussed.

MAJOR CONSIDERATIONS

The major considerations in child custody disputes involve the process employed to arrive at the custody determination, the criteria used in determining custody, and the types of possible custody arrangements.

How Should Child Custody Be Decided?

Disputes regarding the custody of children, for the most part, originate in the interpersonal conflicts between the adult caregivers. On occasion, however, disputes may be intergenerational. A parent may be feuding with his or her own parent and refuse to allow that grandparent to see the grandchildren. A former son- or daughter-in-law with sole custody may deny a disliked grandparent access to the children, forcing the grandparent to petition the court for visitation. It should be noted that, in most states, grandparents have legal standing to seek visitation. In New York, both grandparents and siblings may petition the court for visitation (New York Domestic Relations Law §71 and §72; Wulach, 1993).

In the best of all worlds, however, people who have or had caregiving responsibility for a child or a caring relationship with a child would be able to put the child's interests before their own. When they are able to do so, the custody issue does not emerge. Fortunately, only a small percentage of children become the focus of custody disputes (Maccoby & Mnookin, 1992).

When people find that they cannot agree on their own how care for the children should be shared, they must seek outside assistance. There are four primary processes available for resolving the conflict. First, they may turn to a mental health professional to help them develop a working relationship with regard to the children. In this situation, the goals of the psychological intervention are to reduce the level of conflict between the parties, to separate their feelings for each other from their children's needs, and to redefine their relationship as one that focuses on their love for their children and, therefore, on their mutual concern for the children's needs. This process is less intrusive than the others because the ultimate decision making remains entirely with the parties themselves.

Second, the parties may enlist their lawyers in an attempt to negotiate a resolution of the dispute. Most custody arrangements are decided by the parties themselves or with the assistance of their attorneys. Only a minority of cases go to court.

Third, the parties may seek mediation when other attempts to agree on custody arrangements have been unsuccessful. In certain cases, parties who wish to avoid the adversarial process may seek a mediated agreement prior to consulting with attorneys. Mediation as a means of resolving child custody disputes has been growing in popularity and importance over the last 20 years. Mediators, who serve an impartial function, can be legal or mental health professionals. Although the goal of mediation is to help the parties reach agreement, the mediator may play a more direct role than a mental health professional does in a counseling or therapeutic context and can offer options for the parties' consideration. Saposnek (1983) describes the mediator's style as "active, assertive, goal-oriented, and businesslike" (p. 32). Thus, while the final decision still rests with the parties, one or both parties may feel pressure to comply.

In contrast to litigation, the basic principles of mediation, such as cooperative problem solving and empowerment, are consistent with the practice of marital and family systems therapy (Kaslow, 1988). Mediation, however, is not therapy and should not be confused with it (Schwartz & Kaslow, 1997). Mediation requires specific training as well as the acquisition of knowledge about the psychology of divorce and family law.

As an alternative to litigation, mediation offers several advantages. It can sometimes lead to a resolution without increasing hostility or the excessive costs that often result from litigation. According to Ahrons (1994), mediation can help the parties learn to work cooperatively in resolving their conflicts. The time that the family members, particularly the children, spend in custody limbo, a significant source of stress for all, may be significantly reduced. Research on the results of mediation is also promising. An important finding of a number of studies is that the parties are more satisfied with the financial and custody arrangements following mediated agreements than following litigated cases (Bautz & Hill, 1991; Schwartz & Kaslow, 1997). In the Charlottesville Mediation Project, families disputing custody were randomly assigned to either mediation or the court process. Only 11% of the mediation group did not settle through mediation or negotiation, whereas 72% of the court group went on to a custody hearing (Emery, 1994). Thus, mediation significantly reduced the incidence of litigation for this sample of already disputing families. Emery (1994) summarizes other positive findings, such as quicker resolution of the dispute and greater compliance with the terms of the agreement. A follow-up of this project, reported by Schwartz and Kaslow (1997), found better interparental communication and more frequent contact between noncustodial parents and children after an average of 9 years.

The question of whether mediation poses a disadvantage to women and an advantage to men has been raised. Some studies have reported that husbands, in contrast to wives, indicate greater satisfaction with mediation than with litigation (Emery, Matthews, & Kitzmann, 1994) or that husbands' satisfaction compared to wives' satisfaction increases (Mathis & Yingling, 1992). Emery (1994) concludes that there is no evidence that mediation favors men more than women, although women may do better in litigation.

As Schwartz and Kaslow (1997) point out, not all families are candidates for mediation. Some parties may refuse to participate in mediation and prefer to have their day in court. Others may be too angry to agree to mediation. For mediation to achieve its goal—an agreed-upon settlement that is fair to both parties—there cannot be a significant power imbalance (Ahrons, 1994; Schwartz & Kaslow, 1997). For many mediators, a history of abuse disqualifies the couple. Emery (1994) discusses conditions for deciding between cooperative and competitive resolution strategies.

Fourth, the parties may formally enter the court system by filing a petition for custody. The presiding judge will make the decision. At any time during the process, the parties may settle the dispute on their own, through their attorneys, through mediation, or with the help of a mental health professional. The judge still must review their decision and retains ultimate authority to make the final ruling. This avenue for resolution is the most intrusive because it removes the decision from the parties. It is not, however, a final decision, as a dissatisfied party may re-petition the court at any time (Houlgate, 1988). One of the inherent problems with the legal system is that one of the parties may prolong the dispute interminably by filing petitions and appeals, thus delaying implementation of a stable plan for the children.

There have been many debates regarding the appropriateness of the legal system for determining who will care for children (see Emery, 1994, pp. 69–72). From a psychological perspective, the court is not the best arena to decide how a child should be raised. Custody of children, however, is a legal matter in the United States and is dictated by individual state civil law. The court may get input from mental health professionals, but the final decision rests with the judge.

LEGAL CRITERIA FOR CUSTODY DETERMINATION

A brief history of the criteria for custody determination can provide perspective for the current state of judicial decision making. From an historical viewpoint, disputes over the custody of children are a recent phenomenon. Until the mid-19th century, around the time of the Industrial Revolution, children were considered to be the property of the father. The Talfourd Act, passed by the English Parliament in 1839, gave mothers the right to custody of children less than 7 years of age, leading to the predominance of the "tender years doctrine" (Elkin, 1987). Following this parliamentary act, preference for the custodian gradually shifted from father to mother. Elkin also notes the co-occurrence of women obtaining the right to own property and changes in society's attitudes toward children. Freud's views of the importance of the mother–child relationship also came into prominence (albeit amid controversy) at the turn of the century (Kelly, 1994). These influences worked together to make the tender years doctrine the overwhelming presumption throughout the first half of this century. Custody was likely to be awarded to fathers or other guardians only if the mothers were found to be unfit, promiscuous, alcoholic, or mentally ill, or followed an alternative lifestyle questioned by the courts.

Houlgate (1988) reported that the Alaska Supreme Court rejected the tender years doctrine as an appropriate criterion for determining the best interests of the child. The court considered warmth, consistency, and continuity of the relationship as the important aspects of "mothering" rather than the sex of the individual performing those functions. Despite such rulings, as well as laws that require gender neutrality and reliance on the "best interests of the child," the tender years doctrine remains a strong influence for many judges who believe that mothers are better suited than fathers to care for young children.

At present, all states incorporate aspects of the best interests of the child as the standard for custody decision making (Buehler & Gerard, 1995). While this concept was probably introduced by Justice Brandeis as early as 1925 (Kaslow & Schwartz, 1987), it is only in the last 25 years that it has become predominant. This standard is supposed to treat all parties equitably and consider the child's needs as paramount.

The Uniform Marriage and Divorce Act (1979), which has been adopted by many states, cites five criteria considered relevant in determining the best interests of the child:

1. The wishes of the child's parent or parents as to custody
2. The wishes of the child
3. The interaction and interrelationship of the child with the parent or parents, siblings, and any other person who may significantly affect the child's best interests
4. The child's adjustment to home, school, and community
5. The mental and physical health of all individuals involved

The act further states that any conduct that does not affect a person's relationship to the child should not be considered. In usage, however, judges may apply any factors that they consider to be pertinent. The end result is that these five criteria are used only as general guides for determining what is in the best interests of the child and are subject to an infinite number of interpretations that may be manipulated by parents, judges, and lawyers (Fineman, 1996).

Another standard that influences custody decisions is the identification of the primary caretaker. Some courts look to the person who has had the major responsibility for the day-to-day care of the child (Buehler & Gerard, 1995; Kelly, 1994). While this consideration tends to favor women because of their child care role in our society, the standard itself is gender neutral because either a man or a woman may be the primary caretaker. (For a further discussion see Melton, Petrila, Poythress, & Slobogin, 1997.)

Willingness to share the child and encourage the relationship between the child and the other relevant parties is also a factor in custody determinations. Both Florida (§61.13[2]; Schutz, Dixon, Lindenberger, & Ruther, 1989, p. 21) and New York (Wulach, 1993) have incorporated this variable into their laws regarding custody. Thus, a judge would be unlikely to grant primary custody to a parent who interferes with the relationship between the children and the other parent, either by preventing visitation or denigrating the other parent.

PSYCHOLOGICAL CRITERIA FOR CUSTODY DETERMINATION

Although the determination of child custody by the courts may be a legal decision, the criteria upon which it is based are, for the most part, psychological ones. The Uniform Marriage and Divorce Act (1979) essentially presents psychological issues, such as psychological adjustment, interpersonal family relationships, and mental and physical health, in defining the best interests of the child.

Over the years, mental health and legal professionals have attempted to establish what criteria, in fact, are used when custody is decided. While certain factors have been considered relevant in determining custody (see Schutz et al., 1989), the particular circumstances of each situation will give weight to some factors over others. In their survey of 201 experienced psychologists, Ackerman and Ackerman (1997) found that certain factors rated as most significant for sole custody differed from those rated as most significant for joint custody. For example, parenting skills and emotional bonding with parents were among those rated as most important for sole custody whereas parents' ability to separate interpersonal difficulties from parenting decisions and amount of anger and bitterness between the parents were among those rated as most important for joint custody. For both sole and joint custody, presence or absence of substance abuse and the psychological stability of parents were selected as the key variables. Ackerman and Ackerman (1997) also reported that parental cooperation was rated as a major variable in considering sole or joint custody. According to Maccoby and Mnookin (1992), California law holds that when parents cannot agree, the preferences of the more cooperative parent should be considered. The assumption is that the cooperative parent would be more supportive of the other parent's involvement with the child.

TYPES OF CUSTODY ARRANGEMENTS

The view of custody as ownership makes the term *custody* an unfortunate one to use in representing the care of children. Although there are movements to substitute more "humane" terms, such as *parenting arrangements* instead of *custody*, or *access* instead of *visitation*, or *periods of physical placement* instead of *physical custody* (Ackerman, 1995; Ackerman & Kane, 1989), *custody* is still the most widespread term and is used in this chapter, despite its negative connotation to some.

In an intact family, parents work out a division of labor involving care and responsibility for the children. When parents do not live together, this division must necessarily be specified and concrete. Many variations of legal and physical custody have been adopted by parents or guardians through negotiation and agreement or by court decree.

On one end of the continuum, sole legal and physical custody may be given to one parent. In this situation, the noncustodial parent may have little or no input and either minimal contact or no contact with the child. This arrangement represents an extreme that is becoming less common because it essentially disenfranchises the noncustodial parent from having a significant presence in the child's life. It may be unavoidable, in certain situations, as when one parent has a military career and is assigned to overseas posts for extended time periods. Many situations do exist in which a liberal visitation schedule is granted the noncustodial parent along with sole legal and physical custody to one parent. Although this provides for more interaction between the noncustodial parent and the child, it may afford the noncustodial parent little say in the child's life.

The more frequent arrangement is one in which both parents share legal custody, but one parent is the primary residential parent. The noncustodial parent has temporary physical custody during visitation periods. Under this situation, the parents need to confer with each other regarding major decisions in the child's life.

At the other end of the continuum, the parents share both legal and physical custody. Shared or joint physical custody does not necessarily mean that the time is divided on a 50-50 basis, but that the child lives with each parent part of the time rather than living with one and visiting the other. Joint physical custody may be structured in many ways. For example, when the parents do not live in the same school district, the child may live with one parent during the week for the school year and with the other parent during the summer vacation. Maccoby and Mnookin (1992) report, however, that joint custody actually functions like sole physical custody. Even when joint physical custody has been granted, most children actually reside with their mothers, regardless of the nature of the court decision. For the most part, children in joint custody have a home base with one parent (Bray, 1991, p. 421). Little (1992) reported that the most common custody order in a sample from the Los Angeles County Conciliation Court was joint legal custody with sole maternal physical custody. Furthermore, sole maternal physical custody arrangements tended to remain stable over time, whereas only 36% of the joint physical custody awards were still maintained 6 years later.

Joint custody, or *shared parenting*, as some prefer to call it, is considered to be the option of choice *if* the parents are amicable, the children have strong attachments to both parents, and both parents have been actively involved in the children's lives. In addition, when the arrangement involves living with the parents during alternating weeks, geographic proximity is essential. For school-age children, this requires that both parents live in the same school district.

Regardless of the type of custody arrangement, parents have financial responsibilities for their children. For the most part, fathers have had the primary financial burden prior to dissolution of the family unit, when much of the responsibility may shift to the custodial mothers (Maccoby, Buchanan, Mnookin, & Dornbusch, 1993). The economic status of custodial mothers and their children usually declines after separation. While some have reported that there is a positive relationship between support payments from the noncustodial parent and contact with that parent (Lamb, Sternberg, & Thompson, 1997), others have concluded that the effects of income are basically indirect and are not primary (Hetherington, Bridges, & Insabella, 1998).

PREVAILING POSITIONS

Questions concerning appropriate roles for psychologists and other clinicians and the issues of joint custody, parental conflict, and contact with noncustodial parents generate diverse views within the child custody debate.

BEST INTERESTS OF THE CHILD

The *best interests of the child* standard, as defined by the Uniform Marriage and Divorce Act (1979), is the prevailing legal criterion in the United States (Buehler & Gerard, 1995; Kelly, 1997; Schretter-Drazen, 1992). In theory, a best-interests criterion focuses attention on the needs of the particular child in a specific case. As noted previously, the Uniform Marriage and Divorce Act provides only general guidelines. This lack of specificity of the best-interests standard represents both its strength and its weakness.

This standard can be applied to the individual case but leaves open which factors or "interests" of the child are to be considered. Although the act states that any conduct that does not affect a person's relationship to the child should not be considered, the personal values and opinions of the particular judge may define the variables used to determine the child's best interests. Sexual orientation is a case in point. There is no empirical evidence that a homosexual lifestyle is detrimental to a child, yet that has been used as a basis for a custody determination (Fowler, 1995). In a highly publicized case, Sharon Bottoms lost her appeal for custody of her son when the Virginia Supreme Court ruled that "active lesbianism practiced in the home" could stigmatize her son ("Lesbian's Appeal," 1995). In the brief filed in support of Ms. Bottoms, the American Psychological Association (APA), along with other organizations, stated that no significant differences had been found between children raised by lesbian mothers or gay fathers and those raised by heterosexual parents (American Academy of Child and Adolescent Psychiatry, APA, National Association of Social Workers [NASW], and Virginia Chapter of the NASW, 1995).

In the APA custody evaluation guidelines (APA, 1994), the best-interests criterion is the standard to be used by psychologists conducting custody evaluations in the context of divorce proceedings. The legal term *best interests of the child* and *psychological best interests of the child* seem to be used interchangeably. The legal standard includes the psychological "best" interests of the child as well as other "best" interests, such as financial or medical. A mental health professional can address the best interests of the child only from a psychological perspective.

Both the best-interests standard and the APA guidelines have been criticized for their sole focus on the child's needs and their neglect of the larger family system (Gindes, 1995b; Saunders, Gindes, Bray, Shellenberger, and Nurse, 1996; Wall & Amadio, 1994). The guidelines state that the child's "interests and well-being are paramount" and should take precedence over parental interests. In contrast, the standards adopted by the Association of Family and Conciliation Courts (1994) state that the primary purpose of the custody evaluation is to assess the family. While it is unlikely that anyone would advocate that parental concerns should dominate over the child's needs, consideration of the family context is essential. Gardner (1987, 1989) uses the phrase "best interests of the family" to take this into account. As Saunders et al. (1996) note, in discussing child custody assessment the goal "is to *preserve* what is sound and successful within any given family system . . ." (p. 32). Furthermore, because children generally continue to view both parents as their family, regardless of the legal outcome, the interests of the entire family, including the parents and, frequently, other children, and, sometimes, other parties who may have significant relationships with the youngsters must be an integral consideration in any custody dispute. If these interests are ignored, there may be negative consequences for all members of the family system.

The emphasis on "the child" does not provide any guidance for reconciling the potentially disparate needs of siblings who are at different developmental levels and for whom identical custody arrangements may be psychologically inappropriate. For example, an adolescent may be more comfortable with a laissez-faire father than with a stricter and more structured mother. In contrast, the preadolescent sibling with a learning disability may fare better living with the mother. Similarly, overnight visits may be fine for a 5-year-old but not for an infant or toddler. From both theoretical and practical points of view, the developmental family systems perspective of Hetherington and Clingempeel (1992), Kaslow and Schwartz (1987), and Saunders et al. (1996) offers the most useful approach to custody issues.

JOINT CUSTODY

Joint custody came into vogue in the early 1980s when some states added a presumption for joint custody to their statutes. California was one of the first states to do so, in 1979 (California Family Code §4600.5; Schutz et al., 1989, p. 120). In principle, joint custody (legal and physical) appears to be the ideal solution, but research and experience have since found that it is appropriate only in a minority of cases (Steinman, 1981; also see Folberg, 1991). The indiscriminate granting of joint legal and physical custody, when it is not suitable, has resulted in increased caution in its usage and greater consideration of the conditions under which joint custody succeeds and fails. As a result, some states (e.g., California; see Maccoby & Mnookin, 1992) have modified their presumption of joint custody, while other states (e.g., New York) prefer agreement by both parties in order to grant joint custody.

As noted earlier, there is an important distinction to be made when talking about joint custody. In joint *legal* custody, both parents retain their parental rights, and each is the legal custodian of the child. Each parent retains a sense of continuity as a parent and the child involved sees both parents as having parental authority. Neither parent is disenfranchised. It also may provide the child with a greater sense of security and may reduce his or her sense of loss of one or both parents. Joint legal custody, however, has several disadvantages. First, this arrangement may increase conflict and dissension for the adults and children concerned when the parents or guardians cannot agree on child-rearing matters. Second, it may be unclear where to draw the line on the decisions that fall within the joint legal custody provision. Disputes have occurred over minor and major issues, ranging from which musical instrument a child should learn to play and the permissibility of sleepovers to religion and school selection. Third, in some situations, when children know that their parents have to agree on decisions, they may play their parents off against each other. While children in intact households may do this as well, when parents are not living together, a child's manipulation can pose another source of potential disruption to what may be a tenuous arrangement.

Joint physical custody presents a different set of positive and negative features. On the positive side, it may afford the child significant amounts of time with both parents. Many children report that they want to live an equal amount of time with each parent because they want to be fair. Joint physical custody may decrease a child's loyalty conflicts and anxiety over the parents. On the negative side, some shared parenting arrangements are disruptive and confusing, especially for young children, who have difficulty shifting from Mom's house to Dad's house frequently (Ricci, 1980), for children who do not yet have a good sense of time, or for children with special needs. In some situations, rather than feeling that they have two homes, some children may feel that they have no home—that they do not belong in either place or that neither parent really wants them. In addition, the physical homes may not be close enough for the children to have the same friends or same afterschool activities at both residences.

The pragmatic and psychological difficulties involved in implementing joint physical custody are reflected in practice. According to Emery (1994), joint legal custody is becoming the norm and is more frequently awarded than joint physical custody. This assertion is supported by the 1997 survey of custody evaluation practices by Ackerman and Ackerman (1997). In their sample of experienced professionals, 46% recommended joint legal custody with primary residence with one parent and 17% recommended joint legal custody with shared physical placement. As cited earlier, even when joint physical custody is awarded, the reality is that most of these children reside primarily with their mothers (Maccoby & Mnookin, 1992).

Many factors have to be examined when considering joint versus sole custody, such as the ages of the children, the geographic proximity of the parents, the level of conflict between the parents, and the preference of the children. The research literature comparing types of custody arrangements is both limited and problematic. Studies are often not comparable with regard to populations, types of custody, or methodology. Most of the findings come from cross-sectional studies and samples of Caucasian families (Lamb et al., 1997). Conflicting research results have led some writers to conclude that joint custody is better than sole custody (Richards & Goldenberg, 1985; Bender & Brannon, 1994) and others to conclude that there is no definitive evidence whether joint or sole custody leads to better outcomes for children (Buchanan, Maccoby, & Dornbusch, 1992; Elkin, 1987; Maccoby & Mnookin, 1992) or for their relationships with their parents (Donnelly & Finkelhor, 1992). Despite the problems in the literature, however, Irving and Benjamin (1991) report that a minority of children exhibit difficulty adjusting to shared parenting. They present the view that many, if not most, mental health professionals hold: When appropriate, joint legal custody should be awarded, and when the circumstances are optimal, joint physical custody may be awarded as well.

A vocal group, however, opposes joint or shared custody unless it is mutually agreed upon by both parties. For a vehement argument by an attorney against court-imposed joint custody, see Kuehl, (1989). Consensus has not yet been reached regarding the advantages of one type of custody over another, and it is doubtful whether this will occur in the foreseeable future.

CONFLICT

One of the most consistent findings in the psychological research is that a high degree of conflict between parents has negative consequences for the children (Amato, 1993; Camara & Resnick, 1989; Johnston, 1994; Lamb et al., 1997). The degree of dissension is a determining factor in the adjustment of children, the resolution of custody, and the success of joint legal and physical custody. In a study comparing mediation and litigation as methods for resolving custody disputes, Kitzmann and Emery (1994) found that parental conflict was the differentiating variable, not the process of custody resolution. Similarly, in a comparison of joint and sole physical custody, parental conflict, not type of custody, was one of the variables associated with the adjustment of the children (Kline, Tschann, Johnston, & Wallerstein, 1989; Wallerstein & Kelly, 1980). In an early study, Hetherington, Cox, and Cox (1982) found that children in high-conflict intact families had more problems than children in low-conflict divorced families.

Kelly (1993), however, notes other studies indicating that the impact of conflict may not be as clear, direct, or as widespread as previously thought. Parental adjustment, expression of conflict, and conflict resolution strategies may alter the impact of the conflict. Johnston (1994), in a review of the effects of high-conflict divorce, reports that the quality of the parent–child relationship can affect the impact of parental hostility. While noting that results of many studies on conflict are correlational and should be viewed as tentative, she states that the findings are, however, fairly consistent. "Interparental conflict after divorce . . . and the custodial parent's emotional distress are jointly predictive of more problematic parent–child relationships and greater child maladjustment" (Johnston, 1994, p. 176). In addition, the association between joint physical custody and poorer child adjustment was present in high-conflict divorces only. She suggests that joint legal and physical custody arrangements are inappropriate for high-conflict families because of the need for frequent parental communication and because the children continue to be entangled in the parental animosity.

The potential for parents to change appears limited. Maccoby and Mnookin (1992) found that parents who showed overt initial conflict and anger were unlikely to become cooperative with each other later. Many variables may contribute to the intractable nature of interparental conflict. For some people, continued conflict serves as a justification for the divorce or separation. For the rejected or hurt party, it may help in dealing with being left. In addition, because the parties do not live together any longer, there is usually little motivation for working through the conflicts with each other.

A paradoxical implication of these findings is that joint legal custody, which has become the norm in many jurisdictions, may, in fact, exacerbate conflict to a greater degree than does joint physical custody. A joint physical custody arrangement may impose less actual interaction and contact between the parents than a typical visitation plan in a sole physical custody arrangement. Joint legal custody, however, requires the parents to discuss and agree upon matters of significance. If no mechanism, such as joint counseling or parent education, is in place for them to reconcile their differences with regard to child rearing, the probability of success is very low. More contact between the child and the nonresidential parent and less contact between the parents might result in the best outcome for all.

CONTACT WITH PARENTS

The general lore has been that it is in the child's best interest to maintain frequent contact with the nonresidential parent, except under extreme circumstances. This principle has been called into question by mixed research results (Lamb et al., 1997). The optimal amount of contact the child has with both parents appears to be related to several variables, including the degree of conflict between the parents, the nature of the parent–child contact, the gender of the nonresidential parent, and parental characteristics. Some studies have found that where there is high interparental conflict, little child–nonresidential parent contact is related to better child adjustment, especially for boys (Amato & Rezac, 1994; Hetherington et al., 1982). The less the child sees of the nonresidential parent, the fewer opportunities the parents have for open hostility in front of the child. While this is not the ideal resolution, for certain children it may be preferable to being exposed and reexposed to their parents' hostility and anger toward each other.

What the nonresidential parent and the child do together may have more influence on the child's well-being than how often they see each other. Sharing the everyday activities, such as doing homework, watching TV, shopping, and school events, is associated with children's well-being (Clarke-Stewart & Hayward, 1996; Lamb et al., 1997). For girls, this type of contact is the only family variable that is a significant predictor of well-being. These findings suggest that children need parents who *act* like parents and share with them the ordinary events of life as well as special events.

The gender (and behavior) of the nonresidential parent has been found to be associated with psychological well-being in children. Some researchers have reported that children in their father's custody do better than children in their mother's custody (Clarke-Stewart & Hayward, 1996). In addition, there is evidence that noncustodial mothers maintain more contact with their children than noncustodial fathers do. Herrerias (1995) reported that after 5 years, 97% of noncustodial mothers still maintained relationships with their children, a much higher figure than for noncustodial fathers. Nonresidential mothers tend to be more supportive to their children and more effective in parenting behaviors than are nonresidential fathers (Hetherington et al., 1998). Furthermore, children who have a positive relationship with their nonresidential mothers fare better psychologically than those who do not (Clarke-Stewart & Hayward, 1996; Maccoby et al., 1993). While some may be tempted to conclude that father custody presents the best solution for children because their mothers are more likely to remain involved with them, several caveats must be noted. First, the category of father-custody families, while growing rapidly, probably accounts for only 10% of the sole custody population. Second, custodial fathers generally constitute a self-selected group and may have different characteristics from those fathers who do not seek custody. Third, custodial fathers are likely to have higher incomes and more emotional and childcare support from friends and family members than custodial mothers (Clarke-Stewart & Hayward, 1996). Fourth, the research support is still limited and not always consistent.

Under certain circumstances, little or even no contact with one parent may be fitting. For instance, no interaction may be appropriate when one parent suffers from a serious mental illness or is violent toward the other parent or the child. Other factors that may warrant reduced contact include substance abuse and physical or sexual abuse (Schwartz & Kaslow, 1997). Minimal contact may be the prudent choice when the other parent is incapable of providing adequate care and supervision for the child or engages in criminal activity. Supervised visitation may be established in these situations. Although it may be in the child's best interest, the cessation of all contact with a parent for any reason can result in confusion and feelings of abandonment and rejection. The custodial parent often does not know how to deal with the absence of the other parent and may be unable to offer the child an explanation for the absence. Explanations should be offered to the child in a sensitive and age-appropriate manner.

THE ULTIMATE ISSUE

Perhaps no question generates as much discussion or controversy in forensic psychology as whether mental health professionals should address the ultimate legal issue, defined by Melton et al. (1997) as "the conclusion that the fact finder must ultimately draw" (p. 9). In the case of a custody dispute, the ultimate issue refers to the custody determination; that is, who should have the child? Of the experienced psychologists surveyed by Ackerman and Ackerman (1997), 65% said that psychologists should be permitted to testify to the ultimate issue. A number of writers (Kaslow & Schwartz, 1987; Melton et al., 1997; Weithorn, 1987) maintain that psychologists and other mental health professionals should never address the ultimate question. Kaslow and Schwartz (1987) state that the report to the court should contain the findings of the evaluation but not a recommendation with regard to custody. According to this position, a recommendation or opinion regarding the custody determination is a matter of law, not of psychology. Kaslow and Schwartz contend that psychologists have specialized knowledge on issues, such as psychological functioning and interpersonal interactions. They may provide opinions regarding those areas only, not regarding the ultimate issue of who shall have custody, which is the purview of the judge.

Other writers (APA, 1994; Bricklin, 1995; Schutz et al., 1989), perhaps in an attempt to be moderate, assume a middle position. According to the APA custody evaluation guidelines (1994), psychologists should be aware of the controversy surrounding the issue of recommendations for custody. The guidelines provide a number of qualifiers if psychologists choose to make recommendations, such as basing the recommendations on "sound psychological data" and "the best interests of the child in the particular case" (p. 679). Schutz et al. (1989) state that a custody evaluator should not answer the ultimate question but later note that "conclusions presented in such a fashion may come remarkably close to a recommendation for a specific custody arrangement" (p. 96). A sample report in the book offers the following sentence: "In fact, on the dimensions of the parent–child relationship assessed by this evaluator, Ms. Evans is the preferable parent" (p. 186).

Still other writers, including this author, take the position that psychologists may provide the court with an opinion or recommendation regarding custody arrangements, when appropriate (Gardner, 1987; Gindes, 1995b; Stahl, 1994). Ackerman (1995) states that it should be labeled as an opinion. For Stahl (1994), "the main purpose for using mental health experts to do a custody evaluation is to provide recommendations to the family, attorneys, and court, giving direction for resolving the conflicts and providing an opportunity for the family to end the litigious process" (p. 97).

The Specialty Guidelines for Forensic Psychologists emphasize that the expert's role is to assist the trier of fact. The guidelines further differentiate between the psychologist's "professional observations, inferences, and conclusions" and "legal facts, opinions, and conclusions" (Committee on Ethical Guidelines for Forensic Psychologists, 1991, p. 665). The distinctions between opinions and conclusions are not very clear.

In fact, mental health experts can make a recommendation or provide an opinion only on the basis of the psychological material obtained. The judge, who is the fact finder and with whom the decision-making power resides, has before him or her information beyond the psychological report that is not accessible to the custody evaluator. The evaluator's recommendation is, therefore, not a recommendation for a custody determination based on all the facts and information before the judge, but rather a recommendation relating to the psychological data only. The competent evaluator will also furnish sufficient documentation to "provide the judge with a frame of reference for weighing the factors and deciding if the recommendations are warranted" (Gindes, 1995b, p. 49). In this way, the evaluator is not answering the ultimate question but is offering one part of the data necessary for the judge to do so. Evaluators who provide recommendations need to be aware of the risks involved. Generally, each parent who engages in custody litigation believes that he or she is the better parent. The parent who is not favored in an evaluation may believe that it is only because the evaluator was biased, incompetent, or unethical, and may sue the evaluator or file a complaint with a licensing board or a professional association.

The evaluator also has a responsibility to interpret the psychological information for the legal professionals and to convey the implications for the adjustment of the children. For example, if a psychologist reported that one parent was less sensitive to the child's needs but was physically more available whereas the other parent was more sensitive to the child's needs but was physically less available to the child, a judge might not know how to interpret the relative importance of these statements (Gindes, 1995b). The psychologist or evaluator is the expert trained to provide the implications of these types of statements both for the child's well-being and for custody.

Except in situations where a child may be at risk, mental health professionals who are therapists, not evaluators, should not make recommendations because they have not gathered the necessary data upon which to base a recommendation. Therapists need to be especially cautious when they have had less contact or no contact with one of the parents.

IMPACT ON FAMILIES

Because children are raised within some variant of a family structure, child custody disputes always have an impact on families. The nature of the families may, however, vary significantly from one dispute to another. Kaslow and Schwartz (1987) approach divorce by integrating the family systems and developmental perspectives. As noted previously, this approach provides the most sound context for understanding child custody issues as well.

DEFINITION OF A FAMILY

Before addressing the impact of these issues, the definition of the family needs to be explored. The traditional notion of a nuclear family with two parents and their biological children can no longer be assumed. Some children never experience their parents as a family unit living together. Other children may be raised by relatives, such as grandparents. On the basis of a housing ordinance that only one family could occupy an apartment, East Cleveland had sought to exclude a grandmother who was caring for two of her grandchildren, who were cousins, not siblings. In 1977, the U.S. Supreme Court determined that East Cleveland's definition of a family was too narrow and the grandmother and her grandchildren could live there (*Moore v. East Cleveland*, 1977, as reported by Derdeyn, 1989). Other children may live with a biological mother and the mother's female partner. The State of New Jersey recently passed a bill opening the door for gay couples to adopt children (Smothers, 1997). In some cases, a child may still consider the two biological parents to be his or her family, even if they never lived all together. The key may be whether the child experiences emotional ties to the parents. Stepfamilies, foster families, and adoptive families add to the broadening definition of what constitutes a family.

Within the context of divorce, a family unit had been created and then was altered. In one sense, the original family has ceased to exist. Families, however, are not static but are constantly changing through life events with greater or lesser impact that may be positive or negative, such as learning to walk and talk, the birth of another child, and the death of a family member. Divorce is a family life event of monumental consequence to the family unit. Divorce and child custody disputes eradicate the current structure and dynamics of the family. What constitutes the family after divorce is not always apparent.

Macklin (1980) regards the family after divorce as being reorganized rather than dissolved. Emery describes the divorced family as being defined by shared relationships, rather than a shared residence (Emery, 1994). Ahrons (1994) introduced the concept of the binuclear family, which is made up of two households, with the child living in both. According to her, the family continues to be a unit, although it now has a binuclear structure. She provides a binuclear family diagram with the child as the focal point. This diagram includes stepparents, stepsiblings, and even former spouses of stepparents, as well as parents, full siblings, and half-siblings. While this may seem excessively broad, children are aware of all these members of their binuclear family. Although there may not be direct interaction between a stepfather's former wife and his stepchild, what happens to each of them may have an impact on the others. In that sense, they are all part of the same extended family system. Support for an inclusive definition of the family is provided in a study by Crosbie-Burnett (1989) which found that there was less competition between stepfathers and fathers when the stepfathers had their own biological children. Although her study had sampling problems, her findings are provocative and warrant further exploration.

Children and their parents or caretakers often perceive their families very differently. Many children, when asked to draw a picture of the people in their family, draw their biological parents, who may never have lived together, along with themselves and siblings. Other children may include the partners of both parents or grandparents with their biological parents. Still others may include adoptive or foster parents. Children, particularly young ones, express fantasies about their parents reuniting, even when parents were never married or have already remarried (see Wallerstein & Kelly, 1980; Bray, 1991).

One parent, however, may not consider the other parent to be part of his or her family and may not be aware of either the child's inclusion of the other parent within his or her family constellation or of the child's reunification fantasy. At the same time that the old family constellation has drastically changed, a new family unit may form that is based on the parent's relationship with another adult, not the child's relationship with that person. As such, the parent may be introducing the equivalent of a stranger to the child's home. Many parents do not realize that the person with whom they are intimate is not only a stranger to their child but also an interloper who may have displaced the absent biological parent. While preschool children may find solace in their fantasies of reunification, older children may retreat to anger and rejection of the residential parent or the new partner.

PSYCHOLOGICAL IMPACT

As previously discussed, the prevailing notion is that custody of a child should be determined by the best interests of the particular child, the goal being to ensure the child's well-being. The body of literature regarding the impact of divorce on children indicates, however, a small but persistent overall difference in the well-being of children from divorced families and of children from intact families (Amato, 1993, 1994; Lamb et al., 1997). Children from divorced families tend to have more psychological difficulties than do children from continuously intact families. Amato (1994) notes that there is considerable overlap between the two groups, with some children from divorced families having better adjustment scores than some children from intact families.

While there are inconsistencies across studies because of sampling and methodological differences, the consensus is that several factors mediate these results: parental presence or absence, mental health and parenting ability of the custodial parent, interparental conflict, and changes in economic status (see Amato, 1994; Hetherington & Clingempeel, 1992; Lamb et al., 1997; Wallerstein & Blakeslee, 1989).

There is no consensus, however, regarding the best custody arrangement for children, other than, perhaps, that when both parents are well-adjusted, cooperative, and amicable, the children should have frequent contact with both parents. In this scenario, joint custody is most likely to succeed (Abarbanel, 1979; Jacobson & Dvoskin, 1992; Steinman, 1981). For the most part, however, no one type of custody has been found to be superior to another with regard to both boys and girls under varying conditions. For example, Crosbie-Burnett (1991) found that, in remarried families, joint custody was generally associated with better adolescent adjustment but that boys in joint custody reported more anxiety than boys in sole custody. In contrast, Kline et al. (1989) reported no relationship between type of custody arrangement and adjustment in children ages 3 to 14.

Once the custody of a child becomes an issue, the members of the family have already experienced a crisis or stressor. While Lamb et al. (1997) identify divorce as a "psychosocial stressor ... with long-term repercussions for many" (pp. 395–396), any separation from a parent or caretaker would fit that definition. Amato's (1993) consideration of all the resources and stressors in divorce can also be applied to other custody situations. According to Amato, when the resources diminish and the stressors increase, one would expect a negative result. For example, when a child experiences the absence of a parent and other family members, when the living situation deteriorates, when the custodial parent enters a casual relationship with another adult, when severe conflict between parents persists, or when unusual circumstances prevail, long-term detrimental effects may be antici-pated. In one case, a mother petitioned the court to remove her grandchild from her own daughter, the child's mother. The family disruption, both prior to and during the custody dispute, was extreme and other members of the family became part of the family conflict. In some instances, children with strong internal resources are able to mobilize and become more realistic and self-sufficient even in the face of increased family stress and disruption.

On the other hand, in those situations where more positive circumstances pre-vail (where parents cooperate; where members of extended families have comfort-able interactions with the child and parents; where the parents are stable, psychologically and financially), few serious psychological problems should be anticipated.

HOW CHILD CUSTODY ISSUES
MAY MANIFEST IN THERAPY

The fact that there is a high incidence of children from one-parent or nontradi-tional homes seen in clinics or in therapy should not be taken as indicative of a serious negative psychological impact of such situations for all children. Most chil-dren are able to cope with their parents' divorce and remarriage (Hetherington et al., 1998). The findings reported in the preceding section acknowledge the signifi-cant but small disadvantage that children from divorced families have with regard to adaptation and well-being. A number of researchers (Amato, 1994; Hethering-ton, 1989; Lamb et al., 1997) embrace the view that children's reactions to family change are diverse, with only some children requiring therapeutic intervention. In contrast, a bleaker picture is presented by Wallerstein & Blakeslee (1989), who report serious and long-lasting negative effects of divorce. The clinical study upon which the book is based was comprised of a self-selected sample of divorced fam-ilies, who were offered short-term therapy for their participation. No comparison sample was used. It may be that the Wallerstein and Blakeslee sample represented the more disturbed portion of the continuum. In the context of the overall litera-ture on the effects of divorce on children, the theme of a diversity of reactions appears to be the most plausible.

Furthermore, the greater presence of these children in therapy may be, in part, an artifact of the realization by most people that separation, divorce, death of a parent, abandonment by a parent, or a dispute over custody represent significant stressors and crisis situations. People who would not ordinarily enter treatment or bring their children for therapy may do so when they perceive their family to be in crisis.

PSYCHOLOGICAL DISTRESS

Custody disputes generate psychological distress throughout the family system. Loss is experienced by many of the people involved, especially the child, who loses a parent or significant caretaker. Even in the best of circumstances, the cus-tomary daily interactions that promote familiarity and closeness are inevitably curtailed when a parent figure ceases to live with the child. In addition, the child may lose contact with aunts, uncles, cousins, or family friends who have been an important part of the extended family constellation.

If the parents had an ongoing relationship, even if it had not been positive, they may experience the loss of the structure that the relationship provided. Sometimes, loneliness or being burdened with family responsibilities accentuates the sense of loss. For the adults, the loss also may involve relatives of the absent parent, who may have been a source of support.

Parents may need help in learning how to care for the child within the new family structure. A consistent finding is that the frequent decline in parenting skills following a divorce can have a negative impact on the child. Parents may be dealing with their own depression, anger, and resentment, and may be unable to care for the child adequately. Depending on the circumstances, the parents and the children may experience guilt, fear, anger, a decrease in self-esteem, and increased stress. The exodus of one person from the family home changes the family dynamics, and the remaining family members have to redefine their relationships, which are often strained for a time. In certain situations, the quality of parenting improves. Fathers, for example, may spend more time with their children than they did while they were living in a difficult marriage. The removal of a hostile and critical parent may diminish the stress of the remaining parent and enable her or him to focus more attention and love on the children.

Regardless of the circumstances surrounding the child custody situation, conflict and change will be present. The child is placed in a less familiar and, often, more ambiguous situation, where his or her future is unknown and under the control of others. Often, the first manifestation of the disruption of the child's sense of security and stability is that a physical move is necessitated. A requirement that the family home be sold is included in the resolution of many custody disputes. The consequences for children can be very strong, as seen in the adolescent boy who reported to an evaluator that he would sit in the yard of his former neighbors so he could think while looking at his old home. Unless maintaining the family home will impose considerable financial hardship, most clinicians recommend that one parent and the children remain in the family home for a period of time following the breakup of the family.

PSYCHOLOGICAL ISSUES UNIQUE TO CUSTODY

There are particular issues that are unique to custody situations. Some parents, particularly those in high-conflict situations, have difficulty in differentiating their own relationship with each other from their relationship with the child. They assume that the former parent treats the child in the same way that he or she treated him or her. For example, a father might assume that because the mother may be demeaning and rejecting toward him, she would treat the child in a like manner. It is often difficult for parents to understand that the other parent can have a better relationship with the child than with them. Some parents even become more involved and closer to their children after the couple relationship ceases and being close to the children no longer entails being involved with the other parent. The parent who previously had the caretaking responsibility may feel that his or her relationship with the child is threatened or that the other parent's interest in the child is not genuine. Many parents honestly believe that the other parent would not be a good primary caretaker. These assumptions frequently raise the intensity level of custody disputes.

Another problem that may manifest in therapy occurs when a parent sees the hated characteristics of the estranged parent in the child. Some of the parent's anger toward the other parent may then be directed at the child.

Occasionally, children become allied with one parent to the degree that they refuse to have any contact with the other parent. The term *parental alienation syndrome* was initially coined by Gardner (1987) to indicate the situation in which the children express hatred for a nonresidential parent, presumably reflecting the feelings of the primary parent. The criticisms sometimes acquire a rote characteristic, as when two or three parental transgressions are repeated over and over again. The feelings and criticisms may have no justification in reality, as with the young child who said that she did not want to see her father because he was mean to her. When asked how he was mean, she said that he called her "silly" one time. This pattern is more common in high-conflict than in low-conflict divorces. (See Gardner, 1992; Garrity & Baris, 1994; Johnston & Roseby, 1997 for more extensive discussions.) Parental alienation may be the result of deliberate manipulation by a parent or the unconscious communication of the parent's own feelings toward the alienated parent. Gardner (1987) acknowledges the contribution of the child, who may see a noncustodial parent as a threat to the custodial or loved parent.

These children are therapeutic challenges, as they do not think that there is anything wrong with their feelings. They experience their feelings as being justified because they believe the alienated parent to be a terrible person. The custodial or loved parent often expresses helplessness because the children refuse to visit, and the custodial parent does not want to force them to go. The longer the situation prevails, the more difficult it is to change, and the greater the risk for pathological development (Garrity & Baris, 1994; Schwartz & Kaslow, 1997).

A more common therapeutic issue arises when the child, who loves both parents, feels torn between the two. For some children, having fun at Mom's evokes a feeling of guilt and betrayal with respect to Dad, and vice versa. These children are caught in a system that cannot be reconciled, because the children love and are loyal to both parents but the parents do not love each other. Furthermore, children may worry that their parents could stop loving them as they stopped loving each other.

WHAT THE THERAPIST NEEDS TO KNOW

Any therapist who has clients involved in legal proceedings must be cognizant of the differences between legal and psychological processes, should be aware of his or her ethical and legal obligations, and must understand the implications of becoming involved in the legal process.

THE LEGAL SYSTEM AND PSYCHOLOGICAL PROCESSES

Despite the increasing interaction of mental health professionals and the legal system, inherent dilemmas still exist. Lawyers and psychologists may enter the same arena, but they do so with widely divergent perspectives and goals. For clinicians, the goal is to use the body of psychological knowledge and accumulated clinical experience to resolve distress and conflict and to seek a win–win agreement, often through understanding, adaptation, and compromise. For lawyers, however, the professional and ethical charge is to have the client's position prevail, through the adversarial process in which one side wins and one side loses. This view is succinctly reflected in a 9-year-old child's question to an evaluator: "Do you know who is going to win yet?"

ETHICAL AND LEGAL OBLIGATIONS OF THERAPISTS

Therapists may become involved in the legal proceedings in a number of ways. They may be asked to talk to a court-appointed custody evaluator, to testify at a deposition or hearing, or to write a letter on behalf of one party. How the therapist responds depends in part on who the client in treatment is and on the therapist's own theoretical orientation. Some therapists tell clients from the outset that they will not become involved in the legal process. While this may be a wise stance therapeutically, it may not be successful in the legal arena. Therapists (or their records) may be subpoenaed by the court. Before responding to a subpoena, therapists should be familiar with state law and local precedent, as well as their ethical obligations. Consultation with an attorney, the state psychological association or licensing board's legal counsel, or the APA Ethics Office can often be useful. The complexities of these issues are beyond the scope of this chapter. (For more detailed information, see APA, 1994, 1996; Committee on Legal Issues, 1996; also Schaffer, 1996a, 1996b; Tranel, 1994.)

In order to protect themselves legally and professionally, therapists should be conversant with the APA Ethical Principles of Psychologists and Code of Conduct (APA, 1992). Perhaps the most relevant principle is that of *confidentiality* (APA, 1992, 5.05), which requires informed consent through written permission from the client to testify or talk to anyone about the parties involved. In the case of custody disputes, the therapist must get a release from the party who actually has custody of the child, as well as from any other parties seen in sessions.

Whether a therapist should testify in a custody case poses serious questions. The APA Ethical Principles do not explicitly prohibit a therapist from giving an opinion, provided the therapist clarifies his or her role appropriately and acts in accordance with the Ethical Principles (Standard 4.03b; APA, 1992, 7.03).

Other guidelines that may be relevant for the therapist who finds himself or herself drawn into the legal battle are the previously mentioned custody evaluation guidelines (APA, 1994), guidelines for forensic psychologists (Committee on Ethical Guidelines, 1991), guidelines from the American Academy of Child and Adolescent Psychiatry (1997), and the standards for evaluation from the Association of Family and Conciliation Courts (1994).

IMPACT ON THE THERAPEUTIC PROCESS

A therapist's involvement in a court case can have a negative impact on the therapeutic process. The therapist treating a child who is the subject of a custody dispute may be that child's only safe haven, a sea of neutrality, independent of the battle that surrounds the child. Once the therapist becomes a participant in court, that safe haven is lost to the child and the therapy can be seriously undermined. Moreover, the parents of the child may each attempt to get the therapist on their side.

Sometimes, one parent may claim to bring the child for "therapy," when, in truth, the parent is looking for a psychologist to testify on his or her behalf. It is important that the therapist pays attention to the red flag raised when the parent of a prospective child client mentions that he or she is in the middle of a custody dispute. The therapist must ascertain the legal status of the case and present to the client or parent, in writing, the therapist's position with regard to involvement with the legal case. As previously noted, this might not prevent a subpoena, but the therapist should establish the terms of the therapeutic contract with the client or client's parent or guardian from the beginning. Some therapists require that the client sign a copy of a therapeutic contract.

The therapist who is working with a family cannot testify in court and retain his or her value as a therapist. As court-appointed evaluators have discovered, once a therapist says anything about the parties to the case, the therapist is no longer seen as impartial and objective and one, if not both, of the parties is likely to be displeased with what the therapist has to say. Even if the therapist does not intend to make negative comments about the parties, he or she may be asked questions that result in the unwanted disclosure of information that neither the therapist nor the parties anticipated. Similarly, the therapist may be asked about a particularly sensitive topic that he or she does not want to discuss in order to protect the client.

Child therapists sometimes inadvertently get caught between two warring parties. This is especially likely to occur when the clinician sees one party as being the better parent. The parent may then attempt to convert the clinician into an active ally with respect to the legal situation. The other parent may seek to remove the therapist because of favoritism. From a therapeutic, ethical, and professional perspective, being between two combatants is unadvisable. Some therapists do not talk to either party alone in order to avoid the appearance of being biased.

The therapist often has a substantial amount of information about the family and sometimes long-term observations that would serve the court well (Saunders et al., 1996). For the therapist, the dilemma is in weighing the potential harm to the therapeutic relationship or to the therapists' own status against the positive value of providing the information. Certainly, for instance, if a child's therapist knew that one parent was endangering the child, that therapist would be obligated to report it.

THERAPEUTIC INTERVENTION

Therapists can play significant roles in helping parents and other caretakers deal with issues of custody. Therapists who work with children, adults, or families that may be involved in legal proceedings can help their patients cope more effectively with the frustration, stress, anxiety, and confusion associated with the legal process as well as with the trauma of custody conflicts. Those who work with children can provide an opportunity for them to voice their bewilderment, worries, fears, and, often, anger, as well as help them understand what is happening around them.

Therapeutic work can reduce or prevent emotional trauma by helping parents work through their own separation issues and develop new roles vis-à-vis each other and their children. The role of extended family members is often ignored in custody decisions but could be considered within a therapeutic environment. Therapists need to be aware of who is absent or excluded from the treatment situation. A therapeutic intervention that includes the parents or caretakers along with the children may be possible, even ideal, in some instances. It is, however, more likely that conditions such as a high level of interparental conflict, a history of violence, or geographic distance may interfere with the participation of all parties. Who is included in the therapy depends, in part, on the particular family constellation and relationships. For young single parents who are living with their own parents, the therapeutic issues may involve their relationship with their parents, not with the other parent of their child.

Where there is severe conflict between parents, it is often beneficial for them to enter therapy that focuses on developing ways to work together with regard to their children. The goal is to repair the rift in their relationship in the service of helping them be better parents. Conflicts over parenting plans can be discussed. The therapist can assume an educational role by reporting research on child development and parenting skills as well as by helping them anticipate problems and keep them in perspective. Most parents, for example, overreact to children refusing to visit the other parent or to children evidencing a temporary or minor disruption upon returning from a visit. Once parents understand that these are not unusual occurrences, they often react more sensibly. Two positive side benefits result when parents or caretakers engage in joint therapy. It sends a message to the children that their parents are sufficiently invested in their happiness and well-being that they are willing to go to a therapist to learn how to be better parents and that they are able to put aside their differences and be together, now and in the future, for special events in the children's lives.

SUMMARY AND RECOMMENDATIONS

As may already be clear, custody arrangements and the families that need them vary considerably. The complex structures of families and relationships today preclude the identification of one prototypical situation that results in a custody dispute.

The literature provides some guidance for psychologists working with members of families with custody concerns. First, clients involved in questions of custody need to be viewed from a developmental or life-cycle family perspective. The definition for child custody evaluations proposed by Gindes (1995a) includes the appropriate context for considering these clients: as "individuals at different developmental stages in the context of a separating family" (p. 278). Even if the parents or caretakers do not live together or have already been divorced and remarried, the process of separating needs to be seen as ongoing within the family system. The family members may be physically separated, but they are not unconnected.

Second, the psychological well-being of the parties involved may be enhanced by reducing open parental conflict. The literature on divorce may well apply to other caretakers or guardians involved in caring for children.

Third, in the absence of exceptional circumstances, children are generally better adjusted when both parents continue to be involved in their lives and when those parents have positive interactions with each other.

As previously noted, when custody problems surface, the adults may pursue several methods to resolve them. The most intractable disputes become part of the legal system, which is adversarial in nature. Many legal and mental health professionals agree that the question of where children should live does not belong in the courtroom. The problem is that there is no other place for it to go, at present. The movement toward mediation and other alternative dispute resolution (ADR) processes is promising, but the availability of these processes, standards for defining them, and agreement on who is qualified to conduct them need to become more widespread. In addition, research on ADR needs to explore who would benefit from it and compare the long-term results of ADR and litigation on the adults and children involved.

Mental health professionals can play both preventive and therapeutic roles during all phases of child custody negotiations. They can help families deal with issues of custody and separation in adaptive and constructive ways, help them learn techniques to reduce open conflict, and, when necessary, help them handle the added stress of the legal proceedings. Therapists can also help parents work together on issues of child rearing.

While convoluted, complex, and acrimonious cases may still require legal determinations, most custody situations can be resolved by the parties themselves or with the assistance of psychologists, other mental health professionals, or mediators.

New language is needed in this field to describe the relationships between parent and child and between parent and parent. This new language should convey the responsibilities and concerns of parents for their children and the needs of children for loving and protective parental figures, willing to cooperate on behalf of their children's physical and psychological well-being.

REFERENCES

Abarbanel, A. (1979). Shared parenting after separation and divorce: A study of joint custody. *American Journal of Orthopsychiatry, 49,* 320–328.

Ackerman, M. J. (1995). *Clinician's guide to child custody evaluations.* New York: John Wiley & Sons.

Ackerman, M. J., & Ackerman, M. (1997). Custody evaluation practices: A survey of experienced professionals (revisited). *Professional Psychology: Research and Practice, 28,* 137–145.

Ackerman, M. J., & Kane, A. W. (1989). *How to examine psychological experts in divorce and other civil actions.* Eau Claire, WI: PESI.

Ahrons, C. (1994) *The good divorce: Keeping your family together when your marriage comes apart.* New York: HarperCollins.

Amato, R. (1993). Family structure, family process, and family ideology. *Journal of Marriage and the Family, 55,* 23–28.

Amato, P. R. (1994). Life-span adjustment of children to their parents' divorce. In *The Future of the Children: Children and Divorce* (Vol. 4, pp. 143–164). Los Altos, CA: Center for the Future of Children; David and Lucile Packard Foundation.

Amato, P. R., & Rezac, S. J. (1994). Contact with non-residential parents, interparental conflict, and children's behavior. *Journal of Family Issues, 15,* 191–207.

American Academy of Child and Adolescent Psychiatry. (1997). Practice parameters for child custody evaluation. *Journal of the American Academy of Child and Adolescent Psychiatry, 36* (Suppl., 57S–68S).

American Academy of Child and Adolescent Psychiatry, American Psychological Association, National Association of Social Workers, & Virginia Chapter of the National Association of Social Workers. (1995). Brief of Amici Curiae for Appellant; S. Bottoms; Bottoms v. Bottoms, Supreme Court of Virginia.

American Psychological Association. (1992). Ethical principles of psychologists and code of conduct. *American Psychologist, 47,* 1597–1611.

American Psychological Association. (1994). Guidelines for child custody evaluations in divorce proceedings. *American Psychologist, 49,* 677–680.

American Psychological Association. (1996). Committee on Psychological Tests and Assessment. *American Psychologist, 51,* 644–648.

Association of Family and Conciliation Courts. (1994). Model standards for practice for child custody evaluation. In P. Bushard & D. A. Howard (Eds.), *Resource guide for custody evaluators: A handbook for parenting evaluations.* Madison, WI: Author.

Bautz, B. J., & Hill, R. M. (1991). Mediating the breakup: Do children win? *Mediation Quarterly, 8,* 199–210.

Bender, W. N., & Brannon, L. (1994). Victimization of non-custodial parents, grandparents, and children as a function of sole custody: View of the advocacy groups and research support. *Journal of Divorce and Remarriage, 21,* 81–114.

Bray, J. H. (1991). Psychosocial factors affecting custodial and visitation arrangements. *Behavioral Sciences and the Law, 9,* 419–437.

Bricklin, B. (1995). *The custody evaluation handbook: Research-based solutions and applications.* New York: Brunner/Mazel.

Buchanan, C. M., Maccoby, E. E., & Dornbusch, S. M. (1992). Adolescents and their families after divorce: Three residential arrangements compared. *Journal of Research on Adolescence, 2,* 261–291.

Buehler, C., & Gerard, J. M. (1995). Divorce law in the United States: A focus on child custody. *Family Relations, 44,* 439–458.

Camara, K. A., & Resnick, G. (1989). Styles of conflict resolution and cooperation between divorced parents: Effects on child behavior and adjustment. *American Journal of Orthopsychiatry, 59,* 560–575.

Clarke-Stewart, K. A., & Hayward, C. (1996). Advantages of father custody and contact for the psychological well-being of school-age children. *Journal of Applied Developmental Psychology, 17,* 239–270.

Committee on Ethical Guidelines for Forensic Psychologists. (1991). Specialty guidelines for forensic psychologists. *Law and Human Behavior, 6,* 655–665.

Committee on Legal Issues. (1996). Strategies for private practitioners coping with subpoenas or compelled testimony for client records or test data. *Professional Psychology: Research and Practice, 27,* 245–251.

Crosbie-Burnett, M. (1989). Impact of custody arrangement and family structure on remarriage. *Journal of Divorce, 13,* 1–16.

Crosbie-Burnett, M. (1991). Impact of joint versus sole custody and quality of co-parental relationship on adjustment of adolescents in remarried families. *Behavioral Sciences and the Law, 9,* 439–449.

Derdeyn, A. P. (1989, May–June). The post-divorce family, legal practice, and the child's needs for stability. *Children Today,* 12–14.

Donnelly, D., & Finkelhor, D. (1992). Does equality in custody arrangement improve the parent-child relationship? *Journal of Marriage and the Family, 54,* 837–845.

Elkin, M. (1987). Joint custody: Affirming that parents and families are forever. *Social Work, 32,* 18–24.

Emery, R. E. (1994). *Renegotiating family relationships: Divorce, child custody, and mediation.* New York: Guilford Press.

Emery, R. E., Matthews, S. G., & Kitzmann, K. M. (1994). Child custody mediation and litigation: Parents' satisfaction and functioning one year after settlement. *Journal of Consulting and Clinical Psychology, 62,* 124–129.

Fineman, M. A. (1996). Child custody decision making and the politics of child advocacy. In B. D. Sales & D. W. Shuman (Eds.), *Law, mental health, and mental disorder* (pp. 532–537). Pacific Grove, CA: Brooks/Cole.

Folberg, J. (Ed.). (1991). *Joint custody & shared parenting* (2nd ed.). New York: Guilford Press.

Fowler, J. G. (1995). Homosexual parents: Implications for custody cases. *Family and Conciliation Courts Review, 33,* 361–376.

Gardner, R. A. (1987). *The parental alienation syndrome and the differentiation between fabricated and genuine child sex abuse.* Cresskill, NJ: Creative Therapeutics.

Gardner, R. A. (1989). *Family evaluation in child custody mediation, arbitration, and litigation.* Cresskill, NJ: Creative Therapeutics.

Gardner, R. (1992). *Parental alienation syndrome: A guide for mental health and legal professionals.* Cresskill, NJ: Creative Therapeutics.

Garrity, C. B., & Baris, M. A. (1994). *Caught in the middle: Protecting the children of high-conflict divorce.* New York: Lexington Books.

Gindes, M. (1995a). Competence and training in child custody evaluations. *American Journal of Family Therapy, 23,* 272–278.

Gindes, M. (1995b). Guidelines for child custody evaluations for psychologists: An overview and commentary. *Family Law Quarterly, 29*(1), 39–50.

Herrerias, C. (1995). Noncustodial mothers following divorce. [Special issue: Single parent families: Diversity, myths and realities: 1.]. *Marriage and Family Review, 20*(1–2), 233–255.

Hetherington, E. M. (1989). Coping with family transitions: Winners, losers, and survivors. *Child Development, 60,* 1–14.

Hetherington, E. M., Bridges M., & Insabella G. M. (1998). What matters? What does not? Five perspectives on the association between marital transitions and children's adjustment. *American Psychologist, 53,* 167–184.

Hetherington, E. M., & Clingempeel, W. G. (1992). Coping with marital transitions. *Monographs of the Society for Research in Child Development, 57*(2–3, Serial No. 231).

Hetherington, E. M., Cox, M., & Cox, R. (1982). Effect of divorce on parents and children. In M. E. Lamb (Ed.), *Nontraditional families: Parenting and child development* (pp. 233–288). Hillsdale, NJ: Erlbaum.

Houlgate, L. D. (1988). *Family and Law: The philosophy of family.* Totowa, NJ: Rowman & Littlefield.

Irving, H. H., & Benjamin, M. (1991). Shared and sole-custody parents: A comparative analysis. In J. Folberg (Ed.), *Joint custody & shared parenting* (2nd ed., pp. 114–131). New York: Guilford Press.

Jacobson, L. S., & Dvoskin, A. G. (1992). Is joint custody in the child's best interest? *Maryland Bar Journal, 25,* 11–14.

Johnston, J. R. (1994). High-conflict divorce. In *The Future of the Children: Children and Divorce* (Vol. 4, pp. 165–182). Los Altos, CA: Center for the Future of Children: David and Lucile Packard Foundation.

Johnston, J. R., & Roseby, V. (1997). *In the name of the child: A developmental approach to understanding and helping children of conflicted and violent divorce.* New York: Simon & Schuster.

Kaslow, F. W. (1988). The psychological dimension of divorce mediation. In J. Folberg and A. Milne (Eds.), *Divorce mediation* (pp. 83–103). New York: Guilford Press.

Kaslow, F. W., & Schwartz, L. L. (1987). *The dynamics of divorce: A life cycle perspective.* New York: Brunner/Mazel.

Kelly, J. B. (1993). Current research on children's postdivorce adjustment: No simple answers. *Family and Conciliation Courts Review, 31,* 29–49.

Kelly, J. B. (1994). The determination of child custody. In *The Future of the Children: Children and Divorce,* (Vol. 4, pp. 121–142). Los Altos, CA: Center for the Future of Children; David and Lucile Packard Foundation.

Kelly, J. B. (1997). The best interest of the child: A concept in search of meaning. *Family and Conciliation Courts Review, 35,* 377–387.

Kitzmann, K. M., & Emery, R. E. (1994). Child and family coping one year after mediated and litigated child custody disputes. [Special section: Contexts of interparental conflict and child behavior]. *Journal of Family Psychology, 8,* 150–159.

Kline, M., Tschann, J. M., Johnston, J. R., & Wallerstein, J. S. (1989). Children's adjustment in joint and sole physical custody families. *Developmental Psychology, 25,* 430–438.

Kuehl, S. J. (1989). Against joint custody: A dissent to the General Bullmoose theory. *Family and Conciliation Courts Review, 27,* 37–45.

Lamb, M. E., Sternberg, J., & Thompson, R. A. (1997). The effects of divorce and custody arrangements on children's behavior, development, and adjustment. *Family and Conciliation Courts Review, 35,* 393–404.

Lesbian's appeal for custody of son rejected. (1995, April 22). *New York Times,* p. A6.

Little, M. A. (1992). The impact of the custody plan on the family: A five-year follow-up [Executive review]. *Family and Conciliation Courts Review, 30,* 243–251.

Maccoby, E. E., Buchanan, C. M., Mnookin, R. H., & Dornbusch, S. M. (1993). Postdivorce roles of mothers and fathers in the lives of their children. *Journal of Family Psychology, 7*(1), 24–38.

Maccoby, E. E., & Mnookin, R. H. (1992). *Dividing the child: Social and legal dilemmas of custody.* Cambridge, MA: Harvard University Press.

Macklin, E. D. (1980). Nontraditional family forms: A decade of research. *Journal of Marriage and the Family, 42,* 905–916.

Mathis, R. D., & Yingling, L. C. (1992). Analysis of pre and posttest gender differences in family satisfaction of divorce mediation couples. *Journal of Divorce and Remarriage, 17,* 75–85.

Melton, G. B., Petrila, J., Poythress, N. G., & Slobogin, C. (1997). *Psychological evaluations for the courts* (2nd ed.). New York: Guilford Press.

Moore v. East Cleveland (1977), 431 U.S. 494.

New York Domestic Relations Law §71 and §72. (1989). *Family law of the state of New York* (pp. 251–252). Flushing, NY: Looseleaf Law Publications.

Ricci, I. (1980). *Mom's house, Dad's house: Making shared custody work.* New York: Macmillan.

Richards, C. A., & Goldenberg, I. (1985). Joint custody: Current issues and implications for treatment. *American Journal of Family Therapy, 13,* 33–40.

Saposnek, D. T. (1983) *Mediating child custody disputes.* San Francisco: Jossey-Bass.

Saunders, T. R., Gindes, M., Bray, J. H., Shellenberger, S., & Nurse, A. R. (1996). Should psychotherapists be concerned about the new APA child custody guidelines? *Psychotherapy Bulletin, 31,* 28–35.

Schaffer, S. (1996a). Dealing with subpoenas, Part 1. *NYSPA Notebook, 8*(2), 15.

Schaffer, S. (1996b). Dealing with subpoenas, Part 2. *NYSPA Notebook, 8*(3), 6.

Schretter-Drazen, J. (1992, January). Counsel for children in a custody dispute: What is in the best interest of the child? *National Trial Lawyer: Rights of Children,* 60–64.

Schutz, B. M., Dixon, E. B., Lindenberger, J. C., & Ruther, N. J. (1989). *Solomon's sword: A practical guide to conducting child custody evaluations.* San Francisco: Jossey-Bass.

Schwartz, L. L., & Kaslow, F. W. (1997). *Painful partings: Divorce and its aftermath.* New York: John Wiley & Sons.

Smothers, R. (1997, October 23). Court lets two gay men adopt child. *New York Times,* p. B5.

Stahl, P. M. (1994). *Conducting child custody evaluations: A comprehensive guide.* Thousand Oaks, CA: Sage.

Steinman, S. (1981). The experience of children in a joint-custody arrangement: A report of a study. *American Journal of Orthopsychiatry, 51,* 403–414.

Tranel, D. (1994). The release of psychological data to nonexperts: Ethical and legal considerations. *Professional Psychology: Research and Practice, 25,* 33–38.

Uniform Marriage and Divorce Act (UMDA). (1979). *Uniform laws annotated,* 402.

Wall, J. C., & Amadio, C. (1994). An integrated approach to child custody evaluations: Utilizing the best interest of the child and family systems frameworks. *Journal of Divorce and Remarriage, 21,* 39–57.

Wallerstein, J. S., & Blakeslee, S. (1989). *Second chances: Men, women & children a decade after divorce.* New York: Ticknor & Fields.

Wallerstein, J. S., & Kelly, J. B. (1980). *Surviving the breakup.* New York: Basic Books.

Weithorn, L. A. (Ed.). (1987). *Psychology and child custody determinations.* Lincoln, NE: University of Nebraska Press.

Wulach, J. S. (1993). *Law & mental health professionals/New York.* Washington, DC: American Psychological Association.

CHAPTER 14

Parental Abduction

CHRIS HATCHER, COLE BARTON, and LOREN BROOKS

FEW ISSUES in recent years have generated as much legislative activity, media activity, and public interest group activity as the problem of missing children (Finkelhor, Hotaling, & Sedlak, 1991; Hatcher, Barton & Brooks, 1990, 1992a, 1992b; Hegar & Grief, 1991; Lippert & Hatcher, 1995). The U.S. Congress and almost every state legislature have passed legislation to increase the responsiveness of law enforcement to child abduction cases. The publicity of the search for missing children has become a common part of television news broadcasts, and missing children's photographs appear on milk cartons, grocery bags, airport and department store flyers, and on the Internet. A substantial number of nonprofit public interest groups have been created to assist in searches and to promote preventive education programs that have become an accepted part of the curriculum in school districts throughout the United States. The National Center for Missing and Exploited Children (NCMEC) provides a central point for information and assistance to families who have had a child abducted. State police agencies, such as the Illinois State Police I-SEARCH Unit, have served to enhance local investigative effectiveness. The Federal Bureau of Investigation has established a special unit to investigate child abductions. The U.S. Department of State has a special unit to assist parents in dealing with international abductions and recovery attempts through the Hague Convention agreement. Every county district attorney's office in California now has full-time investigators assigned to parental abduction cases. These positive changes in law enforcement response have resulted in the recovery of many parentally abducted children.

However, the attitudes and responses of U.S. law enforcement agencies and the courts to family kidnapping vary considerably among jurisdictions. In many parts of the country, family abduction, the specific focus of this chapter, remains pri-

This chapter has been supported in part by a research grant entitled "Families of Missing Children: Psychological Consequences" from the Office of Juvenile Justice and Delinquency Prevention, U.S. Department of Justice.

marily a civil, rather than a criminal matter (Gridner & Hoff, 1992). As illustrated in the following profiles of the experiences of four parents (Creighton, 1995), the psychological, legal, and practical problems in these cases are very substantial:

SANDY KEARNS

On the night of December 30, 1993, Sandy Kearns waited in vain in a gas station parking lot for Noel Kearns, the father of her 3-year-old son, Joshua, to appear. As time went on, she began to feel that neither father nor son was going to show up that night. Sandy called the state police and told the dispatcher on duty that her baby son had been kidnapped by his father. After consulting with a shift supervisor, the dispatcher returned and told Sandy that this was a civil, not a police matter. For Sandy, the abduction of her son was not a new experience. Noel had previously abducted Joshua, evading detection for 2 weeks. With the help of friends, Sandy's parents found Noel and Joshua, and the police did then arrest Noel. However, both the legal and practical consequences of the abduction were not over. Soon after his arrest, Noel was able to obtain court-ordered supervised visitation. Next, a court-ordered psychiatric evaluation cleared the way for unsupervised visitation. The 5 months of postrecovery legal maneuvers had cost $10,000. Of greater concern were Joshua's comments: "My daddy doesn't like you. He's going to shoot you."

This time, Sandy and her parents were not going to wait. They kept calling and eventually reached a local assistant district attorney who stated that she would try to obtain police assistance. Later that day, two state police officers appeared at the Kearns' residence with the news a left-behind parent fears most. Noel's pickup truck had been found by hunters. Three-year-old Joshua had been asleep in the cab of the truck when his father shot him in the head.

Joshua would never be coming home.

CYNTHIA SMITH

Julian was taken by his father when he was 2. For the next 5 years, Cynthia, his mother, dedicated her entire life to finding and recovering her son. To finance the search, she had to sell her home and her mother's jewelry. When Julian was recovered in Florida, the reunification of mother and son was not a totally happy event. As a consequence of physical and sexual abuse by his father and the fugitive lifestyle, Julian was a very disturbed child. He had watched his father drown a pet cat in an aquarium. He was secretive, wanted to steal things, urinated down heat ventilator shafts, repeatedly tried to injure the family's dog, did not know what Christmas or Halloween meant, and attacked a baby in a doctor's waiting room. Despite this, Julian's father spent only 6 months in jail while awaiting trial on charges of custodial interference. He was found not guilty on those charges, but a separate civil proceeding did bar him from contact with Julian for a while.

Cynthia knows it will be a long time before her son recovers from the abduction. However, occasionally, her son will offer reinforcement for the effort when he says: "Daddy told me you were dead, but I always wished on the stars that you were waiting."

JEFF YOUNG

Jeff, Autumn's father, was in the midst of difficult legal battle with Autumn's mother. When the court case seemed to go against the mother, she grabbed Autumn and shoved her into a car. Jeff initially jumped on the hood of her car, but could not hold on and slipped off. Jeff would not see his daughter again for 5 years.

Jeff spent his savings on lawyers and detectives without result. Finally, he remarried, and 1 week after their new baby was born, the FBI called to indicate that Autumn had been found as the result of an unrelated investigation of the Florida house where she, her mother, and her grandmother had been living.

The moment of reunification was difficult. Autumn was 7, quite dirty, her clothes were soiled and worn, and her skin was extremely white, the result of a fugitive lifestyle which had kept her hidden inside a house for almost 5 years. Jeff and his new wife cried, but Autumn did not. She simply went with these adults whom she did not now know, clutching her stuffed doll "Little Foot." When they arrived home, Autumn had to have 4 rotten teeth pulled and 17 cavities fixed. She was 15 pounds underweight, was not used to wearing shoes, and could not ride a bicycle.

Looking at their situation now, father Jeff states: "What was done to me, I can get over, but what was done to her, I cannot forgive." Autumn says: "My mom was a stripper. She was never around; never sent me to school. It's good now to be with two people who know what they're doing."

STEVE FENTON

After 8 years and a son, Steve Fenton's marriage broke up in 1990. There was no difficulty with shared custody for 2 years. Then, just before Christmas in 1992, Steve's ex-wife wanted to take their 6-year-old son, Stephen, to Jalapa, Mexico, for a winter vacation. Steve agreed, signed an agreement for the 3-week visitation, and even gave mother and son a ride to the airport. However, things did not go well in Jalapa, and 2 weeks later, Stephen called his father, crying, and asked his father to come get him. Steve engaged a lawyer, then contacted the State Department, where a staff member indicated that he should not worry as the return rate from Mexico is 90 percent. But Steve's efforts to get his child back through international legal channels were not successful.

Desperate, Steve made a decision to hire a private paramilitary team to find and bring back his abducted son. The fee was $51,000. If the Mexican police caught them, they would be jailed. But the only risk factor to Stephen would be having to remain in Mexico with his mother. Steve agreed. The agreement eventually led him to a small street in a little Mexican town. Steve was waiting for a school van that would be taking Stephen to school. When the van appeared, Steve ran up, pulled open the door, displayed a handful of custody documents to the van driver, and stated: "Good morning, we are here to recover the abducted child, Stephen Fenton." Little Stephen became frightened, not recognizing his father through the disguise of beard and sunglasses. Driving rapidly through the town, Steve tried to find a way to get his still-frightened son to recognize him: "Stephen, do you remember the time I took you camping? When we were fishing, you fell in the lake and I pulled you out. Do you remember?" Stephen replied: "Mom said you won't send any money to take care of us." His father could only respond: "I never stopped looking for you."

As father and son approached the small airfield where the chartered plane was standing by, the airfield guards passed them through. The guards' cooperation had been secured by gifts the previous day. As the plane took off, Steve began to give his son left-behind items that he hoped might be meaningful. Steve had brought along a toy killer whale, a Leggo toy, and a dozen baseball cards. Stephen was going home to California. Reviewing Stephen's case, a State Department staff member later said: "Obviously, we do not condone reabductions. But if it were my child, I can't say what I would not have done to get him back."

In each of the preceding cases, both the human tragedy and the complexity of parental abduction is illustrated.

On one end of the range of outcomes in parental abduction cases is the death or serious injury of the child. Such cases are rare, but frequently involve an abducting parent who barricades him- or herself and the child in a house or car. Police hostage negotiation teams have learned that such cases have a higher potential for child murder immediately followed by parent suicide than do other types of barricade and hostage cases.

In the midrange of outcomes, the abducting parent takes the child into a fugitive lifestyle, with new identities, no school attendance, inadequate health care, and stories designed to convince the child either to be fearful of the left-behind parent or that the parent has died.

At the opposite end of the range of outcomes, the abducting parent tells the child that this is a surprise vacation and lavishes the child with attention, gifts, and fun activities. Active support for the abductor by relatives is very common, adding to the amount of attention placed upon the child. While the children recovered from this situation are not physically harmed or subjected to clear psychological abuse, they routinely report great confusion over parental motives: Did all of this happen to protect me or was I just a pawn in one parent's anger and revenge toward the other parent? When another parent or authority figure tells me something, who am I to trust? When I get married, will my mate also abduct my child if there is enough anger in our relationship?

This chapter aims to assist the mental health provider and legal professionals to better understand the impact of parental abduction on children and parents, and to provide an introduction to a model for analyzing and communicating about these complex cases. First, the chapter presents an overview of parental abduction in literature and history. Second, it examines changes in American society that have led to the breakup of the two-biological-parent family unit, the resulting child custody problems, parental abduction as a response option, and finally parental abduction as a serious social problem of the 1990s. Third, it presents a model for identifying common variables across different types of parental abduction cases. In addition to its clinical and forensic utility, this model (Burr, 1973) has also been employed by the authors of this chapter in implementing a 6-year, large-sample-size, federally funded research project that will be the subject of forthcoming publications. Fourth, the chapter presents a complex parental abduction case narrative and analyzes it by model variables, illustrating clinical and forensic applications for the mental health professional.

PARENTAL ABDUCTIONS IN LITERATURE

The theme of a child being kept from a loving parent has appeared in literature since antiquity. For example, child loss followed by the parent's joy upon child recovery has appeared in popular children's stories such as the tales of Pinocchio, Hansel and Gretel, and the Lost Son. Parental abduction, however, has been less frequently portrayed.

While Euripides' Greek tragedy of Medea is most readily remembered for its chilling depiction of maternal infanticide, it is also a timeless story that reveals many themes common to contemporary families experiencing a divorce or marital separation.

As the play opens, Medea has been left by her husband, Jason, with their two sons. Jason has left the family in order to marry the young daughter of Creon, the king. Jason's conduct is condemned by the remaining members of the household staff, but it is also understood. He is described by the family nurse as an enemy to those he should have loved. Medea is a wife who feels she has given up everything of meaning in her own life in order to allow her husband to become a man of heroic proportions. She has sacrificed the life of her brother in order to save her husband, and given up her country, social position, and family of origin in order to follow her husband to Corinth. Her sacrifice results in bitterness and resentment about being cast aside by her husband.

Jason's new father-in-law orders Medea and her children into exile as a way of protecting his daughter. Medea meets with Jason and confronts him with his actions, which combine divorce with substantial consequences to the children. Jason responds by assuring Medea that he only wants to provide what is best for their children. Medea rejects this explanation and accuses him of wanting a young virgin for a wife. Medea then develops her plot for retaliation against her husband. She agrees to allow the children to live with their father, who says he can offer them a better life because of his new marriage. Medea uses the children to seek revenge on Jason and her rivals, his new bride and her family, by having the children deliver a gift of an incinerating cloak which destroys Jason's new wife. Medea's desperation is contained in the statement: "I kill my sons—my own—/No one shall snatch them from me."

Medea continues on her course of revenge, rejecting the pleadings of all, and takes the children from their father's house to her house and kills them, stating: "It is the supreme way to hurt my husband."

Even in death, the children of this tragic union continue to be used as weapons to inflict further pain. Jason returns to Medea's household to seek his sons and is told they are dead. He pleads to be able to touch the bodies of his dead sons and is rebuffed by Medea. He begs to be able to take the bodies and bury them. Medea's response is, "Never!" Jason responds that he would rather the children had never been born than to have witnessed their destruction. The intense emotions experienced by parents around issues of divorce and child custody have rarely, if ever, been more compelling in their depiction than in the tragedy of Medea. The universality of human emotion links this ancient Greek tragedy with modern-day parents who wrestle with an age-old dilemma.

This tragedy is unusual in its early emphasis on the continuation of maternal interests following a marital breakup. The rights of mothers to the company or custody of their children is a modern legal and social concept. The father's right to retain the children of a marriage was an unquestioned historical precedent throughout most of history (Derdeyn, 1978). This may account for the scarcity of family abduction as a literary theme. Prior to the 1900s, mothers had no independent right to custody, and no forum for the pursuit of maternal interests existed.

In the 18th century, Mozart told "The Tale of the Magic Flute," which contains two characters who were both veterans of abductions: one abducted by a stranger, and the other abducted by a parent. The princess, Pamina, is carried off by a demon, and her mother, the queen, describes the anguish of the parent of a missing child by singing: "I die a thousand deaths each moment without my daughter by my side, and all my joy is torment." Pamina is eventually able to outwit her abductor and escape. Another character, Papageno, was raised by an old man identified as his putative father. He has no memory of his mother and knows only that she was a servant. Papageno states that he never knew his mother and did not know what had become of her. It is interesting to note that Papageno, who was abducted by his father in infancy and never knew his mother, is written as a very fearful character. On the other side, Pamina, who was more mature when abducted, becomes a more heroic figure who uses a number of coping strategies to find a way home.

PARENTAL ABDUCTIONS IN U.S. HISTORY

One of the earliest documented parental abductions in the United States is referenced in a letter dated February 27, 1885, to the sheriff of Santa Barbara County, California, from W. A. Pinkerton, of the famous Pinkerton National Detective Agency in Chicago, Illinois. The letter tells of the agency's involvement in aiding a mother to secure the return of her daughter, a child named Mary Reeves. Pinkerton informs the sheriff that the child was abducted from her mother by her father at New Haven, Connecticut, about 8 months prior to the date of the letter. The father, described as "a man about 5 feet 8 inches high, heavy built, rather sallow complexion, dark eyes and dark hair, and one shoulder higher than the other," is characterized as a "very pleasant talker." At the time of the correspondence, the whereabouts of the girl are unknown, although the father is described as being incarcerated in Chicago. Pinkerton, writing from Chicago, states that the mother has had an "intimation" that the girl is with a banker or his relatives in Santa Barbara, most likely taken there by friends of the father. A photograph of the child was sent to the sheriff, who apparently recovered the child.

Alix (1978), in a review of the *New York Times Index* from 1874 to 1974, found references to cases of "child stealing" and "domestic relations kidnapping" extending back to the 1840s. Alix reported locating 1,703 cases of both adult and child kidnapping, covering all possible motives. Of this group, 17% were noted as child stealing, and 8% were noted as domestic relations kidnapping.

While parental abduction has existed throughout literature and history, it has received the most attention in the second half of the 20th century. Media and anecdotal accounts describe the abducting parents as having one or more of the following motivations:

1. A desire to have sole custody of a child, whether by legal means or otherwise
2. A desire to deprive the other parent of contact with the child
3. A belief that existing legal systems are insufficient to protect the child from abuse by the other parent

As more and more parents began to use abduction as a response option, the incidence rate escalated faster than family law and court systems could adapt. This resulted in inconsistent laws and overlapping jurisdictions among states, and between the United States and other countries, as well. Abducting parents found that such legal inconsistencies could be used to their advantage. Even if the abducting parent and child could be located, existing law could be used to continue to deny the left-behind parent contact with the child. Further, law enforcement agencies found it difficult to determine if family abduction was a civil or criminal matter, or at what point the abducting parent's behavior became a criminal matter.

PARENTAL ABDUCTION IN SOCIAL SCIENCE

Although definitions of parental abduction vary in the social science literature, there is a general consensus that an abduction has occurred when a parent or guardian who has legal custody or right of access to a child is deprived of that access by the actions of the other parent (Agopian, 1981; Gridner & Hoff, 1992; Finkelhor, Hotaling, & Sedlak, 1990; Hegar & Grief, 1991). Parental abduction is often an extension of parental conflict associated with the termination of a marital or quasi-marital relationship. Thus, it has been viewed by many as a less serious domestic matter associated with divorce or separation (Agopian, 1981), rather than as a significant social problem warranting the attention of mental health professionals and social scientists.

Increased awareness of parental abduction as a serious problem came from three sources:

1. Contemporary changes in family systems and social policy about children evidenced in concern about rising divorce rates and increased interest on the part of fathers in custody rights, which has put increasing numbers of children at risk for family abduction (Agopian & Anderson, 1981; Finkelhor et al., 1990)
2. Estimates of the incidence of family abduction that show this phenomenon to be a problem of much greater magnitude than was previously believed (Finkelhor et al., 1990)
3. An accumulation of anecdotal evidence that family abduction can produce negative psychological reactions in children and remaining parents (Agopian, 1984; Forehand, Long, Zogg, & Parrish, 1989; Lewall, 1993; Schetky & Haller, 1983; Senior, Gladstone, & Nurcombe, 1982; Terr, 1983)

CONTEMPORARY CHANGES IN FAMILY SYSTEMS

Family abduction is a phenomenon linked to postseparation marital conflict. Therefore, changes in the divorce rate directly affect the number of children at risk for family abduction. Population statistics indicate that there was an increase in the divorce rate from 3.5 per 1,000 to 5.2 per 1,000 population during the decade from 1970 to 1980. While the divorce rate declined slightly during the 1980s (from 5.2 in 1980 to 4.8 in 1988), the absolute number of families involved in divorce has continued to rise to over 1 million divorces annually in the United States (U.S. Bureau of the Census, 1990).

As the divorce rate increased, radical changes occurred in the awarding of child custody. Child custody standards evolved from an early standard of *paternal preference*, to a *maternal preference* standard, and most recently, to a *gender-neutral* standard that is supposed to consider the child's best interests (Kaslow & Schwartz, 1987).

Prior to the 20th century, the legal standard for child custody was sole male parental custody unless the child was a nursing infant, or it was determined that the father was unfit. For most mothers, access to children of the marriage was terminated with the divorce. As fathers were legally responsible for the care and maintenance of their children, they were also deemed to be the appropriate custodians and beneficiaries of the children's labor.

The parental preference doctrine then gave way to the granting of custody to the "innocent" party in divorce proceedings. Accordingly, mothers gained an advantage in the retention of custody, as husbands were more often designated as the party "at fault" in the failure of the marriage. It came to be presumed that mothers were the natural caretakers of children following divorce, particularly where the children were of a "tender age." For the major part of the 20th century, the *tender years doctrine* (i.e., under 7 years of age) was in common use in most states. This doctrine held that a young child should be in the care of the mother, unless she was shown to be unfit. Unfitness for motherhood was judged by moral criteria, of which adultery, alcoholism, and mental illness were the primary transgressions (Derdeyn, 1978).

Although mothers are still awarded custody in approximately 90% of divorce cases, a preference for maternal custody is no longer automatic. The greater involvement of mothers in full-time employment and changes in social attitudes toward greater involvement on the part of fathers in day-to-day caregiving activities have resulted in the assertion by some fathers that paternal custody will serve the child's best interests (Weitzman, 1985). Child custody also remains a bargaining chip in the settlement of divorce issues (especially support issues), as joint custody or sole custody has very substantial financial implications for both parents.

In the past 15 years, there has been a distinct legal trend away from a formal maternal preference standard in the determination of custody, toward a best interests of the child standard. Today, most states have gender-neutral child custody statutes. Options other than maternal custody are more actively championed, as there is an assumption, based on research findings, that the best interests of children are served through maintaining close contact with both parents following marital separation. Preference, therefore, may be given to joint custody, or to the parent who is willing to insure ample visitation with the other parent (Brennan, Huizinga, & Elliott, 1978; Schwartz & Kaslow, 1997).

For mothers, the changes in societal attitudes have not been parallel to those taking place for fathers. There has been a slight improvement of attitude toward noncustodial mothers, based on an understanding that mothers do not have to be "unfit" in order to lose a custody battle. However, women who do not fight for custody are still likely to experience strong social censure and a judicial attitude that assumes the worst about them (Grief & Hegar, 1992, 1993; Grief & Pabst, 1988).

Major social and legal changes in the 1970s resulted in an increasing number of mothers in full-time employment. At the same time, divorce law reforms made it possible for marital partners to terminate a marriage with greater ease. As no-fault divorce laws and equitable distribution of marital property statutes became more common, the division of property was no longer an accepted mechanism for rewarding the "virtuous" marriage partner (Weitzman, 1985). Child custody, however, remained a stage upon which unresolved parental hostility could continue to be played out. This dynamic, combined with a lack of objective information regarding what really constitutes the best interests of a specific child, set the stage for a custody determination system often characterized by confusion and strife.

CHILD CUSTODY AND FAMILY ABDUCTION

As most children abducted by family members are children whose parents have divorced or separated, the issues of divorce, child custody, and abduction are inexorably linked. The 1980s and 1990s have generated much interest on the part of social scientists seeking to study the effects of family dissolution on developing children. Forty percent of children in the United States will experience a parental divorce before they reach the age of majority, and for many children the experience of divorce will be a repetitive one (Hetherington & Martin, 1986). Children of divorce constitute the target population of children likely to be the victims of a family abduction.

DEFINING AND MEASURING PARENTAL ABDUCTION

As the problem of missing children became a significant issue during the early and mid-1980s, efforts were made to estimate incidence rates of missing children. Early nationwide estimates of nonfamily abduction ranged from a low of 67 estimated by FBI spokespersons to a high of 50,000 (National Center for Missing and Exploited Children, 1985). Initial estimates of annual incidence of family abduction ranged from 25,000 to as high as 750,000 (Gelles, 1984).

The National Incidence Study of Missing, Abducted, and Thrownaway Children in America (NISMART) addressed this problem by using a two-level definition of parental abduction (Finkelhor et al., 1990). The basic definitions used in the NISMART study were *broad scope* and *policy focal* abduction:

> *Broad scope* refers to parental abduction as defined by the family. It includes both serious and minor episodes.
> *Policy focal* refers to parental abduction as defined by law enforcement or social services official involvement. It includes only incidents of a serious nature in which there is a need for immediate intervention. Policy focal cases are thus a subset of broad scope cases.

Within the category of parental abduction, broad scope cases refer to situations in which family members take a child in violation of a custody decree or agreement, or fail to return a child following a period of visitation. Whether a custodial or noncustodial parent takes a child, the event can be considered an abduction.

Policy focal cases refer to more serious cases characterized by one or more of the following features:

1. An attempt is made to conceal the taking or location of a child.
2. A child is taken to another state.
3. Evidence indicates that the abductor intends to keep the child or permanently change custody.

Using these definitions, the NISMART study resulted in the following parental abduction incidence rates (Finkelhor et al., 1990, p. vii):

ESTIMATED NUMBER OF FAMILY ABDUCTED CHILDREN IN 1988

Broad scope	354,100
Policy focal	163,200

As no follow-up incidence study of missing children has been commissioned, the NISMART remains the best index of the extent of the family abduction problem to date.

THE ABCX MODEL APPLIED TO PARENTAL ABDUCTION

The ABCX model (Burr, 1973; Hill, 1958; McCubbin & Patterson, 1981, 1983) provides an effective means of organizing the complex amount of information in parental abduction cases. This model incorporates many aspects of the trauma response experience, including: (a) *temporal variables,* such as pre- and post-trauma risk factors; (b) *coping style variables,* such as approach versus avoidance, which influence emotional and behavioral response before, during, and following trauma; and (c) *family context variables* that are also known to influence children's reactions to traumatic events.

Hill's original ABCX model focused on precrisis variables that accounted for differences in family vulnerability to a stress (i.e., abduction) and the degree to which the outcome represents a crisis for the family. McCubbin and Patterson's updated and expanded version is a more dynamic model that includes both pre- and post-crisis variables. This allows for a view of both family and individual efforts over time in adapting to the crisis through the use of different resources and perceptions.

The addition of postcrisis variables is important in that they describe: (a) the additional life stresses and changes that may make family adaptation more difficult to achieve; (b) the critical psychological and social factors that families can call upon and use in managing crisis situations; (c) the processes that families engage in to achieve satisfactory resolution; and (d) the outcome of these family efforts (McCubbin & Patterson, 1981, 1983). In this model, the following definitions are used:

Factor A　The stress event, the crisis to which the family has been exposed.

Factor a　Additional life stresses that are present in the family, but are unrelated to Factor A (the stress event).

Factor Aa　The combination of the stress event and additional unrelated stresses.

Factor B　Pre-event family coping resources. These include the behavioral responses of family members, and the collective family unit, to eliminate stresses, manage the hardships of the situation, resolve intrafamilial conflicts, and acquire coping resources. *Coping* refers to the family's efforts to develop and use resources from within the family (leadership skills, role sharing, income, bonds of family unity, etc.) and from the community (friendships, support groups, professional assistance, etc.).

Factor b   Postevent coping resources. These may include new resources (individual, family, and community) that have been developed in response to the crisis, or improvements in precrisis resources.

Factor Bb   The combination of pre-event family coping resources and post-event family coping resources.

Factor C   Pre-event family perceptions. These include the way in which the family perceives the predictability of the crisis, responsibility or guilt for involvement in these events, and their effectiveness in coping with new events.

Factor c   Postevent family perceptions. These include new perceptions that have been developed in response to the crisis as well as changes in precrisis perceptions. Adaptive families respond to a crisis by redefining the situation in more manageable terms and continuing to keep up with basic daily family tasks. Maladaptive families redefine the situation in unmanageable terms, escalating the failure to maintain basic daily family tasks.

Factor Cc   The combination of pre-event family perceptions and postevent family perceptions.

Factors Aa, Bb, and Cc interact with each other to produce *Factor Xx*, which is defined as the combination of Factor X (the immediate postevent stress experience of the family) and Factor x (the intermediate and long-term stress experience of the family). Taken together, these factors all influence the family's vulnerability to parental abduction.

Overall, the ABCX framework provides a means of systematically identifying and more fully describing select critical variables that appear to shape the course of family adaptation to the stress of parental abduction.

PARENTAL ABDUCTION CASE NARRATIVE AND THE ABCX MODEL

This section examines the historical background of child abduction by a family member, presents a detailed case history, and analyzes the complex information in the case according to the ABCX model.

MOTHER'S HISTORY

Beth Franz was born in the Midwest to working-class parents. Her family was of Western European origin and traditionally had been Protestant. She was the second of two children, a brother having been born 2 years before her. Her mother and her brother's family continue to live in the midwestern community where she grew up. She describes herself as not having been close to her brother, as she felt that her brother was treated as the favored child by her father. Her father died from a rapidly progressing illness shortly before her own son, Sean, was born.

Beth attended public schools and describes herself as having been an average student who did well in the classes she liked. Her special interests were art and athletics, and she excelled in these areas. Beth's participation in school activities served as an escape from family tensions, as well as a way to express and develop her interests and talents and socialize with other students. As she became older, she became more aware of the dysfunctional nature of the relationships in her family. She was most acutely aware of her father's direct and frequent expressions of anger toward her mother. Her mother's response was a submissive one: This and other problems within the family were never discussed. Beth, too, learned to placate her father in an attempt to control his anger. The family situation, however, was stable as the family structure remained intact and there was no discussion of separation. Beth saw her mother as being unable to stand up to her father and was anxious about becoming like her mother. She chose to emulate her aunt instead, as she felt that her aunt was a stronger person, who was better able to stand up for herself.

Following high school, Beth attended an extension program of the state university. She planned to enter teaching or human services, but completed only 2 years of college before terminating her education to marry a fellow student, Otto Franz.

THE COURTSHIP OF BETH AND OTTO

Beth and Otto first met in the student lounge at the extension program. Beth was 18 and Otto was 19. Both were living at home with their respective parents. A male student friend of Beth's encouraged her to join the chess club, of which Otto was a member. Otto had a self-confident manner and an Old-World quality that set him apart from the other young men at the school. Beth found Otto to be arrogant and aloof, but she remembers that this only made him seem like a greater challenge to her. Beth responded to this challenge by arranging her schedule so that she and Otto would have some classes in close proximity and they could attend to school demands at the same time. Otto and Beth soon began to date.

Late one evening, Beth and Otto returned home from a date and Beth's father threatened to expel her from the house. Otto was upset by Beth's father's reaction and tried to impress her father with the statement that he was not trying to use or take advantage of Beth, as he was planning to marry her. Beth now believes that Otto meant the comment more to reassure her father than as a declaration of his actual intentions at that time. The confrontation with Beth's father, however, served as a marker in the couple's relationship, as the question of marriage had been brought out in the open.

Initially, both sets of parents responded negatively to the couple's engagement. Beth's parents had hoped she would marry another boy whom they saw as a better "catch" for their daughter, as his family was more acculturated and prominent in the community. Beth's mother initially voiced her objections and then acquiesced to her daughter's wishes. The response from Otto's family was also not supportive, as Otto's father offered to send him back to his country of origin, in order to get him out of the impending marriage. Otto's mother acquiesced to her husband's authority in family matters.

During the engagement period, the two families began to adjust to the situation and met socially on occasion. Otto, however, had difficulty coping with both parental pressure and the impending marriage. He arranged to take a trip to California with a close male friend and was gone for 6 months, returning 4 weeks before the wedding. Beth understood Otto's need to distance himself from his close relationship with his mother, and tried to accept the fact that he chose to spend their period of engagement at such a distance from her also. Because Otto always traveled with a passport, Beth had some concerns that he might bolt and not return for the wedding. She was relieved when he returned to the midwest and took it to be a sign of commitment to their relationship, diminishing the doubts that she had let build up during his absence.

During Otto's absence, Beth had busied herself with plans for a formal, expensive wedding. She came to an agreement with her father about the expenses she would assume and those her family would pay.

The July weather was hot and humid during the honeymoon trip. Beth realized there was something wrong on this trip, as she felt that Otto did not enjoy being alone with her. She found the hot weather oppressive, and this discouraged her from sleeping close to her new husband. Beth reports not having been sexually experienced at the time of her marriage, and she was not aware of how sexually experienced or inexperienced her new husband was. Tension from this and other issues between the couple was not resolved on the trip, and Beth was left with the feeling that the marriage was not beginning on secure grounds.

After returning from their honeymoon, the couple moved in with Otto's parents for the remainder of the summer. Otto became a full-time student at the state university that fall, while Beth worked to support them. Their social group was composed mainly of Otto's single friends, who were in favor of the use of recreational drugs. Beth was uncomfortable with this, and this difference remained a source of conflict between them. Beth remembers feeling lonely and socially isolated during this time, as Otto chose to spend a great deal of time away on the campus, complaining that he could not study in the apartment with her around.

After graduation, they moved to the vicinity of their respective families, where Otto began working for one of Beth's relatives. Otto became closer to Beth's family and Beth came to see that her husband and her father actually held many attitudes in common. One attitude that was especially disturbing to Beth was their shared belief in the inferiority of women.

The couple had a dream of beginning a life for themselves in the West. Otto contacted a personnel recruiter for assistance in locating a position in that part of the country, but instead was told of a good opportunity with a company in another midwestern community. Otto interviewed for the job and the couple liked the area (a college town): They quickly made the decision to take the job and remain in the Midwest. They bought an old house and moved in with plans to remodel it. House remodeling became the focus of their time together. They went out rarely and had few married friends. Otto began to use alcohol regularly, and Beth describes shutting down emotionally to cope with the ongoing marital tension.

TRANSITION TO PARENTHOOD

Beth became pregnant with Sean, their only child, after 8 years of marriage. The pregnancy was not planned. Beth was not sure that she wanted children. She was also not sure whether Otto would make a very good father, as he didn't seem to her to really like children.

Beth broke the news of her pregnancy to her parents first, as her father was ill and she knew that he wanted very much to have a grandson. Her father's condition rapidly worsened, and he died during Beth's fifth month of pregnancy. Beth spent the month following his death managing the details of his affairs and providing emotional support for her mother.

Beth was disappointed with Otto's response to the pregnancy and describes him as not wanting to be involved, as he continued to work long hours. He attended childbirth classes and the labor and delivery, but Beth sensed that he was not really interested. Preparations for the baby were not complete when Beth went into labor. Otto's interest seemed to be engaged only at the time of the actual birth; then he seemed to be fascinated by the process.

Sean weighed over 8 pounds at birth and appeared to be a healthy and attractive baby. From the beginning, he was difficult to care for as he did not sleep or eat with any regularity. Beth was at home full time and Otto became the sole financial supporter of the family. As Otto needed to be at work every day, Beth was careful not to awaken him at night when the baby cried. After several weeks, Beth felt exhausted and returned to her mother's house with Sean so that her mother could help with the baby at night while she got some rest.

With the transition to motherhood, Beth coped with the couple's marital problems largely by involving herself with raising Sean. Otto worked long hours at his job (60 to 80 hours a week) and didn't come home until late at night. Beth became increasingly dissatisfied with her life after Sean's birth. However, she didn't feel there was sufficient reason to justify leaving the marriage until she discovered that Otto was having an affair with a coworker. Beth confronted Otto with her suspicions, and he denied that he was romantically involved. She suggested that they seek counseling, but Otto was not interested. His reason for refusing counseling was that Beth would not change sufficiently, and he believed that as soon as the counseling was discontinued, Beth would again fail to meet his expectations as a housekeeper and a lover.

Beth reported that Otto continued to contact the woman he was involved with, and she came to feel that the situation was intolerable. She talked with an attorney and decided upon a separation. She eventually was able to obtain a court order that required Otto to vacate the house. Rather than hire an attorney of his own to fight the injunction, Otto moved out into an apartment.

CUSTODY AND VISITATION

After the separation, Otto saw Sean on an informal basis, usually in the evenings while Beth was working part time. He would come to the family residence where Sean and Beth continued to live and would spend the evening with their son while Beth was at work. Otto brought up the subject of joint physical custody, meaning a 50-50 sharing of time. Beth rejected the proposal, as she did not feel it was a workable arrangement. Communication between Otto and herself was not good and she had heard many of her friends talk about the difficulties of trying to work out joint custody. In responding to his proposal for joint custody, Beth found herself questioning Otto's motivation for wanting to spend more time with Sean, in light of what she interpreted as his previous lack of interest in their son or in assisting with his care during their marriage.

Beth described several instances that she felt illustrated Otto's ineptness as a parent. When she returned home after work on the evenings that Otto was staying with Sean, she would find that their son had not been bathed or put to bed, even though it was around 10 P.M. Friends reported to Beth that Otto seemed to make no attempt to control Sean's behavior, so that strangers had to discipline Sean when he misbehaved in public. She also believed that Otto, on occasion, did not require Sean to use a seat belt while riding in the car. And once, while making a purchase, Otto reportedly left Sean unsupervised in front of the shop.

Beth began to suspect that Otto's attempts to spend more time with Sean were laying the groundwork for a custody battle and that Otto wanted to strengthen his case. Beth became increasingly anxious about Otto's chances in court and the possibility of an abduction.

After Beth refused Otto's plan for joint custody and complained to him about his violations of their visitation arrangement, she noticed a change in Otto's behavior. He hired a well-known custody attorney. When she began getting letters from his attorney, her own lawyer withdrew from the case. It alarmed Beth that her attorney seemed to be intimidated by Otto's attorney.

When she learned that Sean had been to see a psychologist hired by Otto, Beth began to develop suspicions that Otto intended to mount a campaign to discredit her as a parent. The report that the psychologist submitted to the court said that Sean "had trouble relating to his mother." Beth was upset by the content of the report, as she had never met with the psychologist. When the report was presented during the custody hearing, Beth felt compelled to agree to see the psychologist for evaluation. Upon completion of the psychologist's evaluation, a hearing was scheduled and Beth was awarded temporary sole custody.

Following the custody hearing, Otto had Sean every Tuesday and Thursday evening and every other weekend, as well as alternating holidays. Beth describes these visitations as being very difficult. When Otto brought Sean back to the house, he would have extreme difficulty handling the transition. Sean would tell Beth that his father said that she was a bad mother, that she was sick, that the judge had made a mistake, and that he was supposed to be with his father. During this time, Beth reported, Otto told Sean that he was actually living with him and only visiting Beth.

Sean began calling his mother "Beth" and calling Otto's girlfriend, Shirley, "Mom," as he had been instructed to do, whenever he was with Otto for visitation. Beth felt that these maneuvers were, in fact, efforts to prepare Sean for being away from her permanently. When Sean was with her between visitations he would calm down, but the transitions were always stormy. Beth describes herself as suffering enormously during this time, as she knew that all of this was painful and confusing for Sean, as well. Twice Sean had been taken for medical care for injuries that Otto claimed were inflicted by Beth. In both cases, reports were filed and the complaints were investigated, but were found to be unsubstantiated. Beth reported that Otto never seemed to understand how harmful all of this was for Sean. During this time she began to believe that Otto was trying to break her emotionally and that the legal system would not be able to protect her or her child.

Around this time, Beth also began to perceive changes in Otto's behavior, toward a more aggressive posture vis-à-vis custody, which generated a sense of helplessness in her. When she learned that Otto had gotten Sean a passport, she tried to get possession of it through the courts, but was unsuccessful. In response to feeling threatened by her husband's actions, Beth hired another attorney whom she felt was better prepared to represent her interests in court.

Beth said that she had previously thought of herself as someone who was very emotional and made decisions on an emotional basis. When she saw her husband acting in ways she thought were irrational in regard to the custody of Sean, she began to think of him as someone who was being driven by his emotions and began to see herself, by contrast, as more able to make decisions on a rational basis.

CIRCUMSTANCES OF THE ABDUCTION

Sean was taken by Otto during a prearranged extended visitation. Beth described being apprehensive prior to the visitation as she had noticed a hardening of her husband's position on the matter of custody, and she had always been concerned that Otto would take Sean to Germany to raise him. A vagueness in Otto's plans for the scheduled vacation and a resistance to talking about topics that were previously discussed openly only heightened Beth's apprehension.

When Otto did not show up with Sean at the agreed-upon time for the end of the visitation, Beth remembers thinking that he might not bring him back this time. The first thing Beth did was call Otto's parents. She was told by Otto's mother that Otto and Sean were not there. Beth's immediate assumption was that Otto had abducted Sean. Beth remembers feeling angry toward Otto, and her first action was to call her lawyer, who advised her to file a police report. Beth made a police report, and the police sent an officer out to her house who reviewed the custody order and previous complaints made against Otto in regard to violations of the visitation agreement. After the police left, Beth remembers feeling very alone and unable to sleep. She was awake the rest of the night and called her husband's place of employment the next morning.

That evening Beth received a call from her mother-in-law stating that she had received a call from Otto's boss. Otto had informed him in a letter that he had taken Sean and was not returning to work. Beth immediately called her lawyer, who gave her the name of a private missing child organization in her state, which provided her with information including the name of a private investigator who worked exclusively on abduction cases. The following morning, Beth met with the private investigator and began the search for Sean. Beth continued to work with the police and informed them of the letter sent to Otto's company, documenting that he did not plan to return with Sean. Beth called Otto's employer and told him not to destroy anything, as the documents were needed in the investigation. That same day, the police went to Otto's former place of employment and obtained the original letter and recent telephone records.

During this period of initial contact with both the police and the private investigator, Beth recalled her feelings as a combination of anger and helplessness. Her thoughts were that Otto had a 2½-week head start, and, therefore, there was a chance that she might not see her son again. Beth considered the most important factor in regaining confidence that Sean would be recovered to have been the private investigator's record of success in other cases.

Beth pointed out that an unanticipated result of Sean's abduction was finding out that several dedicated people would go out of their way to assist her. Other parents of missing children, a day care worker, the police investigator, and a private investigator were among those who went beyond the requirements of their jobs in order to assist her in the search for Sean. In spite of disappointment and frustration during the search, Beth was able to function on her job and develop what resources she could to keep the search effort going. She distributed fliers, spoke before groups, appeared on television, and gave media interviews.

During the time Sean was missing, Beth's financial support came from her job and from a prior business investment. As her husband was still a fugitive, the court allocated part of the investment income to Beth. In this way, she was able to meet her living expenses and finance the search. She estimated the dollar cost of the search to have been $50,000, including the bill for the services and expenses of the private investigator, which amounted to $30,000. Beth was always able to maintain hope as new leads and resources continued to appear. The private investigator persisted in tracking down leads developed from phone calls made by Otto prior to the abduction and other information left behind by Otto and Shirley.

Several clues uncovered during the investigation turned out to be significant. First, it became known that Otto and Shirley had auctioned off their belongings prior to the abduction. This indicated that the abduction had been thoroughly planned, and that they could afford to move frequently, if necessary, to avoid detection. Second, before the school year had ended, Shirley had sent her son to be with her parents in Atlanta, planning to soon join him with Otto and Sean. Third, the couple had moved into a hotel during the period immediately prior to the abduction. When Otto picked Sean up for the beginning of what was supposed to be a brief vacation, Beth was not aware that Otto had already given up his permanent place of residence and that his plan to abduct Sean was under way.

Upon leaving Shirley's parents' home in Atlanta, Otto, Sean, Shirley, and Shirley's son proceeded to travel through the southern and southwestern United States, Central America, the Caribbean, and Canada, eventually settling in Ottawa.

RECOVERY AND REUNIFICATION EVENTS

At the time Sean was recovered, Otto, Shirley (now his wife), her son, and Sean were living in Canada. Beth reported that almost 2 years after Sean was abducted, an anonymous phone caller contacted the local police department, asking to speak to the sergeant assigned to investigate her case. When told that the sergeant was not in, the caller asked whether the department had an ongoing case with the name Franz; when told that it did, the caller said that Otto could be found living in Ottawa, Canada. The caller also revealed the fictitious name Otto was using and the address where he was residing. The dispatcher asked the caller if he wanted to call back and talk to the sergeant, or leave a number. The anonymous caller declined and hung up.

With the information from the anonymous tip, the Royal Canadian Mounted Police (RCMP) began surveillance on the house and verified that Otto and Sean were living there. They knew from Beth that Otto's gun was not listed among the items the couple had sold at the auction of their belongings, and so they assumed that he might be armed. The RCMP then assembled a SWAT team and a K-9 unit to approach the house. The RCMP talked to Beth on the phone just before the recovery and told her that they were prepared to go in to get Sean. They asked her not to come to Canada until they could report that he was in custody. Beth was both frightened and elated at the news. She had some concerns for Sean's safety but also feared that with delay, Otto might be given time to flee. Late at night, the RCMP approached the house, and Otto answered the door. They addressed him by his assumed name and also asked him if he was Otto. When they knew they had the right parties, the RCMP arrested Otto and Shirley and took the children into protective custody.

A social worker was present with the team at the recovery and arranged to have the children transported together to a foster home that night. Shirley's son was soon released to his grandparents and left Canada. Sean was then transferred to another foster home, as Shirley's son knew the location of the original foster home in which Sean was placed and could have disclosed information regarding Sean's whereabouts to members of Shirley's family.

Beth also consulted with Sean's therapist to let him know that Sean had been found, and they discussed ways of approaching the reunification with Sean in order to make it as easy as possible. The therapist agreed that it would be a good idea to take along someone that Sean had known before the abduction and was likely to trust. Beth had some ideas on how to approach Sean, such as letting him take the lead and not rushing him or expecting too much too soon, as she had been meeting with the therapist occasionally while Sean was gone to keep him apprised of the case and to discuss her thoughts and concerns about reunion.

Beth, Sean's former day care worker, and the private investigator got on the plane for Canada the day after Sean was recovered by the RCMP. They went directly to the Social Services office to meet with the social worker assigned to Sean's case. A meeting was arranged at which Beth would finally see Sean. She described herself as being very nervous, afraid of saying or doing the wrong thing.

The first meeting was held in a conference room and was attended by Sean, his social worker, Beth, the child care worker, and the private investigator, Carl. Initially, Sean sat holding his social worker's hand and then began to talk comfortably to the men in the room. He eyed Beth warily and did not make any effort to touch her or be comforted by her. At the end of the meeting when they stood up to leave, Sean looked at his mother and told her that his father had said that she was dead. Beth calmly reaffirmed that she had been alive all along, and that ended the first meeting. Beth remembers that she didn't try to touch Sean or talk to him a lot, but rather let him talk or draw pictures so that he could feel in control and could stay as relaxed as possible. Her goal for the reunification was to make it as easy for Sean as possible.

The next visit was arranged to let Sean take them sightseeing. He took them around the city on a tour bus, and then showed Beth and Carl places that were familiar to him. Sean got to be the tour guide, which gave him a sense of control in the situation. That day, he let Beth touch him on the shoulder, but then quickly pulled away. A couple of times during the outing, he would let her briefly touch him and then would move away.

The third visit was at a restaurant, and Sean let his mother put her arms around him to have a picture taken. This was the first time he actually let her get close to him. On the fourth visit, they spent time in Beth's hotel room, and had 5 hours together that Beth remembered as being wonderful. By that day, Sean was comfortable enough to crawl underneath the blankets on the bed and snuggle up against his mother while they read books and played games. When it was time to leave, Sean became very upset because he didn't want to leave.

While the series of meetings allowed Beth and Sean to get used to being together again, they also were characterized by a separation at the end of each visit. In order to protect Sean, the social worker decided not to have another visitation until a decision was made in court regarding the release of Sean to his mother's custody.

It was another 5 days before a hearing was scheduled and Beth was given custody and allowed to leave the country. When she saw Sean that day, he seemed happy and ready to return home. The 3-week stay in Canada was hard on Beth emotionally and financially, but gave her time to learn more about the facts of the abduction and to gradually begin to reestablish a parenting relationship with Sean.

Beth learned that Sean and Shirley's son had been attending private school and that Otto and Shirley had both been working for a company under assumed names without Canadian work permits. They had been depositing money directly into their bank account and were paying no taxes. The car they were using was leased under a false company name and their housing was directly paid for by the company where they worked. They avoided putting anything in their own names.

The motivation of the caller who revealed the information that led to Otto's arrest stemmed from Otto's attempts at a hostile takeover of the company where he and Shirley were employed. His actions angered the members of the board of directors, and they began looking for a way to get him out of Canada. A director reported Otto to Canadian immigration authorities and placed the call to the police. The bottom line to Otto's arrest, says Beth, was money.

The anonymous caller turned out to be someone who had been contacted by the police very soon after the abduction because his telephone number was on a list of calls that Otto or Shirley had made. At that time, the person had denied that he had any information. The same person had called Beth anonymously some months after Sean's abduction and said that he was going to mail her some information, but she had never received anything. The caller was not heard from again until he contacted the police to report Otto's whereabouts.

In addition to allowing Beth to gradually become Sean's caretaker again, Beth's prolonged stay in Canada also benefited Sean by giving him a chance to adjust to the changes that had taken place suddenly and unexpectedly following the arrest of his father. He had the support of a social worker he could talk with and also was able to become reacquainted with a trusted person from his former day care setting. Upon returning to his home in the Midwest, Sean responded immediately to a picture of himself with his mother, taken before he was abducted, and to the objects that had remained untouched in his room. Beth feels that these familiar objects helped Sean to recall memories from his life before the abduction. Beth also realized that it was important not to say anything negative about Otto, Shirley, or her son. Regardless of her feelings about any of them, they had been Sean's family for nearly 2 years. When they came back to the Midwest, Beth took two important actions to help Sean adapt to his life back in that community. First, she contacted Sean's therapist so that he would be available to see Sean right away. As Beth had met with him several times during Sean's absence, he was familiar with the details of the case and could avoid having to obtain the information from Sean. Second,

Sean was enrolled in school as soon as possible, in order to get him back into the life of a normal 8-year-old child.

After she and Sean had been back home for several months, Beth rated the reunification process as exceedingly good. Even though she would have liked to bring Sean home as soon as possible, she feels there were benefits to the extra time they spent in Canada together. The time it took to obtain permission to return to the United States with Sean gave her and those who went along to assist time to visit some places that were familiar to Sean. This gave them a shared sense of what Sean's life was like while he was living with his father in Canada. Upon returning home, Beth and Sean were then able to talk about the places he remembered as places with which they both had some positive associations. Visiting the location of the house where Sean had been staying, his school, and other sites familiar to him made her a part of his experience there. She feels that this aided in the reunification process, which continues now that Sean is home.

POSTABDUCTION ADAPTATION

The period of adjustment following Sean's return home has been stressful at times. Beth's mother had been living with her during the period just prior to Sean's recovery, but left following Sean's return because she found it difficult to deal with Sean's aggressive behavior toward Beth. Beth relates that Sean still shows signs of not trusting what people tell him. She feels that this is the result of being lied to by his father and being forced to live as if those lies were true. Sean frequently asks his mother if she really likes him, and questions what she tells him. When this happens, Beth encourages Sean to call other adults to verify what he is being told, and he usually seems satisfied after he does this.

Sean also continues to make claims of having been abused by his mother. He believes that he was locked in the closet by his mother while he was living with her, although Beth has pointed out to him that it could not have happened because there were no doors on the closets at that time. Beth continues to provide Sean with evidence that these events could not have happened. Beth would like to remain in her present community, as she reports feeling safer where she knows the police and where they know Sean and Otto. She anticipates that she would feel less secure if she had to trust the police in another community, as she still feels that Otto would be capable of abducting Sean again.

Beth describes her concerns about being a single parent and her desire to meet someone with whom she can have a permanent relationship. During the time that Sean was gone, she wasn't emotionally available to meet anyone as she was preoccupied with bringing about his return. Now that Sean is home, Beth feels that a man would have a lot to deal with coming into the situation. There are still three major sources of stress in her life: (a) the psychological aftermath of the abduction still felt by Beth and Sean; (b) the reentry of Otto into her life, with the upcoming trial and anticipated ongoing custody dispute; and (c) Sean's need for services to assist with his present learning, behavioral, and emotional problems.

Beth has not sought professional help for herself, as she claims that she is functioning well enough. She has been warned by Sean's therapist that she may yet have a delayed stress reaction. As she has been continually drawing on all of her coping resources since she first began to feel that Otto wanted to take Sean away from her, she sometimes wonders if she might experience a crisis after Otto's trial is over. She also is aware that she did not have time to recover from the stress of Sean's abduction before having to deal with his recent diagnosis of Tourette's syndrome, a neurological condition marked by tics, involuntary movements, and verbal outbursts. She has received information about a support group for parents of children with Tourette's syndrome and is considering attending in the future.

In regard to Sean's adjustment, the aggression and behavior problems he showed after his return to his mother's custody have been related to Tourette's syndrome. He has recently been put on medication, and his symptoms have shown improvement. Prior to the abduction, Sean had been identified by his school as needing special education services for Attention Deficit Disorder (ADD). He will continue to receive special education services with the more recent diagnosis.

So far, Beth is satisfied that the school is able to handle Sean's academic and behavioral problems. Sean now sees his therapist on a regular basis and is monitored by a pediatric psychiatrist for dosage and side effects of the medication prescribed for Tourette's syndrome. Considering all that he has been through, Beth states that she is amazed that Sean has done as well as he has.

Beth does not believe that her life has returned to normal since Sean has come back, and doubts that it ever will, as she anticipates that Otto will continue to fight for custody. Beth continues to be concerned about the possibility of a reabduction and doesn't feel that she can ever regain either the trust she has lost or the time that Sean was away from her.

Otto decided to plead guilty to the charge of abducting Sean. He agreed to enter a guilty plea with a recommendation of no jail time and no state prosecution of his wife Shirley. The county probation officer has recommended that he receive a 6-month prison sentence, perform community service, serve 3 years probation, and make restitution for the cost of the search and recovery, which Beth reports is in excess of $50,000. Beth is aware that enforcing a restitution award in a parental abduction case is very difficult.

Otto is requesting visitation in family court, but the court order on visitation stands. Otto will be allowed to see Sean only with the recommendation of Sean's therapist. Supervised visitation will be conducted only in the presence of Sean's therapist.

Beth is hoping that something positive will come out of the case. Her attorney is proposing legislation to restrict the use of the defense that the abducting parent took the child to protect the child from abuse by the other parent. This legislation would require a more thoroughly documented history of abuse, and proposes penalties for parties who withhold information regarding the whereabouts of the child or who perjure themselves before investigating parties.

FAMILY ABDUCTION CASE ANALYSIS WITH THE ABCX MODEL

The narrative of Beth and Otto's case is compelling. It illustrates the interplay of premarriage variables, couple relationship dynamics, parenting conflicts, retaliatory anger, extended family involvement with the abduction, the response of the criminal justice system, the response of the family court system, and postrecovery psychological issues.

Mental health professionals must begin to understand how the relative contribution of preabduction stress experiences and perceptions of coping with stress influence how a parent initially copes with an abduction. Becoming knowledgeable about the unique problems and obstacles that confront a left-behind parent after an abduction is also helpful for the therapist, as such knowledge reduces the sense of distance, confusion, and isolation that the left-behind parent has already experienced in the child search process. Further, effective treatment planning is enhanced by identifying how the abduction and postrecovery events have influenced the parent's and child's perceptions of the world as being safe rather than unsafe, and predictable rather than unpredictable.

Forensic practitioners and legal professionals must understand the motivations of abducting parents and their rationales or justifications for taking the law into their own hands. In accomplishing such a task, it is equally important to see if the parent bases a decision to abduct upon values shared with the grandparents or if such values have been developed by the parent on his or her own with little or no input from others. What, if anything, made this an abduction in the best interests of the child rather than one motivated by a primary parental need for retaliation or revenge? Was the child lied to about the left-behind parent? Did the abducting parent draw the child into a fugitive lifestyle? After recovery, would the abducting parent consider doing this all over again if the opportunity presented itself? How would these behaviors be presented as mitigating versus aggravating factors in a presentencing court report or in postrecovery custody hearings?

The ABCX model provides a convenient method for organizing and addressing these variables and issues:

FAMILY ABDUCTION CRISIS EVENT (FACTOR A)

- Beth rejects joint custody.
- Beth obtains temporary sole custody.
- Otto violates visitation agreement.
- Otto sells belongings.
- Sean not returned from visitation.

As can be seen with the Franz family crisis event (Factor A), the abduction of Sean by his father was a crisis event outside of the family's normal range of experience. After the Franzes' divorce, Beth assumed that she would continue to be Sean's primary parent and that Otto would be required to cooperate with the court-ordered custody and visitation agreements. Although Otto's failure to strictly adhere to the visitation agreement was annoying and even threatening to Beth, she was unaware of Otto's extensive preparations for abducting their son. Only in hindsight was Beth able to relate isolated cues, such as Otto's move to a temporary residence, to the subsequent abduction.

Although Beth was often suspicious of Otto's motives or behaviors, she tended to interpret these in light of the past event of the couple's divorce. It was not until after Sean was abducted by his father that Beth was able to perceive the overall meaning of Otto's actions. Beth then felt that her trust in Otto had been misplaced. Her emotional response was not only grief and anxiety in response to Sean's disappearance, but also a sense of betrayal and anger at the court for not protecting her and her child, and at herself for placing unwarranted trust in Otto.

Left-behind parents in a family abduction are often judged as overreacting to the abduction, as the child is still in the company of a parent. In contrast to a non-family abduction, the child in a family abduction is usually not taken with the specific intent of exploiting or harming the child. For the left-behind parent, however, there is often a powerful emotional response with an overlay of guilt and a sense of having been betrayed.

FAMILY STRESS OTHER THAN THE ABDUCTION (FACTOR A)

- Ongoing parental conflict
- Sean diagnosed with ADD
- Otto's affair with coworker during marriage

The Franz family had experienced moderate to high levels of stress prior to the abduction, primarily related to their problematic marital relationship and the circumstances of the separation. An additional source of stress for Beth came from difficulties with Sean's development that had been noted but not effectively addressed. There was also disagreement between the parents as to the seriousness of Sean's problems and unfounded accusations of child abuse made against Beth by her ex-husband.

FAMILY PREABDUCTION COPING RESOURCES (FACTOR B)

- Beth's role as family crisis manager
- Adequate financial resources

Although the Franz family had experienced multiple stresses prior to the abduction, they were also a family with an active style of coping. Beth was able to terminate an unsatisfactory marital relationship and considered herself to be the family crisis manager. This was a role she had played in her family of origin and continued to play during her marriage. Due to the financial resources accrued during the marriage and the absence of other children, Beth was able to devote considerable time and energy to the search for Sean.

FAMILY POSTABDUCTION COPING RESOURCES (FACTOR B)

- Immediate access to legal help
- Referral to specialized resources
- Social support from family members
- Social and financial support from the community
- Unexpected financial windfall

Beth was fortunate to live in a community in which there was a high level of awareness of specialized resources for families of missing and abducted children. She was also able to use family and community resources for emotional support and in carrying out the actual work of the search effort. A search effort requires considerable organization, labor, and material resources for activities such as flyer preparation and distribution, answering phones, and media contact. It is a challenge for most families to develop an effective search strategy while coping with the emotional impact of the abduction and meeting the ongoing needs of all family members. This may be possible only with high levels of sustained external support.

PERCEPTUAL DEFINITION OF FAMILY CRISIS EVENT (FACTOR C)

- Beth's fears of abduction confirmed
- Cooperation of private and police investigators

In the Franz case, the abduction was an extension of a sustained parental power struggle. Beth had felt that Otto was attempting to gain control of Sean and feared that he would be willing to flee the country in order to gain this control. Beth had asked the court to retain Sean's passport as a means of protecting herself and Sean from this action. Beth had previously used the courts and legal resources effectively during the divorce and custody proceedings and viewed the abduction as a violation of her legal rights as a parent. She was initially less concerned about Sean's physical well-being, as Otto had sufficient resources with which to provide for Sean's physical needs.

PERCEPTUAL DEFINITION OF FAMILY CRISIS EVENT (FACTOR C)

- Knowledge of other successful recoveries
- Otto's history of attention-calling behavior
- Constant discovery of new leads
- Media interest in case

The perceptual definition following the crisis event was consistent with Beth's view of herself as an effective crisis manager. This positive belief in her ability to cope effectively was reinforced by the assurances she received from the individuals and agencies involved with Sean's case that children are recovered even after long absences.

Beth had a continuing positive belief in her ability to recover her child. This stemmed in part from her knowledge of her husband's previous behavior. She knew him to be a person who engages in high-profile activities and knew that he would find it difficult to live a life in hiding or anonymity. Although Beth experienced emotional lows, she was generally convinced that her personal and financial resources would allow her to persist until she could locate her child.

IMMEDIATE EXPERIENCE OF STRESS DUE TO ABDUCTION (FACTOR X)

- Fear that child would be taken from United States
- Time to recovery approximately 2 years
- Concerns for Sean's welfare
- Unaccustomed public visibility

Although Beth's style of actively coping with crisis situations and the continued support from family and community resources allowed her to mount an effective search effort, she was not prepared for the length of time it would take to recover Sean. Beth assumed that her immediate response to Sean's abduction would bring him home quickly. The frustration and grief that a family experiences when the child is not recovered rapidly contribute greatly to the family's experience of stress. The longer the child is missing, the more anniversary events occur in the child's absence, such as the child's birthday or the anniversary of the child's abduction.

The level of stress experienced is affected by previous sources of stress in the family. In the Franz case, Beth's anxiety was increased by her knowledge of Sean's special educational needs and Otto's lack of acknowledgment of these needs, as she feared that Sean would not be placed in an educational environment that would support his continued development.

The need to keep media attention focused on her case required Beth to quickly contact her attorney and the local police. She was immediately directed to specialized resources, and because of the family's financial resources, she was able to mount an effective media campaign. However, this required her to develop the skills necessary to become a media figure. This change from her previous role as wife and mother was a source of personal stress, as well as a strain on relationships with extended family members.

IMMEDIATE AND LONG-TERM EXPERIENCE OF STRESS DUE TO ABDUCTION
(FACTOR X)

- Sean's psychological diagnosis
- Changes in parent–child relationship
- Pressure of trial on abduction charges
- Anticipation of ongoing custody dispute
- Fears of reabduction

The Franz case illustrates many of the stresses faced by families experiencing a family abduction, such as the absence of knowledge of the child's whereabouts for a period of many months or years. The emotional and financial cost of continuing an effective search is an ongoing stress for the remaining family members. Reunification, while joyful, can be difficult for the family and child as well, as the child has not only experienced the trauma of the abduction, but may have adapted to the new situation. The child may have also changed, so that he or she may seem to be a different child from the one the recovering parent remembers. Often, the abducted child has been told that the left-behind parent does not want him or her or is dead. For a child such as Sean who may already be psychologically vulnerable, the additional trauma of the abduction may alter the child's basic sense of trust and safety. Such children may continue to mistrust their parents for extended periods after reunification, and the family may need professional help in order to be able to function well as a unit.

Parents also retain a fear of reabduction, in part realistic and in part as a reaction to their sense of betrayal by the other parent. It is difficult for the parents to reestablish trust following reunification, as they are likely to continue to be involved in judicial proceedings around custody, visitation, and criminal charges stemming from the abduction.

In the Franz case, the process of recovery from the abduction was further complicated by Sean's subsequent diagnosis with a serious neurological disorder. The family was confronted with a new crisis event before its members could resolve the issues of the abduction to any degree of satisfaction. This underlines the importance of evaluating a family crisis event in light of the coping resources and styles of its members. The life of the family does not end or even pause significantly with the recovery of the abducted child. The family must be able to confront additional challenges as they arise, while simultaneously recovering from the abduction. Effective assistance given at the time of the reunification can help families to avoid being overwhelmed by the magnitude of the pressures in their lives and allow them to proceed with an adaptive recovery.

SUMMARY AND RECOMMENDATIONS

While parental abductions can be documented throughout history and across a variety of cultures, the increased incidence of this phenomenon appears to be related to the major changes in family life of the latter part of the 20th century. These changes include a broadening of the traditional family roles for men and women, the increased mobility of families, divorce, the extension of family court influence in child custody and support decisions, domestic violence, and drug and alcohol abuse. The divorce process, and more specifically, determination of custody, may have left a residue of impressions, experiences, and expectations related to the ineffectiveness of the legal system in resolving family disputes. For a significant number of mothers and fathers, these changes in the current legal and social system are not compatible with their vision of themselves as parents and their attachments to their children. For them, parental abduction has become a viable and morally defensible option. In many cases, other relatives, friends, and even organized support groups believe in the actions of the parental abductor and will support this decision to abduct and go underground.

The psychological risks to children and parents involved in parental abduction are substantial, as children are separated from custodial parents under false pretenses, often for extended periods of time, and with almost no utilization of mental health resources. Children recovered from parental abduction are likely to experience a wide range of psychological symptoms upon return. In some cases, these symptoms remain for extended periods of time after the reunion occurs. The ABCX model provides one method for clinicians, forensic practitioners, and legal professionals to organize the complex array of information present in parental abduction cases in order to conduct more effective treatment and make better recommendations to the court.

Initial efforts to understand the impact of parental abduction on the abducted child, the abducting parent, the left-behind parent, and the extended family have now been completed (Hatcher, et al., 1992a). Further efforts at effectively reunifying the child recovered from parental abduction with the left-behind family (Hatcher et al., 1992b) and provide for subsequent therapy (Lippert & Hatcher, 1995) have also been implemented on a national level. Regrettably, these developments have not yet resulted in the wide availability of knowledgeable mental health services to these children and families, who must frequently attempt to cope alone with both the abduction and the recovery.

Although set in the context of a growing concern for all missing children, the problem of family abduction needs to be examined as a significant social and legal problem in its own right. Family abduction might be viewed as a nonhazardous form of abduction, as compared to stranger abduction cases that result in homicide and sexual assault. However, family abduction represents one of the most extreme expressions of marital hostility and family conflict, in which the needs of the dependent child are ignored. As this chapter illustrates, family abduction of children in marital and postmarital battles is anything but benign.

REFERENCES

Agopian, M. W. (1981). *Parental child stealing.* Lexington, MA: Lexington Books.

Agopian, M. W. (1984). The impact on children of abduction by parents. *Child Welfare, 63*(6), 511–519.

Agopian, M. W., & Anderson, G. L. (1981). Characteristics of parental child stealing. *Journal of Family Issues, 2*(4), 471–483.

Alix, K. R. (1978). *Ransom kidnapping in America.* Carbondale, IL: Southern Illinois University Press.

Brennan, T., Huizinga, D., & Elliott, D. S. (1978). *The social psychology of runaways.* Lexington, MA: Lexington Books.

Burr, W. R. (1973). *Theory construction and sociology of the family.* New York: John Wiley & Sons.

Creigton, L. (1995). Parental abduction. *U.S. News and World Report.*

Derdeyn, A. P., (1978). Child custody: A reflection of cultural change. *Journal of Clinical Child Psychology, 7,* 169–173.

Finkelhor, D., Hotaling, G., & Sedlak, A. (1990). *Missing, abducted, runaway and thrownaway children in America. First report: Numbers and characteristics: National incidence study.* Washington, DC: U.S. Department of Justice, Office of Juvenile Justice and Delinquency Prevention.

Finkelhor, D., Hotaling, G., & Sedlak, A. (1991). Children abducted by family members: A national household survey of incidence and episode characteristics. *Journal of Marriage and the Family, 53,* 805–809.

Forehand, R., Long, N., Zogg, C., & Parrish, E. (1989). Child abduction: Parent and child functioning following return. *Clinical Pediatrics, 28,* 311–316.

Gelles, M. (1984). Parental child snatching. *Journal of Marriage and the Family, 46*(3), 735–740.

Greif, G., & Hegar, P. (1992). Impact on children of abduction by a parent: A review of the literature. *American Journal of Orthopsychiatry, 62,* 599–604.

Greif, G., & Hegar, R. (1993). *When parents kidnap: The families behind the headlines.* New York: Free Press.

Greif, G., & Pabst. (1988). *Mothers without custody.* Lexington, MA: Lexington Books.

Gridner, L., & Hoff, P. (Eds.). (1992). *Obstacles to the recovery and return of parental abducted children.* Washington, DC: Office of Juvenile Justice and Delinquency Prevention, U.S. Department of Justice.

Hatcher, C., Barton, C., & Brooks, L. (1990). *Reunification of missing children project assessment report.* Washington, DC: Office of Juvenile Justice and Delinquency Prevention, U.S. Department of Justice.

Hatcher, C., Barton, C., & Brooks, L. (1992a). *Families of missing children: Psychological consequences final report.* Washington, DC: Office of Juvenile Justice and Delinquency Prevention, U.S. Department of Justice.

Hatcher, C., Barton, C. & Brooks, L. (1992b). *Reunification of missing children: Final report.* Washington, DC: Office of Juvenile Justice and Delinquency Prevention, U.S. Department of Justice.

Hegar, R., & Greif, G. (1991). Parents whose children are abducted by the other parent: Implications for treatment. *American Journal of Family Therapy, 19,* 215–219.

Hetherington, E. M., & Martin, B. (1986). Family factors and psychopathology in children. In H. Quay & J. Werry (Eds.), *Psychopathological disorders of childhood* (3rd ed.). New York: John Wiley & Sons.

Hill, R. (1958). Generic features of families under stress. *Social Casework, 39,* 139–150.

Kaslow, F. W., & Schwartz, L. L. (1987). *The dynamics of divorce: A life cycle perspective.* New York: Brunner/Mazel.

Lewall, B. (1993). Domestic violence and parental kidnapping. *National District Attorneys Association Bulletin, 11*(6), 9.

Lippert, J., & Hatcher, C. (1995). *Model treatment programs for recovered missing children: Final report*. Washington, DC: Office of Juvenile Justice and Delinquency Prevention, U.S. Department of Justice.

McCubbin, H. I., & Patterson, J. M. (1981). *Systematic assessment of family stress, resources and coping: Tools for research, education, and clinical intervention*. St. Paul, MN: University of Minnesota.

McCubbin, H. I., & Patterson, J. M. (1983). The family stress process: The Double ABCX model of adjustment and adaptation. In H. McCubbin, M. Sussman, & J. Patterson (Eds.), *Advancements and developments in family stress theory and research*. New York: Haworth Press.

National Center for Missing and Exploited Children. (1985) *Background information on missing children*. Washington, DC: National Center for Missing and Exploited Children.

Schetky, D. H., & Haller, L. H. (1983). Child psychiatry and law: Parental kidnapping. *Journal of the American Academy of Child Psychiatry, 22*(3), 279–285.

Schwartz, L. L., & Kaslow, F. W. (1997). *Painful partings: Divorce and its aftermath*. New York: John Wiley & Sons.

Senior, N., Gladstone, T., & Nurcombe, B. (1982). Child snatching: A case report. *Journal of the American Academy of Child Psychiatry, 21,* 579–583.

Terr, L. (1983). Children of Chowchilla: A study of psychic trauma in a group of "normal" children. *Journal of the American Academy of Child Psychiatry, 22*(3), 221–230.

U.S. Bureau of the Census. (1990). *Statistical abstract of the United States, 1990*. Washington, DC: U.S. Department of Commerce.

Weitzman, L. J. (1985). *The divorce revolution: The unexpected social and economic consequences for women and children in America*. New York: Free Press.

CHAPTER 15

Family Decision Making, Civil Commitment, and Treatment

PETER ASH

Half an hour before a family appointment, the mother telephones your office and says that her 15-year-old son refuses to get in the car to come to the appointment. "What should I do?" she asks.

Jimmy, a 12-year-old in special education classes, wants to be moved back to a mainstream classroom. An education program planning meeting with the school has been set up, and his parents are unsure how strongly they should advocate for their son's return to a regular class.

A family comes to treatment because Joanne, 15, has lost both her kidneys to a rare infection, and her sister Elaine, 13, has been identified as the best-matched potential kidney donor. The family is trying to figure out whether Elaine should donate one of her kidneys to her older sister.

A family describes how the father has become more and more reclusive, sits in his room for hours, and spends considerable time cleaning his guns. In response to all of the therapist's questions, he just slowly mumbles, "I'm fine."

In the context of legal rules, there is a continuum of decision making about participating in treatment. At one end, there are those choices that are governed by clinical issues and that the law clearly leaves to the patient: For example, if a father decides to stop coming to family therapy sessions, that, legally, is the end of the matter. The therapist and the rest of the family may try to persuade the father to participate, but the decision is up to him, and there is no recourse to the legal system. At the other end of the continuum are those situations in which legal involvement is automatic. If a therapist decides a mother is so suicidal as to warrant civil commitment and she refuses voluntary hospitalization, the therapist has a duty to institute civil

314

commitment procedures that will lead to a judicial hearing. Between these two poles there is an array of issues which fall in the shadow of the law, issues which a family and a clinician will first attempt to address clinically while recognizing that if the family can not arrive at a satisfactory resolution, there is recourse to legal rules and processes that can enforce a solution. This chapter addresses the interplay between family decision making and legal regulations and processes on issues of participating in treatment. This chapter does not focus on the issue of what constitutes valid or informed consent, as that issue is covered in detail elsewhere in this book.

WHO DECIDES?

From a legal perspective, the first question in decision making is who decides. Only if the answer to this is someone outside the family (such as a judge or a therapist) does the legal system approach the second question of what values the decision maker should use in deciding. Legal principles envisage a sole, legally competent decision maker, such as an adult, emancipated minor, or judge, depending on the situation. Family matters, however, tend to emphasize joint decision making. There is a certain tension, therefore, between external legal principles and internal family processes.

There are two basic principles regarding designating the legal decision maker. First, competent adults decide for themselves, and may refuse treatment, including life-saving treatment. Second, legally incompetent people (minors, demented elderly people, some severely retarded or severely mentally ill adults) need to have their decisions made for them by an appropriate, competent decision maker. For example, the Supreme Court has held that the Constitution permits a parent to have a child admitted to an inpatient psychiatric unit over the minor's objection if a doctor agrees it is indicated (*Parham v. J.R.*, 1979), although some states allow minors to object.

There are, however, some exceptions to these two basic principles, which are listed in Table 15.1 and discussed in detail in the remainder of the chapter. The reader should be aware that there is considerable variation among the states regarding the applicability of these exceptions. Rozovsky (1990) and Morrissey, Hofmann, and Thrope (1986) have cataloged state statutes on many of these points.

In individual treatment, the legal emphasis on a sole decision maker makes it clear how decisions get made. The patient, or the person legally empowered to decide for the patient, decides. The therapist may advise, but the decision clearly belongs to the individual decision maker, unless the therapist believes it is necessary to pursue involuntary commitment. Family treatment is rather different in that the legally designated individual decision maker may not be the actual decision maker, because much family treatment emphasizes shared decision making and family treatment supports and fosters children's autonomy where appropriate. Families think differently than judges do.

ASSESSING CHILDREN'S DECISION-MAKING CAPACITY

While parents legally decide many issues for their children, there are instances in which parents wish to include children in making choices. Including children in

Table 15.1   Who Gives Consent for Treatment

General Principles
1. Competent adults decide for themselves.
2. Incompetent persons (minors, incompetent adults) have decisions made by a designated decision maker (parent or guardian).

Exceptions
Classes of minors can make decisions.
Emancipated minors.
Mature minors.*
Minors can make certain types of decisions.
Obtain treatment for substance abuse, sexually transmitted diseases.
Mature minors can obtain abortion.
Begin individual outpatient psychotherapy.*
Assent of minor needed in addition to informed consent of parent.
Federally funded research.
Do not resuscitate orders.*
Judicial review needed in addition to assent of minor and informed consent of parent.
Child as organ donor for transplant.
Emergencies.
Patient cannot give consent (unconscious, incompetent).
Treatment necessary to protect others (e.g., tranquilization of violent patient).
Civil commitment.
Dangerous to self (suicidal).
Dangerous to others.
Unable to care for self.*

*Exception exists in some states only.

decision making recognizes their capacities and desires in the family and promotes the growth of normal autonomy. For example, if a child objects to participating in treatment, the family may want to explore the child's thinking, and, perhaps, defer to his or her judgment. When parents of a child in special education classes are going to a meeting with the school to develop an individualized educational program (IEP, required by the federal Education for All Handicapped Children Act of 1975, as amended) they may want to take the views of their child into account. Or, when facing certain complex medical decisions (see following), the child may have actual legal authority to decide. In these and many other instances, the capacity of children to make reasonable decisions becomes a significant issue.

Because these capacities are complex to assess, but do correlate roughly with age, chronological benchmarks have evolved as the predominant way of formulating rules. Ages that approximate multiples of 7 have been used in civil and religious law, with the age of 7 being considered the end of infancy, 13 to 14 as marking the beginning of adult responsibilities, and 21 (now usually 18) as the age of majority and the granting of all adult rights and privileges (Group for the Advancement of Psychiatry, 1989). Ages 7 and 14 also correspond with Piagetian theories of cognitive stages. For relatively normal children of average intelligence, most studies have found that children age 14 and up make decisions similarly to how adults do (see Adleman, Lusk, Alvarez, & Acosta, 1985, re decisions about psychoeducational interventions; Grisso, 1981, re waiving *Miranda* rights; Weithorn & Campbell, 1982, re decisions about consenting to health care). These findings have been challenged by some recent work which suggests that children's judgment in nonlaboratory situations is more impaired than adults' (Scott, Reppucci, & Woolard, 1995; Steinberg & Cauffman, 1996).

The limited research on preadolescents suggests that for decisions on issues *within their experience,* preadolescents make reasonable choices, compared to those of older youngsters or adults, but are typically unable to explain the reasons that underlie their decisions (see Garrison, 1991, re preferences about custody in hypothetical divorce situations; Lewis, Lewis, Lorimer, & Palmer, 1977, re decisions on issues of minor health care; Taylor, Adleman, & Kaser-Boyd, 1985, re psychoeducational placement decisions).

Decision-making capacity is most variable and difficult to assess in the age range of normal 10- to 14-year-olds. Also problematic are those children with developmental delays and psychopathology which render general age guidelines inappropriate. Assessing the child's decision-making capacity can clarify for all members of the family the issues involved in the decision and the weight to be given to the child's preference. While a full discussion of techniques of assessing children's decision-making capacity is beyond the scope of this chapter, the most salient issues are highlighted (for fuller discussion, see Ash, Jurkovic, & Harrison, 1998).

For many children, their experience has been that their parents make major decisions for them; they may assume that they do not have a choice, or that their only choice is to agree to a decision their parents have already made. They may defer to parental pressure (Scherer, 1991). Family therapists are generally experienced in supporting appropriate autonomy for children.

Good decisions are predicated on knowledge of alternatives and their consequences. Experience with the situation in question is generally of more import than the results of IQ tests. If the child does not know the range of alternatives ("What will my life be like if I give one kidney to Jamie and have to go on with just one kidney in me?"), the clinician must assess whether information or education will remedy the situation.

The assessment of children's reasoning is a complex process. It involves assessing the following:

- The youngster's ability to think and reason generally, including the abilities to imagine oneself in a future situation, to understand causal connections, to hypothesize about a variety of consequences, and to evaluate various alternatives.
- The child's reasoning about the particular issues involved.
- The presence of developmental tendencies that affect reasoning, such as adolescent egocentrism, risk taking, impulsivity, and susceptibility to peer pressure.
- Emotional conflicts that interfere with the utilization of existing capacities, such as depression or unrealistic fantasies.

Causal thinking can be assessed by observing whether the child spontaneously links action and consequences. While most preadolescents can connect a cause with an effect, such as a particular misbehavior and its punishment, they may have difficulty considering the effects of mediating events.

> Jeanie, 10, has repeatedly gotten into trouble with her parents for talking back. When her parents became completely fed up with her, they said the next time she talked back, she would lose all television for a week. When Jeanie did talk back and the television was withheld, she was outraged, and thought that the punishment was disproportionate to her "just saying I didn't want to pick up my clothes."

Jeanie had difficulty appreciating that the punishment was connected to her parents being fed up with her chronic oppositional behavior. If she were facing an important decision which had a number of interrelated variables, her impairment in considering mediating events would be important to consider.

In evaluating consequential thinking, the clinician should consider whether a youngster spontaneously considers a range of possible outcomes. Thus, a prospective kidney donor who is sure that "I'll never have any problems with just one kidney" is demonstrating poor consequential thinking. The clinician can assess evaluative thinking by asking how the child has decided that a particular outcome is best.

Important choices are highly emotionally charged, and strong affects may cloud decision-making capacity. Talking to a child about hypothetical situations that are similar in their logical complexity but removed from the current situation may help differentiate whether the child's difficulty reflects emotional interference or developmental limitations in reasoning capacity. This distinction is important in assisting the child. Emotional interferences are dealt with by helping the child understand the emotional fantasies and conflicts involved; cognitive limitations are dealt with by bolstering the child's reasoning by highlighting causes, likely effects, connections, consequences, alternatives, and possible pros and cons.

A child's decision making will be affected by talking over the issues with a clinician. Discussion with an empathic clinician should help a youngster clarify preferences, consider new possibilities, become aware of areas of incomplete information, and sharpen reasoning skills. Further, the youngster's ability to make use of the clinician's input provides additional data regarding decision-making capacity. Finally, conducting such an assessment in a family context clarifies for the parents the extent to which the child's thinking should be considered in a decision which they may ultimately need to make.

MEDICAL DECISIONS THAT CHILDREN CAN MAKE

Although the general rule is that parents speak for their children and provide informed consent for medical treatment, the courts have increasingly recognized that many youths, particularly older adolescents, have the cognitive capacity to give informed consent. An emancipated minor is, for most legal purposes, an adult. Emancipation is generally reflected in the child's being self-supporting, married, or engaged in military service. Living separately is usually involved, although living separately per se does not constitute emancipation. A minor can be treated as emancipated without a court declaration of emancipation if the facts are clear. Because emancipation indicates a separation from parents, emancipated minors only rarely are involved in family therapy with their parents. Being a student living away at college but supported by one's parents does not usually constitute emancipation. Nor, generally, would a 14-year-old unwed mother living at home with her own mother and infant be considered emancipated. (An interesting legal wrinkle is that such a 14-year-old mother, in some jurisdictions, could give legal consent for an operation on her baby as a parent, but could not, as a minor, give legal consent for an operation on herself.)

Some states have adopted a *mature minor* rule (for a court's discussion, see *Cardwell v. Bechtol*, 1987) that gives "mature minors" the right to consent. The problem for the clinician is that *mature minor* is not clearly defined (it is sometimes defined circularly as having the capacity to give consent; sometimes it is limited to children near the age of majority). Whether a particular adolescent is "mature" is often decided only during litigation after an adverse result and a lawsuit by the parents. In certain areas, the courts have increasingly afforded children input into certain medical decisions. For example, many states allow minors over a certain age to initiate a limited number of sessions of individual mental health treatment without their parents' knowledge or consent. (Problems may arise when the parents, who are generally legally liable for the child's debts, receive the bill.) Most states also allow minors to personally initiate treatment for sexually transmitted diseases and substance abuse, based on society's particular interest in promoting treatment of these conditions.

Abortion and access to contraceptives (*Carey v. Population Services International*, 1977) are the clearest examples of national minimal standards being set, because the rules derive from U.S. Supreme Court holdings that have found a constitutionally protected privacy interest in access to an abortion in the wake of *Roe v. Wade* (1973). In *Planned Parenthood of Central Missouri v. Danforth* (1976), the Court struck down a statute that required parental notification before a minor could have an abortion, and introduced a judicial bypass procedure that allowed an adolescent to circumvent her parents and obtain court permission. In *Bellotti v. Baird* (1976), the Court held that a mature minor could decide for herself whether to obtain an abortion, but left undefined just what a *mature minor* was. In *Hodgson v. Minnesota* (1990) the Court allowed an abortion with notification of one parent, rather than two, and maintained judicial bypass procedures for those adolescents who did not want parental involvement. Clinical issues raised by these holdings are covered in Chapter 8.

The Court's holdings that many adolescents can rightfully decide about abortion for themselves and the publicity attending the Court's findings has spurred a general legal trend toward acknowledging adolescents as more responsible. The Uniform Health-Care Decisions Act permits mature minors to make advance directives, and many courts have allowed mature minors to refuse life-sustaining treatment. In *Rosebush v. Oakland County Prosecutor* (1992), the court utilized statements made when the girl was 10 years of age to form a substituted judgment regarding her wishes for life-sustaining treatment when she was 16 years old and in a persistent vegetative state.

ATTENDING OUTPATIENT TREATMENT

Parents decide whether a minor child will participate in family treatment. Thus, when a parent calls to say that his or her child does not want to come, the therapist may and can reinforce the principle that the parent has the authority to require the child to come. This authority extends to obtaining the help of neighbors or the police to bring the child to treatment. Children's refusal to come usually plays to the parent's ambivalence about exerting his or her authority. The appropriate clinical intervention is to empower the parent so that he or she feels supported in exerting his or her authority. Once a parent insists that the child is coming, and makes it clear that he or she is prepared to use whatever means are necessary to effect attendance, the child generally acquiesces. "You're going. If I have to call the police to drag you to the car, so be it. Get your coat," said in a sufficiently firm tone of voice, cuts through a great deal of oppositionalism. The parent may add, "Nobody can make you say a word while you're there, but you're going to be there," and thereby point to an alternative route for oppositional behavior, and underline who is in control of what.

With a spouse, adult child, or emancipated child, the situation is different. As an adult, such a person cannot be made to attend family sessions, although various forms of cajoling and persuasion can be tried. There are limited situations in which minors can also refuse outpatient mental health treatment. Nebraska and Nevada allow minors to refuse treatment unless a significant risk is perceived (Rozovsky, 1990). States that have adopted a mature minor rule arguably also afford a mature minor rights to refuse treatment.

While for most situations involving treatment of minors the consent of one parent is sufficient, problems arise if one parent consents, but the other explicitly refuses the treatment on behalf of the child. Few general rules can be given for these situations; the outcomes depend on the nature of the proposed treatment (emergency versus routine versus cosmetic) and local jurisdictional rules. It is usually not the prerogative of the therapist to determine which parent's view should prevail, and legal advice should be sought as to how to proceed. Postdivorce conflicts in which there is joint legal custody are the most common situations in which these disputes arise; the safest course for the therapist is to ask the parent who wishes treatment to seek a court order for treatment or a judicial determination that one parent's consent is sufficient.

FAMILY DECISION MAKING
IN COMPLEX MEDICAL CONTEXTS

Some medical decisions require family deliberation and may be considered during family therapy sessions. A girl who has told her parents she is pregnant but who disagrees with her parents over what to do faces a family crisis. Family treatment to help the family come to a consensual decision supportive of the girl's course of action can be very helpful (see Chapter 8).

When a child is the identified best donor of a body organ, such as bone marrow or a kidney, the family confronts a serious dilemma. First, the parents must consent to the donation and transplant. If the child is able to understand the risks and benefits, then the consent of the child should also be obtained. Family therapists may be consulted to help families decide and feel comfortable with these difficult choices. The benefits to the child donor are largely psychological in nature. A minor's assent or dissent to being a donor may be an important clue as to whether the minor will experience later satisfaction. When children do dissent, investigation into the basis of their concerns may allow correction of misconceptions. For minors who do consent, it is important to examine the voluntariness of the consent. Although the research on the psychological benefits of organ donation is scanty, Simmons, Marine, and Simmons (1987) found that those who donated a kidney to a family member experienced minimal regret and took great satisfaction in helping a family member to live. Because the parents of a potential donor are not presumed to have solely the best interests of the donor in mind, physicians routinely obtain court authorization for a serious procedure. The ethics code of the American Medical Association (American Medical Association, 1997, para. 2.167) requires that physicians obtain a court order authorizing utilizing a minor as an organ donor when there is serious risk (such as when donating a kidney), although not for donations of moderate risk (such as bone marrow, where the risk is primarily that of general anesthesia, but the tissue can be expected to regrow). Court review also reduces the burden of making the decision and possible guilt the parents might feel toward the donor because they have made the needs of the recipient child their priority.

When a child or adolescent is in the hospital and is likely to die, families face a tragic situation. Decisions to terminate life-sustaining care are excruciatingly difficult for families to make. While in many states parents can consent to termination of life support, in Georgia, for example, if a minor of any age can understand the choice, a do not resuscitate order cannot be written without the minor's assent (Official Code of Georgia, Annotated [O.C.G.A.] 31-39-1 to 31-39-9).

FAMILIES WHO REFUSE MEDICAL TREATMENT

Parents sometimes refuse to consent to recommended medical treatment. Such treatment refusals generally stem from one of three sources. First, parents may have a religious objection to the recommended treatment. The classic cases are of Jehovah's Witness parents who object to blood transfusions, or Christian Scientist parents who decline all treatment because they believe in faith healing. Second, parents may have a philosophical disagreement with a particular recommendation, such as parents who want to use herbal remedies instead of standard treatment. Finally, parents may disagree in cases where extraordinary care is recommended: They may refuse lifesaving treatment that is likely to lead to a very reduced quality of life, or high-risk procedures with an overall poor prognosis, as in surgery for congenital defects that may itself leave the child severely impaired, or cancer treatments that have debilitating side effects and are unlikely to lead to a cure. In such cases, the disagreement is between the parents and the physicians, rather than among family members, and so family therapists are seldom involved unless the family is ambivalent about what course to follow and is seeking help in clarifying its thinking. In the event that the physician cannot resolve the dispute, he or she may either seek a court order (generally in emergency situations, by telephoning a judge, such as when an order to transfuse blood is needed), or file a report of medical neglect against the parents with the county child protection agency, which will then take the matter to court. If the court finds medical neglect, the court may then take temporary custody of the child and consent to treatment after considering the child's best interests.

RESEARCH INVOLVING CHILDREN

The Department of Health and Human Services has developed regulations governing institutional review boards (IRBs) that review research proposals to ensure adequate safeguards for human subjects. Any institution that sponsors federally regulated or funded research (universities, governmental agencies, drug companies, etc.) must have an IRB (sometimes also referred to as a *human subjects review committee*). Although the federal regulations technically apply only to federally funded or regulated research, they are generally followed by IRBs in all their reviews and so have become de facto standards for all research. The 1983 regulations and their subsequent amendments (45 Code of Federal Regulations [C.F.R.] 46.408) essentially hold that for research involving children of any age who can understand the nature of their research participation, the assent of the child, in addition to the informed consent of the parents, must be obtained. Thus, a 7-year-old who does not want to have blood drawn for research purposes "because it will hurt" or complete a questionnaire "because it's boring" can veto his or her participation in a research study. From a legal perspective, this is probably the high-water mark of children's competency: Most children who have even minimal understanding are deemed competent to refuse or assent. The exceptions are essentially those that would not require informed consent in the case of an adult (such things as obtaining anonymous quantitative chart review data). Another exception is if the research is an integral part of treatment undertaken to benefit the child (such as additional monitoring for an experimental treatment for which the parents have consented). These regulations apply to research that poses only minimal risk. Research that engenders moderate risk (rare in family therapy research) comes under more stringent safeguards.

INVOLUNTARY INPATIENT TREATMENT OF MINORS

When a therapist recommends inpatient treatment of a minor, generally the parents need to consent to the treatment. On clinical grounds, the decision also must be discussed with the minor. Parents may exert considerable pressure on their child to go along with the admission. When the Supreme Court considered the question of admission of minors, they found that the parents' consent, plus a physician's concurrence, are all that is constitutionally necessary to proceed with hospitalization (*Parham v. J.R.*, 1979). The minor's liberty interest is not sufficient to require civil commitment or judicial review. Some states, however, have granted adolescents due process rights to object to hospitalization; these potentially make accessible different mechanisms for children of different ages, including appointment of an attorney to represent the minor. When judicial review occurs, the standard is generally less stringent than that used in civil commitment, and more often centers around the youth's need for treatment. The dynamics of oppositional adolescents hospitalized by their parents often play out in an interesting way. It is fairly common for adolescents who are told they have a right to object to file a formal objection, but it is also common for such adolescents to withdraw their objection shortly before the hearing, sometimes leaving an inexperienced court-appointed attorney feeling quite deflated. Once the youngster is in the hospital, generally parental consent is all that is necessary to administer treatment, although some states afford certain categories of adolescents more decision-making power or rights to judicial review.

Children who are wards of the state often come under somewhat different rules, because the presumption that a parent or guardian is deciding in the best interests of a child is much weaker when applied to a child protection agency worker. Foster parents do not generally have the authority to consent to psychiatric hospitalization; such a decision regarding a foster child is either made by a juvenile court judge, a parent whose rights have not been terminated, or, in some circumstances, the child protection agency that legally has custody of the child.

In those cases in which the therapist believes that inpatient treatment is warranted but the parents do not consent to such treatment, the minor cannot be hospitalized unless civil commitment criteria are met.

CIVIL COMMITMENT

There are times when an adult patient refuses treatment but the therapist, or in some cases the family, believes that involuntary treatment is necessary. In these cases, family decision making has failed, and external coercion becomes necessary. In the past, some states have allowed *need for treatment* as a grounds for involuntary commitment. However, the U.S. Supreme Court has ruled that need for treatment is not sufficient to override a patient's liberty interest in staying out of the hospital (*O'Connor v. Donaldson*, 1975). While states have worded their legal tests somewhat differently, generally a patient must (a) have a mental illness, and (b) be dangerous as a result of that mental illness. *Dangerous* in this context means either dangerous to others, dangerous to self, or, in most states, so gravely disabled that one is unable to care for oneself. The mental illness requirement usually means that people who are dangerous by virtue of their criminality or psychopathic traits alone do not meet the threshold test for commitment. Some states have additional requirements, such as *imminent danger* or dangerousness evidenced by *recent overt acts*, which further narrow the grounds for commitment. It is important that the clinician be aware of the specific test in his or her state: Frequently the decision to commit comes up in an emergency situation, and there is limited time to check the law when a patient in the office has expressed clear suicidal or homicidal ideation. However, a quick telephone call to the police or a psychiatric emergency room can elicit the specific criteria.

State statutes specify who may institute a commitment. Psychiatrists are always listed. Psychologists are usually listed, and, increasingly, so are social workers, nurses, and other mental health clinicians. Statutes often also specify just what constitutes a member of the discipline (i.e., a psychiatric resident with 1 year of experience, a psychologist with a PhD and an unlimited license, etc.) It is important that therapists know whether they are eligible to institute civil commitments. For therapists who are not authorized to initiate commitment proceedings, the possibilities are to refer the patient to another clinician with commitment authority or to an emergency room (assuming there is a reasonable likelihood the patient will go), to solicit the help of the police, or to encourage the family to apply for commitment to the probate court. A family member can file an affidavit with the probate court, and, on appropriate evidence, a judge will then issue an order for the sheriff to take the person to a designated place for mental health evaluation. This latter route is important to remember for those times when someone telephones and describes an explosive situation, but the therapist has not evaluated the person in question. Being taken to the hospital by the police under duress is usually an unpleasant experience and may engender great resentment in the patient against his or her family and the therapist.

Filing the initial commitment document sets in motion a sequence of events which varies in detail among jurisdictions, but follows similar lines. Typically, there is a state-approved form to be filed which allows a single clinician to hospitalize a patient, or at least have the patient taken to an evaluating facility and held in the hospital for a time-limited period (up to several days). It is essentially an emergency initiating document. Before the expiration of the first form, a second form documenting a continuing need for hospitalization must be completed. This second form usually requires completion by at least one psychiatrist, and, commonly, examination by a second clinician as well. The second form sets in motion the scheduling of a formal commitment hearing to take place within a specified time (generally 2 to 3 weeks). An attorney is appointed to represent the patient, if the patient does not have one. At the hearing, the judge will rule whether commitment should be continued. The U.S. Supreme Court has held that at least *clear and convincing evidence* is required that the patient meets the statutory test for commitment (*Addington v. Texas*, 1979). This burden of proof is less than the *beyond a reasonable doubt* standard needed to convict someone of a crime, but more than the *preponderance of the evidence* necessary in most civil trials. If the judge commits the patient, the commitment will be for a specified period, at which time it will be reviewed at another hearing.

At any point, based on the judgment of the attending physician, the patient may be discharged or, if the patient agrees to hospitalization, converted to voluntary status. A request by the patient to convert to voluntary status does not require the physician to do so. It is also important to recognize that commitment is seen legally as depriving the patient of liberty for the patient's own or society's protection. Commitment does not give the physician the authority to treat the patient over the patient's objections.

The commitment of minors or other legally incompetent persons follows a similar process.

CLINICAL ASSESSMENT FOR COMMITMENT

There is considerable research to suggest that mental health professionals do not have the ability to make accurate long-term predictions (Monahan, 1981). This is so in large part because both suicide and homicide are relatively rare events and have multiple causes. The assessment of dangerousness for commitment purposes is essentially an analysis of risk. That is, while a clinician is unlikely to accurately predict whether a person in a given situation will actually kill him- or herself, there is some evidence that clinicians have some expertise in evaluating short-term risk (McNiel & Binder, 1987). In testifying in a commitment hearing, it is important that the clinician keep in mind that he or she has assessed risk, not made a medically certain prediction that the patient would carry out a dangerous act.

Risk factors can be divided into static or dynamic factors. For example, having a history of prior violence or an antisocial personality disorder are positive *static risk factors* for dangerousness toward others, while a recent onset of paranoid psychosis or making a specific threat are *dynamic factors*. Dynamic factors may be amenable to treatment, while static factors are not.

An assessment of risk should include a general clinical evaluation, in addition to assessment of specific risk factors. Clinicians should consider the possibility that a patient is withholding information or minimizing symptoms. For this reason, obtaining information from family members is often important in making a complete assessment. Other records may also be useful, although these are seldom available in outpatient emergency assessments.

The issues of informed consent in evaluations for commitment are complex. Does the patient need to be informed that confidentiality may be lost? Should the patient be warned that anything he or she says may be used for commitment purposes, if relevant? Does the patient need to consent to the evaluation? The strict legal answers to these questions vary by situation and jurisdiction, and are not always clear (for discussion, see Perlin, 1989, pp. 265–280). The concern, of course, is that issuing *Miranda*-like "right to remain silent" warnings or other legalistic-sounding injunctions will cause the patient to stop talking: The clinician will not then be able to identify grounds for commitment, and harm will result. In a family treatment context, the question of commitment most commonly arises during the course of treatment when symptoms of dangerousness begin to come to light, and voluntary hospitalization remains an option. Once it appears that there is a reasonable possibility that the patient (a) may meet commitment criteria and (b) may refuse voluntary hospitalization, one ethical way to proceed is for the clinician to express concern about how the patient is thinking and feeling and indicate that they need to assess these symptoms together, adding that if there is serious risk of harm and the patient does not want to go into the hospital, the clinician may need to reveal enough of the interview to have the patient hospitalized. If the clinician has discussed confidentiality with the patient earlier in the treatment and has made clear that dangerousness to self or others is an exception to maintaining confidentiality, then a "reminder" notice is probably not required. Consent for continuing an outpatient interview can generally be inferred from the patient's continuing to talk, as long as he or she is not told that participation is mandatory. How the clinician has handled the notice and consent issue should be documented in the patient's chart to forestall the patient from successfully invoking the patient–therapist privilege at a commitment hearing.

RISK FACTORS IN SUICIDE ASSESSMENTS

There is an extensive literature on suicide and risk factors. Over 70% of patients who commit suicide have suffered from either depression or alcoholism; overall, the risk of dying from suicide if a patient has a major depressive disorder is about 15% (Roy, 1995). However, among the cohort of depressed patients, no factors have as yet been identified that statistically predict which patients will kill themselves (Goldstein, Black, Nasrallah, & Winokur, 1991). Research from the NIMH Collaborative Program on the Psychobiology of Depression (Fawcett et al., 1990) found that seven factors mostly related to anxiety in depressed patients were associated with suicide in the year following assessment (these are noted as exacerbating factors under "Depression" in Table 15.2.) There are no methodologically satisfactory studies assessing risk in the short term, because one cannot conduct a study that involves releasing patients thought to present a high risk.

This data forms the backdrop of emergency suicide assessment. Given the statistically low level of association of risk factors with completed suicide, suicide risk assessment remains a clinical task with the goal of assessing *imminent* risk of suicide, that is, suicide within the next several days. The threshold issue is an assessment of current intent. A combination of high risk factors in the context of a believable denial of current or recent suicidal thinking is unlikely to warrant commitment. Table 15.2 lists some of the key items to be considered. Intent does not depend solely on the verbalizations of the patient: A report by a family member that a person has been talking of "ending it all" is evidence of intent. Suicidal intent then needs to be evaluated in the context of other risk factors noted in Table 15.2. For example, low-level intent (occasional thoughts of killing oneself, but no

Table 15.2   Key Factors in Assessing Suicide Risk

Suicidal Intent
Current thoughts about killing oneself
Chronicity of suicidal thinking
Suicidal thoughts expressed to others
Formed plan
Availability of means
Steps taken to initiate plan
Actions taken in anticipation of death
Recent attempt
Depression, Especially If Recent Exacerbations Of
Panic attacks
Psychic anxiety
Loss of pleasure
Alcohol abuse
Depressive turmoil
Diminished concentration
Global insomnia
Discharge from psychiatric hospital within 3 months
Hopelessness
Psychosis
Risk highest in first 3 years after onset of schizophrenia
Comorbid depressive symptoms and anxiety
Hallucinations commanding suicide
Recent Stressors
Divorce or other loss
Job loss
Physical illness
Static Factors
Family history of suicide
History of depression
Previous attempts
Demographics: increased age, male, white
Living alone, social isolation

plan) in the context of recent onset of severe depression, high anxiety, and hopelessness during a divorce would be more worrisome than higher-level intent ("Oh, I'd probably take some pills") in a chronically mildly depressed but otherwise calm patient who frequently toys with fantasies about suicide and who has suffered no recent stressors. Recently diagnosed psychotic patients present risk, in part, because their level of anxiety is difficult to assess and they are unpredictable in responding to command hallucinations. Protective factors, such as the willingness of a family member to stay with the patient, certain religious beliefs, and the nature of the therapeutic alliance, must be considered. The willingness of the patient to make a so-called suicide contract—that is, to agree to contact the therapist before making a suicide attempt—is evidence of some therapeutic alliance, but should not be relied upon to deter suicide. Finally, reasons not to proceed with hospitalization, such as its tendency to foster regression in certain patients, must be considered. After the data is obtained, a judgment of overall risk is made. There is no clear formula for how to weigh the various risk factors. A person seriously thinking about carrying out a specific plan that has at least moderate lethality generally warrants commitment. The more complex judgments tend to involve patients with general thoughts about suicide in the context of other significant risk factors and patients who are chronically at some risk due to moderate depressive symptoms coupled with more severe, acting-out personality disorders. (For more detailed discussions of assessing suicide risk see Bongar, 1992; Chiles & Strosahl, 1995; Group for the Advancement of Psychiatry, 1996; Roy, 1995; Simon, 1992.)

Risk Factors in Assessments of Dangerousness toward Others

In the general population, the best predictor of future violence is a past history of violence (Klassen & O'Connor, 1988). The peak age for the onset of violent behavior is around age 15 to 16 (Elliott, 1994) although the peak onset age in psychiatric patients is in the mid-20s (Swanson, Holzer, Ganju, & Jono, 1990). As might be expected, antisocial personality disorder and psychopathy, when coupled with a history of violence, are bad prognostic signs.

In family treatment, the most common situations in which questions of dangerousness to others arise are when one spouse has an antisocial personality disorder or paranoid psychotic decompensation, or there is a question of spouse abuse, child abuse, or postdivorce stalking. In inpatient settings, dangerousness is most often an issue with paranoid psychotic patients. For child and spouse abuse, the question is generally not a predictive one, but a determination of whether abuse has taken place. At times, therapists are asked to determine whether it is now safe for an abuser to return to live with the victim (such as following treatment). Abuse issues are dealt with in the chapters on those subjects. In stalking cases, the stalker is seldom involved in family treatment with the victim, so the stalker is rarely accessible to the family clinician for assessment, and presents special difficulties (see Meloy, 1997).

In assessing imminent dangerousness towards others, current homicidal intent (including homicidal command hallucinations) coupled with a history of past violence is the most worrisome situation. All threats need to be taken seriously. Of particular note, it is important to inquire as to how well planned the threat is. What is the affect? Fear of the target is quite common in addition to anger. Actions taken to avoid the target out of fear (such as barricading one's room) raise risk significantly. If the patient is paranoid, it is often useful to ask what he or she would do if confronted by the perceived persecutor (Resnick, 1997). Psychotic patients who describe threat/control-override symptoms (e.g., belief that thoughts are being put into one's head or that one is being followed) are more likely to be assaultive (Borum, Swartz, & Swanson, 1996). Alcohol or other drug intoxication is often implicated in violent acts because of associated impulsivity and decreased judgment, so substance abuse needs to be carefully assessed (Murdoch, Pihl, & Ross, 1990).

If the clinician has been given a history of violent behavior, it is important to obtain a detailed history of the violent acts themselves. Some specific areas worth inquiring into are noted in Table 15.3. Wack (1993) has developed a protocol for obtaining a detailed history. If the patient has been violent a number of times, patterns running through the events should be looked for. Meloy (1987) has distinguished between affective violence, violence taken in response to a perceived threat, and predatory aggression, which is planned, purposeful, and emotionally detached. Predatory aggression is highly dangerous because there are not behaviors which precede it. A detailed history will also illuminate what dynamic factors play a role in triggering violence. For example, a history of fighting with men in bars during periods when a patient is depressed does not suggest high risk to a spouse when the patient is euthymic and not intoxicated. Finally, a clinician's gut feelings are important. Dangerous patients raise considerable anxiety in most clinicians; this is an arena in which such feelings may well reflect actual risk, even if the clinician is hard pressed to fully explain the concern. There is a considerable literature on assessing danger to others which provides more detailed discussion (Brizer & Crowner, 1989; Meloy, 1987; Monahan & Steadman, 1994; Tardiff, 1989).

In those states that have adopted a duty to protect likely victims (a so-called Tarasoff duty, see Chapter 22), commitment of a dangerous patient generally fulfills the duty and an additional warning is not necessary. Warning a potential victim may become an issue as the patient approaches discharge.

EVALUATING AND DOCUMENTING RISK

How much risk does the clinician need to find before instituting civil commitment proceedings? In most cases of dangerousness, a clinician will first recommend voluntary hospitalization, and will resort to commitment only if this option is refused. The threshold for commitment is higher than that for a simple recommendation for hospitalization. At a commitment hearing, a judge will need to find by at least clear and convincing evidence that the patient is dangerous. This does not mean, however, that the clinician must find that there is more than a 50% chance that the patient will kill him- or herself. In fact, it is very unclear just how certain the clinician must be. Commentators have spoken about "significant risk" and "being able to sleep after deciding." Most clinicians will tolerate a higher level of risk in the case of a suicidal patient than they would for a homicidal patient. If things go wrong and the clinician is later sued for malpractice, the plaintiff will likely claim either that the patient should have been committed, but wasn't (and went on to assault someone or kill himself), or that the patient was improperly detained. In either case, the clinician will be held to the malpractice standard: what

Table 15.3 Key Factors in Assessing Homicide Risk

Dynamic Factors
Current threats
Nature and lethality of threat
Degree of planning
Fear of victim
Weapons availability
Psychosis
Paranoid thinking
Hallucinations commanding violence
Avoidance of perceived persecutor
Threat/control-override symptoms
Fantasies of violence
Substance abuse
Current presence of factors associated with previous violence

Static Factors
History of violence: Obtain a detailed history of episodes
Frequency
Precipitants
Relationship to victim
Weapons
Affective versus predatory
Association with psychosis
Intoxication
Degree of injury
Remorse
Antisocial traits
Childhood abuse

a reasonable clinician would have done under the circumstances. The test is not what a judge would have ruled at a commitment hearing.

A great deal of malpractice liability stems from work with dangerous patients. There are a number of things the clinician can do to minimize malpractice liability. The first, of course, is to conduct a comprehensive assessment of risk. Second, careful documentation of the assessment is important. This is not the time to write a brief note. Rather, the note should list the pertinent positive and negative risk factors, both the factors that suggest dangerousness and the factors that mitigate against it. In addition to the risk factors, the clinician should note other factors that go into the decision. For example, for a chronically suicidal patient, hospitalization may exacerbate regressive or manipulate behaviors and so complicate later treatment. In addition to noting the relevant data, written documentation of how the clinician weighed the factors, the reasoning that led from the data to the conclusion of whether to commit, is important. This reasoning component is probably the aspect of documentation that is most frequently missing in records, but it is crucial in validating that the clinician went through a reasonable process in reaching a decision. Finally, in complicated cases in which the risk is unclear, a good rule is: "When in doubt, shout!" (Rappeport, 1984). Get a second opinion, and have it documented. Malpractice cases turn on hindsight. It is all too easy to find an expert to testify that if he or she had been there assessing the patient, clearly he or she would have had the patient committed. The best way to avoid retrospective arguments is to have a second clinician. Then one's defense is: "I asked a reasonable clinician to look at the situation at the time, and this is what that clinician found." Because the standard of practice is what a reasonable clinician should have done, the testimony of a second reasonable clinician who saw the patient at the time is much more compelling than that of the Monday-morning quarterbacking of a hired expert who wasn't there.

OUTPATIENT COMMITMENT

Many states have passed statutes allowing for outpatient civil commitment. The threshold standard of dangerousness is generally the same, but outpatient commitment may be appropriate for patients who can be treated in a less restrictive environment. Such procedures are rarely used in initial commitments, because the risk of dangerousness requires more intensive supervision of the patient. Outpatient commitment has become fairly common as a step-down measure for committed inpatients. The most common situation is that of a patient who improves on medication in the hospital, but who is thought to be at significant risk of going off medication and again becoming ill as soon as he or she is discharged. Outpatient commitment in these situations is used to enforce compliance with treatment, usually pharmacologic treatment. If a patient does not comply with treatment, the outpatient commitment allows for involuntary rehospitalization without all the cumbersome due process that inpatient commitment entails. Outpatient commitment is often used as a quasi–plea bargain at a commitment hearing for a patient who has made some gains in the several weeks of hospitalization prior to the hearing. Court-ordered outpatient treatment may also be utilized by the criminal justice system (such as treatment being a condition of probation). Outpatient commitment to family therapy is unusual.

SUMMARY AND RECOMMENDATIONS

The ideal, for families and therapists, is to reach consensus on participation in treatment through family discussion without recourse to legal processes. Engaging in legal actions tends to undermine family and individual autonomy and family cooperation. For these reasons, shifting decision making to the legal system is to be avoided whenever possible. However, it is often important to know how the legal system is likely to decide, if it were to rule. Knowing the potential legal outcome reduces uncertainty, which reduces the likelihood of legal involvement. The clinician should be cautious, however, about injecting knowledge of potential legal outcomes prematurely. The message "I can have you committed" may finally persuade an objecting patient to accept a recommendation for voluntary hospitalization, but the same message given too early in the discussion may be seen as an emotional abandonment and an uncaring act by the therapist, which will reinforce opposition to treatment and interfere with the therapeutic alliance. Clinical approaches should be tried first; legalistic approaches are the court of last resort.

REFERENCES

Addington v. Texas (1979), 441 U.S. 418.

Adelman, H. S., Lusk, R., Alvarez, V., & Acosta, N. K. (1985). Competence of minors to understand, evaluate, and communicate about their psychoeducational problems. *Professional Psychology Research and Practice, 16,* 426–434.

American Medical Association. (1997). *Code of medical ethics: Current opinions with annotations.* Chicago: Author.

Ash, P., Jurkovic, G., & Harrison, S. I. (1998). Observation, interview, and mental status assessment (OIM): Competence for independent decision making. In J. D. Noshpitz, S. I. Harrison, & S. Eth (Eds.), *Handbook of child and adolescent psychiatry: Clinical assessment and intervention planning* (Vol. 5, pp. 518–525). New York: John Wiley & Sons.

Bellotti v. Baird (1976), 428 U.S. 132.

Bongar, B. M. (1992). *Suicide: Guidelines for assessment, management, and treatment.* New York: Oxford University Press.

Borum, R., Swartz, M., & Swanson, J. (1996). Assessing and managing violence risk in clinical practice. *Journal of Practical Psychology and Behavioral Health,* 205–215.

Brizer, D. A., & Crowner, M. (Eds.). (1989). *Current approaches to the prediction of violence.* Washington DC: American Psychiatric Press.

Cardwell v. Bechtol (1987), 724 S.W.2d 739 (Tenn.).

Carey v. Population Services International (1977), 431 U.S. 678.

Chiles, J., & Strosahl, K. (1995). *The suicidal patient: Principles of assessment, treatment, and case management.* (1st ed.). Washington, DC: American Psychiatric Press.

Code of Federal Regulations (1998), 45 C.F.R. § 46.408.

Education for All Handicapped Children Act of 1975, as amended, 20 U.S.C. §§ 1400 *et seq.* (1998).

Elliott, D. S. (1994). Serious violent offenders: Onset, developmental course, and termination—the American Society of Criminology 1993 Presidential Address. *Criminology, 32*(1), 1–21.

Fawcett, J., Scheftner, W. A., Fogg, L., Clark, D. C., Young, M. A., Hedeker, D., & Gibbons, R. (1990). Time-related predictors of suicide in major affective disorder [see comments]. *American Journal of Psychiatry, 147*(9), 1189–1194.

Garrison, E. G. (1991). Children's competence to participate in divorce custody decision-making. *Journal of Clinical Child Psychology, 20,* 78–87.

Goldstein, R. B., Black, D. W., Nasrallah, A., & Winokur, G. (1991). The prediction of suicide. Sensitivity, specificity, and predictive value of a multivariate model applied to suicide among 1906 patients with affective disorders. *Archives of General Psychiatry, 48*(5), 418–422.

Grisso, T. (1981). *Juveniles' waiver of rights: Legal and psychological competence.* New York: Plenum Press.

Group for the Advancement of Psychiatry, Committee on Child Psychiatry (1989). *How old is old enough?: The ages of rights and responsibilities.* New York: Brunner/Mazel.

Group for the Advancement of Psychiatry, Committee on Adolescence. (1996). *Adolescent suicide.* Washington, DC: American Psychiatric Press.

Hodgson v. Minnesota (1990), 497 U.S. 417.

Klassen, D., & O'Connor, W. A. (1988). A prospective study of predictors of violence in adult male mental health admissions. *Law & Human Behavior, 12*(2), 143–158.

Lewis, C. E., Lewis, M. A., Lorimer, A., & Palmer, B. (1977). Child initiates care: The use of school nursery services by children in an "adult free" system. *Pediatrics, 60,* 449–507.

McNiel, D. E., & Binder, R. L. (1987). Predictive validity of judgments of dangerousness in emergency civil commitment. *American Journal of Psychiatry, 144*(2), 197–200.

Meloy, J. R. (1987). The prediction of violence in outpatient psychotherapy. *American Journal of Psychotherapy, 41*(1), 38–45.

Meloy, J. R. (1997). The clinical risk management of stalking: "Someone is watching over me . . ." *American Journal of Psychotherapy, 51*(2), 174–84.

Monahan, J. (1981). *The clinical prediction of violent behavior.* Rockville, MD: National Institute for Mental Health.

Monahan, J., & Steadman, H. J. (1994). Violence and mental disorder: Developments in risk assessment. *University of Chicago Press, 324*(11), 11.

Morrissey, J. M., Hofmann, A. D., & Thrope, J. C. (1986). *Consent and confidentiality in the health care of children and adolescents: A legal guide.* New York: Free Press.

Murdoch, D., Pihl, R. O., & Ross, D. (1990). Alcohol and crimes of violence: Present issues. *International Journal of the Addictions, 25*(9), 1065–1081.

O'Connor v. Donaldson (1975), 422 U.S. 563.

Official Code of Georgia, Annotated (1998), O.C.G.A. 31-39-1 to 31-39-9.

Parham v. J.R. (1979), 442 U.S. 584.

Perlin, M. L. (1989). *Mental disability law: Civil and criminal* (Vol. 1). Charlottesville, VA: Mitchie.

Planned Parenthood of Central Missouri v. Danforth (1976), 428 U.S. 52.

Rappeport, J. R. (1984, May). *Malpractice prevention.* Paper presented at the Spring Grove State Hospital Center, Catonsville, MD.

Resnick, P. J. (1997, October). *Risk assessment for violence.* Paper presented at the Forensic Psychiatry Review Course, Denver, CO.

Roe v. Wade (1973), 410 U.S. 113.

Rosebush v. Oakland County Prosecutor (1992), 491 N.W.2d 633 (Mich. Ct. App.).

Roy, A. (1995). Psychiatric emergencies. In H. I. Kaplan & B. J. Sadock (Eds.), *Comprehensive textbook of psychiatry* (6th ed., Vol. 2, pp. 1739–1752). Baltimore: Williams & Wilkins.

Rozovsky, F. A. (1990). *Consent to treatment: A practical guide* (2nd ed.). Boston: Little, Brown.

Scherer, D. G. (1991). The capacities of minors to exercise voluntariness in medical treatment decisions. *Law & Human Behavior, 15,* 431–449.

Scott, E. S., Reppucci, N. D., & Woolard, J. L. (1995). Evaluating adolescent decision making in legal contexts. *Law & Human Behavior, 19,* 221–244.

Simmons, R. G., Marine, S. K., & Simmons, R. L. (1987). *Gift of life: The effect of organ transplantation on individual, family, and societal dynamics.* New Brunswick, NJ: Transaction Books.

Simon, R. I. (1992). Clinical risk management of suicidal patients: Assessing the unpredictable. In R. I. Simon (Ed.), *Review of clinical psychiatry and the law* (Vol. 3, pp. 3–63). Washington, DC: American Psychiatric Press.

Steinberg, L., & Cauffman, E. (1996). Maturity of judgment in adolescence: Psychosocial factors in adolescent decision making. *Law & Human Behavior, 20,* 249–272.

Swanson, J. W., Holzer, C. E., Ganju, V. K., & Jono, R. T. (1990). Violence and psychiatric disorder in the community: Evidence from the Epidemiologic Catchment Area surveys. *Hospital & Community Psychiatry, 41*(7), 761–770.

Taylor, L., Adelman, H. S., & Kaser-Boyd, N. (1985). Minors' attitudes and competence toward participation in psychoeducational decisions. *Professional Psychology Research and Practice, 16,* 226–235.

Tardiff, K. (1989). A model for the short-term prediction of violence potential. In D. A. Brizer & M. Crowner (Eds.), *Current approaches to the prediction of violence* (pp. 3–12). Washington DC: American Psychiatric Press.

Wack, R. C. (1993). The ongoing risk assessment in the treatment of forensic patients on conditional release status. *Psychiatric Quarterly, 64*(3), 275–293.

Weithorn, L. A., & Campbell, S. B. (1982). The competency of children and adolescents to make informed treatment decisions. *Child Development, 53,* 1589–1598.

Part Three

WHEN FAMILIES IN TREATMENT INTERFACE WITH LEGAL AND JUDICIAL SYSTEMS

The Postlaunching Years

CHAPTER 16

Succession Planning in the Family-Owned Firm

Psycholegal Concerns

SAM KIRSCHNER and DIANA ADILE KIRSCHNER

SUCCESSION, the process of handing over power at the top of the company, seldom works as smoothly in the family business as it does in the nonfamily business. Often it involves a protracted debilitating struggle between the generations or between the siblings that can seriously weaken, if not destroy, the company. Surveys show that only 30% of family-owned businesses endure into the second generation, while only 10% survive into the third (Beckhard & Dyer, 1983).

There are four typical complications that the family business must confront if it is to successfully deal with succession (Davis, 1991). First of all, the founder or chief executive is frequently reluctant to let go. The fears the founder experiences as he or she looks at stepping aside not only delay handing over the power but also may make real planning for succession an impossibility.

Furthermore, it is difficult, if not impossible, to know how good the next generation will be when they take over. They may have been working for years under the founder's shadow or may have been sabotaged by jealous nonfamily employees. Thus, their true talents can never really be assessed until they have the chance to be fully responsible for the top job.

Third, moving from one generation to the next usually produces a complex management dilemma. For example, the parent with several children faces a company transition from a situation in which power is clearly centralized in one person, to one in which the ambitions of several aspirants to power and the top position must be mediated while a selection is made from among them. The parent with some children who work in the business and some who do not may be well advised to create a new class of stakeholders (family owners who are not working in the company) to try to accommodate everyone's needs, albeit differentially.

Finally, through selection and attrition, the key employees take on personas that allow them to survive with the family members who are in power. For example, a hard-driving entrepreneurial founder will often be surrounded with a passive, compliant senior management. These managers may not be the ones to support the next generation. Succession may necessitate other changes in top-level management and an eventual reorganization of the company.

ORGANIZATIONAL DYNAMICS IN THE FAMILY FIRM

In the family firm, organizational behavior is often greatly influenced by the quality of the family's relationships, and these, in turn, are influenced by powerful unconscious forces. In some businesses, brothers seek to dominate brothers, fathers need to be stronger than their sons or daughters, and women are devalued and demeaned. These types of aggressive or destructive behaviors adversely impact upon the whole organization. When personal issues arise, disguised as business issues, they may really be part of the dysfunctional emotional agenda of the family played out in the work sphere. As a result, lines are drawn, positions are taken, and rationalizations are developed, resulting in stalemates and the constant repetition of familiar battles.

ORGANIZATIONAL CULTURE

What gives rise to the organizational behavior often seen in family firms? Most management and organizational experts would agree that organizational behavior is mostly determined by the culture of the organization, the source of which, according to Schein (1990), is the set of norms that are collectively and unconsciously held by employees, including family members. These norms shape employee behavior by limiting choices among options by defining what is appropriate and what is not.

In the family firm, the founder originally shapes the organizational culture. As Schein notes, the founder passes on "a pattern of assumptions that has worked well enough to be considered valid and, therefore, to be taught to new members as the correct way to perceive, think, and feel" (Schein, 1983, p. 14). The founder's values and beliefs provide a foundation that, in successful businesses, provides stability and security. Yet, the founder's underlying beliefs and attitudes are informed by the legacies instilled by the founder's family of origin (Bowen, 1978). Davis and Stern (1980) sum up this process well:

> The legend of the founder entrepreneur may often serve as a symbolic distillation of espoused norms and values. Family folklore and mythology seem to be key ingredients in the maintenance of cohesion and continuity. (p. 321)

These guiding myths, then, contribute to forming the foundation of the family firm's organizational culture. Furthermore, they are instilled in the children both in the home and in the workplace. No wonder it is so difficult for the next generation to free itself from the generally unexamined intergenerational legacies (Kaslow, 1993).

Consider a real-life case study in which apparent legacies were played out in the organizational culture of a large family firm, ending with the destruction of the family and with it almost the entire business. In 1990, the *Wall Street Journal* reported that Mr. Farah, the "King of pants-making," had ruled his firm with an iron fist and had turned back several attempts by his three sons to succeed him. The article went on to say that "his three sons, who grew up with a vision of carrying on the family business, have been driven out after clashes with the family patriarch. His daughter, the only family member still on the board, voted to oust her father as chairman" (Corchado, 1990, p. 1). The banding together of the siblings (who always had been played off against each other by their father in a divide-and-conquer strategy) to "kill" the patriarch is reminiscent of the great Greek tragedies of Euripides (1972).

In *Iphigenia in Aulis* and the later play *Electra*, the legacies of hate and murder are repeated through three generations. Electra and her brother Orestes band together to kill their mother, Clytemnestra, who has killed her husband and their father, Agamemnon. And what was Agamemnon's sin? He killed his oldest child, Iphigenia. This pattern of destroying one's children and then being avenged began with Agamemnon's father (Euripides, 1972).

One can only speculate on Mr. Farah's upbringing. But surely the tragic ending of his life with no family or business is a cruel and profound example of how unconscious legacies can organize the culture and behavior in the family firm (see Kirschner, 1992).

Sibling Relationships

Sibling dysfunction is typically not as extreme as in the Farah case. However, siblings in the family firm do carry their own conscious and unconscious legacies such that they are frequently plagued with rivalries and jealousies. When siblings are raised in families that do not own a business, they grow up and move out of the house, emerging, to some extent, from parental control. They are apt to find a common ground and develop some camaraderie, since they no longer regularly vie for parental attention and support. This is especially true for those adult children who are able to become economically self-sufficient and therefore to be less dependent on the parents.

However, children who are raised in a family that owns a business experience a very different kind of maturation process, especially if they choose to enter the family firm. In this case, the parent, who is also the boss, continues to hold power over the children, who are subordinates on the job long after they reach adulthood. The children remain dependent on the parent's good will and generosity and are therefore, to some extent, put into a no-win situation. For example, if they express normal feelings of anger and disappointment, or express disagreement with how facets of the business are being handled, they run the risk of being disliked by the boss, with possible consequences for salary increases, promotion, and ultimately succession. As a result, children and their parents in family firms often find it very difficult to communicate honestly and openly, even at home, because of the possible consequences at the office (Carroll, 1988).

Naturally, this problem is greatly exacerbated when the home and the business are at the same address. Despite this lack of appropriate boundaries, many family business CEOs operate under the assumption that what is good for the business is good for the family. Rosenblatt, Demick, Anderson, and Johnson (1985) identify this syndrome well:

> As symptom, the statement that "what is good for the business is good for the family" is simply an indication that the person holding the belief lives with unclear boundaries between business and family. As cause, believing that what is good for the business is good for the family may lead one to do things that reduce boundary clarity, such as bringing work home, using home as a workplace, exploiting family members in service of the business, and seeing them as extensions of one's self. Believing that what is good for the business is good for the family also leads to reduced boundary clarity if it means one rationalizes subordination of family priorities to business priorities. (p. 136)

Power struggles in both business organizations and families are normal and at times beneficial. Family businesses provide a very fertile ground for these battles. For example, children in the family business must necessarily engage in conflict with parents as a part of gaining autonomy and asserting their ideas and values. They may proffer that they know more about today's business climate because they have more formal education than their parents. Children also have power in the simple fact that without their cooperation, there will be no continuation of the family business into the next generation.

Conversely, the parent/boss will want the power of his or her accumulated knowledge, experience, and expertise to be respected by the younger generation. Also, the parents, on some level, must be relieved to know that at least one of the siblings is strong enough to stand up to conflict. Still, the everyday testing that family members put each other through is magnified when a business is at stake.

A common family power struggle that Alcorn (1982) has observed in her consultation with business families concerns the infighting among multiple heirs. In what Alcorn calls the *Cain and Abel syndrome*, each sibling attempts to place him- or herself in the dominant position in the family and business hierarchy and thus relegate the others to a subordinate position. Rivalries with the parent/boss take place simultaneously as each sibling presents his or her challenge. Because many of these families have very loose boundaries, the infighting will also be brought home to spouses or other siblings, who will enter into the feud.

Spouses, in particular, can help maintain or even exacerbate tension between the siblings. Jealousy and greed often play a role in feeding the flames of discontent. For example, in one family firm, the father had named the younger of two brothers to be his successor. While the older brother's stock remained the same as his brother's, his salary would be less. The older brother had long ago accepted that his temperament was more suited for running the manufacturing plant while his younger brother was clearly born to lead. Initially, he supported the plan, but by the time the father stepped down, open warfare had broken out between the brothers. As is so often the case, the two families stopped socializing with each other.

The parents then called in the lead author of this chapter to resolve the conflict. After interviewing all concerned parties, he discovered that the wife of the older brother had never accepted the succession plan and had berated and demeaned her husband almost daily to "get what he deserved from the father." In addition, she made it more difficult for her in-laws to have access to the grandchildren. The older brother found himself caught between loyalty to his wife and to his family of origin. In order to preserve his marriage, he joined her camp and declared war on the brother, which eased tensions in his own home and family of procreation.

This case illustrates how the succession issue fosters rivalry not only between the siblings but also with their spouses. Usually, however, it is the parent/boss who tacitly plays sibling against sibling in the hopes of finding the "right" successor. Alcorn (1982) comments on this tendency:

> Unfortunately, far too many entrepreneurs contribute to the existing sibling rivalries with what could be called "seductive secrecy." They fail in the management structure to designate the position and responsibilities of the sibling employees. Subconsciously, they are probably pitting employee against employee and dangling a carrot (the presidency of the company) before each of the sons. Dad encourages competition with the idea that it will make better men of both of them.

This struggle is exacerbated if there are more than two heirs, and if some are female and outshine their brother(s) in competence or qualifications. When dysfunctional rivalry persists into adulthood, it is evidence that the parents have not been able to foster cooperation in the sibling system (Kahn, 1988). Thus, it is the children who must instigate shifts in the balance of familial power once they recognize that they cannot remake the behavioral styles and emotional makeup of the parents. It is up to the adult siblings themselves to seek means of reconciliation and cooperation; this is more apt to occur when they realize that commonality of interest and economic gain can be achieved by doing so. These potential advantages can be powerful inducements to work together. Later in this chapter, the subsection "Preparing and Evaluating the Next Generation" discusses how the family business consultant works with the sibling subsystem.

DAUGHTERS AND SUCCESSION

Until recently, daughters were not seriously considered as heirs apparent in the succession process. For example, Rosenblatt et al. (1985) found that fathers were reluctant to give daughters training and experience in their businesses. The tendency to overlook daughters grows out of a strong historical tradition. As Barnes (1988) points out, throughout human history, parents have used hierarchy and primogeniture to determine succession in both kingdoms and commerce. The rule has been that the eldest or only son is the first in line to assume the seat of power.

This tendency toward a phallic structure in which males are valued, prized, and empowered, while females are devalued, disenfranchised, and used mainly for service and caretaking of others is still alive and well in many family businesses. Because of this, even if a female child is more talented and competent for taking over the business, she may not be considered a real "contender to the throne."

Sons are typically the preferred choice in succession planning. Often in these families there are gender-based alliances—that is, there are alignments between same-sex parents and children. This type of coalition is based not simply on common interests, but may also have roots in a shared hatred or mistrust of the opposite sex. This "us versus them" or common-enemy approach to childrearing can create great chaos, strife, and tension in the family at the time of succession—it can even tear the family apart. (For a case example in which the lead author had to overcome strong cultural prejudices against the female members in a family business in order to effect a daughter's successful ascension to the top, see Kirschner, 1992.)

PRESENTING PROBLEMS: WHAT BRINGS FAMILY BUSINESSES TO CONSULTANTS?

Family business owners typically seek consultation at a number of key crisis points in the family life cycle, the business life cycle, or both. Sometimes the crisis involves serious illness or sudden death, most often, of course, involving the older generation. A member of the younger generation may be having a psychological or physiological problem, such as depression or anxiety. Other crises revolve around conflicts among the siblings, in-laws, or cousins, or breakdowns in the relationship between the older and younger generations.

Another crisis point concerns conflict in the relationship between members of the older generation, as when two siblings who are the founders of the company disagree about whose children shall be their successors. Lawsuits between family members or the resignation of key nonfamily managers can also precipitate a crisis, as can the commencement of estate planning. Finally, marital problems or divorce and its accompanying financial settlement in either the older or the younger generation can lead the family to seek help. Ultimately, however, regardless of the presenting problem, it usually becomes clear as the consultation progresses that the family is most concerned with succession issues, ownership issues, or financial issues.

These concerns, succession in particular, surface family and individual problems that are typical of nodal points in the family life cycle. In earlier work, we have posited that throughout the life span there is a biphasic pattern of family development called *progressive abreactive regression* (PAR; Kirschner & Kirschner, 1991). PAR describes a cycle of progression in new challenges, such as leaving home, getting married, being promoted to a new job, or beginning retirement, which are followed by a reexperiencing of old fears, doubts, and a need for regressive contact with a secure and trusted figure. When managed properly, the regressive process, in turn, is followed by further progress in the domains of work, parenting, and marriage. In family businesses, the succession issue arouses the most profound PAR reactions in most of the family members. Thus, most of the presenting problems described in this chapter can be viewed in a holistic context as part and parcel of the larger PAR process. Management of PAR, as it manifests in family firms, is therefore a key to fruitful family business consulting.

ROLE OF THE FAMILY BUSINESS CONSULTANT

The role of the family business consultant is not that of the family therapist, but rather that of the sophisticated organizational consultant (Borwick, 1986). Because emotional issues and interpersonal conflicts are very strong forces in the family business, it is important that the consultant have a solid knowledge base about the family life cycle, family dynamics, and the unique characteristics of the family business. The consultant does not target family dysfunction for remediation. Rather, he or she uses this knowledge to educate family members and will refer them out as needed for marital, family, or individual therapy. However, as Kaslow (1993) points out, psychologists and other therapists who have a background in individual and family therapy as well as organizational work bring a uniquely valuable expertise and skill set to the consulting role.

Succession issues in the family business pose difficult sets of problems for the family business consultant. Often the client family can be vague or unclear about their own goals or objectives (Dreux & Goodman, 1997). Therefore, the consultant must be *equipped with both relational skills and business acumen* in order to bond with the key family members and create a workable consulting contract and climate.

There are four broad phases that must be addressed in consulting to the family-owned business; both the older- and the next-generation members must be enabled to go through them in order to effect a viable succession plan:

1. Getting outside support
2. Preparing the older generation to relinquish control
3. Evaluating and preparing the next generation to assume their new roles and responsibilities
4. Devising and implementing the succession plan

These phases do not occur in a linear fashion, but rather tend to overlap in time. The consultant often plays a crucial role in each of these phases. He or she functions as an educator, confidante, coach, and mediator with various family members, with the overarching goal being a win–win outcome for all concerned.

GETTING OUTSIDE SUPPORT

The management of succession is not easy. Designing the right roles and organizational structures to support the process is critical to success. As Peter Drucker (1994) noted in the *Wall Street Journal*, "Getting outside help is the best way to insure a successful transition of power in the family business." The family business consultant can function directly as a mentor or buffer or can help select other appropriate advisors to play these roles. He or she works together with these other advisors, helping to orchestrate both the succession plan and the estate planning for the family. The consultant may also play an important role in creating two other organizational structures that can facilitate the succession plan: the board of directors and the family council.

The next generation usually needs mentoring by individuals who can guide them and support their development. Only rarely should mentors be parents or other employees. Preferably, they should be experienced outsiders who are respected by the next generation, who can tell the children the truth when they are not performing well, give them unqualified support, and provide direct counsel and advice. Mentors can be attorneys, accountants, or other trusted business associates.

Buffers or mediators also can play significant roles. At times, the family business consultant can serve as the mediator between the strong-willed parent/CEO and the heir apparent son or daughter. At other times, a trusted key nonfamily employee can serve as the buffer. The succession process at IBM between the founder, Tom Watson, Sr., and his son, Tom Watson, Jr., provides an excellent example of how a key nonfamily employee can function as a mediator. In his memoir, Watson (1991) acknowledges the role played by his father's number-two man, Charley Kirk, as mentor and buffer.

As previously mentioned, the consultant can help establish or strengthen two institutional structures that can be invaluable in supporting the management of succession: an effective board of directors and a family council. Many family boards do not include sufficient outside representation, that is, people who are not friends and associates of the founder or chair. When this does not occur, the decision making of these boards lacks objectivity. For example, board members may not speak out when they believe that the CEO's leadership is ineffective or that it is time for the CEO to retire. A board that includes members with fresh thinking can both represent and encourage continuity as the baton is passed from one generation to the next. The board should be comprised of the firm's owners and executives from other companies with considerable business experience. Most next-generation family members, therefore, will not qualify to be board members. In some instances, if needed, the family business consultant might serve as a board member during the transition phase of the succession.

If some family members do not qualify to be on the board of directors, a family council can be established to provide a forum for all family members to meet regularly (say, quarterly) and discuss the relationship of the *family* to the business. The family council might concern itself with family estate and financial planning and the rules for entry of family members into the business. A council allows for educating family members about the business—its mission, goals, and progress; its challenges and financial affairs—and creates a sense of ownership among the family members. The council might decide on the formation of a family foundation to channel funds into carefully chosen philanthropic endeavors, and it can use the foundation as another vehicle to teach younger family members a sense of fiscal and communal responsibility.

PREPARING TO LET GO

The leader of a midsized family business consulted the lead author not long ago about the way his deteriorating relationship with his son and daughter was hurting the business. After a brief discussion, his anger over the situation erupted, and he shouted: "To heck with them, they can have the business, I'm going to Florida. Let them figure it out."

Succession handled in this escapist manner seldom works. The children are usually not prepared: There may be deep conflicts between them, and those in managerial positions are not ready to support them. Succession works best when the generation letting go has laid tracks for the next generation, has carefully selected the best candidates for leadership positions, and has deliberately managed a gradual exit.

One key factor in resolving these dilemmas in a smooth, efficacious fashion is the positive resolution of various developmental life-cycle tasks. Using the life-cycle view, one can understand the developmental context in which succession issues arise. Adapting Erikson's individual model (1950) to the family life cycle would posit that the older generation, the parent/CEO, is facing the integrity/despair crisis, while the next generation entering adulthood is facing the generativity/stagnation stage. Many an owner/parent will avoid despair by maintaining control of the business because the business is his or her life (Kaslow & Kaslow, 1992). Turning the business over is experienced as akin to a psychological and creative death. No longer having a defined place of status and stature may loom as a devastating loss. The parent's resistance to leaving frustrates the younger members, who then feel stagnant, stymied, and noncreative. How can this scenario be avoided?

Succession in a healthy family business must be planned for and envisioned by the parent/CEO. The parent/CEO must create and allow for two new stages of self-actualization—that of integrity for him- or herself and that of generativity for the younger members. The parent/CEO's needs for identity and belongingness must be transformed from being rooted in the family business to being rooted in the larger community or other activities from which he or she derives gratification and a continuing sense of high self-esteem. A key figure in facilitating this transition often is the CEO's spouse. Nowhere is the marriage more critical in relation to family business matters than in the domain of succession. Where there is a strong and loving marriage based on mutual acceptance and respect and the couple can together envision a fulfilling retirement future, the power transfer process can be accomplished with greater ease. Where there is emptiness or strife in the marriage, particularly with regard to the children, there are problems with succession. If the marriage is extremely dysfunctional, the consultant may refer the couple out for marital therapy, so that they can resolve their differences and hopefully prepare for a mutually fulfilling retirement life together.

Laying tracks for the next generation is important groundwork that must be in place several years before the reins are formally handed over. There are two components of this process: (a) cleaning up and strengthening the organization so that it effectively supports the next generation, and (b) resolving conflicts and grievances between members of the generation currently in power so that these conflicts and grievances are not passed on to their offspring. The family business consultant assists in both of these tasks.

Over the years, the founder may have hired nonfamily managers who have risen to key positions in the company. While most managers may be performing well on the job, there will usually be several who have ceased to perform at an appropriate level, given their job titles and expected performance. These managers are usually protected because of their longevity of service and their loyalty to the older generation and vice versa. Successful transition planning requires the determination of who will remain on the management team and in what capacity. In particular, non- or low performers need to be supported in setting goals and being responsible for following through or be helped to develop successful exit strategies. The family business consultant can assist in setting performance standards and criteria for these employees and/or supporting their win–win exits. The generation in power should not pass on the problem of nonperformers as an unwelcome inheritance for their successors.

Conflicts that are unresolved in the older generation will usually show up as grievances in the next generation. If two siblings are battling over stock ownership in the older generation, one can expect that there will be major ownership conflicts in the next generation. Or if these two siblings are in contention over leadership issues, there will be other major struggles over leadership in the future. Therefore, issues between members of the older generation must be resolved before handing over the reins of power. Resolution of these issues does not necessarily require agreement. It does, however, require that the emotionally charged issues be defused so that these dilemmas can be discussed rationally and, ultimately, compromises can be reached. The consultant conducts family meetings aimed at resolving these conflicts with the various warring factions.

PREPARING AND EVALUATING THE NEXT GENERATION

If members of the next generation were to make it on their own in the outside world, they would be forced to deal with the normal developmental challenges of growing up. They would need to look for a job and test their own marketability against others. They also would have to find a place to live and establish a lifestyle consistent with their earnings, gradually develop skills and make career choices, and put together a support structure of friends, colleagues, and mentors to help them.

Many next-generation family members who join the family business early in life never have to do any of these things. They therefore miss out on the learning gained by meeting these developmental challenges. It is important, therefore, that parents help their children learn to manage their careers effectively and that growth challenges be included as part of their development. A model of optimal career development for the young adult children of family business owners is useful in helping families accomplish these goals (Kirschner & Kirschner, 1986). This model contains several key points. Young adults need to go through a breaking away phase. Living away at college or away from home may facilitate this process. They also need to go through a period of adulthood in which they begin to make career decisions on their own. A period of, say, 3 to 5 years working for someone outside of the family firm is helpful in permitting this phase to unfold. This exposure to the real world, without family protection and surveillance, provides an opportunity to test the children's mettle and adds to their knowledge base, skills, and wisdom.

Young adults also need to be concerned about mastering a specific skill set. This may be a specific functional skill, such as selling, manufacturing, or accounting. They may also seek to obtain a graduate degree in law or some aspect of business, such as marketing, public relations, accounting, or finance. At some point, however, it is wise to bring the next-generation members into the business so that they can learn its inner workings and begin to take their places as managers.

Establishing a climate in which young family members can develop themselves effectively is a most critical variable in succession planning. If the children are not trained, capable, and experienced, it is a disservice to them and to the family to turn over the business to them. The older generation needs to be sure that the special knowledge that is so essential to the success of the company is passed on to the adult children who will work within the business. This knowledge may include customer relationships, contract negotiation skills, selling philosophies, product knowledge, team-building skills, organizational development and expansion, or developing new markets. The next generation needs to be frequently and intensively coached on these matters so that they can continue to create wealth for the family and contribute to the larger community. The consultant furthers this process by ensuring that appropriate mentors are in place for the successors and sometimes by encouraging them to develop a mission statement that encompasses the values and purposes of the firm as a cornerstone for all actions.

Another aspect in preparing the next generation is resolving the dysfunctional aspects of the siblings' relationships. Siblings in the family firm need to work together toward recognizing and embracing their differences in order to discover win–win solutions to existing and future problems. In addition, each sibling should be encouraged to find a position either inside or outside the firm in which he or she feels competent, creative, and validated.

To this end, the family business consultant meets with the siblings and encourages the strategic use of third parties, such as the family attorney or the consultant, to help them recognize their commonality of interests, examine their childhood patterns of interaction, and improve their conflict-resolution and problem-solving skills. The aims of such interventions are to transform the siblings' conflict into a springboard for psychological as well as economic progress in the family firm.

Responsibility for overcoming the debilitating consequences of pathological adult sibling rivalry in family firms ultimately rests with the siblings, not with the parents. For parents to pass on the mantle of familial leadership with grace and with blessings for the next generation is to create conditions in which the siblings can peacefully coexist and thrive. If the parents have failed to foster positive sibling relationships during their offspring's childhood, then it is not likely that they will be able to create them in the present. Consultants can assist the parents by minimizing their involvement and by working directly with the adult siblings and their spouses (see Kirschner, 1992, for a case example and a more complete description of intervening with siblings). The focus of the intervention is to legitimize the siblings' competitive strivings, to help them recognize how present-day conflict-handling skills may reflect ancient patterns of interaction that are no longer necessary or useful, and to free them to develop productive careers either inside or outside of the family firm.

SELECTING THE HEIR APPARENT

If the next generation is to take over senior management of the company, they will probably want to do so between the ages of 40 and 50. For most companies, by the time the next generation reaches this age, succession becomes a hot issue in the family and the need for implementing a succession plan becomes critical.

Some choices have to be made by the older generation that is still in power that are too difficult to be shouldered by the next generation. Among these are decisions around leadership and ownership. After members of the next generation have had an opportunity to demonstrate their capabilities, the founder or CEO, with input from the board of directors and top management, must, at the appropriate time, select and appoint a leader from the next generation. The children who are not selected must then be supported to develop career plans that will allow them to develop their own potential. The family business consultant can help determine who is the most competent family member (if any) to succeed as chief executive at this juncture in the business's history, and can help outplace those family members who will not stay in the business. The heir's personality and talents must fit well with both the demands of the position and the stage of the business's life cycle.

EXAMINING OTHER OPTIONS FOR THE DISPOSITION OF THE BUSINESS

If a suitable heir cannot be found within the family to assume the top position in the company, the family business consultant helps the CEO examine other options for the disposition of the business. These include appointing a nonfamily member as the new CEO, the sale of the business, or merger with another company. Consideration of all the options happens again each time that succession issues come to the fore, that is, in each successive generation.

DISTRIBUTION OF OWNERSHIP

Another task of the older generation is to take responsibility for the distribution of ownership. It is frequently not the best option to leave each child with an equal share of common stock in the company (Davis, 1991). For example, giving the heir apparent the lion's share of the voting stock not only supports his or her authority but also is often a more satisfactory solution for the founder's (and spouse's) estate tax plans. Announcement of who is to be the heir apparent should not be made until decisions have been finalized about ownership, career opportunities for the other children, and the future of nonfamily management personnel. Appropriate legal contracts should be drawn up and explained to all family members. The family's attorney, together with the family business consultant, often will facilitate these discussions, answering questions and mediating potential conflicts and disagreements between and among the generations.

IMPLEMENTING THE SUCCESSION PLAN

The implementation of a win–win succession usually takes several years and involves four key steps, each of which is facilitated by the family business consultant when necessary. These include developing performance criteria for the top positions, developing career plans for other key individuals, creating a plan for succession in ownership, and turning over the reins of power. Each step has profound emotional, legal, financial, and tax implications.

Step 1.   Developing Performance Criteria for the Heir Apparent

This involves determining the remaining hurdles that the heir needs to overcome before making it to the top. The succession plan needs to be very specific, with clear performance and assessment criteria, as delineated and evaluated by outside board members, the consultant, and the CEO.

Step 2.   Development of Possible Career Paths for Other Key Individuals

The career opportunities for the children not chosen need to be addressed. Some may choose to leave. Others may elect to work in senior management positions, perhaps as vice presidents of divisions, or managers of stores or branches, while others may not want to be in management and would prefer part-time roles. The purpose of this phase is to open up opportunities and also to clearly specify the limitations. If a sibling is not chosen to become chief executive officer, he or she should know what other top positions might be available in the future, such as chief financial officer or vice president of sales.

Similarly, senior nonfamily managers need to know what the opportunities are for their career advancement. The CEO may hold back from announcing that a son or daughter will eventually take over because of a fear of losing key nonfamily managers who may not want to work under someone much younger or less experienced than themselves. Most often, nonfamily managers already know what the situation is regarding the top spot. The family business consultant can often help resolve this unsettled situation by making the succession plan clear and helping the nonfamily managers to make more effective plans for their own futures, including accepting and supporting the new leadership.

Step 3.   *Creating a Plan for Succession in Ownership*

In most cases, for tax reasons, planning of succession in ownership begins when the next generation members are quite young. However, plans need to be crystallized as part of this effort so that a complete succession package covering management and ownership is developed.

The planning for succession in ownership may be a complex matter requiring a good understanding of tax laws and financial planning. In general, in transferring ownership the older generation is handing over inheritance rights in four areas: (a) the rights to a claim on existing equity, (b) the rights to future income, (c) the rights to future appreciation of equity interests, and (d) the rights to control of the corporate entity (Davis, 1991).

The parent may pass on these rights as a gift or may offer them for sale in a buy-sell agreement between the generations. There are a variety of financial instruments that embody these rights or combinations of them. These include common stock, income-generating preferred stock, voting preferred stock, and promissory notes. The planning of succession of ownership requires the matching of the assigning of these rights to (a) the needs of each member of the next generation, (b) the needs of the older generation, (c) the needs of the business, and (d) the demands of the Internal Revenue Service.

For example, the older generation may assign the common stock to those members of the next generation who will work in the business. A buy-sell agreement between members of the younger generation may be enforced to require those members who leave the company to sell their stock to those who remain in the business. Children who elect not to work in the business can receive preferred stock with buyout provisions (Davis, 1991).

Frequently, the older generation has need for a continuing income from the business, and this *must* be provided for and honored over time. Written buy-sell and consulting agreements may be signed in regard to obligations from one generation to the next, and payments may be adjusted to the cash-flow needs of the business and of the retired members of the firm. All too often, however, these agreements are violated, evoking resentment, disappointment, or financial hardship for the formerly proud and trusting parents. Thus, formal agreements should be drawn up by an attorney, duly signed, and notarized.

The development of an effective ownership succession plan often requires a significant investment in outside technical expertise. The family business consultant must work closely with the family's attorney and accountant to understand the legal and financial labyrinth that engulfs the family business. These meetings also must focus on the senior generation's estate plans. Thus, knowledge of family dynamics and processes is certainly necessary but not sufficient to function as an effective family business consultant.

Step 4.   Turning Over the Reins of Power

The last step in implementing the win–win succession plan is when the CEO turns over the reins of power to his or her successor. This step is often accompanied by a great deal of emotionality as well as celebration in the family. Some companies honor their retiring founder or CEO with a farewell party, while others prefer to signal the change with only a modest announcement and get-together. In situations where the family, consultant, and other advisors have been working together for a number of years to implement the plan, this transfer of authority signals the end of the current succession process and the beginning of the next era for the company and the family.

SUMMARY AND RECOMMENDATIONS

Succession in the family business is a complex and demanding process. It must be carefully planned over a period of years and be implemented rigorously and with discipline. This chapter discusses the phases of succession planning that should be considered and the various roles of the family business consultant. The most difficult part of succession is dealing with the emotional issues that arise and become a roadblock to systematic judicious planning and implementation. The fears of letting go are very real and intense. The fears of the next-generation members about running the business are equally real and intense, despite their eagerness to ascend to the helm. Both generations need to acknowledge these fears for what they are and, if necessary, get outside support in dealing with them.

Succession planning is one of the most difficult management problems that is confronted in the family firm and requires great skill, wisdom, and maturity to implement effectively. A well-trained and knowledgeable family business consultant can be an invaluable asset at this critical time in the life of the family business and of the extended family outside of the business realm, as the decisions and actions in either segment have an enormous impact on the other. He or she can deal with the schisms, hostilities, and factions in either world, and thus influence all concerned parties, their partners, and their children for decades to come.

REFERENCES

Alcorn, P. (1982). *Success and survival in the family-owned business.* New York: McGraw-Hill.

Barnes, L. B. (1988). Incongruent hierarchies: Daughters and younger sons as company CEOs. *Family Business Review, 1,* 9–21.

Beckhard, R., & Dyer, W. (1983). Managing continuity in the family-owned business. *Organizational Dynamics, 12,* 5–12.

Borwick, I. (1986). The family therapist as business consultant. In L. C. Wynne, S. McDaniel, & T. Weber (Eds.), *Systems consultation: A new perspective for family therapy* (pp. 423–440). New York: Guilford Press.

Bowen, M. (1978). *Family therapy in clinical practice.* New York: Jason Aronson.

Carroll, R. (1988). Siblings and the family business. In M. D. Kahn and K. G. Lewis (Eds.), *Siblings in therapy: Life span and clinical issues* (pp. 379–398). New York: W. W. Norton.

Corchado, A. (1990, August 10). Family business: Patriarch of Farah Inc. loses his company—And his children too. *Wall Street Journal,* p. 1.

Davis, P. (1991, March). *Passing the baton.* Paper presented at the Wharton Family Business Network, University of Pennsylvania, Philadelphia.

Davis, P., & Stern, D. (1980). Adaptation, survival, and growth of the family business: An integrated systems perspective. *Human Relations, 34,* 207–224.

Dreux, D. R., & Goodman, J. M. (1997). *Business succession planning and beyond.* Chicago: American Bar Association.

Drucker, P. F. (1994, August 19). How to save the family business. *Wall Street Journal,* p. 1.

Erikson, E. (1950). *Childhood and society.* New York: W. W. Norton.

Euripides. (1972). *Orestes and other plays.* Baltimore: Penguin Books.

Kahn, M. D. (1988). Intense sibling relationships: A self-psychological view. In M. D. Kahn and K. G. Lewis (Eds.), *Siblings in therapy: Life span and clinical issues* (pp. 3–24). New York: W. W. Norton.

Kaslow, F. W. (1993). The lore and lure of family business. *American Journal of Family Therapy, 21,* 3–16.

Kaslow, F. W., & Kaslow, S. (1992). The family that works together: Special problems of family businesses. In S. Zedeck (Ed.), *Work, families and organizations* (pp. 312–361). San Francisco: Jossey-Bass.

Kirschner, D. A., & Kirschner, S. (1986). *Comprehensive family therapy.* New York: Brunner/ Mazel.

Kirschner, S. (1992). The myth of the sacrifice of the daughter: Implications for family-owned business. *American Journal of Family Therapy, 20,* 13–24.

Kirschner, S., & Kirschner, D. A. (1991). The two faces of change: Progression and regression. In R. C. Curtis & G. Stricker (Eds.), *How people change* (pp. 117–127). New York: Plenum Press.

Rosenblatt, P., Demik, L., Anderson, R., & Johnson, P. (1985). *The family in business.* San Francisco: Jossey-Bass.

Schein, E. (1983). The role of the founder in creating organizational culture. *Organization Dynamics, 12,* 13–38.

Schein, E. (1990). Organizational culture. *American Psychologist, 45,* 109–119.

Watson, T. J. (1991). *Father, son & co.: My life at IBM and beyond.* New York: Bantam Books.

CHAPTER 17

Children Who Sue Parents

A Legal Route for Family Destruction?

FLORENCE W. KASLOW

Thou shalt honor they father and mother.
—THE TEN COMMANDMENTS

Do CHILDREN really sue parents? And if so, why, and under what circumstances? These are perplexing and distressing questions because the concept of children suing parents runs counter to some very deep rooted and treasured beliefs— notably, that parents invariably want what is best for their children and act accordingly. If this assumption were in fact true, children would have no reason to challenge their parents by entering into a legal battle. How can children honor parents, as they are admonished to do in such revered moral documents as the Ten Commandments, whom they believe have acted in ways that are abusive, negligent, and otherwise reprehensible? This raises a query central to deliberations on morality on the eve of the millennium, as has also been true in preceding centuries and no doubt will be for centuries to come; that is, is the decalogue to be construed as absolute and infallible, or are there extenuating circumstances that lend credibility to positing a more relativistic than absolute standard? Perhaps this chapter can shed some light on this extremely complex subject.

In the preceding three decades, the legal doctrines of intraspousal and interfamily immunity have been weakened or stricken in many states. Spouses are now permitted to testify against one another, and children are sometimes, under law, permitted to sue parents. This is a cutting-edge arena of grave concern, as intrafamily lawsuits intensify existing strife and contribute to the irreparability of cutoffs in families (Bowen, 1988; Kerr & Bowen, 1988), a relational condition many family clinicians seek to prevent or reverse.

This chapter initially presents a brief history of the legal origins of intrafamilial lawsuits. Next, it elaborates eight extant categories of child-against-parent lawsuits. What becomes apparent is that when children of any age resort to suing parents, the conflicts and schisms in the family are severe and deep-seated, and the lawsuit often makes the gulf permanent.

LEGAL PRECURSORS: CHILDREN AS PROPERTY

Historically, children could not and did not sue their parents; children were considered chattel, the possession of their fathers. This philosophy is traceable to ancient Roman times, when a father was granted almost absolute authority over his children under the doctrine of *patria potestas* (*Bill of Rights in Action*, 1973, p. 9). Until the current century, in the United States as in almost every other civilization, children were deemed to be valuable property: They could work on farms and in shops, and their earnings belonged to their fathers. Children were expected to obey their elders and be subservient; they were not to question or challenge their parents. To do so was to incur great wrath and, often, corporal punishment. There are still areas of the globe, such as some parts of the Arab world, in which this is the prevailing philosophy and such practices still occur; otherwise documents such as those on the rights of children promulgated by the United Nations would not have been necessary. Even in the Western world, remnants of this attitude linger in certain ethnic groups that endow the parents, particularly the father, with great power and control as the indisputable head of the household.

In the United States, children had few, if any, rights under law in the first half of the 20th century. They were still considered property, as illustrated in the case of *Rule v. Geddes* (1904). In this case, when the teenage daughter requested a legal hearing before her father could send her away to reform school, the court opined that *she had no right to ask for a hearing because a child had no right to control her own actions or to select her own course of life, and therefore, had no legal right to be heard at the proceedings.*

The Ninth Amendment of the U.S. Constitution specifically recognizes basic personal rights, which are generally extended to include a family's right to privacy and to protection from intrusion by any agent of the state. This is coupled with the fact that, under law, parents traditionally have been entitled to discipline their children for misbehavior and disobedience, including by the utilization of corporal punishment. Until recently this was interpreted as sanctioning the use of physical action, such as spanking and other behaviors now considered to be child abuse by many mental health professionals, physicians, and legislators (Ceci & Hembrooke, 1998). Also, physical child abuse, molestation, and incest were tolerated in the past, because many adults believed they could do whatever they wanted with their property, and children were considered to be property (see Buchanan, 1996, and Green, 1988, on cycles of child maltreatment for excellent contemporary overviews on the child sexual abuse literature). Except under dire circumstances, the right to privacy (see *Katz v. United States*, 1967) is guaranteed to everyone in our democratic society. The complicated issue is where one draws the line between what constitutes an appropriate and acceptable type of punishment, and how severe it should be when the safety and well-being of a child may be at stake, before the state can and should intrude on the privacy and sanctity of the family to protect children from harsh and cruel punishment, as well as from other forms of physical and sexual abuse.

Another longstanding assumption that undergirds the legal preference for non-interference previously mentioned is that parents act in the best interest of their children. This ideal is still frequently articulated, despite statistics that show spiraling amounts of child abuse and incest—clearly not parental behaviors motivated by the best interest of the child (MacFarlane, Waterman, Conerly, Damon, Surfee & Long, 1986; Oates, 1986; Shetky & Green, 1988).

An additional factor is that the state traditionally has been loath to act as if it can determine, better than the parents can, what is best for a particular child. In reality, few lawyers or judges are trained in child or developmental psychology, and therefore they are not equipped to make such an evaluation by objective means. Loving, rational parents are clearly the best judges of this. However, angry, violent, unloving, or dysfunctional parents are *not*. They do what the impulse of the moment spurs them to do, provoking great animosity in the child, which may be expressed later in a variety of ways, including a lawsuit.

THE CONTEMPORARY LEGAL MILIEU: RESPONSIBILITIES AND RIGHTS

Parents still have primary rights regarding their children, along with the primary responsibility to provide for them. This responsibility includes, but is not limited to, providing the basic essentials of food, clothing, shelter, medical care, an education, and a wholesome environment. The amount or level of support is not clearly established nor regulated; rather broad and vague phrases like "minimum standard of living" and "necessities of life" abound (Kaslow, 1990, p. 152).

Beyond the basics, all parents are free to determine what they want to make available to their children; this is perceived as a personal matter. Once a child reaches his or her legal majority, parents do not have a continuing legal responsibility to provide for him or her financially, although many voluntarily choose to do so. A grown child cannot legally compel a reluctant, disgruntled, or poor parent to pay for a college education or for debts that he or she has incurred after reaching the age of 18. Nor are affluent parents obligated to support or supplement the income of their children, once they reach the age of legal majority or become emancipated minors.

In postdivorce families, if a petition is filed in court by one parent, usually the primary residential (custodial) parent (see, for example, Florida Dissolution of Marriage Act, 1987) against the other, wealthier parent for an increase in child support, the court will hear the petition based on the idea that children should be maintained at a standard of living as close to the predivorce standard as possible. This principle also applies only until the child reaches the age of legal majority, for it is then that parental financial responsibility ceases to exist, unless otherwise specified in an enforceable provision of a divorce decree.

In the post–World War II years, a more permissive psychosocial context regarding children's behavior has evolved. There is a widespread belief that children should be encouraged to express their needs, feelings, and thoughts, and to discuss their sometimes terrible experiences in the family. Nevertheless, parents have continued to be granted almost all rights regarding their children. This is considered necessary for promoting a healthy family system in which the parents are the "architects and executives" in charge (Minuchin, 1974). Usually, unless charges are filed and a parent is proven to be "unfit," which is rather difficult to do, parents are entitled to custody of their offspring and are given the power to make decisions that shape their child's environment and impact significantly upon his or her well-being. Under law and through tradition, parents have the right to have their children live with them, to have the pleasure of their company, to expect them to help with household tasks, and to contribute in other ways to the overall functioning of the family. Parents are entitled to the wages that minor children earn. If a child was born out of wedlock and lives with his or her mother, she, not the father, has the entitlements specified here. Because parents are expected by society to regulate their children's behavior, as previously indicated, until recently they were permitted to use corporal punishment to discipline their children for misbehavior (*Bill of Rights in Action*, 1973, p. 10).

The point at which physical punishment becomes child abuse has been defined by law in an increasing number of states. Generally, malicious intent or willfully hurting or permanently injuring a child must be proven before a parent is held in violation of child abuse or assault and battery laws. States traditionally have been reluctant to intervene in domestic relations matters; rather, the idea that "A man's home is his castle" has served to exclude family behavior from the realm of public scrutiny. The family is regarded as having some boundaries that separate it from the external world; yet, when the well-being of a child is at stake, there are times when these dividing lines should become permeable. In fact, because the state recognizes that not all parents are committed to fostering the well-being of their children, it can intervene under the doctrine of *parens patriae* in situations in which parents are allegedly not fulfilling their responsibilities, but instead are perceived as being negligent or abusive, just as the state can in child custody disputes between two parents, between parents and other concerned relatives, or between parent and state (Kaslow, 1990, p. 5).

When family disputes come before the court, the trier of fact has to balance two conflicting doctrines: (a) the family's right to privacy, and (b) the state's right to intervene to protect the interests of the child (*Bill of Rights in Action*, 1973, p. 9). In a multicultural and multiracial society such as ours, there are diverse interpretations of what constitutes the best interests of the child. So, too, attitudes and values about discipline utilized in child rearing and about the point at which punishment is deemed to be emotionally or physically abusive and a violation of the child's well-being and safety also vary across a wide spectrum.

Because almost all states have enacted, and are enforcing, child abuse reporting statutes, the number of cases alleged and investigated has climbed upward. More children are being asked to testify in court regarding allegations of abuse and neglect. First, the child must be deemed competent to be a witness—a complex process (Melton, 1981). The child should be treated respectfully and should not be further traumatized by the deposition or the court appearance (Shetky & Green, 1988). Child witnesses should be helped to understand the seriousness of the courtroom procedures and the potential impact of their testimony. They should not be encouraged to lie to protect someone or to help anyone retaliate against someone else; to be credible witnesses, they must be able to comprehend the "moral obligation to tell the truth" (Melton, 1981, p. 75). Although in such cases the child is not suing his or her parent(s), he or she may be an important witness against them. Such legal proceedings do not contribute to healing a family's tensions any more than does the denial of, and secrecy about, abuse. This poses a significant double-bind dilemma (Watzlawick, 1963). If children do not testify, they continue to harbor the repressed knowledge of the repugnant behavior and are plagued by the emotional sequelae of shame, and perhaps guilt, from presumed collusion; if they are involved in pressing charges and testifying, at some level they perceive themselves (and others may perceive them) as committing a sin of disloyalty (Boszormenyi-Nagy & Spark, 1973/1984), and perhaps as contributing to having a parent sent to prison or placed on probation—heaping additional embarrassment on the already troubled family. This is a destructive lose–lose scenario, whichever way the drama unfolds. When expert witnesses, such as psychologists, are brought in to testify in such murky cases, the terrain is treacherous, and the evidence controversial (Ceci & Hembrooke, 1998).

In the 1990s there has been much more discussion in law journals regarding the efficacy of viewing children's rights as separate from parental rights. For example, Federle (1995) criticizes current rights theories for their inability to protect children. She proposes that we should think more about children's rights in terms of children's current powerlessness. She promulgates an *empowerment rights perspective* that would transfer rights to the disempowered, specifically youngsters. Her article applies this perspective to divorce, custody, and child welfare proceedings to exemplify how such a perspective would better protect children's interests and provide them with more meaningful entrée for participation in legal processes.

Similarly, Minow (1995) examines the history of children's rights and where they are likely to be headed. She believes the promises of the 1960s have remained virtually unfulfilled, and traces the history of the children's rights movement and the difficulties it has encountered. She endorses the position that those concerned about children should challenge the imposition of adult rights and agendas, and instead focus on children's needs and society's (including parents') responsibilities to them.

In a third article on a related topic, which also appeared in the middle of the 1990s, Wu (1996), an attorney who represents children in dependency cases, posits that the general duties of the lawyer should be modified when the client is a minor. He concludes that children need their own advocates and that the attorney should defer to a child client's wishes. Although I would add that the child must be cognitively and emotionally able to express his or her wishes and understand the consequences of being granted what he or she is requesting, being entitled to separate representation by a sensitive and competent attorney acting as a child advocate would mark a major advance in the pro–children's rights movement. It might also lead to a dramatic increase in the number of intrafamily lawsuits, if attorneys were willing to handle these cases on a pro bono or contingency fee arrangement.

Viewed together, these three articles reflect the slowly changing sociocultural and legal climate regarding the distinctiveness of children's rights and present a backdrop for the issues and cases that are discussed in the following section.

FAMILY DYNAMICS, STRUCTURE, AND FUNCTIONING

In healthy, optimally functional families (Kaslow, 1981; Lewis, Beavers, Gossett, & Phillips, 1976; Olson, 1996; Walsh, 1982) there are clear and definite boundaries between members of the several generations. Parents, as a couple, create a new family unit; they become its architects and serve as its leaders in carrying out its functions (Minuchin, 1974), which include having and rearing children. This overall role category assumes a commitment to fulfilling all parental responsibilities to provide the material necessities of life, such as food, clothing, and shelter, as well as the emotional necessities of love, affection, protection, guidance and limit setting, a growth-enhancing environment, "and a framework for meaning and value. To these, many would add a comprehensive secular and religious education" (Kaslow, 1990, p. 154).

Healthy couples undertake this kind of parenting with a tremendous sense of dedication and loyalty to their children. They impart to them age-appropriate ways of communicating, a knowledge of tasks to be mastered and executed, problem-solving skills, ways to cope with life's exigencies, and encouragement to share in shaping their reality and in making decisions. Such parents respect their children's abilities and rights, their increasing need for individuality and autonomy, and their wish to be a vital and contributing member of the family.

Children who are raised by parents who are emotionally and intellectually healthy, affectionate, attentive, and who have a sense of the absurdity of life are fortunate (Keith & Whitaker, 1978). Usually, in return, they love and respect their parents and realize that their own desires and needs are heard and dealt with fairly by the significant adults in their lives. They feel and demonstrate a reciprocal loyalty (Boszormenyi-Nagy & Spark, 1973/1984).

When inevitable parent–child tensions occur in optimally functioning families, family members discuss the problems and feelings surrounding the issue at hand (Kaslow, 1981). Each person has an opportunity to state their ideas and desires; the others listen attentively and then answer. They ponder numerous alternative solutions, and consider what the best resolution of the conflict for all involved is likely to be. If, however, the discussion and problem-solving efforts result in an impasse, family rules clearly specify that the final decision-making authority rests with the parents. And children, even older adolescents, are apt to feel secure and safe in the knowledge that their views have been listened to and that their parents are capable of acting wisely to protect them from actions that would be detrimental to their own well-being.

By contrast, adults who abdicate this executive authority to their children are frequently only nominally at the rudder of a dysfunctional family unit. Children who garner too much power over their own lives too early in their own developmental process often become parentified children or dictatorial despots. The invisible but essential generational boundary line is crossed, and the children are prematurely given the privilege of being included in the parental/adult subsystem. When this happens, children are robbed of their childhood and adolescent roles—to play, to learn, to experiment within a safe range, and to love in accordance with their own developmental level. Likewise, it is deleterious to the long-term functioning of the family when the grandparent generation (except on a short-term or emergency basis) acts in loco parentis, perpetuating the fiction that they (or he or she) are the parents, pushing the real biological or adoptive parents to the sidelines, or to older sibling status. (For example, this may happen when the mother is an unwed teenager and her mother takes on the main parental role and responsibilities.) When this occurs, the birth parents are not accorded adult status and the grandparents may usurp or sabotage the parents' decision-making role with their own children.

SEEDS OF DISCONTENT

Chaotic, disengaged, enmeshed, and other dysfunctional families (Beavers, 1977; Kaslow, 1981) are often characterized by intense warfare and a blurring of generational boundaries; for example, a father may become overly enmeshed with his daughter, particularly if he has primary custody after divorce, and ultimately may establish a pathological codependency or long-term symbiotic relationship with her. Or, a needy, immature, or selfish parent may violate the taboo against incest and sexually molest his or her child. Parents who are angry at everyone in general, and at those they live with specifically (because they feel undervalued or exploited), and who have poor impulse control, may take their rage and despair out on their children, who then become victims of their parents' aggression and fury. Sometimes the emotional, physical, or sexual damage inflicted on children when they are very young, during adolescence or young adulthood, is quite subtle; other times it is very overt. After years of being tormented and having no recourse but to take it or run away and live on the streets if they do not yet have jobs, the children may crave some form of retribution, or a way to retaliate.

SEEKING LEGAL REDRESS

Whatever the area of conflict, children over age 18 who cannot reach an acceptable and viable resolution of the perceived wrongs perpetrated by their parents through a family effort at problem solving increasingly turn elsewhere. They see themselves as victims entitled to compensation. Prior to the past few decades, when the extended family form was pervasive, a child might have asked a respected relative, beloved friend, or clergyperson to intervene. Or parents and child might have had a major quarrel that resulted in a long-term family schism (Kaslow, 1990, p. 155) and emotional distancing. Some parents maintained control by disinheriting the rebellious or disrespectful child; some resorted to disowning the child; or the child might have moved far away and severed all contact, in effect disowning the parents. This sometimes happened when a young adult child married outside of the family's ethnic, racial, or religious group and the choice was considered totally untenable to the parents.

Yet throughout history, many intergenerational family wars have been fought inside the family around money, power, and control issues. But children did not sue parents; it would have been unthinkable until recently. Today, given so many changes in the nature of families and of society, more and more self-directing young people, or those with friends who are lawyers who urge them to sue, are turning outside of the family and its personal extended network when disputes arise that seem impossible to resolve and are seeking legal solutions from an impartial and uninvolved judicial system. It is my belief that if and when someone chooses to pursue legal remedies to family conflicts, the family relational system is already fraught with great animosity and disequilibrium, and that the legal battle exacerbates rather than diminishes the schism and pathology, often to the point of no return—it becomes irreparable, regardless of the decision rendered and the so-called justice meted out.

TYPOLOGY OF LAWSUITS

Several illustrative case examples follow. Three of the cases were reported by young adult children of the families involved, who appeared on Phil Donahue's television show in March 1988, a show entitled "Children Who Sue Parents," on which I was the psychological consultant.[1] Cases 1 and 5 had been tried previously on Judge Wapner's television show. Case 2 had not yet gone to trial; I was especially fascinated by this one as it ties in with my ongoing clinical involvement in understanding the dynamics of those engaged in family businesses and the type of interventions utilized to resolve conflicts that arise in this relationship context. Cases 4 and 5 are drawn from clinical cases shared with me by a plaintiff involved in each case.

This section is included in an effort to expand clinicians' knowledge of this recently increasing phenomenon and to provide information that may influence the shaping of future relevant legislation.

The types of cases of children suing parents[2] that I have been able to locate can be organized into the following eight categories:

I.   Disputes over property
II.   Family business controversies
III.   Disagreements over inheritances
IV.   Disputes over child support
V.   Assault and battery cases: Seeking damages for being a child abuse or incest victim
VI.   Kidnapping and deprogramming from cults
VII.   Children suing to divorce their parents
VIII. Injuries sustained for which parents are covered by insurance (for a car or other accident)

CATEGORY I.   DISPUTES OVER PROPERTY

In the first case presented on the Donahue show, deep animosities bubbled over in response to what others might consider a minor dispute.

Case 1.   An Unreturned Possession

Sometimes a young adult child temporarily leaves an item in the home of a parent while going off to live elsewhere. Miss J went back to reclaim a stereo set that she had left with her mother several years earlier. Her mother refused to return it. The daughter stated that her mother believed that long-term possession of the stereo entitled her to keep it. Enraged, the daughter took the issue to small claims court, hoping to humiliate and punish her mother, as well as get the stereo back. She was shocked and infuriated when the judge ruled in favor of her mother.

Several years later, the daughter still harbored much antagonism toward her mother for this "theft," and the chasm between them had expanded. The daughter's attachment to her father, long divorced from her mother, had grown stronger during the preceding years, in opposition to their common enemy, the mother. The judge served as the "trier of fact," not as a healer of the family duel.

A cursory assessment suggested that the lawsuit represented the culmination of a long-standing acrimonious mother–daughter dyadic interplay. In my on-the-spot analysis of this brief case vignette, it seemed that Miss J, like many others who perceive themselves to be victims, saw her mother as the perpetrator solely responsible for her misery and their relational strife. She saw herself as an innocent victim, not a contributor to a two-way negative interaction.

The systems thinking that permeates family therapy is not usually adapted as germane to law. Instead, in law, Aristotelian logic dominates. Therefore, in the resolution of a dispute, one party is pronounced innocent while the other is adjudicated guilty. The innocent party is held to be the victor and receives either the item in contention (in this case, the stereo) or some form of compensation. It is this extreme difference between the systemic thinking of family clinicians and the linear thinking of legal professionals that is a hallmark of legal arguments and judicial opinions that makes it so hard for therapists to help some patients comprehend and grapple with the legal system and the principles on which it is predicated. Those who turn for succor to the courts want to blame others for their problems and seek retribution and vindication, just as Miss J did. They probably would devalue systemic thinking and find it alien or ego-dystonic, just as legal philosophy does.

CATEGORY II.   FAMILY BUSINESS CONTROVERSIES

Case 2 involved an extremely successful family business founded, owned, and operated by the patriarch father.

Case 2.   It Belongs to Me

According to the plaintiff and his lawyer, the plaintiff's brother functioned in much the same way that his conservative father did, and those two worked well together. Mr. X, the person in the center of the storm, had a much more flamboyant lifestyle and wanted to do things his own way. Originally his father had underwritten a venture for him by providing the financial means to launch a subsidiary corporation while still retaining an ownership interest in the subsidiary. Mr. X, a good-looking, debonair man, probably in his early 40s, posited that he had piloted "his" business into a thriving and lucrative operation.

Mr. X decided he wanted a divorce, an action that his father strongly disapproved. The controlling father supported his daughter-in-law's position against his son's and thought she should have primary custody of the children, if his son pursued the divorce. The father threatened to take the business away from his son, and proceeded to do so when Mr. X did not settle down and agree to stay married. Outraged at these power machinations, Mr. X sued his father for both loss of income and loss of his business. Because they all lived in California, a community property state with regard to the division of assets in a divorce, and given that the ante at stake involved millions of dollars, Mr. X engaged the services of a high-profile, high-priced attorney. A horrendous legal battle ensued. I became aware of this case when Mr. X, his attorney, and I were all participants on the aforementioned Donahue show.

Several questions from me to Mr. X brought out the following facts: From the time he was very young, he had experienced a great deal of conflict with his parents. They viewed him as a troubled child. He had been taken to see therapists throughout his childhood and adolescence—ostensibly to help him become less recalcitrant and more acquiescent. He had considered himself assertive and determined to do things his own way; his parents regarded him as oppositional and unappreciative (Kaslow, 1990, p. 157–158).

In response to my query about whether the family had considered mediating the disputed business issues, we were informed that they had not. Mr. X said that he did not think any kind of mediation would have been successful. He was not interested in compromise; he wanted a complete victory. He also seemed very dependent on his attorney, who was reputed to enjoy major battles—that is, he was perceived as a gladiator lawyer.

My preliminary diagnostic impression, albeit based on scant data, was that, like his attorney, he relished the limelight and the notoriety. He seemed to thrive on the fray. In my opinion, in seeking to satisfy his narcissistic needs and desire for control, he spoke of being eager to triumph over his parents, and implied that he wanted to hurt and humiliate them publicly. He seemed to believe that if he won the court battle, he finally would emerge victorious over his perceived archenemy, his father.

His attorney stated that he thought his client had a strong case and he was encouraging him to pursue the matter in court. Mr. X held that, despite the fact that his father's money had enabled him to begin the business, he was the one who had made it run successfully; therefore, it belonged to him; thus, he could not be fired. Significantly, Mr. X did not seem to care "that the lawsuit was causing him further estrangement from his family; family closeness had apparently long eluded him and was not an outcome he consciously valued." At this point, he indicated that what he wanted was twofold (Kaslow, 1990, p. 157):

1. Financial—an enormous settlement for damages
2. Emotional—the ego gratification of being declared the winner

(I do not know what happened when this case went to court; it was not possible to ask Mr. X or his attorney to keep me apprised.)

Subsequently, two clients that I have seen in my private therapy practice in the last 5 years were struggling with similar issues surrounding lawsuits against parents emanating from disputes within and about the family business. A short summation of these should serve to further illuminate the deleterious events preceding and subsequent to taking legal action against one's parents or in-laws in a family business matter. I believe these three cases are representative of the kinds of cases brought to court in this category.

Case 3.   How Could You Do This to Us?

In 1994, Mrs. Janine Le Bec began therapy, as she was very distressed about her deteriorating relationship with her parents. Like them, she and her husband had a home in Connecticut and one in the Palm Beach area. They all belonged to the same country clubs and churches; both couples lived in small communities and socialized in the same circles. At the time she entered therapy, her parents were ignoring her whenever they saw each other in the community, and this hurt her enormously. The story that unfolded was about her husband, Pierre. He had worked in her parents' business for many years. Janine and Pierre both believed he had been treated unfairly—in fact, they believed that they had been robbed of their share of the business through creative accounting procedures, and had not received their share of the proceeds when the business was sold. When reasoning and attempts at negotiation failed, they had filed suit against her parents. The suit was still wending its way through the legal mill when she first contacted me.

They had all been unable to separate personal family matters from the contentious feud over the family business (Kaslow & Kaslow, 1992). Her parents treated them with icy disdain whenever they saw them. She also had become aware that she had been cut out of any inheritance in both of her parents' wills. What made the personal situation even more distasteful was that Janine had two teenagers who had been close to their maternal grandparents. The grandparents continued to call the house; if Janine or Pierre answered, they immediately asked to talk with one of the children. They would invite their grandson and granddaughter to go out with them to dinner or to play golf. Initially Janine and Pierre had permitted this to continue, as they did not wish to disrupt this part of the intrafamilial relationship. Also, the grandparents previously had verbally promised to help pay for the children's college education, and because they were counting on this assistance so the children could attend Ivy League universities, they did not wish to alienate her parents further. Despite the almost intolerable myriad tensions then extant in the relationship, they did not back out of the suit because they thought that they were right, that they had been caused undue suffering, and that they deserved to collect for damages caused. In therapy it was agreed that they should continue to allow their children to maintain contact with her parents, as it seemed still to be mutually beneficial and outside the realm of the family business dispute.

The final blow that led to severing of the grandparent–grandchild ties came when on several occasions the grandparents tried to tell the two teenagers what horrible parents they had and to turn them against Janine and Pierre. They came home confused and distraught, particularly because their parents had tried to shield them from the details. Janine and Pierre could not tolerate what her parents were trying to do, and went along with the children's request not to have to visit any more. At that point Janine and Pierre came to terms with the loss of the large annual tax-free cash gifts the children had traditionally received from her parents and the fact that they would renege on the payment of college tuition. Janine worked on her sadness about the multiple losses—particularly the loss of parents she had been close to and had relied on. All came to understand that strong actions taken generate strong reverberations, and that by asserting their rights in the legal arena and making the family feud public, they had challenged her father's powerful grip on everyone in the family. He retaliated by disowning and disinheriting his children and grandchildren.

Janine finally decided to give up her maiden name and take on her husband's name, signifying in this case a new and symbolic, fuller commitment to her husband and family of creation. Pierre went into his own business and liked being accountable only to himself. He and Janine were encouraged to communicate more openly with their daughter and son about what was transpiring in ways that were age appropriate, so they could grasp the situation and understand why their grandparents would no longer be part of their lives.

This family was ripped asunder when someone challenged the patriarch's authoritarianism in the family business and resorted to legal action to redress their grievances. Now, 5 years after the suit was filed and some sizeable damages were awarded to Janine and Pierre by the judge, the two parts of the family remain estranged. The lawsuit took them to the point of no return.

Case 4.   I'll See You in Court

Larry and Jill came to my office for marital therapy. Despite the fact that they lived in an affluent area and their children attended a tony private day school, both were obese and slovenly, he much more so than she. Everything about him seemed out of control. Jill resented that he was very loyal to his mother and a chronically ill brother. After almost 20 years of marriage, she still could not understand that when his parents divorced, he literally had been assigned the role of "man in the house," including protecting and supporting his mother and brother. He had stayed in his father's then-lucrative import-export business, and he continued to be pulled between his parents. He saw his father engage in many illicit activities, and deplored it. As a shareholder and stakeholder he tried to protest and was told, "I got rid of your mother and I can get rid of you." Finally, in sheer desperation Larry decided that because he could not change the way the business was operated, he had to resign, and asked his father to buy him out. His father laughed in his face and dismissed him. Infuriated, Larry sued his father in what sounded like a prolonged and nasty battle. Larry still harbored enormous resentment, as he had never resolved his issues about his father's "crooked and unfair behaviors," nor about the terribly unnerving lawsuit. In the ensuing 20 years he had never trusted an older male business associate or partner, always being afraid he would be shafted.

Conversely, Jill came from a close-knit family that couldn't understand this type of family contention and its long-term continuing repercussions. They insisted that Larry's father be invited to the wedding and Larry's mother concurred that it was the right thing to do, as she had come to terms with the divorce and believed that the myth of a good family should be promulgated to make Larry seem more desirable. He had resented all the pressure, but buckled under to it. For him the wedding was a fiasco of pretense that started the marriage off on a poor track; he fought against being dominated by Jill and her family. However, he became quite attached to Jill's father for a number of years, and then once again became disillusioned when his father-in-law invited him to become involved in a shady business venture. When he told Jill what was occurring, she had retorted, "My father would not do such a thing; you are trying to belittle him so he looks as bad as your father." Once again Larry felt misunderstood (he had probably assessed the situation accurately) and unappreciated, and this had driven another wedge between him and Jill.

At the time that they came for therapy he was again involved in a business-related lawsuit, this time against a man who manufactured a product he used in his stores, as he believed he had misrepresented what it could do and that it was defective. Larry was totally preoccupied by this financially and emotionally, as if replaying the drama with his father from 25 years earlier. He was also considering suing Jill's sister over some business dealings in which he felt he had been cheated. Jill was livid, as she did not want to have to choose between her husband and her family of origin, and implored him not to do this (Kaslow, 1995). He was devastated, feeling that she was siding with them against him.

Unfortunately, Larry had created a legacy for himself of resorting to legal action as a way to resolve disputes, and seemed to conceptualize family relationships as competitive win–lose struggles. He was obsessed with being triumphant and having a judge dispense justice in his favor to show everyone he was right. No matter what it took, this seemed the only way he had been able to bolster a poor self-image and justify his existence. The cost in anguish, cutoffs from family members, internal tension, and marital strife had not been sufficient to offset whatever he viewed as the benefits that could be derived from an intrafamily lawsuit.

One therapeutic intervention did succeed in having him reconsider the action against Jill's sister and the possibility of contemplating alternative dispute-resolution strategies. He dearly loved his children and when I talked about the model (of suing) he was setting, several times over, and the likelihood that they might replicate it in the future, he was horrified. He saw his son as very like him in many ways—curious, defiant, independent, and strong-willed. He resonated to the possibility that "if my son comes into my business, history could well repeat itself." At this point in time, he is willing to try (voluntarily) mediation of the dispute with his sister-in-law instead, and has begun to comprehend why his behavior has been so repugnant to Jill. She, in turn, is trying to be more supportive and affectionate. Both are attempting to get their lives in shape, which includes losing weight and being less preoccupied with lawsuits. Larry still has a long way to go, as being combative seemed so necessary for his early survival. The damage of rejection lingers on, along with the desire for retribution. Like Mr. X, he had considered himself assertive and determined to do it his own way; his parents regarded him as oppositional and unappreciative (Kaslow, 1990, p. 157–158). Throughout his life, he had felt unloved and undervalued; this is slowly changing in therapy.

Category III.   Disagreements over Inheritances

Case 5 is the third case from the Donahue show.

Case 5.   I Want "My" Inheritance

A young woman stated that she had been due an inheritance of $800 on her 18th birthday. When she went to her father to get it, he told her that he had needed the money and so had spent it; now he was financially unable to replace it. Furious and hurt, and believing that her rights had been insensitively trampled upon, she sought restitution through the legal system. She did not think her father was honorable enough to ever give her what was owed to her on his own.

The judge ordered the man to pay his daughter; thus, "justice" was done. However, her father, stepmother, and stepsiblings all felt betrayed and embarrassed, especially because the unhappy daughter had made the family fight public on television (originally on Judge Wapner's program). As often happens, they saw the girl's reaction and not the father's provocative action as the cause of the problem.

She was estranged from the family subsequent to this suit, and came to rue the action she had taken. She indicated that she had felt isolated and alone, cut off from her family of origin and floating without any anchor. Although she continued to think that what her father had done was wrong, in retrospect she decided that "winning" and being awarded the $800 were not sufficient recompense for the loss of family connectedness. Eventually, the daughter contacted her family and apologized for seeking recourse through legal channels instead of trying to work out a repayment plan within the family unit. They superficially accepted her overtures to rejoin the family and the schism seemed to have been bridged. Nevertheless, several years later there was still uneasiness and distrust between her and her family; she wished she had been able to find a less acrimonious route to resolution. Obviously, the action she had taken had further undermined the level of trust between family members and seriously impaired the family's sense of cohesion (Kaslow, 1990, p. 157).

Another case illustrates the diversity of issues within the categories of lawsuits children are waging against parents or parent surrogates. This story was conveyed to me by a mental health professional acquaintance when I was collecting data for this chapter. It resembles numerous similar cases I have heard in clinical practice.

Case 6. What Happened to My Inheritance?

Mr. R had three children and lived in Virginia. He had been told repeatedly by his father that he and his two sisters would inherit his father's estate, the majority of which was invested in corporate stocks. When his divorced father remarried, Mr. R did not realize that this promise would soon evaporate. His father's new wife nursed him during a prolonged illness. Secretly the father disinherited his three children several months prior to his death, and bequeathed his total estate to his much younger second wife.

Mr. R's emotions of rage, anguish, and despair escalated when he realized that his father had abandoned him in death, as he purportedly had in life. The only things his father had ever given were tangible, and now that financial legacy had also vanished, and another commitment had been broken. This left him vulnerable to his mother's taunting remarks that he and his sisters should sue the "stepmother for their 'fair share' of the estate." They decided to do just that, wanting a monetary settlement to help alleviate their hurt, fury, and sadness at their father's financial betrayal. He felt, as he had on many prior occasions, that he was bereft of his father's love and loyalty and of a solid place in his father's heart. The three children all believed that they were entitled to an inheritance on the basis of their having been conceived voluntarily by their father, and because they had played an active role in his life for 40-plus years. By contrast, his young wife had only been involved with him for 10 years.

Therefore they filed suit, claiming their rightful share of the estate and questioning their father's testamentary capacity at the time the recent changes to the will had been made (see Chapter 20). They derived a modicum of satisfaction from tying up their stepmother's access to the funds while the case wended its way through probate. This second wife allegedly had implied that she would leave their father, ill and alone, if he did not accede to her wishes and change his will to name her the sole beneficiary. Seeing no other viable option and not wanting to be deserted, he had complied. The children wanted revenge, and resented her greedy demands. They hoped the court would recognize their entitlement under law. Nonetheless, the court ultimately decided in favor of his widow, leaving the children completely disgruntled and furious with the selfish stepmother whom they believed had coerced their father into bequeathing all of his wealth and possessions to her.

This case illustrates the same theme that emerged in the prior cases. Positive family bonds were tenuous. Much estrangement had already characterized the family of origin over a long period of time before the suit was filed. The family members' level of mutual trust and their ability to communicate candidly and responsively were quite minimal.

CATEGORY IV.   DISPUTES OVER CHILD SUPPORT

Cases in this category present a very different issue and set of circumstances. This case example is condensed from the clinical files of another Florida psychologist who had seen a patient who had sued her parents. Dr. W checked with this patient to ascertain if she would be willing to be interviewed by me by telephone. She agreed, and I conducted an hour-long telephone interview with her (August, 1988).

Case 7.   The Child Support Belongs to Me

Miss G was then age 28. She had sued her mother 10 years earlier when she turned age 18. Both of her parents were alcoholics. They had divorced when she was age 12 and her mother had been awarded child support, to be paid by the father until the children were age 18 or until they had completed undergraduate college. When Miss G was between ages 16 and 18, her relationship with her mother had become highly conflictual. Eventually her mother insisted that she move out of the house, permanently. At this juncture, "Miss G reasoned that her mother was no longer entitled to the child support since she (Miss G) was now completely self-supporting" (Kaslow, 1990, p. 158).

The young woman sought legal counsel and found an attorney in Miami who was willing to handle this atypical case (1978). The dispute was settled out of court in Miss G's favor and the $62.00 child support, every other week, was forwarded to Miss G thereafter. Initially, she was exuberant; she desperately needed the money and thought it was a justified verdict. Her decision to sue evolved out of her long-accumulated misery, which eventuated from her parents' inebriation, their frequent arguments, their attempts at drawing her into taking sides, and their divorce. She had been her father's favorite; nonetheless, her mother had tried to enlist her assistance in having him "thrown into jail" when he had defaulted on paying her child support. Such manipulations had enraged and estranged her from both parents.

Miss G remained alienated from her mother for 2 years postsettlement. Her siblings pressured her to reunite with the family. She contacted her mom, who had "run into hard times," and finally "rejoined the family." Her mom died several years after their reunion; Miss G regretted the time lost in not having a friendly relationship.

As might be expected, after the reconciliation animosity and distrust still pervaded family members' feelings and behaviors toward her, because she had "gone out of the family" to seek a legal resolution of the conflict. Years later she still senses lingering resentment from her siblings, which she attributes to the legal action she took many long years ago.

Miss G went on to become an attorney. In retrospect, she wishes she and her mother had been able to "talk things out rationally" prior to her going to a lawyer. Despite residual feelings of guilt, she still thinks she was right and would repeat the action she took *if* it appeared to be the only viable pathway to getting money earmarked for her. Mother and daughter were each locked into a fixed stance; Miss G still does not believe their dispute could have been mediated, as neither would have "listened to anyone." For Miss G, taking legal action apparently was a way of getting "unstuck". Others, with a different perspective, seek to do this in therapy or mediation.

CATEGORY V.   ASSAULT AND BATTERY CASES: SEEKING DAMAGES FOR BEING A CHILD ABUSE OR INCEST VICTIM

There is still a lack of clarity regarding the statute of limitations on retroactive suits. This is a relatively new arena for legal action by adult children against a parent, and the issue is, how long after the abuse occurred can a grown child sue parents for damages inflicted years earlier? The time frame is central. Does the statute of limitations pertain to time of commission of the act; to time of recall of repressed memories of the fact, after layers of camouflage are slowly stripped away in a safe experience, such as a good love relationship or therapy; or to the time of recognition of the very damaging impact of the behavior? As more suits have reached the courts and legal opinions have been rendered and published on this topic, there have been retroactive lawsuits filed by purportedly brutally beaten children against their abusive parents. What was not expected when this trend began was the enormous controversy that would be evoked. Accused parents have vehemently defended themselves and denied the allegations. Therapists have been sued for precipitating the recall of false memories (Loftus, 1994), and a foundation has been established to dispute the plentitude of supposed evidence against parents based on memories recovered many years after an event occurred. Nonetheless, such tales continue to surface in therapists' offices (Courtois, 1988; Kirschner, Kirschner, & Rappaport, 1993), and the delayed, embittered dramas have been played out in courtrooms across the country.

What becomes apparent in reading about such cases is that the legal action is not the cause of the family's disintegration. Rather, family relationships were disturbed and strained for a long time; the seeds of the severe conflicts had been germinating throughout many years. The filing of the suit represents an external, public display of deep personal pain and angst, and a desperate, even misguided, attempt to redress victimizations and find a sense of peace that the participants in the dispute are unable to engineer on their own. The suit is an attempt to culminate the disastrous interaction cycle. Often, previous interventions by therapists, human service workers, clergy, and others have brought little or no relief from the pain nor ended the abusive behavior. Rarely would one resort to litigation to humiliate or tear apart a family if it has been a well-intentioned, well-functioning unit.

Such assault and battery cases are usually tried in criminal court. The defendant(s), if adjudged guilty, may be sentenced to a prison term. When this transpires, the adult offspring who filed the charges has to face the reality that "not only was his or her parent abusive, but that the parent now is also a convicted felon." The horror of this situation is magnified if one knows that he or she has contributed to exacerbating the ordeal by making the matter public in the courts, thereby leading to the conviction. The distress is increased if siblings denigrate the legal action because they perceive it to be an unforgiveable betrayal of a family secret, or if the denial of the alleged egregious behavior persists. The victim-turned-accuser is further victimized if he or she is blamed for the family's disgrace (Kaslow, 1990, pp. 159–160), and may also face expulsion from all family contact, rather than receiving any support or validation.

The procedure usually followed when allegations of child abuse are reported is that an investigation is conducted by the state agency delegated that responsibility. If the investigators believe the charges are well founded, the case goes to court. If the accusations are validated, the offending parent may be sentenced to prison, or placed on probation and mandated to attend treatment, often group therapy with other abusive parents. Even when the court appoints a guardian *ad litem* to represent a child's interest, children are rarely apprised of the right to sue for assault and battery retroactively when they reach the age of legal majority. One wonders if they should be. Is the knowledge that they can do so apt to relieve or increase their level of pain and suffering?

Another explosive pertinent arena of concern revolves around incest cases. What if a parent has forced an incestuous relationship on a child and as a result of this the child contracts a venereal disease or AIDS? There is no doubt that irreparable harm has been done—sometimes under the veil of demonstrating affection. In this type of situation, what constitutes "damages"? And what damages should the innocent child victim be entitled to? It is almost impossible to comprehend how anyone who becomes aware of such cases can still posit that the parent was acting in the best interest of the child. In such situations personal behaviors must be subjected to public scrutiny and some form of negative sanctions should be imposed. We must examine whether the systemic explanations emanating from some family therapy theorists are applicable here, or whether, as the law attests, the adult parent has victimized the unsuspecting young child and a linear explanation that assigns responsibility (and the concomitant blame and guilt) is a more realistic one.

CATEGORY VI.   KIDNAPPING OUT OF AND DEPROGRAMMING FROM CULTS

During the 1960s, 1970s, and 1980s, scores of older adolescents and young adults were recruited or mesmerized into joining pseudoreligious cults such as Hare Krishna (Iskcon), the Church of Scientology, the Unification Church (Moonies), Divine Light Mission, Bagwan Sri Rajneesh, and others. Through such techniques as "heavenly deception," "love bombing," repetitive lectures, and totally immersing prospective members into the cult's philosophy and lifestyle, the young people were (and are) gradually coerced into adopting the cult family as a replacement for their personal families (Schwartz & Kaslow, 1982). Frequently they are almost spirited away to retreat settings to live in relative isolation from familiar home and college contexts and taught that nonbelievers (to the cult's ideology) are of Satan. Through such brainwashing methods, these young people are made to succumb to the cult's leadership, belief system, and proscribed expectations. The conversion process is carefully overseen and includes daily worship rituals, poor diet which eventually modifies cognitive processes, a structured living routine, promulgation of blind-faith acceptance of dogma, and minimal or no contact with loved ones.

Once parents realize that their children have become engulfed by a cult, they have virtually no avenues to pursue to get them out. The legal argument used successfully by cult leaders has been that the young person is over 18 years of age and, under the Constitution of the United States, is guaranteed freedom of religion (Fourth Amendment).

Desperate to have their children back in their lives, and determined to set their children's minds free from a coercively imposed lifestyle and belief system (Hershell & Hershell, 1982), many parents resort to kidnapping children back from the cults. When and if they succeed in bringing the child back with them, frequently against the child's wishes initially, they seek to have the child *deprogrammed.* Some of these young adults later return to the cult, infuriated at their parents for having intruded in the life they (think they) have selected; some, at the urging of cult leaders, have sued their parents for infringement of their right to freedom of religion (Schwartz & Zemel, 1980).

In our research (Kaslow & Schwartz, 1982, 1999), we identified several variables that increase vulnerability to cult appeal, including an external locus of control, that is, seeking an outside authority figure who determines right and wrong, and a prior weak relationship to one's own father. In addition, although many ex-cult members come from physically intact families, the majority indicate that something vital was missing for them spiritually or emotionally at home. Many of their fathers believe they have "given them everything," but this tends to mean material goods.

Category VII. Children Suing to Divorce Their Parents

As indicated at the beginning of this chapter, children's rights under law, as separate and distinct from those of their parents, is a relatively new legal concept. The fact that children even have the right to engage their own legal counsel, even if they are under 18, is a radically new phenomenon that seems to have emerged only in the 1990s.

The case of Gregory K is probably a harbinger of a turning of the tide in favor of greater recognition of children's rights, including the right to retain counsel. On April 9, 1992, an 11-year-old, then known as Gregory K (now Shawn Russ) filed a petition in his own name. He had privately retained legal counsel and sought to end the parent–child relationship with his birth parents. He also sought declaratory relief regarding his constitutional and other legal rights:

> Gregory K had been adjudicated dependent by the Department of Health and Rehabilitative Services (DHRS) and had been in the foster care system almost continually

since September 26, 1989. Exactly three years later, on September 25, 1992, Judge Thomas Kirk granted his petition for termination and allowed his adoption by his foster parents. (Russ, 1993, p. 365)

Gregory K was a young boy whose maturity seemed to exceed that of his parents, who sought to exercise their "rights" over him. His birth parents had abused, abandoned, and neglected him during his entire lifetime with them. Gregory, born July 28, 1980, was the oldest of three children born to Ralph and Rachel Kingsley; his parents separated when he was 4. He spent most of his early years in the care of his biological father, who had a severe substance abuse problem that contributed to his abusive and negligent behavior of his son.

After police filed a neglect complaint in 1989, the Florida DHRS removed Gregory from his father's custody and placed him with his mother. Five months later, in September 1989, Rachel voluntarily placed Gregory and one of his brothers in foster care. In 1990 he was returned to his mother's care for a few months; she then told DHRS that she could no longer cope with her children. Rachel suffered from substance abuse, paid little attention to her offspring, left them alone and unsupervised, and was involved in abusive adult relationships during much of Gregory's life. Gregory was in and out of foster care many times.

In January 1991, Gregory's mother requested no further visits with him and sent no letters or cards:

In June 1991, the trial judge in the dependency action ordered DHRS to transfer the case to their adoption unit and seek termination of parental rights. Gregory was placed with the Russ family in October 1991. In February 1992, DHRS finally decided to proceed with termination and informed Gregory's foster parents. When Gregory was advised of this fact, he was elated. He had been asking to be adopted by his foster family since he first came to their home. This was his dream come true. (Russ, 1993, pp. 367–368)

About 6 weeks later, without explanation and in violation of the Florida statutes, DHRS reversed its position and sought to reunite Gregory with his biological parents. A guardian *ad litem* had been appointed but had not met Gregory nor talked with him during the 22 months following the appointment.

When Gregory heard about the reunification plan, he reacted with disbelief, anger, and frustration. He threatened to run away, or to make his parents despise him so that they would not want him to stay with them. His foster father told him that he might have certain legal and constitutional rights, which, although not yet fully recognized under the law, might be obtainable. Because the guardian *ad litem* failed to bring an action on his behalf, and neither the DHRS nor any adult would seek the termination of his parents' rights, Gregory retained Jerri Blair as his lawyer and filed a petition to terminate his parents' rights. His father voluntarily gave up rights shortly thereafter, so the only rights left were those of his mother. Although Gregory was the person who obviously had the greatest stake in the result, the key question was whether the court would allow him to present his case.

While state protective agencies periodically file petitions to terminate parental rights, it is most unusual to allow a child to file the action. Many think that, in fact, Gregory K may have been the first minor child to be granted standing to bring such an action based on his asserted constitutional right to do so, in the same way that an adult does. The court entered an "order on standing," which stated that "minors have the same constitutional rights as adults to due process, equal protection, privacy, access to the courts, and the right to defend life, liberty, and to pursue happiness" (Russ, 1993, p. 366).

Despite the fact that an appellate court recently found that Gregory did not have the capacity to bring the action, the Gregory K case has stimulated a national and international debate as to whether children should have access to the courts and about the wisdom and consequences of granting that access. National children's rights organizations have credited this case with generating increased momentum toward the reform of child protection laws. The Gregory K case has resulted in a call for legislative reform in numerous states. One child advocate organization has speculated that this case will trigger a national movement for legal aid for children.

Criticisms of Granting Children Standing

As previously indicated, critics of the children's rights movement protest that children are too immature to have rights, that the movement is destroying families by infringing on the rights of parents and weakening parental authority, and that the result will be an abundance of frivolous lawsuits. Others believe that "these criticisms result from hundreds of years of ignorance and false perceptions regarding the nature of children and the role they play in our society and they are not supported by credible factual data" (Russ, 1993, p. 390). It falls to family mental health professionals to help bridge these two disparate positions and encourage attention to what is the best interest of the child in any specific case.

Good Omens

Since the Gregory K case, another 12-year-old Florida minor has been granted the same constitutional right of standing, and other constitutional rights, in the context of a postdissolution custody battle. The child has obtained the right to intervene in her own name, with independent counsel, for the purpose of bringing a petition to change custody from her biological father to her maternal grandmother. In this case, the court made the additional finding that the young woman involved was an indispensable party to the proceedings, given that she was the one that had the most to gain or lose. A similar ruling permitting standing to a minor child to seek to terminate her biological parents' rights was granted in April 1993 and reaffirmed in September 1993 by a Michigan court, based on the Michigan Constitution.

The Gregory K case has been highly publicized and has aroused much attention to the dilemma of balancing the rights of biological parents and those of their children when the former do not fulfill the responsibilities that should accompany their rights and privileges:

> Although legal recognition of standing for children to bring actions to terminate the parent/child relationship and to be parties to disputed custody cases will not end the massive problem of abuse, neglect, and abandonment of children in this country, such changes are a necessary precondition for children being able to defend themselves and for the child protective system becoming part of the solution instead of part of the

problem. The complete answer will be found in the correction of a myriad of social deficiencies. (Russ, 1993, p. 392)

Perhaps some day soon the Supreme Court will address the substantive standard to be applied to the child in custody disputes between a genetic parent and an adult with no biological connection who claims de facto parenthood, that is, who has become the psychological parent. This must be done for the sake of the hundreds of thousands of children not properly being cared for or protected by our legal system, or who are being threatened with return to biological parents who do not love them, do not care for them, and do not meet their needs, while a much more devoted and accessible family is willing to do so.

CATEGORY VIII.   INJURIES SUSTAINED FOR WHICH PARENTS ARE COVERED BY INSURANCE

When a child is injured in a car accident and a parent is driving, a special situation arises. If the parent carries insurance, the child is eligible to sue for damages, due to negligence. When this happens, the child sues the parent in order to be reimbursed by the parent's insurance carrier. The possibilities for collusion between parent and child are readily apparent. Cases in this category take a slightly different turn and are probably not as destructive to the family as the other kinds of cases discussed earlier (*Ard v. Ard*, 1981). In fact, they can conceivably draw the family members closer as they unite against the insurance company, and might all emerge wealthier.

COMPLEX AND DISTRESSING ISSUES: WHAT LIES AHEAD

When one first contemplates the reality that a child can decide to sue his or her parents, this potential course of action looms as one that will cause irreparable disruption and damage to the family, as cutoffs are almost invariably harmful (Bowen, 1988). The vast majority of family clinicians would posit that such legal action will bring the family to the point of no return, truncating all the loyalty bonds that are supposed to unite families even in times of enormous turbulence tantamount to intrafamily warfare (Boszormenyi-Nagy & Spark, 1973/1984). Also, the family hierarchy with the parents as the architects and executives of the family (Minuchin, Lee & Simon, 1996) is turned topsy-turvy, with children accruing far too much power over their parents, as all are aware that they can resort to lawsuits against their progenitors. Therefore, many believe that such actions should be avoided in all circumstances; rather, alternative dispute resolution strategies such as family mediation should be utilized to resolve conflictual issues.

What has become apparent as I have delved into the legal literature pertinent to the topic of children who sue parents is that some legislators and judges have addressed this thorny subject, but that mental health professionals have not. Some of society's greatest legal minds have long understood that intrafamily lawsuits could, and probably would, wreak havoc on the family. Traditionally, in addition to the aforementioned concept of *patria potestas* and the doctrine of the family's right to privacy, there have been corollary doctrines of intraspousal and intrafamily immunity, which were originally established to preserve the integrity of the family unit. Although most states no longer have such statutes on their books, they did exist until about three decades ago. Courts have recognized, sagaciously, I think, that "The primary disruption to harmonious family relationships is not the lawsuit brought for damages after injury but the injury itself" and have held that "the argument that parental immunity is necessary to preserve the tranquility and harmony of domestic life misconceives the facts of domestic life" (Verezzio, 1985).

Only since the termination of intrafamily immunity statutes have the eight kinds of cases this chapter discusses become potential grist for the legal mill. Today, in all states, children over age 18 can sue; in many states, however, unemancipated minors still cannot. Many mental health and family professionals dreaded the probability that the abrogation of the parent–child immunity doctrine for unemancipated minors would unleash a Pandora's box of legal actions predicated on not getting one's way or on being extremely obstinate and rebellious. Nonetheless, since *Gibson v. Gibson* (1971), when the California Court struck down the doctrine of parental immunity and substituted the *reasonably prudent parent standard* instead, there has not been a rash of lawsuits, and the pessimistic predictions have not materialized.

REPETITIVE THEMES AND LONG RANGE CONSEQUENCES

In each of the cases discussed previously, except Category VIII, family relationship bonds were extremely tenuous prior to the initiation of the lawsuits. Longstanding, intense animosities and rifts existed. It is quite possible that each of the plaintiffs, feeling they had never been given sufficient, consistent unconditional love and affection from their parents, unconsciously hoped they could redress this emptiness by being awarded a sum of money. Neither they nor the judge could mandate parents to be loving and nurturing; thus, there is a futility experienced, regardless of outcome, because what they really were longing for is still not forthcoming and never will be.

Usually these plaintiffs are not knowledgeable about contemporary alternative dispute resolution techniques, such as mediation or arbitration, which are being employed in place of litigation in various types of civil disputes. In mediation, particularly, a win–win rather than a win–lose result is sought through negotiation, compromise, trade-offs, and other problem-solving techniques. Such strategies are much more congruent with what professionals treating families hope to accomplish—repair and reworking of conflictual relationships and prevention of rejection between members (Erickson & Erickson, 1988; Schwartz & Kaslow, 1997). The emphasis might well be placed on the existential fact that, at the most basic level, good relationships are much more crucial to survival and a satisfying quality of life than are material possessions, fame, or money. Although some reconciliation was achieved in several of the cases, it eventuated under a continuing veil of suspicion, hostility, and mistrust. Thus, the reunion was far from satisfying to anyone. In the other cases, the accumulated fury, distrust, and resentment made rapprochement impossible.

Hopefully, mediation will be employed much more often in resolving seemingly irresolvable family disputes, so that more harmonious family bonds can be forged. Families that utilize dispute resolution strategies do not seem to become as bruised and decimated. It is perhaps in mediation, conducted by a neutral but objective and empathic third party, that the confluence of law and the behavioral sciences approaches its zenith and serves to foster a cooperative settlement. When this happens, none of the parties to the dispute is hurt further and a more complete legal and emotional resolution can be accomplished.

Another alternative lies, of course, in therapy. When patients convey to a therapist that they are considering or have already filed a lawsuit against another family member, a sensitive therapist can address the feelings and thoughts that have culminated in such an action. While accepting the severe distress that is a precipitant, they can also explore with the patient the likely implications of such legal action. They can convey that, rather than serving a curative or healing function, except in Category VII cases such as Gregory K's, moving completely outside of the family to the judicial system will probably exacerbate the schism. They might suggest holding one or several multigenerational family therapy sessions (Framo, 1992) to determine if there is a less adversarial and less destructive route to a co-evolved, mutually agreed-upon resolution predicated on increased understanding, acceptance, and even forgiveness.

Children who sue parents are, indeed, dealing a deadly blow to their family of origin. This constitutes a nonphysical homicide, a form of "murder in self-defense" without the use of deadly force. When the bonds are irreparably destroyed through devastating legal action, the lifelines in the family are severed. All members suffer from the family internecine warfare and experience a profound sense of confusion, loss, and grief when the legal battle is over. The family, as a viable entity for all members, is killed; it becomes a corpse (Kaslow, 1990, p. 162). Family lawsuits constitute a less violent, more insidious form of family destruction than physical homicide, but the end result is still lethal, and to be avoided whenever possible. Such lawsuits clearly are not in keeping with the commandment to "Honor they father and mother," but does the behavior of the parents in some of the situations described really merit such honoring?

NOTES

1. These three vignettes are not confidential, as they were provided on national television. Nonetheless, I have refrained from mentioning names of the principals. The interpretations are attributable to this author only.

2. Some of these categories were first articulated in my article, "Children Who Sue Parents: A New Form of Family Homicide" (Kaslow, 1990). The sequence has been changed, some categories have been renamed and expanded, and two new categories have been added.

REFERENCES

Ard v. Ard (1981), 395 So.2d 585.

Beavers, W. R. (1977). *Psychotherapy and growth: A family systems perspective.* New York: Brunner/Mazel.

Bill of Rights in Action Newsletter (1973), pp. 9 & 10. Los Angeles: Constitutional Rights Foundation.

Blair, J. A. (1993, June). Gregory K. and emerging children's rights. *Trial, 29*(6), 22–27.

Boszormenyi-Nagy, I., & Spark, G. (1984). *Invisible loyalties.* New York: Brunner/Mazel. (Original work published 1973. New York: Harper & Row.)

Bowen, M. (1988). *Family therapy in clinical practice* (2nd ed.). Northvale, NJ: Jason Aronson.

Buchanan, A. (1996). *Cycles of child maltreatment: Facts, fallacies and interventions.* Chichester, England: John Wiley & Sons.

Ceci, S. J., & Hembrooke, H. (1998). *Expert witnesses in child abuse cases: What can and should be said in court.* Washington, DC: American Psychological Association.

Courtois, C. A. (1988). *Healing the incest wounds: Adult survivors in therapy.* New York: W. W. Norton.

Erickson, S., & Erickson, M. (1988). *Mediation casebook.* New York: Brunner/Mazel.

Federle, K. H. (1995). Looking ahead: An empowerment perspective on the rights of children, *Temple Law Review, 68,* 1585.

Florida Dissolution of Marriage Act, 61.001-61.30 Fla. Stat. (1987) or 61.13 Fla. Stat. (1987).

Framo, J. L. (1992). *Family of origin therapy: An intergenerational approach.* New York: Brunner/Mazel.

Gibson v. Gibson (1971), 3 Cal. 3d 914, 92 Cal. Rptr. 288, 479 P.2d 648.

Green, A. H. (1988). *Child sexual abuse.* New York: Brunner/Mazel.

Hershell, M., & Hershell, B. (1982). Our involvement with a cult. In F. W. Kaslow (Ed.), *Cults and the family* (pp. 131–140). New York: Haworth Press.

Kaslow, F. W. (1981). Profile of a healthy family. *Interaction, 4,* 1–15.

Kaslow, F. W. (1990). Children who sue parents. *Journal of Marriage and Family Therapy, 16*(2), 151–163.

Kaslow, F. W. (1995). *Projective genogramming.* Sarasota, FL: Professional Resource Press.

Kaslow, F. W., & Kaslow, S. (1992). The family that works together: Special problems of family businesses. In S. Zedeck (Ed.), *Work, families and organizations* (pp. 312–351). San Francisco: Jossey-Bass.

Kaslow, F. W., & Schwartz, L. L. (1983). Vulnerability and invulnerability to the cults: An assessment of family dynamics, functioning, and values. In V. Bagarozzi, A. Jurich, & R. W. Jackson (Eds.), *Marital and family therapy: New perspectives in theory, research, and practice* (pp. 165–190). New York: Human Sciences Press.

Kaslow, F. W., & Schwartz, L. L. (1999, in press). The cult phenomenon: A turn of the century update. In M. Sussman (Ed.), *Marriage and Family Review* (20th Anniversary ed.). New York: Haworth Press.

Katz v. United States (1967), 389 U.S. 347.

Keith, D. V., & Whitaker, C. A. (1978). Struggling with the impotence impasse: Absurdity and acting in. *Journal of Marriage and Family Counseling,* (4)1, 69–78.

Kerr, M., & Bowen, M. (1988). *Family evaluation.* New York: W. W. Norton.

Kirschner, S., Kirschner, D. A., & Rappaport, R. L. (1993). *Working with adult incest survivors.* New York: Brunner/Mazel.

Lewis, J., Beavers, W. R., Gossett, J. T., & Phillips, V. A. (1976). *No single thread: Psychological health and the family system.* New York: Brunner/Mazel.

Loftus, E. F. (1994). The repressed memory controversy. *American Psychologist, 49*(5), 443–445.

MacFarlane, K., Waterman, J., Conerly, S., Damon, L., Surfee, M., & Long, S. (1986). *Sexual abuse of young children.* New York: Guilford Press.

Melton, G. B. (1981). Children's competency to testify. *Law and Human Behavior, 5,* 73–86.

Minow, M. (1995). Children's rights: Where we've been, and where we're going. *Temple Law Review, 68,* 1573.

Minuchin, S. (1974). *Families and family therapy.* Cambridge, MA: Harvard University Press.

Minuchin, S., Lee, W.-Y., & Simon, G. M. (1996). *Mastering family therapy.* New York: John Wiley & Sons.

Oates, K. (1986). *Child abuse and neglect: What happens eventually?* New York: Brunner/Mazel.

Olson, D. H. (1996). Clinical assessment and treatment interventions using the family circumplex model. In F. W. Kaslow (Ed.), *Handbook of relational diagnosis and dysfunctional family patterns* (pp. 59–80). New York: John Wiley & Sons.

Rule v. Geddes (1904), 23 App. #D.C. 31.

Russ, G. H. (1993). Through the eyes of a child, "Gregory K": A child's right to be heard. *Family Law Quarterly, 27,* 365–393.

Schwartz, L. L., & Kaslow, F. W. (1982). The cult phenomenon: Historical, sociological, and familial factors contributing to their development and appeal. In F. W. Kaslow & M. Sussman (Eds.), *Cults and the family* (pp. 3–30). New York: Haworth Press.

Schwartz, L. L., & Kaslow, F. W. (1997). *Painful partings: Divorce and its aftermath.* New York: John Wiley & Sons.

Schwartz, L. L., & Zemel, J. L. (1980). Religious cults: Family concerns and the law. *Journal of Marital and Family Therapy, 6,* 301–308.

Shetky, D. H., & Green, A. H. (1988). *Child sexual abuse.* New York: Brunner/Mazel.

Virezzo, D. M. (1985). Child vs. parent. *Florida Bar Journal,* 49–51.

Walsh, F. (1982). *Normal family processes.* New York: Guilford Press.

Watzlawick, P. (1963). A review of the double bind theory. *Family Process, 2,* 132–153.

Wu, C. N. (1996). Conflict of interest in the representation of children in dependency cases, *Ford Law Review, 64,* 1857.

CHAPTER 18

The Impact of
Recovered Memories

KENNETH S. POPE and O. BRANDT CAUDILL, JR.

IT IS more likely than not that a therapist will work with at least one patient for whom recovered memories of abuse are an issue, and there is a small but not insignificant chance that the patient, therapist, or both will wind up in court.

National survey research suggests that almost three-fourths (73%) of therapists encounter at least one patient who reports recovering a memory of abuse (Pope & Tabachnick, 1995). Half of these therapists indicated that there was external validation for the abuse in at least one case; about one out of five (21%) judged that the recovered memory was false (for at least one patient); and 12% indicated that at least one such patient later decided that the memory was false. A substantial minority of these cases entered the forensic arena. About 15% of these therapists indicated that at least one client who reported recovered memories of abuse filed a civil or criminal complaint.

This national survey also examined another population of patients affected by recovered memories of abuse. About 15% of the participants indicated that they had encountered at least one patient who had been accused of child sex abuse on the basis of someone else's recovered memories. About 21% of these clinicians judged the memory to be false in at least one case. About 6% of the clinicians indicated that there was external validation for at least one report of recovered memories. A significant number of these cases also entered the forensic arena: About 6% of these clinicians indicated that there was at least one case in which a civil or criminal complaint had been filed against the client.

This chapter provides information about the rapidly evolving legislation and case law relevant to therapy when recovered memories are at issue, and highlights a few areas of practice that warrant special attention.

LEGISLATION AND LITIGATION

This section reviews recent legal history concerning recovered memory issues.

STATUTES ALLOWING DELAYED CLAIMS

If an adult recovers a memory of having been sexually abused as a child, the customary statute of limitations may prohibit a lawsuit against the alleged perpetrator. While a prospective plaintiff might make a legal challenge to the statute of limitations or establish some valid reason that the statute should be tolled (i.e., a reason that the "clock" should not begin to run at the time when the alleged offense originally occurred), some states have enacted legislation that allows delayed claims. For example, section 340.1 of the California Code of Civil Procedure provides that the time for commencing a suit against an alleged molester must be within 8 years of the date when the plaintiff attained the age of majority or 3 years of the date the plaintiff discovered, or reasonably should have discovered, the psychological injury or illness occurring after the age of majority which was caused by the sexual abuse, whichever period expired later. This statute provides that where a plaintiff was 26 years of age or older at the time the lawsuit was filed, certificates of merit had to be filed by the attorney and by a licensed mental health professional attesting to the merit of the claim. A mental health professional in California is required to state that he or she is licensed, practices in the state, and is not treating and has not treated the plaintiff. The mental health professional must attest that he or she has interviewed the plaintiff and is knowledgeable of the relevant facts and issues involved and has concluded based on his or her knowledge that in his or her professional opinion there is a reasonable basis to believe the plaintiff had been subject to sexual abuse.

Pope and Brown present a listing of each state's statutes regarding delayed memories and delayed realization, the length of time allowed for filing suits, and other information (1996, pp. 271–275). On the Internet, a web page maintained by attorney Susan Smith also presents this information for each state at www2.imagine.com/smithlaw (see also http://idealist.com/memories).

LEGISLATION AUTHORIZING THIRD-PARTY SUITS

In August, 1994, a draft Mental Health Consumer Protection Act was prepared, which was jointly sponsored by the Illinois False Memory Syndrome (FMS) Society, the Ohio Parents Falsely Accused, the Texas Friends of FMS, the Minnesota Action Committee, and Florida Friends of FMS. This original proposal called for model legislation to be introduced in each state which would specifically create standing for nonpatients to sue therapists if they were injured by "negligent therapy," the goal being to ensure that "all reasonably foreseeable victims of the willful and/or reckless use of hazardous therapy techniques or procedures (e.g. families of patients subjected to 'recovered memories' therapy) shall have a cause of action for legal redress or malpractice suits" ("Proposal to Finance Preparation of Model Legislation Entitled Mental Health Consumer Protection Act," p. 6). As of this writing, no legislation has been adopted that specifically authorizes third-party suits in regard to delayed memories. However, a number of suits have been brought (see the following subsection, "Third Party Suits in the Courts") on the basis of existing general statutes and case law. Missouri has recently enacted a statute that gives standing to parents and other interested third parties to file licensing complaints concerning psychologists, but only if the third party is financially responsible for the therapy (Missouri Psychology Practice and Rules Act, 1995, Section 337.035).

Allowing third parties to sue therapists when sex abuse is at issue raises a variety of complex legal and clinical issues. The *Harvard Law Review* published a detailed examination of some of these issues, providing a good starting place for those interested in this topic (Bowman & Mertz, 1996b; see also 1996a). For an analysis of what is now labeled the Truth and Responsibility in Mental Health Practices Act, see Hinnefeld and Newman (1997).

THIRD-PARTY SUITS IN THE COURTS

Where a nonpatient is suing the therapist, the first issue that is generally raised by the defense is that there is a lack of duty to the third party because the therapist has traditionally been held to owe a duty only to his or her patients. This third-party duty argument has been successful in the defense of therapists in a number of cases. However, there has been a series of cases that have carved out exceptions to the general rule that no suit can be brought by someone who is not a patient. In *Truman v. Genesis Associates* (1996), the parents of a patient sued their daughter's therapist alleging that their daughter had gone to the therapist for treatment of an eating disorder. However, they alleged that during the course of therapy she had recovered memories of sexual and satanic abuse by them. While the court held that the parents could not assert malpractice claims, the court nonetheless allowed them to maintain breach of contract and intentional infliction of emotional distress claims because they were paying for the therapy.

In *Sullivan v. Cheshire* (1995), the parents of a psychologist's patient sued him alleging that he caused estrangement of her from her family because under hypnosis she recovered memories of sexual abuse by a sibling. The federal court held that the estrangement of the patient from her family gave rise to certain claims but that the parents could not sue for malpractice committed against their child. The court noted that under Illinois law the only circumstance where a parent could sue over malpractice committed against the child was where the child's death resulted from the malpractice.

Courts in Vermont and Colorado have found third-party duties running from therapists to the parents of child patients where abuse has been alleged (*Montoya v. Beebensee*, 1988; *Wilkinson v. Balsam*, 1995). However, Texas has refused to find such a duty (*Bird v. W.C.W.*, 1994).

RETRACTOR SUITS AGAINST THERAPISTS

Third-party suits raise the question of what duties, if any, a therapist has in regard to third parties. Whether the therapist bears a duty to the plaintiff is not an issue if the plaintiff has received clinical services from the therapist. In various instances, the plaintiff is a patient who recovered memories of abuse during therapy and later retracted them. The largest monetary figures to date in repressed memory cases have come in retractor cases. On November 4, 1997, United Press International (UPI) reported that a woman had agreed to accept a settlement of $10.6 million in her suit against a clinician and medical center, for "an experimental treatment that implanted false memories of a satanic cult that abused children"

("Woman Wins $10M in False Memory Suit," 1997). According to the UPI report, "the treatment, which included drug therapy and frequent hypnosis, left her believing she was a high priestess of the supposed cult." The *Houston Chronicle* reported a previous case in which a jury awarded $5.8 million to a woman who claimed that psychotherapy had caused her to develop false memories of satanic ritual abuse (Smith, 1997).

IS TESTIMONY ABOUT RECOVERED MEMORIES ADMISSIBLE?

Recovered memories serve as a focus not only of suits by patients and third parties against therapists but also of criminal and civil cases against alleged perpetrators. In such cases, a central issue tends to be: Does testimony based on recovered memories meet the legal standards for admissibility?

The criminal cases and the cases involving suits by patients against alleged abusers have frequently featured motions by the alleged abusers to exclude all testimony based on delayed memories on the grounds that such evidence is inadmissible. Frequently this takes the form of a motion *in limine*, which is a motion that is filed on the eve of trial to exclude evidence that would otherwise be too prejudicial to be heard by a jury. Generally, most courts in the United States have followed some form of test regarding scientific evidence which requires that an initial showing be made of the reliability of the evidence before a lay jury is allowed to hear it. The seminal case in this area was *Frye v. United States*, a case decided by the U.S. Court of Appeal for the District of Columbia Circuit in 1923. Generally, the *Frye* standard required that for the admission of the testimony to be allowed the following criteria must be met: (a) the subject matter must be beyond the knowledge of an average juror or judge; (b) the field in which the expert is testifying must be sufficiently advanced that the testimony could be considered reliable; (c) once the field has been determined to have sufficient reliability, the individual expert must be established as having sufficient competency to testify; and (d) the specific techniques or devices relied on by the expert must meet standards of scientific accuracy and reliability, that is, be generally accepted in the scientific community. A number of states adopted the *Frye* standards in various ways. For example, in *People v. Kelly* (1976) the California Supreme Court adopted the rationale of *Frye v. United States* specifically, thereby creating the test in California known as *Kelly-Frye*.

The U.S. Supreme Court returned to the issue of scientific admissibility and "junk science" in the case of *Daubert v. Merrell Dow Pharmaceutical, Inc.* (1993). At that time the Supreme Court held that the Federal Rules of Evidence had superseded the *Frye* standards. In the eyes of at least one federal appellate court, the Ninth Circuit Court of Appeal, the new test announced by the Supreme Court in *Daubert* imposes a substantially greater duty on trial courts to ascertain what the liability is of scientific evidence before it is admitted.

The factors to be taken into account under *Daubert* are as follows:

1. Whether the proferred scientific knowledge or technique has been or can be tested.
2. Whether the scientific theory or technique has been submitted to peer review and publication.

3. The known potential error rate of the technique.
4. Whether the theory or technique has gained general acceptance in the relevant scientific discipline.

Using these standards, a series of cases at the criminal and civil levels have excluded testimony of repressed memories of sexual abuse.

In *State v. Hungerford* (1997), the Supreme Court of New Hampshire concluded that a recovered memory which previously had been completely absent from a witness's conscious recollection was suspect because it could not be separated from the process that may have facilitated the recovery of the memory. The New Hampshire Supreme Court held that because of the ongoing debate about how repression occurs, how the process of retrieval occurs, and whether accurate retrieval is possible, the trial courts must have hearings to consider whether such evidence is properly admissible in front of lay juries. In so doing, the New Hampshire Supreme Court relied in part on a decision by the Supreme Court of Rhode Island in *State v. Quattrocchi* (1996). In *State v. Quattrocchi,* a defendant had been sentenced to concurrent sentences of 60 years in jail for sexual abuse of a girl who was described in the decision by the fictitious name of Gina. Gina was age 19 at the time of trial. When Gina was approximately 17 she was admitted to a hospital twice in rapid succession for depression and suicidal thoughts. She had been experiencing deteriorating mental problems for a period of 2 years prior to her hospitalization. While in the hospital she experienced flashbacks during which she recalled incidents of abuse by the criminal defendant, who was her stepfather. The hospital staff thought that she was exhibiting symptoms of Post-Traumatic Stress Disorder (PTSD) and reassessed a former diagnosis of Bipolar Disorder.

The Supreme Court of Rhode Island found it to be particularly significant that while at the hospital Gina had complained about being molested by another patient. After release from the hospital, Gina explored pursuing a civil suit against the defendant but chose not to. The criminal trial was based in large part on the testimony of her treating physician and of a psychiatric nurse. The Supreme Court of Rhode Island concluded that when testimony based on repressed memories is offered, including testimony relating to PTSD which includes flashbacks, the trial court must exercise a gatekeeping function and hold a preliminary hearing to determine whether the evidence is reliable and whether the expert testimony should be admitted. The Supreme Court of Rhode Island accepted most of the *Daubert* guidelines, and reversed the defendant's conviction.

After reviewing the *Quattrocchi* decision, the New Hampshire Supreme Court in *State v. Hungerford* announced eight factors that trial courts need to consider regarding repressed memories:

1. The level of peer review and publication on the phenomenon of repressed memories.
2. Whether the phenomenon has been generally accepted in the psychological community.
3. Whether the phenomenon can be empirically tested.
4. The potential or known rate of falsity of the memory.
5. The particular witness's age at the time of the alleged repressed event.

6. The length of time between the alleged event (or abuse) and the recovery of the memory.
7. The presence or absence of objective and verifiable corroboration that the event took place.
8. The circumstances regarding the recovery of the memory, including whether the witness was in therapy.

Based on these criteria, the New Hampshire Supreme Court reversed the *Hungerford* conviction.

In addition to these criminal cases, several civil cases have led to the exclusion of such testimony. In one California case, *Schall v. Lockheed Missiles & Space Company, Inc.* (1995), the issue was repressed memories of sexual harassment in the workplace. The plaintiff had undergone "light hypnosis" which was not for the purpose of accessing her memories. She began gradually remembering her manager's sexual harassment behavior while undergoing the hypnosis. There was no independent evidence that she had complained of such harassment prior to therapy. The California Appellate Court extended to this civil case a California Supreme Court case that had held that hypnotically refreshed memory is unreliable and inadmissible in criminal cases, absent compliance with certain safeguards.

The U.S. Court of Appeal for the Second Circuit in *Borawick v. Shay* (1995) dealt with the question of whether to allow an action to proceed against a woman's aunt and uncle on her assertions that they had sexually abused her and she had repressed the memories for 20 years. The case was complicated by the fact that the plaintiff had undergone hypnosis through an unlicensed hypnotist who used a form of regression therapy. The memories that were recovered included anal object penetration and her aunt inserting a cap pistol in her vagina. The trial court had excluded the testimony based on a motion *in limine*. The Court of Appeal upheld the decision after a thorough review of a number of cases discussing the impact on witnesses' reliability of hypnosis. The court concluded that while hypnosis may be a valid technique for therapeutic purposes, there was no evidence that it is a consistently effective means to accurately retrieve repressed memories of traumatic past experiences. The court stated that it was highly skeptical of the belief in a clinician's ability to weed out groundless claims in part because childhood sexual abuse seemed to fit like a tailor-made glove to certain types of psychiatric disorders. However, the court did not adopt a per se rule of admissibility or inadmissibility but instead adopted a rule that requires the district court to consider all of the circumstances in a particular case, determining whether to allow the testimony to be admitted.

In *Ramona v. Superior Court* (1997), a California appellate court upheld the trial court decision excluding the testimony of Holly Ramona in an action brought against her father because she had undergone sodium amytal interviews before first asserting that there had been some type of incestuous contact.

One of the few cases holding that delayed memories may be offered into evidence and are not some form of new technique is the U.S. District Court for the District of Massachusetts decision in *Shahzade v. Gregory* (1996).

These cases taken as a whole suggest that courts tend to be extremely cautious in allowing testimony based on delayed memories into evidence, particularly in a criminal case and when there is no independent corroboration of any nature.

SPECIAL CONCERNS FOR THERAPISTS

The following topics represent areas that may be especially problematic for some therapists and that warrant special concern.

LEGAL AWARENESS AND HUMILITY

It is important that therapists remain aware of the evolving legislation and case law governing practice related to recovered memories in their jurisdiction. But it is equally important that they not attempt to "play lawyer." Clients may have numerous pressing questions when recovered memories are at issue, such as, "Is it too late to bring legal action against the alleged perpetrator?" But clinicians must resist any temptation to function as attorneys providing clients with legal opinions and advice.

AWARENESS OF THE THERAPIST'S HISTORY

Research suggests that this topic may be not only of professional interest but also of personal immediacy for many therapists. A national survey of psychologists found that of the nearly one-quarter who reported a personal history of child abuse, about 40% reported a time during which they could not remember some or all of the abuse (Feldman-Summers & Pope, 1994; see also http://idealist.com/memories/history2.shtml). Amnesia occurred for both sexual and nonsexual forms of abuse. The reported "forgetting" of abuse was statistically unrelated to the age or sex of the participants but was related to severity (i.e., the more severe the abuse, the more likely to have undergone a period of forgetting). About half of the psychologists who reported having experienced a period of forgetting the abuse also reported finding external corroboration that the remembered abuse actually occurred.

Therapists must be aware of how their own history of abuse—perhaps including recovered memories—or their absence of such a history may influence their work. There is no research demonstrating that better therapy is done by those who have no history of abuse (e.g., that they might be more "objective") or by those who have an abuse history (e.g., that they might tend to be more empathetic toward abuse survivors or have a better understanding of the dynamics of abuse). While avoiding such unfounded stereotypes, therapists need to be aware of their own unique history and how it affects their work. It is the responsibility of each therapist to examine the ways in which personal factors may create bias, blind spots, or barriers to effective responses to those who seek their help when recovered memories are at issue.

EVALUATING CLAIMS ABOUT RESEARCH, THEORY, AND PRACTICE

Therapists who work with patients when recovered memories are at issue must remain abreast of the literature discussing research, theory, and practice in this arena. But it is important that such claims not be accepted passively and reflexively, without active consideration and questioning. It is the opinion of the authors (which, of course, readers should also challenge) that many of the most basic issues in this area are far from settled, despite various authoritative claims to the contrary. Here are five examples.

Child Sex Trauma as Typical in Women's Histories

There have been claims that child sex abuse typically occurs in the histories of women. Blume (1990), for example, wrote that "it is not unlikely that *more than half of all women* are survivors of childhood sexual trauma" (p. iv; italics in original). It is important to question such statements in light of the empirical data, especially the absence of any general population study published in a peer-reviewed scientific or professional journal that supports this claim.

Tests That Show Child Abuse Occurred

Pope and Vasquez (1998) discuss claims that certain "signs" on standardized tests warrant the conclusion that child abuse occurred, emphasizing that such claims lack empirical support. One such claim asserted that a particular response to a Rorschach card infallibly revealed a history of child abuse. Such claims should always be carefully examined in light of their empirical support, if any.

> Whenever standardized psychological tests are used as part of an assessment, it is essential that the tests be adequately normed for the relevant population and adequately validated for the task to which they are put. Unfortunately, standardized tests may often be misused in the area of sexual abuse. Especially in forensic assessments but also in other contexts, a test or test battery may be put forth as showing that a person did experience a certain instance of abuse or did not experience a certain form of abuse . . . all in the complete absence of any successful attempt to validate the test or test battery for that purpose. (Pope, 1994, pp. 106–107; see also Pope, Butcher, & Seelen, 1993)

The responsibility to carefully question claims about standardized psychological tests such as the MMPI-2 or the Rorschach in light of the empirical support also extends to claims about checklists. No checklist should be accepted without adequate evidence that it has been validated for its intended purpose (see, e.g., Olio, 1996).

Recovered Memories as False Per Se

There have been claims that recovered memories are per se false. For example, the False Memory Syndrome Foundation (FMSF) noted in 1992 that: "Psychiatrists advising the Foundation members seem to be unanimous in the belief that memories of such atrocities cannot be repressed. Horrible incidents of childhood are remembered" (FMSF, 1992a, p. 2). Such amnesia is, according to such claims, a scientific impossibility because the brain lacks any mechanism that would enable it to function in this way. In an amicus brief argument to the court, FMSF (1997) claimed that no known cognitive mechanism is considered capable of even contributing to an amnesia of a traumatic event: "Although a broad range of mechanisms are known to produce various kinds of memory disturbance and have been examined by memory researchers and theorists, none are, at present, considered capable of contributing to a supposed amnesia for traumatic events" (p. 17). But if they are not actual memories, by what function do recovered memories of abuse arise? Miller (1997) described the growing amount of evidence supporting the claim that recovered memories "are the artifact of the constructive and suggestible nature of our memories (e.g., Lindsay & Read, 1994; Loftus, 1993)" (p. 250). Fraser (1997) noted the effects of such authoritative claims, writing that one consequence of the work of FMSF is "that many . . . members of the public have been persuaded to believe that all recovered memories are bogus" (p. D14).

But rather than reflexively accept such claims that atrocities cannot be repressed, that horrible incidents of childhood are remembered, that there are no cognitive mechanisms that might enable such amnesia, and that recovered memories are artifacts, it is useful to examine them in light of, for example, the studies published in peer-reviewed scientific and professional journals of such amnesia occurring in various populations (e.g., general population, therapy patients, and therapists). Such population studies, some of them prospective, meeting the criterion of peer-reviewed publication include: Andrews et al. (1995); Briere and Conte (1993); Burgess, Hartman, and Baker (1995); Cameron (1994); Dalenberg (1996); Elliott (1997); Elliott and Briere (1995); Feldman-Summers and Pope (1994); Golding, Sanchez, and Sego (1996); Herman and Schatzow (1987); Hovdestad and Kristiansen (1996); Leavitt (1997); Loftus, Polonsky, and Fullilove (1994); Melchert (1996); Polusny and Follette (1996); Pope and Tabachnick (1995); Roe and Schwartz (1996); Roesler and Wind (1994); van der Kolk and Fisler (1995); Widom and Morris (1997); Widom and Shepard (1996); and Williams (1994).

Similarly, Professor Ross Cheit maintains a recovered memory archive at his web site (www.brown.edu/Departments/Taubman_Center/Recovmem/Archive.html), listing publicly available documents supporting the validity of 35 individual cases of recovered memories of abuse. These cases meet the following criteria for admission:

1. *Cases must be verifiable.*   To be included on this list, cases must be identified with sufficient specificity to facilitate independent examination by others. Proper names are favored, and cases without proper names must nevertheless be verifiable. The only cases involving pseudonyms are those so treated by a court, and those cases can be located and reviewed (although obtaining access to all of the records would require judicial approval). There is at least one citation for each case on this list. . . .

2. *Cases must include strong corroborative evidence.*   To be included on this list, the recovered memory at issue must be corroborated by at least one of the following sources:
   a. confession, guilty plea, or self-incriminatory statement,
   b. testimony from other victims (or from an eyewitness to the abuse), or corroborative documentary evidence that is vitally relevant to the charges at issue, or
   c. corroboration of significant circumstantial evidence

Note: Almost all cases in the Archive have more than one form of corroborative evidence. With the exception of a few cases set within a family, the multiple victim cases all have corroboration from more than one additional victim. The cases based on circumstantial corroboration all include favorable judicial decisions on the facts as well (Cheit, 1997).

It is important to note that such additional sources of data must themselves be carefully scrutinized and questioned. The point is not to arrive at some clear and definitive answer, but rather to emphasize the need for continuous, rigorous questioning of claims, no matter how authoritative their source or how numerous their advocates.

Easily Implanted Memories of Child Abuse

There have been claims that, in the words of FMSF amicus briefs: "The available data indicate the relative ease with which psychotherapy can mistakenly persuade clients that they were sexually abused as children" (e.g., FMSF, 1995, pp. 33–34; 1997, p. 41). This claim, originally made to the court in 1995, may be traced back to a famous study conducted by a member of FMSF's Scientific and Professional Advisory Board and to an expansive view of memory's suggestibility. In Loftus's original "shopping mall" experiment (variations of which were later conducted), a person is convinced, on the basis of false statements from a family member who was supposedly there at the time, that many years ago he or she was lost in a shopping mall (Loftus & Ketcham, 1994; see also Crook & Dean, 1999a, 1999b; Loftus, 1999). This experiment became the basis for claims that it is easy to implant complete and detailed memories for traumatic events that never occurred.

> When challenged with the assertion, "But it's just not possible to implant in someone's mind a complete memory with details and relevant emotions for a traumatic event that didn't happen," Loftus responded: "But that's exactly what we did in the shopping mall experiment." (Loftus & Ketcham, 1994, p.212)

This claim of experimental proof of the ease with which false memories of childhood trauma can be implanted reflects sweeping claims about how any memory can be completely shaped.

> If handled skillfully, the power of misinformation is so enormous and sufficiently controllable that a colleague and I recently postulated a not-too-distant "brave new world" in which misinformation researchers would be able to proclaim: "Give us a dozen healthy memories . . . and our own specified world to handle them in. And we'll guarantee to take any one at random and train it to become any type of memory that we might select . . . regardless of its origin or the brain that holds it." The implications for the legal field, for advertising, and for clinical settings are far reaching. (Loftus, 1992, p. 123)

Questioning such claims in historical perspective can be useful. The claims are essentially those made more than a half-century earlier by Watson (1939), who asserted that numerous scientific experiments had proven learning theory to be so powerful that psychologists with sufficient resources could randomly select a dozen individuals and produce literally any kind of people and behavior they might select. The Watsonian claims were enthusiastically embraced by many in the scientific community. It was only as time passed and more objective assessments were gradually given consideration that the claims about the almost absolute power of learning theory were acknowledged to be false. It was not just that people failed to fall helplessly under the sway of conditioning: Even docile animals frequently failed to follow the proclaimed "laws" of conditioning (e.g., Breland & Breland, 1961).

When considering the shopping mall experiment as demonstration that false memories of child abuse are easily implanted in therapy patients, perhaps one question concerns stimulus validity: Is the childhood experience of being briefly lost in a setting such as a shopping mall sufficiently like the experience of being repeatedly raped by a parent to justify generalization? Pezdek (1995; see also Pezdek, Finger, & Hodge, 1996, 1997) has suggested that such an analogy may not be valid in the area of implanting false memories. Using what she suggests might be a somewhat more analogous scenario—that of a suggested false memory of a rectal enema—her experimental attempts at implantation of a suggestion had a 0% success rate.

Again, the goal in presenting this material is not to encourage the view that a particular claim has been proven but rather to encourage a careful, open, active questioning of all claims in this area in light of the full range of research and theory, and a willingness to acknowledge the complexity of these issues and the possibility that simple, easy, clear answers may not be warranted by the data.

Suspecting Child Abuse on the Basis of Symptoms

Kihlstrom (1995; see also Olio, 1995), who set forth the definition of false memory syndrome that FMSF cites in its amicus briefs, has claimed that "it is not permissible to infer, or frankly even to suspect, a history of abuse in people who present symptoms of abuse." Reviews of state laws suggest that almost half use a form of the verb *suspect* (e.g., "suspect that a child has been abused") in legislation requiring therapists to report suspected child abuse (Kalichman, 1993). Such claims that it is impermissible to form suspicions based on presenting symptoms may affect clinicians' decisions about whether to file mandated reports of suspected child abuse.

Kihlstrom's claim that it is impermissible "even to suspect" is based on the argument that there is no specific association between any symptom and child abuse and to do so would be to commit the logical error of affirming the consequent. One approach to questioning this claim is to distinguish between the syllogistic proof of deduction and the formation of diagnostic hypotheses. (For a discussion of affirming the consequent fallacy in assessment, see Pope & Brown, 1996; Pope, Butcher, & Seelen, 1993.)

When conducting a clinical assessment, especially in the initial sessions, therapists must begin developing hypotheses in light of incomplete data. As new data emerge, they provide evidence that contradicts, supports, or refines initial hypotheses as well as suggesting new hypotheses. Therapists conducting an assessment in the early stages may legitimately form suspicions about numerous diagnostic, etiologic, or prognostic possibilities. Varied options may be added to the rule-out list during the process of differential diagnosis. Extensive research and theory support and describe this process of professional decision making in the face of uncertainty (e.g., Bell, Raiffa, & Tversky, 1988; Dowie & Elstein, 1988; Kahneman, Slovic, & Tversky, 1982; Wolf, Gruppen, & Billi, 1985). An array of incomplete information such as presenting symptoms may form an adequate, reasonable basis for suspecting that a patient may have been abused while forming an inadequate, fallacious basis for determining that abuse must have occurred.

An array of presenting symptoms such as dizziness, shortness of breath, heaviness in the chest, and an aching arm or jaw illustrates this essential distinction between deductive proof and provisional hypotheses. Informed and qualified health care professionals would never accept such symptoms as proof that the patient is having a heart attack. These symptoms—taken singly or in combination—do not have a specific or pathognomonic relationship with a heart attack; the symptoms—singly or in combination—can be caused by an almost infinite variety of biological or psychological factors. But it is not only permissible but also responsible practice for heath care professionals to suspect a heart attack as a possible cause and to address this hypothesis during differential diagnosis.

If it is considered malpractice to suspect child abuse on the basis of presenting symptoms, then we are drawn back to the period not so long ago when presenting symptoms per se never led to a provisional hypothesis of child abuse and additional data were not sought that might contradict, support, or refine the hypothesis. Caffey (1946), for example, described cases in which health care professionals encountered infants whose presenting symptoms were chronic blood clots in the brain and broken arms and legs. The infants' parents and other witnesses volunteered no reports of accidental or intentional trauma as a possible cause of the symptoms. Caffey described the bafflement experienced by clinicians of that period at what possible causes might have led to these symptoms. Should clinicians be prohibited from suspecting that one possible cause of such presenting symptoms in infants might be child abuse? In her analysis of Kihlstrom's (1995) claim that clinicians must never suspect a history of child abuse on the basis of the patient's presenting symptoms, Olio (1995) presented a hypothetical example: a 3- to 5-year-old girl, one of whose presenting symptoms is infection by the gonococcus bacterium, *Neisseria gonorrhoeae*.

Case Presentations and Source Data

When reading and evaluating case presentations, clinicians must avoid overreliance on secondary sources. Clinicians must be prepared to examine primary sources of data on which case discussions are based. For example, a discussion by Schooler, Bendiksen, and Ambadar (1997) of the scientific status of recovered memories presents the case history of Ross Cheit as a public case for which there appeared to be reasonable corroborative evidence. Schooler et al. characterize a 1993 *U.S. News & World Report* article (Horn, 1993) as providing "multiple sources of indirect corroboration of the event. Specifically, the author of this article was able to find other individuals who had independently recorded instances of Farmer's sexual improprieties, both before and after Cheit's recovered memory experience" (p. 261). The reasoning is that because there were some people (other than Cheit) who had alleged that Farmer had sexually abused other individuals (i.e., other than Cheit), it is possible that Farmer may have sexually abused Cheit as well. Consequently, the available evidence is inconclusive in regard to whether Cheit was abused. "Although these sources of evidence do not conclusively demonstrate that Cheit himself was the victim of abuse, their implication of Farmer as a sexual abuser clearly supports the possibility that he may have abused Cheit as well" (p. 261).

The indirect and inconclusive evidence supporting the possibility that Cheit may have been abused comes, according to Schooler et al. (1997), from a questionable source and may reflect the personal biases of its author. "It should be noted that the reporter who investigated this case was a friend of Cheit's. While such an affiliation need not invalidate the evidence provided, it is possible that the evidence was not collected in a completely unbiased manner" (p. 261). Calling into question the credibility of the article's author, Schooler et al. set forth no facts to support the notion that the author collected or presented the evidence in a biased manner.

Those who rely on Schooler et al. to learn about the nature, sources, and credibility of evidence relevant to Cheit's report of recovered memories of abuse may conclude that there is only this indirect evidence, collected by a reporter of questionable fairness. However, Schooler et al. do not disclose that the *U.S. News & World Report* article that they cite as their source also discusses a taped confession: "For nearly an hour, Cheit held Farmer on the phone, a tape recorder running all the while. Farmer admitted molesting Cheit in his cabin at night. . . ." (Horn, 1993, p. 62). Other reporters have also listened to the tape; Wagner (1993) published quotes from the tape and later (1994, p. B7) wrote, "At that time, Farmer admitted molesting Cheit, according to the tape." This taped confession, along with other evidence, was also heard and considered by the court in Cheit's civil suit against Farmer, resulting in a "judgment from said defendant in the sum of $457,000" (*Cheit v. Farmer*, 1994, p. 1). The taped confession was also noted in a letter of public apology to Cheit issued by the sponsors of the camp at which Farmer was camp director. The sponsors expressed to Cheit and his parents that they were "deeply sorry for the harm that came to them while Ross Cheit attended the Chorus's summer camp in 1968 and wishes to assure them that the Chorus is doing everything possible to prevent child molestation at the Chorus and at the summer camp" (San Francisco Boys Chorus, 1994, p. 2). (For additional accounts of this case, see, e.g., Butler, 1994; McNeil-Lehrer, 1995; Stanton, 1993, 1995.)

It is, of course, possible to take the position that no combination of taped confession, legal judgment, and the other sources of information could ever conclusively establish that Cheit's report of recovering memories of repeated abuse after decades of not being aware of the abuse is accurate. But it is worth considering the impact and implications of a chapter published in 1997 (Schooler, et al.) presenting the case study of Cheit as if these other sources of information, which were publicized in 1993 and 1994 as well as in subsequent years, did not exist. This example underscores the importance of avoiding an overreliance on secondary sources. But it is important to consider what impact such case presentations may have on the person (i.e., Cheit) whose experiences they publicly describe and examine, on other people with similar experiences (who may fear that sources of information relevant to their claims about abuse may be denied, discounted, or ignored in the scientific literature, and who may therefore decide to remain silent), on the body of scientific literature to which it contributes, and on the beliefs and attitudes of scientists, therapists, policymakers, and the lay public.

This example serves as a reminder of essential responsibilities beyond that of avoiding overreliance on secondary sources. When making public presentations of case studies, clinicians have a significant responsibility to ensure that information is presented accurately and fairly. Presentations must not, through omission of important data, unintentionally mislead scientists, clinicians, and others into believing that additional sources of information do not exist. Clinicians have a similar responsibility when documenting their work with patients. They must ensure that the record they provide of the patient's history, informed consent, assessment, treatment plan, and response to treatment adequately reflects the information available.

THE AD HOMINEM FALLACY AND FALSE ACCUSATIONS

When controversy arises, thoughtful statements may unfortunately give way to ad hominem, personal attacks disparaging the character, integrity, or motivation of someone who disagrees. The shift in focus from considering the nature, validity, or implication of ideas to circulating false statements attacking the character, ethics, motivation, or other personal attributes of someone who disagrees may produce varied consequences (e.g., influencing public opinion, affecting reputations, or silencing dissent) but rarely plays a useful role in the scientific process.

An example of this shift in focus is the frequent labeling as *True Believers* those who disagree with the False Memory Syndrome Foundation and its board. One of the most widely cited books on the topic of recovered memories uses this True-Believer label to underscore the claim that those who have resisted the senior author's conclusions are motivated by prejudice and fear rather than disagreeing on the basis of evidence, reason, and good faith (e.g., "I know the prejudices and fears that lie behind the resistance to my life's work"; Loftus & Ketcham, 1994, p. 4). This book splits the profession into two groups: "On one side are the 'True Believers,'. . . . On the other side are the 'Skeptics,' . . ." (Loftus & Ketcham, 1994, p. 31). The book makes clear its source for disparaging those who disagree with its thesis by quoting from Hoffer's well-known text, *The True Believer* (1951/1989).

True Believers, as Hoffer wrote, insulate themselves from facts and ignore a doctrine's validity, valuing its ability to protect from reality (1951/1989, p. 80). Hoffer emphasized the True Believer's passionate hatred and fanaticism, and described how "the acrid secretion of the frustrated mind, though composed chiefly of fear and ill will, acts yet as a marvelous slime to cement the embittered and disaffected into one compact whole" (p. 124).

In the history of science, use of statements that disparage the character or other personal attributes of someone who disagrees has been identified as a logical fallacy. It is illogical to conclude that because we have discredited the motivation, integrity, or worth of someone who articulates an idea, we have thus discredited the idea expressed by the person.

While ad hominem attacks have tended to emerge in the heat and spontaneity of face-to-face debates and in behind-the-scenes gossip, this current controversy seems noteworthy for the degree to which the ad hominem appears prominently in formal scientific writings (for discussion of diverse examples, see Pope, 1995a, 1995b, 1997; Pope & Brown, 1996). Disparaging the character of those with whom one takes issue may not only be a major theme of a book, as in the preceding example, but may even define the work by serving as the book's title. One book devoting a section to recovered memory issues leaves no doubt about the abhorrent character of those on the other side: *Whores of the Court: The Fraud of Psychiatric Testimony and the Rape of American Justice* (Hagen, 1997).

Traditionally, peer-reviewed scientific journals have remained relatively free of such attacks because journal editors and peer reviewers have recognized the ad hominem fallacy and rejected such tactics. In some peer-reviewed scientific journals, however, ad hominem argument has become an acceptable part of scientific discourse. An author's use of the term *True Believers* characterizing those who disagree, for example, now appears in the American Psychological Society's journal *Psychological Science* (Crews, 1996, p. 66).

In a more extreme example involving one of this chapter's authors, Elizabeth Loftus published a false accusation that someone with whom she disagreed was wildly reckless in an important area of ethics. Her claim was later carefully investigated, reviewed, and evaluated in light of the facts by the American Psychological Association (APA) journal that had published this charge and by the APA structure responsible for the content of this journal. Her claim was found to be false. The Fall 1997 issue (vol. 4, no. 3) of *Clinical Psychology: Science and Practice* contains, prior to the first article, a page headed "Correction Notice and Apology." The journal describes and documents the relevant statements and facts in detail, provides a correction, and specifically apologizes for this "false statement disparaging Dr. Pope's ethics."

It is likely that many, if not all, of us have, in the heat of controversy, been tempted to resort to ad hominem tactics. But such approaches detract and distract from scientific discourse and often misinform readers. The process of scientific deliberation is better served when attacks on character and false accusations are avoided.

INFORMED CONSENT

Providing patients with informed consent and informed refusal is one of therapists' fundamental legal and ethical responsibilities (Pope & Brown, 1996; Pope & Vasquez, 1998). According to a news report (Smith, 1997) of the $5.8 million jury award in a false memory case previously described, jurors later said that one of their primary concerns during deliberations was the lack of informed consent, that the therapists failed to provide adequate information about the nature and possible effects of the treatment.

The following list of consent issues is from Pope and Brown (1996, pp. 285–288; copyright © 1996 by the American Psychological Association. Reprinted with permission).

INFORMED CONSENT ISSUES FOR PROVIDING THERAPY TO A PATIENT WHEN RECOVERED MEMORIES ARE AN ISSUE

Informed consent is best viewed as a process rather than a static formality. The process is likely to occur differently and to possess different content according to whether the therapy is, say, cognitive-behavioral, psychodynamic, feminist, existential, systems, or gestalt. Aside from differences of theoretical orientation and technique, each therapist, patient, and situation are unique, and the process of informed consent must be shaped to respect and take account of that uniqueness.

The process, both oral and written, will vary significantly from therapist to therapist, patient to patient, and setting to setting, but certain issues seem central to this process. What follows is a list of some of the most significant issues that tend to be a part of the informed consent process. It may be useful for the therapist to review this list periodically and consider the degree to which each issue may be essential to a particular patient's providing or withholding informed consent. Because both informed consent and therapy itself are processes, the list may be useful not only at the beginning of therapy but also in subsequent stages as the patient's situation, therapeutic needs, and treatment plan change.

- Is there any evidence that the person is not fully capable of understanding the information and issues relevant to giving or withholding informed consent?
- Are there any factors that would prevent this person from arriving at decisions that are truly voluntary?
- Does the person adequately understand the type and nature of the services that the therapist is offering?
- Are there other methods (that might replace or supplement the therapy that you provide) that the person might use to effectively address the relevant issues of concern? If so, is the person adequately aware of them?
- If the degree of the therapist's education, training, or experience in the area of providing clinical or forensic services to patients reporting recovered memories would be relevant to the person's decision about whether to begin or continue work with the therapist, does the person have the relevant information?
- Does the person understand that the therapist is not an attorney and cannot provide legal counsel or representation?
- Does the person understand whether the therapist is licensed (or is, for example, an unlicensed intern); the nature of that license (e.g., psychology, psychiatry, social work); and how the license status may affect such issues as types of services provided (e.g., medications), confidentiality, privilege, etc.?
- If any information about the person or the treatment will be communicated to or will be in any way accessible to others in your setting (e.g., administrative staff, utilization review committees, quality control personnel, clinical supervisors) either orally (e.g., supervision, case conferences) or in writing (e.g., chart notes, treatment summaries, treatment reports), is the person adequately aware of these communications and modes of access and their implications?
- If information about the person or the treatment will be communicated to any payment source (e.g., an insurance company, a government agency), is the person adequately aware of the nature, content, and implications of these communications?
- Have any potential limitations in the number of sessions (e.g., a managed care plan's limitation of 10 therapy sessions, an insurance plan's limitation of payments for mental health services to a specific dollar amount) or length of treatment (e.g., if the therapist is an intern whose internship will conclude within 3 months, after which the therapist will no longer be available) been adequately disclosed to the person and the potential implications been adequately discussed?
- Does the person adequately understand the therapist's policy regarding missed or canceled appointments?

- Has there been adequate disclosure and discussion of any information about the therapist that might significantly affect the person's decision to begin or continue work with the therapist?
- Does the person adequately understand limits to accessibility to the therapist (e.g., will the therapist be available to receive or return phone calls during the day, during the evening, or on nights, weekends, or holidays)? Does the person adequately understand limits to the extent of such accessibility between regularly scheduled sessions (e.g., will phone contacts be limited to brief periods of 5 or 10 minutes, or will the therapist allow longer phone consultation)? Are fees for such services clearly defined?
- Does the person adequately understand what steps to take and what resources are (and are not) available in case of a crisis, emergency, or severe need?
- If the person or the treatment is to be used for teaching or related purposes, does the person adequately understand the nature, extent, and implications of such arrangements? If the person or the treatment is to be used for research or related purposes, does the person adequately understand the nature, extent, and implications of such arrangements?
- Does the person adequately understand limitations to privacy, confidentiality, and privilege, particularly those related to discretionary or mandatory reports by the therapist and to any legal actions?
- Does the person adequately understand the degree to which treatment notes and any other documents in the chart will be made available to the patient and/or to the patient's attorney?
- Does the client understand the implications of the use of such treatment modalities as hypnosis or amytal interviews, if these are contemplated? Are the effects of these treatments on a client's potential rights to pursue litigation outlined? Has the therapist considered the use of an additional, separate consent form for such techniques?

INTRUSIVE ADVOCACY AND FORGIVENESS

The issue of informed consent raises more subtle issues of the therapist's influence. Therapists may, however unintentionally, act in ways that intrude on deliberations and decisions that are rightly in the domain of the patient. If a client discloses a recovered memory, the therapist may move in to convince the patient that the memory must be true or must be false. The therapist may attempt to direct the patient's response to the memory, perhaps instructing the client to cut off all contact with the alleged perpetrator. Maneuvers like these represent what might be called *intrusive advocacy* (Pope, Sonne, & Holroyd, 1993) and may cause great harm. Intrusive advocacy is the therapist's "tendency to want to guide, direct, or determine a patient's decisions about what steps to take or what steps not to take in regard to a perpetrator" (p. 116).

A central issue occurring in the treatment of many patients who have recovered memories of abuse and that may be subject to intrusive advocacy is that of forgiveness. Like instructions that the client must cut off all contact with the family or at least with the abuser, the message that the client must forgive an abuser also seems to be a form of intrusive advocacy (Pope et al., 1993). While forgiveness may seem an essential step in recovery to some therapists, it may be useful to consider Olio's (1992) discussion of what she terms the three myths of mandated forgiveness, which are excerpted in the following (reprinted with permission of the author).

Myth 1.   Forgiveness Makes You a Better Person

Olio notes that:

> This myth originates with the difficulties we all have in facing and acknowledging the ugly act of child abuse. Especially when we contemplate its possibility in our own homes, child abuse calls into question many of our hopes and beliefs of the world as a fundamentally decent and safe place. It is, of course, natural to want to do everything possible to make the hurt go away. It is a well-meaning mistake that is often made to hope that by encouraging the survivor not to think about the abuse, it will stop bothering him or her. . . . In addition, I believe this myth reflects a fear and a misunderstanding of anger. In this myth anger, outrage, and revenge are all used interchangeably, with no distinction drawn between the emotion itself and the various options available to express it. It seems important to remember that anger is a feeling, and feelings themselves do not damage anyone. Feelings of anger are a natural response to abuse, and as Bass and Davis (1988) point out, anger can sometimes be the "backbone of healing" the damage caused by sexual abuse.

Myth 2.   Forgiveness Must Be All-Encompassing

Olio comments that:

> I imagine this concept of linking self-forgiveness to the forgiveness of others comes from the belief that, if we can acknowledge both the good and evil in others and forgive their mistakes, then we can more easily accept the good and evil in ourselves, and thus achieve self-forgiveness. Although this idea has theoretical merit, it would seem to apply more to the general development of a capacity to forgive rather than to the decision to forgive in a particular situation. The recognition that forgiveness can be a valuable process does not necessarily lead to the conclusion that forgiveness must be given in all instances. . . .
>
> Self-forgiveness, or what might be more aptly titled self-acceptance, is an essential step in the integration of the abuse experiences. Survivors may have to forgive/accept that they did have needs, that they were small and powerless, that they had feelings in response to the abuse (pain, fear, rage, and in some cases even pleasure), and that it has taken time to heal. However, the idea that this self-forgiveness is somehow contingent on forgiving the abuser is troublesome, as it suggests the necessity of a merging with the person who is to be forgiven. . . .
>
> Adults whose physical and psychic boundaries have been violated by childhood sexual abuse have difficulty enough maintaining a healthy sense of separation from the abuser. Especially in those cases where the abuser is someone, perhaps the only one, by whom the child has felt loved, the child may feel sorry for and/or have a deep need to protect the abuser. . . .
>
> The belief that forgiveness must be total to be effective implies that there is only one kind of "good enough" forgiveness. In reality the meaning and degree of forgiveness varies from person to person. Each person, as he or she is able to reconnect to his or her own experiences without the use of denial and dissociation, must find the type of forgiveness that fits for that unique person. If forgiveness is to be meaningful, it must be given out of free choice, which necessarily implies the freedom not to give it.

Myth 3. Failure to Forgive Maintains Helplessness

Olio comments that:

> Myth #3, which addresses issues of helplessness and responsibility, has been heavily influenced by the recovery movement and 12 step programs. Faced with the powerlessness experienced by individuals who abuse alcohol and the resulting enmeshed, codependent relationships, recovery programs have stressed the importance of each person's taking responsibility for him or herself. This has provided individuals with an understanding of the need to take charge of changing their lives, regardless of others' behaviors. Many people have experienced a great relief with the realization that they don't need to change anyone else in order to get on with their own lives. Forgiveness has been a central component of this approach. . . .
>
> This issue of empowerment is a tremendously important one for survivors of sexual abuse. Empowerment develops as the individual is able to fully acknowledge the painful realities of childhood, while simultaneously integrating an updated reality of grown-up strength and options. Forgiveness may be part of this process for some individuals; for others it will not be. The fact remains, however, [that] although forgiveness may result in a shift in the experience of victimization for some survivors, there is no evidence to suggest that survivors cannot come to an experience of empowerment and effectiveness through other means as well. (Olio, 1992, pp. 73–79)

THE STRESSES AND DISTRESSES OF THE WORK

Therapy itself can be stressful work, involving intense emotions, and sometimes therapists themselves may be in need of therapy (Kaslow, 1984, 1986; Pope & Tabachnick, 1993, 1994). Trauma work may bring its own special stresses. For example, to sit and listen as a patient describes a horrifying event may sometimes cause what has come to be called a vicarious (or secondary) traumatization in the therapist. It is important that therapists monitor their responses to working with patients when child sexual abuse or other forms of violence, oppression, or horror are at issue; ensure that they have the personal and professional resources to continue such work effectively; and take prompt steps in any instance when they, as therapists, become so distressed that they cannot work safely and effectively. Books by McCann and Pearlman (1990), Pearlman and Saakvitne (1995), Saakvitne, Pearlman, et al. (1996), and Salter (1995) may be particularly useful in this regard.

In addition to the work done in the consulting room, therapists may encounter challenges such as their patients being forced to cross picket lines to obtain legal mental health services (Pope, 1996, 1997). This activity was mentioned by the False Memory Syndrome Foundation as early as 1992. In a newsletter article entitled "What Can Families Do?" the first activity mentioned after the rhetorical title question was picketing (FMSF, 1992b). In his order granting summary judgment in favor of defendant trauma therapist Charles Whitfield, MD, whom Pamela Freyd and Peter Freyd had sued for alleged defamation, U.S. Judge Benson Legg mentioned many aspects of FMSF activities, including picketing. He wrote:

> In response, the Freyds mounted a public campaign, challenging the validity of such recovered memories. In 1992, they formed the False Memory Syndrome Foundation ("FMSF"), aggressively contesting the existence of traumatic amnesia and repressed memories. . . . Plaintiffs relied on various fora to publicize their foundation and "to

debunk this preposterous theory," including . . . the picketing of therapists' homes. (*Pamela Freyd et al. v. Charles L. Whitfield*, 1997, pp. 1–2)

(For a discussion of this case, see Becker, 1997, p. 39.)

A symposium on these tactics and their effects on patients, therapists, and others was presented at the 1997 annual meeting of the American Psychological Association. Among the presenters and their topics were: Jennifer Hoult, "Silencing the Victim: The Politics of Discrediting Child Abuse Survivors"; Ross Cheit, "False Representations about True Cases of Recovered Memory"; Jennifer Freyd, "Science in the Memory Debate"; Anna Salter, "Confessions of a Whistle Blower: Lessons Learned"; and David Calof, "Notes from a Practice Under Siege" (Sidran Foundation, 1997).

Former American Psychological Association (APA) president Ron Fox, presenting the results of an APA task force study, emphasized that the research showed that "state licensure and grievance procedures have been used to harass and make unfounded charges against psychologists who provide psychotherapy to abuse victims" (Seppa, 1996, p. 12). According to the *APA Monitor*, " 'There are some groups that have taken [recovered] memories as prima facie evidence of poor therapeutic practice,' Fox said. Some groups have mailed out newsletters instructing people how to make complaints to ethics boards to harass therapists, he said" (Seppa, 1996, p. 12). Fox noted that some therapists have consequently altered their practice in response to such tactics, and others have stopped serving this very distressed population.

Therapists must candidly and continually assess their own responses to such tactics and to the consequences of an increasing number of therapists refusing to treat this population. It is a fundamental responsibility of a therapist to address immediately any stress or distress that might interfere with providing competent and helpful services.

SUMMARY AND RECOMMENDATIONS

Therapists responding to reports of recovered memories of abuse face complex challenges: the rapidly evolving legal structure, the unresolved scientific questions, and the stresses and distresses of work in this area. When therapists fail to meet these challenges adequately, people suffer. "It is worth emphasizing that some therapists engage in incompetent, unethical, or well-meaning but misguided behaviors, sometimes with disastrous consequences for patients (see, e.g., Pope, 1990, 1994; Pope, Simpson, & Weiner, 1978). In some instances, these behaviors include using unvalidated, misleading, or bizarre methods for assessing whether a patient was sexually abused as a child (Pope & Vasquez, 1991)" (Pope, 1996, p. 961; see also http://idealist.com/memories/science.shtml). Such unsupported and inappropriate methods would include, for example, using a particular response to a Rorschach card, a specific MMPI profile, a style of clothing, or a client's constellation of concerns as a pathognomonic sign that sex abuse must have occurred. This chapter attempts to provide information useful for therapists who are attempting to stay abreast of the legal, scientific, and clinical aspects of recovered memories, and to highlight some of the special pitfalls or concerns.

REFERENCES

Andrews, B., Morton, J., Bekerian, D. A., Brewin, C. R., Davis, G. M., & Mollon, P. (1995). The recovery of memories in clinical practice: Experiences and beliefs of British Psychological Society practitioners. *The Psychologist, 8*, 209–214.

Becker, E. (1997, December). Court upholds free speech rights in memory debate. *American Psychological Association Monitor*, p. 39. Internet: www.apa.org/monitor/judno.html.

Bell, D., Raiffa, H., & Tversky, A. (Eds.). (1988). *Decision making: Descriptive, normative, and prescriptive interactions*. Cambridge, England: Cambridge University Press.

Bird v. W.C.W. (1994), 37 Tex.Sup.Ct. 329, 868 S.W. 2d 767 (Tex.)

Blume, E. S. (1990). *Secret survivors: Uncovering incest and its aftereffects in women*. New York: John Wiley & Sons.

Borawick v. Shay (1995), 68 F.3d 597 (2d Cir.), *cert. denied* 116 S. Ct. 1869, 134 L. Ed. 2d 966 (1996).

Bowman, C. G., & Mertz, E. (1996a). A bias in the flow of information? *American Bar Association's Judges' Journal, 35*, 13.

Bowman, C. G., & Mertz, E. (1996b). A dangerous direction: Legal intervention in sexual abuse survivor therapy. *Harvard Law Review, 109*, 549–639.

Breland, K., & Breland, M. (1961). The misbehavior of organisms. *American Psychologist, 16*, 681–684.

Briere, J., & Conte, J. R. (1993). Self-reported amnesia for abuse in adults molested as children. *Journal of Traumatic Stress, 6*, 21–31.

Burgess, A. W., Hartman, C. R., & Baker T. (1995). Memory presentations of childhood sexual abuse. *Journal of Psychosocial Nursing, 33*, 9–16.

Butler, K. (1994, September 1). S.F. Boys Chorus settles abuse case. *San Francisco Chronicle*, p. A2.

Caffey, J. (1946). Multiple fractures in the long bones of infants suffering from chronic subdural hematoma. *American Journal of Roentgenology, 56*, 163–173.

Cameron, C. (1994). Women survivors confronting their abusers: Issues, decisions, and outcomes. *Journal of Child Sexual Abuse, 3*, 7–35.

Cheit, R. (1997). Recovered memory archive. Internet: www.brown.edu/Departments/Taubman_Center/Recovmem/Archive.html.

Cheit v. Farmer (1994), Case # 954272 Superior Court of the State of California for the County of San Francisco, Judgement, November 14.

Crook, L. S., & Dean, M. C. (1999a). "Lost in a shopping mall"—A breach of professional ethics. *Ethics & Behavior, 9*, 39–50.

Crook, L. S., & Dean, M. C. (1999b). Logical fallacies and ethical breaches. *Ethics & Behavior, 9*, 61–68.

Crews, F. (1996). The verdict on Freud. *Psychological Science, 7*, 63–68.

Dalenberg, C. J. (1996). Accuracy, timing and circumstances of disclosure in therapy of recovered and continuous memories of abuse. *Journal of Psychiatry & Law, 24*, 229–275.

Daubert v. Merrill Dow Pharmaceutical, Inc. (1993), 113 S. Ct. 2786, 509 U.S. 579 [125 L. Ed. 2d 469].

Dowie, J., & Elstein, A. (Eds.). (1988). *Professional judgment: A reader in clinical decision making*. Cambridge, England: Cambridge University Press.

Elliott, D. M. (1997). Traumatic events: Prevalence and delayed recall in the general population. *Journal of Consulting and Clinical Psychology, 65*, 811–820.

Elliott, D. M., & Briere, J. (1995). Posttraumatic stress associated with delayed recall of sexual abuse: A general population study. *Journal of Traumatic Stress, 8*, 629–647.

False Memory Syndrome Foundation. (1992a). *Legal aspects of false memory syndrome*. Philadelphia: Author.

False Memory Syndrome Foundation. (1992b, October 5). What can families do? *False Memory Syndrome Foundation Newsletter*, p. 4.

False Memory Syndrome Foundation. (1995). Amicus curiae brief filed with the Supreme Court of Alabama in the case of McDuffie v. Sellers-Bok (No. 1940524).

False Memory Syndrome Foundation. (1997). Amicus curiae brief filed with the Supreme Court of Illinois in the case of M.E.H. and D.M.H. v. LH. and OH. (Appeal No. 81943).

Feldman-Summers & Pope. (1994). The experience of "forgetting" childhood abuse: A national survey of psychologists. *Journal of Consulting & Clinical Psychology, 62,* 636–639.

Fraser, R. (1997, January 25). Abuse wars: Whose memory matters? *Toronto Globe and Mail,* p. D14.

Frye v. United States (1923), 293 F.1013.

Golding, J. M., Sanchez, R. P., & Sego, S. A. (1996). Do you believe in repressed memories? *Professional Psychology: Research & Practice, 27,* 429–437.

Hagen, M. A. (1997). *Whores of the court: The fraud of psychiatric testimony and the rape of American justice.* New York: HarperCollins.

Herman, J. L., & Schatzow, E. (1987). Recovery and verification of memories of childhood sexual trauma. *Psychoanalytic Psychology, 4,* 1–14.

Hinnefeld, B., & Newman, R. (1997). Analysis of the Truth and Responsibility in Mental Health Practices Act and similar proposals. *Professional Psychology: Research & Practice, 28,* 537–543.

Hoffer, E. (1989). *The true believer.* New York: Harper Perennial. (Original work published 1951.)

Horn, M. (1993, November 29,). Memories lost and found. *U.S. News & World Report,* 52–63.

Hovdestad, W. E., & Kristiansen, C. M. (1996). A field study of "false memory syndrome": Construct validity and incidence. *Journal of Psychiatry & Law, 24,* 299–338.

Kahneman, D., Slovic, P., & Tversky, A. (Eds.). (1982). *Judgment under uncertainty: Heuristics and biases.* Cambridge, England: Cambridge University Press.

Kalichman, S. C. (1993). *Mandated reporting of suspected child abuse: Ethics, law, & policy.* Washington, DC: American Psychological Association.

Kaslow, F. W. (1984). *Psychotherapy with psychotherapists.* New York: Haworth Press.

Kaslow, F. W. (1986). Therapy with distressed psychotherapists: Special problems and challenges. In R. R. Kilburg, P. E. Nathan, and R. W. Thoreson (Eds.), *Professionals in distress: Issues, syndromes, and solutions in psychology* (pp. 187–209). Washington, DC: American Psychological Association.

Kihlstrom, J. (1995, January 24.). On checklists. Internet posting on witch-hunt.

Leavitt, F. (1997). False attribution of suggestibility to explain recovered memory of childhood sexual abuse following extended amnesia. *Child Abuse & Neglect, 21,* 265–272.

Loftus, E. F. (1992). When a lie becomes memory's truth: Memory distortion after exposure to misinformation. *Current Directions in Psychological Science, 1,* 121–123.

Loftus, E. F. (1999). Lost in the mall: Misrepresentations and misunderstandings. *Ethics & Behavior, 9,* 51–60.

Loftus, E. F., & Ketcham, K. (1994). *The myth of repressed memory: False memories and allegations of sexual abuse.* New York: St. Martin's Press.

Loftus, E. F., Polonsky, S., & Fullilove, M. T. (1994). Memories of childhood sexual abuse: Remembering and repressing. *Psychology of Women Quarterly, 18,* 67–84

MacNeil/Lehrer news hour. (1995, February 2). Transcript #5155.

McCann, I. L., & Pearlman, L. A. (1990). *Psychological trauma and the adult survivor: Theory, therapy and transformation.* New York: Brunner/Mazel.

Melchert, T. P. (1996). Childhood memory and a history of different forms of abuse. *Professional Psychology: Research & Practice, 27,* 438–446.

Miller, L. A. (1997). Teaching about repressed memories of childhood sexual abuse and eyewitness testimony. *Teaching of Psychology, 24,* 250–255.

Missouri Psychology Practice Rules Act. (1998). *Missouri Revised Statutes,* Chapter 337, Section 337.035. (L. 1977 H.B. 255 § 6, A.L. 1981 S.B. 16, A.L. 1989 H.B. 738 & 720, A.L. 1997 S.B. 141).

Montoya v. Beebensee (1988), 761 P.2d 285 (Col.App.).

Olio, K. A. (1992). Recovery from sexual abuse: Is forgiveness mandatory? *Voices: The Art and Science of Psychotherapy, 28,* 73–79.

Olio, K. (1995). Het voorschrift van Kihlstrom; over de verdenking van seksueel misbruik bij kinderen aan de hand van hun symptomen [Kihlstrom's prescription: On the suspicion of sexual abuse of children on the basis of their symptoms]. *Directieve Terapie, 15,* 194–195.

Olio, K. A. (1996). Are 25% of clinicians using potentially risky therapeutic practices? A review of the logic and methodology of the Poole, Lindsay et al. study. *Journal of Psychiatry & Law, 24,* 277–298.

Pamela Freyd et al. v. Charles L. Whitfield (1997), Civil Case No. L-96-627 in the U.S. District Court for the District of Maryland, Judge's order dated July 18.

Pearlman, L. A., & Saakvitne, K. (1995). *Trauma and the therapist.* New York: W. W. Norton.

People v. Kelly (1976), 17 Cal.3d 24.

Pezdek. K. (1995. November). *What types of false childhood memories are not likely to be suggestively implanted?* Paper presented at the annual meeting of the Psychonomic Society, Los Angeles.

Pezdek, K., Finger, K., & Hodge, D. (1996, November). *False memories are more likely to be planted if they are familiar.* Paper presented at the annual meeting of the Psychonomic Society, Chicago.

Pezdek, K., Finger, K., & Hodge, D. (1997). Planting false childhood memories: The role of event plausibility. *Psychological Science, 8,* 437–441.

Polusny, M. A., & Follette, V. M. (1996). Remembering childhood sexual abuse: A national survey of psychologists' clinical practices, beliefs, and personal experiences. *Professional Psychology: Research & Practice, 27,* 41–52.

Pope, K. S. (1994). *Sexual involvement with therapists: Patient assessment, subsequent therapy, forensics.* Washington, DC: American Psychological Association.

Pope, K. S. (1995a, August). *Memory, abuse, and strange science: Therapy, forensics, and new research.* Award for Distinguished Contributions to Public Service address presented at the 103rd Annual Convention of the American Psychological Association, New York. (Audiotape No. APA9S-245 available from Sound Images, Aurora, CO; telephone [303] 649-1811.)

Pope, K. S. (1995b). What psychologists better know about recovered memories, research, lawsuits, and the pivotal experiment. *Clinical Psychology: Science and Practice, 2,* 304–315.

Pope, K. S. (1996). Memory, abuse, and science: Questioning claims about the false memory syndrome epidemic. *American Psychologist, 51,* 957–974.

Pope, K. S. (1997). Science as careful questioning: Are claims of a false memory syndrome epidemic based on empirical evidence? *American Psychologist, 52,* 997–1006.

Pope, K. S., & Brown, L. (1996). *Recovered memories of abuse: Assessment, therapy, forensics.* Washington, DC: American Psychological Association.

Pope, K. S., Butcher, J. N., & Seelen, J. (1993). *The MMPI, MMPI-2, & MMPI-A in court: A practical guide for expert witnesses and attorneys.* Washington, DC: American Psychological Association.

Pope, K. S., Sonne, J. L., & Holroyd, J. (1993). *Sexual feelings in psychotherapy.* Washington, DC: American Psychological Association.

Pope, K. S., & Tabachnick, B. G. (1993). Therapists' anger, hate, fear, and sexual feelings: National survey of therapists' responses, client characteristics, critical events, formal complaints, and training. *Professional Psychology: Research & Practice, 24,* 142–152.

Pope, K. S., & Tabachnick, B. G. (1994). Therapists as patients: A national survey of psychologists' experiences, problems, and beliefs. *Professional Psychology: Research & Practice, 25,* 247–258.

Pope, K. S., & Tabachnick, B. G. (1995). Recovered memories of abuse among therapy patients: A national survey. *Ethics & Behavior, 5,* 237–248.

Pope, K. S., & Vasquez, M. J. T. (1998). *Ethics in psychotherapy and counseling: A practical guide* (2nd ed.). San Francisco: Jossey-Bass.

Proposal to finance preparation of model legislation entitled Mental Health Consumer Protection Act. (1994). Unpublished document.

Ramona v. Superior Court (1997), 57 Cal.App.4th 107, 66 Cal.Rptr.2d 766 (2d Dist.).

Roe, C. M., & Schwartz, M. F. (1996). Characteristics of previously forgotten memories of sexual abuse: A descriptive study. *Journal of Psychiatry & Law, 24,* 189–206.

Roesler, T. A., & Wind, T. W. (1994). Telling the secret: Adult women describe their disclosures of incest. *Journal of Interpersonal Violence, 9,* 327–338.

Saakvitne, K. W., Pearlman, L. A., & Staff of the Traumatic Stress Institute. (1996). *Transforming the pain: A workbook on vicarious traumatization.* New York: W. W. Norton.

Salter, A. C. (1995). *Transforming trauma: A guide to understanding and treating adult survivors of child sexual abuse.* Thousand Oaks, CA: Sage.

San Francisco Boys Chorus. (1994, September 9). Public letter of apology in the matter of Ross Cheit.

Schall v. Lockheed Missiles & Space Company, Inc. (1995), 37 Cal.App.4th 1485 [44 Cal.Rptr.2d 191].

Schooler, J. W., Bendiksen, M., & Ambadar, Z. (1997). Taking the middle line: Can we accommodate both fabricated and recovered memories of abuse? In M. A. Conway (Ed.), *Recovered memories and false memories* (pp. 251–291). Oxford, England: Oxford University Press.

Seppa, N. (1996, April). Fear of malpractice curbs some psychologists' practice. *APA Monitor,* p. 12.

Shahzade v. Gregory (1996), 930 F. Supp. 673 (D. Mass.) & 923 F. Supp. 286.

Sidran Foundation. (1997). *Science and politics of recovered memories* [Cassette recording]. Symposium conducted at the annual meeting of the American Psychological Association; G. Koocher, chair. (Telephone [410] 825-8888; fax [410] 337-0747; e-mail sidran@access.digex.net.)

Smith, M. (1997, August 15). Jury awards $5.8 million in satanic memories case. *Houston Chronicle.*

Stanton, M. (1993, October 5). S.F. Chorus hit with molestation suit. *San Jose Mercury News,* p. 5B.

Stanton, M. (1995). Bearing witness (a 3-part series). *Providence Journal-Bulletin,* May 7. pp. A1, A18–A19; May 8, pp. A1, A8–A9; May 9, pp. A1, A6–A7.

State v. Hungerford (1997), 697 A.2d 916.

State v. Quattrocchi (1996), 681 A.2d 879 (R.I.).

Sullivan v. Cheshire (1995), 895 F. Supp. 204 (N.D. Ill.).

Truman v. Genesis Associates (1996), 935 F. Supp. 1375 (E.D. Pa.) & 894 F. Supp. 183 (E.D. Pa. 1995 WL124740).

van der Kolk, B. A., & Fisler, R. (1995). Dissociation and the fragmentary nature of traumatic memories: Overview and exploratory study. *Journal of Traumatic Stress, 8,* 505–525.

Wagner, M. G. (1993, October 7). He confronts memory—and alleged molester. *Sacramento Bee,* p. A1.

Wagner, M. G. (1994, July 14). Ex-leader of boys camp held in molest: Charges brought decades later based on "recovered memory." *Sacramento Bee,* p. B7.

Watson, J. B. (1939). *Behaviorism* (2nd ed.). Chicago: University of Chicago Press.

Widom, C. S., & Morris, S. (1997). Accuracy of adult recollections of childhood victimization: Part 2. Childhood sexual abuse. *Psychological Assessment, 9,* 34–46.

Widom, C. S., & Shepard, R. L. (1996). Accuracy of adult recollections of childhood victimization: Part 1. Childhood physical abuse. *Psychological Assessment, 8,* 412–421.

Wilkinson v. Balsam (1995), 885 F. Supp 651 (D.VT.).

Williams, L. M. (1994). Recall of childhood trauma: A prospective study of women's memories of child sexual abuse. *Journal of Consulting & Clinical Psychology, 62,* 1167–1176.

Wolf, F., Gruppen, L., & Billi, J. (1985). Differential diagnosis and the competing-hypothesis heuristic: A practical approach to judgment under uncertainty and Bayesian probability. *Journal of the American Medical Association, 253,* 2858–2862.

Woman wins $10M in false memory suit. (1997, November 4). United Press International Wire Service.

CHAPTER 19

Elder Abuse

Families, Systems, Causes, and Interventions

THOMAS H. PEAKE, JAMES R. OELSCHLAGER, and DANIEL F. KEARNS

People who live long,
who will drink the cup of life to the very bottom,
may expect to meet some of the dregs.
—BENJAMIN FRANKLIN

THE CONCEPT of elder abuse conjures up an image of neglect of or cruelty to older adults. This chapter focuses on the usual meaning and also on the abuse of families who care for seniors. Health care systems and other agencies can indirectly create iatrogenic pressures on families. The legal system may also complicate the problems. A systems perspective is valuable in reminding us that problems of abuse (like other interpersonal maladies) are an interactive production with multiple causation. Often the victim is an incidental casualty. Structural and strategic patterns can be understood and addressed for remediation, if not prevention. Stereotypes about older adults affect the victim, the family, agencies, and health care providers who can honor or neglect those in life's "third age."

The causes of seniors' mistreatment include the following suggested dimensions (Quinn & Tomita, 1997, p.87):

1. Those that focus on the victim's dependency (e.g. physical and mental impairment)
2. Those that emphasize the effect of stress on caregivers
3. Those that suggest unique pathology of families who solve problems by intimidation and violence
4. Those that emphasize the individual problems of the abuser

Special thanks to Lori Sorum for her preparation of the manuscript.

5. A society that casts older adults in the role of being unimportant because of ageism, sexism, or destructive attitudes toward the disabled, poor, and unattractive

6. Greed and financial gain

Ageism is both subtle and blatant. Aside from Dychtwald and Flower's book *The Age Wave* (1989), there is not much in the popular media to make Americans enthusiastic or hopeful about the prospects of getting older. The most ageist factions in society include older adults' negative views of themselves and the portrayal of seniors in news and entertainment media, as well as the perceptions of health professionals and the health care system (Estes and Binney, 1989). Many seniors view themselves as destined to decline, having poor or uncertain expectations about their physical health. Articles in respected journals regularly document that old age alone is a risk factor for poor medical care. For example, an article in the *Journal of the American Medical Association* describes age as a risk factor for inadequate treatment (Wettle, 1989).

America's culture and media portrayals too rarely honor or seek the wisdom of older adults unless they are vastly accomplished or wealthy. Chinen (1989) sampled many cultures and discovered that America has few legends or folk tales that portray seniors as a resource rather than a burden, unlike other cultures which venerate the elderly, such as many Oriental cultures. On a related theme, Dr. Seuss, the author of humorous children's books, in his wise and entertaining way caricatures the ways in which health care can be uncaring. The reader who has not had the pleasure of laughing lately with Dr. Seuss will find his book *You're Only Old Once* (1986) an entertaining way to understand the meaning of the word *iatrogenic:* when health care harms rather than helps. Another important family pressure is embodied in the concept of the *sandwich generation:* people born post–World War II (baby boomers) who are now caught between the pressures of their adult children and their own senior parents. The later and earlier generations often must depend on their "50-something" breadwinners. The cross-generational system pressures become clearer when one considers the variety of interactions that can occur.

The following section considers these and other causes of elder abuse to augment the readers' understanding and suggests ways to improve the outlook for healthier aging.

THE NATURE OF ELDER ABUSE

Elder abuse is a serious problem which, until the late 1970s, had gone largely unnoticed. The earliest reports of elder abuse and neglect were documented in the United Kingdom in the 1970s. These dramatic case reports horrified the public and the medical community and were labeled *granny battering* (American Medical Association [AMA], 1992). In the mid 1970s a U.S. Senate special committee on aging released several reports addressing abuse and neglect that originated in institutional settings such as nursing homes (AMA, 1992) The first reported cases of abuse of the elderly in the United States were documented by Steinmetz (1978). Awareness of the problem spread based on a subsequent article by Rathbone-

McCuan (1980). These reports suggested a prevalence rate for elder abuse nearly as high as for child abuse. This statistic was disturbing because many of us are raised with the notion that we are to respect our elders. A U.S. Senate select committee established in the early 1990s estimated that approximately 2 million older Americans experience elder abuse or neglect annually (U.S. Congress, 1991). Because abuse and neglect are frequently underreported, these statistics may not accurately assess the magnitude of this problem. Needless to say, it has become increasingly apparent that as people age they are afforded less respect and fewer rights. This constellation of stereotypical attitudes and behaviors toward the aged has been termed *ageism* (Butler, 1969) and can contribute to incidents of elder abuse.

Research is accumulating that helps determine whether consistencies exist, across studies, in the characteristics of the abused elderly and the perpetrators of elder abuse. A general profile is emerging as somewhat "typical" of the elderly abuse victim. Most are female, over 65 years of age, and dependent upon others for the fulfillment of their daily needs. Descriptors of the abusers are not as specific. A study by Homer and Gilleard (1990) described alcohol abuse and abuse by the patient as being significantly associated with physical abuse by the caregiver. A significant majority of the caregivers in this study also lived with those they were caring for. Other factors thought to be related to abuse are preexisting personality characteristics of the caregiver; degree of financial dependence; history of conflictual relations between the patient and caregiver; stress level experienced by the caregiver; and degree of medical, functional, and cognitive disability of the elder.

From its first appearance in the literature, there has been continuing debate surrounding the proper definition of elder abuse. Amendments made in 1987 to the 1975 Older Americans Act resulted in federal definitions of elder abuse, exploitation, and neglect. Although this definition provides general guidelines for identifying elder abuse, state laws and state definitions are utilized for enforcement purposes. State laws and definitions of abuse, however, may vary greatly. This, along with significant underreporting of elder abuse, has made it nearly impossible to determine accurate prevalence rates. The situation is further complicated by the many subtypes of elder abuse and the difficulty in assessing them.

TYPES OF ELDER ABUSE

The earliest studies on elder abuse addressed mainly neglect and physical abuse. (Block & Sinnott, 1979; Clark, Mankikar, & Gray, 1975). Since then, emotional, sexual, and financial abuse increasingly have been the focus of research (Blunt, 1993; Ramsey-Klawsnik, 1991). The National Center on Elder Abuse collected data in 1994 from state adult protective service agencies throughout the nation (Tatara & Kuzmeskus, 1996). Figure 19.1 illustrates the types of domestic elder abuse reported based on this study.

Neglect emerges as a relatively common form of elder abuse. Despite its prevalence, neglect may not always be obvious to the observer, nor immediately be considered as abuse. Significant weight loss could indicate that the older person is not eating well-balanced meals and may be eating fewer than three meals a day. Bed

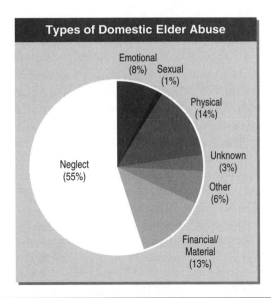

Figure 19.1 Types of domestic elder abuse. (Data from National Center on Elder Abuse; Tatara & Kuzmeskus, 1996).

sores from remaining sedentary for long periods of time are often hidden from view by clothing. Some of the more obvious signs of neglect include unkempt appearance, stains on clothing, malnutrition, dehydration, and unpleasant odor due to a failure to maintain proper hygiene.

Physical abuse is most often perpetrated by males in younger populations. However, in examining elder abuse in comparison to that of younger individuals, new evidence suggests that elder husbands are abused twice as often as elder wives. In addition, the abusers are generally dependent on the individual they abuse (American Psychological Association [APA], 1997). Indicators of physical abuse include bruises on the face or extremities, untreated injuries in various stages of healing, signs of being restrained, scalp injuries, sprains, dislocations, and the caregiver's refusal to allow others to evaluate or consult with the elder separately. Physicians and medical professionals may have a tendency to attribute these physical injuries to an elderly person's physical frailty or falls.

Emotional abuse is a fairly common form of elder abuse that typically coexists with other forms of abuse. This type of abuse significantly hampers the older person's ability to perform activities of daily living and can present as or exacerbate existing symptoms of dementia. Emotional abuse can include verbal insults, threats of harm or abandonment, isolation from others, treating the elder like a child, withdrawal of privileges (television, reading material, etc.), or confinement to the home or bedroom. Signs of emotional abuse may include extreme withdrawal, depression and agitation, and expression of ambivalent feelings toward nonfamily or family caregivers (AMA, 1992).

Financial abuse is an increasingly more common form of elder abuse and may involve as many as 2.5% of all dependent elders (Pillemer & Wolf, 1986). In cases of financial abuse, caregivers may use undue influence to gain access to the financial resources of older persons under their care. They may promise lifelong care and the avoidance of nursing home placement in exchange for money or property rights. Some caregivers are unaware that such behavior is illegal and considered abusive. They may feel that the difficulty of the caregiving task entitles them to some type of material compensation. The cognitive deficits associated with dementia and depression in the elderly may allow manipulation at the hands of unscrupulous caregivers. The chances of financial abuse going undetected increase significantly when there are few surviving relatives or acquaintances available to protest. A case example provides a look at the subtleties of financial abuse:

> Mary is a 76-year-old woman who was seen at a local clinic for memory evaluation. She was accompanied by a 43-year-old man named Fred, whom she described as a friend. Fred said that he had known Mary for the past 3 years and had been taking care of her since then. He reported that her only living relative was a daughter who resided out of state. He said that she held power of attorney. Fred said that he wanted Mary to have her memory evaluated because he had become worried that she was spending money in an eccentric manner. He said that she had been donating large sums to charities she had seen on television. The clinician assigned to Mary became suspicious of Fred's interest in her financial matters and noticed that he never mentioned his concerns in Mary's presence. When questioned, Mary was not exactly sure why she was participating in this evaluation. The results of the memory evaluation revealed that Mary suffered some mild memory deficits that would warrant referral to a neurologist. When the clinician contacted Mary's daughter to inform her of her mother's condition, the daughter said that she had no knowledge of Fred. She went on to say that she did not, in fact, have power of attorney for her mother. Mary's daughter hired a lawyer to investigate further. It was discovered that there had been several small withdrawals from Mary's bank account over the preceding 2 years. When questioned about this, Fred insisted that the money was used for the fulfillment of Mary's needs. Further, he admitted that he had used some of the money for his own needs, but saw nothing wrong with this because of all the time he spent taking care of Mary. Mary's daughter pursued prosecution with a favorable resolution for her mother. The process helped them connect and helped her mother to get appropriate care.

Sexual abuse is far less common in elders than other types of abuse and is very difficult to detect (Ramsey-Klawsnik, 1991, 1993). The presence of unexplained venereal disease or genital infections in the client or the observation of inappropriate, flirtatious behavior by the caregiver toward the client should raise suspicions of sexual abuse. The older person must be interviewed alone to reduce any feelings of embarrassment and to prevent retaliation from the perpetrator. It is exceedingly difficult to elicit reports of sexual abuse from older adults, particularly if the abuse has never been spoken of previously. Appropriate time and care should be taken in the development of a trusting and therapeutic relationship before the subject is broached. The patient and the suspected abuser should be separated as soon as it becomes established that sexual abuse has taken place. This strategy requires a systems approach rather than just a focus on the individual.

The various types of elder abuse mentioned earlier obviously have a significant impact on the emotional and physical well-being of the older individual (see Table 19.1). The symptoms cover a broad spectrum ranging from anxiety, in response to the actions of an inconsistent caregiver, to death resulting from severe physical abuse or neglect. Anxiety and depression stemming from emotional abuse can

Table 19.1 Impact of Abuse on Physical and Mental Health

Presenting symptom	Chronic pain syndromes
	Headache
	Atypical chest pain
	Abdominal pain
	Functional gastrointestinal complaints
	Muscle or joint pain
	Hyperventilation
	Pelvic pain
	Recurrent vaginal infections
	Sleep, mood, and appetite disorders
Mental health problems	Alcohol and drug abuse
	Anxiety
	Depression
	Suicide attempts
	Post-traumatic stress disorder
	Post-concussive disorder
Delayed physical effects	Visual and hearing defects
	Arthritis
	Dysphagia
	Recurrent sinus infection or dental problems
	Dyspareunia or recurrent GU infections
	Hypertension
	Heart disease

SOURCE: University of Miami School of Medicine, *Opening Pandora's Box: A Physician's Guide to Identifying and Treating Victims of Abuse*, 1995. Reprinted with permission.

cause significant cognitive deficits and functional decline in the elderly. In addition, the potential for cumulative traumatic brain injury sequelae from physical abuse is significantly high in domestic violence environments, particularly for the elderly (Oelschlager and Cauffield, 1997). Hence, a vicious cycle can result wherein the emotionally abusive caregiver becomes frustrated at the older person's compromised cognitive capacities, interpersonal withdrawal, lack of energy, and loss of appetite related to the depression and emotional reactions resulting from the abuse.

CAUSES OF ELDER ABUSE

A good deal of research has focused on the causes of elder abuse in an effort to develop strategies of prevention. Dowd (1975) investigated the role of exchange theory (Homans, 1961) in elder abuse. Exchange theory deals with the ways in which the exchange of rewards and punishments in social interactions affect behavior. In relation to elder abuse, it appears that when a power differential exists and younger family members are dependent upon their elders, the probability of abuse increases. A study by Pillemer (1985) provided evidence in support of the application of exchange theory in cases of physical abuse of the elderly. This also occurs in cases of financial abuse in which dependent individuals divert money from elders for whom they are caring.

Quinn and Tomita (1997) incorporated aspects of the preceding findings on exchange theory while expanding the spectrum of possible causative factors. The six factors they extrapolated are mentioned at the beginning of the chapter. The variety of problems, causes, and solutions includes individuals; couples; families; health care, legal, and social service systems; communities; and government regulating and funding agencies. Interventions must be derived from a systems perspective and clinicians who work with elder abuse must conceptualize the situation beyond the confines of their offices.

The earliest theories about the etiology of elder abuse concern the dependency of the victim (Hickey & Douglass, 1981; Steinmetz, 1978). The idea here is that elderly victims are in a state of physical and mental frailty and are unable to defend themselves against potential abusers. While this may be true, it does not adequately explain why the abuse occurs. The focus is on the victim, rather than the abuser. An interactive systems perspective must be considered.

Few people are truly prepared for the responsibilities entailed in assuming the role of caregiver for an older adult, particularly when that individual is suffering from significant physical or emotional disabilities that render him or her unable to attend to the activities of daily living. This lack of preparedness in approaching what can often be a frustrating and time-consuming task creates significant enduring distress in the caregiver. Individuals suffering from dementia can exhibit behavioral problems that are extremely difficult to manage. These include wandering, physical aggression, and sexually inappropriate behavior. The caregiver who is not skilled in behavior management and has not learned appropriate methods to cope with his or her own stress will not respond in a manner conducive to the care of the elder and may resort to abusive behavior.

Long-standing patterns of family interaction are exacerbated when the stressors of caring for an elder are added to the mix. If family members have habitually reacted to adversity with the expression of hostility, it is likely that this pattern will continue in the face of the difficulties associated with caregiving. Lingering resentments from years past can also have an impact on the behavior of an adult child toward an infirm parent.

Preexisting personal problems of caregivers can increase the likelihood of abusive behavior toward older persons in their care. These include substance abuse, emotional problems or personal pathology, and financial hardship. Studies have found a strong positive correlation between alcohol abuse and abusive behavior in caregiving situations (Anetzberger, Korbin, & Austine, 1994; Bristowe & Collins, 1989). The possibility of financial abuse increases in cases where the abuser is financially dependent upon the elder person or requires a steady flow of cash to finance a drug habit. Emotional problems, such as depression, have also been found to contribute to elder abuse. It has also been documented that more than 50% of family caregivers who live with an Alzheimer's patient will have a clinical depression themselves (Cohen & Eisdorfer, 1986; Mace & Rabins, 1991). More chronic forms of psychopathology, such as sociopathy, obviously can be contributory factors in cases of elder abuse as well. The presence of any emotional disorder makes it more difficult for caregivers to appropriately communicate and manage the stresses related to their role.

As previously mentioned, the stereotypical attitudes of society toward older adults constitute yet another antecedent of elder abuse. *Ageism* has been defined as a system of false assumptions and beliefs about older adults (Butler, 1969). The elderly have long been perceived as irritable, rigid, opinionated, physically frail, and senile. Such stereotypical characterizations heighten the potential for abuse (Peake, Rosenzweig, & Williamson, 1996).

Greed is a prime motivator in situations involving financial abuse. The abuser is typically dependent upon the older person and may excuse any financial liberties that are taken by rationalizing the behavior in the context of a give-and-take relationship. As mentioned earlier, drug or medication abuse by the caregiver increases the possibility of financial exploitation.

Other important factors must be considered when dealing with the victim of abuse. A national study of domestic elder abuse conducted by the National Center on Elder Abuse (Tatara & Kuzmeskus, 1996) indicated that adult children are the most frequent abusers of the elderly. The spouse of the elder victim is the next most likely abuser, with other family members being the third most frequent abusers. Being confined with the incapacitated senior may lead to a sense of claustrophobia and heighten the resentment of having one's own life and activities severely curtailed.

Paid nonfamily caretakers may also be abusive; their performance and financial expenditures should be monitored by someone concerned about the welfare of the elder. Family members may be unwilling to confront a paid caretaker for fear of losing their services and having to replace them or take over personally.

Some facts about abuse include that 31% of elderly married women experience violence in the relationship, and that elder abuse is usually a continuation of a long-standing pattern (Ramsey-Klawsnik, 1993). However, in a smaller number of cases it is a new phenomenon triggered by external stressors such as a new role conflict, forced retirement, or illness (Deitch, 1993).

In actuality, situations of abuse and the factors contributing to them are rarely clear-cut. Often, there is an interaction between two or more of the previously mentioned factors. The complex nature of elder abuse makes it difficult to tease out individual causative factors. An interactive systems perspective is crucial for prevention, identification, intervention, and treatment of the problem.

CULTURAL CONTEXTS OF ELDER ABUSE

Most of the literature on elder abuse deals with Caucasians. However, the ethnic distribution of U.S. citizens has become quite diverse. Despite increased research activity in the area of elder abuse, only a handful of studies have addressed the issue in other racial or ethnic groups (Cazenave & Straus, 1979; Hall, 1986; Krassen-Maxwell & Maxwell, 1992; Stein, 1991).

Difficulties in conceptualizing elder abuse are magnified when cultural variations are introduced. Are definitions of elder abuse that have been formulated with the use of primarily Caucasian samples (Omer & Gilleard, 1990) generalizable to members of other cultures? Cross-cultural differences in intrafamilial communication, caregiving practices, and sociocultural considerations could render accepted definitions obsolete (Tomita, 1982). Krassen-Maxwell and Maxwell (1992) described poor economic conditions as contributing to differences in the incidence of elder abuse in two Plains Indian tribes. Tomita (1994) outlined the complex pattern of intergenerational communication in Japanese families in an effort to direct future research efforts.

Despite the shortage of cross-cultural research into elder abuse, it is clear that important differences exist in perceptions of and responses to abuse across cultures (Baltes & Baltes, 1990). A study conducted by Moon and Williams (1993) found a sample of elderly Korean American women to be more conservative than elderly African American and Caucasian women in their assessments of abuse and less likely to seek formal support systems when confronted with abuse scenarios.

Adding to the confusion of cross-cultural assessment of elder abuse has been the conflicting research regarding prevalence rates. Some early studies (see e.g., Cazenave & Straus, 1979) reported higher rates of elder abuse for Caucasians than for African Americans. Subsequent research has challenged these findings (Steinmetz, 1990). As with prevalence rates, there is a problem in obtaining accurate support utilization rates (Johnson & Barer, 1990; Sokolovsky, 1985; Taylor & Chatters, 1986). The limitations of some of the previously listed studies (e.g., small samples and underrepresentation of males) and seemingly contradictory findings underline the need for additional cross-cultural research. Only through comprehensive, inclusive research can we arrive at an acceptable conceptualization of elder abuse and appropriate interventions for the abused elderly.

As a rule, where interventions are required and professionals are not available from the ethnic or cultural background of an abused elder, the services of paraprofessionals from the population served in conjunction with the services of a professional person should be used to sensitize law enforcement personnel or social service or legal agents regarding the cultural subtleties of the clients and their families. The more this kind of information can be made available, the more likely that further inadvertent (though well-meaning) abuse by the helping systems can be prevented.

LEGAL ISSUES AND MANDATORY REPORTING

The Older Americans Act of 1975 (OAA), with amendments in 1987 and 1992, has had a significant impact on addressing elder abuse issues (Quinn & Tomita, 1997). This federal legislation mandates states to develop a variety of programs related to preventing and reducing elder abuse, including public education, outreach activities, and support of research and training programs. The act has also resulted in the development of an ombudsman program to investigate and resolve nursing home complaints. In addition, this act mandates states to develop policies, procedures, and programs to accept and investigate reports of elder abuse.

Institutional abuse issues have been addressed by specific laws in numerous states. National standards of care for nursing homes are contained in federal legislation in the Nursing Home Reform Act of 1987 (AMA, 1992). This act is part of the Omnibus Budget Reconciliation Act (OBRA), and became effective in 1990. Broadly stated, the intent of this act is to promote high-quality care and prevent abuse, neglect, and substandard care of residents in nursing homes (AMA, 1992).

It specifically protects the elderly from Medicaid discrimination, assures the right to participate in decisions related to health care, mandates a reduction in the use of physical and chemical restraints, and assures access to a personal physician, long-term care ombudsman, and other advocates relating to elder issues.

Following the OBRA implementation, the federal government also enacted the Patient Self-Determination Act in December 1991 (Quinn & Tomita, 1997). All institutions that receive reimbursement from Medicare, Medicaid, or both are required to comply with this act. The intent of the law is to increase patient involvement, when appropriate, in decisions regarding life-sustaining treatment. Essentially, the act assures the right to refuse any and all medical interventions, including life-sustaining measures. The act requires health care providers in hospitals, skilled nursing facilities, home care agencies, hospice programs, and HMOs to: (a) develop written policies concerning advance directives, (b) inquire whether new patients have prepared an advanced directive and have incorporated this information in the patient's chart, (c) provide patients with written materials regarding the facility's policy on advance direction and the patient's right to prepare such documents, (d) educate staff and the community about advance directives (Ferri & Fretwell, 1992). Currently, the two types of advance directives in use are the *living will* and the *health care proxy* or *durable power of attorney for health care*. The living will allows a terminally ill individual to have life-sustaining intervention withheld or withdrawn, even though the individual is unable to communicate this to the physician. The health care proxy or durable power of attorney for health care transfers the decision-making power to a designee to act in the individual's behalf if the individual is unable to speak or act in the future. Clinicians working with elderly clientele should be familiar with these acts and know how to assist patients and their families to access what they are entitled to based on these laws.

Although the federal government has clearly been a leader in addressing elder abuse issues, abuse and neglect continue to occur in institutional settings as well as in the home. Quinn and Tomita (1997) raised concerns that the federal government is relinquishing the aggressive leadership role it has exhibited in addressing elder abuse. In part this appears to be related to funding issues and an attempt to encourage government at the state level to take on this responsibility. Unfortunately, some states appear to have lax enforcement of legislated standards (AMA, 1992), and, as mentioned, the stringency of elder abuse laws varies from state to state. Furthermore, the U.S. General Accounting Office estimates that about 80% of the 6 million dependent elders are being cared for at home (APA, 1996). As a result, elder legislation that is created for institutional settings optimally should be extended to health care professionals who provide in-home services. In addition, despite the federal legislation reviewed here, stringent laws regarding nursing home staffing ratios are lacking. In fact, a recent General Accounting Office report indicated that 50% of the suspicious deaths evaluated in California nursing homes were the result of neglect, including not preventing or treating dehydration and malnutrition ("Health Care," 1998). Inadequate staffing ratios, supervision of care, and lack of training in elder care are causative factors. More extensive federal legislation and a higher degree of accountability on the part of the nursing home industry are necessary. Clinicians with expertise in geriatric issues can contribute to the process of developing more stringent guidelines by becoming active with state and federal legislative bodies.

The State of Florida has fairly progressive laws regarding elder abuse that provide a model against which to measure other states' laws. Not surprisingly, Florida has a higher proportion of elder residents (23% of the population is over age 60) than any other state in the nation (AMA/Administration on Aging, 1997).

Florida's Adult Protective Service Act (APSA) mandates reporting of abuse, neglect, or exploitation of disabled adults or elderly persons. It is robust in that it mandates bank and savings and loan employees, spiritual healers, and home care staff (in addition to physicians, nurses, mental health professionals, criminal justice employees, and law enforcement officers) to report suspected abuse, neglect, and exploitation. The Florida APSA also mandates background checks on all employees working with the elderly in institutional settings as well as in home health care agencies. The addition of attorneys to the list of those mandated to report abuse, neglect, and exploitation, however, would enhance Florida's APSA.

The legislative intent of the Florida APSA includes the goal of encouraging the constructive participation and involvement of families in the care and protection of elderly persons. A variety of services, including protective supervision, placement, and in-home and community-based services, are available to intervention specialists. One provision stresses that short-term psychological treatment (no more than 6 months duration) must be available to those elders who have been abused, neglected, or exploited and are in need of psychological intervention.

Quinn and Tomita (1997) raised concerns that many states' reporting laws related to elder abuse overlook or fail to include psychological abuse and neglect. However, Florida's definition of abuse effectively includes not only physical and sexual but also psychological injury. The law defines *psychological injury* as "an injury to the intellectual functioning or emotional state of a disabled adult or an elderly person as evidenced by an observable or measurable reduction in the disabled adult's or elderly person's ability to function within that person's customary range of performance and that person's behavior." This broad definition takes into account the effects of emotional abuse and neglect on an elder.

Currently, mandatory reporting laws regarding elder abuse exist in 42 states (APA, 1996), requiring many professionals to report suspected cases of abuse, neglect, and exploitation. However, the issue of what types of abuse to report, timing of the report, who has to report, and consequences for not reporting vary from state to state. Generally, the adult protective services agency in each state is the designated agency to receive and investigate these reports. Once reported, this agency is also responsible for providing the victim and caregivers treatment and protective services as necessary. In addition, some states mandate in-service training in domestic violence. As a result, practitioners need to be familiar with state laws regarding reporting requirements and current trends in regard to domestic violence continuing education training.

The AMA (1992) indicates that there is considerable debate as to the effectiveness of mandatory reporting laws in identifying elder abuse cases. A 1992 study conducted by the U.S. General Accounting Office attempted to examine this issue (AMA, 1992). However, the conclusion at that time was that a meaningful comparison between states with and without mandatory reporting laws could not occur.

It also pointed out that the previously mentioned variability between states in investigation protocols and definitions of abuse and neglect had made it difficult to evaluate this issue. The AMA (1992) does cite a survey of protective service officials that concluded that increasing public and professional awareness regarding elder abuse and neglect has had more impact than any legislative requirements developed by the states in regard to mandating elder abuse reporting.

EVALUATION AND TREATMENT ISSUES

Searching for treatment options for abused elders shows that specific counseling techniques are scarce and viable models are just beginning to emerge (Ramsey-Klawsnik, 1993, 1995). One model of pertinent principles applicable to elder abuse issues is the concept of *neutralization* (Minor, 1981; Sykes & Matza, 1957), which helps professionals understand the behaviors of the abuser, the abused, and the clinician. The relevant processes include the following:

1. *Denial of responsibility.* "It was an accident" or otherwise out of the perpetrator's control.
2. *Denial of the injury.* "It didn't cause significant harm."
3. *Denial of the victim.* The elder is cast as the wrongdoer instead.
4. *Condemnation of the condemners.* Protective service agents have grudges or "pick on us."
5. *Appeal to higher loyalties.* "If you love me, you won't turn me in."
6. *Defense of necessity.* The elder has been "kept in line" in some way, such as by removing money from his or her bank account so it won't be squandered.
7. *The metaphor of the ledger of balances.* People who commit illegal acts may feel that they have been sufficiently "good" that occasional bad acts can be excused in the balance.

These concepts show how people rationalize their behavior.

In an interesting study in Massachuchusetts, Godkin, Wolf, and Pillemer (1989) found that members of abusive families were more likely to have emotional problems, which contributed to interpersonal difficulties in other arenas also. Abused elders were not more dependent on caregivers for their daily needs. However, the abused elders and their caregivers became increasingly interdependent prior to the onset of abuse. This was related to the loss of other family members and subsequent increased social isolation, along with increased financial dependence of the perpetrators on the senior victim. These findings underscore the recurrent theme that the problems are frequently systemic rather than centered on an individual.

One general consideration is worth mentioning before describing specific treatment strategies. Healthy aging involves the task of preserving a sense of self (Kaufman, 1986; Peake, 1998) and continuity of personal identity in the face of changes, losses, and life's surprises. Borrowing a quote from John Lennon, "Life is what happens to you when you're planning something else." The therapy task is, therefore, an exercise in preserving a sense of identity in the face of events that challenge the meaning of one's life story (or the story of one's relationships with those close to one). How much work preserving that identity requires depends on the history of relationships with family or caregiver. Also, if physical illness, dementia, or financial calamities create overwhelming shock or stress, there may be no safe place to sort through this process of rewriting the story of who one is.

Treatment must involve a thorough consideration of the big picture, including:

1. Who and what variables are involved?
2. What are the victim's history and resources?
3. What has recently changed?
4. Who are the other people involved?
5. What are the legality and confidentiality issues?
6. What parameters (and authorities, if necessary) can be used to create a safe environment for treatment?

The most effective way to answer these questions is to develop a treatment plan and intervention based on a comprehensive psychological and systems assessment. Such an assessment is particularly relevant for the elderly because neuropsychological issues and processes are frequently woven into the clinical presentation. At a minimum, APA's guidelines contained in *Violence and the Family* provide a viable model to follow in assessing victims of neglect and abuse (APA, 1996). These recommendations include a clinical interview with mental status examination, psychosocial history, standardized psychological assessment instruments, neuropsychological screening, and clinical observation. Relevant legal and medical documents should be obtained in order to assist in the assessment, intervention, and case management process. In addition, collateral contacts and interviews with other people in the family or system are essential in order to corroborate accusations of neglect and abuse.

In evaluating multiple family members or caretakers, it is essential to interview the victim or alleged victim alone without the presence of the caretakers or alleged abuser. Further, the victim who is the identified patient should be evaluated first. Strong resistance on the part of family members or caretakers to allow a professional to evaluate the victim in this manner may be a red flag warning of an abuse-and-control issue wherein the abuser is afraid of the potential outcome of a private one-on-one meeting with the victim. In some cases the victim may prove to be an unreliable historian due to a dementing condition, to inappropriate medication dosages by caretakers, or to emotional distress from the neglect and abuse and resulting cognitive impairment. However, even in these situations it behooves the clinician to make a concerted effort to obtain collateral information from individuals who are not presumed to be a perpetrator of abuse or neglect.

Providing the alleged victim with a physically and emotionally safe environment to conduct an initial evaluation is critical, as it is with any trauma victim. Developing rapport and asking questions in a manner that does not place responsibility for the neglect and abuse on the patient is the essential starting point for the initial contact. A useful guide for such evaluations is the *Elder Mistreatment Guidelines for Health Care Professionals: Detection, Assessment, and Intervention* (1988). This guide encourages the healthcare professional to ask the alleged victim direct questions such as the following: Has anyone in your home ever harmed you? Has

anyone ever touched you without your consent? Have you ever signed any documents that you did not understand? Are you afraid of any one at your home? Has
anyone ever failed to help you take care of yourself when you needed assistance?
Obviously, any positive answer to these questions would require more detailed
evaluation of who, where, and when. Clinicians who agree to evaluate suspected
elder abuse and neglect in private practice or on an emergency basis must allow
sufficient time to conduct a comprehensive intake, so as to assure the safety of the
client and to notify appropriate agencies and family members. They also should be
aware of the possibility that they may later be called to testify if legal proceedings
are initiated.

Comprehensive record documentation of the initial and subsequent contacts
is particularly relevant in all cases of domestic violence or abuse evaluations.
Legal investigative processes will occur as the result of reports of neglect and
abuse, and a detailed record of events and clinical observations provides support
to initiate and facilitate legal action. Hirst and Miller (1986) caution that a diagnosis of elder abuse or neglect must be based on the facts and resulting objective
data, not on personal feelings. Optimally, consultation with other healthcare professionals or colleagues regarding the alleged abuse or neglect, including caretaker or family dynamics and objective data (including physical signs), should
occur before a final opinion is rendered. Frequently, reports of abuse and neglect
by an elder are inappropriately attributed to paranoia secondary to dementia or
medical illness (AMA, 1995). As a result, clinicians need to remain objective and
cautious in reaching a conclusion. Family therapists without training or experience in neuropsychology and neurological disorders associated with aging are
strongly encouraged to develop a professional relationship with a neuropsy-
chologist and neurologist in order to appropriately evaluate an elder victim for
abuse or neglect.

The AMA (1992) provides a valuable model for developing screening and intervention strategies in working with elderly clients when neglect and abuse is suspected (see Figures 19.2 and 19.3).

In using the decision tree that appears in Figure 19.3, the AMA (1992) recommends choosing interventions that will result in the least restriction of the elderly
client's independence and decision-making responsibilities, while at the same
time fulfilling state-mandated reporting requirements. Table 19.2 provides a
cogent overview of the continuum of care, from least restrictive to most restrictive.
Due to the complex needs of elder victims, the clinician should be cognizant of
available community resources and support services. The APA Presidential Task
Force on Violence and the Family (APA, 1996) divides the intervention tools available to the clinician into: (a) protective services, (b) treatment, and (c) support services. Issues related to protective services laws and resources have already been
reviewed.

Treatment models for elder abuse continue to emerge. Likewise, psychotherapeutic strategies for trauma victims is also a developing field (Enns, Campbell, &
Courtois, 1997). Currently, treatment for elder victims of neglect and abuse are
similar to those for adult trauma victims. APA (1996) identifies the central treatment components as ensuring safety and empowering the victim. Once safety and

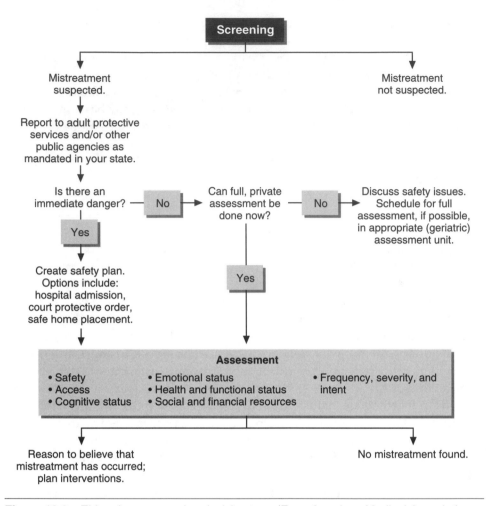

Figure 19.2   Elder abuse screening decision tree. (From American Medical Association, *Diagnostic and Treatment Guidelines on Elder Abuse and Neglect,* 1992, Chicago: Author. Copyright © 1992 by American Medical Association. Adapted with permission.)

placement issues are addressed, decisions can be made about treatment. Interventions need to be flexible and creative, based upon understanding the causative factors and long-range goals. Clinicians trained in a family systems approach to intervention are in a good position to integrate the complex factors previously reviewed. However, family therapy interventions are sometimes contraindicated in working with abuse victims (Walker, 1994). As a result, flexible interventions may include individual therapy to explore systems issues that led to the abuse or neglect; psychoeducation for family members or paid companions, nurses, or aides; institutional staff responsible for the care of elderly; and group treatment. Walker (1994), in her development of *survivor therapy,* outlines the principles of intervention with abuse victims as: safety, empowerment, validation, emphasis on strengths, education, expanding alternatives, restoring clarity in judgment when possible, understanding oppression, and making one's own decisions. In order to achieve these goals, APA (1996) identifies the following essential ingredients of intervening utilizing survivor therapy:

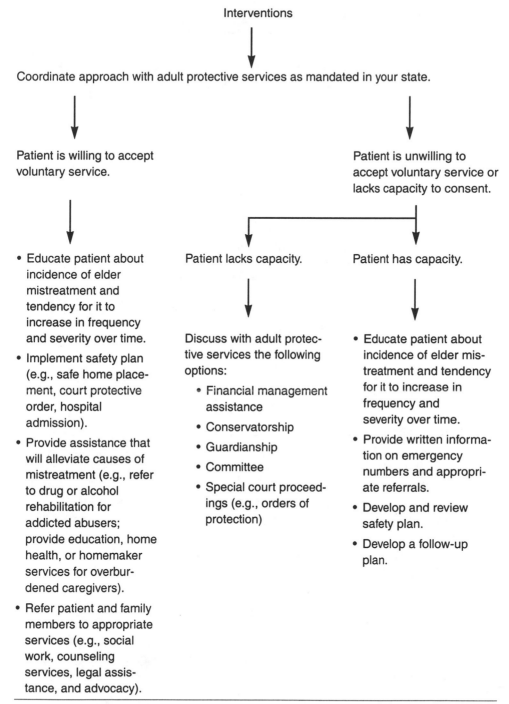

Interventions

Coordinate approach with adult protective services as mandated in your state.

Patient is willing to accept voluntary service.

Patient is unwilling to accept voluntary service or lacks capacity to consent.

Patient lacks capacity.

Patient has capacity.

- Educate patient about incidence of elder mistreatment and tendency for it to increase in frequency and severity over time.
- Implement safety plan (e.g., safe home placement, court protective order, hospital admission).
- Provide assistance that will alleviate causes of mistreatment (e.g., refer to drug or alcohol rehabilitation for addicted abusers; provide education, home health, or homemaker services for overburdened caregivers).
- Refer patient and family members to appropriate services (e.g., social work, counseling services, legal assistance, and advocacy).

Discuss with adult protective services the following options:
- Financial management assistance
- Conservatorship
- Guardianship
- Committee
- Special court proceedings (e.g., orders of protection)

- Educate patient about incidence of elder mistreatment and tendency for it to increase in frequency and severity over time.
- Provide written information on emergency numbers and appropriate referrals.
- Develop and review safety plan.
- Develop a follow-up plan.

Figure 19.3 Elder abuse intervention decision tree. (From American Medical Association, *Diagnostic and Treatment Guidelines on Elder Abuse and Neglect,* 1992, Chicago: Author. Copyright © 1992 by American Medical Association. Adapted with permission.)

Table 19.2   Continuum of Care

Diagnosis and Intervention		
Full legal process and all due process rights	Prison	Most restrictive
	Civil commitment	
	Conservatorship of person	
	Nursing homes	
	Skilled	
	Intermediate	
	Group home living	
	Group home for elderly	
	Retirement home	
	Independent living	
	Assisted living	
	24-hour live-in homemaker	
	In-home support services	
	Meals-on-wheels	
	Homemaker several times per week	
	Visiting nurse	
	Case management by practitioner	
	Information and referral	
Little or no legal process	Living in own home with no assistance	Least restrictive

SOURCE: Modified from Consortium for Elder Abuse Prevention, *Protocols*, 1983, San Francisco: UCSF/ Mount Zion Center on Aging.

1. Emphasize the victim's positive qualities rather than his or her weaknesses.
2. Attempt to break the victim's isolation and relieve underlying depression.
3. Treat other mental health or substance abuse issues, if present.
4. Recognize and counter power and control issues.
5. Assist the victim in achieving appropriate economic independence.
6. Increase assertiveness.
7. Deal with anger and rage.
8. Distinguish between oppression and personal circumstances.
9. Meet the needs of the victim (and family members when possible).

Although survivor therapy was developed out of feminist theory and trauma theory, the concepts and principles apply well to male and female elder abuse victims. However, despite Walker's contribution to providing therapy to abuse and neglect victims, the complexity of issues that play a role in elder neglect and abuse issues underscores the need for an even more integrated conceptualization and intervention approach.

Lazarus's multimodal therapy approach provides a useful paradigm for clinicians working with the elderly. Lazarus's recent contribution (1997) is a helpful reference for clinicians not familiar with this approach. He states that the multimodal therapy framework "provides clinicians with a comprehensive template that permits them to pinpoint salient problems that call for corrections." Lazarus contends that psychotherapy approaches are trimodal, typically intervening in the affect, behavior, and cognition. By intervening in each domain, a more comprehensive and positive treatment outcome may be achieved. Essentially, multimodal therapy evaluates excesses and deficits across behavior, affect, sensation, imagery, cognition, interpersonal, and drugs/biology (BASIC ID). Although the modalities are discrete, they are interactive with each other.

Following is an example of a problem list for the BASIC ID with a 65-year-old male patient experiencing the early signs of cognitive decline that his physician has diagnosed as Alzheimer's. The patient also has a relevant abuse history; his daughter-in-law has slapped him several times due to his episodes of agitation and suspicion. Currently the patient is living alone; his son and daughter-in-law, who live in the same town, are his caretakers. The family and patient pursued the evaluation and treatment of their father on a voluntary basis, and no elder abuse agencies had been contacted.

MULTIMODAL PROBLEM LIST

Behavior	Mild memory difficulties and agitation when forgetful
	Interpersonal isolation due to difficulty remembering names
	Difficulty organizing and paying bills on time
Affect	Episodic anxiety
	Depressed mood due to awareness of cognitive changes
	Fear regarding who will care for him as the Alzheimer's progresses
	Fear that he may be physically abused again
Sensation	Multiple somatic concerns
	Hearing difficulty never evaluated
Imagery	Flashbacks of his daughter-in-law slapping him several times
Cognition	Negative self-statements due to cognitive decline
	Slowed thinking and concentration difficulties
Interpersonal	Reduced social participation
	Increased suspicion of others
	Increased conflict with son and daughter-in-law, who are caretakers, over role changes
	Caretakers exhibiting feelings of being overwhelmed and fear of the future
Drugs/biology	Insomnia
	Self-medication with 2 to 3 drinks of alcohol daily
	Antianxiety medication prescribed by family physician
	Reduced activity level

A review of the BASIC ID problem list guides comprehensive intervention with elderly patients. (Lazarus, 1997.) A cognitive-behavioral approach, family systems intervention, or psychopharmacological intervention alone would not adequately address the complex symptom presentation this patient exhibits. The following is an example of possible intervention points with this patient:

Behavior	Refer patient to a memory disorder clinic for neurological and neuropsychological evaluation to confirm diagnosis of Alzheimer's and assist with treatment plan development.

	Instruct patient in compensatory techniques for memory difficulties.
	Refer patient to elder day treatment program to increase socialization opportunities with peers.
	Refer patient and caretakers to a bank to establish automated bill payment for regular bills.
Affect	Conduct individual therapy with patient to explore emotions related to cognitive decline and future needs.
	Have memory disorder clinic reevaluate current use of antianxiety medication and consider antidepressant that may address both symptoms.
	Interview caretakers to determine extent of abuse issues and determine reporting needs.
	Facilitate family discussion to assist members in developing more adaptive redirection or deescalation techniques.
Sensation	Reevaluate antianxiety medication, as somatic preoccupation is likely the result of depression.
	Refer patient to audiologist as hearing impairment may be contributing to behavioral issues such as suspicion and reduced social participation. Determine if hearing aid is needed.
Imagery	Utilize guided imagery or eye movement desensitization therapy (Shapero, 1989) to reduce intensity of flashbacks and gain control.
Cognition	Consider psychoeducation for patient and family to frame the cognitive decline experience.
	Consider cognitive restructuring and RET techniques to reduce negative self-statements (Ellis, 1970).
	Recommend a support group for patient with other peers at similar cognitive level to assist the patient in reframing his experience.
Interpersonal	Consider day treatment program to increase socialization opportunities with peers, provide respite for family, and provide cognitive stimulation.
	Refer patient for audiology evaluation to determine hearing impairment's contribution to patient's suspicion.
	Recommend family therapy to address role changes and plan for future while patient is less impaired.
	Recommend caretaker support group for family members.
Drugs/Biology	Refer patient to day treatment program with mental and physical activity to enhance sleep.
	Consider psychoeducation and family intervention to address self-medication with alcohol.
	Reevaluate antianxiety medication due to amnestic side effects and underlying depression with sleep difficulties.
	Pending neurological evaluation from memory disorder clinic, consult with neurologist and family regarding medication that slows progression of Alzheimer's.

In examining the intervention treatment points, it is clear that the intervention needs should be prioritized. As mentioned, safety issues are of immediate concern and a comprehensive neurological and neuropsychological evaluation is the second priority to determine actual diagnosis and then implement the treatment plan. Lazarus (1997) notes that by intervening in a specific modality, a ripple effect may occur in other modalities. Treatment intervention that may result in the greatest ripple effect rapidly is desirable. This aspect of the therapy relies on the art, experience, and creativity of the therapist.

Ferguson and Beck (1983) recommend that the therapist involve the family when possible to assure that dependency needs are balanced or shared. They also recommend using role theory to realign family responsibilities, to encourage the personal growth of each family member, and to develop clear boundaries and expectations. Educating families about normal aging and ageist stereotypes is also crucial.

Support services integrated into the treatment of elder clients may include legal advocacy, financial planning and guardianship programs, respite care, caretaker support groups, group homes, day care programs, and socialization services. The goals of such programs should be to increase the victim's independence and self esteem, reduce feelings of social isolation, provide an appropriate level of cognitive stimulation, and provide caretakers an opportunity to share their experiences, pressures, and issues related to the role of caretaker. Support services vary from state to state (Harway, Hansen, Rossman, Geffner, & Deitch, 1996). When services such as caretaker support groups are not available, clinicians have an excellent opportunity to develop such programs as part of their practice (Wolfe & Pillemer, 1994).

TRAINING IMPLICATIONS

Training in the areas of assessing and treating domestic violence can significantly improve the detection of elder abuse, providing an opportunity for intervention. Unfortunately, without appropriate training for health care professionals and increased public awareness, statistics have indicated that only 1 out of 14 cases of violence against elders is reported (Harshbarger, 1993). Warshaw (1989) found that physicians' discharge diagnoses correctly indicated spouse abuse in only 8% of the cases, despite the fact that explicit information regarding the abuse had been recorded in the medical charts. Currently, numerous states require continuing education in the area of domestic violence during licensure renewal periods. However, the issues and dynamics of elder abuse are generally overlooked, with greater focus on nonelderly female victims and the abuse effects on children in the victim's family. As the proportion of elderly adults continues to dramatically increase in the United States, a movement in the direction of mandatory training in elder abuse by health care professionals should be considered (Lachs, Berkman, Fulmer, & Gorwitz, 1994).

Previous research supports the notion that health care training in domestic violence improves detection rates; it also appears that ongoing training ensures that health care professionals will continue to evaluate for these issues in their clinical work. A follow-up study conducted at a hospital emergency room revealed that detection rates reverted back to pretraining rates after 8 years when ongoing in-service training was not provided (McLeer, Anwar, Herman, and Maguiling, 1989). As a result, mandatory training for those treating any elderly clients during each licensure renewal period may be an effective route to pursue.

Salber and Taliaferro (1995) addressed reasons why physicians and health care providers fail to inquire about domestic violence:

- Fear of offending the patient
- Belief that domestic abuse and violence does not occur in the patient population they serve
- Inadequate training in domestic abuse issues
- Time required to address the issue
- Not knowing what to do if they uncover the abuse or belief that it is the job of other professionals (i.e., social workers)
- Holding a belief that the victim provoked or deserved the abuse
- Belief that what happens in the home, in terms of domestic abuse, is a private matter and therefore should not be discussed
- Belief that victims can remove themselves if they choose to
- Knowing the assailant and believing that he or she is incapable of being abusive
- Knowing what to do, but believing it won't help; belief that patients will go back to the abusive environment

Past researchers have also documented the reluctance of primary care physicians to address any form of family violence (AMA, 1992). In addition to the preceding factors, physicians state that the time-consuming nature of an evaluation that requires physical examination and detailed histories from the patient, the alleged abuser, and other family members is a significant barrier. In addition, managed care policies do not allow reimbursement for such labor and "cognitively intensive" evaluations (AMA, 1992). Because the issues and dynamics of elder abuse are complex, the AMA has made recommendations for the utilization of multidisciplinary geriatric teams when available to effectively evaluate and intervene.

The importance of comprehensive training for health professionals regarding domestic violence and elder abuse cannot be overstated (Peake & Philpot, 1991). In a survey conducted by Brendtro and Bowker (1989), the majority of the women who successfully ended an abusive relationship had sought help from their physician or other health professionals. Unfortunately, in this same survey, the victims stated that medical professionals were the least effective source of help. Education in medical and professional schools should make training about elder abuse a required part of the curricula. Figure 19.4 illustrates that 22.5% of elder abuse reports were made by a physician or health care provider. This again emphasizes the importance of training these professionals in recognizing and treating elder abuse. The federal Administration on Aging and the AMA prepared *Diagnostic and Treatment Guidelines on Elder Abuse and Neglect* (AMA, 1992). This document sensitizes clinicians to issues of elder abuse as well as outlining identification and intervention strategies. It is a concise 44-page document that is useful for all health professionals.

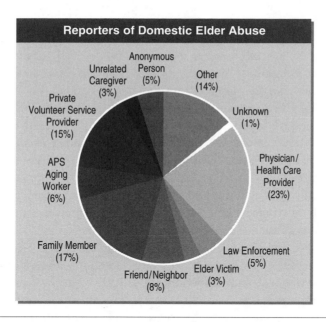

Figure 19.4 Reporters of domestic elder abuse. (Data from National Center on Elder Abuse; Tatara & Kuzmeskus, 1996).

SUMMARY AND RECOMMENDATIONS

The individual or agency clinician must appreciate that elder abuse involves the entire landscape of clinical issues, including developmental, clinical, gerontological, psychiatric, and family systems, plus medical and nursing standards of practice in the climate of managed care. In addition, the clinician must be conversant with various agencies and sometimes conflicting systems, such as legal, law enforcement, health care, mental health, housing, protective services, and not-for-profit resources, which may all be involved with the complex problems of elder health and elder abuse. Not surprisingly, few clinicians elect to work with issues of domestic violence and elder abuse even in light of the rapid "graying of America." Sensitivity and good training are valuable. However, an appreciation for the multisystemic "trip wires" that may detonate and redirect well-meaning interventions are the true sign of a savvy clinician. There is an understandable wish to establish cause or blame and move to intervene decisively. However, knowing the ways that one system venue may clash with another is part of the essential skill and knowledge base.

One useful example is the conundrum of Alzheimer's disease and the specter of abuse (both to and by the patient) that may accompany it. In clinical research settings, this cluster of problems is called *senile dementias of the Alzheimer's type* (SDAT). Alzheimer's disease is diagnosed by eliminating other diseases first. It is a presumptive diagnosis until autopsy. Paveza et al. (1992) began to identify the prevalence and risk factors for families and patients. They found an overall violence rate of 17.4% of the community population sampled in the year after an Alzheimer's diagnosis was made (patients being violent 3 times as often as the caregivers). They identified the risk factors as caregiver depression and living arrangements.

Consider one other problem that families of Alzheimer's patients face: Many people are shocked to find that in the current health care system (with Medicare and Medicaid as the primary insurance), a diagnosis of Alzheimer's disease eliminates the patient's eligibility for many clinical services. This is because the prognosis is deemed so poor that already rationed health benefits are denied. Patients with other acute medical conditions (e.g., heart disease and colon cancer) with a more favorable prognosis get treatment (see Callahan, 1990, 1995). This denial of care for dementia patients presents a dilemma for clinicians who may either avoid the problem ("It's not my job") or learn to be creative in adding other medical or psychiatric diagnoses in addition to Alzheimer's in order to justify the desperately needed extra services for patients and their families. When additional services are not available, a family's caretaking burden can become overwhelming and the risk for depression and abuse escalates.

Although abused children are not considered capable of determining what is in their best interest, elders have the right to remain in their own homes and the right to privacy. These rights are threatened in the delicate balance of suspected abuse. The threat of being put into a nursing home or institution may be viewed by abused elders as being worse than the abuse. This prospect intensifies their feelings of hopelessness, helplessness, or powerlessness. Consequently, abuse charges are often dropped in an attempt to preserve what is left of their autonomy and family connectedness (Deitch, 1993). Although not a procedure to prevent abuse in every respect, the concept of a living will may help in certain aspects of preserving an older adults' wishes when their competence to make decisions for themselves is in jeopardy. A valuable resource on this topic is Collins and Weber (1991).

As one ponders the complexities of all the agencies involved in the problems of elder abuse (nursing homes and the statutes that govern them, health care providers, protective services, legal considerations regarding competency and estate settlement, not to mention driving and the division of motor vehicles, etc.), one gains an appreciation of the ageist and daunting terrain that awaits elders and their professional and lay caregivers. Perhaps the coming throng of baby boomers (who have been vocal, demanding, and omnipresent in every other stage of their lives) may create the pressure to see the problem and risk of elder abuse as broader than an individual or family affair. Meanwhile, professionals working with this sizable population must become a force to be reckoned with (Carstensen, Edelstein, & Dornbrand, 1996), blending compassion and good clinical skills (in individual, family, and systems approaches) with assertive uncovering of injustices and a role of advocacy and education to reverse the worst kind of ageism—elder abuse.

REFERENCES

American Medical Association (1992). *Diagnostic and treatment guidelines on elder abuse and neglect.* Chicago: Author.

American Medical Association (1995). *Diagnostic and treatment guidelines on mental health effects of family violence.* Chicago: Author.

American Medical Association/Administration on Aging (1997). *Profile of older Americans.* Chicago: American Medical Association.

American Psychological Association (1996). *Violence and the family.* Washington, DC: Author.

American Psychological Association (1997). *What practitioners should know about working with older adults*. Washington, DC: Author.

Anetzberger, G. J., Korbin, J. E., and Austine, C. (1994). Alcoholism and elder abuse. *Journal of Interpersonal Violence, 9*(2), 184–193.

Baltes, P. B., & Baltes, M. M. (Eds.). (1990). *Successful aging: Perspectives from the behavioral sciences*. Cambridge, England: Cambridge University Press.

Block, M. R., & Sinnott, J. D. (Eds.). (1979). *The battered elder syndrome: An exploratory study*. College Park, MD: University of Maryland Center on Aging.

Blunt, A. (1993). Finacial exploitation of the incapacitated: Investigation and remedies. *Journal of Elder Abuse and Neglect, 5*(1), 19–32.

Brendtro, M., & Bowker, L. (1989). Battered women: How nurses can help. *Issues in Mental Health Nursing, 10*, 169–180.

Bristowe, E., & Collins, J. B. (1989). Family mediated abuse of noninstitutionalized frail elderly men and women living in British Columbia. *Journal of Elder Abuse and Neglect, 1*(1), 45–64.

Butler, R. (1969). Ageism: Another form of bigotry. *The Gerontologist, 9*, 243–246.

Callahan, D. (1995). *Setting limits: Medical goals in an aging society*. Washington, DC: Georgetown University Press.

Callahan, D. (1990). *What kind of life? The limits of medical progress*. New York: Simon & Schuster.

Carstensen, L. L., Edelstein, B. A., & Dornbrand, L. (1996). *The practical handbook of clinical gerontology*. Thousand Oaks, CA: Sage.

Cazenave, N. A., & Straus, M. (1979). Race, class, network embeddedness and family violence: A search for potent support systems. *Journal of Comparative Family Studies, 10*(3), 280–300.

Chinen, A. B. (1989). *In the everafter: Fairy tales for the second half of life*. Wilmette, IL: Chiron.

Clark, A. N. G., Mankikar, G. D., & Gray, I. (1975). Diogenes syndrome: A clinical study of gross neglect in old age. *Lancet, 1*(790), 366–368.

Cohen, D., & Eisdorfer, C. (1986). *The loss of self: A family resource for Alzheimer's disease*. New York: Penguin.

Collins, E. R., & Weber, D. (1991). *The complete guide to living wills: How to safeguard your treatment choices (forms and guidelines for every state)*. New York: Bantam Books.

Consortium for Elder Abuse Prevention. (1983). *Protocols*. San Francisco: Goldman Institute on Aging.

Deitch, I. (1993). *Alone, abandoned and assaulted: Elder abuse and the family*. Paper presented at American Psychological Association, Toronto, Canada.

Dowd, J. J. (1975). Aging as exchange: A preface to theory. *Journal of Gerontology, 30*, 585–594.

Dychtwald, K., & Flower, J. (1989). *The age wave: Challenges and opportunities of an aging America*. Los Angeles: Tarcher.

Elder mistreatment guidelines for health care professionals: Detection, assessment and intervention. (1988). New York: Mount Sinai/Victim Services Agency, Elder Abuse Project.

Ellis, A. (1970). *The essence of rational psychotherapy: A comprehensive approach to treatment*. New York: Institute for Rational Living.

Enns, C. Z., Campbell, J., & Courtois, C. A. (1997). Recommendations for working with domestic violence survivors, with special attention to memory issues and post-traumatic processes. *Psychotherapy, 34*(4).

Estes, C. L., & Binney, E. A. (1989). The biomedicalization of aging: Dangers and dilemmas. *The Gerontologist, 29*, 587–596.

Ferguson, D., & Beck, D. (1983). H.A.L.F.—A tool to assess elder abuse within the family. *Gerontological Nursing, 4*(5), 301–304.

Ferri, F. F., & Fretwell, M. D. (1992). *Practical guide to the care of geriatric patient*. St. Louis, MO: Mosby.

Florida Adult Protective Service Act. (1989). State of Florida Public Law.

Godkin, M. A., Wolf, R. S., & Pillemer, K. A. (1989). A case-comparison analysis of elder abuse and neglect. *International Journal of Aging and Human Development, 28,* 207–225.

Hall, P. A. (1986). Minority elder mistreatment: Ethnicity, gender, age, and poverty. *Journal of Gerontologic Social Work, 9*(4), 53–72.

Harshbarger, S. (1993). From protection to prevention: A proactive approach. *Journal of Elder Abuse and Neglect, 5*(1), 41–55.

Harway, M., Hansen, M., Rossman, B. R., Geffner, G., & Deitch, I. (1996). Families affected by domestic violence. In M. Harway (Ed.), *Treating the changing family* (pp. 163–190). New York: John Wiley & Sons.

Health care: Tales of neglect and abuse. (1998, August 3). *Time,* 42–43.

Hickey, T., & Douglass, R. L. (1981). Neglect and abuse of older family members: Professionals' perspectives and case experience. *Gerontologist, 21*(4), 171–176.

Hirst, S. P., & Miller, J. (1986). The abused elderly. *Journal of Psychosocial Nursing, 24*(10), 28–34.

Homans, G. C. (1961). *Social behavior: Its elementary forms.* New York: Harcourt, Brace, and World.

Homer, A., & Gilleard, C. (1990). Abuse of elderly people by their careers. *British Medical Journal, 301,* 1359–1362.

Johnson, C. L., and Barer, B. M. (1990). Families and networks among older inner-city blacks. *The Gerontologist, 30,* 726–733.

Kaufman, S. R. (1986). *The ageless self: Sources of meaning in late life.* New York: Meridian.

Krassen-Maxwell, E., & Maxwell, R. J. (1992). Insults to the body civil: Mistreatment of elderly in two Plains Indian tribes. *Journal of Cross-Cultural Gerontology, 7*(1), 3–23.

Lachs, M., Berkman, L., Fulmer, T., & Gorwitz, R. (1994). A prospective community-based pilot study of risk factors for the investigation of elder mistreatment. *Journal of the American Geriatric Society, 42,* 169–173.

Lazarus, A. (1997). *Brief but comprehensive psychotherapy: The multimodal way.* New York: Springer.

Mace, N. L., & Rabins, P. V. (1991). *The 36-hour day: A family guide to caring for persons with Alzheimer's disease, related illnesses and memory loss in later life.* Baltimore: Johns Hopkins Press.

McLeer, S. V., Anwar, R. A. H., Herman, S., & Maguiling, K. (1989). Education is not enough: A system's failure in protecting battered women. *Annual of Emergency Medicine, 18,* 652–653.

Minor, W. (1981, July). Techniques of neutralization: A reconceptualization and empirical examination. *Journal of Research in Crime and Delinquency,* 295–318.

Moon, A., & Williams, O. (1993). Perceptions of elder abuse and help-seeking patterns among African-American, Caucasian-American, and Korean-American elderly women. *Gerontologist, 33*(3), 386–395.

Oelschlager, J., & Cauffield, C. (1997). Treating domestic violence: Issues and symptoms of traumatic brain injury. In R. Fry (Ed.), *Eighth National Forum on Issues in Vocation Assessment* (pp. 235–241). The Rehabilitation Resource, Stout Vocational Rehabilitation Institute, University of Wisconsin, Stout, Menomonie, WI.

Omer, A., & Gilleard, C. (1990). Abuse of elderly people by their carers. *British Medical Journal, 301,* 1359–1362.

Paveza, G., Cohen, D., Eisdorfer, C., Freels, S., Semla, T., Ashford, J., Gorelick, P., Hirschman, R., Luchins, D., & Levy, P. (1992). Severe family violence and Alzheimer's disease: Prevalence and risk factors. *The Gerontologist, 32,* 493–497.

Peake, T. H. (1998). *Health aging, healthy treatment: The impact of telling stories.* Westport, CT: Praeger/Greenwood.

Peake, T. H., Rosenzweig, S. G., & Williamson, J. M. (1996). Aging problems and family solutions. In M. Harway (Ed.), *Treating the changing family* (pp. 79–96). New York: John Wiley & Sons.

Peake, T. H., & Philpot, C. (1991). Psychotherapy with older adults: Hopes and fears. *The Clinical Supervisor, 9,* 185–202.

Pillemer, K. (1985). The dangers of dependency: New findings on domestic violence against the elderly. *Social Problems, 33*(2), 146–157.

Pillemer, K., & Wolf, R. (1986). Elder abuse and neglect: Conflict in the family. Dover, MA: Auburn.

Quinn, M. J., & Tomita, S. K. (1997). *Elder abuse and neglect: Causes, diagnosis and intervention strategies* (2nd ed.). New York: Springer.

Ramsey-Klawsnik, H. (1991). Elder sexual abuse: Preliminary findings. *Journal of Elder Abuse and Neglect, 3*(3), 73–90.

Ramsey-Klawsnik, H. (1993). Interviewing elders for suspected sexual abuse: Guidelines and techniques. *Journal of Elder Abuse and Neglect, 5*(1), 17–90.

Ramsey-Klawsnik, H. (1995). Investigating suspected elder maltreatment. *Journal of Elder Abuse and Neglect, 7,* 41–67.

Rathbone-McCuan, E. (1980). Elderly victims of family violence and neglect. *Social Casework, 61*(5), 296–304.

Salber, P., & Taliaferro, E. (1995). *The physician's guide to domestic violence.* Volcano, CA: Volcano Press.

Seuss, Dr. (1986). *You're only old once!* New York: Random House.

Shapiro, F. (1989). Efficacy of the eye movement desensitization procedure in the treatment of traumatic memories. *Journal of Traumatic Stress, 2*(2), 199–223.

Sokolovsky, J. (1985). Ethnicity, culture, and aging: Do gerontology differences really make a difference? *Journal of Applied Gerontology, 4*(1), 6–17.

Stein, K. F. (1991). *Working with abused and neglected elders in minority populations: A synthesis of research.* Washington, DC: National Aging Resource Center on Elder Abuse (NARCEA).

Steinmetz, S. K. (1978). Battered parents. *Society, 15*(15), 54–55.

Steinmetz, S. K. (1990). Elder abuse: Myth and reality. In T. H. Brubaker (Ed.), *Family relationships in later life.* Newbury Park, CA: Sage.

Sykes, G., & Matza, D. (1957). Techniques of neutralization: A theory of delinquency. *American Sociological Review, 22,* 664–670.

Tatara, T., & Kuzmeskus, M. A. (1986). *National Center on Elder Abuse adult protective services statistics.* Washington, DC: National Center on Elder Abuse.

Taylor, R., & Chatters, L. (1986). Patterns of informal support to elderly black adults: Family, friends, and church members. *Social Work, 31*(6), 432–438.

Tomita, S. K. (1982). Detection and treatment of elderly abuse and neglect: A protocol for health care professionals. *Physical and Occupational Therapy in Geriatrics, 2*(2), 37–51.

Tomita, S. K. (1994). The consideration of cultural factors in the research of elder mistreatment with an in-depth look at the Japanese. *Journal of Cross-Cultural Gerontology, 9,* 39–52.

United States Congress, House Select Committee on Aging. (1991). *Elder abuse: What can be done?* Washington, DC: U.S. Government Printing Office.

University of Miami School of Medicine (1995). *Opening Pandora's box: A physician's guide to identifying and treating victims of abuse.* University of Miami Continuing Education.

Walker, L., (1994). *Abused women and survivor therapy.* Washington, DC: American Psychological Association.

Warshaw, C. (1989) Limitations of the medical model in the care of battered women. *Gender Sociology, 3,* 506–517.

Wettle, T. (1989). Age as a risk factor for inadequate treatment. *Journal of the American Medical Association, 258,* 516–518.

Wolfe, R. S., & Pillemer, K. A. (1994). What's new in elder abuse programming? Four bright new ideas. *The Gerontologist, 1*(34), 126–129.

CHAPTER 20

Wills and Trusts

Family Planning

STUART B. KLEIN

PREPARATION OF a will or trust requires very careful consideration of legal, financial, and psychological issues. The questions of who to leave what to and who will make vital decisions at critical times require an enormous amount of financial analysis, legal preparation, and the exploration and sometimes resolution of family and emotional conflicts. This chapter presents a brief review and discussion of wills and trusts. It addresses some of the legal, ethical, and planning dilemmas confronted by professionals who must consider the desires of the person who wishes to create a will or trust and the legacy that person chooses to bequeath. This chapter defines wills and trusts and explains how these instruments are effective estate planning instruments. It also examines the dilemmas faced by attorneys and other professionals when dealing with incapacitated clients who have a desire to create a will or trust. Further, this chapter addresses the potential impact of the various choices that family members can make and how these choices affect the estate planning process as well as the persons involved with it.

WILLS

A *will* is a document that becomes effective upon one's death and is the formal means by which a person can direct the disposition of his or her property. A will is used to dispose of both real and personal property, as well as tangible and intangible property. In many states, any person who is age 18 or older and is of sound mind may make a will (Fla. Stat. Ann. § 732.501, West 1998). Each state has its own statutes a person must comply with and that provide certain formalities required to make a will valid. For instance, in Florida, a will must be in writing and exe-

The author wishes to thank Mr. Carlton Smith and Ms. Atyria Clark for their assistance in the preparation of this chapter.

cuted by the testator (the person creating the will) or by another person directed by and in the presence of the testator on his or her behalf. Some states require that the will contain an acknowledgment stating that the testator signed the will and that the will be signed in the presence of at least two attesting witnesses (Fla. Stat. § 732.502(2), West 1998). Statutes may also require that the witnesses themselves sign in the presence of the testator, in the presence of each other, and in the presence of a notary public who can attest to the fact that the testator and witnesses signed in the notary's presence.

While most states require that the will be in writing and be signed by the testator in the presence of at least two witnesses, some states allow for certain variations of these formalities. Many states recognize holographic and nuncupative wills. A *holographic will* is a will that is completely written and signed in the handwriting of the testator and is usually unwitnessed. A *nuncupative will* is an oral will (New York Est. Powers & Trusts Law Ann. § 3-2.2(b)(1)-(3), McKinney, 1998). Both holographic and nuncupative wills are invalid in Florida; however, Texas and New York do recognize these types of wills. In New York, a nuncupative or holographic will is valid only if made by a member of the armed forces of the United States engaged in armed conflict, by a person who serves with or accompanies an armed force engaged in armed conflict, or by a mariner at sea (New York Est. Powers & Trusts Law Ann. § 3-2.2(b)(1)-(3), McKinney, 1998). In Texas, a holographic will is valid merely if it is written in the testator's handwriting. (Tex. Prob. Code Ann. § 60, Vernon, 1998). A nuncupative will is valid if it is made on the deathbed of the testator and at the testator's home or anyplace that he or she has resided for at least 10 days. Formal wills and codicils (special amendments to the will), however, must be executed with the same specific formalities as the original will (Fla. Stat. Ann. § 732.504, West, 1998). Thus, if a person writes an original will and later wants to make changes to or add provisions to that will, these changes or additions must follow the same formalities as those required by statute to make a valid will.

Some states provide for a *self proof affidavit.* A self proof affidavit is attached to the will at the time of execution and is required to avoid having the witnesses later testify as to the proper execution of the will upon the testator's death. Each witness must be *competent*—age 18 or older and of sound mind—in order for the affidavit to be valid (Fla. Stat. Ann. § 732.503, West, 1998).

The purpose of preparing a will or a trust is to ensure that the individual's intentions are carried out upon his or her death as to the distribution of the decedent's property and any other provisions regarding important matters that affect the decedent's survivors. Thus, a will or trust can create provisions for the maintenance and protection of minors, or others who are cherished, including family pets. It can also specify certain distributions to named charities. If no will or trust is put into place, then the laws of intestate succession determine the distribution of the estate. *Intestate succession* occurs when any part of the decedent's estate is not effectively disposed of by will or trust. The intestacy laws in a particular state set forth the beneficiaries of the estate based upon what the state presumes the decedent would have wanted. This order is based largely upon the degree of familial relation to the decedent. For instance, under Florida intestacy statutes, if there is a surviving spouse but no lineal descendants of the decedent and that surviving spouse, then the surviving spouse gets the entire estate. If there is a surviving spouse and lineal descendants of the decedent and the surviving spouse, then the surviving spouse gets the first $20,000 of the estate plus half the balance of the remainder, with the other half going to the lineal descendants, who equally share that half (Fla. Stat. Ann. § 732.102(b), West, 1998). If there are no lineal descendants and no surviving spouse, then the decedent's father and mother, or the survivor of either, inherit the estate. If none of the foregoing is living, then the decedent's brothers and sisters share in the estate equally (Fla. Stat. Ann. § 732.103(c), West, 1998).

California, on the other hand, is a community property state and has different intestacy provisions. *Community property* is the property that a husband and wife share equally during their marriage and split equally upon divorce. A surviving spouse is entitled to the other spouse's half of the property upon that spouse's death (Cal. Prob. Code § 6401(a), West, 1998). As for separate property held by the deceased spouse, under California's intestacy statute, a surviving spouse will inherit the entire separate estate if there are no lineal descendants, no parents, and no siblings or children of the deceased person's siblings (Cal. Prob. Code § 6401(c)(1), West, 1998). However, a surviving spouse will get only half of the decedent's separate property if the decedent leaves one child, or if the decedent leaves no children but is survived by either parents or siblings or nieces and nephews (Cal. Prob. Code § 6401(c)(2), West, 1998). If the decedent leaves more than one child or leaves grandchildren, then the surviving spouse will get only a third of the decedent's separate estate (Cal. Prob. Code § 6401(c)(3), West, 1998). A properly prepared will or trust avoids the sometimes confusing and perhaps misguided intestacy provisions and allows an individual to distribute his or her estate according to the way that he or she in fact wants the property divided. Therefore, suppose a person has an estate worth $500,000 at the time of his or her death and leaves behind a wife and one child. If the decedent dies intestate (without a will), then, in Florida, the wife would inherit the first $20,000 of his estate plus half of the remaining $480,000. The other $240,000 would go to the child. In California, if the $500,000 is the value of the decedent's separate property, then the wife would inherit one-half of the estate ($250,000) plus all of the community property that the husband and wife shared during the marriage. But if the decedent despised his wife and was planning to divorce her, but unexpectedly died before obtaining a divorce and did not leave a will, the loathed wife would get $250,000 to $260,000 from the estate (depending on the state), whereas the decedent probably would have preferred that the survivor get nothing. In this case, the decedent should have had a will that specifically stated that someone else would inherit the estate and ensured that the spouse would inherit nothing, or at least no more than the statutory minimum or elective share. A person might also consider preparing a trust.

TRUSTS

A trust, in contrast to a will, becomes effective upon its formal and proper execution. The use of the revocable *intervivos trust*, commonly referred to as a *living trust*, has proliferated over the past 20 years in many states, especially in Florida. The perceptions of many people concerning living trusts are inaccurate. Many people obtain information about the living trust by attending seminars offered on the subject. These seminars often explain that the trust will save money, time, and delay in realizing the assets. People are also led to believe that a living trust saves taxes and avoids the sometimes horrid probate process. A typical intervivos trust provides for the individual's property to be titled in the settlor's name. The *settlor* is the person who creates the trust and can also be the trustee and beneficiary of the trust property. Thus, the property is merely *titled* in the name of the trust rather than in the individual's name. The settlor then possesses both *legal title*, as the trustee of the estate, and *equitable title*, as the beneficiary of the estate. The property is transferred into a formal written document in which the settlor is the trustee with legal obligations to himself or herself. There is little difference between individual and trust ownership as a practical matter. In reality, the settlor retains equitable title with legal title placed in the trust. The settlor also maintains the power to revoke, amend, withdraw, and otherwise control the assets and the trust property. Essentially, in a typical living trust the settlor is the trustee *and* the beneficiary under the trust.

However, there are other types of trusts that can serve various functions. These trusts include *support trusts, discretionary trusts,* and *spendthrift trusts* and are usually designed to name a third party as the beneficiary and some person other than the settlor, as the trustee. Under these forms of trusts, the settlor relinquishes both legal and equitable title to the property. The trustee holds legal title for the benefit of the beneficiary, who holds equitable title. The settlor may own nothing after the execution of the trust. However, this chapter addresses only intervivos trusts.

Under an intervivos trust, the trustee holds legal title to the trust property and has fiduciary obligations to the beneficiary(s). The trust instrument should be very specific as to the duties and obligations of the trustee. Although the trustee, settlor, and beneficiary may all be one and the same, it is essential to specify the requirements, duties, and obligations when there is a successor trustee who will administer the trust on behalf of the beneficiary. The amount of discretion given to the successor trustee is critical and requires an accurate evaluation of that person's capacities and capabilities.

There are many key differences between a will and a trust and many misunderstandings as to the effect of the two documents on taxes, probate, and the ability to act for an incapacitated person. A popular misconception is that a trust will save the decedent's heir from estate taxes. This notion is not correct. Section 2031 of the Internal Revenue Code provides that the value of all assets held by a decedent in his or her own name is includable in his or her gross estate under a will (26 U.S.C. § 2031, 1998). The same is true for all assets held in a living trust at the decedent's death, under Section 2035 of the Internal Revenue Code (26 U.S.C. § 2035, 1998). Under Section 2035, estate taxes begin at 37% and quickly rise to 55% for federal estate taxes. In addition, most states also impose their own taxes above any federal tax. (See, for example, Tex. Prob. Code § 427, Vernon, 1998.) Presently every taxpayer is entitled to make lifetime taxable gifts and transfer at death a gift which totals $625,000 without being subject to an estate or gift tax. This amount will increase gradually each year between 1998 and 2006. In 2006, the exemption reaches $1 million pursuant to the Taxpayer Relief Act of 1997. The following is the schedule of increases in the estate tax exemption: $650,000 in 1999; $675,000 in the years 2000 and 2001; $700,000 in the years 2002 and 2003; $850,000 in 2004; $950,000 in 2005; and $1 million in 2006. A person can gift present and future donations up to $10,000 per calendar year to any number of donees without affecting this lifetime exception. Married couples can gift $20,000 per donee (26 U.S.C.

§ 2012, 1998). Thus, with a carefully planned gifting program to children and grandchildren, a person can significantly reduce the size of his or her estate (that is, subject to tax) and actually experience his or her money being utilized by loved ones.

Another misconception is that with the living trust the fiduciaries' fees will be significantly less expensive. Many people are under the impression that a living trust allows for the avoidance of fees and costs in the distribution process. Although a will can provide that fiduciaries serve without a fee, the personal representative (the one administering the estate under a will) and a trustee are both entitled to statutory fees under most state laws, as is the lawyer for each. Fees for representing the trustee may be somewhat less than the legal fees to represent the personal representative, but not significantly less. For instance, in Florida, the statute provides for a 25% difference in the amount of fees for representing the trustee than for the personal representative (Fla. Stat. § 733.6171, West, 1998). States typically allow attorneys fees for representing the personal representative as well as the trustee. Therefore, the total amount of actual costs to administer a will or a trust differ considerably less than is usually believed.

Another reason for the promotion of the living trust is that it ensures greater privacy of the estate's assets. At the time of one's death, a will becomes a matter of public record, although the inventory of property is not subject to inspection unless ordered by a court for good cause. While there is more privacy of the actual assets held in a trust upon one's death, the Florida legislature will probably eliminate this privacy difference in the near future.

A living trust also makes it easier for a settlor to disinherit someone. In *Friedberg v. Sunbank Miami* (1994), the Court of Appeals reviewed whether a spouse had the right to take an elective share against the assets of a revocable intervivos trust established by the deceased's spouse. The court ruled that a state statute effectively eliminated the elective share protection from the trust estate. Normally, a spouse would receive at least 30% of the net probate assets of an estate under the elective share provision, even if a will specifically disinherited that spouse (Fla. Stat. Ann. § 732.201, West, 1998). However, if all of the decedent's assets are in a trust, then these assets are not subject to probate and the surviving spouse would not be able to get his or her 30 percent. So, referring back to the hypothetical case where the husband dies leaving a wife he despises and whom he intended to divorce before his unexpected death—if the husband dies, but does leave a will that bequeaths nothing to the wife, she can still take an elective share against the $500,000 estate and would get at least $150,000 of the husband's estate. However, if the husband put the $500,000 into an intervivos trust, then the wife would not be entitled to receive an elective share because there will be no assets in probate. Therefore, one can use trusts to limit the funds a spouse receives and to possibly retaliate against a spouse for years of conflict, disrespect, and emotional abuse.

Another advantage of the living trust, and one that an attorney must carefully consider, is the effect on a client who becomes disabled prior to death. With the will, the assets must be managed and administered by a court-appointed guardian unless the incapacitated person has executed a durable power of attorney, giving control and the ability to act for the incapacitated person to another. With a living trust, a person's incapacity may have no effect on its validity or continued operation. The trust can provide for a clear indication of who should be the successor trustee in the event that the present trustee becomes incapacitated. In addition, the trust may provide a mechanism for determining when a successor trustee shall be appointed without the need for a determination by a court. For instance, the trust may require that when, in the opinion of the settlor's physicians, the settlor cannot manage his or her affairs, the successor trustee shall step in and administer the trust. Litigation to determine the competency of the person may still occur, but it is less likely. This author has found that one of the most painful things to witness is an elderly person whose family must obtain an incapacity adjudication so that a family member can be appointed to act as guardian to take care of the infirm person's affairs. The stress, guilt, and resentment experienced by the parties can be devastating. The infirm person can view even the best of intentions as a betrayal. Under a trust, the successor trustee may then manage the assets of the living trust without interference or approval of the court, allowing for uninterrupted continuity. This is the one advantage of the trust that an attorney should consider for estate-planning purposes, especially when planning for the infirm.

LIVING WILLS

In many states an individual can compensate for the incapacity differences in a number of ways. For instance, under a *living will*, a competent individual may declare his or her intentions for termination of life support systems upon meeting certain criteria under terminal circumstances. Under a living will there is a written instrument with prior notification to the health care providers and to other significant individuals. This notification details what the hospital should do in the absence of recovery prospects for the maker of the living will (Fla. Stat. Ann. § 765.302, West, 1998). In addition, some states allow for a *durable power of attorney* statute, which provides for an appointed attorney-in-fact to act for the incapacitated person. Often the law requires a very close family member to act in the capacity of attorney-in-fact for the incapacitated person. Under Florida law, there is also a health care surrogate provision that allows one to appoint a health care decision maker under certain circumstances.

For the very elderly, who may hold all of their assets in a limited number of accounts and perhaps own a home, a living trust is not too cumbersome to create or maintain. However, when the settlor is of an age at which he or she engages in many transactions and has fluidity in his or her financial life, often some of the assets do not actually get titled in the name of the trust. Thus, ultimately the need for probate arises. In addition, there can be substantial transactional costs for placing all of the assets into the trust. Therefore, when there are clients with limited transactions and holdings and when there is a trusted family member to act as the successor trustee, the living trust should be seriously considered. However, an attorney should be careful when creating a living trust for someone who partakes in numerous transactions and has a large number of different assets.

CAPACITY AND INCAPACITY

In most states a person age 18 or older on the date of execution can make a will (Fla. Stat. Ann. §. 732.501, West, 1998). Nevertheless, the testator must also have the mental capacity to make a will. This requires that he or she know and understand the nature and extent of his or her property, the persons who are the natural objects of his or her bounty, and the nature of the disposition he or she is making. All circumstances existing at the time of the execution, as well as evidence relating to the testator's state of mind shortly before and after the preparation and signing of the will or trust, are relevant and pertinent to the determination of the testator's capacity.

A will or trust can still be valid despite the fact that the testator is very old or physically frail, has a failing memory, is a habitual drunk or addicted to drugs, or is even adjudicated incapacitated and under the care of a guardian. These matters do not completely eliminate a finding of *testamentary capacity*, although strong contrary evidence would be needed to support a finding that the person did not lack capacity. In the case of *In re Estate of Zimmerman* (1956), the court found that the precise condition of a decedent's mental health at time of execution may be established in more ways than one. While an adjudication of incapacity may create a presumption of the lack of testamentary capacity, this presumption may be overcome by showing that the testator has met certain specific criteria as set forth previously.

Duress and undue influence can also affect the validity of a will or trust. If a will or trust is obtained through duress or undue influence, then that will or trust will be invalid (Fla. Stat. Ann. § 732.5165, West, 1998). Undue influence occurs when a person uses force or persuasion over the settlor or testator, which is sufficient to destroy the free agency and desires of the testator. Duress is similar to undue influence and occurs when a person uses blackmail, violence, or some other type of force to make the testator design a trust or will. For instance, suppose the wife in the previous hypothetical case discovers that the husband has written a will that leaves little to her. Suppose further that the husband is a prominent public official and the wife has damaging information about the husband's character that can destroy his career. The wife threatens to use this information to demand that the husband rewrite the will, leaving everything to her. The husband, fearing that his wife will act on the threat, does rewrite the will and then dies shortly after the will is validly executed. In this scenario, the will may be invalid if someone can prove that the wife threatened the husband and the husband rewrote the will because of coercion. If this were a recent marriage and there was a great disparity as to the ages of the parties, the case might be bolstered further.

Proof of undue influence can also invalidate a will. In the case of *In re Dunson's Estate* (1962), the court articulated that the burden of proving undue influence is on the person contesting the will and that such person generally must show that the testator was susceptible to undue influence or domination. The contesting person must also show that such person had a disposition to influence for the purpose of personal benefit and that the provisions of the will appeared to be unnatural and the result of such influence. A presumption of undue influence and duress is raised when a testator makes a gift in his or her will or trust to a person with whom the testator has a *confidential* relationship. For example, suppose a man in his late 70s is very sick and has a 30-year-old nurse helping him. He eventually marries this woman, and after 2 or 3 months of marriage, she strongly suggests that he rewrite his will to leave his entire estate to her. The man reluctantly rewrites the will out of "love" and then dies a year later. Under these circumstances, a court can find that the will was invalid because of undue influence. The disparity in age may raise eyebrows, but that fact alone is insufficient to void a will. The totality of the circumstances must be viewed and analyzed.

The case of *Carpenter v. Carpenter* (1971) establishes that when an opponent to a will raises the presumption of undue influence, said person has only the burden of showing a reasonable explanation for his or her active role in the preparation of a will. In this specific case, the decedent had left her entire estate to her daughter and had left nothing to her three sons. The sons contested the will, arguing that the total bequest had been procured by undue influence. The trial court ruled that the will was invalid because the court determined that there had been a confidential relationship between the decedent and the daughter; therefore, amongst a number of other circumstances, the trial court found that the will had been made under undue influence. The appellate court, however, reversed the lower court's judgment and held that the will was valid. It also held that although there was sufficient evidence to raise a presumption of undue influence, this presumption did not shift the burden of proof to the proponent to disprove the existence of such manipulation. The court ruled that the burden remained with the contestants to show facts that supported a finding of undue influence, and in this case, the contestants could not do that. Therefore, the will remained valid.

Practical considerations for the determination of undue influence include presence of the beneficiary at the execution of the will, presence of the beneficiary on occasions when the testator expressed a desire to make a will, recommendation by the beneficiary for the attorney who draws up the will, the beneficiary's knowledge of the contents of the will before it is signed, the beneficiary's giving of instructions to the attorney who drafts the will, the securing of witnesses to the will by the beneficiary, and safekeeping of the will by the beneficiary subsequent to execution. Despite the ostensible good intentions of family members, I find that a great deal of candor and prudence is required when the family begins to orchestrate the execution or any changes in the person's documents. Repeated assurance that the elderly or infirm client knows what he or she is doing and why, bolstered by the evaluation and counsel of a health care professional, is critical. In addition to making sure that the person is protected and may carry out his or her wishes, prudence will also help keep the attorney and the health care providers from having to testify as witnesses in court.

DEALING WITH THE POTENTIALLY INCAPACITATED CLIENT

One area affecting attorneys as well as other participating professionals involving incapacitated as well as potentially incapacitated clients is the matter of creating or changing documents that affect the estate-planning needs of that client. When professionals, including attorneys, accountants, and mental health providers, have questions concerning the capacity or incapacity of a client, these questions present a myriad of issues. The client still maintains the right of privileged and confidential information, but now the information he or she presents to the attorney may have a serious impact on others and may in fact place into question not only the needs of the client, but those of potential beneficiaries as well. There is little guidance provided to attorneys concerning how to deal with an impaired client. Under the Model

Rules of Professional Conduct, the American Bar Association merely provides that when a client's ability to make decisions is impaired, because of minority, mental disability, or some other reason, the lawyer shall, as far as is reasonably possible, maintain a "normal" client–lawyer relationship with the client (American Bar Association, 1998, Rule 1.14a). The rule further provides that the lawyer can seek the appointment of a guardian, but only when the lawyer reasonably believes that the client cannot adequately act in the client's own interest (American Bar Association, 1998, Rule 1.14b). Thus, in the event that a potentially incapacitated client directs a lawyer to prepare a document that materially affects either a joint client (a spouse, for example) or even a person who is close to the client but not a joint client (such as an heir), the issue of whether the attorney can go forward with the preparation of the documents presents a very difficult dilemma. Here, the law often creates contradicting remedies. In such cases, issues of confidentiality, privacy, and freedom of choice clearly come head to head with the issues of incapacity, vulnerability, and the need to do "right" for the maker of the document and his or her heirs.

In the case of *Vignes v. Weiskopf* (1949), the Florida Supreme Court opined that it was appropriate for an attorney to go forward with the execution of a will even though the client-testator did not read the will and did not know of the will's contents. Furthermore, the witnesses were unaware that the testator did not know the contents of what he was signing and that he lacked mental capacity. The court held that it would have been unfaithful to an old client for the lawyer to act otherwise. This is certainly a confused and convoluted approach, but this is the only guidance many states have to follow. As a practical matter, an attorney must wrestle with his or her own values and conflicts. If the client insists upon a change in the document and execution, but the attorney (who has long been representing that client) feels that the changes are misguided, the attorney could easily alienate and lose that client, only to have the client easily accomplish his or her goals elsewhere.

Unfortunately, most attorneys are not in the position to promptly evaluate whether a client has the capacity to go forward with a will or a trust. In an ambiguous case, the lawyer is likely to go forward with the instrument and leave the determination of validity to the consideration of the court after proper consideration of all surrounding facts and other circumstances. The attorney may not even have much information about the client and his or her life circumstances. One possible choice for the lawyer is to go ahead and draft the will or trust and then document his or her observations and preserve evidence so that a court can later make the determination. Unfortunately, this author has had the recent experience of a key Florida District Court of Appeals ruling that attorney fees were not recoverable in a contested guardianship and estate matter. The guardianship and later the estate were contested, and the attorney fees were also then contested, despite the fact that the trial court and the appeals court found that the services had been properly rendered. The numerous hours expended to collect the fees were not compensated as billable (*Rivera v. Klein*, 1997). In the event of undue influence, when a spouse or important other is exercising influence to impose his or her will over the testator's, an attorney needs to ascertain whether and how it may be possible to isolate the latter individual from such a domineering influence.

In the event an attorney is placed in the position of determining the capacity of a client, he or she may find that this situation poses a significant problem. Most attorneys probably lack the skill and training to make such a psychological or psychiatric decision, and the courts and state statutes offer minimum guidance in this area. Reliance upon mental health professionals for an opinion based on a complete evaluation would be helpful here; however, often these professionals do not want to get involved with such cases and may hedge their opinions for fear of getting caught up in a lawsuit or contested will. If such a professional is willing to assist, it is best for the attorney to retain the services of an impartial expert who is not already involved with the client or the client's relatives, and who can render objective findings.

An attorney may be faced with potential malpractice exposure if he or she does not go forward with the execution. This becomes a conflict raising both legal and ethical issues concerning what an attorney could or should do for the client and how to handle the possibility of a grievance or malpractice suit in the event that there is a death in the interim. On the other hand, if the attorney does go forward with the execution of the will or trust and this adversely affects some or all of the beneficiaries, the attorney might be faced with a malpractice, or other suit. This situation creates a frustrating dilemma—heads you lose, tails you lose.

Under these circumstances, an attorney should consider certain important tactics when drafting a will or trust for someone who lacks mental capacity or for someone the attorney feels is being pressured by a manipulative or dictatorial potential beneficiary. One tactic involves the video- or audiotaping of the actual execution whereby the testator or settlor is asked a series of detailed questions concerning his or her capacity and his or her intentions in creating the will or trust. This tactic may be a two-edged sword in that the development of evidence could go either way as to the proof that the person had or did not have the ability to create a will or trust. It also presents a potential concern about the preservation of evidence and whether the questions should be scripted. There is also the danger of a panic reaction by the testator as to the necessity of the taping. Furthermore, this tactic presents the issue of whether the individual should be taped professionally or by the office as part of a standard operating procedure. Nonetheless, the problem still remains that lawyers are typically not trained to adequately assess a person's mental competency. Even a lawyer with training in the field of mental health is limited in the amount of information available to him or her concerning the familial background and current circumstances of the client's mental status and would probably have to perform a very thorough and perhaps costly investigation and evaluation in order to arrive at a high degree of certainty in the determination of the client's capacity.

Other problems facing attorneys when drafting a will or trust include fraud and mistake. *Fraud* generally occurs when there is evidence of willful intent to deceive. In the case of a will or a trust, fraud occurs when there is a deception as to the character or content of the instrument or as to the facts and circumstances that led to the drafting of the will or trust. For instance, suppose a person pretends to be the long-lost cousin of the testator or settlor, and the testator or settlor, believing this person to be a relative, executes a will or trust that leaves part of the estate to this supposed relative. If someone later discovers that the person is not a relative and instead intentionally deceived the testator or settlor, a court may invalidate the will or trust because of fraud.

Mistake may occur when the wrong document is executed. Mistake invalidates a will or trust because the person does not possess the requisite testamentary intent to create the particular instrument that was wrongly signed. Although the execution of a will creates a strong presumption that the testator knew of its contents, if the testator is in fact ignorant of the document's contents, then the document will not be admissible. Mistake usually happens when there is an omission of a material provision in the will or trust. However, if a testator mistakenly omits a certain provision or person from a will, generally no relief will be granted to the omitted beneficiary. Even if a testator is mistaken as to the existence or nonexistence of a material fact, which if known to the testator would not have resulted in the execution of the will as written, the will still cannot be invalidated on these grounds (*Forsythe v. Spielburger*, 1956). Thus, mistakes as to the legal effect of a provision of a will or trust, even when produced with the advice of an attorney, cannot be corrected by the court.

PSYCHOLOGICAL EFFECTS OF A WILL OR TRUST ON FAMILY RELATIONSHIPS

While wills and trusts are excellent estate-planning devices that allow for a means to distribute a person's property upon death, and, in the case of a trust, perhaps during life, the wishes expressed in these instruments may have a significant emotional and psychological impact on familial relations. These tools may be used by some as emotional and psychological weapons to control or punish family members. They may also be used to reward others, both for sound and for misguided reasons. This "carrot" is especially risky in view of the fact that the bequest becomes effective only upon the death of the testator, and it can be changed at any time prior to death. Even in the case of a revocable trust, the settlor can make changes at any time preceding his or her demise. A person could easily use the promise of a provision in a will or trust to manipulate a potential beneficiary. For instance, a person could write a trust for his or her child that would become effective only if that child performs or meets a certain condition or criterion. That trust could provide that the child will get $500,000, but if and only if he or she goes to a particular college. This provision would cause tremendous pressure on a child to go to the college designated in the will, even if that child has his or her heart set on attending another college or does not want to go to college at all. Another example of control exerted through a will or trust occurs when the instrument provides that the beneficiary shall inherit a property only so long as he or she does not marry someone of a particular race or religion. This provision can significantly restrict a person's freedom of choice and allows a third party to interfere with that beneficiary's own personal life.

Problems can also arise when a will or trust favors one or several beneficiaries or family members over other beneficiaries or family members. This situation can definitely cause a great deal of tension and animosity among siblings or other relatives and may lead to psychological trauma and feelings of worthlessness in the sibling who is disadvantaged. This may lead to family feuding and possibly to a malpractice suit against the attorney who implemented the instrument. This author has too often viewed the hurt and confusion of an individual who has been left out of a will or has been left less than was expected. The beneficiary unfortunately cannot fully reconcile the disappointment and rejection resulting from the actions of the decedent and rarely wants to consider what he or she had done that antagonized or alienated the progenitor of the will. In addition, potential beneficiaries and legatees may spend significant time and effort to ingratiate themselves with the maker of the will or trust in order to place themselves in a favored position. This situation places the elderly person in a position to receive a lot of attention and gain a feeling of importance, and a potential beneficiary's behavior may substantially change in order that he or she will receive a larger portion of the estate, often to the detriment of other family members. This posturing and concurrent power shifts and manipulations should be closely monitored and evaluated by any therapist working with the family.

Another problem arises when a decedent leaves an enormous amount of his or her estate to a charity or to a pet animal and leaves nothing or little to anticipating family members who have been expecting to receive a large financial bequest as an affirmation of affection. If these family members have gone out and squandered large sums of money in anticipation of inheriting a significant fortune, this situation may lead to a financial disaster or a bad credit rating for them. It might possibly jeopardize a person's life. Very often such individuals project the blame onto the testator and do not want to take responsibility for behaving as if their fantasy of largesse were factual.

An attorney must take all of these circumstances into consideration when designing an estate plan for someone. Perhaps the attorney can suggest that the testator or settlor thoroughly discuss his or her intentions with family members and other potential beneficiaries before drawing up the will or trust, although this approach could certainly complicate matters. The attorney may suggest that the testator and his or her family members partake in psychological treatment or consultation before executing the instrument. The client may even obtain counseling when it appears that he or she has serious conflicts with family members. This method would allow a testator or settlor to evaluate his or her reasons behind creating the specific provisions of the will or trust. If those reasons are vindictive or retaliatory, perhaps the conflicts leading up to that attitude can be resolved in therapy rather than having a will or trust adversely affect the beneficiaries and cause further problems down the line. Whatever the situation, an attorney should always try to encourage clients to use estate-planning methods in positive ways that will carry out their own well-thought-out intentions. Once an individual dies, the remaining family members are left without the ability to resolve matters directly with the decedent. Sadly, no one initiated the needed dialogue prior to the person's demise. Often haunting questions and conflicts highlighted by the contents of the will linger on and contribute to continuing family turmoil. During the aftermath of the death, relatives will sometimes finally seek the kind of family therapy that has been needed all along.

Finally, an inheritance can significantly change the power alignments in the family structure. For instance, a mother who has normally had a lower power position may garner more respect and exercise greater authority after she comes into an enormous amount of wealth. The sons, who had emulated the now-deceased father who held the higher power position, may feel resentment and despair when the mother comes into control of the finances and no longer caters to them or deprives herself of the luxuries of life. This is just another situation that attorneys and mental health practitioners must consider when dealing with families and anticipating the aftermath of the distribution of the testator's assets.

REFERENCES

American Bar Association. (1998). *Model rules of professional conduct*. Chicago: Author.

California probate code. (1998). St. Paul, MN: West.

Carpenter v. Carpenter, 253 So. 2d 697 (Fla. 1971).

Florida statutes annotated. (1998). St. Paul, MN: West.

Friedberg v. Sunbank Miami, 648 So. 2d 204 (3rd Fla. Dist. Ct. App. 1994).

Forsythe v. Spielburger, 86 So. 2d 427 (Fla. 1956).

In re Dunson's Estate, 141 So. 2d 601 (2d Fla. Dist. Ct. App. 1962).

In re Estate of Zimmerman, 84 So. 2d 560 (Fla. 1956).

New York estate powers & trusts law annotated. (1998) McKinney.

Rivera v. Klein, 698 So. 2d 329 (4th Fla. Dist. Ct. App. 1997).

Texas probate code annotated. (1998). Bellevue, WA: Vernon.

United States code. (1998). Volume 26. Washington, DC: U.S. Government Printing Office.

Vignes v. Weiskopf, 42 So. 2d 84 (Fla. 1949).

CHAPTER 21

Euthanasia Decisions

DOROTHY S. BECVAR

ONE OF the most challenging issues with which we currently must come to terms, whether in our work with clients as mental health professionals or as private individuals, is the manner of our death and the degree to which as dying persons we may control the final moments of our life. In fact, according to some,

> society stands at an unprecedented juncture regarding end-of-life issues: the convergence of modern technology with ancient religious beliefs. On either side of this intersection, both medical doctors and "soul doctors"—psychologists, clergy, and meditation teachers—are pondering a set of moral riddles never before confronted. (Peay, 1997, p. 34)

These moral riddles have arisen in the context of heated debates regarding the individual's right to end his or her own life, or to be assisted in this process by a physician. The controversy surrounding euthanasia was brought to a head in January 1997, when the U.S. Supreme Court took up the matter of "whether the Constitution gives terminally ill people a right to commit suicide with a doctor's help, or whether the government's stake to protect life is strong enough to outweigh whatever individual right may exist" ("Before the Court," 1997, p. 4E). After much debate, the Court ruled that laws banning physician-assisted suicide are neither unconstitutional nor do they violate the Fourteenth Amendment's equal protection clause. Left open by the Court's decision, however, are questions regarding the right of individual states to enact legislation permitting physician-assisted suicide (Brodeur, 1997).

Indeed, there are many questions at many levels that must be addressed when considering the complex area of euthanasia. For, as medical technology has succeeded in extending life in the face of what previously would have been fatal illness, a problem has emerged in terms of being able to distinguish between a so-called natural death and life that is artificially sustained. For example, one must consider when it is appropriate for life support systems to be removed, how much physical or emotional suffering a person should have to endure, the ramifications of the use of narcotics which may relieve physical pain but dull consciousness, and the appropriateness of allowing a person to die by refusing food and liquids (Peay, 1997). Further, as author M. Scott Peck (1997, p. 18) queries:

> Is euthanasia solely an act committed by someone—physician or family member—on someone else who is ill or dying? Or can the term also be used for someone who is ill or dying who kills himself without the assistance of another? Does euthanasia require the patient's consent? The family's consent? Is it separable from other forms of suicide or homicide? How does it differ from simply "pulling the plug?" If one type of euthanasia consists of refraining from the use of "heroic measures" to prolong life, how does one distinguish between those measures that are heroic and those that are standard treatment? What is the relationship between euthanasia and pain? Is there a distinction to be made between physical pain and emotional pain? How does one assess degrees of suffering? Above all, why are ethical issues involved, and what might they be?

As is immediately apparent, the topic of euthanasia decisions moves us into the realms of ethics, morality, philosophy, religion or spirituality, and medicine, as well as public policy and the law. Central are considerations about the meaning of life and death; individual rights; the medical view of such issues as pain, suffering, treatment, and cure; and where the responsibility lies for providing adequate care for the dying.

Despite the fact that there has been much public debate over these issues, Conwell (1994) notes that mental health professionals, who have a great deal of relevant clinical and research experience, have nevertheless contributed relatively little to the discussions about physician-assisted suicide. However, as Albright and Hazler (1992) state, it is imperative that mental health professionals understand the complexity of the issues involved as well as the differences between voluntary, involuntary, passive, and active euthanasia; between mercy killing and assisted suicide. Further, these authors believe it essential for mental health professionals to create ethically informed positions for helping clients make end-of-life decisions. Thus, it is more than timely and appropriate to be contributing to and becoming actively involved in this important public health and policy debate. Given the likelihood that at some point mental health professionals will be called upon to help some clients come to terms with some aspect of the euthanasia issue, it is essential that they be familiar with its complexities. In order to do so in an informed manner, first consider the meaning of some terms.

DEFINITIONS

The Netherlands State Commission on Euthanasia has defined *euthanasia* as "the intentional termination of life by another party at the request of the person concerned" ("Final Report," 1987, p. 166). *Assisted suicide* has been defined by the same group as "intentionally helping a patient to terminate his or her life at his or her request" (Scheper & Duursma, 1994, p. 4). While in both cases there is assistance from an outside party, the distinction lies in who actually terminates the life of the dying person.

In discussions regarding the role of medical personnel, euthanasia also has been classified as either *voluntary active euthanasia* (VAE) or *physician-assisted suicide* (PAS; Watts, 1992). VAE refers to instances in which the physician administers medication or otherwise intervenes at the patient's request with the intention of causing death. In PAS, the physician provides information, means, or direct assistance in order that the patient may take his or her own life. Another classification is *physician aid in dying*, or discontinuance of treatment at the patient's request (Celocruz, 1992).

Relative to the discontinuance of treatment at the patient's request, an important aspect of euthanasia decisions are the so-called advance directives. These include the *living will* and the *health care proxy*. Now a concept common enough to be included in some dictionaries (Lush, 1989),

> The term "living will" was coined by Luis Kutner in 1969 to describe a document in which a competent adult sets forth directions regarding medical treatment in the event of his or her future incapacitation. The document is a will in the sense that it spells out the person's directions. It is "living" because it takes effect before death. (Annas, 1991, p. 1210)

By contrast, a health care proxy refers to the designation of a health care agent to make treatment decisions for a person should that person become unable to make such decisions for him- or herself. The mechanism for this designation is the *durable power of attorney*. It is interesting to note that,

> Although new laws are not necessary in any state (because of existing laws regarding the assignment of a durable power of attorney), the current trend in the United States is for states to enact additional proxy laws that specifically deal with health care. (Annas, 1991, p. 1211)

The use of advance directives was supported by the enactment of the federal Patient Self-Determination Act (PSDA), part of the 1990 Omnibus Budget and Reconciliation Act, which went into effect in December 1991. This act requires health care providers (primarily hospitals, nursing homes, and home health agencies) to give patients information about their right to make advance directives under state law. While the substance of the law governing advance directives is left to the states, the PSDA also requires providers to have written institutional policies regarding advance directives and to document whether or not a patient has executed one (Choice in Dying, 1991).

Advance directives may focus on either the clinical condition or the *values history* (Doukas & McCullough, 1991; McLean, 1994). In the former case, the individual defines the medical conditions with which he or she would not want to live. The questions thus focus on medical decisions to be made in the event of decisional incapacity. In the latter case, the individual describes the circumstances in which continued life is not preferred, even if all medical options have not yet been exhausted. In this instance, "the questions focus on the premises and processes the person uses, and would like used, when deciding on medical treatment" (Lambert, Gibson, & Nathanson, 1990, p. 210). Regardless of their form, such advance directives "are becoming an increasingly important component of medical decision making for incompetent patients" (McCrary & Botkin, 1989, p. 2411). Further, while they play a part, they represent some of the least controversial aspects of the euthanasia debates.

HISTORICAL CONTEXT

According to common law as well as legislative policy in several states, both suicide and assisted suicide were prohibited not only during the early years of this country's existence but also at the time that the Fourteenth Amendment to the Constitution was ratified ("Before the Court," 1997). Today, one state allows physician-assisted suicide while none of the states prohibits suicide or attempted suicide. However, according to the Hemlock Society (1997), 36 states have statutes that explicitly criminalize assisted suicide, 7 states criminalize assisted suicide through the common law, and in 6 states the law is unclear concerning the legality of assisted suicide.

However, in the 1990 case of *Cruzan v. Director, Missouri Department of Health*, a limited constitutional right to refuse unwanted medical treatment was recognized. In the 1992 case of *Planned Parenthood v. Casey*, the constitutional right to abortion, first articulated in the 1973 case of *Roe v. Wade*, was reaffirmed ("Before the Court," 1997). The core issues of concern in these cases are individual rights to free choice in private matters as well the right to equal protection under the law (Will, 1997).

While only Oregon allows physician-assisted suicide, in 1976 California became the first state to pass legislation that directly addressed decision making on behalf of incompetent patients. The California Natural Death Act allowed individuals, in certain circumstances, to plan in advance for their treatment at the end of life (Choice in Dying, 1991). While many states have enacted living will statutes or acts that deal with life-prolonging procedures (Lush, 1993), there are no minimum standards for states that choose to legalize any form of euthanasia. Moreover, in August 1997 the American Bar Association (ABA) refused to participate in the creation of such standards and approved a resolution stating that assisted suicide "should be left to be resolved by state legislatures and their electorates." However, the ABA did recommend close monitoring of any legalized practices (Prodigy, 1997).

CURRENT CONTEXT

Because of incredible advances in medical technology in recent years, we now have cures for most illnesses, women generally do not die in childbirth, and even the failure of a major organ such as the liver or the heart does not mean certain death. As a result, people tend to live much longer than previously was the case and their dying is a much slower process. This, of course, is a mixed blessing, bringing with it the kinds of issues and questions previously posed. Given the progress in medical science, the new field of bioethics, or biomedical ethics (Beauchamp & Childress, 1994), has responded to the need to be able to make prudent life and death decisions at an institutional level. Further, the realities of our aging population require that every individual seriously consider personal end-of-life decisions. For example, it is estimated that Alzheimer's disease, which seriously impairs cognitive functioning, occurs in slightly more than 10% of the total population of people age 65 or older and in 47% of those 85 and older living in the community (Webber, Fox, & Burnette, 1994). Thus,

> As more and more of our population live into extreme old age and suffer from cognitive and functional disabilities that impair their ability to eat without assistance, decisions about enteral [tube] feeding and other medical treatments will assume greater importance. (Krynski, Tymchuk, & Ouslander, 1994, p. 36)

Additional euthanasia-related dilemmas emerge as a function of what happens in the real world of physicians, hospitals, and dying patients, a context that has been described as a system of "winks and nods." As Goodman (1997, p. 7B) notes, "It is not unusual, under existing bans [against PAS], for doctors to withdraw nutrition. It's not unusual to prescribe 'terminal sedation' and place patients in a barbiturate coma that eases the pain of a slow death by starvation or dehydration." Thus, while the letter of the law may be observed, physician assisted suicide actually is practiced often.

In a more global context, assisting suicide is not a crime in either Germany or the Netherlands (Battin, 1992a, 1992b). Euthanasia also has become a frequent topic of public discussion in Canada. According to Hoffmaster (1994), the principal moral and social considerations surrounding the debate in Canada include the following arguments in support of assisted suicide: (a) the relief of pain, (b) the relief of suffering, (c) respect for autonomy, (d) lack of a moral difference between withdrawing life support and assisted suicide, (e) discrimination against the physically incapable, and (f) harmful consequences inherent in euthanasia's prohibition. Arguments against the legalization of assisted suicide include: (a) the possibility of abuse, (b) potential backlash in the wake of possible abuses, (c) undermining of efforts to develop more effective pain control and better palliative care, (d) the burden of choice, (e) the proliferation of nonvoluntary euthanasia, and (f) economic imperatives resulting in euthanasia for cost defrayal.

These are the same issues that comprise much of the debate in the United States, where, according to one survey, more than half of 1,311 adults age 18 and older indicated they would consider euthanasia if all hope of recovery were gone and they were suffering great pain (Battin, 1992a). A more recent study in Washington State (Back, Wallace, Starks, & Pearlman, 1996) revealed that 26% of physicians had had at least one request for some form of euthanasia. Those requesting euthanasia were more likely to be male and to be suffering from AIDS or cancer than from heart disease, even when the prognosis was similar. Voigt (1995) notes that physicians in general are less likely to receive such requests than are family physicians with large HIV-positive populations.

EUTHANASIA AND THE CONCERNS IT RAISES

Interestingly, physical pain is not the primary issue underlying most euthanasia requests. Rather, the most crucial concerns are more related to becoming a burden, financial or otherwise, and to losing one's sense of independence, control, and dignity (Peay, 1997). Thus, the concept of euthanasia elicits concerns related not only to legal and policy ramifications but also to various moral questions. According to Heintz (1994, p. 1656), "It makes no sense to discuss euthanasia in terms of being for it or against it. The basic question is whether we accept the right of human beings to decide for themselves how their lives will end." Stated somewhat differently, we are challenged to consider the following two questions:

> Do our mortal lives belong to us alone or do they belong to the communities or families in which we are embedded? Will this new right give the dying a greater sense of control over their circumstances, or will it weaken our respect for life? (Carter, 1996, p. 29)

In response to the latter question, the so-called slippery slope argument has been advanced. That is, there is a great fear on the part of some that if euthanasia were legalized, human life would increasingly be devalued as assisted suicide was requested for an ever-expanding and less valid array of reasons. To illustrate, in a study of the Dutch experience, Hendin (1995) describes a culture in which legalized euthanasia encourages the choice of death on the part of seriously ill patients and leads to complications when it is considered for those who are not physically ill, or allows physicians to feel that they can end the life of a terminally ill patient without his or her consent. On the other hand, others would argue against such a position, stating that:

> The ultimate success or failure of these slippery slope arguments depends on speculative predictions of a progressive erosion of moral restraints. If dire consequences will in fact flow from the legal legitimation of assisted suicide or voluntary active euthanasia, then the argument is cogent, and such practices are justifiably prohibited. But how good is the evidence that dire consequences will occur? Does the evidence indicate that we cannot maintain firm distinctions in public policies between patient-requested death and involuntary euthanasia? Scant evidence supports any of the answers that have been given to these questions, so far as we can see. (Beauchamp & Childress, 1994, p. 231)

Another set of concerns raised by the euthanasia debate relates to the way we as a society think about death. According to Jung, "To the psyche death is just as important as birth and, like it, is an integral part of life" (Wilhelm, 1962, p. 124). Similarly, Cousins (1989, p. 25) notes, "Death is not the ultimate tragedy in life. The ultimate tragedy is to die without discovering the possibilities of full growth." However, we Westerners are challenged by the fact that we live and work in a death-denying society (Becker, 1973). Thus, while awareness of mortality undoubtedly has existed as long as human beings have had the capacity for self-reflection, in the present era the common response to death is terror and a reluctance to consider it until one has no other choice (Foos-Graber, 1989).

Until recently, death has been a taboo subject, rarely talked about, and then, "discussed in hushed, solemn tones" (Hainer, 1997, p. 1D). As a society we have pathologized death, and nowhere has this been more apparent than in the medical world. According to physician Ira Byock (1997, p. 35), "Modern clinical training, procedures, record-keeping, and economics constrain doctors and force them to approach dying as if it were strictly a set of medical problems to be solved." He suggests that we recognize the growth, or like Loewy (1994), the healing that can occur in the context of dying and focus on what he calls the crisis in end-of-life care. In a similar vein, Callahan asks:

> What if medicine once and for all accepted death as a limit that cannot be overcome and used that limit as an indispensable focal point in thinking about illness and disease? The reality of death as a part of our biological life would be seen, not as a discordant note in the search for health and well-being, but as a foreseeable endpoint of its enterprise, and its pacification as a proper goal of medicine from the outset. What if the aim of scientific medicine was not an endless struggle against death, with the fight against disease as the token of that struggle, but helping humans best live a mortal, not immortal life? (1993, pp. 33–34)

Part of the task of the mental health professional thus involves coming to terms with his or her own mortality and being able to discuss the topic comfortably with clients. It also involves being aware of possible differences in the way death may be perceived as a function of the developmental stage of the client. For example, one study indicates that while young adults are more likely to fear death, older adults are more concerned about the circumstances of their dying (Vries, Blueck, & Birren, 1993). Further, we must acknowledge the possibility of controversy regarding the definition of death and the willingness of family members to accept that it has or has not occurred. Consider the following distinctions between brain death and a vegetative state:

> [W]hen a patient is brain-dead, the patient is dead, all spontaneous vital functions have ceased because the brain stem has ceased to function and so the whole brain has ceased to function as well. A patient in a vegetative state, although unconscious, is alive, the vital function of spontaneous breathing is still present, there is no need for ventilation and so the brain-stem is alive and functioning. (Iglesias, 1995, p. 54)

Despite definitions such as the preceding, it is important to be aware that while both life and death are biological states, their meanings are social creations (Markson, 1995). Thus, for some, the loss of the ability to be productive, the reality of being a financial or emotional burden, or the experience of intractable pain may constitute the end of life, despite the fact that death has not officially occurred. Indeed, the need for more effective pain control for terminally ill patients was one of the driving forces in the creation of the international hospice care movement (Kastenbaum, 1993). And it was out of concern that a Florida AIDS patient might be "forced to die a miserable and degrading death" that a circuit court judge granted the man the right to request that his physician assist him in dying ("Florida Court," 1997, p. 23).

THE MAJOR ISSUES

Ultimately, the Florida Supreme Court overturned the decision just noted, consistent with the historical stance against legalizing physician-assisted suicide. The legal issues around euthanasia are anything but clear. For example, there are many who question the distinction between the withdrawal of life support systems, or *passive euthanasia*, as opposed to taking direct action to cause death, or *active euthanasia:*

> We conclude that the distinction between killing (suicide, homicide, etc.) and letting die suffers from vagueness and confusion. It is conceptually impossible to classify many acts as instances of letting die without also classifying them as instances of killing. We have also seen that the language of killing is so confusing—causally, legally and morally—that we should avoid it in discussions of euthanasia and assistance in dying. It is often morally and conceptually more satisfactory to discuss these issues exclusively in the language of optional and obligatory treatments, dispensing altogether with killing and letting die. (Beauchamp & Childress, 1994, p. 224)

A second issue concerns the degree to which the legalization of euthanasia would constitute pressure, however subtle, to choose to give way to this right ("Before the Court," 1997). Thus, as Battin (1992b, p. 136) suggests:

> Not all family life is harmonious, and underlying pathology can often be exacerbated by the stresses a family member's terminal illness brings. "All right, Granny, it's time to go" is a message we can imagine being conveyed in a variety of ways, exhibiting an entire range from the faintest suggestion to outright coercion.

A third issue relates to the area of autonomy and the notion that laws restricting the individual choice to die threaten one's personal liberty (Faust, 1995). Thus, while we may control our fertility and we are urged to monitor our health and take personal responsibility for it, the process of dying is to be "left to nature" (Tindall, 1995). The further, perhaps tragic, irony noted in this regard is that:

> [T]he law produces the apparently irrational result that people can choose to die lingering deaths by refusing to eat, by refusing treatment that keeps them alive, or by being disconnected from respirators and suffocating, but they cannot choose a quick, painless death that their doctors could easily provide. (Dworkin, 1993, p. 184)

A fourth issue relates to the assumption that moral appropriateness constitutes sufficient reason for legal sanction. However, it also has been argued that:

> [T]he judgment that an act is morally acceptable does not imply that the law should permit it. For example, the thesis that active euthanasia is morally justified if patients face uncontrollable pain and suffering and request death is consistent with the thesis that the government should legally prohibit active euthanasia because it would not be possible to control abuses if it were legalized. We are not here defending particular moral judgments about the justifiability of such acts. We are maintaining only that the connections between moral action-guides and judgments about policy or law or legal enforcement are complicated and that a judgment about the morality of acts does not entail a particular judgment about law and policy. Factors such as the symbolic value of the law, the costs of a program and its enforcement, and the demands of competing programs must also be considered. (Beauchamp & Childress, 1994, p. 10)

In addition to legal dilemmas, much of the controversy surrounding euthanasia is focused on moral and ethical issues. For example, it is argued that maintaining existence is not always the most humane or moral option (Weir, 1992). Further, the duty of physicians to care for their patients sometimes requires the ability to participate in the termination of the patient's life, and refusal to do so "renders them as liable for their omissions as for their acts (McLean, 1996, p. 262). According to Battin (1994), medical practitioners have long seen themselves as moral agents having the positive duty of beneficence and recognizing that relief of pain is the most universal and least disputed moral obligation. At the same time, it is often argued that the prohibition against maleficence contained in the Hippocratic Oath constitutes a prohibition against euthanasia. However, even here there is confusion.

Beauchamp and Childress (1994) note that the principle of nonmaleficence requires that harm not be inflicted intentionally and that in medical ethics this principle usually is wrongly associated with the maxim *primum non nocere,* meaning "above all (or first) do no harm":

> Often proclaimed the fundamental principle in the Hippocratic tradition of medical ethics, it is not found in the Hippocratic corpus, and a venerable statement sometimes confused with it—"at least, do no harm"—is a strained translation of a single Hippocratic passage. Nonetheless, an obligation of nonmaleficence and an obligation of beneficence are both expressed in the Hippocratic Oath: "I will use treatment to help the sick according to my ability and judgment, but I will never use it to injure or wrong them." (Beauchamp & Childress, 1994, p. 189)

In either case, the specific responsibilities of physicians may be interpreted in different ways. Physicians' basic obligation is "for the benefit of the sick." However, the assistance of a physician in the suicide of a patient may be viewed as providing a benefit for the patient. What the Hippocratic Oath specifically prohibits is physician assistance in the suicide of a patient for the purpose of benefiting either the physician or other institutional or societal goals (Battin, 1994).

Another issue relates to the ethics of the current context, described previously as a system of nods and winks. According to Shavelson (1995), whatever the knowledge that has accrued regarding the best methods for ending the life of a person who is terminally ill, it has been gathered in secrecy and is anecdotal at best. It therefore lacks scientific credibility and precision and leads to a situation in which:

> [N]ot a single physician has ever assisted in the death of a patient while following set rules, nor under the observation of her peers, nor under the watchful eyes of the law. Yet surveys of doctors have found that up to 37% have, in secrecy, aided in the death of a terminally ill patient. While the public expresses fear of abuse of assisted suicide, no one is overseeing those physicians who have already made aid in suicide part of their medical practice. (Shavelson, 1995, p. 103).

Yet other dimensions of the moral and ethical debate include the possibility that our basic respect for human life will be undermined if the fundamental rule in our moral code against causing the death of another person is violated (Beauchamp & Childress, 1994). Some fear the escalation of the right to choose death to include others than those who are terminally ill (Carter, 1996; Chapman, 1997). A further dilemma emerges as one begins to see patients as existing in the context of families

(Hardwig, 1990, 1995); that is, in the process of focusing on the individual rights of the patient, the family and other caregivers may be ignored as a legitimate force in ethical decision making. However, if autonomy truly is a value, then it must have relevance for everyone involved. The issue of whether it is possible to create one policy that has the potential to be equally appropriate for all persons must be considered (Maltsberger, 1994; Young & Jex, 1992).

According to one view, "more than anything else, our differing beliefs about the existence or nonexistence of the human soul make euthanasia a subject for passionate ethical and moral debate" (Peck, 1997, p. 18). Not surprisingly, therefore, the consideration of moral and ethical issues related to euthanasia often moves into the realm of religion and spirituality: "Many in the death and dying field believe that it is the medical profession's lack of spiritual support for terminally ill patients and their families that has opened up the subject for debate" (Hainer, 1997, p. 1D). Here again, the waters are muddy and the guidelines both within single traditions and between various religious and spiritual groups often conflict. For example, Keown and Keown conclude that it would be "immoral from a Buddhist perspective to embark on any course of action whose aim is the destruction of human life, regardless of the agent's motive" (1995, p. 267). In rebuttal, Perrett (1966) notes that Buddhism contains many schools but no central body of precepts and practices and states that "it is important to recognize that Buddhist attitudes to suicide have always been much less harsh than Christian ones." The Dalai Lama is quoted by Perrett as saying that, according to one Buddhist tradition, the termination of life may be permitted in some extreme situations. However, according to Kapleau, "Buddhism is emphatic in its opposition to suicide" (1989, p. 131). Kapleau notes:

> Over the centuries various religious faiths have taken every conceivable view of suicide, from recommending it to resolutely and uncompromisingly opposing it. Euthanasia has often not been differentiated from suicide. There have been civilizations where the suicide of a wife or servant following the death of a husband or master was expected. . . . St. Augustine, it is reported, felt that suicide for whatever reason is a crime because "suicide is an act which precludes the possibility of repentance, and . . . it is a form of homicide, and therefore a violation of the sixth commandment ["Thou shalt not kill"], not justified by any of the exceptions, general or special, to that commandment." Orthodox protestantism has been just as forceful. . . . Judaism too has repudiated self-destruction in no uncertain terms. (1989, pp. 130–131)

Despite the stance of various religious traditions regarding euthanasia, considering death as an essential aspect of a spiritual growth process has not been a mainstream focus in modern society. One writer states:

> American culture contrasts sharply with that of ancient Egypt, whose enigmatic civilization revolved entirely around the mysteries of death; medieval Europe with its Christian contemplation of the suffering, crucifixion, and resurrection of Christ; and Tibet, which produced a *Book of the Dead* that mapped out richly detailed landscapes of the afterlife. Aware that death was a central organizing principle of inner and outer life, these cultures did not expect the dying to make the final passage unaided. Instead, priests, priestesses, monks, and nuns provided spiritual and psychological

assistance. . . . What was once a royal road traversed by saints and sinners, the powerful and the humble alike, has become a narrowly defined passage involving only the physical dissolution of the body. (Peay, 1997, p. 34)

From a spiritual perspective (Becvar, 1996), such a view is expanded. Accordingly, we may be challenged to consider what is most appropriate—not right or wrong—at the deepest level of the being of everyone involved. Being sensitive to the impact of various cultural stories about death and suicide, it may become useful to consider the possibility that we participate in choosing our life's circumstances, including the manner and time of our death, and that these present opportunities for growth and learning at a soul level (Becvar, 1997).

Further, while the intent of those who would assist another to commit suicide may be compassion, it also may be important to ask whether this is truly the most loving response. Mental health professionals would do well to familiarize themselves with the concepts of conscious dying (Byock, 1997), or deathing (Foos-Graber, 1989), which enable one to understand death as an important transition that can be moved through, even in the most trying circumstances, with grace and healing. Consistent with an Eastern spiritual perspective, we may encourage the recognition that the only thing permanent about our life is its impermanence (Sogyal, 1992).

Ironically, a spiritual perspective, one that aims at providing the most humane support not only for those who are terminally ill but also for everyone involved, is consistent with the rationale employed by both supporters of hospice care and advocates for the legalization of euthanasia (Tindall, 1995). However, while in each case a "good death" is the goal, the processes or policies involved are very different. Hospice care involves the alleviation of pain in order that the dying person may deal with such end-of-life issues as completing worldly affairs, bringing to a satisfactory resolution both personal and professional relationships, examining the meaning of life and love, considering the existence of a transcendent dimension, accepting death, and surrendering to the unknown (Byock, 1997). It involves the creation of a support system to aid the patient throughout the dying process, however long that may take. On the other hand, according to the Dying Well Network (1996, p. 1):

> Acceptance of death often leads to an increased quality of the life the terminally ill person has remaining. A terminally ill person lives better knowing that he or she may gain control over the physical pain, the psychological agony and the financial devastation of dying. Many terminally ill persons who have had control over their living expect to have control over their dying.

Consistent with this philosophy regarding euthanasia, and in order to avoid possible abuse, Physicians for Mercy, a group of Michigan doctors and specialists, promulgated the following guidelines for physician-assisted dying on December 4, 1995:

1. The request for patholysis must be made voluntarily by the patient.
2. The request must be in writing, dated, and signed by the patient, and by any physician involved in the request, as well as signed by two competent adults as witnesses having no financial relationship with the patient, and no

financial interest in the patient's life or death. The signatures of the witness must be notarized.

3. The request thus validated is to be forwarded to a qualified OBITIATRIST who will refer the patient for medical consultation to:
   • A specialist dealing with the patient's specific affliction
   • A specialist in pain management (if pain is a major factor)
   • A psychiatrist (in every case)

4. The above consultations must verify the patient's mental competence with regard to making an independent, informed decision, and verify that the affliction is incurable, that the agony cannot be relieved or controlled, and/or that the side effects of pain management or medical therapy are intolerable for the patient.

5. Completed reports of all consultations must conform to current medical standards. The reports are to be sent to the obitiatrist who will arrange for their review by the patient jointly with the obitiatrist, or with the requesting physician, or with another physician designated by the patient.

6. The time and site of the final patholytic procedure are to be decided solely by the patient. This decision must be made within three weeks after review of the consultation reports. The decision must be documented as an informed consent in writing, dated, *timed,* and signed by the patient under conditions set forth in paragraph (2) above.

7. The final patholytic procedure must be performed within seventy-two (72) hours of the time of signing of the informed consent, but no sooner than twenty-four (24) hours from the date of such signing.

8. The entire process from the initial request to the final patholytic procedure shall be constantly under the control of the patient who may stop it at any time.

9. Every physician involved at any time in the entire process delineated herein (except the obitiatrist) may be present to observe or console, but will not participate actively in the final procedure of patholysis.

10. The final action is to be performed only by an obitiatrist and there will be no professional fee for the service.

PREVAILING POSITIONS ON EUTHANASIA

However, despite policies such as the preceding, which is but one example, it is not likely that the controversy over euthanasia will be resolved in the foreseeable future. Given the nature and the complexity of the issues involved, it is not surprising to find that there are three major positions relative to this issue: (a) those who support euthanasia, (b) those who oppose it, and (c) those who take a middle-ground position.

The typical viewpoint of those who advocate legalizing physician-assisted suicide is that it is the most humane response, allowing the fatally ill person to die with dignity (Hemlock Society, 1997; McLean, 1996; Weir, 1992). The sanctity of life is not being rejected or denigrated by those who choose a quick, more peaceful death for themselves or their relatives (Dworkin, 1993). Rather, such a choice is understood to be more respectful of life. Crisp (1994) suggests that doctors should be seen as carers rather than as either curers or killers. The argument is that sometimes curing is not possible and most of the time doctors do not kill. It is only in special circumstances that killing becomes part of proper caring. Markson (1995) notes that the decision to die is not necessarily irrational, psychotic, or delusional, but may be pragmatic. Solomon (1995, p. 69) states, "Having seen the simple logic of euthanasia in action and witnessed the comfort of that control, what astonishes me is how many people die by other means."

Those who oppose euthanasia generally see it as an illegal or immoral action. For example, according to Wellman (1995, p. 255) there are two moral reasons for the prohibition against killing a human being: "One is that the act of killing a human normally results in grievous harm, the loss of a life and thereby the loss of every other value that constitutes that person's well-being." The fact that it is also invasive engenders negativity against the killer, "because his act of killing reveals him to be one who is at least callous and probably hostile and malicious as well as arrogant in the sense of arrogating to himself another's choice whether to live or die" (Wellman, 1995, pp. 255–256), also represents a moral prohibition against such an act. Another argument against euthanasia is the potential for physicians to act out of their own fear of death as well as the possible negative impact that assisting a suicide may have upon the doctor (Miles, 1994).

The middle ground is represented by those who, like Celocruz (1992), argue for allowing physician aid in dying but continuing to prohibit physician-committed voluntary active euthanasia because of the affront of the latter to life and personal autonomy. Similarly, Gostin (1993) proposes an incremental adjustment in the line drawn by the law regarding assisted suicide, together with safeguards necessary to ensure that the line holds relatively firmly until the next development in ethical thought and public opinion. Under this proposal, law and medical ethics would continue to maintain the moral distinction between letting die and killing, and physician-assisted suicide would not be unlawful given specific criteria and procedures, with suicide being included in the continuum of medical treatment.

THE IMPACT OF VARIOUS ISSUES ON INDIVIDUALS, COUPLES, FAMILIES, AND THERAPISTS

The Society for Healing and Human Values Task Force (1995), comprised of health professionals and teachers concerned about the value dimensions of medicine, conducted an in-depth examination of the moral status of suicide, its clinical and epidemiological aspects, the relevance of voluntary choice, the nature of professional duty, and the social implications of various choices. The conclusion reached was that medical education should introduce students to the skills of palliative and hospice care and all methods of sharing control over medical decisions with patients and their families. The group believed that educators should address the full range of questions related to assisted suicide rather than only those oriented toward a single position. Certainly this seems a sound recommendation as well for those working in the mental health field.

Exploring the ramifications of potential choices on the part of clients is obviously an important part of client conversations focused on end-of-life decisions. Others include the issue of who decides what and how various members are to be included in the decision-making process. Consideration must be given to the stories of family members about illness (Kleinman, 1988) as well as about the meaning of life and death. Another concern is how to handle divergent positions between family members as well as ambivalent beliefs within individuals. However, before any of these conversations can take place, therapists must be clear about their own biases and beliefs as well as their ability to work effectively with clients around this issue. They must be cognizant of conflicting positions with regard to the legal and judicial systems not only for their clients, but also for themselves.

For example, marriage and family therapists are advised to consult an attorney regarding state laws before working with clients on euthanasia-related issues (Daw, 1996). It is important to know whether it is legal even to provide information, and if so, to what extent. Legal risks could be incurred by having knowledge of a client's intent to hasten death. A decision of guilt in a case involving assisted suicide would constitute a violation of the Code of Ethics of the American Association for Marriage and Family Therapy (1991). This might also be the case relative to licensure laws in various states.

Callahan (1994) discusses assisted suicide from a social work perspective and finds it to be unethical. This conclusion is based on research which indicates that the judgment of most suicidal people is impaired as a result of depression or other mental illness. While acknowledging that truly "rational" suicide may exist, Callahan considers it to be quite rare. Callahan further concludes that legalized assisted suicide may lead to increased rates of suicide in the general population, especially among young people, as a function of the contagion phenomenon as well as of destigmatization of the concept.

While many psychologists have similarly argued against legalizing assisted suicide, also seeing it as a symptom of mental illness, others have joined a group that recently submitted an amici curiae brief to the Supreme Court. The latter group believes "that suicide can be a rational act and that psychologists and other mental-health professionals should be allowed to help such patients without fear of legal or professional repercussions" (Clay, 1997, p. 1). In a recent article, Farberman (1997) notes that the American Psychological Association does not take a position either for or against assisted suicide but does support quality of care at the end of life and supports informed decisions about end-of-life issues that reflect correct and complete assessment of the patient.

Kiser (1996) notes that given the shift in current beliefs regarding legalizing physician-assisted suicide, counselors must be prepared to counsel clients who have decided to end their lives. However, a reevaluation of standards may be required in order to avoid violating the ethical guidelines established by the American Counseling Association. Thus, in all cases, mental health professionals are urged to be well informed and to take precautions to avoid violation of either the law or the ethical standards of their various professional organizations.

INTERVENTIONS

Interestingly, Graber (1993, p. 88) suggests that "a physician's willingness to consider voluntary active euthanasia as an option is likely to enhance trust, and refusal even to entertain such requests may be viewed as inhumane and uncaring." This may hold true for therapists as well. In cases where it is deemed legally and ethically appropriate to work with clients regarding the consideration of euthanasia, Bloch and Billings (1994, p. 2039) recommend exploration of "the adequacy of symptom control; difficulties in the patient's relationships with family, friends and health workers; psychological disturbances, especially grief, depression, anxiety, organic mental disorders, and personality disorders; and the patient's personal orientation to the meaning of life and suffering."

Also to be considered is the possibility of a transference phenomenon (Maltsberger, 1994) in which therapists are enlisted as accomplices in suicide in order either to punish oneself, to punish another person, or to destroy a self experienced as worthless. Battin (1994) suggests that 17 questions should be asked:

1. Is the person making a request for help? For example, when somebody wants assistance in suicide is it in fact cloaking some other aspect or some other solution which may be found?
2. Why is the person consulting a physician or mental health professional? Has the consultation been sought because the person has certain expectations from the professionals?
3. What has kept the person from attempting or committing suicide so far? Is it fear of consequences, or that given advanced illness or physical limitations the person simply cannot obtain the means of causing death? Is the time for suicide not yet right? Or is the person seeking some sort of approval?
4. Is the request for help in suicide a request for someone else to decide?
5. How stable is the request? Has this been part of a long-term decision, or a short-term response as a result of some traumatic event, such as diagnosis of serious illness, or death of a friend or relative? Also, when the person thinks of suicide, does someone else come to mind? Does the person frequently change his or her mind about suicide?
6. Is the request consistent with the person's basic values? If there is a discrepancy, can the discrepancy be justified?
7. How far in the future would the suicide take place? Is it intended to solve a future problem, to resolve the eventual onset of intractable pain or mental deterioration, or to put an end to current problems?
8. Are the medical facts cited in the request accurate?
9. How accurate are the other nonmedical facts cited in the request, for example, that others who assist in an attempt may be subject to criminal penalties, or that life insurance coverage will benefit others?
10. Is the suicide plan financially motivated? Is it intended to avoid catastrophic medical expenses?
11. Has the person considered the effect of his or her suicide on other persons, and the stigma associated with suicide?
12. Does the person fear becoming a burden? Is he or she being manipulated by family members or others, or has there been frank and open communication between the person and his or her loved ones?
13. What cultural influences are shaping the person's choice? Are religious beliefs or prejudices, especially against the handicapped and aged, contributing to a feeling of worthlessness?
14. Are the person's affairs in order?
15. Has the person picked a method of committing suicide? Does the person know what kinds of injuries are likely to result if the attempt is not fatal?

Does the person want to stick to this one method only? If the person hasn't chosen one method, does this make them ambivalent about committing suicide at all, or is it simply lack of information?

16. Would the person be willing to tell others about his or her suicide plans?
17. Does the person see suicide as the only way out?

In other words, the client's decision must be rational, autonomous, and not motivated by depression (Weir, 1992). And the role of the mental health professional is to assess and facilitate therapeutic conversations relative to each of these areas. Should there be a need, appropriate referral, collaboration, and follow-up are essential.

Somewhat less precarious in terms of the legal and ethical mine field, but no less complex, is the area of advance directives. Obviously, in the best-case scenario, either living wills or health care proxies are created well in advance of a medical crisis. Hospitals may or may not have mechanisms for assisting patients in learning more about the creation of such documents (McCrary & Botkin, 1989). Further, hospitals may impede the process of good decision making through a focus on the paperwork rather than on the way in which decisions are made (Annas, 1991). For example, according to Docker (1996, p. 189), "Most attempts at living will documentation so far have been notable for their blandness, almost as if they were designed for lawyers and academics rather than lay members of the community who might have ailing health and poor eyesight."

Even when made in advance, clients should be advised that some hospitals do not have formal policies regarding the implementation of such directives (McCrary & Botkin, 1989). Virmani, Schneiderman, and Kaplan (1994) found that physicians frequently are unaware of their patients' advance directives and that such directives typically are not associated with enhanced communication between doctors and patients regarding end-of-life treatment decisions. In the case of health care proxies, the evidence suggests that the decisions made by others may not match what patients would have chosen (Lambert, et al., 1990).

Although such provisos should be taken into consideration, mental health professionals must also be aware of the following therapeutic opportunities relative to the creation of advance directives:

> As important as such documents may become in the future, perhaps even more important will be the process individuals go through defining what quality of life means to them by specifying their values and beliefs to their families and physicians before they face a crisis situation. (Hoffman, 1994, p. 229)

What is more, should clients opt for a health care proxy, choosing someone to act on their behalf not only offers a context for confronting their mortality but also requires a careful consideration of friends and relatives in an effort to determine who to have make decisions for them should they become unable to do so themselves (Annas, 1991).

When working with clients to create advance directives, the following elements are considered to be essential: *competence, disclosure, understanding, voluntariness,* and *consent* (Beauchamp & Childress, 1994). Sensitivity to *ethnic and cultural differ-*

ences also is crucial. For example, "In many Chinese and Japanese communities, autonomy has different connotations. In these communities, 'autonomy' is to be expressed by the family as a whole rather than by a single designated proxy" (Young & Jex, 1992, p. 112). In addition, the final document should be internally consistent and should not include dimensions that fall outside the scope of the standards of medical practice (VA Medical Center, 1993).

There are certainly limitations in the world of advance directives. In order to improve the process, some have suggested a focus on the use of stories to assess values:

> Story-based value assessments and directives and other narrative methods that employ the development, evaluation, and integration of stories into a person's own life story are an alternative to traditional directives. Since story-based assessments and directives do not provide ready-made recipes for medical intervention, they challenge good clinical practice to integrate value assessment with medical assessment and improved physician-patient interaction into on-going stories of cure and care. (Kielstein & Sass, 1993, p. 313)

Similarly, the rationale for the use of a values history is that "While we cannot predict our future, we can at least explain ourselves now. The explanation may help ensure that the person we are, and hope to be, is respected by others who must stand in our stead" (Lambert, et al., 1990, p. 211).

SUMMARY AND RECOMMENDATIONS

Indeed, the issue of respect—for fundamental beliefs, for individuals, for the moral and ethical fabric of society—seems to be what the debate and concerns around euthanasia are about, regardless of one's stance on the issue. In the words of two biomedical ethicists:

> If it is morally permissible to unplug respirators and detach intravenous lines knowing that death will eventuate, the logic of our present situation is that we are struggling to preserve as many traditional restraints against killing as we can, consistent with taking a humane approach towards seriously suffering patients and respecting their rights. (Beauchamp & Childress, 1994, p. 234)

As mental health professionals, our task seems to be to become as familiar as possible with the issues at the various levels of all systems involved; to engage in self-exploration regarding our own ability to work with these issues; to operate with knowledge of ethical and legal constraints on participation with clients regarding end-of-life decisions; and to be prepared to engage with clients in appropriate therapeutic conversations, including the possibility of referral. As the overview provided in this chapter hopefully makes clear, we are sailing in largely uncharted waters, and even where there are charts, they are often confusing at best and conflicting at worst. Our most useful role may be one of offering information and support, recognizing both that we are all somewhat at sea and that we all ultimately will be affected by the way euthanasia decisions are made.

REFERENCES

Albright, D. E., & Hazler, R. J. (1992). A right to die?: Ethical dilemmas of euthanasia. *Counseling and Values, 39*(3), 177–189.

American Association for Marriage and Family Therapy. (1991). *AAMFT Code of Ethics.* Washington, DC: Author.

Annas, G. (1991). The health care proxy and the living will. *New England Journal of Medicine, 324*(17), 1210–1213.

Back, A. L., Wallace, J. I., Starks, H. E., & Pearlman, R. A. (1996). Physician-assisted suicide and euthanasia in Washington state: Patient requests and physician responses. *Journal of the American Medical Association, 275*(12), 919–925.

Battin M. (1992a, March/April). Assisted suicide: Can we learn anything from Germany? *Hastings Center Report,* 44–51.

Battin M. (1992b). Voluntary euthanasia and the risks of abuse: Can we learn anything from the Netherlands? *Law, Medicine & Health Care, 20*(1–2), 133–143.

Battin, M. (1994). *The least worse death.* New York: Oxford University Press.

Beauchamp T., & Childress, J. (1994). *Principles of biomedical ethics* (4th ed.). Oxford, England: Oxford University Press.

Becker, E. (1973). *The denial of death.* New York: Free Press.

Becvar, D. (1996, October). Assisted suicide: A spiritual perspective. *Family Therapy News,* p. 15.

Becvar, D. (1997). *Soul healing: A spiritual orientation in counseling and therapy.* New York: Basic Books.

Before the court, the sanctity of life and of death. (1997, January 5). *New York Times,* p. 4E.

Bloch S., & Billings, A. (1994). Patient requests to hasten death: Evaluation and management in terminal care. *Archives of Internal Medicine, 154,* 2039–2047.

Brodeur, D. (1997, August 31). Examining the American way of dying. *St. Louis Post Dispatch,* p. 3B.

Byock, I. (1997). *Dying well.* New York: Riverhead Books.

Callahan, D. (1993, July–August). Pursuing a peaceful death. *Hastings Center Report,* 33–38.

Callahan, J. (1994). The ethics of assisted suicide. *Health and Social Work, 19*(4), 237–244.

Carter, S. L. (1996, July 21). Rush to a lethal judgment. *New York Times Magazine,* 28–29.

Celocruz, M. T. (1992). Aid-in-dying: Should we decriminalize physician-assisted suicide and physician-committed euthanasia? *American Journal of Law and Medicine, 18*(4), 369–394.

Chapman, S. (1997, January 8). Opening the way to a right to kill. *St. Louis Post Dispatch,* p. 7B.

Choice in Dying, Inc. (1991). *Refusal of treatment legislation—A state by state compilation of enacted and model statutes.* New York: Author.

Conwell, Y. (1994). Physician-assisted suicide: A mental health perspective. *Suicide and Life-Threatening Behavior, 24*(4), 326–333.

Clay, R. (1997). Is assisted suicide ever a rational choice? *APA Monitor, 28*(4), 1, 43.

Cousins, N. (1989). *Head first: The biology of hope.* New York: E. P. Dutton.

Crisp, R. (1994). Reasonable care? Some comments on Gillett's reasonable care. *Bioethics, 8*(2), 159–167.

Cruzan v. Director, Missouri Department of Health (1990), 497 U.S. 261, 262.

Daw, J. (1996, October). *Assisted suicide: The facts.* 14, 28.

Docker, C. (1996). Advance directives/living wills. In S. McLean (Ed.), *Contemporary issues in law, ethics and medicine* (pp. 179–214). London: Dartmouth Press.

Doukas, D., & McCullough, L. (1991). The values history—The evaluation of the patient's values and advance directives. *Journal of Family Practice, 32*(2), 145–150.

Dworkin, R. (1993). *Life's dominion—An argument about abortion and euthanasia*. London: HarperCollins.

Dying Well Network. (1996). *Helping people die well*. Spokane, WA: Author.

Farberman, R. K. (1997). *Terminal illness and hastened death requests: The important role of the mental health professional*. Washington, DC: American Psychological Association.

Faust, J. J. (1995). The human right to die with dignity: A policy oriented essay. *Human Rights Quarterly, 17*(3), 463–487.

Final report of the Netherlands State Commission on Euthanasia: An English summary (Anon. Trans.). (1987). *Bioethics, 1*(2), 163–174.

Florida court OKs assisted suicide. (1997, February 8). *St. Louis Post Dispatch*, p. 23.

Foos-Graber, A. (1989). *Deathing: An intelligent alternative for the final moments of life*. York Beach, ME: Nicolas-Hays.

Goodman, E. (1997, January 8). Deciding on death is a crucial freedom. *St. Louis Post Dispatch*, p. 7B.

Gostin, L. O. (1993). Drawing a line between killing and letting die: The law, and law reform, on medically assisted dying. *Journal of Law, Medicine and Ethics, 21*(1), 94–101.

Graber, G. (1993). Assisted suicide is not voluntary active euthanasia, but it's awfully close. *Journal of the American Geriatrics Society, 41*(1), 88–89.

Hainer, C. (1997, August 11) At peace with death. *USA Today*, pp. 1D–2D.

Hardwig, J. (1990, March/April). What about the family? *Hastings Center Report*, 5–10.

Hardwig, J. (1995, July/August). SUPPORT and the invisible family. *Hastings Center Report* [Special suppl.] G22–G25.

Heintz, A. P. M. (1994, 25 June). Euthanasia: Can be part of good terminal care. *British Medical Journal*, 1656.

Hemlock Society. (1997, August). *Legislative Matters*. 1–6.

Hendin, H. (1995). Assisted suicide, euthanasia, and suicide prevention: The implications of the Dutch experience. *Suicide and life-threatening behavior, 25*(1), 193–204.

Hoffman, M. (1994). Use of advance directives: A social work perspective on the myth versus the reality. *Death Studies, 18*, 229–241. [Supports values histories.]

Hoffmaster. (1994). Dragons in the sunset: The allure of assisted death. *Yearbook of Access to Justice, 14*, 269–299.

Iglesias, T. (1995). Ethics, brain-death, and the medical concept of the human being. *MLJI*, 51–57.

Kapleau, P. (1989). *The wheel of life and death*. New York: Doubleday.

Kastenbaum, R. (1993). Dame Cicely Saunders: An Omega interview. *Omega: Journal of Death and Dying, 27*(4), 263–270.

Kielstein, R., & Sass, H. (1993). Using stories to assess values and establish medical directives. *Kennedy Institute of Ethics Journal, 3*(3), 303–325.

Kiser, J. D. (1996). Counselors and the legalization of physician-assisted suicide. *Counseling and Values, 40*(2), 127–131.

Kleinman, A. (1988). *The illness narratives: Suffering, healing & the human condition*. New York: Basic Books.

Keown, D., & Keown, J. (1995). Killing, karma and caring: Euthanasia in Buddhism and Christianity. *Journal of Medical Ethics, 21*, 265–269.

Krynski, M., Tymchuk, A., & Ouslander J. (1994). How informed can consent be? New light on comprehension among elderly people making decisions about enteral tube feeding. *Gerontologist, 34*(1), 36–43.

Lambert, P., Gibson, J., & Nathanson, P. (1990). The values history: An innovation in surrogate medical decision-making. *Law, Medicine and Health Care, 18*(3), 202–212.

Loewy, E. (1994). Physicians, friendship, and moral strangers: An examination of a relationship. *Cambridge Quarterly of Healthcare Ethics, 3*(1), 52–59.

Lush, D. (1989). Living wills. *Law Society's Gazette, 12,* 21–25.

Lush, D. (1993). History of living wills. *Exchange on Aging Law and Ethics, 1*(2), 4–8.

Maltsberger, J. T. (1994). The psychotherapist as an accomplice in suicide. *Giornale Italiana di Suicidologia, 4*(2), 75–81.

Markson, E. W. (1995). To be or not to be: Assisted suicide revisited. *Omega: Journal of Death and Dying, 31*(3) 221–235.

McCrary, S., & Botkin, J. (1989). Hospital policy on advance directives: Do institutions ask patients about living wills? *Journal of the American Medical Association, 262*(17), 2411–2414.

McLean, S. (1994). Paper given to International College of Surgeons, London, November 14.

McLean, S. (1996). End-of-life decisions and the law. *Journal of Medical Ethics, 22,* 261–262.

Miles, S. H. (1994). Physicians and their patients' suicides. *Journal of the American Medical Association, 271*(22), 1786–1788.

Peay, C. (1997, September/October). A good death. *Common Boundary,* 32–41.

Peck, M. S. (1997, March 10). Living is the mystery. *Newsweek,* 18.

Perrett, R. W. (1996). Buddhism, euthanasia and the sanctity of life. *Journal of Medical Ethics, 22,* 309–313.

Physicians for Mercy. (1995, December 4). Approved guidelines for patholysis (medically-assisted suicide). Internet: www.rights.org/~deathnet/kevorkian_guidelines.html

Planned Parenthood v. Casey (1992), 505 U.S. 833.

Prodigy. (1997, August 1–31). American Bar Association "ducks issue" of assisted suicide. *U.S. News Bulletins.*

Roe v. Wade (1973), 410 U.S. 113.

Scheper, T., & Duursma, S. (1994). Euthanasia: The Dutch experience. *Age and Aging, 23,* 3–8.

Shavelson, L. A. (1995). *Chosen death: The dying confront assisted suicide.* New York: Simon & Schuster.

Society for Healing and Human Values Task Force. (1995). Physician-assisted suicide: Toward a comprehensive understanding. *Academic Medicine, 70*(7), 583–590.

Solomon, A. (1995, May 22). A death of one's own. *The New Yorker.*

Sogyal, R. (1992). *The Tibetan book of living and dying.* New York: HarperCollins.

Tindall, G. (1995, March 4). *New York Times Magazine.*

VA Medical Center. (1993). *Advance directives—making decisions about your health care.* Seattle, WA: Author

Virmani, J., Schneiderman, J., & Kaplan, R. (1994). Relationship of advance directives to physician-patient communication. *Archives of Internal Medicine, 54,* 909–913.

Voigt, R. (1995). Euthanasia and HIV Disease: How Can Physicians Respond? *Journal of Palliative Care, 11*(2), 38–41.

Vries, B., Blueck, S., & Birren, J. (1993). The understanding of death and dying in a lifespan perspective. *Gerontologist, 33*(3), 366–372.

Watts, D. T. (1992). Assisted suicide is not voluntary active euthanasia. *Journal of the American Geriatrics Society, 40*(10), 1043–1046.

Webber, P., Fox, P., & Burnette, D. (1994). Living alone with Alzheimer's disease: Effects on health and social service utilization patterns. *Gerontologist, 34*(1), 8–14.

Weir, R. F. (1992). The morality of physician-assisted suicide. *Law, Medicine and Health Care, 20*(1–2), 116–126.

Wellman, C. (1995). The inalienable right to life and the durable power of attorney. *Law and Philosophy, 14,* 245–269.

Wilhelm, R. (Trans.). (1962). *The secret of the golden flower.* San Diego, CA: Harcourt Brace Jovanovich.

Will, G. (1997, January 6). A broad reading of privacy rights. *St. Louis Post Dispatch,* p. 7B.

Young, E., & Jex, S. (1992). The Patient Self-Determination Act: Potential ethical quandaries and benefits. *Cambridge Quarterly of Healthcare Ethics, 2,* 107–115.

PART IV

GENERAL FORENSIC ISSUES

CHAPTER 22

Professional Ethics, Regulatory Licensing, and Malpractice Complaints

ROBERT HENLEY WOODY

TODAY, EVERY couple and family therapist faces an unprecedented degree of risk of being the respondent to an ethical, regulatory licensing, or legal complaint. This chapter describes the contemporary framework for practice, identifies the precedents for the escalation of legal actions and other types of complaints, states the incidence of complaints, sets forth the causes of actions, reveals the psychological and financial consequences for the practitioner, clarifies the role of professional training and professional associations in the current ethical and legal scene, and offers practical guidelines for minimizing the possibility of a complaint.

THE CONTEMPORARY FRAMEWORK FOR PRACTICE

Providing mental health services to couples and families imposes a high risk on the practitioner. Contemporary societal conditions have contributed to tenuous marital and familial relations, as witnessed by the high incidence of divorce, custody and visitation disputes, allegations of spousal and child abuse, destructive or illegal conduct by children and adolescents, and many more dysfunctional behaviors. Stressed by disturbed family relations, individuals often attempt to reduce the pressure on the self through use of ego defense mechanisms. In a divorce situation, the pressure on the self is profound. Walsh, Jacob, and Simons (1995) have noted that divorce "sets in motion a number of difficult transitions" (p. 348) and "has a profound impact on an individual's sense of self" (p. 349). Consequently, the couple or parents faced with a legal problem associated with their marriage or family may look for explanations that would minimize self-responsibility and bolster their flagging sense of self.

Further complicating matters for the marriage and family therapist are the two primary therapy approaches used with couples and families. First, *brief therapy*

461

and *solution-focused therapy,* the darlings of managed care organizations, often produce a patchwork result. Consequently, when another problem comes to the foreground, such as anger being added to distancing between spouses, consumers (formerly known as clients or patients) tend to believe that the therapy provided to them has been ineffective and that the therapist should be held accountable. The second approach, *systems therapy,* is also risky. As Maddock (1993) puts it:

> In short, the willingness to bring social systems into the domain of mental health care has created added layers of ethical and legal complexity never envisioned by the original architects of the psychotherapeutic process, just as physicians of a century ago could not have imagined the moral and legal dilemmas to be faced as a result of recent advances in biotechnology. (p. 116)

One of the most common pitfalls in systems therapy concerns defining who is the client (Monahan, 1980). For example, defining and maintaining confidentiality becomes complicated when a therapist insists on sessions involving various family members. For example, complaints often arise from a parent's belief that the therapist has improperly refused to tell the parent everything that the child has said to the therapist, revealed confidential information to favor the other parent, or given confidential information to an insurance company or a court to the detriment of the parent. Such issues produce ethical dilemmas that leave many couples and family therapists feeling overwhelmed and defensive, qualities which impact negatively on the therapeutic relationship and process. They may then purchase consultation from attorneys "to define their legal limits of liability, hoping to reassure themselves that mental health care need not be as burdensome as it often feels or as risky as it presently appears" (Maddock, 1993, p. 116). Regrettably, this search for protection yields no assured comfort or safety zone.

THE ESCALATION OF LEGAL ACTION

There is no denying that society has thrown open the doors of the courthouse to accommodate legal actions against health care providers, and some would say especially mental health professionals. Reaves and Ogloff (1996) indicate:

> The amount of ongoing litigation in the United States has reached appalling proportions, and although the growth in litigation has not been as severe in Canada, often the response to problems or differences among people is the initiation of a lawsuit. Although many people seem to abhor this growing trend, the fact remains unaltered. (p. 117)

To be sure, some complaints are well justified by misconduct or malpractice by the therapist. A significant number of complaints, however, reflect psychopathological processes in the client. As a result, even the most conscientious therapist is vulnerable to a complaint. Although professionals may "think that others might be accused of ethics violations, but not themselves" (Chauvin & Remley, 1996, p. 563), no one is safe from this risk.

There are three basic types of complaints: (a) ethics, (b) regulatory (or licensing), and (c) malpractice.

In a nutshell, an *ethics complaint* is one that is submitted to a professional association. If the subject of the complaint, the practitioner, is not a member of the association, there can be no direct disciplinary action on the complaint.

A *regulatory complaint* is filed by a consumer to a state regulatory agency, commonly an investigative unit that serves a professional licensing board. Of course, a regulatory agency has jurisdiction only over licensees, and possibly over someone who encroaches on the realm of licensure, such as an impostor or quack (note that any legal principle is subject to the laws unique to the particular jurisdiction). Today's society seems to favor holding service providers accountable through governmental regulation; and as with all complaints against a practitioner, some regulatory or licensing complaints are well founded, while others reflect a client's pathological retaliation or abuse (e.g., coming from a paranoid mind state or borderline character disorder).

The most common legal action against a practitioner involves alleged *malpractice*, which is predicated on professional liability. That is, the service provider is alleged to have damaged a consumer through failing to provide services within the prevailing standard of care for the profession, and thereby failing to satisfy a legal duty. For example, the practitioner may have diagnosed a child in a manner that led to a special education intervention, provided an evaluation for a child custody case that disappointed or angered one of the parents, or provided an intervention that did not halt the progression of pathology. Because the viewpoint expressed by the practitioner did not please the consumer, malpractice is alleged.

Moreover, there are certain causes for complaint that could result, depending on the jurisdiction, in an alleged violation of criminal law. For example, a number of states have criminal statutes that allow for prosecution of a therapist who engages in sexual misconduct with a client. Reaves and Ogloff (1966) state: "Although mental health professionals may enter practice concerned that they may someday be a defendant in a civil lawsuit, most never consider the possibility that they may face criminal charges or loss of their licenses" (p. 117). The fact is that while "there are more professionals sued civilly, criminal and license-related cases are far more serious" (p. 117).

In keeping with the notion that license-related cases are potentially more serious than other forms of complaints, there is ample reason to believe that the regulatory system, overall, is biased against the therapist facing a complaint (Woody, 1993). Because the regulatory system (including the licensing board) is intended primarily for consumer protection, there is definitely a prosecutorial atmosphere. Many respondents allege that they have felt "guilty until proven innocent," and even then the playing field is not level. Some therapists have stated that when they have faced complaints, their professional associations have abandoned them in favor of catering to consumers' interests, a practice which again imposes inequitable treatment.

Often the uneven playing field is due to personal factors. For example, one practitioner was appointed by the court to provide therapy to a teenager; one of the parents continued to oppose the therapy, made demands of the therapist that were contradictory to the interests of the teenager (and the court order), and filed a complaint that alleged all sorts of practice violations with the state regulatory agency. The prosecuting attorney assigned to the case engaged in a number of telephone and written exchanges with the complainant that revealed advocacy for personal reasons (e.g., a bond between the prosecuting attorney and the complainant rooted in their personal histories of abuse). Even when the judge expressed support for the practitioner, the prosecutor continued the investigation.

A more pervasive inequity arises from the career aspirations of agency personnel. As representatives of consumer protection, more favorable annual reviews of job performance are gained by disciplinary actions against practitioners, as opposed to dismissed complaints. Personal experience supports for example, that, attorneys prosecuting licensing complaints aspire for promotion up the governmental legal ladder.

Seeming injustices toward mental health and medical professionals by regulatory (licensing) agencies have led to, among other things, formation of a national organization that seeks to counter false accusations against therapists and obtain regulatory equity. (For additional information, contact the Professional Advocacy Network [PAN], 6230 Wilshire Boulevard, Suite 110, Los Angeles, CA 90048.)

THE SPAWNING OF ADDITIONAL COMPLAINTS

It should be noted that a single complaint can spawn additional complaints (based on the same incident) that may include ethical, regulatory (licensing), civil (malpractice), and criminal investigations. A disgruntled, disturbed patient can seek to discredit a therapist in every possible channel. The outcome from one source can influence the outcome in other sources. For example, a malpractice lawsuit can (and quite likely would) be reported to the state licensing board and to the ethics committee of the practitioner's professional association.

THE INCIDENCE OF COMPLAINTS

It is impossible to give precise numbers of complaints or statements about the probability of a complaint being filed. While insurance companies, ethics committees, and licensing boards can report the number of cases that were under their aegis in a given year, those numbers do not tell the full story.

Many complaints are resolved by a demand letter from the complainant's attorney, to which the therapist makes a financial settlement. To further obfuscate the degree of risk, although a legal case may actually be filed with a court, a negotiated settlement may lead to the dismissal of the case. Similarly, a case before a trial court (where the therapist does not rely on malpractice coverage and no ethics or licensing complaints are filed) may not be reported to any source (e.g., most court cases do not appear in printed form for mass distribution, such as in a state or regional reporter). Thus, statistics do not reflect anywhere near all of the complaints filed.

The incidence of complaints seems to be increasing. Peterson (1996) reports an increase in ethical, regulatory, and legal (malpractice) actions against psychologists: "Available data clearly indicate that there has been a significant increase in disciplinary and legal actions against psychologists for unprofessional and unethical conduct" (p. 71). No doubt, the same can be said for the other mental health disciplines. Disciplinary actions by regulatory agencies have increased 500% over the past 10 years for some types of alleged misconduct by psychologists, and the number of ethics complaints filed with the APA against psychologists "doubled in a 5-year period (1984–1989), with a similar increase in the number of sanctions by the association" (p. 71).

There is a noteworthy trend for ethics codes to be highly specific; the language used is both elaborate (i.e., broad) and restrictive (i.e., detailed). Historically, ethics codes were purposefully general, setting forth principles from which the practitioner could deduce practical guidelines for self-regulation. Concurrent with the escalation of legal liability, ethics codes have been revised to be significantly more specific about conduct. Instead of principles and concepts, the ethics codes establish prescriptive and proscriptive standards for professional and personal conduct, thereby diminishing the decision making that can be exercised by the practitioner. This trend is, of course, in accord with the micromanagement that is imposed by state licensing agencies.

An analysis of three years of complaints against psychologists submitted to the Florida Department of Business and Professional Regulation (DBPR) concluded:

> Given the total number of licensees in each of the years, it means that, in the respective years, 5.3%, 4.6%, and 6.7% of Licensed Psychologists had a formal complaint against them. While it is known that some psychologists have more than one complaint in their past, let us assume that it is a small number. Thus, the foregoing percentages suggest that over, say the next five years, about one-third of Licensed Psychologists will be the subject of a DBPR formal complaint. (Woody, 1994, p. 19)

Whether data for Florida is comparable to that for other states or for disciplines other than psychology is unknown; however, it is obvious that regulatory complaints create a substantial risk and appear to be increasing. Clinicians are concerned about their vulnerability, and this adds another stressor to the many others that they experience in their professional lives; of course, the stress flows over to personal lives as well.

CAUSES OF ACTION

A cause of action refers to the legal bases or principles from which a complaint can ensue. The reasons for a cause for complaint vary according to the jurisdiction and the type of action (i.e., ethical, regulatory, or legal). Maddock (1993) believes that the most visible complaint is "the sexual exploitation of clients, although other violations also exist: inappropriate crossing of social boundaries, involvement in multiple roles with clients, working outside of established areas of competence, or providing treatment under conditions of impaired judgment" (p. 118). While seemingly generalizable to all mental health practitioners, Reaves and Ogloff (1996) identify the following causes of action for psychologists:

- Professional negligence
    - Failure to warn or protect
    - Failure to properly supervise hospitalized patients
    - Negligent release of dangerous patients
    - Negligent prescription of contraindicated drugs
    - Negligence of auxiliaries (i.e., other personnel associated with patient care)

- Sexual relations with clients
- Faulty record keeping
- Inappropriate or negligent release of records
- Lack of informed consent
- Failure to satisfy the duty to inform (e.g., to notify a subsequent care provider of a patient's history of suicide attempts)
- Assault and battery
- Employer–employee relations (e.g., sexual harassment and age and gender discrimination)

As relevant to malpractice actions against social workers, Besharov indicates that the top ten types of claims are the following (1985, see p. 3):

1. Sexual impropriety
2. Incorrect treatment
3. Improper child placement
4. Breach of confidentiality
5. Improper death of patient or others
6. Child placement removal, including custody disputes
7. Violation of civil rights
8. Bodily injury to client
9. Defamation, including libel and slander
10. Failure to supervise client properly, causing injury to client or others

Hogan's early analysis (which covered all mental health specialties) specified 25 causes of action used in malpractice cases against psychotherapists, including the following (1979, see p. 7):

- Involuntary servitude
- False arrest
- Trespass
- Malicious infliction of emotional distress
- Abuse of process
- Loss of liberty
- Misrepresentation
- Libel
- Assault and battery
- Malicious prosecution
- False imprisonment

Obviously, potential causes of action go well beyond a simplistic notion of malpractice per se.

In a sense, trying to delineate the cause of action is futile. Multiple volumes define (and provide forms for) legal causes of action. Any attorney, on receiving negative comments about a couples and family therapist from a disgruntled consumer, could locate numerous causes of action that would potentially apply to the consumer's expressed problem. Moreover, an enterprising attorney can exercise ingenuity and create seemingly new causes of action tailored to the particular case.

THE PSYCHOLOGICAL CONSEQUENCES
OF A COMPLAINT

Over the last three decades, the possibility of a complaint being filed has increased, to the point that some practitioners experience *litigaphobia* and *litiga-stress* (Brodsky, 1983; Turkington, 1987). A complaint about a therapist's professional conduct is an assault on the inner core of the therapist's self-esteem. As might be expected with any denigration of self-esteem, the complaint can lead the practitioner to experience depression, tension, anger, and symptoms of physical illness; and there can be adverse effects on marital and familial relations, career motivation, and general satisfaction with life (Charles, Wilbert, & Kennedy, 1984).

The elevated threat of ethical, regulatory, and legal complaints that cause a therapist emotional distress can be severe enough to lead to exaggerated defensive practices and unhealthy personality adaptation. Practicing by a risk management plan is not illogical. Any complaint, even one that is frivolous, false, or malicious can irreparably damage the professional reputation—and thus the income—of the therapist. The prudent therapist should always maintain legal safeguards in every interaction with a client or collateral source.

THE FINANCIAL CONSEQUENCES OF A COMPLAINT

The cost to a couple and family therapist goes well beyond money paid in damages to the complainant. Ethical and regulatory complaints do not generally involve a payment of money to the complainant. Some situations, however, can lead to a requirement that restitution be paid to the complainant, and some licensing boards impose costs or what amounts to a fine.

The majority of professional liability complaints (i.e., malpractice) are settled for "nuisance" amounts of money; if the therapist is insured, this payment is likely to come from the insurance carrier. On the other hand, some insurance companies will seek to have the insured pay all or part of the settlement, depending upon the cause of action, the evidence of wrongdoing, and the exclusions or reservations of rights that apply to the particular situation. For example, an insurance company was pressuring the defendant therapist to agree to settle a claim, but the company did not want to spend the full amount being required by the plaintiff. In an obvious attempt to capitalize on the defendant therapist's anguish about the case, the insurance company proposed that the practitioner pay half of the settlement amount. While there is no legal basis for this position, it reveals how an insurance company may opt to preserve its financial assets at the expense of the therapist. (Incidentally, this example is not an isolated incident.)

Of special concern to the therapist, a settlement can carry two financial penalties. First, it is common for insurance companies to reserve the right to select the attorney used in the malpractice case and to negotiate a settlement with the complainant. While attorneys selected by insurance companies are honorable in their intentions to advocate the interests of the insured (i.e., the therapist), their directions come from fiscally oriented monitors affiliated with the insurance carrier. To clarify the process, it is common for an insurance carrier to have attorneys and accountants who track the progress of cases and issue recommendations, which are often worded more like demands, that settlement or some other strategy be implemented. Thus, the attorney hired by the insurance company to represent the defendant therapist may be ordered to settle a case, regardless of the therapist's innocence and the impact that it may have on the therapist's career.

Of special importance for the therapist faced with the possibility of settling a case, some jurisdictions require that settlements (perhaps over a certain amount) be reported to a governmental agency. This step could lead to an investigation by the regulatory agency affiliated with the licensing board. A further result might be a report to the Disciplinary Data System (DDS), a computerized national registry developed and maintained by the Association of State and Provincial Psychology Boards (ASPPB, 1996) for possible regulatory action in other states where the therapist is (or wants to be) licensed or to a professional association for an ethics complaint. Malpractice insurance does not always cover regulatory complaints, unless this additional specialized coverage has been purchased. Having to hire a personal attorney can prove expensive and increase the emotional pressure.

The fact that the attorney for the therapist is being paid by the insurance carrier could easily have an effect on how the therapist's defense is handled. The earlier comment about the insurance carrier's potential influence on (or direction of) the attorney whom it is paying must be considered. Stated bluntly, any attorney being paid by an insurance carrier is potentially subject to influence, consciously or unconsciously, or blatant direction to resolve the case primarily for the financial benefit of the insurance carrier, with only a modicum of concern about the negative effects for the therapist. To many therapists, having to settle implies an admission of guilt.

Given the aforementioned influence of the insurance carrier and the differing interests between the insurance carrier and the therapist, the therapist in this instance also may need to incur the costs of a personal attorney, which would be paid out of pocket. The personal attorney would represent and advocate the therapist's interests and work in collaboration with the attorney who was hired by and on behalf of the insurance company.

In the event that there is a settlement, judgment, or disciplinary action against the therapist, it will have to be self-reported to a variety of sources, such as managed health care companies, facilities granting service privileges, employers, professional associations, national registries, certification bodies, and licensing agencies—not just in the immediate future, but potentially during one's entire career. Needless to say, this sort of report could be viewed as negative by any of the aforementioned sources. Incidentally, even settlements that include "confidentiality for the terms included" have a surprising way of circulating through the professional community, with the result being a tainting of the professional's reputation and possibly decreased referrals.

THE ROLE OF PROFESSIONAL TRAINING AND PROFESSIONAL ASSOCIATIONS

With the surge in regulatory licensing and professional liability law that occurred in the mid-1970s, the importance of and reliance on professional ethics for protecting consumers was reduced. Two interesting concomitants developed, which involve professional training and professional associations.

Professional training sources, such as university faculty members, have tended to ignore the rise in control over professions imposed by governmental regulatory agencies: "Among internal obstacles one may note the essential stasis and inflexibility of faculty-owned curricula which particularly resist innovative proposals for instructional design; criteria for faculty promotion and tenure; faculty ignorance of the changing imperatives of the world of work; competency and resources shortfall with programs; and the inappropriate expectations of new trainees" (Troy & Schueman, 1996, p. 75). Instead, the notion is that the academy is the foremost decision maker of what is and is not acceptable professional practice. While this would be the ideal, it is not the reality.

At this time, the distrust of health care providers in general (Starr, 1994) and of the efficacy of mental health services in particular leads consumers to give primary importance to governmental regulations and to rely on prosecutors rather than professional societies to discipline errant practitioners: "With increased public awareness and increased willingness by aggrieved individuals to face the ordeal of bringing charges, licensing boards in many professions have many more cases to adjudicate" (Sinclair, Simon, & Pettifor, 1996, p. 12). Consequently, the legislatures and licensing boards have promuglated statutes and rules that clearly reflect micromanagement of clinical practices. This authority cannot be superseded by even the most esteemed or well intentioned professor or practitioner.

The nature of today's mental health professions is considerably different than in the past (which may well be where many senior trainers and leaders in professional associations are rooted). Today mental health professionals are viewed by society as being part of the health care industry, and deserving of governmental and legal regulation (Cummings, 1996).

Nonetheless, professional trainers have remained amazingly ignorant of the commercial marketplace in which mental health professionals now operate. It is the rare training program that provides nominal coverage of how to practice in the era of managed health care, the importance of managed care organizations for the success of many mental health practices (Cummings, 1996), and the problems associated with managed care for patients and therapists. This void is not without legal implications; Applebaum (1993) has aptly pointed out that working under the rubric of a managed care organization creates additional legal liability for service providers. As an example of ethical risk (which could extend to legal liability as well), when the managed care organization curtails reimbursement and forces a cessation of services, the practitioner remains vulnerable to allegations of wrongdoing, such as abandonment or failure to adequately address the financial issues.

The national mental health professional associations, perhaps in an effort to recapture some of their once-omniscient position with practitioners, have asserted increasing definitions of what should and should not occur in practice, along with strict procedures by which complaints against their members will be processed. If one is not a member, an ethical complaint cannot be adjudicated, which leads many practitioners to avoid memberships in professional associations. Also, many practitioners wonder why they should pay membership dues to an association that appears not to represent their interests. They see the guidelines as advocating the interests of consumers over the interests of members. This viewpoint, along with other factors, may perhaps account for the decrease in membership of some professional associations (proportionate to the pool of potential members).

Due to inadequate training, some therapists are ill prepared to deal with complaints of any kind. The prevailing notion in mental health training programs seems to be that when a complaint is voiced or threatened, the practitioner should confront the dissatisfied client and attempt to deal with the situation in a therapeutic manner. This could (and some training sources say should) include the therapist's owning his or her share of responsibility for the problem. While this might have a salving effect on ethics, it would be an *admission against interests* in a legal situation; that is, the therapist's owning of a failure or problem would likely be tranformed into adverse evidence.

When dealing with a complaint—be it ethical, regulatory, or legal—the wise therapist acknowledges not having the expertise for legally safe conflict resolution. Also, it may be strategically unwise to try to interpret to the patient that his or her complaints are part of a negative transference or typical pattern of projecting blame onto others. Although writing a decade and a half ago, Wright (1981) provided sage information that should be heeded by every mental health practitioner:

> Our training and our personal philosophies tend to emphasize the importance of the individual and our obligation as a helper/practitioner to evidence humanistic concerns or attempt "conflict resolution." We find it hard to believe that our virtue is unappreciated, so we attempt to follow our ethical admonitions to resolve conflict and discover to our subsequent dismay that the plaintiff's attorney made our virtuous and well-meaning efforts appear to be an attempt to "cover up" or "cop out." (p. 1535)

Notwithstanding the financial expense of an attorney, professional survival requires astute and steadfast legal defense and recognition that nurturance and altruism cannot exist without business acumen and sound risk management.

ADOPTING HEALTHY DEFENSIVENESS

The contemporaneous legal liability and risk of complaints that permeate the practice of couple and family therapy can be distressing. Being a professional is, however, a noble calling, and necessitates adopting a positive, but realistic, outlook for practice. Therefore, the following five recommendations are offered.

1. *The prudent couple and family therapist should recognize that legal situations (and often ethical situations as well) require expertise that goes beyond the professional's training in mental health services.* Unfortunately, therapists who face an ethics complaint "are often unprepared to respond in a rational, cautious, and appropriate manner" (Chauvin & Remley, 1996, p. 563). Malpractice attorneys commonly believe that many times a therapist's worst opposition is self-created.

   For couple and family therapists, being a highly intelligent, well-defined professional can be both a blessing and a curse. Such a person may be able to assist the attorney in the preparation of the case by offering information on academic substance, professional standards, and insights from personal experience with the opposing litigants. On the other hand, the therapist as legal client may hold an inflated sense of competency to understand and manage a legal case. An attorney told Wright (1981):

> Heaven protect me from intelligent, sophisticated clients. While they're "helping" me win my case, they can find ways I never dreamed of to mess things up. The smarter they are the more ways they can find to botch it. (p. 1535)

LaNoue and Lee (1987) provide numerous examples of how professors have tried to dictate the manner in which their alleged discrimination cases were handled, ultimately to their own detriment.

All too often, a mental health professional responds to a complaint with a therapeutic response, and in the process makes statements that are transformed into admissions against interests. That is, by the time the complaint has been issued, the consumer, now turned into a complainant or party litigant, has in all likelihood talked with an attorney or involved a state prosecutor in directing the situation; consequently, the therapist's attempt to avoid legal action is too late and ill advised. Indeed, Stampelos and Jones (1990) indicate that when a complaint is filed, the professional "should state he will be represented by an attorney and that he will respond through his attorney" (pp. 69–70) and refrain from further discussions "without first consulting counsel" (p. 70). Similarly, Chauvin and Remley (1996) point out that therapists who receive a complaint "should be careful to respond in an appropriate manner from the first moment they are notified" (p. 567) and should immediately act to obtain legal advice and emotional support.

Because mental health professionals are verbally oriented, in a tension-provoking situation, such as a legal proceeding, they often will say too much. Unbridled verbiage and ignoring the advice of counsel call to mind the World War II slogan, "Loose lips sink ships." To avoid being on the sinking ship, that is losing the legal case, the prudent couples and family therapist should always rely strictly on the objectivity and expertise of his or her attorney and recall and heed the old saw, "When you serve as your own lawyer, you have a fool for a client."

2. *The prudent couple and family therapist should recognize that professional services, despite their historical identity with benevolent and human services, are now considered to be in the commercial marketplace.* Therefore, the previously sacrosanct therapeutic alliance has been altered drastically; much of the humanism that pervaded therapeutic services in the past is now inappropriate and carries unnecessary legal liability. The therapeutic relationship should be conceptualized as an exchange (payment for expertise), and a written contract for services should be entered into and signed at the end of the first session if further therapy is to be undertaken. Services should be provided according to contractual terms and should be carefully calculated to maximize benefits for both the consumer and the therapist. Unyielding adherence to high professional standards benefits both the consumer and the therapist. Noncompliant consumers (e.g., those who will not follow an individual treatment plan) should neither be accepted nor continued; the clinical

interests of the consumer and the risk management of the therapist do not allow for nonadherence to the therapist's policies and practices.

3. *The prudent couple and family therapist should keep extensive records.* Record keeping is surpassed only by high professional standards as a source of protection against complaints.

Professional ethics and position statements, state regulatory laws and rules, other statutory laws, common law, and policies from third-party payment sources establish irrefutably that records must be kept; records must be comprehensive (exact contents are commonly prescribed by one or more of the foregoing sources); and an individualized treatment plan must be established and followed (preferably reflected in the notes for *every* session). It should be noted that these disciplinary bodies do not necessarily maintain an unassailable view. For example, numerous regulatory sources have defined what should be included in mental health records, such as notes about psychotherapy, yet well-known clinicians believe otherwise (e.g., that no treatment notes are necessary; Bergantino, 1997).

4. *Because of the high-risk complaints emanating from divorce, custody, visitation, and abuse contexts, the prudent couple and family therapist must be cautious in releasing records and offering testimony in legal proceedings.* Many complaints are founded on alleged breach of confidentiality. Following the guidelines for child custody evaluations (American Psychological Association [APA], 1994) or some similar authoritative document (e.g., a position statement from a professional society or a scholarly publication) is advisable; this will, at least, provide a professional basis for asserting that a prevailing standard of care has been fulfilled.

5. *The prudent couple and family therapist should be well versed in professional ethics codes and position statements from his or her primary and other relevant professional associations.* All couples and family therapists, regardless of mental health discipline, should be familiar with the ethical information provided by the American Association for Marriage and Family Therapy (1991); American Association of Sex Educators, Counselors and Therapists (1992); American Counseling Association (1995); American Psychiatric Association (1992); National Association of Social Workers (1993); and particularly the publications from the American Psychological Association about record keeping (APA, 1993), child custody evaluations (APA, 1994), disclosure of test data (APA, 1996a), and coping with subpoenas or compelled testimony for client records of test data (APA, 1996b); as well as Burke's (1995) ideas about how to honor confidentiality following the death of a client. Because there are some differences between mental health disciplines relevant to the application of this APA information, adaptations must be made according to the couple and family therapist's professional discipline.

The preceding five recommendations create a framework for legally safe practice of couple and family therapy. Further study is advisable; additional information is available in Woody (1988a, 1988b, 1991, 1997).

As a final caveat, a decade ago Woody issued the following admonition:

For centuries, sages have sermonized on how spiritual progress will be destroyed by the seven deadly sins: pride, covetousness, lust, anger, gluttony, envy, and sloth. These sins are potentially no less fatal to career progress. (1988a, pp. 130–131)

In the intervening years, the author has been extensively involved as an attorney, with several hundred complaints against mental health practitioners. Inspection of the cases reveals that, perhaps more than ever, the warning to "guard against the seven deadly sins" (p. 130) is still good advice for the prudent couple and family therapist.

REFERENCES

American Association for Marriage and Family Therapy. (1991). *AAMFT code of ethics.* Washington, DC: Author.

American Association of Sex Educators, Counselors and Therapists. (1992). *1992 revised code of ethics.* Chicago: Author.

American Counseling Association. (1995). Code of ethics and standards of practice. *Counseling Today, 37*(11), 33–40.

American Psychiatric Association. (1992). *The principles of medical ethics (with annotations especially applicable to psychiatry).* Washington, DC: Author.

American Psychological Association. (1993). Record keeping guidelines. *American Psychologist, 48*(9), 984–986.

American Psychological Association. (1994). Guidelines for child custody evaluations in divorce proceedings. *American Psychologist, 49*(7), 677–680.

American Psychological Association. (1996a). Statement on the disclosure of test data. *American Psychologist, 51*(6), 644–648.

American Psychological Association. (1996b). Strategies for private practitioners coping with subpoenas or compelled testimony for client records or test data. *Professional Psychology: Research and Practice, 27*(3), 245–251.

Applebaum, P. S. (1993). Legal liability and managed care. *American Psychologist, 48*(3), 251–277.

Association of State and Provincial Psychology Boards. (1996). Disciplinary data system pilot project kicks off. *ASPPD Newsletter, 17*(1), 1, 4.

Bergantino, L. (1997). Note taking and psychotherapy. *PAN Observer, 3*(1), 11.

Besharov, D. J. (1985). *The vulnerable social worker: Liability for serving children and families.* Silver Spring, MD: National Association of Social Workers.

Brodsky, S. L. (1983). Litigaphobia: The professionals' disease [Review of B. Schutz, *Legal liability in psychotherapy*]. *Contemporary Psychology, 28,* 204–205.

Burke, C. A. (1995). Until death do us part: An exploration into confidentiality following the death of a client. *Professional Psychology: Research and Practice, 26*(3), 278–280.

Charles, S. C., Wilbert, J. R., & Kennedy, E. C. (1984). Physicians' self reports of reactions to malpractice litigation. *American Journal of Psychiatry, 141,* 563–565.

Chauvin, J. C., & Remley, T. P., Jr. (1996). Responding to allegations of unethical conduct. *Journal of Counseling & Development, 74*(6), 563–568.

Cummings, N. A. (1996). The resocialization of behavioral healthcare practice. In N. A. Cummings, M. S. Pallak, & J. L. Cummings (Eds.), *Surviving the demise of solo practice: Mental health practitioners prospering in the era of managed care* (pp. 3–10). Madison, CT: Psychosocial Press (International Universities Press).

Hogan, D. B. (1979). *The regulation of psychotherapists: Vol. 3. A review of malpractice suits in the United States.* Cambridge, MA: Ballinger.

LaNoue, G. R., & Lee, B. A. (1987). *Academics in court: The consequences of faculty discrimination litigation.* Ann Arbor, MI: University of Michigan Press.

Maddock, J. W. (1993). Ecology, ethics, and responsibility in family therapy. *Family Relations, 42*(1), 116–123.

Monahan, J. (Ed.). (1980). *Who is the client?* Washington, DC: American Psychological Association.

National Association of Social Workers. (1993). *Code of ethics of the National Association of Social Workers.* Washington, DC: Author.

Peterson, C. (1996). Common problem areas and their causes resulting in disciplinary actions. In L. J. Bass, S. T. DeMers, J. R. P. Ogloff, C. Peterson, J. L. Pettifor, R. P. Reaves, T. Rétfalvi, N. P. Simon, C. Sinclair, & R. M. Tipton (Eds.), *Professional conduct and discipline in psychology* (pp. 71–89). Washington, DC: American Psychological Association; and Montgomery, AL: Association of State and Provincial Psychology Boards.

Reaves, R. P., & Ogloff, J. R. P. (1996). Liability for professional misconduct. In L. J. Bass, S. T. DeMers, J. R. P. Ogloff, C. Peterson, J. L. Pettifor, R. P. Reaves, T. Rétfalvi, N. P. Simon, C. Sinclair, & R. M. Tipton (Eds.), *Professional conduct and discipline in psychology* (pp. 117–142). Washington, DC: American Psychological Association; and Montgomery, AL: Association of State and Provincial Psychology Boards.

Sinclair, C., Simon, N. P., & Pettifor, J. L. (1996). The history of ethical codes and licensure. In L. J. Bass, S. T. DeMers, J. R. P. Ogloff, C. Peterson, J. L. Pettifor, R. P. Reaves, T. Rétfalvi, N. P. Simon, C. Sinclair, & R. M. Tipton (Eds.), *Professional conduct and discipline in psychology* (pp. 1–15). Washington, DC: American Psychological Association; and Montgomery, AL: Association of State and Provincial Psychology Boards.

Stampelos, C. A., & Jones, D. P. (1990). What your client should do when the Department of Professional Regulation investigates him. *Florida Bar Journal, 64*(4), 68–70.

Starr, P. (1994). *The logic of health care reform.* New York: Whittle Books (Penguin).

Troy, W. G., & Shueman, S. A. (1996). Program redesign for graduate training in professional psychology: The road to accountability in a changing professional world. In N. A. Cummings, M. S. Pallak, & J. L. Cummings (Eds.), *Surviving the demise of solo practice: Mental health practitioners prospering in the era of managed care* (pp. 55–79). Madison, CT: Psychosocial Press (International Universities Press).

Turkington, C. (1987). Litigaphobia. *American Psychological Association Monitor, 17*(11), 1, 8.

Walsh, F., Jacob, L., & Simons, V. (1995). Facilitating healthy divorce processes: Therapy and mediation approaches. In N. S. Jacobson & A. S. Gurman (Ed.), *Clinical handbook of couple therapy* (pp. 340–365). New York: Guilford Press.

Woody, R. H. (1988a). *Fifty ways to avoid malpractice: A guidebook for the mental health practitioner.* Sarasota, FL: Professional Resource Exchange.

Woody, R. H. (1988b). *Protecting your mental health practice: How to minimize legal and financial risk.* San Francisco: Jossey-Bass.

Woody, R. H. (1989). *Business success in mental health practice: Modern marketing, management and legal strategies.* San Francisco: Jossey-Bass.

Woody, R. H. (1991). *Quality care in mental health services: Assuring the best clinical services.* San Francisco: Jossey-Bass.

Woody, R. H. (1993). Regulatory equality for clients and psychotherapists. *Voices: The Art and Science of Psychotherapy, 29*(2), 87–92.

Woody, R. H. (1994). Being realistic about legal complaints. *Florida Psychologist, 44*(2), 19–20.

Woody, R. H. (1997). *Legally safe mental health practice: Psycholegal questions and answers.* Madison, CT: Psychosocial Press (International Universities Press).

Wright, R. H. (1981). What to do until the malpractice lawyer comes: A survivor's manual. *American Psychologist, 36*(12), 1535–1541.

CHAPTER 23

Serving as an Expert Witness

Evaluations, Subpoenas, and Testimony

STANLEY L. BRODSKY and STEPHEN J. ANDERER

THIS CHAPTER describes the knowledge, skills, and situational competencies needed to be effective as an expert witness in depositions and in courtroom testimony.

PREREQUISITES TO BE AN EXPERT

The starting points in discussing the prerequisites of experts are the important elements of *competence, specialized knowledge,* and the *forensic ethic,* each of which is discussed in turn. The three most important factors that cut across these elements of working as an expert in litigation are *preparation, communication,* and *anticipation.* Therefore, much of the expertise should be present and work should be done before an actual hearing.

THE REQUISITE COMPETENCE

All too often, mental health professionals are willing to work and testify beyond their competence, notwithstanding the relevant ethical prohibitions on such conduct. As managed care has produced a vocal cohort of resentful and unhappy clinicians, a noticeable number of independent health practitioners have moved into forensic work and testimony as an alternative or supplementary career path; for some of them, the move has been precipitous. Forensic evaluations and testimony are free from the intrusions into independent decisions regarding treatment that are present in much therapy reimbursed by managed care or other third-party payers. Some of these new experts, as well as some long-active forensic practitioners, so want their practices to be financially successful and to build up their referrals that now and then they go beyond their actual knowledge base.

Responsible actions are to decline cases beyond one's competence or to throw oneself seriously into extending one's professional expertise into new subject areas. Some senior forensic practitioners offer telephone consultation to new forensic psychologists who are looking for guided supervision in acquiring new competencies. This consultation is often exciting to offer because the recipients are willing to listen, to work hard, and to receive critical feedback. By virtue of seeking consultation, they acknowledge their limitations. The professionals who do not pursue needed additional knowledge and skills are the problem.

The most frequent public demonstration of competence lapses is in response to direct examination questions. Sometimes the knowledge of the expert witness is obsolete. Sometimes the conclusions do not follow. Sometimes the expert just misses the target on how the assessment should have been done. The other side of this problem occurs during cross-examination, when witnesses extrapolate from their own areas of deficient knowledge through guesses and through strong assertions that "that is what I found, and that is the nature of this person."

In an unrelated context, Robert Heinlein (1973) once observed that "You can't teach a pig to sing; it only wastes your time and annoys the pig." Note that this statement was made well before the release of the film *Babe*. The underlying principle is one that applies equally well to attorneys' choice of expert witnesses: They are far better off selecting the right person than trying to transform the wrong person into someone closer to "right." Who do attorneys choose when considerable choice is available? A few attorneys do seek the least experienced, or most gullible, or most malleable professionals who will produce the opinions the attorneys desire. Responsible attorneys seek experienced, poised individuals who are alert and proactive. Working in court cases involves a situational competency in which presentation of the substantive case improves with skillful self-presentation.

SPECIALIZED KNOWLEDGE NEEDED

As the knowledge base has expanded in the multitude of areas about which psychologists may be called to testify, it has become impossible for mental health professionals to maintain a high level of expertise in every subcategory within their professions. As a result, the expert must determine what specialized knowledge is needed in a particular case. For example, if a psychologist is going to conduct a child custody evaluation, he or she should have specialized training in such evaluations, including the requisite forensic assessment skills. (For examples of the needed training and substantive skills, see the guide to custody evaluation by Gould, 1998.) In some cases, a professional may be needed for a purpose other than a comprehensive custody evaluation (e.g., to determine whether children need psychotherapy, to determine the best school for a child with a learning disability), and an expert other than a custody evaluator may be appropriate. In other cases, an appropriate expert will have specialized training and experience with custody evaluations and with certain other relevant areas (e.g., sexual abuse, very young children, adolescents, etc.). In some jurisdictions, practical considerations may make it difficult to get someone other than a generalist to conduct an evaluation, but that expert should make an effort to educate him- or herself to the extent necessary. Toward such goals, Gould (1998) has described the multifaceted nature of child developmental guidelines, of parenting capabilities, and of information drawn from collateral sources (see also Chapter 13).

A FORENSIC ETHIC

Clinical practitioners, in particular, have a markedly different way of approaching clients than do forensic psychologists. Clinicians have primary loyalties to the welfare of their clients. Forensic experts have primary responsibilities to the court and to the impartial inquiry into such questions as custody, injury, and competencies. A necessary step to be able to act ethically is to master a forensic frame of reference. Greenberg and Shuman (1997) have identified irreconcilable conflicts that divide the clinician from the forensic assessor. They point out that the forensic expert, compared to the clinician, is more structured and evaluative, seeks collateral sources, views the retaining attorney as the primary client, and acts towards the parties in litigation with a neutral and objective attitude rather than an accepting and empathic interpersonal mind-set.

If the professional does not have such a forensic ethic, the process of educating the expert can be exasperating at worst, and time-consuming at best, for the retaining attorney. As the fields of forensic psychology, social work, and psychiatry have emerged, it has been an ethical expectation that experts will be knowledgeable about the legal processes, issues, and procedures that relate to their work. How can one acquire such expertise? Some paths include membership in the American Psychology-Law Society, the American Academy of Forensic Psychology (open only to those board certified in forensic psychology), the American Academy of Psychiatry and Law, or other similar organizations; reading psychology-law or psychiatry-law journals and books; and seeking postdoctoral or continuing education training in psychology or psychiatry as applied to legal issues.

Even if the expert is not primarily a forensic mental health professional, he or she should be familiar with applicable legal standards, ethical codes, and practice guidelines. For example, all psychologists involved in child custody evaluations should be familiar with the American Psychological Association's (APA's) Ethical Principles of Psychologists and Code of Conduct (1992), the APA's Guidelines for Child Custody Evaluations in Divorce Proceedings (1994), and the APA Division 41 Specialty Guidelines for Forensic Psychologists (Committee on Ethical Guidelines for Forensic Psychologists, 1991). State licensing boards also may have promulgated ethical guidelines and regulations that a psychologist practicing in that state must know. Psychiatrists conducting child custody or child abuse evaluations should be familiar with documents such as the American Academy of Child and Adolescent Psychiatry's (AACAP) Practice Parameters for Child Custody Evaluations (1997) and the Practice Parameters for the Forensic Evaluation of Children and Adolescents Who May Have Been Physically or Sexually Abused (1997).

There has been an increase in the number of ethical complaints against professionals based on their child custody evaluations; therefore, this point is particularly salient. Testimony about adherence to professional codes and guidelines is an essential element of testifying during direct examination, particularly when an opposing expert has violated the codes or guidelines. Such a violation can be a powerful line of attack during cross-examination. Two examples of such violations are the expert who works on a contingency fee in violation of the Specialty Guidelines for Forensic Psychologists, or one who barters therapy services for a client's housepainting or carpentry, in violation of the APA ethical guidelines.

EXPERIENCE ALONE NOT ENOUGH

Despite the inclusion of experience in the Federal Rules of Evidence (and most states' rules of evidence) as a basis for qualifying experts, a substantial research review by Garb (1989) and a related chapter by Faust (1994) have suggested that experience by itself is unrelated to diagnostic competence. Our explanation for this is that some psychologists (like some physicians and some attorneys) simply do not learn from experience. Good experts have a sound knowledge base, a good conceptual frame of reference, competence directly relevant to the issues at hand, and a grounding in scientific approaches, and are conversant with legal and scientific expectations and processes. Experience is probably important when accompanied by exposure to events, studies, or inquiries that actually deepen the expert's understandings of the issues. To make a critical judgment about the worth of one's own experience is not easy, but we advise thinking through experience-related issues such as identifying the major ways that learning from outside experience assists your approach to this work and what further sources of competence and knowledge you bring to this work as a result of your experience. Inexperienced experts should prepare themselves by maintaining close links between the scholarly literature and their emerging career activities, as well as by observing hearings and trials and seeking out critical and directed feedback about their forensic activities.

FACT WITNESS OR EXPERT WITNESS?

The forensic task may bring a mental health professional to court or to a deposition (a procedure in which testimony is taken by opposing counsel outside of the courtroom and is transcribed and possibly videotaped for discovery purposes or for later use at trial). In either case, it is important to clarify whether one is being called as a *fact witness* or as an *expert witness*. When mental health professionals are called as fact witnesses, they may be asked to testify regarding facts or events that they have personally observed. This fact testimony does not require any special forensic expertise. Treating professionals who are serving as fact witnesses might be asked questions about whether they met with a client on certain specified dates, how much the client paid, or what the client's physical appearance or psychological state was on a certain date.

At times, the distinction between expert witness and fact witness may not be clearly drawn. For example, a treating therapist who is called to testify regarding the facts surrounding a client's therapy may also be asked about the client's diagnosis and whether the client improved during the course of treatment. These latter questions may call for further opinions to be offered. One legitimate option for the treating therapist is to decline to offer an opinion, explaining that the nature of the therapeutic contact was not to evaluate the issue in question (e.g., whether the client is a good parent). Depending on the nature of the case, attorneys may seek to qualify the treating professional as an expert to allow opinions to be offered.

Fact witnesses are not required to offer *evaluative* opinions and are not necessarily paid for their time. Although no obligation is incurred by attorneys to pay treating professionals who are called as fact witnesses, many times payments are indeed made. The payments reflect the attorneys' respect for the time and status of the experts and also may have the subtext of influencing the witnesses to feel that they are allies of the attorneys. Many professionals called as fact witnesses routinely bill for their court time. More frequently than not, and fully at the option of the attorneys who call them, the bills are honored and paid. No legal recourse is available for pursuing unpaid bills by professionals who have been fact witnesses.

Expert witnesses are allowed to testify regarding their opinions on matters requiring specialized education, training, or experience, whereas ordinary lay witnesses are not. Experts need not have personal knowledge of the case itself, in which instance they may be "pure experts," testifying about scientific findings. Such pure experts sometimes testify on topics such as eyewitness identification limitations (e.g., Loftus & Ketchum, 1991) or the nature of minimally adequate parenting. However, before giving an opinion, expert witnesses must demonstrate that they have the qualifications to serve as experts as defined by the law and the courts. This qualification or credentialing generally happens during a process that occurs before the witnesses give testimony about substantive issues. Only after the judge has determined that the witness is qualified as an expert can he or she proceed to testify about the substantive issues in the case.

Although the requirements vary somewhat from jurisdiction to jurisdiction, the general rule is that experts must demonstrate that they are qualified by specialized training or experience to render opinions that will assist the fact finder, whether the judge or a jury. It generally is not difficult to qualify as an expert witness, but questions may arise as to the scope of the professional's expertise. For example, is the general psychologist qualified as an expert in the psychological evaluation of children, or is the family therapist qualified as an expert in the evaluation of Post-Traumatic Stress Disorder? How specific the expert's qualifications need to be varies from locale to locale and from judge to judge. It is common for retaining counsel to submit the expert's curriculum vitae to the judge and to comment on the particular forensic training or achievements of the expert. At this time retaining counsel typically moves for acceptance of the witness as an expert. The exception to this abbreviated procedure is during a jury trial, when the attorney wishes to have the training and accomplishments stated aloud to impress the witness's expertise on the jury.

Individuals who are going to testify as experts should make sure that they have exactly the credentials they claim. Unfortunately, resume exaggeration is not uncommon. The credentials listed always should be legitimate. For example, the expert who prominently notes on a resume that he or she is an "adjunct" faculty member may lose credibility when required to acknowledge that he or she does not teach any courses or supervise any students, and that the appointment is in fact ceremonial. The expert's publications can also provide information that may be used in direct or cross-examination, so prepared experts should be able to answer any questions that are based on their own writings and be able to indicate why their views have changed, if, indeed, they have.

Even if the witness demonstrates that he or she is qualified as an expert, the opinions offered must meet the standard that has been established for the admission of opinion testimony. It may be possible to prevent the psychologist from testifying at all if the expert's testimony is within the ken of the average layperson (see Suplee, Woodruff, & Winkelman, 1993, pp. 137–138). Depending on the jurisdiction, if the experts are proffering testimony that is speculative rather than scientific, technical, or other specialized knowledge, and their opinions are derived from such speculative knowledge, the testimony may not meet the standard for admissibility. The law is still developing in the area of determining whether testimony is scientific, technical, or other specialized knowledge and whether opinions derived from such knowledge should be admitted. At the federal level, there was a major change when the Supreme Court decided *Daubert v. Merrell Dow Pharmaceuticals, Inc.* (1993) and announced a new standard for determining the admissibility of expert testimony. The prior standard of general acceptability of methodology and knowledge was supplemented with a more stringent test calling for judicial assessment of whether the underlying theory or methodology can be and has been tested and subjected to peer review and publication, and examination of known and potential error rates and related safeguards. Some expert testimony by mental health professionals may be susceptible to this form of challenge to credentials, which takes the form of a separate *Daubert* hearing preceding or during the trial itself.

CONTRACTING WITH ATTORNEYS

Long before one enters the courtroom, the foundations of one's testimony will have been profoundly shaped by how the case is understood. That understanding begins with developing an explicit working agreement with the attorneys.

AN EXPLICIT WORKING AGREEMENT

Working relationships between attorneys and experts succeed or fail for simple reasons. For example, the initial contacts should produce explicit understandings of the nature of the professional arrangement. Some aspects of the relationship may depend on whether the psychologist is hired by one side or is jointly retained or court appointed. Other aspects of the relationship may be dictated by specific state or local rules. However, during the initial contacts, the attorney and the psychologist should be in agreement, preferably in writing, about the following eight issues:

1. *What communication there will be with each attorney.* If the expert is jointly retained or court appointed, as in some custody or termination of parental rights evaluations, it should be agreed whether there will be ex parte (private) communication with either attorney.
2. *Whether communications with the attorney are covered by the attorney work-product privilege or are otherwise privileged against disclosure to opposing counsel or the court or the jury.* Attorney work products are stringently protected by law. Many experts and attorneys prominently identify all pages of all letters, notes, and faxes to each other as attorney work product in an effort to avail themselves of this privilege.
3. *Whether the mental health professional may be listed as an expert by retaining counsel.* Such a listing does not compel counsel to call the expert, but puts such information on the record so that pretrial discovery may proceed.

4. *Retainers and billing: how much, at what point, for what services, and from whom.* Our recommendation is that all fees be in the form of advance retainers paid only by counsel and not by the party involved in the litigation. On occasions when the retainer is about to be exceeded, it is customary to "refresh" the retainer to cover the additional anticipated time. This arrangement clarifies that the expert is being engaged in a professional relationship by the attorneys and is not financially beholden to the party to the litigation. When the expert is jointly retained, it may be appropriate to divide the responsibility for payment of the fee equally between the parties to avoid any appearance of a motive for bias.

5. *How the theory of the case fits into the psychologist's expertise.* It is an ethical mandate to practice within the boundaries of one's expertise (Standard 1.04, Boundaries of Competence, APA, 1992).

6. *What assessment or consultant steps will be taken.* It is not unusual for attorneys to need substantial guidance in preparing cases involving psychological or psychiatric issues, and attorneys may hire mental health professionals as consultants, or to help plan trial strategy, and not as evaluators. The role of the consultant may be inconsistent with the objectivity required in an assessment. Therefore, assessors should not be consultants and vice versa.

7. *Whether reports will be initially delivered orally or in writing.* Court-appointed and jointly appointed experts tend to deliver reports in writing. Experts retained by one side sometimes deliver oral reports, after which the retaining attorneys decide whether to use the expert and thus to request a written report.

8. *The timetable for the evaluation and report.* Some cases go for years before a hearing or trial. In other instances, a discovery deadline is days away and an opinion is needed on short notice.

PROTECTING IMPARTIALITY

If the case involves a psychological evaluation, attorneys often attempt to persuade the experts during the initial contact that their side is correct and otherwise attempt to bring the experts onto their side. This effort can compromise the necessary impartiality of the experts in any evaluation. A skilled expert will resist these efforts. However, the appearance of inappropriate influence may remain. Indeed, we recommend that experts ask retaining counsel to gather and send all of the materials that support opposing counsel's position, so that a fair and objective assessment may be conducted. If such materials are not sent, it is easy for opposing counsel to present these heretofore unrevealed materials during cross-examination and use them to undermine the expert's opinion.

When an expert is to be retained by one side, it may be appropriate to work within a sequence of steps so that attorneys can ascertain which opinions the expert is likely to develop. For this reason, it may be helpful for an attorney to send the expert full copies of all written case materials along with a check for the anticipated hours of reviewing time to be expended. At this point it may be possible for the expert to give a sufficiently clear preliminary opinion that the attorneys can decide whether they wish to proceed in working with the expert.

HELPING THE ATTORNEY BECOME
PSYCHOLOGICALLY MINDED

Mental health professionals can assist lawyers by helping them to become more psychologically minded. Some attorneys who work in family law do become sophisticated in the psychological issues inherent in divorce, custody, and termination of parental rights matters. It seems obvious to assert that family law attorneys should be masters of these issues, yet many lawyers are not well versed in them. Some get so caught up in the adversarial aspects of their work that they cannot conceptualize the nature of the human experiences and emotions with which they are working. Other attorneys are averse to psychological understandings, explaining that their work is stressful, that they deal with demanding people in nasty situations, and that they struggle to keep their heads above water in the legal proceedings they need to shepherd.

We think of the process in an alternative way. Personal construct theory (Kelly, 1963) argues that people organize their experiences and perceptions around major constructs. Intellectually limited people have only two or three simple constructs, such as good-bad, safe-dangerous, or difficult-easy, around which their lives are structured. However, the sign of an effective personality is to have a variety of constructs available around which one can organize life experiences, because the more constructs available, the more finely differentiated is the ability to see, think, and experience. In an area such as family law, there is so much intersection of emotions and legal issues that the successful attorney is the psychologically wise and conceptually differentiated attorney.

Particularly in family law litigation, the attorney who can see the complexity of the issues involved—rather than seeing the litigation as win–lose, all-or-none—will be in a better position to make use of the psychologist expert witness. In the average child custody case, a well-qualified psychologist is unlikely to find all observations 100% in favor of one side; psychologically minded attorneys can build on that portion of the psychologist's opinion that favors the client's position, or they can forge a consensus somewhere in the middle ground. Therefore, we seek to move the attorney to a psychologically sound foundation of knowledge and skills. This objective means educating attorneys in the underlying theories, practices, and understandings of psychology related to families and the process of divorce (Schwartz & Kaslow, 1997).

SUBPOENAS

Subpoenas may be issued to require mental health professionals to present themselves or designated records (in the case of a *duces tecum* subpoena) at court proceedings or, in some cases, to attorneys who are engaging in the pretrial process known as *discovery*. Although procedures vary somewhat from state to state, a subpoena may be prepared by an attorney and sent to a mental health professional without any oversight by a court. Therefore, mental health professionals must exercise caution in responding to subpoenas. The attorney who prepares the subpoena may be representing a client whose interests conflict with the interests of the clinicians or their clients.

Mental health professionals who receive a subpoena do have a duty to respond to that subpoena; it is not good policy to ignore it. Of course, if the subpoena has been issued in a case in which a professional has already been retained as an expert, the proper response is to consult with retaining counsel. If a professional unexpectedly receives a subpoena relating to a client who was treated or evaluated in a non-forensic context, the professional should contact the client whose records or information are being sought. Before disclosing information or records, the professional may have a duty to raise the client's right to confidentiality and the privilege that exempts certain communications and documents from production in court proceedings and discovery.

If the nonforensic mental health professional or the client does not want the information or documents to be released, then the professional, the client, or, preferably, the client's lawyer may ask a court to invalidate or *quash* the subpoena or issue a protective order limiting the information that is released. It may ultimately be a battle to fight against the disclosure of the information, and the mental health professional and the client should have the right and opportunity to fight that battle.

PRIVILEGE

Mental health professionals should familiarize themselves with the applicable law on confidentiality and privilege in their jurisdiction. For example, does the privilege not to release information or documents extend to anyone engaging in therapy or mental health evaluations, or does it extend only to specific licensed mental health professionals such as psychologists or psychiatrists? Does the privilege apply in cases of couples counseling or group therapy, or is the privilege waived because information is given to additional parties in those settings? Does the jurisdiction have specific rules for the steps to be followed in accessing psychiatric records, substance abuse records, or records that disclose HIV status? Are there special rules that apply to court-ordered evaluations, counseling, or mediation? If the mental health professional is engaged in work that is related to court proceedings, the scope and limits on the privilege should be clarified in advance.

In general, the client controls the privilege. If the client authorizes the release of the documents or information and is competent to do so, then the mental health professional may release the information unless there is some other independent reason for withholding the information (e.g., the client was engaged in marital counseling and the partner has not authorized the release of information). The clinician should make sure that any authorization to release records is *informed* by telling the client the nature of the information to be released and the risks that might be entailed in disclosing the information. If the client may have a negative emotional reaction to something that is in the records, the therapist might want to take some precautions against that reaction (e.g., meet with the client to discuss the information contained in the records).

Mental health professionals dealing with children need to know what the statutes are in that state with regard to children's treatment or evaluation information. For example, at what age does the child control the privilege rather than the parents or guardians? What if the parents—whether they are separated, divorced, or together—disagree about disclosure of information relating to the child?

In some cases, subpoenas may be particularly intrusive. Such intrusive requests may range from demands for therapy notes about a party in litigation unrelated to the therapy, or to the experts' own divorce records, income tax records, or case notes for other clients with similar problems. In such cases, the therapists should initially consult with the retaining lawyer or the client's lawyer. The lawyer may be able to block the request for information by raising the right to confidentiality and the privilege that exempts certain communications and documents from production in court proceedings and discovery.

The release of information need not be a question of all information being released or none. In some cases, a balancing of interests may dictate that some information be released while other information remains privileged. For example, the court or the parties to a dispute may accept a compromise whereby treatment summaries or admission and discharge summaries are released but progress notes detailing day-to-day statements made by the client are not. If there is particular information that is irrelevant to the issue at hand and that might be damaging if released (e.g., information about sexual experiences or HIV status), the mental health professional may propose limits on the release of the information. Of course, the mental health professional should recognize that many attorneys will balk at limits being placed on the information they are given, and these issues are properly resolved by the court.

Release of Raw Data and Notes

Another issue that arises is whether evaluating professionals—most often psychologists—should release raw test data, including the test questions themselves. Some psychologists have taken the position that to protect the integrity of the tests or to prevent misinterpretation of tests by unqualified persons, they should release test data only to other similarly trained professionals. This issue is still being debated. The rules and procedures for discovery of raw data—including test results, test manuals, interview notes, and all materials reviewed by the expert—vary from jurisdiction to jurisdiction. Attorneys may insist that discovery of such raw data may be helpful to direct examination and may be essential for effective cross-examination. Major guides for managing such requests have been issued by the Committee on Legal Issues (1996) and the Committee on Psychological Tests and Assessment (1996) of the APA. Our position is that evaluation notes and results are reasonable targets for discovery requests. Test manuals and normative information may be seen as doing opposing counsel's work for them, and that issue may call for rulings by the court regarding privilege and discovery.

Working Assumptions

Evaluating experts should assume that all of the assessment information in their files, except attorney work products as defined in their jurisdiction, may eventually be revealed to the parties, the attorneys, and the court. Such information includes interview notes and all materials reviewed by the expert. Often errors can be found in the administration, scoring, and interpretation of test results. Reviewing raw data, we have found mistakes in simple addition as well as more sophisticated errors that have affected the scoring and interpretation of test results. We have discovered interview notes that conflict with the expert's report. In some cases, we have found inaccurate materials that were supplied by one party to the expert and on which the expert relied heavily, and we have found materials provided by other parties that were completely ignored. Thus, careful attention to procedures in assessments and a thorough and fair balancing of information from both sides are essential steps in preparing not just for subpoenas, but for all stages of legal scrutiny.

THE REPORT

The type of report that is anticipated should be discussed in the explicit working agreement between the attorney and the mental health professional. Sometimes attorneys will ask for an oral report before any written report is prepared. After receiving the oral report, the attorney may decide not to have a written report prepared. Generally, the mental health professional will not be called to testify if he or she did not prepare a written report, although there may be occasions when a psychologist or psychiatrist testifies after having given only an oral report or without having given any report in advance. In the majority of circumstances, there should be a written report that is seen by the attorneys in advance of testimony. This report should be prepared carefully, because it may provide a blueprint for direct and cross-examination.

The report may reveal whether the mental health professional's opinion is well supported or is vulnerable to attack. It may reveal the strengths and weaknesses of the opinions offered. For example:

- Did the expert rely on biased or erroneous information or on objective data (e.g., did the expert rely too heavily on unsubstantiated reports from one party, or use unreliable, invalid, or obsolete tests)?
- Did the expert make errors in his or her factual findings?
- Do the expert's opinions follow from the factual findings?
- Do the expert's recommendations follow from the factual findings and opinions?
- Are the expert's opinions and recommendations supported by clinical consensus or widely accepted reviews of research?

GOING TO COURT

There are limits on the extent to which the attorney can prepare a jointly retained or court-appointed expert. However, in most cases it is desirable to meet with the attorney who will conduct the direct examination to prepare for actual testimony and, if possible, to prepare for cross-examination. Also, the attorney may want the expert's assistance in preparing to cross-examine the opposing side's expert.

NEGATIVE TRAITS IN TESTIFYING

It is far easier to state what is counterproductive in an expert than it is to state what is desirable. The negative actions are more clear and vivid than the positive ones. Here is what we deem inappropriate in an expert witness and what one should try to avoid in preparing to testify:

1. *Defensiveness instead of clarity and openness.* Even among well-prepared and knowledgeable experts, the perception of being under attack during cross-examination sometimes brings out a wide-ranging, pervasive, and stubborn defensiveness. They refuse to give an inch, even when it is apparent that the facts call for an admission. This defensiveness is especially true about admitting any points that contradict one's conclusions. The neutral observer in the courtroom might be tempted to shout: "For goodness sake, give in on this point!" The coauthor of this chapter had the experience of examining an expert who was so defensive that he refused to acknowledge that he was male and not female. Such defensiveness reduces witness credibility.

2. *Overexplaining.* Maybe it is because the witness box is rather like a pulpit. Perhaps it is because of anxiety. Whatever the cause, some witnesses never allow a statement to stand unelaborated. They say it; then, before the next question is asked, they say it in a slightly different way; then they say it again, each answer piggybacking awkwardly atop the prior answer. Eyes in the courtroom glaze over as the points become diffused by their repetition. This particular behavior occurs with little awareness on the part of the witness. When we have replayed videotapes of testimony in expert witness workshops, the participants are startled by how much they repeat themselves and how markedly it diminishes the power of their messages.

3. *Backing down during cross-examination.* When we see a knowledgeable witness wither or shrink back in anxiety during cross-examination, we always feel concern. Both traits and states contribute to this process. The traits and states together yield excessive sensitivity to criticism combined with a professional self-concept that has elements of vulnerable inadequacy. Sometimes these good clinicians and scientists fail to obtain professional respect because they do not assertively, confidently restate their findings. These losses in presentation of oneself when attacked diminish the worth of the testimony.

   Of course, the expert is much less likely to be in this position if he or she stays within the limits of his or her competence and does not go beyond the data and the conclusions that can be drawn from the data with a reasonable degree of professional certainty. Moreover, the expert is less likely to feel personally attacked if he or she maintains a neutral, professional stance and realizes that his or her task is to present objective evidence to the court, not to be an advocate for one side or the other.

POSITIVE TRAITS IN TESTIFYING

1. *Thorough preparation and knowledge, with specific generalization of existing knowledge.* Seating opinions in scholarly literature allows experts to meet

two levels of responsibility: (a) to the retaining parties to be current and competent, and (b) to the demands of rules of evidence for material that goes beyond speculation and is scientifically supported.

2. *Clear and compelling testimony.*   The best expert witnesses are lucid in their responses and organized in their thoughts. Good responses to attorneys' questions follow a logical order and build a cogent rationale for the general issues, the specific methods, the findings, and the conclusions that follow from the findings.

3. *Self-knowledge and comfortable "I do not know" responses.*   Good witnesses are aware of the limits of their competence. When attorneys ask questions that test the limits of competence, it is important to be able to say that one does not know an answer. By nondefensively stating that they do not know everything related to their field, witnesses often build credibility for what they do know.

4. *Openness and admitting weaknesses.*   This trait is the opposite of the defensiveness noted earlier under negative traits. The open expert describes in a matter-of-fact manner the findings that did not support the opinions, and gives to the court the full range of information, including weaknesses in the field of practice, that influence such professional or scientific conclusions.

5. *Speaking to the whole courtroom.*   Some experts become visually bound to the attorney who is asking the questions. We encourage experts to scan the courtroom as they speak, making eye contact with all of the participants in the legal matter. When this kind of eye contact occurs, everyone listens, and experts appear more empowered and masterful.

6. *Teaching without pontificating.*   Much of what experts do is teach, whether they conceptualize their testimony in those terms or not. Both juries and judges want to learn what the expert knows, and, like all good teaching, good testimony involves explanation in terms that the audience understands and can process meaningfully.

7. *Likability.*   The good expert is credible in what she or he says. People believe witnesses they like, as well as witnesses who are confident in their testimony. Witnesses who have a tendency to be argumentative, caustic, or sharp in other contexts are advised to moderate such attitudes on the stand. Visible goodwill does aid the witness in a multiplicity of ways.

DIRECT EXAMINATION

Direct examination can be an opportunity for experts to present straightforward expositions of their credentials, their experience, the nature of their evaluations or therapy, their findings, and their best professional opinions. This may go awry when communications between attorneys and experts are flawed, when the experts are inexperienced in these roles, or when the aims of the two parties are not consonant.

It is a cliché to say that communication breakdowns occur regularly between attorneys and experts. Nonetheless, clichés do not rule out underlying truths. As a minimum preparation, a clear understanding should be established regarding the questions the attorneys intend to ask and the answers the experts intend to give.

With no surprises, the possibility exists that the experts will be able to develop their findings.

Credibility is the bottom line. As already observed, triers of fact believe expert witnesses who are substantively sound, who are confident, and who are likable. The substantive soundness should have been taken care of well before the witnesses ever enter the courtroom. Competence in one's area of practice is an ethical sine qua non for forensic practitioners. Confidence comes about in part from long-term, persistent traits of personality, and in part from the situational influences of knowing what to expect.

Likability is less obvious as an issue. Our position is that feisty, irritable, and anxious mental health professionals should be especially attentive to self-presentation in the courtroom. Whether the same admonition applies to attorneys is less clear, but we lean toward *probably*. The hazard comes about when experts find that their natural ways of letting themselves be seen as likable (as, we opine, is characteristic of most mental health professionals) become covered up by the performance demands of courtroom testimony. But how does one stay true to one-self when the unfamiliar demands of the legal situation tend to bring out different attitudes and behaviors? In part, the solution lies in acclimatization, in part in mastery of the courtroom role through concerted attention and practice, and in part through realization that most witnesses' fears are only rarely actualized.

Three partners in the coauthor's firm (Suplee et al., 1993) have put together a checklist of topics that are normally covered during the direct examination of an expert witness:

1. The expert's qualifications
2. The expert's knowledge of the facts of the case
3. The steps that the expert has taken in forming an opinion
4. Whether, on the basis of knowledge and the work done on the case, the expert has formed an opinion to a reasonable degree of professional certainty on the question(s) at issue
5. The expert's opinion
6. The reasons and bases for the expert's opinion

CROSS-EXAMINATION

In domestic relations court cases, in particular, cross-examination tends not to have the ferocity that can appear in criminal and personal injury litigation. In fact, a ferocious cross-examination can backfire by arousing sympathy for the expert or hostility toward the cross-examiner, particularly when the expert is well known to the judge and is well respected. More effective attorneys try to moderate the expert's opinion or even turn the psychologist to support the attorney's position. With proper pretrial preparation, experts should be in a position to be aware of which strategy is being tried.

Good witnesses know how to handle attorneys who prepare inadequately but make up for it by blustery, demeaning cross-examinations, as well as how to deal with skilled attorneys who slowly build crosses by using the experts' own expertise against them. (See Brodsky, 1991 for more development of these themes.) Once on the stand, experts should be able to anticipate where a line of questioning in a cross-examination is going; avoid being trapped in narrowly constructed content areas that mislead the triers of fact; maintain a sense of professional power and personal control on the stand; stand up for and articulately defend findings and opinions in a way that serves to advocate for the findings, not for counsel; and, finally, give the court that to which it is entitled—nondefensive, truly expert, objective presentation of relevant psychological knowledge.

Drawing again from Suplee et al. (1993), here is a checklist of topics that may be covered during the cross-examination of an expert witness:

1. Limits on the expert's qualifications
2. The expert's interest or bias
3. The expert's status as a professional witness, if appropriate
4. The contents of the expert's file
5. The facts on which the expert bases his or her opinion and how that opinion would differ if certain assumed facts were changed
6. Any admissions or impeaching statements from the expert's testimony in the case at hand or other cases, from the expert's writings, or from treatises conceded to be authoritative

Any suggestions of violations of professional guidelines or ethical codes may provide fodder for cross-examination. Errors in psychological testing or errors in clinical decision making (whether obvious or hypothesized by the attorney) also provide valid avenues for cross-examination. Good cross-examining attorneys listen carefully to the direct examination and to the answers received on cross-examination.

If the witnesses have prepared thoroughly and anticipated the potential questions, they will be in a better position to address even aggressive cross-examinations. If the case is important enough, we advise practicing cross-examination with the retaining attorneys. Let them help anticipate what questions the witness is likely to receive during a thorough deposition or cross-examination.

REFERENCES

American Academy of Child and Adolescent Psychiatry. (1997). Practice parameters for child custody evaluations. *Journal of the American Academy of Child and Adolescent Psychiatry, 36,* Supplement, 57S–68S.

American Academy of Child and Adolescent Psychiatry. (1997). Practice parameters for the forensic evaluation of children and adolescents who may have been physically or sexually abused. *Journal of the American Academy of Child and Adolescent Psychiatry, 36,* Supplement, 37S–56S.

American Psychological Association. (1992). Ethical principles of psychologists and code of conduct. *American Psychologist, 47,* 1597–1611.

American Psychological Association. (1994). Guidelines for child custody evaluations in divorce proceedings. *American Psychologist, 49,* 677–680.

Brodsky, S. L. (1991). *Testifying in court: Guidelines and maxims for the expert witness.* Washington, DC: American Psychological Association.

Committee on Ethical Guidelines for Forensic Psychologists. (1991). Specialty guidelines for forensic psychologists. *Law and Human Behavior, 6,* 655–665.

Committee on Legal Issues (1996). Strategies for private practitioners coping with subpoenas or compelled testimony for client records or test data. *Professional Psychology: Research and Practice, 27,* 245–251.

Committee on Psychological Tests and Assessment. (1996). Statement on the disclosure of test data. *American Psychologist, 51,* 644–648.

Daubert v. Merrill Dow Pharmaceuticals, Inc. (1993), 509 U.S. 579.

Faust (1994). Are there sufficient foundations for mental health experts to testify in court? In S. A. Kirk & S. D. Einbinder (Eds.), *Controversial issues in mental health.* Boston: Allyn & Bacon.

Garb, H. N. (1989). Clinical judgment, clinical training, and professional experience. *Psychological Bulletin, 105,* 387–396.

Greenberg, S. A., & Shuman, D. W. (1997) Irreconcilable conflict between therapeutic and forensic roles. *Professional Psychology, 28,* 50–57.

Gould, J. W. (1998). *Scientifically crafted child custody evaluations.* Thousand Oaks, CA: Sage.

Heinlein, R. A. (1973). *Time enough for love.* New York: Putnam.

Kelly, G. A. (1963). *Theory of personality: The psychology of personal constructs.* New York: W. W. Norton.

Loftus, E., & Ketchum, K. (1991). *Witness for the defense.* New York: St. Martin's Press.

Schwartz, L. L., & Kaslow, F. W. (1997). *Painful partings: Divorce and its aftermath.* New York: John Wiley & Sons.

Suplee, D. R., Woodruff, M. S., & Winkelman, N. (1993). *The expert witness: Law and practice.* Harrisburg, PA: Pennsylvania Bar Institute.

CHAPTER 24

Consulting and Collaborating with Attorneys

MICHAEL C. GOTTLIEB

When considering forensic consultation, most mental health professionals think of playing the role of expert witness (e.g., Blau, 1984; Brodsky, 1991; Shapiro, 1984). While this role is most visible, mental health professionals may consult and collaborate with family lawyers in numerous ways regarding a wide variety of issues. Rapid social change plus an explosion of knowledge over the last 25 years have brought the fields of law and mental health in contact with each other in fascinating and challenging ways. This chapter considers current opportunities for consultation and collaboration as well as future possibilities.

More specifically, this chapter explores some of the roles one may play as a forensic consultant or collaborator in the area of family and mental health law today. Some of the pitfalls that arise in the process are also featured. Later, some contemporary developments are presented that pose vexing social policy challenges for both professions but that also afford opportunities for them to move toward a better working relationship.

In this discussion, the following assumptions are made: first, that the reader has sufficient experience to be familiar with relevant legal terminology and procedures; second, that the reader is conversant with his or her profession's code of ethics as well as guidelines relevant to forensic consultation in family law (e.g., American Academy of Child and Adolescent Psychiatry, 1997; American Psychological Association [APA], 1992; Committee on Ethical Guidelines for Forensic Psychologists, 1991; Committee on Professional Practice and Standards, 1994); third, that the reader is a conscientious professional who is mindful of remaining within her or his boundaries of competence (e.g., APA, 1992, Sect. 1.04, p. 1600); and finally, that the reader understands, respects, and adheres to appropriate professional roles and boundaries in dealing with attorneys and their clients.

THE THERAPIST

Functioning as a therapist and refusing work as a forensic consultant do not immunize one from exposure to the legal process. It is understandable that some therapists prefer to avoid becoming involved based on the reasonable assumption that testifying in open court could harm the client and the therapeutic relationship. While this may be true in certain cases, the therapist may not be able to assert his or her client's privilege to avoid testifying. In Texas, for instance, there is a specific statutory exception to the confidentiality statue with regard to matters involving the parent–child relationship. Therefore, a therapist who is called to testify regarding his or her client will be faced with numerous ethical and clinical dilemmas.

SUBPOENAS

When a therapist receives a subpoena from an attorney, he or she must respond in some fashion. However, unlike a court order, this does not mean that the requested information must necessarily be revealed. (For further information on coping with subpoenas, see Committee on Legal Issues, 1996; and Chapter 23 of this handbook.)

A common circumstance arises when the client has signed a release and the therapist receives a subpoena from his or her attorney. The therapist may take the opportunity to consult with the attorney, discuss the relevant issues, and explain how testifying might affect the client. If the therapist feels that testifying would be harmful, the attorney may decide to forego the testimony and dismiss the therapist. On the other hand, the attorney and the therapist may disagree. For example, the attorney may override the therapist's input, deciding that his or her testimony will be more helpful than harmful. In such a case the therapist has few options. If the therapist agrees to testify, it is vital that he or she take whatever time is necessary to prepare the client for what will be said as a matter of informed consent (see "Testimony" subsection following). In this way, the client will not be hearing the therapist's testimony for the first time when sitting in the courtroom. Alternatively, the therapist could hire his or her own attorney to have the subpoena quashed or file a protective order. This alternative will involve time and expense, but if the therapist feels that the testimony will be sufficiently damaging to the client, it may be the only alternative. Unfortunately, there is no guarantee that a judge will agree, and the therapist may be forced to testify, regardless of his or her best efforts.

A more complex problem arises in the following example. A therapist is treating a man who is involved in a custody dispute. The therapist receives a subpoena for records from the attorney of the client's wife. In this case the prudent therapist will notify the client, who may wish to consult with his attorney before the therapist responds. Doing so may remove responsibility for the decision from the therapist while the attorneys argue the issue. The subpoena also may provide an opportunity to consult with the client's attorney. Upon receipt, the therapist might consider obtaining written informed consent from the client in order to speak with his attorney. In this way, the subpoena may provide an opportunity for the therapist to collaborate with the attorney to the client's benefit. For example, the client may be seeking treatment due to problems with anger control. The attorney may be unaware of this information, which, if revealed in court, could be harmful to the client's case. Providing the attorney with this information may give him or her greater reason to try to keep the information from being revealed and may lead to a different legal strategy. On the other hand, the attorney may be aware of this information and expect the therapist to testify nonetheless. In this case, the wise therapist will discuss this matter in detail with the client beforehand.

TESTIMONY

In the law there are various kinds of witnesses. Generally, *fact witnesses* are persons who testify regarding their direct observations. *Expert* witnesses, on the other hand, may offer opinions if their *specialized knowledge* will help the trier of fact in determining a relevant issue (Melton, Petrila, Poythress, & Slobogin, 1997). Therapists are typically called as fact witnesses. However, many therapists do not realize that the court may grant a motion to qualify the therapist as an expert regarding the diagnosis, prognosis, and treatment of the client. Therapists should be aware of these different roles and meet with the attorney in advance to clarify boundaries regarding their testimony (see Chapter 23).

Another matter involves preparing the client to hear the therapist's testimony. Because the client is likely to hear things that he or she would not normally have learned were it not for the litigation, it is reasonable to assume that some of the information may be distressing. Therefore, two steps are recommended. First, it is valuable to consult with the attorney. The therapist must know the attorney's legal theory of the case, what he or she plans to ask on direct examination, and what questions can be anticipated on cross-examination. Having this information will help the therapist to testify in the most relevant manner and will help to prepare the client. Second, it is necessary to then meet with and prepare the client as a matter of informed consent. It is desirable for the therapist to devote as much time as necessary to reviewing the content of the meeting with the attorney, explaining his or her role in the legal process, and discussing what material will most likely be revealed. As the meeting proceeds, the alert therapist will watch for signs of distress in the client and will promptly address these as a clinical matter. Also, the therapist should assess the client at the end of the session and determine if further preparation is required. For example, highly anxious clients may require some weeks of practice in advance of trial to learn relaxation and self-soothing techniques to reduce their distress.

An additional alternative may be for the therapist to become more involved in the process. For example, the client may request assistance in learning how to respond to various questions that may be asked. Also, the client may seek information regarding the process that has not been provided by the lawyer. Some clients benefit from the in vivo experience of going to the courthouse, becoming familiar with the environment, and watching other trials. In some cases, therapists may be asked to accompany clients to provide support and assistance with anxiety reduction. Finally, some clients may ask the therapist to remain in the courtroom throughout the trial. Time permitting, all of these strategies may help the client cope more effectively with the courtroom situation. Independent of the clinical advisability and expense of these requests, the client should be reminded that if the therapist is to testify, he or she will not be permitted to remain in the courtroom to hear others' testimony (referred to as *invoking the rule*), because doing so is a violation of procedure and could be grounds for a mistrial.

For the therapist contemplating these latter activities, three notes of caution are offered. First, the therapist should clear any of these activities with the attorney. Thorough and sensitive attorneys often plan such things before trial, and the therapist is well advised to avoid duplication of effort. Second, some of these functions are quasi-legal. It is never appropriate for a mental health professional to offer clients legal advice. Clinical interventions relevant to a legal matter should be approved by the attorney. Third, to the extent that a therapist becomes involved in the preceding functions, his or her role may change vis-à-vis the client. For the more well integrated client, such role shifting may pose no problem. On the other hand, for those clients whose functioning is more compromised, such activities may be inappropriate and even harmful to the client and the therapeutic process. In such cases, these activities are best left to the attorney or to other consultants hired for such purposes.

AFTER LITIGATION

When testimony has been completed, debriefing with the attorney and the client is a sound practice. Because neither the attorney nor the client may be available when the therapist completes his or her testimony, some posit that it is a good idea to call the attorney and obtain feedback regarding the effectiveness of the testimony, the probable outcome of the trial, and his or her observations regarding it. Second, it is desirable to have a prearranged appointment scheduled with the client as soon as possible after the trial. Debriefing will provide opportunities for the client to ask the therapist questions about the testimony, for the therapist to explain his or her answers, and for repairing whatever damage may have been done to the therapeutic relationship.

Following the preceding guidelines will not necessarily keep an unwilling therapist out of court or guarantee that the therapeutic relationship will not be harmed. Unfortunately, such eventualities may occur; however, following the steps outlined here may preclude the necessity of testifying. If a therapist must testify, consulting with the attorney and collaborating with the client may at least enhance the effectiveness of the testimony and reduce the risk of harm to the client. In other cases, participating in the process may provide good grist for the therapeutic mill and promote client gains. For example, a therapist testified regarding her client in a custody dispute. Among other things, the attorney asked the psychologist to discuss the client's background and how it had contributed to some of her personal characteristics. When the therapist and client met after the trial, the client expressed appreciation and commented that she had learned much from the therapist's testimony about how her history related to her contemporary functioning. Having this insight allowed the client to pursue other issues more quickly than she might have otherwise.

THE CONSULTANT

When a mental health professional serves as a consultant to an attorney, the attorney is the client. Mental health professionals may consult in a variety of ways in matters pertaining to mental health and family law, some of which this section describes.

Before proceeding, the reader should know that for attorneys there are two types of consultants. Consulting experts are retained by attorneys to provide them with various types of information. Attorneys are not required to identify such persons or release the information given to them because it is considered part of their work product and is privileged. Therefore, some consultations occur behind closed doors, and the mental health professional may never be identified. In other cases, after obtaining consultation, the attorney may choose to designate the mental health professional as an expert. Only in this case is the information provided discoverable and the consultant designated as an expert who may be called to testify. Generally, such relationships should be clarified at the outset of the consultation.

SPECIFIC AREAS OF EXPERTISE

Mental health professionals who have specialized knowledge may be asked to consult with attorneys regarding a wide variety of matters. Such persons may not examine any of the parties but simply provide information from their areas of expertise. These persons are often scholars who are sometimes referred to as *pure experts*. In the area of family law, a developmental psychologist might opine on the effects of various postdivorce parenting and visitation arrangements depending on the age of a child. Or, a family therapist with expertise in families from different cultures might offer testimony regarding the child-rearing practices of a particular ethnic group in an adoption hearing. Sometimes, such persons will also be asked to answer hypothetical questions that bear on the facts at issue.

Pure experts also may consult to attorneys to help them prepare for depositions or trial. For example, I examined the report of a physician who alleged that a woman was suffering from various psychological problems. In reviewing the material, I realized that the individual was not a board eligible psychiatrist as he had led the attorney to believe. A more detailed review of his credentials placed his credibility in even greater doubt. I provided this information to the attorney, who was pleased to have it in order to impeach the testimony that was harmful to his client.

PERFORMING EVALUATIONS

Attorneys need to know about their clients and may be the first to suspect that a client is experiencing personal problems. As a result, they may ask a consulting mental health professional to perform an evaluation. Such requests may occur early in legal proceedings so that the attorney can better plan his or her strategy. For example, an attorney called a psychologist requesting an evaluation of her client, who was contemplating divorce and admitted to having chronic interpersonal problems. The attorney feared that litigation could lead to a custody battle with the husband, who had taken major responsibility for child rearing over many years. In such a case, the psychologist might perform an evaluation for the attorney to determine the mother's strengths and weaknesses, both personally and as a parent. If the findings were considered favorable by the attorney, she might then move for a court-ordered evaluation, expecting her client to do better than she had originally feared. On the other hand, if she considered the evaluation unfavorable, she might advise her client regarding other alternatives.

REVIEWING DOCUMENTS

Consultation to attorneys invariably involves reviewing documents. Mental health professionals may be called upon to review all manner of materials and provide opinions regarding them. For example, an attorney might request that a social worker review the report of a court-ordered social study in child custody litigation. The attorney might want to know if the report followed appropriate procedures or was flawed or biased in some way. While such questions more frequently arise when the attorney finds the report unfavorable to the client, this is not necessarily the case. I was once asked to review a child custody evaluation, even though the attorney found the conclusions favorable, simply because he wanted added assurance that the document would stand up to the challenge of opposing counsel.

A more complex situation arises when one is placed in the position of criticizing a colleague's work. Many feel that doing so is out of place and only serves to tarnish the reputation of mental health professionals in the eyes of the bar and the judiciary. This position certainly has merit; however, I respectfully disagree.

Having done this work for some time, I have been saddened and sometimes outraged by what can only be considered incompetent work on the part of fellow professionals. When confronted by a judge whose job it is to decide weighty issues, I have no compunction about speaking out when the court has not been well served, noting that it should not rely upon inadequate or incompetent work. For example, I was once asked to testify regarding the work of a court-appointed expert in a custody matter where each parent had accused the other of abusing the children. The court was in a serious dilemma, fearing that sending the children to either parent might be dangerous, and ordered a psychological evaluation of the parties. Unfortunately, at the time of trial, the court-appointed psychologist had not completed his work despite ample time in which to do so. Interviews were not completed, psychological testing had not been finished, there was no written report of his findings, and he did not even make himself available at trial. At the request of one of the parties, who apparently believed that he was leaning favorably in their direction, he sent a very brief letter to the court outlining his preliminary findings that were favorable to the attorney who had requested it. In such a situation I had no difficulty informing the judge that she should not rely upon inadequate and possibly compromised information and made no bones about the fact that the court had not been well served by its appointed expert.

In complex and protracted litigation, the parties may have been evaluated by any number of different professionals. The reader is cautioned to remember that it is appropriate to evaluate only the material for which one is qualified. Psychologists are the only ones who are qualified to evaluate psychological evaluations, but they may not be competent to evaluate the records or opinions of other professionals. When consulting within the legal system, remaining within one's professional areas of competence is absolutely required. To do otherwise courts disaster.

DEVELOPING STRATEGY

Family lawyers know that much of what they do has a heavy psychological component, and they spend a great deal of time considering these matters when preparing for trial. As part of that preparation, they will often ask mental health professionals for advice regarding various aspects of their task. They may wish to know the vulnerabilities of an unfavorable witness or how best to present their client. They may want to discuss whether their client should testify, whether certain persons should be called to testify, or whether certain persons should be called as hostile witnesses. Finally, they may simply wish to talk generally and use the mental health professional as a sounding board.

In performing these roles, it is vital that the mental health professional remember what he or she does *not* know. Sometimes attorneys will assume that their consultants are experienced in the legal system and presume that they have technical legal knowledge. This can be a trap for even the experienced forensic consultant. Lawyers will use *terms of art* that consultants may presume to be commonplace conversation, only to learn later that such terms are being used deliberately and have very specific meaning. For example, when attorneys refer to the *best interest of the child*, they are using a legal term with a specific definition (Melton et al., 1997). Mental health professionals are not lawyers, and lawyers do not expect them to be. As a result, they are always happy to explain the law so that the consultant will be accurately informed, and so that they will receive competent consultation.

If a mental health professional is to testify, it is always advisable to discuss strategy with the attorney as a component of preparation. This is particularly important because the mental health professional may not know the legal theories relevant to the case, required standards of proof (i.e., *beyond a reasonable doubt, clear and convincing evidence,* and *preponderance of the evidence*), or relevant court decisions. In some circumstances, these issues will have little or nothing to do with mental health issues per se, such as jurisdictional disputes, statutes of limitation, and filing deadlines. In other cases, they will have relevance as part of the attorney's legal theory of the case. Therefore, it is always prudent to inquire regarding the relevant legal theories that both the attorney and opposing counsel will use as a basis for their arguments. Once informed regarding these matters, the mental health professional is in a far better position to be helpful. For example, a psychologist completed an evaluation of a man whose ex-wife had filed a motion to terminate his parental rights. It was only when preparing for trial that the psychologist asked about the attorney's legal theory and learned that he wanted to argue that his client was a victim of parent alienation syndrome. (For additional reading see Rand, 1997a, 1997b.)

ATTORNEY COMPETENCE

This chapter emphasizes the need for mental health professionals to function within appropriate professional boundaries and maintain their competence. In an effort to be evenhanded, it is only fair to note that attorneys are not all equally capable and, on some occasions, one is forced to cope with lawyers who do not practice at the highest level of their profession.

On more than one occasion, I have been retained in a case without ever having met with the attorney or spoken with him or her for any length of time, despite my best efforts. This often leads to a phone call the day before the trial with apologies and the question, "How about if we meet at the courthouse early and we can talk then?" On another occasion, an attorney asked me what I thought the legal theory should be in a child custody dispute. I later learned that other forensic consultants no longer would work with him because they felt such questions were inappropriate and were an excuse for not doing his job. Finally, a judge once asked me to make a custody recommendation even though I had not performed a custody evaluation. I respectfully refused to answer her question.

Lawyers are professionally responsible for managing their cases as they see fit and are ultimately responsible to their clients. Consultants cannot control them. On the other hand, mental health professionals do have the obligation to do their part. This involves making every effort to do all they can on behalf of the attorney and his or her client. In some cases doing so may accomplish little, but in others it may prompt the attorney to improve his or her performance as well.

THE COLLABORATOR

Much of this chapter discusses working with lawyers in existing, traditional, and preconceived roles. Collaboration entails looking at the issues from differing perspectives and searching for new ways to work together. This section explores some things that are being done already as well as others that are being planned for the near future. Finally, the last section looks farther ahead at some of the challenges that face mental health and legal professionals over the long term.

EDUCATION

There is much that the mental health professions can teach both the bar and the judiciary, and there is a great deal that can be learned from them. Therefore, a basic means of collaboration is through reciprocal education. First, there is information that would help judges and lawyers reach better decisions for children. For example, they would benefit from learning how children are affected by different visitation agreements depending upon their age, gender, personality, culture, and other key variables. Perhaps one day divorce decrees will take greater account of these variables.

Sometimes attorneys and judges tend to forget that the children will still have the same parents, who must coparent the children once the divorce is over. Teaching general systems theory (e.g., Nichols & Schwartz, 1995), relevant psychopathology (e.g., Ehrenberg, Hunter, & Elterman, 1996), and issues surrounding visitation interference (e.g., Gardner, 1992; Turkat, 1994) would help them understand how conflict arises and may systemically continue after a divorce is granted (Schwartz & Kaslow, 1997). Such knowledge might, for example, encourage the use of alternative dispute resolution strategies, such as mediation, which truly place priority on the best interest of children (Kaslow & Schwartz, 1987).

The bar and bench would also benefit greatly from understanding the professional roles and limitations of mental health professionals. A rich literature has arisen in recent years regarding forensic consultation. This literature addresses a number of issues that most attorneys and judges do not know. For example, they are unfamiliar with the ethical standards of mental health professionals (e.g., American Association of Marriage and Family Therapy [AAMFT], 1991; APA, 1992; National Association of Social Workers [NASW] 1996) and do not know that standards exist regarding forensic consultation (e.g., Committee on Ethical Guidelines for Forensic Psychologists, 1991; NASW, 1997; NASW, undated).

They would benefit from understanding differences between professional roles (e.g., Greenberg & Shuman, 1997; Strasburger, Gutheil, & Brodsky, 1997) and that some mental health professions have guidelines regarding aspects of the legal process (e.g. Committee on Professional Practice and Standards, 1994; Committee on Professional Practice and Standards, in press). They might also be interested in how psychological test data is utilized (APA Ethics Committee, 1997; Tramel, 1994) and evaluated (e.g., Heinze & Grisso, 1996). Such information would make attorneys and judges more sophisticated and critical consumers of mental health professionals' services and would raise the standards of mental health practice within the legal system as well.

On the other hand, understanding mental illness and family dynamics does not mean that one understands the law. Many colleagues do not know the basics of how the legal system operates (e.g., Committee on Legal Issues, 1996), much less how standards for resolution of custody disputes have evolved in our society (e.g., Melton et al., 1997) or how expert testimony is evaluated (e.g., Goodman-Delahunty, 1997).

Involvement in the legal system entails a heavy responsibility for the lives of others who will be affected by the information provided. Therefore, it is vital that mental health professionals be familiar with the legal process before involving themselves in it. Professionals have the obligation of learning this information as a matter of maintaining competence (e.g., AAMFT, 1991; APA, 1992; NASW, 1996). In addition to attending continuing education seminars within one's own profession, another way of increasing one's skills is to be educated by the bench and the bar. When asked, they are generally happy to comply. For example, one might enroll in continuing legal education courses, or even attend law school classes.

PROJECTS OF MUTUAL INTEREST

In addition to education, there are numerous projects that legal and mental health professionals can pursue together. For example, in 1994 the American Bar Association (ABA) and the American Psychological Association (APA), through its Committee on Legal Issues, established a task force to facilitate the development of collaborative projects. Their first accomplishment was a jointly hosted meeting held in Los Angeles in April 1997 by the APA and the ABA Family Law Section. This meeting, attended by over 1,000 attorneys and mental health professionals, was designed to cross-educate one another and address potential sources of conflict. By all accounts it was very worthwhile and generated much enthusiasm. This project was only the first of other joint projects to come. The two groups will sponsor a meeting on criminal law in 1999, and there is active discussion regarding the establishment of a jointly supported think tank to address family law and mental health issues.

Individual attorneys and researchers are also beginning to collaborate on projects of mutual interest. One notable example is Daniel Shuman, Professor of Law at Southern Methodist University. Professor Shuman has noted in jest that "lawyers are psychologists who were afraid of statistics" (personal communication, June 11, 1997). This aphorism is certainly not true in his case because, in addition to being a noted legal scholar, he has authored numerous articles based on empirical research with mental health professionals (e.g., Shuman, Champagne, & Whitaker 1996; Champagne, Shuman, & Whitaker 1996). Shuman represents an example of how professionals can collaborate, support one another, and generate new knowledge at the same time. This kind of collaborative approach is amply illustrated in the coauthorship of chapters in this volume by colleagues drawn from the professions of law and mental health.

At the state level, numerous initiatives are under way to establish closer links between state bar associations and state psychological associations. A leader in this movement is Dr. William Foote, a forensic psychologist in Albuquerque, New Mexico. He has done groundbreaking work in getting the state psychological association and the New Mexico Bar to collaborate on meetings and on joint publications addressing numerous issues that have caused conflict in the past. A similar effort is under way in Colorado under the joint sponsorship of the Colorado Bar Association and the Colorado Medical Society. In Florida, Dr. Florence Kaslow has, since the 1980s, frequently conducted beginning and advanced family mediation trainings with former judge Lewis Kapner and Nancy Palmer, JD, to cross-train attorneys and mental health professionals. Occasionally these presentations have been cosponsored by the Florida Psychological Association and the Florida State Bar Association.

Local professionals can also do their part. In many communities, the local bar association and various mental health professions jointly sponsor directories of attorneys and mental health professionals who work in the area of family law. Local professional associations are now holding joint continuing education programs where both professional groups may obtain credits by studying topics of mutual interest. Finally, groups are forming to meet and discuss issues of mutual concern. Groups of attorneys, judges, and mental health professionals are now actively meeting in Seattle and Dallas. Such efforts cannot resolve all the conflicts that arise between mental health and legal professionals, but they can go a long way toward improving communications and reducing misunderstanding.

FRONTIERS FOR COLLABORATION

The initiatives the preceding section notes are all interesting and helpful beginnings, but they are only beginnings. Changes in society are placing the law and judiciary, policymakers, and the mental health professions in roles no one could have anticipated just a decade ago, and for which many are not prepared. Such changes place all three groups in deeply disturbing circumstances and sometimes put them at odds with one another. This section reviews selected examples of these changes to highlight two issues. First, we live in a complex and changing world that presents serious challenges to our social fabric and legal system and to our definitions of family and mental health. Second, such changes will also provide us with fascinating opportunities for enhanced consultation and collaboration as well as opportunities to learn from one another.

Cultural Diversity

It is no longer news that the United States has become increasingly diverse in recent years due to high rates of immigration from every part of the world. The influx of such a large number and variety of people has raised fundamental political issues regarding how we define ourselves as a nation. The debate is not settled and will continue for some time to come. In the meantime, regardless of how the issue is resolved politically, mental health professionals and family lawyers will be faced with extraordinarily complex issues for which there are no adequate answers. Two examples should suffice to make the point.

Two Muslim Iraqi men were jailed in Nebraska after they had gotten married. Both men, in their early 20s, had agreed to marriages to teenage sisters arranged with the girls' father. Arranged marriage is a common practice in their country and is consistent with their religious traditions. Shortly after the two couples were married, both men were arrested. They were later convicted of child sexual abuse, and the girls' father was ordered by the court to receive counseling. They were expected to know and follow the law, regardless of whether they agreed with it, as are all residents of the country.

A Hmong child named Lia Lee was taken to the hospital at the University of California at Davis (Fadiman, 1997). She presented with a severe seizure disorder. Her physicians became dedicated to her care over the next 4 years of her treatment. As a result, she was hospitalized 15 times and was taken to the emergency room or outpatient clinic 100 times. It turned out that Lia's parents believed that she was possessed by a bad spirit or *dab,* that folk healing would also be helpful to her, and that taking too much of the prescribed medication might be harmful to her. Mrs. Lee said, "If we did a little of each she didn't get sick as much, but the doctors wouldn't let us give just a little medicine because they didn't understand about the soul" ("Doctors and Deities," 1997). As a result, they varied the medication based upon their judgment that it was harming her. It was not long before many of the medical personnel began to view the family as "resistant." At one point, the child was taken from her parents and placed in foster care in order to try to treat her more effectively. When Lia was 5 she experienced two episodes of status epilepticus with a fever of 105. She is now in a persistent vegetative state, and the conflict is over.

It is a fundamental notion in the United States, as well as in most other countries in the world, that one must obey the law and that ignorance of it is no excuse. It is hard to blame the district attorney who felt that his course was clear in acting to protect two young girls from sexual abuse. But, are such laws sufficient to deal with these circumstances, or do they represent oversimplifications in a complex society? When people emigrate from one country to another, are they expected to give up their cultural and family traditions because those in their new homeland do not happen to agree with them? Is there a place for exceptions in the law; if so, what is the implication of creating them? Would it result in chaos and confusion? Would such changes be viewed as preferential treatment? Perhaps mental health professionals can shed some light on this situation and be of assistance to attorneys and the judiciary in understanding such matters at a more complex level where there are no heroes or villains.

ADVANCES IN TECHNOLOGY

Until recently, a *family* was defined as two parents and their biological or adopted children. Later, as divorce rates increased in the post–World War II period, families with parents, stepparents, and step- and half-siblings became commonplace. This development has permanently changed the way in which "family" is constructed. The process of redefining basic family structure is dynamic, not static, and will certainly continue.

Perhaps the best illustration is the now-famous case of *Baby M* ("Hard Questions," 1997; Schwartz, 1991) in which a surrogate mother, Mary Beth Whitehead, fled to Florida with her baby rather than give it up to William and Elizabeth Stern as she had agreed and been paid to do. This case brought national attention to the question of commercial surrogacy, or what the New Jersey Supreme Court called "the sale of a child."

Today there are numerous alternative ways in which one can conceive and bear a child—not only through in vitro fertilization, in which case the people who raise the child are the ones who conceived it, but also through numerous other variations in which other women are used as surrogates and other men donate sperm. Such technology can create children who may never know either of their biological parents and who may view them only as "employees" of the parents who raised them.

Examples such as these make one realize that advances in reproductive biology are creating changes that will perforce redefine the family (see Chapter 3). How will the family be defined in the future? How will the rights of each of the parties be determined when disputes arise? What is the best interest of the child in such a complex situation? Who will have rights to the child, and when there is a dispute, how will it be resolved? There are no simple answers to these complicated questions, but individual cases will work their way through the court system, and case law will be established based upon the facts of the particular cases in question. Is that the best the professions can do? Should mental health professionals abdicate their role and leave it to the legal system, or can they, the policymakers, and the legal and judicial system collaborate in an effort to address some of these vexing issues? Perhaps the APA-ABA joint efforts previously discussed are a step in the right direction.

CHANGING SOCIAL VALUES

Recent years have seen a resurgence of conservative groups that support various political initiatives under the rubric of "family values." In addition to trying to ban abortion and remove sex education and certain works of literature from the schools, many are working to change marriage and divorce statutes. For example, in some states there is a movement to rescind no-fault divorce in the belief that doing so will reduce the incidence of divorce. A variation on this theme occurred in Louisiana recently: A proposal was introduced in the legislature whereby couples could choose to marry under laws that would make divorce more difficult. While these matters remain issues to be faced in the future, one other consequence of this movement has had immediate implications for how *family* is defined.

Recently some studies have shown that as many as two-thirds of teenage girls who become pregnant do so by adult men ("Jail Baiting," 1997). While these statistics have been called into question, the academic debate is of no concern to Kevin Gillson, 19, who was convicted of sexual assault for having sex with his 15-year-old girlfriend, even though he had planned to marry her and raise the baby with her. His young fiancée said, "Thanks to the court system, I have lost the love of my life and the father of my unborn baby." While such an example may have been publicized because it is extreme, one cannot know the true incidence of such cases, and it seems reasonable to assume that such problems arise on a more frequent basis than has been assumed but are simply not publicized.

Here, as in the case of the Iraqi men, the law punished someone who meant no harm, because the state had arbitrarily determined that such behavior is harmful per se. Furthermore, Kevin Gillson's fiancée and her parents now have the responsibility of raising this child while the father remains incarcerated and unable to help them. Is there a way that mental health professionals can aid the legal system in examining these issues from the more complex perspective of social science? Can the professions collaborate to change laws in order to take greater account of extenuating circumstances? Legislators frequently discuss passing laws that will have unintended consequences. Rigid enforcement of statutory law can only add to such unintended outcomes. Perhaps such examples call for laws that may at least allow prosecutorial and judicial discretion in such cases.

ALLEGATIONS OF SEXUAL ABUSE

Perhaps nowhere do the legal system and mental health professionals agree more than on the degree to which allegations of sexual abuse in the context of child custody litigation have intruded into the system. This phenomenon may be attributed to three historical factors (Rand, 1997a). In the 1970s the legal treatment of child custody changed from preference for the mother under the *tender years* presumption to joint custodial arrangements based on the *best interest of the child*. In some states, cocustody is now the legal preference (Schwartz & Kaslow, 1997). Second, as society became aware of the actual incidence of child abuse, legislatures established mandated reporting laws in all jurisdictions. These laws led to a doubling of abuse reports. Third, for many years mental health professionals believed that children do not lie about abuse. As a result, recent estimates suggest that for every bona fide allegation of abuse, two are made (National Coalition on Children's Rights, 1996/1997).

Unfortunately, allegations of abuse have now become the ultimate weapon in child custody matters. While one may understand the historical roots of this behavior, less is known about its causes in individual cases. Much anecdotal data supports the notion that these accusations are made by persons who are extremely vulnerable to narcissistic injury that prevents resolution until the other party is shown to be clearly at fault (Johnson & Campbell, 1988). And it is not surprising that such allegations lead to or become a part of parental alienation syndrome (Gardner, 1985; Palmer, 1988).

WHAT ARE PROFESSIONALS TO DO?

Each of the examples in this section describes complex social and human problems that confront the legal system. I do not propose that all were correctly or incorrectly decided, but I believe they illustrate the extent to which the law, in and of itself, is not adequate to address these problems. Rather, I submit that how professionals construe such situations will determine how they will treat them. In my view, better decisions will be made to the extent that mental health professionals collaborate with lawyers, legislators, and judges to create more enlightened policy based on knowledge drawn from the behavioral and social sciences.

One place to begin may be with allegations of child abuse in custody disputes. Because of the fiduciary responsibility to protect children, all allegations of child maltreatment must be taken seriously. Yet, while professionals are legally and ethically bound to work for the best interest of the child, each attorney is still forced to advocate for his or her client. In such situations thousands of dollars can be spent in polarized and conflictual litigation, and attorneys and mental health professionals can often find themselves at odds. In such situations the best interest of the child may become lost when each seeks to win and to prove that the other is wrong (Johnson & Campbell, 1988). The win–win resolutions sought in mediation are far preferable. This area is a fertile one for collaboration.

SUMMARY AND RECOMMENDATIONS

Some time ago, a small group composed of judges, lawyers, and mental health professionals who were interested in many of the problems this chapter raises began meeting in Dallas. (A similar group met for many years in Philadelphia during the 1970s and 1980s.) The group realized rather quickly that there are numerous areas where mental health concerns and the law diverge and conflict. This chapter tries to point out some of these areas, as well as those of possible convergence, in the hope of reducing differences and conflicts between the two and of engendering respect where differences of goals and procedures must continue. If mental health and legal professionals increase their efforts at consultation and collaboration, perhaps they can generate increased mutual understanding, better laws, and better solutions together.

REFERENCES

American Academy of Child and Adolescent Psychiatry. (1997). Practice parameters for child custody evaluation. *Journal of the Academy of Child and Adolescent Psychiatry, 36,* 57S–68S.

American Association of Marriage and Family Therapy. (1991). *AAMFT code of ethics.* Washington, D.C: Author.

American Psychological Association. (1992). Ethical principles of psychologists and code of conduct. *American Psychologist, 47,* 1597–1611.

American Psychological Association Ethics Committee. (1997, March 21). *Policy statement regarding interpretation of standard 2.02(b).* Washington, DC: American Psychological Association.

Blau, T. H. (1984). *The psychologist as expert witness.* New York: Wiley Interscience.

Brodsky, S. L. (1991). *Testifying in court: Guidelines and maxims for the expert witness.* Washington, DC: American Psychological Association.

Champagne, A., Shuman, D. W., & Whitaker, E. (1996). The problem with empirical examination of the use of court-appointed experts: A report of non-findings. *Behavioral Sciences and the Law, 14,* 361–365.

Committee on Ethical Guidelines for Forensic Psychologists. (1991). Specialty guidelines for forensic psychologists. *Law and Human Behavior, 15,* 655–665.

Committee on Legal Issues. (1996). Strategies for private practitioners coping with subpoenas or compelled testimony for client records for test data. *Professional Psychology: Research and Practice, 27,* 245–251.

Committee on Professional Practice and Standards. (1994). Guidelines for child custody evaluations in divorce proceedings. *American Psychologist, 49,* 677–680.

Committee on Professional Practice and Standards. (In press). Guidelines for psychological evaluations in child protection matters.

Doctors and deities. (1997, October, 13). *The New Republic,* 31.

Ehrenberg, M. F., Hunter, M. A., & Elterman, M. F. (1996). Shared parenting agreements after marital separation: The roles of empathy and narcissism. *Journal of Consulting and Clinical Psychology, 64,* 808–818.

Fadiman, A. (1997). *The spirit catches you and you fall down: A Hmong child, her American doctors and the collision of two cultures.* New York: Farrar, Strauss & Giroux.

Gardner, R. (1985). Recent trends in divorce and custody litigation. *Academy Forum, 29,* 3–7.

Gardner, R. (1992). *The parental alienation syndrome: A guide for mental health and legal professionals.* Cresskill, NJ: Creative Therapeutics.

Goodman-Delahunty, J. (1997). Forensic psychological expertise in the wake of *Daubert. Law and Human Behavior, 21,* 121–140.

Greenberg, S. A., & Shuman, D. W. (1997). Irreconcilable conflict between therapists and forensic roles. *Professional Psychology: Research and Practice, 28,* 50–57.

The hard questions. (1997, October 20). *The New Republic,* 25.

Heinze, M. C., & Grisso, T. (1996). Review of instruments assessing parenting competencies used in child custody evaluations. *Behavioral Sciences and the Law, 14,* 293–313.

Jail baiting. (1997, October 20). *The New Republic,* 12.

Johnson, J. R., & Campbell, L. E. (1988). *Impasses of divorce: The dynamics and resolution of family conflict.* New York: Free Press.

Kaslow, F. W., & Schwartz, L. L. (1987). *The dynamics of divorce: A life cycle perspective.* New York: Bruner/Mazel.

Melton, G. B., Petrila, J., Poythress, N. G., & Slobogin, C. (1997). *Psychological evaluation for the courts.* New York: Guilford Press.

National Association of Social Workers. (1996). *Code of ethics.* Washington, DC: Author.

National Association of Social Workers. (1997). *NASW standards for social work practice in child protection.* Washington, DC: Author.

National Association of Social Workers. (undated). *Standards of practice for social work mediators.* Washington, DC: Author.

National Coalition on Children's Rights, (1996/1997). Data provide relief for false allegations. *Speak out for children* [pamphlet].

Nichols, M. P., & Schwartz, R. C. (1995). *Family Therapy: Concepts and Methods.* Boston: Allyn & Bacon.

Palmer, N. S. (1988). Legal recognition of the parental alienation syndrome. *American Journal of Family Therapy, 16,* 361–363.

Rand, D. C. (1997a). The spectrum of parental alienation syndrome: Part I. *American Journal of Forensic Psychology, 15*(3), 23–52.

Rand, D. C. (1997b). The spectrum of parental alienation syndrome: Part II. *American Journal of Forensic Psychology, 15*(4), 39–92.

Schwartz, L. L. (1991). Psychological and legal perspectives on surrogate motherhood. *American Journal of Family Therapy, 19,* 33–366.

Schwartz, L. L., & Kaslow, F. W. (1997). *Painful partings: Divorce and its aftermath.* New York: John Wiley & Sons.

Shapiro, D. L. (1984). *Psychological evaluation and expert testimony.* New York: Van Nostrand Reinhold.

Shuman, D. W., Champagne, A., & Whitaker, E. (1996). Assessing the believability of expert witnesses: Science in the jury box. *Jurimetrics, 37,* 23–33.

Strasburger, L. H., Gutheil, T. G., & Brodsky, A. (1997). On wearing two hats: Role conflict in serving as both psychotherapist and expert witness. *American Journal of Psychiatry, 154,* 448–456.

Tramel, D. (1994). The release of psychological data to non-experts: Ethical and legal considerations. *Professional Psychology: Research and Practice, 25,* 33–38.

Turkat, I. D. (1994). Child visitation interference in divorce. *Clinical Psychology Review, 14,* 737–742.

CHAPTER 25

Preparation for Forensic Family Therapy Practice

FLORENCE W. KASLOW

PRIOR TO the 1970s, there appear to have been no courses on the interface of legal issues and family therapy practice in medical schools or in the family therapy, psychology, social work graduate school, or institute training programs. Some law schools had family law courses, and even law and psychiatry courses, that included some attention to laws about such areas of life as divorce, child abuse and neglect, child custody, testamentary capacity, and civil commitment. These courses stressed then, and still emphasize, knowledge and interpretation of law and judicial decisions, as well they should. However, little if any attention has been devoted to the impact of these laws on the families whose lives they regulate and influence. As little as 30 years ago there were no joint degree programs in psychology and law (PhD-JD) seeking to bring together the two bodies of knowledge and the very different mind-sets fostered in law schools and in psychology and other mental health graduate programs. This contributed to the awkward situation that clients who concurrently utilized the services of professionals trained in each of these disciplines often received very different and conflicting counsel and information. This frequently led to clients expressing further confusion in an already stressful predicament. For example:

A couple involved in litigating a divorce should each have a separate attorney. Their attorneys will construe their roles as *advocates;* in such cases divorce is perceived to be a win–lose battle in terms of money, property, and children (Kaslow & Schwartz, 1987; Wallerstein & Kelly, 1980). Thus legal counsel revolves around building a case against one's exiting partner, often escalating the fray instead of diminishing it.

While this is occurring, a family psychologist or marriage and family therapist seeing the couple conjointly in divorce therapy may be encouraging them to be as fair to each other as possible (Kaslow, 1994), and to make this painful experience as constructive as they can so as to be able to be proud instead of ashamed of their behavior and to minimize the hurt inflicted on their children (and other family members) by avoiding a nasty, protracted battle. It is hoped that during the anguishing divorce process, they will learn some better coping skills and perhaps gain greater self aware-ness rather than becoming increasingly embittered (Kaslow, 1995).

The attorneys and the therapist each no doubt believe they are acting in their client's best interest. What they are missing is that there are different aspects of the divorce process, and each of them is focusing on some but not all of the variables. The lawyer's primary areas of concern on the client's behalf are the legal and eco-nomic aspects; the therapist is apt to focus on the emotional, the parenting and vis-itation issues and children's needs, and the eventual psychological recovery (Schwartz & Kaslow, 1997).

Only when lawyers and therapists are cognizant of, sensitive to, and respectful of each other's perspectives and disciplines can each work in a manner that optimizes the beneficial outcome of the services they offer to clients. At a time when their lives are being ripped apart, separating couples are usually overly immersed in battle and do not need to have this heightened by the professionals they turn to. If anything, if they can perceive the lawyer and the mental health professional as being coopera-tive, if possible, or at least not combative, the clients can stay focused on the primary issue—completing the divorce process as equitably and peacefully as they can.

ADVENT OF JOINT
PSYCHOLOGY-LAW DEGREE PROGRAMS

Various people scattered around the country bemoaned this sad schism and lack of meaningful interprofessional dialogue and, when ethically permissible, collab-oration. Each of these individuals, initially operating quite separately, decided to attempt, quite actively, to change what they considered to be an unacceptable sta-tus quo. The results of the actions taken by several pioneers are summarized in the following section.

In the early 1970s, a PhD-JD program was started at the University of Nebraska at Lincoln under the leadership of Bruce Dennis Sales, PhD, JD. This was a com-bined program under the aegis of the law school and the department of psychol-ogy. At Stanford University in California, students could take graduate courses in law and psychology, and some integration of what they were learning was con-ducted by faculty. David Rosenhan, PhD, was one of the prime movers in this joint program. A third program was started in Baltimore, Maryland, combining the resources of Johns Hopkins Law School and the University of Maryland Psychol-ogy Department, with Donald Bersoff, PhD, at the helm.

In 1976 and 1977, when I was chief of the Forensic Psychology/Psychiatry Sec-tion at Hahnemann Medical University in Philadelphia, Pennsylvania, in the Department of Mental Health Sciences, I introduced the idea of starting a PhD-JD program to the department chair, Israel Zwerling, MD, PhD. Because he was a knowledgeable and farsighted community, family, and forensic psychiatrist, he responded favorably to the idea.

As Hahnemann did not have a law school, we had to search for a partner outside of our own institution. Through some work I had done as a consultant to the Penn-sylvania Law and Justice Institute, I had had some contact with Dean Charles

O'Brien of Villanova University Law School, and so I approached him to determine his receptivity to the idea. His response turned out to be quite positive. We then moved swiftly through the administrative structures of both universities to get the program approved. In 1979 we admitted the first class of five ultrabright students into a program projected to run 6 years. Students were to spend years 1, 3, and 5 in the psychology program, and years 2, 4, and 6 at the law school. They had to meet the entrance requirements of both programs and fulfill all regular curriculum requirements, plus spend summers in practice and internships that incorporated the interface of psychology and law, such as the guardian *ad litem* unit at the Philadelphia Juvenile Court. Initially I codirected the joint program for several years with Associate Dean Gerald Abraham at Villanova. At both centers, the program was greeted with excitement and enthusiasm, and has continued to flourish for the past 20 years.

In the early 1990s the Hahnemann PsyD program moved to Widener College in Chester, Pennsylvania. Dr. Amiram Elwork, who succeeded me as codirector of the program, relocated to Widener and established a PsyD-JD between Widener's psychology program and its law school. From all reports, this program is faring well.

The PhD-JD program remained at Hahnemann Medical University (in Philadelphia). Now under the leadership of Dr. Donald Bersoff (who had left the Baltimore-based program) and Dr. Kirk Heilbrun, the program has been modified based on findings of periodic reevaluations and changing demands in the psychology-law marketplace. The program has graduated some outstanding students who have gone on to cutting-edge positions, confident in their knowledge of psychology and law as separate disciplines and in the integration of both.

In the ensuing years, both the Stanford and the University of Maryland–Johns Hopkins programs no longer seemed to be in existence. The University of Nebraska at Lincoln program alluded to earlier continues to be a bastion of law and psychology training. Numerous other programs have come into existence. The lists that follow are replicated from the 1998 edition of *Graduate Study in Psychology* (American Psychological Association [APA] 1998, pp. 529, 532, respectively). It is not clear what factors led to inclusion in either specific list. It is also important to note that several are MS-terminal degree level programs only, and that just Hahnemann, Nebraska, and Widener are joint degree programs at the doctoral level.

FORENSIC

California School of Professional Psychology: Fresno (PsyD)
California School of Professional Psychology: Los Angeles (MA-terminal)
City University of New York: John Jay College of Criminal Justice (MA-terminal)
Denver, University of (PsyD)
Nebraska, University of, at Lincoln (JD-PhD)
Pacific Graduate School of Psychology (JD-PhD)
Queen's University (MA, PhD)
Sam Houston State University (PhD)
Simon Fraser University (PhD)
Widener University (JD-PsyD)

LAW AND PSYCHOLOGY

Alabama, University of (PhD)

Arizona, University of (PhD)

California School of Professional Psychology: Fresno (PsyD)

California School of Professional Psychology: Los Angeles (MA-terminal)

Denver, University of (MA-JD-terminal)

Detroit-Mercy, University of (MA-terminal)

Duke University (MA-JD-terminal)

George Washington University (PhD)

Hahnemann Medical University (JD-PhD)

Illinois, University of, at Chicago (PhD)

Nebraska, University of, at Lincoln (JD-PhD)

North Carolina State University (MS, PhD)

The Catholic University of America (MA-JD-terminal)

Toronto, University of (MA, PhD)

Tulsa, University of (respecialization diploma–terminal)

Virginia, University of (PhD)

Clearly, the number of programs offering courses in forensics or law and psychology have proliferated in the past 20 years, reflecting the increased need for and interest in this area of knowledge and practice by psychologists. It is anticipated that the number of programs will continue to increase as more and more people see forensic psychology as a lucrative and stimulating specialty or subspecialty area of practice and teaching.

ACQUIRING REQUISITE TRAINING, EDUCATION, AND SKILLS

For those just embarking on their future career path, and desiring to function well in the forensic arena, enrolling in the kind of PhD-JD (or PsyD-JD) program alluded to earlier is probably the way to acquire the best and broadest foundation and internship experience. The list of such programs available can be found in the aforementioned book (APA, 1998); more detailed information about each program appears under the particular university's listing. Or the American Bar Association can be contacted to secure a list of the law schools that offer joint degree curricular or law-psychology or law–mental health–family courses.

Those at the postdegree level who want to add forensic activities to the other services they render would be wise to become extremely well prepared before venturing into this complex and demanding arena. For here they will be dealing with other skilled forensic mental health practitioners who are possibly offering contradictory testimony, determined-to-win attorney litigators, judges, and no-nonsense criminal justice personnel. If it is not possible to enroll in a graduate PhD-JD program or in a postdoctoral program in forensics, other options might include pursuing a combination of some of the following, depending on one's needs and the gaps in one's knowledge and skills:

- Reading extensively in the forensic literature in all areas in which one wishes to practice or is practicing (see, for example, Stromberg & Associates, 1988; Stromberg, Lindberg & Schneider, 1995).
- Acquiring and digesting the laws in one's state that circumscribe the areas of practice—civil (child custody, Saposnik, 1983; divorce, Kaslow & Schwartz, 1987; civil commitment, personal injury, and testamentary capacity, see Chapter 20) and criminal (evaluating competency to stand trial, malingering, and spouse abuse, Walker, 1990, 1994; rape, etc.).
- Continuing to obtain and be conversant with amendments to the laws and updates on key judicial decisions.
- Keeping said laws and opinions and other items, such as state child support guidelines, handy for easy reference.
- Becoming and remaining knowledgeable about one's professional code of ethics as well as state licensing laws regarding record keeping (Caudill, 1998), confidentiality, duty to protect, and duty to warn (*Tarasoff v. Regents*, 1976).
- Attending relevant courses at a law school, perhaps on a special student basis (i.e., auditing).
- Taking continuing education (CE or CLE) workshops offered by such groups as the American Academy of Forensic Psychology, the American Board of Professional Psychology, one's local bar association or the American Bar Association, or the American Psychological Association or state psychological association in areas pertinent to one's fields of interest.
- Entering a mentoring or consultation arrangement with someone with the requisite expertise.
- Visiting various courtrooms in which different kinds of cases are tried, to observe and become comfortable with courtroom procedures and atmosphere, with what is expected of a fact witness and an expert witness, with how other expert witnesses comport themselves, and with what kind of behavior and testimony are most effective.
- If one is to serve as an expert witness (Blau, 1984; Brodsky, 1991; also see Chapter 23), become extremely well prepared before the deposition and the trial. Go over possible questions that will be asked with the attorney in advance; that is, engage in role rehearsal. Indicate what you would prefer not to be asked, request a copy of your deposition as soon as it is available, and be sure to reread it the night before the hearing or trial so as to avoid inconsistencies and contradictions. (Become aware of other similar pointers to improve your activity in the forensic arena.)
- Become familiar with what psychological tests and evaluative instruments are considered best for conducting assessments that will be utilized for forensic purposes. Know how to interpret the data so that it can be understood by judge and jury. Be able to present current validity and reliability norms (see, for example, Melton, 1998; Pope, Butcher, & Seelen, 1993).
- Be aware of current perspectives regarding the testimony of children (Ceci & Bruck, 1995).
- Remember that judges and attorneys wear clothing appropriate to their roles in the courtroom (i.e., judicial robes and business suits) and lawyers will

advise clients on what to wear to convey a particular image. Mental health professionals should be groomed in accordance with prevailing standards in their community and the impression they want to convey to the judge and the jury.

A list of some of the topics of the workshops being offered under the auspices of the American Academy of Forensic Psychology in 1998 to 1999 appears below. It is provided to offer a broader view of what the field currently encompasses, and the multiple facets of knowledge the forensic psychologist is expected to possess.

- Child Custody Evaluations: Legal, Ethical, and Clinical Contours
- On the Same Page as the Judge: Psychiatric and Psychological Evidence and Testimony Benchbook
- Role of the Forensic Psychologist in Death Penalty Litigation
- Correctional Psychology: Practice, Ethics, and Law
- Ethical Issues for the Forensic Practitioner
- Personal Injury Evaluations: Ethics, Practice, and Case Law
- Brewing a Jury: Scientific and Practical Perspectives
- Advanced Topics in Criminal Forensic Assessment
- The Use of Third Party Information in Forensic Assessment
- Civil and Criminal Forensic Neuropsychology
- Assessing Malingering and Defensiveness

A legal update on forensic psychology (Stromberg et al., 1995) provides another rich source of information on this multifaceted field.

CREDENTIALING AND CREDENTIALS

In 1978 a group of six people met in my office at Hahnemann Medical University to explore the possibility of setting up a board to certify people at the diplomate level in forensic psychology. Part of the impetus came from the fact that the profession of psychiatry had begun moving in this direction, and we did not wish to lose the ground that early forensic psychologists had already staked out in the forensic world and that had been upheld in the Jenkins decision (*Jenkins v. United States*, 1961). Initially it functioned as an ad hoc task force of the American Psychology Law Society (APLS). At this first meeting I was elected chair. All of the officers were highly committed to the task we had identified.

It soon became apparent that APLS was not prepared to move as rapidly as we deemed necessary. Thus, we split off and established and separately incorporated the American Board of Forensic Psychology (ABFP). In 1978 we administered our first batch of examinations (Kaslow, 1989). We also formed the American Academy of Forensic Psychologists as the group to which all diplomates would belong, and as a separate organization to sponsor continuing education workshops.

In the mid-1980s forensic psychology was officially recognized as a separate and distinct specialty by the prestigious American Board of Professional Psychology (ABPP), becoming the fifth specialty to be recognized. Thereafter ABFP became part of ABPP, and its diplomate is now awarded by ABPP. The number of people applying has accelerated markedly in the last decade. The credentials review, review of two work samples, and an oral examination of several hours are part of the lengthy and arduous process of demonstrating one's qualifications to a jury of one's peers. Nonetheless, there are now several hundred forensic diplomates, and the ABFP has celebrated its 20th anniversary. Board certification in forensic psychology has become a well-respected credential which adds to one's status and credibility with attorneys and judges.

The field of psychiatry has a comparable diplomating process, and there are also one or two interdisciplinary forensic organizations in existence.

SUMMARY AND RECOMMENDATIONS

The burgeoning forensic mental health field is a stimulating, challenging, and complex one. Many academicians, clinicians, and researchers have attempted to enter this arena during the 1990s because of these attractive aspects of the field, and also because forensic activities do not fall within the purview of managed care and beckon as a haven that allows greater autonomy. In actuality, forensic practitioners in private practice do negotiate their own fees with attorneys and courts, and fees for forensic services are often billed at rates substantially higher than those that are received for therapy, supervision, or teaching and training. However, there is sometimes a misconception that one can be totally independent in rendering forensic services. One is still governed by the professional code of ethics, state licensing laws, and standards of practice. Further, forensic practitioners are expected to abide by prevailing customs and mores in the legal and judicial context in which they become involved.

With excellent preparation, a broad knowledge base, finely honed skills, and an understanding of the legal and judicial mind-set and milieu, forensic practice can be satisfying and rewarding. As indicated earlier, the highest and most respected credential that one in this discipline can currently acquire is board certification in forensic psychology or forensic psychiatry. It is highly recommended that those who are qualified consider applying and taking the requisite examination. Having this credential of validation and recognition by one's professional peers also often expedites the credentialing process in a courtroom. This is an expanding field and opportunities abound in a multitude of facets and places; the main caveats are to be well prepared; to expect the unexpected; to continue studying and learning, because laws change rapidly; and to recognize that this is not an area in which kindness and empathy abound. Rather, it is ostensibly about truth and justice as defined under law; about the difference between facts and opinions; about guilt and innocence, competence and incompetence, and the willingness to be decisive and not to equivocate. Those who are intellectually astute, self-confident, courageous, and strong in mind and spirit probably fare best.

REFERENCES

American Psychological Association. (1998). *Graduate study in psychology*, Washington, DC: Author.

Blau, T. H. (1984). *The psychologist as expert witness*. New York: John Wiley & Sons.

Brodsky, S. (1991). *Testifying in court: Guidelines and maxims for the expert witness.* Washington, DC: American Psychological Association.

Caudill, O. B. (1998). Notes: The paper shield. *Family Therapy News*, 27–28.

Ceci, S. J., & Bruck, M. (1995). *Jeopardy in the courtroom: A scientific analysis of children's testimony.* Washington, DC: American Psychological Association.

Jenkins v. United States (1961), 307 F.2d 631, 651, 652 (D.C. Circuit).

Kaslow, F. W. (1989). Early history of the American Board of Forensic Psychology: A retrospective account. *Forensic Reports, 2,* 305–311.

Kaslow, F. W. (1994). Painful partings: Providing therapeutic guidance. In L. L. Schwartz (Ed.), *Mid life divorce counseling* (pp. 67–82). Alexandria, VA: American Counseling Association.

Kaslow, F. W. (1995). The dynamics of divorce therapy. In R. H. Mikesell, D. D. Lusterman, & S. H. McDaniel (Eds.), *Integrating family therapy: Handbook of family psychology and systems theory* (pp. 271–283). Washington, DC: American Psychological Association.

Kaslow, F. W., & Schwartz, L. L. (1987). *Dynamics of divorce: A life cycle perspective.* New York: Brunner/Mazel.

Melton, G. B. (1998). *Psychological evaluations for the courts* (2nd ed.). Washington, DC: American Psychological Association.

Pope, K. S., Butcher, J. M., & Seelen, J. (1993). *The MMPI, MMPI-2 and MMPI-A in court: A practical guide for expert witnesses and attorneys.* Washington, DC: American Psychological Association.

Saposnek, D. T. (1983). *Mediating child custody disputes.* San Francisco: Jossey-Bass.

Schwartz, L. L., & Kaslow, F. W. (1997). *Painful partings: Divorce and its aftermath.* New York: John Wiley & Sons.

Stromberg, C. D., & Associates (1988). *The psychologist's legal handbook.* Washington, DC: Council for the National Register of Health Service Providers in Psychology.

Stromberg, C. D., Lindberg, D., & Schneider, J. (1995). *A legal update on forensic psychology* (No. 6). Washington, DC: National Register of Health Service Providers in Psychology.

Tarasoff v. Regents of the University of California, et al. (Calif. 1976), 17 Cal. 3d 425, P. 2d 334, 131 Cal. Rptr. 14.

Walker, L. E. A. (1990). Violence in the family. In F. W. Kaslow (Ed.), *Voices in family psychology* (Vol. 2, pp. 139–158). Newbury Park, CA: Sage.

Walker, L. E. A. (1994). *Abused women and survivor therapy: A practical guide for the psychotherapist.* Washington, DC: American Psychological Association.

Wallerstein, J. D., & Kelly, J. B. (1980). *Surviving the breakup: How children and parents cope with divorce.* New York: Basic Books.

Author Index

Subject Index

Abandonment:
  by mental health practitioner, 469
  by noncustodial parent, 271
  as stalker issue, 136, 138
ABCX model, 295–296
  child abduction application, 296–311
Abduction:
  from cult, 357, 366–367
  by parent (*see* Parental abduction)
  by stranger, 311
Abortion, 142–160
  counseling on, 142, 146, 153–160
  frequency of, 142–143, 159
  funding for, 146
  legal concerns in, 144–146, 159, 160
  minors' right to, 108, 146–147, 157, 158,
    316, 319
  psychological effects of, 150–159
  right to, 53, 106, 144, 442, 502
  therapeutic, 153
Abraham, Gerald, 509
Abuse. *See also specific types of abuse*
  amnesia about, 381–383
  and complaints about therapist, 472
  forgiveness for, 391–393
  history of, 138
  survivors of, 225
Academy of Family Mediators, 245
Adaptation level theory, 130
Addams, Jane, 192
Addington v. Texas, 324
Ad hominem fallacy, 388–389
Adler, Nancy, 150
Administration on Aging, 420
Adoption, 23–39
  closed, 24, 25, 30
  coparent, 169, 180
  fees for, 26

  international, 24, 25, 28–30, 36
  interracial, 24, 26–28, 36
  laws on, 27–29, 36, 50, 52
  of nonrelative, 24, 30
  of older children, 25, 28, 30
  open, 24, 30, 35, 36
  private, 25
  putative father's role in, 33–34
  of relative, 24
  by same-sex couple, 25, 31–32, 36, 167,
    169, 179
  by second parent, 32
  by single parent, 36
  sources for, 25–26, 29, 39
  of special needs children, 25, 28, 30
  standards for, 25–26
  therapist role in, 23, 27, 31, 32, 35–39
Adoption Assistance and Child Welfare
  Act, 65
Adoption and Safe Families Act, 69
Adoptive parents, 23, 32–34, 57, 258
  relationship with biological parents,
    24–25, 30, 37
  in surrogacy, 44, 52, 54, 56–57
Adult Protective Service Act (APSA;
  Florida), 410
Adult protective services agency, 402, 410,
  415
Advance directives, 409, 441–442,
  454–455
African Americans:
  abortion rate among, 62
  and adoption, 26–28
  attitudes toward surrogacy, 49
  and domestic violence, 207
  and elder abuse, 408
  poverty level among, 62
Ageism, 401, 402, 407, 419, 422

533